Anthropology

Asking Questions About Human Origins, Diversity, and Culture

THIRD EDITION

Robert L. Welsch
FRANKLIN PIERCE UNIVERSITY AND
DARTMOUTH COLLEGE (RETIRED)

Luis A. Vivanco
UNIVERSITY OF VERMONT

Agustín Fuentes
PRINCETON UNIVERSITY

OXFORD
UNIVERSITY PRESS

OXFORD
UNIVERSITY PRESS

Oxford University Press is a department of the University of Oxford.
It furthers the University's objective of excellence in research, scholarship,
and education by publishing worldwide. Oxford is a registered trade mark
of Oxford University Press in the UK and in certain other countries.

Published in the United States of America by Oxford University Press
198 Madison Avenue, New York, NY 10016, United States of America.

© 2025, 2020, 2017 by Oxford University Press

For titles covered by Section 112 of the US Higher Education Opportunity
Act, please visit www.oup.com/us/he for the latest information about
pricing and alternate formats.

Library of Congress Cataloging-in-Publication Data
Names: Welsch, Robert Louis, 1950– author. | Vivanco, Luis Antonio, 1969–
    author. | Fuentes, Agustin, author.
Title: Anthropology: asking questions about human origins, diversity, and
    culture / Robert L. Welsch, Franklin Pierce University and Dartmouth
    College (Retired), Luis A. Vivanco, University of Vermont, Agustín
    Fuentes, Princeton University.
Identifiers: LCCN 2023033899 (print) | LCCN 2023033900 (ebook) | ISBN
    9780197666968 (paperback) | ISBN 9780197666982 (ebook)
Subjects: LCSH: Anthropology—Textbooks.
Classification: LCC GN25 .W45 2025 (print) | LCC GN25 (ebook) | DDC
    301—dc23/eng/20230824
LC record available at https://lccn.loc.gov/2023033899
LC ebook record available at https://lccn.loc.gov/2023033900

Printed and bound by Marquis, Canada

Robert L. Welsch:

To Sarah for her love and support, and to my students who have nudged me toward a broader and more complex view of the human condition and humanity's remarkable diversity.

Luis A. Vivanco:

To Peggy, Isabel, Felipe, and Camila for their love and support, and to my students who have taught me much about the importance of inspired teaching and learning.

Agustín Fuentes:

To all the students in my classes, who listened, learned, spoke up, and pushed me to be a better teacher and a more effective scholar.

Brief Contents

Contents

2 Culture:
Giving Meaning to Human Lives 29

3 Human Biocultural Evolution:
Emergence of the Biocultural Animal 49

6 Ancestral Humans:
Understanding the Human Family Tree **145**

7 Human Biodiversity Today:
Understanding Our Differences and Similarities **187**

8 The Body:
Biocultural Perspectives on Health and Illness 217

11 The Rise and Decline of Cities and States:
Understanding Social Complexity in Prehistory 311

PART IV   *Human Social Relations and Their Meanings*

12 Linguistic Anthropology:
Relating Language and Culture 343

13 Economics:
Working, Sharing, and Buying 373

16 Kinship and Gender:
Sex, Power, and Control of Men and Women 451

17 Religion:
Ritual and Belief 479

■ **CLASSIC CONTRIBUTIONS:** Clifford Geertz's Notion of Religion as a Cultural System 484

■ **THE ANTHROPOLOGICAL LIFE:** Is Anthropology Compatible With Religious Faith? 491

■ **A WORLD IN MOTION:** Contemporary Pilgrimage and the Camino de Santiago 496

Epilogue:
Anthropology and the Future of Human Diversity 503

Letter from the Authors

Dear Reader,

Humans are fascinating and complex beings. With our large brains, flexible diets, and ability to get around on two feet, evolutionary history has made us different from other primates and facilitated our adaptation to practically any environment on the planet. At the same time, we are more than our biology, and there is nothing we do that does not involve culture, which encompasses our capacities for symbolic communication, intensive social cooperation, intergenerational learning, and metaphysical thinking.

These points raise some interesting questions: What is it about our humanity that distinguishes us from other species? What is culture and how does it shape our origins, prehistoric pasts, and present? How do we as humans construct meaningful social worlds? What are the reasons for human biological and cultural diversity? Such questions are at the core of the study of anthropology.

The goal of our textbook is to help students develop the ability to pose good anthropological questions and begin answering them, our inspiration coming from the expression "99% of a good answer is a good question." We present problems and questions that students will find provocative and contemporary, and then use theories, archaeological and ethnographic case studies, and applied perspectives as ways of explaining how anthropologists have looked at these topics over time. Our approach emphasizes what is currently known within the study of anthropology and issues that continue to challenge us.

Central to the plan of this book are four underlying principles that guide our approach to anthropology:

- A holistic view of anthropology, emphasizing the complementarity and integration of its subfields.
- Respecting tradition, with a contemporary perspective.
- An emphasis on learning how to ask important and interesting anthropological questions.
- Applying anthropology to understand and solve human problems.

Every chapter, every feature of the book has been written with these principles in mind. We have written a book about anthropology that draws on insights anthropologists have learned during the twentieth century. At the same time, with its cutting-edge content and pedagogy, this is a textbook that provides what students need for the twenty-first century.

For most students, an introductory course in anthropology is the only educational exposure they will have to anthropological thinking. Most readers are unlikely to see anthropological thinking as relevant to their own lives unless we find a way to make it so. This book represents our endeavor to do just that.

Here's wishing you greater appreciation of our discipline and a lifetime of anthropological revelations to come.

Sincerely,

Robert L. Welsch
Luis A. Vivanco
Agustín Fuentes

A note about the turbulent times of the COVID-19 pandemic:

We completed the first draft of this manuscript for the third edition during 2022, a period when, in spite of widespread vaccinations, the COVID-19 pandemic continued to sicken and kill. As we go to press, in the United States, more than 6.2 million people have been hospitalized due to the virus and more than 1.1 million have died.

The senior author of this textbook was an undergraduate in 1970 when student protests across the nation erupted following the National Guard's shooting of thirteen students on the Kent State University campus, killing four students and injuring nine others. Students were sent home at many of these universities and it seemed to many of us that life was so profoundly disrupted that things would never return to anything approaching normal. All three authors were profoundly affected by the events of 9/11, which disrupted international travel for many weeks and likewise deeply affected our students. And nearly all of us were affected in diverse ways by the financial crisis of September 2008, which brought so much economic disruption that is reflected in the economic problems affecting so many families even today.

The COVID-19 pandemic has combined all three of these periods of upheaval, along with a health crisis, a socioeconomic crisis due to the shutdowns, nationwide civil unrest following the murder of George Floyd in Minneapolis at the hands of police, and an attack on the US Capitol after months of false claims of a stolen presidential election. Add to these a war in Ukraine and seemingly relentless inflation in the cost of everyday goods and services, and for many students it will seem that the basic form and character of the world they grew up knowing has suddenly disappeared. There will be many changes that emerge from this turbulent period, and we understand students' worries and anxieties as all of us try to find our way through this uncertain time. From experience, we can attest that life will eventually return to something closer to the patterns we all were used to, even if some aspects of life have likely changed forever.

In response to these health, economic, and social disruptions, we have added a few thoughts into the text that reflect the turbulent times we have all experienced, largely by including new insights from these various crises to show how an anthropological approach can help faculty and students have a better understanding of the world in which we live.

RLW, LAV, & AF

About the Authors

Robert L. Welsch is retired from Franklin Pierce University, where he taught from 2008 to 2019. Previously, he taught at Dartmouth College, from 1994 to 2008. He was an adjunct curator of Melanesian Ethnology at the Field Museum in Chicago for more than two decades. He was trained in the 1970s at Northwestern University and the University of Washington, at a time when anthropologists still focused mainly on non-Western village-level societies, and when cultural materialist, Marxist, structuralist, and interpretive theories dominated the discipline. Welsch has conducted long-term field research in Papua New Guinea and Indonesia, and shorter periods in Alaska, Seattle, and California, on themes related to medical anthropology, religion, exchange, art, and museum studies. Currently he gives occasional guest lectures at Dartmouth and its Hood Museum of Art, where he has curated a number of exhibitions of Melanesian art.

Luis A. Vivanco is Professor of Anthropology and Chair of the Anthropology Department at the University of Vermont. He was trained in the 1990s at Princeton University when post-structuralist perspectives and "studying up" (studying powerful institutions and bureaucracies, often in Western contexts) was becoming commonplace. Vivanco has worked in Costa Rica, Mexico, Colombia, and the United States, studying the culture and politics of environmentalist social movements, the media, science, ecotourism, and urban mobility with bicycles. He has also won four of his university's top teaching awards.

Agustín Fuentes is Professor of Anthropology at Princeton University and a leading figure in multiple areas of biological anthropology, including ethnoprimatology and the biocultural perspective. Trained at Berkeley during the 1990s, his work has focused on cooperation and creativity in human evolution, evolutionary theory, debates about human nature, race and racism, sex and sexuality, primate conservation, and multispecies anthropology. His work on primates has taken him to Gibraltar, Bali, and Singapore. A prolific writer in the public sphere, he is also a *National Geographic* "Explorer."

Preface

What is anthropology, and how is it relevant in today's world? Answering these core questions is the underlying goal of this book.

Anthropology is the most panoramic of the social sciences, focusing on the study of human origins, diversity, and culture, past and present. It provides a powerful framework to organize the intertwined complexities of human biology and evolution, social organization and experience, and symbolic communication and beliefs. It helps us comprehend how our species spread globally, as well as what globalization means for us in the contemporary world. The practice of anthropology also provides knowledge that helps solve some of our most pressing human problems today.

Thinking Like an Anthropologist

Unlike textbooks that emphasize the memorization of facts, *Anthropology: Asking Questions About Human Origins, Diversity, and Culture* teaches students how to think anthropologically. This approach helps students view cultural issues as an anthropologist might. In this way, anthropological thinking is regarded as a tool for deciphering everyday experience and what it means to be human and the confusion and complex world in which we live.

A Cutting-Edge and Integrative Vision of Anthropology

The demands of disciplinary specialization mean that very few—if any—anthropologists can claim to be truly "four-field." Yet many of anthropology's biggest questions require a holistic perspective. Cutting-edge research areas like the biocultural synthesis and materiality—both of which are examined in detail in this book—are meeting the challenges of integration. The structuring of the book into four parts, each with its own introduction that frames the connections between the chapters, is intended to bring subfields together around common concerns.

Organized Around Key Questions

Inspired by the expression "99 percent of a good answer is a good question," each chapter opens with a contemporary story and introduces key questions that can be answered by anthropology. Each main section of a chapter is built around these questions. Through these unique chapter-opening and follow-up questions, students will see how classic anthropological concerns relate to contemporary situations. Those lessons are reinforced at the end of each section with a thought-provoking question ("Thinking Like an Anthropologist"), and at the end of each chapter in the "Reviewing the Chapter" feature. Throughout the book, "Methods Memos"—short, insightful essays about how anthropologists go about answering their questions—also support student learning.

Solving Human Problems

At the heart of *Anthropology: Asking Questions About Human Origins, Diversity, and Culture* is the belief that anthropology can make a difference in the world. We explain how anthropologists have looked at a wide range of human issues over time—mediating conflict, alleviating social problems, contributing to new social policies—through concrete examples, while also recognizing the challenges that remain.

The Past Through a Contemporary Perspective

Anthropology: Asking Questions About Human Origins, Diversity, and Culture represents our effort to close the gap between the realities of the discipline today and traditional views that are also taught at the introductory level. We believe that there is much to be gained, for ourselves and our students, by strengthening the dialogue between generations and subfields of anthropologists. We endeavor to bring classic anthropological examples, cases, and analyses to bear on contemporary questions.

Why We Wrote This Book

In view of how most academic work and life is organized and practiced today, our coauthorship is a somewhat unlikely collaboration. We come from different generations of anthropological training, have taught at different kinds of institutions, do our research in opposite corners of the world, and work on different topics in different subfields. Given the pressures and realities of regional and topical specialization within the discipline, we might not even run into each other at conferences, much less have reason to work together.

But as teachers concerned with sharing the excitement of anthropological findings and thinking with our undergraduate students, we have a lot in common. For one, we believe that there is strength in diversity, and we think our different backgrounds are representative of the breadth of the discipline and who actually teaches introductory courses in four-field anthropology. Because the three of us feel that anthropological thinking is for everyone, we wrote this textbook to appeal to instructors who blend traditional and contemporary views of anthropology and teach students of many cultural backgrounds. We do this by treating the learning experience as a process of actively asking questions about real-world problems and applying theoretical insights to understand them, as nearly all anthropologists actually do.

Thematic Boxes

Five types of thematic boxes are used throughout the book to highlight key themes and principles. *Classic Contributions* boxes consider the history of anthropological thought on a particular topic and provide follow-up questions to promote critical analysis. *Doing Fieldwork* boxes draw upon actual field projects to explore the special methods anthropologists have used to address specific questions and problems. *Anthropologist as Problem Solver* boxes describe cases in which anthropologists have applied disciplinary insights and methods to help alleviate social problems, mediate conflicts, and (re)define policy debates. These cases also provide insights into careers that take advantage of an anthropology background. *A World in Motion* boxes focus on the border-crossing dynamics and global flows of people and objects that characterize and have shaped human lives for millennia. Finally, *The Anthropological Life* boxes provide students with applied illustrations that demonstrate how studying anthropology can provide them with an array of useful insights and tools for living in the world, whatever one's interests, values, or career.

New in the Third Edition

Building on the successful approach established in the first two editions, the third edition of *Anthropology: Asking Questions About Human Origins, Diversity, and Culture* features a number of changes designed to keep the material up to date, relevant, and engaging for students. The following are the most visible changes.

- **A brand new feature**. Nine "**A World in Motion**" boxes interspersed throughout the book focus on border-crossing dynamics such as migration, the peopling of the Americas, medical tourism, art objects, and pilgrimage, among others. Along with Chapter 4 ("Cross-Cultural Interactions") and numerous chapter-opening stories, this feature reinforces the relevance and power of integrative and holistic anthropological thinking for understanding the importance of human mobility, interconnectivity, and globalization.
- **Up-to-date, authorative perspectives on a rapidly changing world**. The last edition of this book came out before the COVID-19 pandemic, the racial justice protests over the police murder of George Floyd, the war in Ukraine, and many other important events that have affected the lives of hundreds of millions. Meanwhile dynamics like climate change, environmental degradation, the rise of cryptocurrencies, among others, continue to evolve, as does scientific research on these matters. Our goal is to show not just how anthropology engages directly with the times, but by drawing on the latest scholarship, show how and why it is relevant to understanding the world in which we and our students live.
- **New chapter-opening stories drawn from real life.** New case studies exploring the effects of COVID-19 on great apes (Chapter 5), hot-off-the-presses discoveries on ancestral humans (Chapter 6), the dilemmas of recreational genetic testing (Chapter 7), the 2019 measles outbreak in Samoa (Chapter 8), efforts to memorialize the deaths of migrants in the Arizona desert (Chapter 9), the role of young women and online communications in driving changes in the English language (Chapter 12), the politics of water access in Mumbai, India (Chapter 15), and the effects of the COVID-19 pandemic on funerals in Pakistan (Chapter 17), each of which will help students relate major themes in each chapter to people's real-world experiences.

In addition to these changes, we have also added new coverage of key topics in various chapters to ensure that students receive a well-rounded introduction to an integrative and holistic anthropology. These additions include the following:

- Chapter 1 features an expanded discussion of early anthropological efforts to understand mass immigration to the United States at the turn of the twentieth century, including A World in Motion box. We also provide refreshed examples of scholars putting their anthropology to work.

- Chapter 3 addresses how topics like COVID-19 and climate change interact with biocultural evolution, and has a new Anthropological Life box on the biocultural dimensions of awe.
- Chapter 4 has a new A World in Motion box on how instant ramen noodles have spread globally and are reshaping local foodways.
- Chapter 5 has new material on the practical contributions of ethnoprimatology to primate conservation.
- Chapter 6 has updated perspectives on paleoanthropology's rapidly changing understanding of ancestral humans, as well as new material on hominin brain development and the effects of climate change on *Homo erectus*. It has a new Classic Contributions focusing on the evolution of hominin social cooperation, and A World in Motion box on the peopling of the Americas.
- Chapter 7 offers new perspectives on the racialization of suffering during the COVID-19 pandemic, a new section on the biocultural dimensions of how humans thrive, and an Anthropological Life box on the biocultural importance of alloparenting.
- Chapter 8 offers new coverage of the social dimensions of the COVID-19 pandemic and vaccine hestitancy. It also has a new Classic Contributions box on Paul Farmer's influential contributions to global health, and A World in Motion box on the phenomenon of medical tourism.
- Chapter 9 has a new Anthropological Life box on working as an ethnographic collections manager in a museum, and A World in Motion box on the transnational circulation of African art objects.
- Chapter 10 has a refreshed opening vignette that brings new angles to the issues raised by the previous edition's opener on the emergence of agriculture in Papua New Guinea, as well as new material on the role of climate change in the Neolithic Revolution in the Fertile Crescent.
- Chapter 11 has an expanded discussion of how archaeologists view social transformation and what it might mean for us in a time when themes like climate change, a pandemic, and war fuel apocalyptic visions of our own society coming to an end. It also has pair of new boxes—A World in Motion, on how archaeologists are reconstructing 2,000-year old trading relationships between East Africa, the Middle East, and Asia, and Doing Fieldwork on a project studying the meaning of sea monsters and sharks for the Classic Maya.
- Chapter 12 has new material on Roman Jakobson's perspectives on how language works, as well as research on two topics of contemporary relevance: the language of racial justice and the effects of social media on language use. It also has a new Anthropological Life box on growing challenges and alternatives to gendered pronouns in English; A World in Motion box on a new emerging language in Australia; and a Doing Fieldwork box on researching language endangerment as both anthropologist and tribal member.
- Chapter 13 has new material on cryptocurrencies and a new Classic Contributions box exploring the influential work of David Graeber on debt.
- Chapter 14 has expanded discussion of cultural anthropology's research on climate change, and A World in Motion box on the relationship between climate change, globalization, and Central American migration to the United States. It also has a new Anthropologist as Problem-Solver box on urban Black food justice.
- Chapter 17 has a new Classic Contributions box featuring Clifford Geertz's influential thinking about religion, and a new A World in Motion box on pilgrimage on the Camino de Santiago.

Oxford Learning Link

This online resource center www.learninglink.oup.com, available to adopters of *Anthropology: Asking Questions About Human Origins, Diversity, and Culture*, offers a wealth of teaching resources, including a test-item file, a computerized test bank, quizzes, PowerPoint slides, and videos. Oxford Learning Link Direct makes the digital learning resources for *Anthropology: Asking Questions About Human Origins, Diversity, and Culture* available to adopters via a one-time course integration.

Adopters also have the option of delivering the learning tools for *Anthropology: Asking Questions About Human Origins, Diversity, and Culture* within a cloud-based courseware platform (Oxford Learning Cloud). Contact your local Oxford University Press representative for a demo of either Oxford Learning Link Direct or Oxford Learning Cloud.

- **Enhanced e-book for *Anthropology: Asking Questions About Human Origins, Diversity, and Culture*:** The enhanced e-book offers numerous opportunities for students to deepen their engagement with the text. The enhanced e-book is available for purchase at RedShelf and VitalSource. For more information, contact your Oxford University Press representative or visit https://learninglink.oup.com/access/welsch-vivanco-fuentes3e.

Ethical Principles for Anthropologists	
This table provides a summarized view of the American Anthropological Association's "Principles of Professional Responsibility" (2012)	
Principle	**Key Ideas**
Do No Harm	A *primary* obligation. Avoid harm to dignity, as well as bodily and material well-being, especially among vulnerable populations. Can supersede goal of seeking new knowledge, even force cancellation of project. Be aware of unintended consequences of one's research. Archaeologists in particular must seek "conservation, protection, and stewardship" of irreplaceable objects.
Be Open and Honest Regarding Your Own Work	Be clear, honest, and open regarding purpose, methods, outcomes, and sponsors of the work. No misleading participants, secret or clandestine research, or omission of significant information that might affect individual's decision to participate. Must consider potential impact of research and its dissemination. Requires explicit negotiation with research partners about ownership of records and access. No plagiarism or data fabrication or falsification (except for use of pseudonyms or other minor modifications to limit informants' exposure to risks).
Obtain Informed Consent and Necessary Permissions	Must obtain voluntary and informed consent of participants, and ensure it was freely granted. Must explain goals, methods, funding, expectations regarding anonymity and credit. Recognizes that consent is dynamic and may need to be renegotiated. Signed consent forms are not automatically necessary; it is *quality*, not format, of consent that is important. All research permissions and permits must be acquired in advance.
Weigh Competing Ethical Obligations Due Collaborators and Affected Parties	Must recognize and weigh competing obligations to participants, students, colleagues, funders, etc. (Usually primary responsibilities are to participants, especially vulnerable ones.) Researcher must be able to distinguish between interdependencies of interests, and also be prepared to be explicit about their ethical obligations. Must not agree to conditions that inappropriately change the research. In a collaboration, open negotiation over credit, ownership, etc., is critical.
Make Your Results Accessible	Results of research must be disseminated in timely fashion, including with participants. Preventing or limiting dissemination, such as to protect confidentiality, may be appropriate.
Protect and Preserve Your Records	Must ensure integrity, preservation, and protection of one's work. Unless otherwise established (such as in collaborations), research belongs to the researcher. Clarity about who owns the records of research is critical. Priority must be given to ensure security and confidentiality of raw data and collected materials, and that these not be used toward unauthorized ends. Must inform participants about uses of records. Interests of preservation outweigh destroying materials for sake of confidentiality.
Maintain Respectful and Ethical Professional Relationships	Must promote an equitable, supportive, and sustainable workplace environment. Must report research misconduct when observed. Must not obstruct responsible scholarly efforts of others. Must provide acknowledgements and credit where they are due.
Source: http://www.aaanet.org/profdev/ethics/	

Acknowledgments

The authors would like to thank the many individuals who have supported this project from its inception to the final stages of production. The impetus for this book lies with Kevin Witt, who had an inspired vision for a new kind of anthropology textbook and the foresight to identify and support the team to write it. In its early stages while this project was with McGraw-Hill, development editors Pam Gordon, Nanette Giles, Susan Messer, and Phil Herbst each played an important role in shaping the manuscript.

At Oxford University Press, Ian Nussbaum and Sherith Pankratz, our Portfolio Managers, and Developmental Editors Thom Holmes (first edition) and Meg Botteon (second and third editions), have managed this project and helped us further refine our vision with exceptional care and expertise. We would also like to thank Content Development Editor, Maeve O'Brien and Assistant Content Editor, Felix Torres. In production, we would like to thank Permissions Manager, Karen Hunter, Senior Production Editor, Ashli MacKenzie, and Copy Editor, Patterson Lamb. And last, but by no means least, we want to acknowledge and thank the hardworking men and women who are marketing this book and getting it into the hands of the students for whom we wrote it. Although the sales and marketing team often go unsung and unacknowledged by many authors, we know their work is critical to the success of a project like this one.

We are grateful to Franklin Pierce University; University of Vermont; Princeton University, University of Notre Dame; Dartmouth College; University of California Berkeley; Central Washington University; the Hood Museum of Art; the Field Museum; the US National Museum of Natural History, a branch of the Smithsonian Institution; and the American Museum of Natural History in New York, all of which have provided support in diverse ways. In particular, we appreciate the support and encouragement of Kim Mooney, Franklin Pierce University president; Andrew Card, former Franklin Pierce University president; Kerry McKeever and Paul Kotila, academic deans at Franklin Pierce; and Jean Dawson and John Villemaire, division chairs of the Social and Behavioral Sciences at Franklin Pierce. At the University of Vermont the Provost's Office and the Office of the Dean of the College of Arts and Sciences have provided important institutional support for this project. The Department of Anthropology at the University of Notre Dame and Mark Roche, former dean of the College of Arts and Letters, provided support and encouragement.

Numerous librarians aided the development of this project at various stages, including Paul Campbell, Eric Shannon, Leslie Inglis, Paul Jenkins, Melissa Stearns, Jill Wixom, Gladys Nielson, Wendy O'Brien, Lisa Wiley, and Amy Horton at Frank S. DiPietro Library at Franklin Pierce University in Rindge, New Hampshire; Laurie Kutner at Bailey-Howe Library at the University of Vermont; Amy Witzel, Fran Oscadal, John Cocklin, and Ridie Ghezie at Baker Library at Dartmouth College; and staff of Alden Library at Ohio University in Athens, Ohio.

We want to especially thank our colleagues Kirk M. and Karen Endicott, Robert G. Goodby, Debra S. Picchi, Douglas Challenger, John E. Terrell, and Robert J. Gordon, all of whom have offered support, encouragement, and insights throughout the various phases of writing this book. Patrick Fazioli, Bob Goodby, and Scott Van Keuren were especially accommodating with helping us frame some of the archaeological issues. Many other colleagues have contributed to this project in direct and indirect ways, including shaping our thinking about various anthropological topics, sparking ideas and being a sounding board about matters of content and pedagogy, and reading and responding to draft chapters. These colleagues include, at Dartmouth College, Hoyt Alverson, Sienna R. Craig, Brian Didier, Nathaniel Dominy, Seth Dobson, Dale F. Eickelman, Kathy Hart, Sergei Kan, Brian Kennedy, Kenneth Korey, Joel Levine, Deborah Nichols, and John Watanabe; and at the University of Vermont, Ben Eastman, Scott Van Keuren, Cameron Wesson, Brian Gilley, Jennifer Dickinson, Teresa Mares, Amy Trubek, Scott Matter, Deborah Blom, Marieka Brouwer-Burg, Chip Zuckerman, and the late Jim Petersen. And we extend our thanks to colleagues Thad Bartlett, Carola Borries, Greg Downey, Hope Hollocher, Lee Gettler, Andrewa Koenig, Kelly Lane, Daniel Lende, James Loudon, Nick Malone, Katherine C. MacKinnon, Thom McDade, Jim McKenna, Rahul Oka, Catherine Panter-Brick, Michael Park, Elsworth Ray, Emily Schulz, Karen Strier, Carel van Schaik, Bob Sussman, Richard Wrangham, Matthew A. Wyczalkowski, and many others for conversations that helped us think through the biological anthropology chapters. Special thanks to Phyllis Dolhinow and David Wake.

Several students at Franklin Pierce, University of Vermont, and Dartmouth College have helped with research during the various stages of writing and rewriting. These include D. Wes Beattie, Christopher Boyce, Justyn Christophers, Brian Dunleavy, Hunter Venture, Brian Kirn, Cooper Leatherwood, Adam Levine, Rebecca Nystrom, Adam Slutsky, Nathan Hedges, Michael Surrett, Scott Spolidoro, Kevin Mooiman, Matthew Dee, Kelsey Keegan, Kyle Brooks, Cory Atkinson, Taber Morrell, Saige Kemelis, Shannon Perry, Catherine Durickas, and Kristin Amato.

We want to thank our students at Franklin Pierce University and the University of Vermont who have test driven various earlier drafts of this book. Their feedback and insights have been invaluable. But in particular we want to thank Courtney Cummings, Kimberly Dupuis, John M. Gass, Kendra Lajoie, Holly Martz, Scott M. McDonald, Lindsay Mullen, and Nick Rodriguez, all of whom were students in AN400 at Franklin Pierce during the fall semester of 2012. Having used drafts of the text in their Introduction to Cultural Anthropology, they reviewed all of the chapters in the book in focus-group fashion and offered useful insights about examples and writing in each chapter.

Last but certainly not least, we would like to thank our families for all the critical emotional and logistical support they have provided over the years to ensure the success of this project. Luis's children Isabel, Felipe, and Camila have aided us in various ways, from prodding questions about the book and anthropology to, at times, comic relief when we needed it. Rob's wife, Sarah Welsch; Luis's wife, Peggy O'Neill-Vivanco; and Agustín's partner, Devi Snively, deserve our deepest gratitude for all their wise counsel at many junctures in the development of this book, their behind-the-scenes support to enable us to research, write, and revise it, and their (long-suffering) patience until finally seeing it finished.

Manuscript Reviewers

We have greatly benefited from the perceptive comments and suggestions of the many talented scholars and instructors who reviewed the manuscript of *Anthropology: Asking Questions About Human Origins, Diversity, and Culture.* Their insight and suggestions contributed immensely to the published work. For their assistance with the preparation of this third edition, we especially thank these:

Katie Marie Ferraro,
Baylor University

Julie Hartman-Linck,
Highland Community College

Joachim Kibirige,
Missouri Western State

Nichol Killian,
Mercer County Community College

Aaron Leo,
Savannah College of Art & Design

Robin O'Day,
University of North Georgia

Donna Rosh,
Central New Mexico Community College

Susan Schalge,
Minnesota State University, Mankato

John Seebach,
Colorado Mesa University

Holly Yatros,
Macomb Community College

We continue to benefit from the generous insights of reviewers of the first and second edition:

Jason Antrosio,
Hartwick College

Anita Barrow,
William Paterson University

Chase W. Beck,
Texas A&M University

Katie M. Binetti,
Baylor University

Renée M. Bonzani,
University of Kentucky

Christine E. Boston,
Lincoln University

Monica Cox,
Auburn University, Troy University

Marni Finkelstein,
John Jay College of Criminal Justice

Kanya Godde,
University of La Verne

Ramie A. Gougeon,
University of West Florida

Renee Gralewicz,
University of Wisconsin–Fox Valley

Adam S. Green,
Georgia State University

Katie Green,
Rappahannock Community College

Christine E. Haney,
University of Nebraska–Lincoln

Diane Hardgrave,
College of Southern Nevada

Jayne Howell,
California State University, Long Beach

Katie Kirakosian,
Northern Virginia Community College

Ludomir Lozny,
Hunter College, CUNY

Dave Matsuda,
California State University, East Bay

Aurelien Mauxion,
Columbia College

Jaclyn McWhorter,
University of Florida

Barbara J. Michael,
University of North Carolina Wilmington

Kathryn T. Molohon,
Laurentian University

Megan D. Parker,
Georgia Perimeter College

Claudine Pied,
University of Wisconsin Platteville

Donald Pollock,
SUNY at Buffalo

Mirjana Roksandic,
University of Winnipeg

Vicki Root-Wajda,
College of DuPage

Larry Ross,
Lincoln University, Missouri

James Sewastynowicz,
Jacksonville State University

B. Katherine Smith,
University of Southern Mississippi

Jesse Todd,
Brookhaven College

Janel Tortorice,
Lone Star College, CyFair

Mary R. Vermilion,
Saint Louis University

Amy Rector Verrelli,
Virginia Commonwealth University

Melissa Vogel,
Clemson University

LuAnn Wandsnider,
University of Nebraska–Lincoln

Donald A. Whatley,
Blinn College

Max E. White,
Piedmont College

Benjamin Wilreker,
College of Southern Nevada

Walter R. T. Witschey,
Longwood University

Catherine S. Wright,
Jefferson State Community College

Lauren A. Wynne,
Utica College

Molly Zuckerman,
Mississippi State University

Brita Wynn,
Sacramento City College

Richard W. Yerkes,
Ohio State University

And seven anonymous
reviewers

Ancillary Co-Authors

Our sincere thanks to the scholars and instructors who aided in the creation of the ancillary materials. Along with the textbook coauthors, they helped create high-quality additional resources specifically for this text:

Jennifer Wies, Eastern Kentucky
University

William Jefferson West, Eastern
Kentucky University

PART I

The Anthropological Perspective

As a discipline, anthropology is concerned with the origins and diversity of human life on the planet, as well as the conditions under which human bodies, technologies, societies, and beliefs change. These concerns bring anthropologists into contact with numerous other disciplines across the natural sciences, the social sciences, and the humanities that share similar concerns, which is one reason it is often said that anthropology is the most interdisciplinary of academic disciplines. But all anthropologists agree that there are certain key concepts and approaches that count more than others. These key concepts and approaches encompass our holistic aspirations and at the same time define the distinctive anthropological perspective.

We begin this part of the book with a broad overview of Anthropology as a four-field discipline, and then follow up with two chapters that introduce two especially important concepts—culture and biocultural evolution, respectively—that provide basic theoretical foundations for the discipline as a whole. Culture clarifies why groups of people around the world think and act in the distinctive ways they do. Bringing this cultural perspective together with the study of human biology reveals the complex ways culture and biology interact to shape our behavior and ongoing evolution as a species. We end this section with a chapter on cross-cultural interactions. The human story, past and present, is characterized by extensive and persistent cross-cultural interactions. Anthropology's perspectives and findings are especially relevant for understanding contemporary patterns of globalization.

Anthropology

Asking Questions About Humanity

HUMAN BEINGS ARE one of the world's most adaptable animals. Evolutionary history has endowed our species with certain common physical characteristics, instincts, and practices that have helped us survive, even thrive, in every conceivable terrestrial environment. Yet no group of people is exactly like another, and as a species we exhibit tremendous variations across groups, variations in our adaptations to the environment, physical appearance, language, beliefs, and social organization.

Humans have always encountered groups of people who look different, speak peculiar languages, and behave in unexpected or unpredictable ways. Although sometimes hostility and wars break out between groups because of such differences, usually people have found ways to get along, often through trade and alliances. To be effective at establishing strong social and political bonds in spite of human differences has always required that people have a practical understanding of human variation.

Some of history's great travelers and explorers developed that practical understanding, among them the Venetian Marco Polo (1254–1324), the Norman cleric Gerald of Wales (1146–1223), the Franciscan missionary William of Rubruck (1220–1292), the North African Muslim Ibn Batuta (1304–1433), and the Chinese admiral

Intercultural Interactions. In 1767 Captain Samuel Wallis and his crew were the first Westerners to reach Tahiti. Their initial interactions were peaceful and included an exchange of gifts between Wallis and Queen Oberea. The cultural differences between Tahitians and the English raised many important questions about human differences and similarities, for both parties-the kinds of dynamics that interest anthropologists today.

Zheng He (1371–1433). These individuals were all deeply interested in other peoples, and their writings express sophisticated understandings of how and why the groups they encountered looked, acted, worshiped, and spoke as they did (Bartlett 1982; Larner 1999; Menzies 2002; Dreyer 2007; Harvey 2007; Khanmohamadi 2008; Fazioli 2014). Similarly, there is a rich historical legacy of intellectual thought about human variation. The great Chinese philosopher Confucius (551–479 BCE) communicated in two of his *Analects* some principles for establishing relationships with *yi* [yee], meaning cultural and ethnic outsiders. A generation later, the Greek historian Herodotus (484–425 BCE), in his seven-volume *Histories*, described the diverse peoples and societies he encountered during his travels in Africa, Southwestern Asia, and India, offering a number of possible explanations for the variations he observed across groups.

While all of these individuals were curious about other peoples and at times quite rigorous in their ways of thinking about human variation, they were not anthropologists as we think of anthropology today. They were not researchers asking systematic questions about humanity, and anthropology as a discipline did not emerge from their writings. Still, their various studies show that getting along with peoples from different cultures has always been important, a point that is sometimes lost on us in the United States, where our international prominence and our preoccupation with American exceptionalism may lead us to think that we don't need to understand people and cultures from other countries. But if we Americans want to be most successful in dealing with people internationally in politics, trade, treaties, and global environmental or health policies, we need to understand in systematic ways the people from other countries and the cultures that guide and motivate them.

These points lead us to our first question, the question at the heart of this chapter: *What is anthropology, and how is it relevant in today's world?* We can answer this question by considering a number of related questions around which this chapter is organized:

How did anthropology begin?

What do the four subfields of anthropology have in common?

How do anthropologists know what they know?

How do anthropologists put their knowledge to work in the world?

What ethical obligations do anthropologists have?

Anthropology is the study of human beings, their biology, their prehistory and histories, and their changing languages, cultures, and social institutions. Anthropology provides a framework for asking questions about and grasping the complexity of human experience, both past and present. Anthropology is about where humans have been, but it also provides knowledge that helps solve human problems today.

1.1 How Did Anthropology Begin?

During the nineteenth century, **anthropology** emerged in Europe and North America as an academic discipline devoted to the systematic observation and analysis of human variation. Three key concerns began to emerge by the 1850s that would shape professional anthropology. These were (1) the disruptions of industrialization in Europe and America, (2) the rise of evolutionary theories, and (3) the growing importance of Europe's far-flung colonies and the vast American West with their large indigenous populations whose land, mineral wealth, and labor Europeans and Americans wanted to control.

- **Anthropology.** The study of human beings, their biology, their prehistory and histories, and their changing languages, cultures, and social institutions.

The Disruptions of Industrialization

Industrialization refers to the economic process of shifting from an agricultural economy to a factory-based one. **Industrialization** disrupted American and European societies by bringing large numbers of rural people into towns and cities to work in factories. The rise of industrial towns and cities raised questions about how society was changing, including how a factory-based economy and the attendant growth of cities shaped society, government, residential patterns, and culture. These were the questions that motivated great social thinkers, in particular German political economists Karl Marx (1818–1883) and Max Weber (1864–1920) and the French anthropologist-sociologist Émile Durkheim (1858–1917), each of whom influenced the rise of anthropology as a social scientific discipline.

- **Industrialization.** The economic process of shifting from an agricultural economy to a factory-based one.

In the beginning of the nineteenth century, most people in Western countries were rural farmers. The rise of factory economies changed such basic aspects of life as the range of people individuals encountered and sometimes married, the activities they spent their days doing, and the role of religion in their lives. In the midst of these upheavals, anthropology developed as a discipline that sought to understand and explain how people organize their communities and how those communities change. It also led scholars to consider how industrialization affected peoples in European colonies in Africa, Asia, Latin America, and the Pacific Islands. Important new questions were posed: Why did these diverse societies organize their lives in the ways they did? Why had the civilizations of China, India, and the Arab world developed social, political, and economic patterns so different from those of Europeans? Asking about how European villages and cities were structured and how they perpetuated their cultures ultimately led to questions about how all sorts of non-Western societies worked as well.

Early scholars also took note of the new patterns of human migration that accompanied these changes. In the United States, millions of immigrants from southern and eastern Europe arrived in the United States between the 1890s and 1914. Many white Americans viewed them as racially inferior and threatening to the social order. In response to the waves of anti-immigrant sentiments that followed, some early American anthropologists sought to promote greater understanding of who these people were through systematic research, as we explain in "A World in Motion: George A. Dorsey and the Anthropology of Immigration in the Early Twentieth Century."

A World In Motion
George A. Dorsey and the Anthropology of Immigration in the Early Twentieth Century

George A. Dorsey was awarded the second PhD in the discipline of anthropology from Harvard University in 1894. After archaeology and bioanthropology research in Peru and ethnographic research among American Indian societies in Oklahoma and the Southwest, he took a job at Chicago's Field Museum. In 1909, he took a leave of absence to collect objects and conduct research overseas. Concerns about emigration from Eastern Europe, Italy, and the Balkans had been rising, so Dorsey proposed to travel to Hungary (then part of the Austro-Hungarian Empire) to study immigrants and their home communities. These were communities that had sent many immigrants to US cities like Chicago and New York. As he explained in the *Chicago Tribune* in 1909: "I shall write of what I see and attempt to give an historical background to the scene, only of sufficient depth, however, to make intelligible the scene itself" (Dorsey 1909: Nov 14:5).

A century after Dorsey's findings were published, it is striking how closely they parallel those of anthropologists studying contemporary migratory flows to the United States. For example, Dorsey found that migrants from Hungary were not necessarily planning on settling permanently in this country but sought to create social mobility back home. As he wrote, "No one ever goes to America the first time with the intention of remaining there. . . . Their object is to acquire a certain amount of money with which to pay

a debt, to buy a house, or to buy land."

Dorsey also observed that social and familial patterns shaped the migratory experience. He described what scholars now call "chain migration," in which individuals travel to destinations where they already knew people. Once an individual's social networks in the United States had grown, they might send for other family members to settle with them. Some villages in Hungary experienced a shortage of labor because so many young people had gone to the United States. But even still, at least one-third of migrants returned to Hungary.

Even in this early period, immigration was not as simple a pattern as public discourses—then or now—may suggest. While there are historical particularities to all migration stories, the patterns Dorsey identified show important commonalities over time and place. His insights further reveal the ways in which anthropology has been useful in applying systematic research to clarify the dynamics of immigration for over a century.

The Theory of Evolution

- **Evolution.** The adaptive changes in populations of organisms across generations.

Evolution refers to the adaptive changes in populations of organisms across generations. English naturalist Charles Darwin (1809–1882) developed a theory of how different species of plants and animals had evolved from earlier forms. He based his ideas on personal observations made during his travels with the British survey ship HMS *Beagle*, as well as his own backyard experiments raising pigeons, among other things. The key mechanism of his evolutionary theory was what he called "descent with modification" (and today we call "natural selection"), a process through which certain inheritable traits are passed along to offspring because they are better suited to the environment.

- **Empirical.** Verifiable through observation rather than through logic or theory.

For Darwin, the question of the origin of species was not a religious one (as many people of his time believed) but an **empirical** one, best answered by observing whether species had changed and whether new species had emerged over time. Thanks to contemporary geologists, Darwin knew that many early species, such as the dinosaurs, had arisen and died out. For him, such changes were evidence that the natural environment had selected some species for survival and that extinction was the outcome for those not well suited to changing environments.

When Darwin published his groundbreaking work, *On the Origin of Species* in 1859, he experienced a backlash, and few scientists accepted Darwin's ideas immediately. But as the century progressed, more scholars came to accept the idea of evolution. Today, scientists no longer view biological evolution as controversial, and nearly all anthropologists and biologists accept evolution as the only way to explain the relationship among animal and plant species and the only way to explain why humans have certain physical abilities and characteristics.

Colonial Origins of Cultural Anthropology

Colonialism is the historical practice of more powerful countries claiming possession of less powerful ones. The Russian empire expanded by claiming and colonizing areas from the Ural Mountains across Siberia to the Pacific Ocean, annexing dozens of indigenous communities across Asia. Although both China and Japan have had colonies, when we think about the development of anthropology, we usually think of colonialism as practiced by Europeans and North Americans.

American seizure of Indian lands is a form of colonialism. Although the colonial period began in the late fifteenth century, the institutionalization of anthropology as an academic discipline occurred during the height of North American and European colonialisms between the 1870s and the 1970s. In these colonial situations, white people established mines, fisheries, plantations, and other enterprises using local peoples as inexpensive labor. Colonies enriched the mother countries, often impoverishing the indigenous inhabitants.

Colonized peoples everywhere had different cultures and customs, and their actions often seemed baffling to colonial administrators, a fact that these officials chalked up to their seemingly primitive or "savage" nature. Colonialists justified their actions—both philosophically and morally—through the **othering** of non-Western peoples, a process of defining colonized peoples as different from, and subordinate to, Europeans in terms of their social, moral, and physical norms (Said 1978). Early anthropologists contributed to othering through the creation of intellectual labeling and classification schemes that were sometimes little more than negative stereotypes (Tuhiwai Smith 2012). At the same time, early anthropologists were developing new social scientific methods of studying non-Western societies, primarily to inform colonial officials how to govern and control such radically different peoples.

Most Europeans and Americans expected their colonial subjects to die out, leading to the urgent collection of information about tribal societies before it was too late. Well into the 1920s, anthropologists pursued an approach known as the **salvage paradigm**, which held that it was important to observe indigenous ways of life, interview elders, and assemble collections of objects made and used by indigenous peoples because this knowledge of traditional languages and customs would soon disappear (Figure 1.1). Of course, today we know that while some Indian tribes, especially along the East Coast, largely died out, many other groups have survived and grown in population. But these Native American cultures have had to adjust and adapt to all the changes that other Americans of different national origins have brought to the continent.

- **Colonialism.** The historical practice of more powerful countries claiming possession of less powerful ones.

- **Othering.** Defining colonized peoples as different from, and subordinate to, Europeans in terms of their social, moral, and physical norms.

- **Salvage paradigm.** The paradigm which held that it was important to observe indigenous ways of life, interview elders, and assemble collections of objects made and used by indigenous peoples.

Figure 1.1 The Salvage Paradigm. Efforts to document indigenous cultures "before they disappeared" motivated anthropologists and others-including well-known American photographer Edward S. Curtis, who took this picture of an Apsaroke mother and child in 1908-to record the ways of traditional people.

Anthropology as a Global Discipline

By the end of the nineteenth century, anthropology was an international discipline, whose practitioners were mainly based in Western Europe and the United States. Although they had some shared concerns, anthropologists in particular countries developed specific national traditions, studying distinct problems and developing their own styles of thought. Throughout the twentieth century, anthropology began to emerge in many non-European countries as well. Many students in colonial territories had gone to European and American universities where they learned anthropology and, in many cases, brought anthropology back home. In these countries, anthropology often focuses on practical problems of national development and on documenting the minority societies found within the country's borders. Today, anthropology is a truly global discipline with practitioners in dozens of countries asking many different kinds of questions about humanity.

THINKING LIKE AN ANTHROPOLOGIST

Can you think of something you do at your college or university that feels "natural" but is probably done somewhat differently at another college? Consider, for example, how your experiences in high school classes may have led you to expect something different from your college classes.

1.2   What Do the Four Subfields of Anthropology Have in Common?

Anthropology has traditionally been divided into four subfields: cultural anthropology, archaeology, biological anthropology, and linguistic anthropology (Figure 1.2).

Cultural anthropology focuses on the social lives of living communities. Until the 1970s, most cultural anthropologists conducted research in non-Western communities, spending a year or two observing social life. They learned the local language and studied broad aspects of the community, such as people's economic transactions, religious rituals, political organizations, and families, seeking to understand how these distinct domains influenced each other. In recent decades they have come to focus on more specific issues in the communities they study, such as how and why religious conflicts occur, how environmental changes affect agricultural production, and how economic interactions create and maintain social inequalities. Today, anthropologists are as likely to study modern institutions, occupational groups, ethnic minorities, and social media in their own cultures as they are to study cultures outside their own.

Archaeology studies past cultures, by excavating sites where people lived, worked, farmed, or engaged in some other activities. Prehistoric archaeologists study prehistory (life before written records), trying to understand how people lived before they had domesticated plants and animals, as well as patterns of trade or warfare between ancient settlements. Prehistoric archaeologists are especially interested in the transition from hunting and gathering to agriculture, and the rise of cities and states. Another branch of archaeology is *historical archaeology*, which studies the material remains of societies that also left behind written and oral histories. Focusing primarily on the past 500 years, historical archaeology supplements what we know about a community or society with studies of recent historical migrations and cultural shifts.

- **Cultural anthropology.** The study of the social lives of living communities.

- **Archaeology.** The study of past cultures, by excavating sites where people lived, worked, farmed, or conducted some other activity.

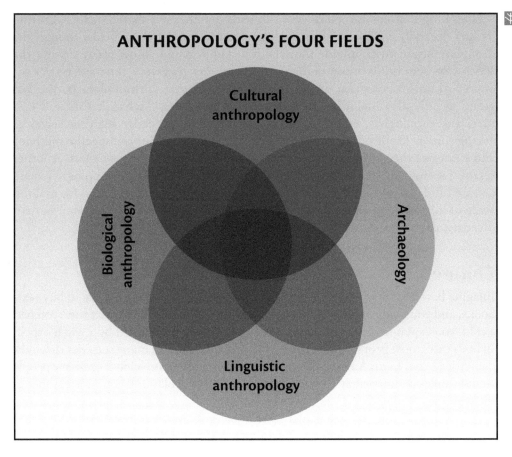

Figure 1.2 Anthropology's Four Fields.

Biological anthropology (also called physical anthropology) focuses on the biocultural aspects of the human species, past and present, along with those of our closest relatives, the non-human primates (apes, monkeys, and related species). A mainstay of biological anthropology has been the attempt to uncover human fossils and reconstruct the pathways of human evolution. By the 1950s and 1960s, biological anthropologists expanded into the study of human health and disease and began to look at the non-human primates (especially monkeys and apes) to determine what is part of our basic primate biology and what comes with culture. Biological anthropology is currently a field of many specializations; in addition to human evolution, health and disease, and primate behavior, researchers also study topics such as human genetics, the impact of social stress on the body, and human diet and nutrition.

Linguistic anthropology studies how people communicate with one another through language, and how language use shapes group membership and identity. Linguistic anthropologists also look at how language helps people organize their cultural beliefs and ideologies. These anthropologists have traditionally studied the categories that indigenous people use in their own languages, attempting to understand how they classify parts of their social and natural worlds.

Anthropology is by nature an interdisciplinary discipline. Its subfields cross into many other academic disciplines across the social and natural sciences. Cultural anthropologists, for example, often draw on sociological and psychological approaches as well as historical and economic data for some projects. Most archaeologists need to understand the principles of geology, including how rock layers form over time and techniques used to date artifacts. Biological anthropology draws heavily on morphology (which deals with the form and structure of organisms), cellular biology, and genetics.

- **Biological anthropology.** The study of the biological and biocultural aspects of the human species, past and present, along with those of our closest relatives, the non-human primates.

- **Linguistic anthropology.** The study of how people communicate with one another through language and how language use shapes group membership and identity.

One thing that keeps such diverse subfields together is a shared history. During its first decades, American anthropologists studied all of these fields, though the discipline began to subdivide into the four subfields we know today during the 1950s. By the 1970s most graduate departments had very separate tracks for biological anthropologists, archaeologists, and cultural anthropologists, the last group usually also including linguistic anthropologists. Archaeologists and cultural anthropologists, especially in North America, generally see themselves as asking similar kinds of questions about human cultures. But the specific methods and strategies they use are somewhat broader than this idea may suggest. Another reason for the persistence of the four-field approach is that anthropologists share certain fundamental approaches and concepts they agree are important for making sense of humanity's complexity. These include culture, cultural relativism, human diversity, change, and holism.

Culture

Imagine how people would react if you went to the university bookstore to buy textbooks, and you haggled over the price at the cash register. Or if the next time you had a cold, you explained to your friends that your sickness was caused by a witch's spell. In both cases most people would think you were crazy. But in many societies throughout Africa, Asia, Latin America, the Pacific, and other regions, a lot of ordinary people would think you were crazy for *not* haggling or for *not* explaining your misfortunes as the workings of a witch.

Every human group has particular rules of behavior and a common set of explanations about how the world works. Within the community, these behaviors and explanations feel totally natural, which is to say, self-evident and necessary. People who behave differently are strange, wrong, or maybe even evil. Yet what feels natural to one group may seem totally arbitrary to another. In anthropology, the term **culture** refers to the taken-for-granted notions, rules, moralities, and behaviors within a social group that feel natural and the way things should be.

- **Culture.** The taken-for-granted notions, rules, moralities, and behaviors within a social group.

The idea of culture is one of anthropology's most important contributions to knowledge. It is also one of anthropology's oldest concepts, its first use commonly credited to British anthropologist Edward Burnett Tylor in the 1870s. In "Classic Contributions: E. B. Tylor and the Culture Concept," we examine his original definition of culture.

Anthropologists believe that people have culture in two senses: the general and the particular. Culture in the general sense refers to humans' possession of a generalized capacity, even necessity, to create, share, and pass on their understandings of things through culture. From this point of view, the development of culture is *the* defining feature of our species' evolutionary history, and thus of great relevance to the subfield of biological anthropology.

Culture in the particular sense refers to the fact that people live their lives within particular cultures, or ways of life. For example, although the "American way of life" is actually culturally diverse, with differences across regions, social classes, and ethnic groups, most Americans share very similar beliefs about such things as the value of a formal education, what kinds of clothes women and men should wear to the office, and which side of the road to drive on. Archaeologists, linguistic anthropologists, and cultural anthropologists tend to study people's lives in the context of a particular culture. In Chapter 2 we explore the concept of culture more deeply, but here it is important to know that when anthropologists use the term *culture* they are nearly always referring to ideas about the world and ways of interacting in society or in the environment in predictable and expected ways.

Classic Contributions
E. B. Tylor and the Culture Concept

LIKE OTHER ANTHROPOLOGISTS of the latter half of the nineteenth century, Edward B. Tylor believed that the social and cultural differences of humanity could be explained as the product of evolutionary forces. Tylor's primary intellectual concern throughout his career was developing an evolutionary sequence that would explain how people evolved from a state of what he called "primitive savagery" to more "advanced" levels of civilization. In his book *Primitive Culture*, published in 1871, he advanced his argument that humans are subject to evolutionary forces in all aspects of their lives, including what he called "culture," offering the now classic definition presented here. Although contemporary uses of the term *culture* have changed since Tylor's definition—mainly because anthropologists today reject Tylor's evolutionary perspective—Tylor's definition is important because it provided a basis for the scientific study of culture that has been central to the discipline ever since.

Culture or Civilization, taken in its wide ethnographic sense, is that complex whole which includes knowledge, belief, art, morals, law, custom, and any other capabilities and habits acquired by man as a member of society. The condition of culture among the various societies of mankind, in so far as it is capable of being investigated on general principles, is a subject apt for the study of laws of human thought and action.... [I]ts various grades may be regarded as stages of development or evolution, each the outcome of previous history, and about to do its proper part in shaping the history of the future. [Tylor 1871:1]

Questions for Reflection

1. How is this definition different from or similar to the notion of culture you had before taking an anthropology course?

2. Tylor believed that people acquire culture as members of a society. But how, specifically, might someone acquire his or her culture?

Cultural Relativism

All human lives are embedded in and shaped by culture. Anthropologists also carry with them basic assumptions about how the world works and what is right or wrong, which typically become apparent when one is studying a culture that makes completely different assumptions. One possible response to the gap in understanding that comes with being in another culture is **ethnocentrism**, assuming our way of doing things is correct, while simply dismissing other people's assumptions as wrong or ignorant. Such a position would render the attempt to understand other cultures meaningless and can lead to bigotry and intolerance. To avoid such negative outcomes, anthropologists have traditionally emphasized **cultural relativism**, the moral and intellectual principle that one

- **Ethnocentrism.** The assumption that one's own way of doing things is correct, while dismissing other people's practices or views as wrong or ignorant.

- **Cultural relativism.** The moral and intellectual principle that one should withhold judgment about seemingly strange or exotic beliefs and practices.

should seek to understand cultures on their own terms and withhold judgment about seemingly strange or exotic beliefs and practices.

Human Diversity

● **Diversity.** The sheer variety of ways of being human around the world.

Another of anthropology's major contributions to knowledge has been to describe and explain human **diversity**, the sheer variety of ways of being human around the world. When anthropologists talk about diversity, they mean something different from the popular usage of the term in the United States, which typically refers to different kinds of art, cuisine, dress, or dance, as well as differences among various racial and ethnic groups.

Defined anthropologically, diversity refers to multiplicity and variety, encompassing both similarity and difference. This idea of diversity-as-multiplicity can shed light on the cultural effects of globalization. For example, people now drink Coca-Cola, wear Levi's jeans, and watch CNN all over the world, leading many observers to believe that the diversity of human cultures is in decline because more and more people are participating in a global economy. Yet cultural differences do not just disappear. In fact, globalization creates many new opportunities for cultural diversity—differences *and* similarities—to thrive.

An example drawn from the southern Mexican state of Chiapas illustrates this point. In Chiapas, some indigenous people have adapted Coca-Cola for use in their religious and community ceremonies. For many generations Tztotzil Mayas [**tso**-tseel **my**-ahs] in the community of San Juan Chamula used alcoholic drinks—particularly fermented corn drinks and distilled sugar cane liquor—in their public and religious rites (J. Nash 2007) (Figure 1.3). To create these rites, traditional Mayan religious leaders blended Catholic and indigenous traditions, combining Catholicism's celebration of saints' days with the Maya belief that consuming intoxicating spirits helps individuals access sacred powers. Alcoholism, however, became a severe problem, and beginning in the 1940s many Maya began converting to Protestant sects that banned alcohol, eroding the power of traditional religious leaders. In the 1980s these leaders began substituting Coca-Cola for alcoholic drinks in ceremonies. Some leaders gained great personal wealth as distributors of Coca-Cola, deepening socioeconomic class

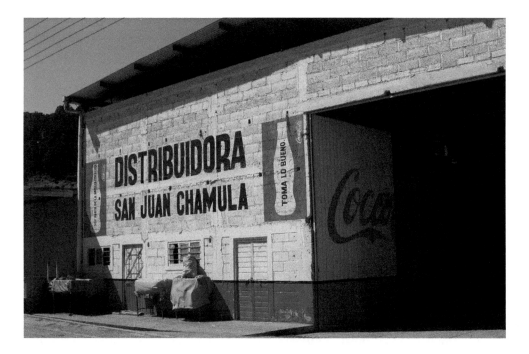

Figure 1.3   San Juan Chamula, Chiapas, Mexico.

divisions in the community (J. Nash 2007). But community members incorporated Coke into their ritual lives easily, accepting the notion that the soft drink's bubbles have powers once associated with alcohol—for example, the ability to help individuals belch out bad spirits residing in their bodies (M. Thomas 2008).

Here is a powerful example of diversity-as-multiplicity: globalization has brought changes to San Juan Chamula that resemble conditions in many other places around the globe, but Maya have imposed their own meanings on the soft drink, using it in ways that reinforce some of their own distinctive cultural traditions.

Change

As the previous example about globalization and Coca-Cola demonstrates, our world is dynamic and constantly changing. Anthropologists in each subfield are specialists in studying human change. For example:

- *Cultural anthropologists* study topics as diverse as how and why religious change happens; the effects of migration on communities that send and receive migrants; and how and why political violence can erupt in societies experiencing rapid social change.
- *Archaeologists* study the effects of climate change on past societies; how changes in material culture reflect ongoing social, economic, and political changes; and the processes through which complex state societies were formed and disintegrated.
- *Biological anthropologists* study the processes of human evolution and how our bodies and genetic makeup change in relation to environmental changes, migration, diseases, and other dynamics.
- *Linguistic anthropologists* study how new languages are formed when different languages come together, and how social changes, such as changes in gender relations, are reflected in and emerge from how people communicate with each other.

Some of these changes, particularly changes in cultural practices, can emerge over a few years or a generation or two. Others, like changes in human biology, can take many generations and are imperceptible to most living observers. Americans, for example, have gotten considerably taller than we were in colonial times, probably because of changes in diet. But this fact is largely unnoticed by modern Americans unless we tour colonial houses from the 1700s, where the doorways are not nearly as tall as those of today.

Anthropology also mirrors the changing world in which it is practiced. As new topics, issues, and problems emerge, anthropologists study things they would not have studied several decades before. Today, for example, archaeologists may study municipal garbage dumps to understand what people actually consume and throw away. Cultural and linguistic anthropologists explore how people create communities and identities and produce new forms of communication and community in cyberspace. Biological anthropologists specializing in primate behaviors design studies to aid wildlife conservation officials.

Moreover, the face of anthropology has changed dramatically in recent decades. Once a discipline dominated by white European and American men, anthropology is increasingly practiced by women and members of many ethnic and racial minority groups. In the United States today, in fact, women constitute the majority of professional anthropologists. Around the world, decolonization of former colonies has brought once excluded indigenous peoples and minorities into universities where many have studied anthropology, further expanding the kinds of backgrounds and perspectives represented in the global discipline.

Holism

In bringing together the study of human biology, prehistory, language, and social life under one disciplinary roof, anthropology offers powerful conceptual tools for understanding the entire context of human experience. The effort to synthesize these distinct approaches and findings into a single comprehensive explanation is called **holism**. It is American anthropology that has strived to be the most holistic, a legacy of German-born Franz Boas (1848–1942), long considered the founder of American anthropology, through his work in the American Anthropological Association and at Columbia University in the early twentieth century. His student Alfred Kroeber once described four-field anthropology as a "sacred bundle" (D. Segal and Yanagisako 2005).

In the discipline's early years, it was possible for individuals like Boas, Kroeber, and some of their students to work in all four subfields because the body of anthropological knowledge was so small. But within several decades, the expansion of the discipline and increasing specialization within its branches forced anthropologists to concentrate on a single subfield and topics within subfields, a continuing pattern today. In the face of specialization and calls to "unwrap the sacred bundle" (D. Segal and Yanagisako 2005)—that is, have the subfields go their separate ways—anthropology has struggled to retain its holistic focus.

And yet many anthropologists are deeply dedicated to holism, citing its ability to explain complex issues that no single subfield, much less any other social science, could explain as effectively (Parkin and Ulijaszek 2007). In "Doing Fieldwork: Conducting Holistic Research with Stanley Ulijaszek," we highlight how one anthropologist conducts research in a holistic fashion.

As Ulijaszek's research demonstrates, no single subfield by itself could address complex research problems. Working together, however, the subfields draw a compelling holistic picture of a complex situation. So how do anthropologists actually come to know such things? We turn to this issue in the next section.

• **Holism.** Efforts to synthesize distinct approaches and findings into a single comprehensive interpretation.

THINKING LIKE AN ANTHROPOLOGIST

Can you suggest ways that you may learn how people in your town or city view college students from your campus?

1.3 How Do Anthropologists Know What They Know?

Anthropology employs a wide variety of methodologies, or systematic strategies for collecting and analyzing data. As we explore in this section, some of these methodologies are similar to those found in other natural and social sciences, including methods that involve the creation of statistics and even the use of mathematical models to explain things. Other methods aimed at understanding different cultures are more closely allied with the humanities.

The Scientific Method in Anthropology

Anthropology often uses the **scientific method**, the most basic pattern of scientific research. The scientific method starts with the observation of a fact or group of facts, a verifiable truth. Next follows the construction of a hypothesis, which is a testable explanation for the fact. Then that hypothesis is tested with experiments, further observations, or measurements. If the data (the information the tests produce) show that the hypothesis is wrong, the scientist develops a new hypothesis and then tests it. If the new tests and the data produced seem to support the hypothesis, the scientist writes a description of what he or she did and found and shares it with other scientists. Other scientists then attempt to reproduce those tests or devise new ones, with a goal of disproving the hypothesis (Figure 1.4).

Note that this way of doing things is a method, not the pursuit of ultimate truths. The goal of the scientific method is to devise, test, and disprove hypotheses. Answering life's big questions—"Why are we here?"—is *not* the goal of science. At best, science can provide a reasonable degree of certainty only about more limited questions, such as "How did our species develop the traits we now have?" Researchers with different intellectual backgrounds and orientations ask different types of questions and look at data in different ways. Scientists tend to see such debates as beneficial to the practice of science because the more questions asked, the more observations made, and the more tests conducted, the more knowledge is produced.

* **Scientific method.** The standard methodology of science that begins from observable facts, generates hypotheses from these facts, and then tests these hypotheses.

Theories Guide Research

Theories, which are tested and repeatedly supported hypotheses, are key elements of the scientific method. A **theory** not only explains things; it also helps guide research by focusing the researcher's questions and making the findings meaningful.

* **Theory.** A tested and repeatedly supported hypothesis.

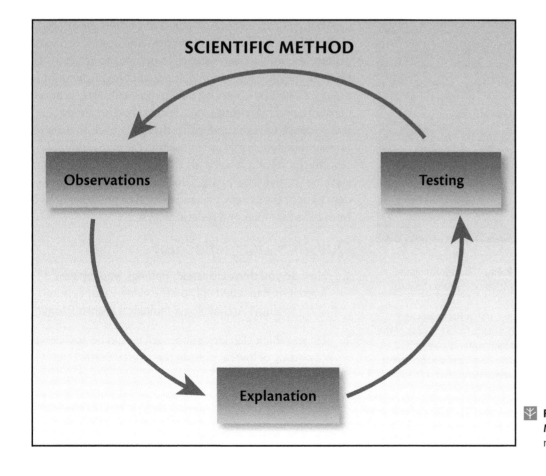

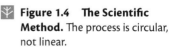

Figure 1.4 The Scientific Method. The process is circular, not linear.

Doing Fieldwork
Conducting Holistic Research with Stanley Ulijaszek

Stanley Ulijaszek is a British anthropologist who has been conducting research for several decades in the swamplands of coastal Papua New Guinea, an island state in the Southwest Pacific. In recent years, he has turned his attention to an interesting question: In this difficult landscape that is unsuited to agriculture, how do people acquire a sufficient, safe, and nutritious food supply? To answer this question properly requires substantial knowledge of the human biology, prehistory, and culture of coastal New Guinea.

At the center of this story is the sago palm, a palm tree that grows abundantly in swamps. Its stem contains starch, a staple food for the people who cultivate it. People cook sago in long sticks resembling dense French bread, eating it with a bit of fish. Sago is not a great staple food, because it is 99.5 percent starch, making it an excellent energy food, but it has few other nutrients. Worse, perhaps, is that sago is toxic when eaten uncooked or improperly prepared. Its toxicity threatens people with a specific genetic mutation that does not allow the red blood cells to carry the toxins out of

the body, a mutation common among coastal New Guinea populations. Thus, because of this toxicity, eating sago presented a risk to these coastal people (Ulijaszek 2007).

It turns out, however, that this same genetic mutation confers some resistance to malaria, a mosquito-borne infectious disease common in the tropics. The key to protecting the people while releasing the nutritional energy of sago is to separate the starch from the pith at the center of the sago palm by washing and straining it, then cooking the starch, all of which reduces its toxicity to safe levels. Archaeological evidence indicates that people in this region figured out this process at least 6,000 years ago, which is when they began leaving behind their hunting-and-gathering way of life to take up agriculture. Ulijaszek concludes that they adapted sago for human consumption by detoxifying it, which in turn allowed people's genetic mutation to survive, thus providing some resistance to malaria in this difficult environment. People then continued to pass on the genetic trait of malarial resistance.

Ulijaszek's research addresses an interesting puzzle about how humans can successfully adapt to a challenging natural environment, and how those changes are intertwined with genetic factors like the resistance to malaria. To achieve this, he drew on the evidence of cultural and linguistic anthropology, gained by observing how people cultivate, process, consume, and talk about sago. He also drew on archaeological evidence of sago production that goes back thousands of years, not necessarily by conducting the excavations himself, but by relying heavily on the evidence archaeologists working in that area had produced. He also drew on evidence about the genetic makeup of local populations drawn from blood samples and genetic analyses.

Cultivating Nutrition from the Sago Palm.   Transforming the pith of the sago palm into food is a complex process. First the pith must be chopped out of the trunk and pulverized using simple cutting and pounding tools, and then the starch must be leached from the dense mass of fiber using a frame made from the base of the leaf stalk in which the starch is pounded with water to release and strain the edible starch, leaving the inedible fiber behind in the frame. Later the sago flour is collected from a basin where it has settled.

Questions for Reflection

1. How do you think Ulijaszek's findings would have differed if he had relied only on the evidence of cultural anthropology? Archaeology? Biological anthropology?

2. Do you think Ulijaszek's approach would be applicable to a study of low-fat diets in the United States? How would you apply it?

While many Americans assume that a theory is some wild hunch or guess, when scientists use the term *theory*, they mean a carefully constructed hypothesis that has been tested and retested. There is rarely any guessing involved.

Quantitative Data Collection

Building and testing hypotheses and theories requires data. Anthropology's subfields employ a number of techniques for gathering and processing data. Some of these techniques use **quantitative methods**, which classify features of a phenomenon, count or measure them, and construct mathematical and statistical models to explain what is observed. Most quantitative research takes place in the subfields of biological anthropology and archaeology, although some cultural and linguistic anthropologists use quantitative techniques as well.

- **Quantitative method.** A methodology that classifies features of a phenomenon, counting or measuring them, and constructing mathematical and statistical models to explain what is observed.

As an illustration of quantitative research, consider the work of one of the authors of this book, Agustín Fuentes. His research examines the nature of human–monkey interactions, and how, when, and why diseases, such as viruses, get passed between these species. Fuentes and his team (including many undergraduate anthropology students) have observed monkeys and humans interacting in Bali, Singapore, and Gibraltar. In each location they recorded quantitative details about interactions: who interacts, how many individuals interact, the length of interactions, whether interactions are aggressive or friendly, whether physical contact between species occurs, and whether food is involved in the contact. They interviewed humans at the locations, sometimes using surveys or administering questionnaires, and collected detailed physical information about the landscape inhabited by the people and monkeys. They also took blood or fecal samples from both the monkeys and the humans, analyzing them for pathogens and parasites. All these variables were considered independently and then compared statistically to see what patterns emerged. Fuentes discovered that human–monkey interactions vary depending on the species of monkey, human cultural patterns, gender differences in humans, and sex differences in the monkeys (Fuentes 2007).

Qualitative Data Collection

Anthropologists also employ **qualitative methods**, in which the aim is to produce an in-depth and detailed description of social behaviors and beliefs. Qualitative research usually involves interviews with people as well as observations of their activities. Research data come in the form of words, images, or objects. In contrast with quantitative methods, qualitative research does not typically use research instruments like surveys or questionnaires. The research instrument is the researcher him- or herself, whose subjective perceptions and experience of the subject matter also become the basis for knowledge. The **ethnographic method**, which involves prolonged and intensive observation of and participation in the life of a community, is a qualitative methodology and is a hallmark of cultural anthropology.

- **Qualitative method.** A research strategy producing an in-depth and detailed description of social activities and beliefs.

- **Ethnographic method.** A prolonged and intensive observation of and participation in the life of a community.

Luis Vivanco, another of this book's authors, is a cultural anthropologist who uses qualitative methods to ask how global environmentalism changes people's relationships with nature in Latin America. In one of his projects, he conducted more than twenty months of research in Monteverde, Costa Rica, a rural community bordering a tropical cloud forest and renowned worldwide as a site of conservation and ecotourism. He interviewed local farmers, environmental activists, ecotourists, and scientists, usually on multiple occasions, sometimes with a tape recorder and notepad and other times in informal conversations at the local grocery store or in some other public setting (Figure 1.5). He observed these people interacting with others and participated in community events, including celebrations and public protests. Working as a volunteer in a nature preserve, he listened to how its managers and the ecotourists

Figure 1.5   Monteverde Bus. In Vivanco's research on environmentalism in Costa Rica, his interest in the social dynamics of ecotourism led him to spend a lot of time among ecotourists, such as the ones shown here arriving in Monteverde by bus.

talked about tropical rain forests. He collected newspaper clippings and reports from local environmental groups and took pictures of people going about their daily lives. His field notes, recordings, images, documents, and personal experiences with environmentalists and farmers have helped him understand environmentalism to be a complex arena of social conflict where people struggle not just over how to protect nature but also how to deal with rapid social changes caused by globalization (Vivanco 2006).

The Comparative Method

Unlike other scientists, anthropologists do not conduct experiments or make predictions. Instead, anthropologists use the **comparative method** (Kaplan and Manners 1972:42–43). The comparative method allows anthropologists to derive insights from careful comparisons of two or more cultures or societies. The actual "method" is nothing like a precise recipe for research, however, but a general approach, which holds that any particular detail of human behavior or particular social condition should not be seen in isolation but should be considered against the backdrop of the full range of behaviors and conditions in their individual social settings.

• **Comparative method.** A research method that derives insights from careful comparisons of aspects of two or more cultures or societies.

Some of the research of another of this book's authors, cultural anthropologist Robert Welsch, illustrates how anthropologists can use the comparative method. Welsch has conducted extended ethnographic research both in Papua New Guinea and in Indonesia (Welsch 2006). One of his research projects explicitly made use of comparative research strategies to understand the social and religious meanings of masks and carved objects in three societies along the Papuan Gulf of New Guinea that are now in museum collections. To conduct his comparative study, Welsch studied the museum collections, pored over published and unpublished accounts of the people who collected the masks, and interviewed older villagers about their traditional practices (Figure 1.6). He learned that although these three societies used the same kinds of objects, their distinct decorative styles expressed differences in the social purposes for which each society used the objects.

Figure 1.6   Boards Inside Longhouse at Naharo. Welsch visited many longhouses to discuss ritual carvings and their meaning as part of his comparative analysis of art and its social contexts in traditional societies of the Papuan Gulf. This image shows boards he was discussing with elders and their families in Naharo village.

When Anthropology Is Not a Science: Interpreting Other Cultures

Not all anthropologists characterize what they do as science. Describing other people requires an understanding of their inner lives and beliefs that no scientific methodology can grasp. Moreover, these days most cultural anthropologists disregard the scientific ideal of the researcher's detachment from the subject of study: the belief that researchers are not supposed to talk about what they feel and experience, or how emotions and experiences influence what they learn and know as anthropologists (Fabian 2001). The work of American anthropologist Renato Rosaldo (b. 1941), who studied headhunting in a Filipino society called the Ilongot [Ill-**lahn**-goht], illustrates this point of view. When Rosaldo (1989) asked the Ilongots to explain why they take heads, they explained that when a loved one dies, their grief turns to rage, and the only way to vent that rage and get on with life is to take the head of a traditional enemy. Rosaldo initially dismissed this explanation, assuming there had to be a "deeper" purpose for headhunting, such as creating group cohesion or allowing young men to prove their worthiness for marriage by showing they could kill an enemy.

Then Rosaldo's wife, Shelly, also an anthropologist, died in an accident during fieldwork in the Philippines. His own devastating loss generated a similar combination of grief and rage. While he was adjusting to Shelly's death, Rosaldo could grasp emotionally what the Ilongot were getting at. Dealing with the death opened his eyes to the force of emotions in social life, something he and most other anthropologists had never really considered. Rosaldo (1989) realized that his training as an anthropologist, which emphasized scientific detachment, accounted for his initial dismissal of Ilongot notions of headhunting. He concluded that his other interpretations of headhunting were not wrong, but they presented an incomplete picture of why Ilongot did it. He also concluded that ethnographic knowledge is an open-ended process; that is, as the ethnographer's own life experiences and knowledge change, so do his or her insights into other cultures.

The Anthropological Life
Anthropologists Are Innovators

In his book, *The Ten Faces of Innovation*, renowned industrial designer Tom Kelley (2006) describes the qualities of innovative people. At the top of his list is the anthropologist. As he says,

> The Anthropologist is rarely stationary. Rather, this is the person who ventures into the field to observe how people interact with products, services, and experiences in order to come up with new innovations. The Anthropologist is extremely good at reframing a problem in a new way, humanizing the scientific method to apply it to daily life. Anthropologists share such distinguishing characteristics as the wisdom to observe with a truly open mind; empathy; intuition; the ability to "see" things that have gone unnoticed; a tendency to keep lists of innovative concepts worth emulating and problems that need solving; and a way of seeking inspiration in unusual places. (*The Ten Faces of Innovation*).

Ethnographers know other cultures from particular points of view. Although they strive to see things from many perspectives—the perspectives of the many people they interview and observe—anthropologists' insights are always partial, indeed, only some of many possible interpretations of culture. But anthropological methods nevertheless produce rigorous and insightful—and, as we highlight in The Anthropological Life, innovative—perspectives on people's lives. Moreover, anthropologists do not just try to understand the world of culture and other human concerns; they also intervene in practical ways, which is an issue we explore next.

THINKING LIKE AN ANTHROPOLOGIST

How might you use a comparative perspective even if you only visit just one country while on vacation? Consider the other cultural contexts you have experienced and how these might provide a comparative framework for experiencing a novel society and culture.

1.4 How Do Anthropologists Put Their Knowledge to Work in the World?

Anthropological research is relevant and useful for addressing many social problems. At some point in their careers, most anthropologists get involved in work with practical, real-world concerns, applying their research skills and knowledge to the creation or implementation of policies, the management of social programs, the conduct of legal proceedings, or even the design of consumer products.

Applied and Practicing Anthropology

Practical applications are such an important component of anthropology that some anthropologists consider them the "fifth subfield." These practical applications include those of **applied anthropology**, anthropological research commissioned to serve an organization's needs, and those of **practicing anthropology**, the broadest category of anthropological work, in which the anthropologist not only performs research but also gets involved in the design, implementation, and management of some organization, process, or product. One reason some consider these two enterprises a fifth subfield is that the numbers of anthropologists doing these things has swelled in recent decades as university budget cuts have diminished job opportunities in academia. But the notion of a fifth subfield sets up a false dichotomy between academic (or theoretical) and practical (or applied) work, which have often been intertwined throughout the history of the discipline (Field and Fox 2007).

Putting Anthropology to Work

Putting anthropological skills and knowledge to work is a challenging enterprise, not least because of tensions it creates with some anthropologists who feel that "we should never forget that a commitment to improving the world is no substitute for understanding it" (Hastrup and Elass 1990:307). In spite of the challenges, however, anthropologists have effectively put their discipline to work addressing difficult social, health, and educational problems, as the following snapshots demonstrate.

Mary Amuyunzu-Nyamongo: Bringing Cultural Knowledge to Health Programs in Kenya

Like many other anthropologists, Kenyan anthropologist Mary Amuyunzu-Nyamongo (Figure 1.7) works on pressing social and health problems confronting her country. As founding director of the African Institute for Health and Development, she uses qualitative research to better understand how to make public health programs work within the specific social conditions and cultural contexts of Kenya where lack of trust in government directives is common. In her work, she emphasizes that impoverished and vulnerable communities should not be approached as sources of poor health practices but as key allies in the promotion of health through various forms of community engagement (Corbin et al. 2021). For example, when COVID-19 arrived in Kenya during 2020, Amuyunzu-Nyamongo coordinated a public health project in a Maasai community that trained respected community members—among them religious and traditional leaders, bus drivers, vendors, and young motorcycle riders—to challenge misinformation circulating about the virus and to promote positive behaviors such as mask wearing, social distancing, and other practices that reduce risks of infection. Wearing distinctive jackets and sashes with the message "#Social Mobilizers #Change Agents," these individuals played a critical role in communicating about COVID in locally meaningful ways that helped keep infection rates low.

Sara Gonzalez: Collaborative Archaeological Research with Indigenous Communities

Historically, archaeological excavation on American Indian lands was perceived by many Tribal nations as disrespectful of their ancestors, a threat to their sovereignty, and an expression of white settler colonialism in the guise of science. Even with the passage of federal and state laws protecting American Indian burial sites and remains in recent decades, this attitude has not necessarily disappeared, and many Tribal

• **Applied anthropology.** Anthropological research commissioned to serve an organization's needs.

• **Practicing anthropology.** Anthropological work involving research as well as involvement in the design, implementation, and management of some organization, process, or product.

Figure 1.7   Cultural Anthropologist Mary Amuyunzu-Nyamongo.

Figure 1.8   Archaeologist Sara Gonzalez.

nations continue to be wary of archaeology's intentions and practices. Given this history, many archaeologists have sought to develop meaningful new ways of working with indigenous communities, including University of Washington archaeologist Sara Gonzalez (Figure 1.8). In one recent project, Gonzalez et al. (2018) developed an archaeological field school in partnership with the Confederated Tribes of Grand Ronde Community of Oregon. Following protocols established by tribal leaders, Gonzalez, her students, and community collaborators used low-impact archaeological methods on Tribal lands to minimize their impact on its cultural heritage resources. They also conducted oral history interviews of Tribal members to contextualize and interpret their findings. Involving members directly in the work of documenting their history contributes to building capacity for the Tribe to effectively protect and manage its cultural heritage, while also building capacity among young non-Native archaeology students to work collaboratively with Indigenous communities.

James McKenna: The Naturalness of Co-sleeping

In much of the Western world, it is considered "healthy" for an infant to sleep in a crib, alone, for long stretches during the night. When a baby wakes frequently or wants to sleep alongside the parents, many see the child as too dependent and not doing well. In our society we also have many deaths from sudden infant death syndrome (SIDS) in which infants die in the night for unknown reasons. After decades examining how humans and their infants share social and physiological space, biological anthropologist James McKenna (1996; Figure 1.9) and his colleagues developed an explanation for how and why many SIDS deaths occur in the United States. Through intensive studies of sleeping mothers and infants around the planet, McKenna and his colleagues found that the frequent stirring of young infants, nursing, and the carbon dioxide and oxygen mix created by bodies close together are important aspects of the healthy development of human babies. Their work shows that co-sleeping assists the infant's development and dramatically reduces the risks of SIDS (see Chapter 3).

Figure 1.9   Biological Anthropologist James McKenna.

Marybeth Nevins: Supporting the Sustainability of Endangered Languages

There are an estimated 6,800 languages spoken in the world today, but many experts expect a great number of them to be gone within the next century. In the face of this problem, linguistic anthropologists have tended to dedicate themselves to the task of documenting endangered languages before their last speakers die. But in recent years, many linguistic anthropologists have also begun to work directly in efforts to protect and maintain endangered languages. Marybeth Nevins (Figure 1.10), of Middlebury College in Vermont, is one such anthropologist. Nevins, who has conducted her research in Arizona on the Fort Apache reservation and with the Susanville Indian Rancheria in California, is critical of the idea that academic linguists can be "superheroes" who come to "save" the local language (Nevins 2013, 2017). Many local language speakers, such as the Apache with whom Nevins works, respond with ambivalence to academic outsiders, whom they see as claiming a privileged authority over their language. In addition, as Nevins explains, in any community of speakers there are distinct cultural dynamics at work that lead to conflicting attitudes toward the language and its use. These matters are further complicated by competing networks of families, religious groups, and political factions that claim authority in and over the language. Nevins argues that instead of promoting what academic linguists determine to be "proper" ways of preserving language, linguists and other language professionals should approach programs as open-ended exchanges with other

Figure 1.10   Linguistic Anthropologist Marybeth Nevins.

members of a language community and support efforts that keep the language in use and relevant to community life. This approach, which she says is driven by the value of "sustainability" (as opposed to "revitalization" or "preservation"), requires outsiders to temper their own ideas about how to maintain the language, by listening to ways that Indigenous language users themselves perceive and represent their linguistic heritage.

These snapshots offer a small sample of the range of ways anthropologists put their discipline to work. In fact, anthropology offers useful perspectives and skills for almost any workplace or career, as we explore in "The Anthropological Life." As we discuss in the next section, anthropology—whether practical or academic in its orientation—raises important ethical issues.

The Anthropological Life
Key Characteristics of Anthropologists in the Workplace

In almost any imaginable workplace, individuals with an undergraduate or graduate background in anthropology are (adapted from Vivanco 2016):

- **Expert learners.** Anthropologists are constantly alert to opportunities to learn something new and connect it to something they already know. They are also habitually curious and willing to question the taken-for-granted, which can lead to innovation.
- **Pattern-seekers.** Anthropologists recognize that even in the most seemingly chaotic situation, there are social, historical, institutional, natural, and cultural patterns at work, and they are deft at identifying and understanding those patterns.
- **Equally Attentive to the Big Picture *and* the Details.** In anthropological research, there is (usually productive) tension between holism and particularism. The advantage for the anthropologist in the workplace is an ability to recognize how the most particular details connect to a big picture.
- **Questioners and listeners.** Based on the adage that 99 percent of a good answer is a good question, anthropologists learn to pose useful and interesting questions that elicit meaningful responses. They are equally good at listening, recognizing that any attempt to understand how and why a group of people think and act as they do requires active and sympathetic listening skills.
- **Accurate and precise.** Anthropologists are very good at identifying and creating accurate and precise evidence to support their claims.

- **Relationship builders.** Anthropologists are effective at identifying, understanding, and using social networks to create relationships and learn about the structure of social groups. As relationship builders, anthropologists recognize the importance of ongoing processes of give-and-take rooted in ethical relations with others.
- **Adaptable.** Anthropologists seek out things that are strange to them, unexpected, and outside their normal experience. Being flexible and adapting without judgment are key elements of anthropological training.
- **Communicators.** Being able to explain to people—especially verbally and in writing—what your research is about and why it's important requires strong communication skills, sometimes in a language other than your native tongue.
- **Effective at working with diversity and difference.** One of the hallmarks of anthropology is cultural relativism, or withholding judgment about people and perspectives that seem strange or exotic. Anthropologists develop a practical relativism based on recognition and respect for people who are different from them.
- **Critical thinkers.** Anthropologists must assess and evaluate on a regular basis the validity of their evidence. Critical reflection on what is known and still unknown are hallmarks of an anthropological education.

1.5 What Ethical Obligations Do Anthropologists Have?

- **Ethics.** Moral questions about right and wrong and standards of appropriate behavior.

Issues of **ethics**—moral questions about right and wrong and standards of appropriate behavior—are at the heart of anthropology, in two senses. First, anthropologists learn about how and why people in other cultures think and act as they do by researching their moral standards. Anthropologists often find out these things in the process of adjusting themselves to that culture's rules of ethical behavior.

Second, doing anthropology itself involves ethical relationships between researchers and others, raising many important and complex issues about the ethical conduct of anthropological research and practice. Ethics in anthropology—the moral principles that guide anthropological conduct—are not just a list of "dos and don'ts." Ethics is organically connected to what it means to be a good anthropologist (Fluehr-Lobban 2003). Here we consider three issues of common ethical concern for all anthropologists: doing no harm, taking responsibility for one's work, and sharing one's findings.

Do No Harm

The Nuremberg trials after World War II revealed that Nazi scientists had conducted harmful experiments on people in concentration camps. Scientists responded by establishing informal ethical codes for dealing with research subjects. But in 1974 abuse of medical research subjects in the United States led Congress to pass a law preventing unethical research with human subjects (Figure 1.11). This new law required research institutes and universities where research was conducted to establish an Institutional Review Board (IRB) to monitor all human subjects–based research. Medical, scientific, and social science organizations, including anthropologists, published codes of ethics emphasizing avoiding harm for people and animals who are the subjects of research.

"Do no harm" continues to be a bedrock principle in anthropology's primary code of ethics, the American Anthropological Association's Principles of Professional Responsibility (see inside front cover). Anthropologists routinely explain to people involved in their research any risks their participation might carry and obtain their "informed consent" to participate. Anthropological publications avoid sharing confidential information and commonly disguise their informants' identities in case those individuals could be targeted for harm because of what they say. Some anthropologists feel the principle of "do no harm" is not enough, asserting that anthropologists have a moral imperative to go further by doing good, by working for social justice and the alleviation of suffering in powerless and marginalized communities (Scheper-Hughes 1995; Fluehr-Lobban 2003).

Figure 1.11   Scandal at Tuskegee. Between 1932 and 1972, the US Public Health Service studied syphilis among white and black men. When scientists learned they could treat syphilis with penicillin, they gave it to the white men but not the black men. This abuse precipitated reform in the use of humans as research subjects in the United States.

Take Responsibility for Your Work

The primary ethical responsibility of anthropologists is to the people, species, or artifacts they study. Whether it is a pottery shard, baboon, or person, anthropologists are expected to side with their subjects. It does not mean that an archaeologist is expected to throw himself or herself in front of a bulldozer to prevent an archaeological site from being destroyed or that a cultural anthropologist should take up arms in defense of informants threatened by the police or the military. It means that anthropologists should take whatever action is possible when their subjects are threatened, short of doing something illegal. Such action might include helping prepare legal paperwork necessary to stop the bulldozer and conserve the artifacts.

What complicates this principle is that anthropologists are also responsible to other parties. For example, anthropologists also have a responsibility to the public, including the obligation to disseminate the findings of their research—even when something that is published can lower public opinion about a group of people. Anthropologists also have responsibilities to their sponsors who fund their research.

Share Your Findings

Historically, anthropologists took blood samples, did long-term ethnographic research, and excavated archaeological sites with little concern for those who might object to these activities, especially in indigenous communities. But during the past several decades, there has been a global sea change in favor of indigenous rights, and nowadays researchers routinely collaborate with native communities affected by their research.

An important ethical question now is who should control anthropological data and knowledge. For cultural anthropologists, the issue of control often relates to questions about who should define the research problem and preserve the data—the anthropologist or the subjects of research. Traditionally, the anthropologist has controlled those things, but communities have increasingly challenged anthropologists to provide them with research skills and information produced by research so they can continue to use them for their benefit after the anthropologist leaves.

> ### THINKING LIKE AN ANTHROPOLOGIST
>
> If you were studying a local Head Start program with few resources and you observed problems with local funding for the facility, what are some ways you might suggest for anthropologists to get involved in helping the organization?

Conclusion

Since the 1850s, anthropologists have been asking questions and developing perspectives on human societies past and present. Their expertise is on culture, diversity, how and why social change happens, the dynamics of human biology, and the ways people communicate with each other. The four subfields of anthropology—cultural anthropology, archaeology, biological anthropology, and linguistic anthropology—sometimes come together to offer powerful conceptual tools for understanding the whole context of human experience, an approach called holism. Together with the range of methodological tools represented in the discipline—sophisticated theories, quantitative methods, qualitative methods, and the comparative method—anthropology offers a highly relevant discipline for today's world.

But because anthropology deals with people, their bodies, and cultural artifacts meaningful to people, nearly everything anthropologists study invokes ethical concerns. Throughout this book we consider the ethics and application of anthropology research as we explore anthropological research in all four subfields. But let us begin our journey toward an understanding of anthropology with a fuller discussion of the concept of culture.

KEY TERMS

Anthropology   p. 5
Applied anthropology   p. 21
Archaeology   p. 8
Biological anthropology   p. 9
Colonialism   p. 7
Comparative method   p. 18
Cultural anthropology   p. 8
Cultural relativism   p. 11
Culture   p. 10

Diversity   p. 12
Empirical   p. 6
Ethics   p. 24
Ethnocentrism   p. 11
Ethnographic method
   p. 17
Evolution   p. 6
Holism   p. 14
Industrialization   p. 5

Linguistic anthropology
   p. 9
Othering   p. 7
Practicing anthropology   p. 21
Qualitative methods   p. 17
Quantitative methods   p. 17
Salvage paradigm   p. 7
Scientific method   p. 15
Theory   p. 15

Reviewing the Chapter

Chapter Section	What We Know	To Be Resolved
How did anthropology begin?	During the nineteenth century, the rise of industrialization, the influence of evolutionary theory, and colonialism generated questions about how cultures operate and interact.	Anthropologists are still fascinated—and challenged—by the contrasts and changes in culture worldwide as a result of globalization.
What do the four subfields of anthropology have in common?	Anthropologists in all subfields share certain fundamental approaches and concepts, including culture, cultural relativism, diversity, change, and holism.	Some anthropologists continue to debate the idea that the subfields, with their distinct methods and specialized research interests, belong together in the same discipline.
How do anthropologists know what they know?	Anthropology has a strong relationship with the scientific method; all anthropologists use theories, collect data, and analyze that data.	While most cultural anthropologists reject the possibility of a completely objective analysis of human culture, other subfields of anthropology, such as archaeology and biological anthropology, are thoroughly committed to the scientific method.
How do anthropologists put their knowledge to work in the world?	All four subfields have both theoretical and applied aspects. Applied research uses the insights of anthropological theory to solve problems.	Most anthropologists see an anthropological approach as providing a better way of understanding people from different backgrounds than any other discipline, but anthropologists continue to disagree among themselves about how to apply that understanding to address human problems.
What ethical obligations do anthropologists have?	Issues of ethics—moral questions about right and wrong and standards of appropriate behavior—are at the heart of anthropology.	Certain ethical issues have no easy resolution, such as the ideal that anthropologists should do no harm, or how to resolve conflicting responsibilities anthropologists have to different communities and publics.

READINGS

Numerous books examine the historical emergence and intellectual history of anthropology. One of the best is the 2007 book *A New History of Anthropology*, edited by Henrika Kuklick (Malden, MA: Wiley-Blackwell). A recent book, *Gods of the Upper Air: How a Circle of Renegade Anthropologists Reinvented Race, Sex, and Gender in the Twentieth Century* (Doubleday 2019) by Charles King, offers a lively history of American anthropology's early decades and its long-term impacts on popular thought.

The 2007 book *Anthropology Put to Work*, edited by Les Field and Richard G. Fox (Oxford: Berg Publishers), offers an introduction to both the opportunities and the disciplinary, social, and political complexities involved in applying anthropological expertise.

For a detailed exploration of the primary ethical concerns and dilemmas involved in anthropological research across the subfields, see Carolyn Fluehr-Lobban's 2003 book *Ethics and the Profession of Anthropology: Dialogue for Ethically Conscious Practice* (Walnut Creek, CA: AltaMira Press).

The 2007 book *Holistic Anthropology: Emergence and Convergence*, edited by David Parkin and Stanley Ulijaszek (New York: Berghahn Books), provides a contemporary perspective on the development of cross-subfield collaborations dedicated to the notion of holism.

Renato Rosaldo's 1989 book *Culture and Truth: The Remaking of Social Analysis* (Boston: Beacon Press) is a classic text that reflects critically on cultural anthropology's complicated relationship with the sciences and objectivity.

Culture

Giving Meaning to Human Lives

IN 2005, the body that governs intercollegiate sports in the United States, the National Collegiate Athletic Association (NCAA), banned teams with American Indian names and mascots from competing in its postseason tournaments. Clarifying the ruling, an official stated, "Colleges and universities may adopt any mascot that they wish. . . . But as a national association, we believe that mascots, nicknames, or images deemed hostile or abusive in terms of race, ethnicity or national origin should not be visible at the championship events that we control" (NCAA 2005). The ruling affected a number of schools with competitive sports programs: Florida State University (Seminoles), University of North Dakota (Fighting Sioux), and University of Illinois (Fighting Illini). Most schools eventually changed their mascot, or received a waiver based on expression of formal support from tribal authorities.

The ruling concluded decades of pressure from American Indians, students, and others who have argued that these mascots stereotype and denigrate Indian traditions. As one Oneida woman expressed, "We experience it as no less than a mockery of our cultures. We see objects sacred to us—such as the drum, eagle feathers, face painting, and traditional dress—being used, not in sacred ceremony, or in any cultural setting, but in another culture's game" (Munson 1999:14). To American Indians, the mascots seem to be just another attack on their cultures by non-Indians—attacks they have endured for several centuries.

Mascot Chief Illiniwek. Chief Illiniwek performs during a University of Illinois football game. In 2007, after a long controversy, the university retired the mascot.

Outraged students, alumni, and political commentators have countered that these mascots honor Indian traditions, pointing to the strength and bravery of Native Americans they hope to emulate in their teams. They also point out that the mascots are part of venerable traditions, part of the living cultures of their universities. Abandoning their mascots is like turning their backs on a part of their own cultural heritage.

This battle of words over college mascots has brewed for decades, with participants on both sides making claims, sometimes exaggerated, about the other side's motivations or intentions. Yet each side in the controversy calls into play an issue of deep concern to them that divides the participants into two opposed groups, each with a radically different interpretation of the issue that often views the opposing point of view as irrational or wrong. In that respect, it is a cultural conflict.

The concept of culture is at the heart of anthropology. *Culture* as anthropologists use the term refers to the perspectives and actions that a group of people consider natural, self-evident, and appropriate. These perspectives and actions are rooted in shared meanings and the ways people act in social groups. Culture is a uniquely human capacity that helps us confront the common problems that face all humans, such as communicating with each other, organizing ourselves to get things done, making life predictable and meaningful, and dealing with conflict and change.

The culture concept provides a powerful lens for making sense of what people do, why they do it, and the differences and similarities across and within societies, a point that leads to a key question: *How does the concept of culture help explain the differences and similarities in people's ways of life?* We can answer this question by considering a number of related questions around which this chapter is organized:

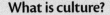

What is culture?

If culture is always changing, why does it feel so stable?

How do social institutions express culture?

Can anybody own culture?

In this chapter, we present an overview of how anthropologists approach culture and explain why it is so relevant to understanding human beliefs and actions. We also offer a definition of culture that informs and shapes the rest of this textbook. We start with the key elements that all anthropologists accept as central to any definition of culture.

2.1 What Is Culture?

Culture has been defined many ways by anthropologists, and there are nearly as many approaches to studying it as there are anthropologists. This lack of agreement does not frustrate or paralyze anthropologists. In fact, most anthropologists see this diversity of perspective as a sign of a vibrant discipline. We will examine the elements of culture in this section, emphasizing the different perspectives that enliven the discipline. A striking fact about this diversity is that most of these definitions emphasize a number of common features.

Elements of Culture

English scholar Sir Edward B. Tylor (1832–1917) was a founding figure of cultural anthropology. He offered the first justification for using the word *culture* to understand differences and similarities among groups of people. He defined culture as "that complex whole which includes knowledge, belief, art, morals, law, custom, and any other capabilities and habits acquired by man as a member of society" (1871:1). Two aspects of Tylor's definition, especially that culture is *acquired* (today we say *learned*) and that culture is a "complex whole," have been especially influential.

Since Tylor's time, anthropologists have developed many theories of culture, the most prominent of which are summarized in Table 2.1. We discuss many of these theories in later chapters and explore in more detail how they have changed over time. One of the most important changes in cultural theory is that early anthropologists

TABLE 2.1 PROMINENT ANTHROPOLOGICAL THEORIES OF CULTURE			
Theory	**Period**	**Major Figures**	**Definition**
Social evolutionism	1870s–1910s	E. B. Tylor (1871), Herbert Spencer (1874), L. H. Morgan (1877)	All societies pass through stages, from primitive state to complex civilization. Cultural differences are the result of different evolutionary stages.
Historical particularism	1910s–1930s	Franz Boas (1940), Alfred L. Kroeber (1916), Edward Sapir (1921)	Individual societies develop particular cultural traits and undergo unique processes of change. Culture traits diffuse from one culture to another.
Functionalism	1920s–1960s	Bronislaw Malinowski (1922)	Cultural practices, beliefs, and institutions fulfill psychological and social needs.
Structural-functionalism	1920s–1960s	A. R. Radcliffe-Brown (1952)	Culture is systematic, its pieces working together in a balanced fashion to keep the whole society functioning smoothly.
Neo-evolutionism	1940s–1970s	Leslie White (1949), Julian Steward (1955)	Cultures evolve from simple to complex by harnessing nature's energy through technology and the influence of particular culture-specific processes.
Cultural materialism	1960s–1970s	Marvin Harris (1979)	The material world, especially economic and ecological conditions, shape people's customs and beliefs.
Cognitive anthropology	1950s–1970s	Ward Goodenough (1965), Roy D'Andrade (1995)	Culture operates through mental models and logical systems.
Structuralism	1960s–1970s	Claude Lévi-Strauss (1961, 1969)	People make sense of their worlds through binary oppositions like hot–cold, culture–nature, male–female, and raw–cooked. These binaries are expressed in social institutions and cultural practices like kinship, myth, and language.
Interpretive anthropology	1970s–present	Clifford Geertz (1973), Victor Turner (1967), Mary Douglas (1966), Roy Wagner (1975)	Culture is a shared system of meaning. People make sense of their worlds through the use of symbols and symbolic activities like myth and ritual.
Post-structuralism	1980s–present	Renato Rosaldo (1989), James Clifford, George Marcus, Michael M. J. Fischer (Clifford and Marcus 1986; Marcus and Fischer 1986)	Not a single school of thought but a set of theoretical positions that rejects the idea that there are underlying structures that explain culture. Embraces the idea that cultural processes are dynamic, and that the observer of cultural processes can never see culture completely objectively.

tended to see the cultures in societies with simple technologies as more fixed and stable than anyone does today. Nevertheless, across all these theories, there are seven basic elements that anthropologists agree are critical to any theory of culture.

Culture Is Learned

Although all human beings are born with the ability to learn culture, nobody is born as a fully formed cultural being. The process of learning a culture begins at birth, and that is partly why our beliefs and conduct seem so natural to us: we have been doing and thinking in certain ways since we were young. For example, the Onge [ahn-**gay**], an indigenous group who live in the Andaman Islands in the Indian Ocean, learn from a very early age that ancestors cause periodic earthquakes and tidal waves. When these natural events occur, Onge have a ready-made explanation for how the world works, guiding their responses so that they do not have to learn how to deal with these things anew every time they occur. Anthropologists call this process of learning the cultural rules and logic of a society **enculturation**.

- **Enculturation.** The process of learning the social rules and cultural logic of a society.

Enculturation happens both *explicitly* and *implicitly*. Your student experience illustrates how enculturation processes have shaped you. Throughout your schooling, your teachers have explicitly taught you many things you need to know to be a productive member of society: to write, to analyze a text, to do mathematics, and so on (Figure 2.1). But you have also learned many other things that are more implicit, or not clearly expressed. These lessons include obedience to authority and respect for social hierarchy, learned, for example, from sitting in class facing forward in rows so the teacher can control your attention and movement. Bells and announcements over the loudspeakers regulated your activities and the flow of your day. By the time you reach college, these patterns are so ingrained that you know more or less exactly what to do when you walk into a classroom. Enculturation hasn't stopped, though; it continues throughout your life.

Culture Uses Symbols

Clifford Geertz (1926–2006), one of the best-known American anthropologists of recent times, proposed that culture is a system of **symbols**—a symbol being something that conventionally stands for something else—through which people make sense of the world. Symbols may be verbal or nonverbal. Symbols are things that people in a given culture associate with something else, often something intangible, such as motherhood, family, God, or country. To illustrate this point, Geertz posed an interesting question: How do we know the difference between a wink and a twitch (Geertz 1973:6–7)?

- **Symbol.** Something—an object, idea, image, figure, or character—that represents something else.

As movements of the eye, winks and twitches are identical, but the difference between them is enormous, as anyone who has experienced the embarrassment of mistaking one for the other can attest. A twitch is an involuntary blink of the eye and generally speaking has no symbolic significance. A wink, however, communicates a particular message to a particular someone, and it takes a lot of implicit knowledge, first, to decide if it is a wink or a twitch, and second, to understand what it communicates.

Figure 2.1 Do You Get It? You were enculturated to read from left to right. But when speakers of Hebrew language are taught to read, such as those who might read this cartoon from a Hebrew language newspaper, they begin on the right and move left.

In an instant, we must consider a number of questions: Is there intent? What is the intent—conspiracy, flirtation, parody, ridicule, or something else? Would it be socially appropriate for this person to wink at me, and under what conditions? Underlying our considerations, which may barely rise to the surface of consciousness, is a shared system of meaning in which we (and the winker) participate that helps us communicate with and understand each other. Interestingly, what sounds like a complex computational process when broken down into these many decision points actually comes quite naturally to the human mind. This is due to the human capacity for learning with symbols and signs that otherwise have little meaning outside a given culture.

Geertz's concept of culture, often called the **interpretive theory of culture**, is the idea that culture is embodied and transmitted through symbols that people interpret to make sense of their experience. This fundamental concept helped anthropologists clarify the symbolic basis of culture, something virtually all anthropologists take for granted today. Because culture is based on symbols, culture is implicit in how people think and act, so they rarely, if ever, recognize culture for what it is; it is simply natural to them. In fact, people express culture in *everything* they do—playing games, speaking a language, building houses, growing food, making love, raising children, and so on (Figure 2.2). The meanings of these things—and the symbols that underlie those meanings—differ from group to group, and, as a result, people do things and organize themselves differently around the world. These differing meanings are what make the Balinese Balinese, Zapotecs Zapotecs, and Americans Americans.

• **Interpretive theory of culture.** A theory that culture is embodied and transmitted through symbols.

Cultures Are Dynamic, Always Adapting and Changing

In a globalized world with high levels of migration across cultural borders, communication flowing in all directions, and social and ethnic mixing, it is often impossible to say with any certainty where one culture or social group ends and another begins. As a result, many anthropologists today talk less about culture as a totally coherent and static *system* of meaning and more about the *processes* through which social meanings are constructed and shared.

Culture is a *dynamic* process. Social groups are not uniform or homogeneous, because not everybody interprets the events of everyday life in the same way, nor do they blindly act out scripts already laid out for them to perform. Cultural processes are emergent, fluid, and marked by creativity, uncertainty, differing individual meaning, and social conflict. Relations of power and inequality routinely permeate these cultural processes.

Culture Is Integrated with Daily Experience

As cultural beings, how we relate to the world seems natural to us, transparent, obvious, inevitable, and necessary. Our sense of passing time, for example, might contrast sharply with that of people in other cultures. In Western cultures, we think of time as an entity that moves from past to present to future. This concept—an element of culture—has a critical influence on our daily lives, because it helps us organize and regulate our activities every day. It also motivates us to make plans, since this concept of time leads us to believe that time must be used or it will be lost.

Understanding that culture comprises a dynamic and interrelated set of social, economic, and belief structures is a key to understanding how the whole of culture operates. The integration

Figure 2.2   It's Like Getting a Joke. When a popular comedian like Trevor Noah tells a funny joke, most of us barely think about what makes it so funny. Like other examples of culture Geertz discussed, we just "get it."

Figure 2.3   Yummy . . . or Not. A meal of insect larvae might make some Americans vomit or retch, which shows how powerful cultural beliefs are: they actually provoke a biological response to something that is perfectly digestible, if not healthy and delicious.

• **Cross-cultural perspective.** Analyzing a human social phenomenon by comparing that phenomenon in different cultures.

of culture across these domains leads to expectations that are specific to a given social group. For example, white middle-class American parents think it is "natural" for their babies to sleep in single beds, often in their own rooms (Small 1998:116–18). They believe that sleeping with their babies creates emotional dependence. In much of American society, which prizes personal independence and self-reliance, such dependence seems damaging to the child. Other societies, however, find these ideas strange and exotic. The Gusii of Kenya, for example, think it is "natural" to sleep with their babies, not to mention holding them constantly during waking hours, precisely because they *want* them to grow up to be dependent on others. For them, proper human behavior means constantly relying on other people.

How we sleep also demonstrates that activities you might think of as "natural"—that is, biologically based, as sleeping is, and therefore universally the same for all humans—are actually culturally patterned (see also Chapter 3). Culture helps shape the basic things all humans must do for biological and evolutionary survival, like eating, sleeping, drinking, defecating, having sex, and so on. There is no better illustration of this fact than food preferences. As omnivores, humans can eat an enormous range of foods. But many Americans' stomachs churn at the thought of eating delicacies like rotten shark flesh (Iceland), buffalo penis stew (Thailand), or dogs (East Asia) (Figure 2.3).

No other animal so thoroughly dwells in artificial, or human-made, worlds of its own creation. Anthropologists stress that a **cross-cultural perspective** (analyzing a human social phenomenon by comparing it to phenomena in different cultures) is necessary to appreciate just how "artificial" our beliefs and actions are, as well as the variety of possible ways of being human. Recognition of that possibility requires an open mind, and it is one reason many notable people have been drawn to the study of cultural anthropology, as we present in "The Anthropological Life."

Culture Shapes Everybody's Life

White middle-class North Americans tend to believe they have no culture, in the same way that most people feel they have no accent. But the other side of the coin is the tendency to view minorities, immigrants, and others who differ from white middle-class norms as "people with culture," as compared to people who have what they understand to be as a fairly general American culture. In the United States, these ideas are tied to social and institutional power: the more "culture," in this sense of the term, one appears to have, the less power one wields; the more power one has, the less one appears to have culture (Rosaldo 1989). This power of mainstream culture over ethnic cultures is about the relationships of power and inequality mentioned earlier. In fact, by differing from mainstream patterns, a group's culture becomes more visible to everyone. It is in this sense that groups with the most obvious cultures tend to be the least powerful. Nevertheless, *all* people's lives are embedded in and shaped by culture.

Culture Is Shared

The notion that culture is shared refers to the idea that people make sense of their worlds and order their lives through their participation in social groups. Culture is not a product of individual psychology or biology, nor is it reducible to either of these things. As a result, anthropologists generally accept that purely psychological and biological explanations of human experience are inadequate.

The Anthropological Life
Cultural Anthropology and Human Possibilities

Many notable people have studied cultural anthropology in college, among them prominent business people, politicians, writers, entertainers, and even cooking show hosts. Reflecting on their interest in anthropology, some of these individuals point to the cross-cultural perspective, and its recognition of the many possibilities for being human, as especially enriching for their lives and work.

Cross-cultural exposure can spark and nurture the imagination and creativity (Kennicott 2011). This is certainly the case for master cellist Yo-Yo Ma, who studied anthropology at Harvard University and observes that he brings an "anthropological spirit" to everything he does as a professional musician, exploring many global musical traditions (Kennicott 2011). This was true of novelist Kurt Vonnegut, as well. He once explained that one of his most famous books—*Cat's Cradle*, for which he was awarded an MA in anthropology from the University of Chicago—"was anthropology, but invented anthropology; in it, I wrote about an invented society" (Vonnegut 2016). A number of prominent science fiction writers also studied or were heavily influenced by anthropology—using its cross-cultural perspective to imagine alternative worlds, galactic universes, and alternative social possibilities—among

them Ursula LeGuin, Samuel R. Delaney, and Michael Crichton of *Jurassic Park* fame. Poets have also traced inspiration from the cross-cultural perspective, such as Gary Snyder, who channeled his undergraduate anthropological training focused on myth and ritual into his writings as a "shaman" communicating nature's insights and lessons.

Cultural anthropology's appreciation for human possibility has also inspired other individuals to be agents of social change. The cross-cultural perspective emphasizes that no human behavior or belief is set in stone, so where there is injustice or social problems, the recognition of humanity as flexible, adaptable, and responsive to circumstances can provide a powerful inspiration. Prominent anthropology-trained activists include Amy Goodman, of *Democracy Now*, who studied the medical anthropology of women's reproductive rights at Radcliffe College, and the environmental activist Michael Shellenberger, founder of various prominent initiatives including the Breakthrough Institute and the organization Environmental Progress. This inspiration extends to activist musicians who sing about political and social causes, among them Tracy Chapman and South African singer Johnny Clegg, who also studied cultural anthropology.

An individual's comprehension of anything is generally based on what his or her group defines collectively as proper and improper. Anthropologists commonly refer to such definitions as **cultural constructions**, which refers to the fact that people collectively "build" meanings through common experience and negotiation. In the debate over college mascots, for example, both sides collectively "constructed" the significance of these images and symbols for both Indians and colleges through their debates, protests, and discussions. A "construction" derives from past collective experiences in a community, as well as lots of people talking about, thinking about, and acting in response to a common set of goals and problems.

• **Cultural construction.** The meanings, concepts, and practices that people build out of their shared and collective experiences.

Cultural Understanding Involves Overcoming Ethnocentrism

One of the key features of culture is that it makes us feel that the ways we do things are correct, that is, that we do things—or think things out—in the "right" way and everybody else thinks and does things incorrectly. As we mentioned in Chapter 1, feeling that everyone else does things the wrong way and that our way of doing things is right is called *ethnocentrism*. For anthropologists, who like all other humans have a culture, ethnocentrism presents a major problem. Overcoming ethnocentrism is the first step to understanding other cultures. Living with a community provides access to understanding what other people do, say, think, and believe, but if we are constantly judging their society and how it does things by our own goals, morals, and understandings, we cannot ever understand them in their own terms.

From the beginning of cultural anthropology in America, anthropologists have argued that the only way to understand other cultures is in terms of that other culture's own goals, ideas, assumptions, values, and beliefs, which is the concept of *cultural relativism*. A relativistic perspective is a central means of overcoming ethnocentrism, and it is a major feature of the anthropological perspective on culture.

But understanding another culture on its own terms does not mean that anthropologists necessarily accept and defend all the things people do. Even though the job of an anthropologist is not to judge other cultures but learn to understand how and why other peoples do things as they do, anthropologists still possess basic values as individuals and as members of their particular societies. A relativistic perspective is simply a useful tool that can help anthropologists overcome ethnocentrism and begin to see matters from the point of view of another culture.

A number of anthropologists, in fact, advocate **critical relativism**, or taking a stance on a practice or belief only after trying to understand it in its cultural and historical context. Critical relativism also holds that no group of people is homogeneous, so it is impossible to judge an entire culture based on the actions or beliefs of a few (Merry 2003). For example, many North Americans practice male circumcision, which other societies consider abhorrent, including people in the German city of Cologne, who banned circumcision in 2012 as a human rights abuse. There is even a small but growing social movement in the United States that condemns the practice along similar lines. But when people from other societies or members of this movement criticize this practice, they are not condemning our entire culture.

Another motive for advocating critical relativism is that, in an extreme form, cultural relativism can be a difficult position to uphold. It can lead to **cultural determinism**, the idea that all human actions are the product of culture, which denies the influence of other factors, like physical environment and human biology, on human behavior. Some critics also argue that extreme relativism can justify atrocities like genocide, human rights abuses, and other horrific things humans do to one another. For some background on the origins of relativism in anthropology, see "Classic Contributions: Franz Boas and the Relativity of Culture."

Defining Culture in This Book

Although all anthropologists agree that these seven elements of culture are critical to any definition of it, in their research, different anthropologists emphasize or interpret these elements differently, which contributes to the diversity of culture theories expressed in Table 2.1. So while we too accept the importance of these key elements to any definition, we do approach culture throughout this book in a particular way. Building on the more general definition provided in Chapter 1, we define culture as *those collective processes through which people in social groups construct and naturalize certain meanings and actions as normal and even necessary*. In whatever manner any group of people does something, their way seems like the only sensible way to people in that community—it seems natural, obvious, and appropriate—even though other people might only scratch their heads, perplexed. No matter how much our culture changes during our lifetimes, our reactions to the people and things around us always seem normal or natural.

This is a constructivist view of culture, by which we mean that culture is not a static set of rules or a totally coherent system of symbolic beliefs that people "have" or "carry" like a toolbox that gets passed down from generation to generation, which have been common views of culture among anthropologists. Culture, in fact, is more dynamic, emergent, and changing than these ideas allow, as cultures intermingle

- **Critical relativism.** Taking a stance on a practice or belief only after trying to understand it in its cultural and historical context.

- **Cultural determinism.** The idea that all human actions are the product of culture, which denies the influence of other factors, like physical environment and human biology, on human behavior.

because of cross-border interconnections such as migration, global media, economic globalization, and other dynamics of our contemporary world. Moreover, culture is emergent and even unstable, responding to innovation, creativity, and struggles over meaning. The power of this definition is that by presenting culture as a dynamic and emergent process based on social relationships, it leads anthropologists to study the ways cultures are created and re-created constantly in people's lives.

Throughout this chapter and in subsequent chapters we illustrate how this approach to understanding culture works. But this definition does raise an immediate question: If culture is a dynamic process, why doesn't it always feel that way to people? We deal with this question in the next section.

Classic Contributions
Franz Boas and the Relativity of Culture

GERMAN-BORN FRANZ BOAS (1858–1942) was a pioneer anthropologist and the major figure responsible for establishing anthropology in America. Although he had a doctorate in physics, he became interested in studying non-Western cultures while conducting research on Baffin Island (Newfoundland) on the color of ice and sea water. He befriended many Inuit (so-called Eskimos) and learned that they thought about the world differently; for example, they did not distinguish between the colors green and blue. From these conversations he learned a valuable lesson that would be at the heart of his work for the rest of his life: to learn about another people's perspective, one has to try to overcome one's own cultural framework. This perspective has come to be known as cultural relativism (see Chapter 1).

Franz Boas. Posing for a museum display about the Hidatsa at the American Museum of Natural History.

The data of ethnology prove that not only our knowledge, but also our emotions are the result of the form of our social life and the history of the people to whom we belong. If we desire to understand the development of human culture we must try to free ourselves of these shackles. This is possible only to those who are willing to adapt themselves to the strange ways of thinking and feeling of primitive people. If we attempt to interpret the actions of our remote ancestors by our rational and emotional attitudes we cannot reach truthful results, for their feeling and thinking were different from ours. We must lay aside many points of view that seem to us self-evident, because in early times they were not self-evident. It is impossible to determine a priori those parts of our mental life that are common to mankind as a whole and those due to the culture in which we live. A knowledge of the data of ethnology enables us to attain this insight. Therefore it enables us also to view our own civilization objectively. [Boas 1940:636; translated from the original German published in 1889 as *Die Ziele der Ethnologie*]

Questions for Reflection

1. Do you think it is really possible to, as Boas said, "free ourselves of these shackles" (our own self-evident points of view)? Why and how? If you do not think it is possible, why not?

2. Do you think we can even know what our self-evident points of view are? How?

> **THINKING LIKE AN ANTHROPOLOGIST: CULTURE**
>
> How can an understanding of the complexities of culture help us make sense of the day-to-day world in which we live? Give an example from your life to illustrate your answer.

2.2 If Culture Is Always Changing, Why Does It Feel So Stable?

Imagine how chaotic life would be if you could not expect the same rules and processes for interacting with others from one week to the next. People need cultural stability. If we always had to stop and think about changes in the rules of social interaction, we could not function in our society. The very power of culture is that its processes feel totally natural and simultaneously predictable. Yet the previous section defined culture in a way that emphasizes its processes as dynamic and emergent. So how does something feel stable if it is so dynamic?

The concept of enculturation—the idea that people have been doing or believing things for much of their lives—only partly explains why culture feels so stable. There are a number of other features of culture—symbols, values, norms, and traditions—that help explain the sense of stability that people feel about it.

Symbols

One way of approaching the issue of cultural stability and change is by examining symbols (Sahlins 1999). A symbol, as we noted, is something that conventionally stands for something else. The relationship between the symbol and what it refers to is arbitrary, based on no particular rhyme or reason (Figure 2.4). Symbols can be more than just images or concepts, however; people also use their bodies as symbols. In Japan, for example, bowing is a form of greeting, but depending on how low one bows, it may also symbolize respect, apology, gratitude, sincerity, remorse, superiority, or humility.

A society will store its conventional meanings in symbols because their meanings tend to be stable. But symbols and their meanings can and do change, sometimes dramatically. For example, during the Spanish conquest of the Peruvian Andes in the sixteenth century, the Spaniards carried banners of their patron saint, Santiago Matamoros, to ensure victory over the Indians. The Indians quickly absorbed Santiago into their native religion. They identified Santiago as their own god of thunder and lightning, Illapa, who they believed was a shape shifter and changed forms. To the Indians, Santiago symbolized the power of their own mountain gods and encouraged resistance against the Spaniards (Silverblatt 1988).

Figure 2.4 Love, Affection . . . and Toilets. Symbols are arbitrary. In the United States and several other countries, the heart conventionally symbolizes love and affection. But in rural Sweden and other parts of Scandinavia people also associate the heart with outhouses, or rustic toilets (Lonely Planet 2014).

- **Values.** Symbolic expressions of intrinsically desirable principles or qualities.

Values

Studying values also helps us understand how change and stability are so closely related. **Values** are symbolic expressions of intrinsically desirable principles or qualities. They refer to that which is moral and true for a particular group of people. For example, "Mom and apple pie" symbolize American core values (values that express the most basic qualities central to a culture), such as patriotism or loyalty to country. In the United States, "Mom" expresses the purity of selfless sacrifice for the greater good.

"Apple pie," a common food since colonial times, expresses Americans' shared heritage. Of course, not everybody eats apple pie and not every mother is loyal to her family, much less sacrifices herself for the greater good. The point is not that these ideals reflect what actually happens in the real world. Rather, they orient thinking about one's obligations as a citizen, like putting aside differences with other Americans and being willing to sacrifice oneself for love of family and country.

Values are conservative in that they conserve prevailing ideas about social relations and morality. Yet this does not mean that a community's values do not change. Nor does it mean that within a society or community people will not have opposing values. It is not uncommon for people to hold conflicting values simultaneously.

Norms

While values provide a general orientation for social relations, norms are more closely related to actual behavior. **Norms** are typical patterns of behavior, often viewed by participants as the rules of how things should be done. In our society, for example, it would be unimaginable to haggle over the price of toothpaste at the grocery store because everyone expects you to pay the listed price. But in many other societies, especially in the Arab world and in Indonesia, the norm is just the opposite: no matter how small the item, it is considered rude to *not* haggle. In such places, taking the first asking price disrespects the seller. For more expensive items, such as a smartphone, buyers and sellers may expect to haggle over the price for an hour.

Norms are stable because people learn them from an early age and because of the social pressure to conform. Norms also tend to be invisible (we're usually not conscious of them) until they are broken, as visitors to a different society or even city often find when they do things the "wrong" way. The scowls or expressions of disapproval you might receive provide a **social sanction**, a reaction or measure intended to enforce norms and punish their violation. Long-established norms may eventually become **customs**, which have a codified and law-like aspect.

Traditions

Tradition usually refers to the most enduring and ritualized aspects of a culture. People often feel their traditions are very old, which justifies actions that make no logical sense in contemporary times. With such justifications, individuals and groups go to great lengths to protect their traditions. The controversy between Indians and NCAA schools over mascots with which we opened this chapter illustrates how powerful such traditions can be.

But anthropologists are aware that where traditions are concerned, appearances can be deceiving (Hobsbawm and Ranger 1983). For example, Scottish people often celebrate their identity with bagpipes and kilts made from tartans, plaid textiles made of stripes of different widths and colors that identify the wearers' clans. But these traditions, while indeed venerable, are not actually ancient. As a matter of fact, these objects, and the sense of a distinctive tradition they symbolize, emerged only during the eighteenth and nineteenth centuries (Trevor-Roper 1983). An English iron industrialist designed the kilt as we know it for his workers in the late 1700s. As the kilt caught on in the Scottish Highlands, textile manufacturers began producing distinctive plaids to expand sales and found willing buyers among clan chiefs. The chiefs wanted to distinguish themselves and their ancestry as unique, so they adopted distinctive designs. When England's King George IV made a state visit to Scotland in 1822, the organizers heavily promoted the use of kilts and tartans to enhance the pageantry of the visit. This occasion legitimized Highlands culture and established the look as a national institution. The power of tartans comes not from their antiquity but from

- **Norms.** Typical patterns of actual behavior as well as the rules about how things should be done.

- **Social sanction.** A reaction or measure intended to enforce norms and punish their violation.

- **Customs.** Long-established norms that have a codified and law-like aspect.

- **Tradition.** Practices and customs that have become most ritualized and enduring.

Figure 2.5   Another "Tradition" That Might Surprise You. Like the use of tartans in Scotland, Sumo wrestling in Japan feels ancient, although key features of it, such as the practice of declaring one person champion, are less than 100 years old.

their association with the clans that have long been central to Scottish Highlander social life. Of course, knowing that a particular tradition may be a recent invention does not mean people are any less protective of it (Figure 2.5).

Historically, anthropologists have emphasized that culture is "shared" among a group of people, implying a kind of uniformity and stability in culture. Clearly, people need a relatively stable and common base of information and knowledge in order to live together. But these different aspects of culture—symbols, values, norms, and traditions—are features that seem stable and common even though they may not be shared by everybody in a society. There is another reason culture feels stable. It is that culture is expressed through social institutions, a theme we turn to next.

THINKING LIKE AN ANTHROPOLOGIST: CULTURE

Most students think it is easy to identify the symbols, values, norms, and traditions that support other people's practices. But they find it more difficult to think about their own daily practices in the same terms. Use any of your own daily practices to illustrate how these four features of culture reinforce your own behavior.

2.3 How Do Social Institutions Express Culture?

• **Social institutions.** Organized sets of social relationships that link individuals to each other in a structured way in a particular society.

The **social institutions** of any society are the organized sets of social relationships that link individuals to each other in a structured way in a particular society. These institutions include patterns of kinship and marriage (domestic arrangements, the organization of sex and reproduction, raising children, etc.), economic activities (farming, herding, manufacturing, and trade), religious institutions (rituals, religious organizations, etc.), and political forms for controlling power. Each culture has its norms, values, and traditions for how each of these activities should be organized and, in each case, they can vary greatly from one society to another because of cultural differences. Here we consider how mid-twentieth-century anthropologists approached culture's relationship to social institutions; we then turn to examine how changes in these institutions can shape cultural patterns, which ultimately transform the social institutions themselves.

Culture and Social Institutions

From the 1920s to the 1960s, many anthropologists understood culture as the glue that holds people together in ordered social relationships. Associated with British anthropologists Bronislaw Malinowski and A. R. Radcliffe-Brown, this theory, known as **functionalism**, holds that cultural practices and beliefs serve purposes for society, such as explaining how the world works, organizing people into roles so they can get things done, and so on. Functionalists emphasize that social institutions function together in an integrated and balanced fashion to keep the whole society functioning smoothly and to minimize social disruption and change.

> • **Functionalism.**
> A perspective that assumes that cultural practices and beliefs serve social purposes in any society.

As an illustration of functional analysis, think back to the case of the Onge, the people who believe their ancestors make earthquakes and tidal waves. A functionalist would focus on how Onge beliefs about their ancestors explain how the natural world works and how these beliefs in turn help shape and are shaped by their migratory hunting-and-gathering existence. Working together with other structures of Onge society, such as political organization, economics, kinship, and so on, these beliefs contribute to the maintenance of an ordered society.

For functionalists, cultures were closed, autonomous systems. But critics insisted, even at its height of popularity, that functionalism's vision of culture was *too* stable. In fact, not all societies function smoothly, and functionalism's static view of culture could not explain history and social change. One of Britain's most prominent anthropologists, E. E. Evans-Pritchard, famously broke with functionalists in 1961 when he said that anthropology should not model itself on the natural sciences but on humanistic disciplines, especially history with its processual focus (Evans-Pritchard 1961).

In spite of its shortcomings, functionalism has left important legacies, especially that of the **holistic perspective**, a perspective that aims to identify and understand the whole—that is, the systemic connections between individual cultural beliefs, practices, and social institutions—rather than the individual parts. This does not mean contemporary anthropologists still see a society as wholly integrated and balanced. Rather, the holistic perspective is a methodological tool that helps show the interrelationships among different domains of a society, domains that include environmental context, history, social and political organization, economics, values, and spiritual life. Thus, the life of a community becomes expressed through the social relationships among its members, organized as they are through their social institutions. To understand how changes in cultural values can lead to changes in social institutions, consider the relationship between diet, industrialization, and sexual deviance.

> • **Holistic perspective.**
> A perspective that aims to identify and understand the whole—that is, the systematic connections between individual cultural beliefs and practices—rather than the individual parts.

American Culture Expressed Through Breakfast Cereals and Sexuality

Let us begin by posing a simple question: Why do so many Americans prefer cereal for breakfast? Most of us today prefer cereal because it is part of a "healthy and nutritious diet" (the standard industry line) or because of its convenience. In any event, eating cereal for breakfast has become a social norm for tens of millions of Americans. It builds on positive cultural values attributed to health and on the symbolism of "healthy food = a healthy body." But Corn Flakes began in the nineteenth century

⅄ **Figure 2.6   The Effects of Masturbation, Circa 1853.** This image comes from a book called *The Silent Friend* about the "horrors of masturbation." At the time, common wisdom held that masturbation would lead to insanity.

as a cure for sexual deviance, masturbation being the most worrisome.

Nineteenth-century religious leaders considered masturbation an abomination, and the emerging scientific disciplines of psychiatry and surgery claimed that masturbation caused shyness, hairy palms, jaundice, insanity, cancer, and murderous behaviors (Figure 2.6). From 1861 to 1932, the US Patent Office issued some two dozen patents on anti-masturbation devices to prevent boys from masturbating, among them a safety pin to close the foreskin of the penis, various kinds of male chastity belts, and an electric bell attached to the penis that would notify parents if their son got an erection during the night. As recently as 1918, a US government brochure advised new parents to prevent their babies from masturbating by tying their hands and legs to the sides of their cribs. Circumcision became the most commonly performed surgery in the United States based on the view that it prevented masturbation.

John Harvey Kellogg (1852–1943), the inventor of Corn Flakes, was a physician from Battle Creek, Michigan. He was a nutritional enthusiast and a follower of the health food movement of vegetarian and dietary reformer Sylvester Graham (1797–1851), who had developed the graham flour used in graham crackers. Kellogg became director of a Seventh-day Adventist sanitarium in Battle Creek, where he built on Graham's ideas, inventing corn flakes and various granolas as food for his patients (Figure 2.7). Both men were concerned with health and sexuality—they especially abhorred masturbation—which they attributed to animalistic passions that were enhanced by a rich, meaty, or spicy diet. Both believed that bland but healthy foods were the way to soothe these volatile and unhealthy sexual urges (Money 1985).

Eating cereal has never prevented masturbation, of course, and no one today would argue that it does. Over time, the meaning of both cereal and masturbation have shifted. In fact, these days, an increasing number of medical professionals embrace masturbation as good for mental health. But the initial assumptions that masturbation was abhorrent and that bland food could curb sexual impulses were enough to create corn flakes.

During the nineteenth century, the American breakfast, like the rest of the diet, was a hearty meal of meat, eggs, fish, biscuits, gravy, jams, and butter. Although

⅄ **Figure 2.7   Happiness Is Wellness in the Bowels.** John Harvey Kellogg's Battle Creek Sanatarium, opened in 1876, served corn flakes, granolas, and yogurts to promote good bowel health. There was also an enema machine that could pump fifteen gallons of water through a person's bowel in seconds. It was a popular and fashionable vacation destination.

farmers worked off the calories in their fields, as America became more urban such rich meals became a sign of prosperity, just as the ideal body type was full-bodied for both men and women. But as American culture began to value healthy eating early in the twentieth century, industrial cereal makers, like C. W. Post and Kellogg's brother William, took advantage of this connection between cereals and good health to market their creations as nutritious foods. By the 1920s the American diet had shifted dramatically along with the ideal body type becoming much thinner. The result was an increased demand from consumers for convenient and tasty breakfast cereals, spawning a giant breakfast cereal industry associated with good taste and health rather than with preventing sexual deviance.

In answering our initial question, we see interrelationships between separate domains like beliefs (about sexual morality, good health), social institutions and power (expert knowledge, medical practices), and daily life (changes in labor organization and economic life, dietary preferences). This is the holistic perspective.

This example also shows the integration of specific domains. For example, beliefs about sexual morality are intertwined with institutions of social authority, such as sanitariums and medical disciplines like psychiatry and surgery, and those institutions, in turn, regulate people's sexual relationships. Similarly, changes in people's economic relationships and work habits help shape, and are shaped by, their ideas about what is good to eat. At any historical moment, these domains feel stable because they are reflected in the other domains, even though some may be highly transitory and dynamic. The values, norms, and traditions in one domain are buttressed and supported by values, norms, and traditions in many other domains.

And herein lies the power of a cultural analysis: it shows how doing something that feels totally "natural" (pouring yourself a bowl of cereal in the morning) is really the product of intertwined "artificial" processes and meanings.

THINKING LIKE AN ANTHROPOLOGIST: CULTURE

The importance of the holistic perspective to anthropology is that it links together lots of things scholars in other disciplines do not routinely think about. Use an example of an object in daily life (e.g., a book or laptop you use in class) to show how it is holistically linked to other aspects of American life.

2.4 Can Anybody Own Culture?

As we have defined culture, the question of owning culture may appear to make little sense. How can somebody own the collective processes through which people construct and naturalize certain meanings and actions as appropriate and necessary? For the most part, owning culture is about power relations between people who control resources and (typically) minority communities who have been kept outside the mainstream. At one level, nobody can own culture, but many will claim the exclusive right to the symbols that give it power and meaning.

The debate over sports teams' Indian mascots is only one example of a conflict over who has the right to use, control, or even "own" symbols, objects, and cultural processes. This conflict is related to the phenomenon of **cultural appropriation**, the unilateral decision of one social group to take control over the symbols, practices, or objects of another. Cultural appropriation is as old as humanity itself. The fact that people adopt

• **Cultural appropriation.** The unilateral decision of one social group to take control over the symbols, practices, or objects of another.

ideas, practices, and technologies from other societies demonstrates the fluidity of social boundaries and partly explains why societies and cultures are changing all the time.

Yet cultural appropriation often involves relationships of domination and subordination between social groups. For American Indians, for example, the pressure to assimilate into dominant white Euro-American society has coincided with the dominant society's appropriation of Indian cultural symbols. That appropriation goes beyond the use of Indian images as sports mascots and includes, among others, kids "playing Indian," New Age religion's imitation of Indian spirituality and rituals, Hollywood's endless fascination with making movies about Indians, and even the use of the Zia Pueblo sun symbol on the New Mexico state flag (Strong 1996; M. Brown 2003). While some Indians do not mind, others find these uses of Indian symbolism degrading and simplistic because they ignore the realities of Indian communities and traditions or because nobody asked permission to use the culturally meaningful objects and symbols.

Some of these conflicts have taken shape as dramatic protests, as in the 2002 case of Australian Aboriginal activists who removed the coat of arms at the Old Parliament House in Canberra. They declared that images of the kangaroo and emu (a large flightless Australian bird resembling an ostrich) on the national seal are the cultural property of Aboriginal people (M. Brown 2003). Other conflicts have happened in courts, such as the highly publicized lawsuit Zia Pueblo brought against the state of New Mexico in 1994, formally demanding reparations for the use of the Zia sun symbol in the state flag (Figure 2.8).

Anthropologists have not escaped indigenous scrutiny and criticism for claiming expertise about native cultures. Anthropologist Kay Warren (1998), for example, studied the rise of the Pan-Maya ethnic movement in Guatemala. When she gave an academic presentation on Maya political activism, Maya intellectuals and political leaders in attendance responded by challenging the right of foreign anthropologists even to study Maya culture. As Warren points out, indigenous movements like Pan-Mayanism reject the idea that anthropological knowledge is neutral or objective. They insist that doing anthropology raises important political and ethical questions: Who should benefit from anthropological research? Why do the people studied by anthropologists not get an opportunity to help define and evaluate research projects?

Figure 2.8   The Cause of Indigenous Rights. Indigenous groups forced the United Nations to establish the Permanent Forum on Indigenous Issues in 2000. The Forum's goal is to address the human, cultural, and territorial rights of indigenous peoples around the world.

Anthropologist as Problem Solver
Michael Ames and Collaborative Museum Exhibits

For several decades indigenous activists in the United States and Canada have criticized museums for mishandling sacred indigenous artifacts and displaying objects without the permission of tribal leaders. Until the 1990s most museums paid little attention to these concerns. They rarely sought indigenous input into museum exhibits, and when they did, it was usually long after planning for an exhibit was complete.

In the United States, the passage of the Native American Graves Protection and Repatriation Act (NAGPRA) in 1990 changed the playing field substantially. The law provides a framework for the return of human remains, burial goods, and religious objects to tribes that can demonstrate a direct connection (M. Brown 2003). At first, museum professionals worried that their collections would be cleaned out by Indian claims. But for the most part museums and Indian tribes have made concerted efforts to find effective solutions to these problems. Anthropologists have played key roles as mediators and advocates—for both museums and Indians—in many of these situations.

One pioneer in creating a partnership between native communities and museums in Canada was Michael M. Ames (1933–2006), who was director of the Museum of Anthropology (MOA) at the University of British Columbia from 1974 until 1997. Ames made several changes in the relationships between museums and their publics, including museum visitors and native peoples. While he was director of the MOA, he put all of the museum's ethnographic collections on display in visible storage so that the ordinary visitor could see everything in the collection. This was a striking shift for a museum, but nothing compared with his efforts in the 1990s to establish a new relationship between the MOA and the local First Nations—as Indian communities are referred to in Canada. He pioneered collaborative exhibitions in the museum.

Two proposed exhibitions dealt with archaeological material excavated on the lands of First Nations communities. Early in the planning process, Ames contacted tribal leaders from the communities, who agreed to participate and wanted to participate fully in managing the exhibitions and interpreting the objects displayed. The tribal leaders insisted on meaningful consultation at every stage of the process, including selection of objects, the final design of the exhibition, interpretation of each object, installation, promotion, and exhibit maintenance.

⚘ **Michael Ames and Margaret Mead.**

Tribal leaders became so involved in developing these exhibits that some museum staff feared that MOA was giving up its scholarly role altogether. After extensive negotiations with tribal leaders facilitated by Ames, First Nations communities acknowledged that museum professionals were experts in research, interpretation, and exhibition design. But they asked that this expertise be used toward the Indians' educational goals (Ames 1999:46). For example, even though the objects displayed were prehistoric and archaeologically significant, they had contemporary relevance for the native groups involved. Ames (1999:48) suggests that these archaeological pieces "have a powerful resonance for the living descendants and thus in a very real sense are contemporary as well as prehistoric" objects, especially since these prehistoric objects and sites are part of their historical record and thus part of their assertion of continuing sovereignty over their territories. These objects have current meaning in much the same way that documents and historic sites from the American Revolution have ongoing meaning for Americans.

Ames's efforts to have real participation by native groups in the museum's exhibitions have changed the museum's relationships with native communities throughout British Columbia. These communities feel that every object in the museum from their area is part of their own cultural patrimony. Museums may hold them, but they do so in trust for the native communities, who made, used, and continue to value these objects. Ames's work helped build bridges where previously there had been little more than suspicion toward anthropologists and museum professionals.

(continued)

Anthropologist as Problem Solver (continued)

Questions for Reflection

1. From the perspective of museum curators, what might be lost if they make indigenous peoples partners in an exhibition?

2. What are the possible benefits to the museum of accepting indigenous input?

3. Even though museums may purchase cultural artifacts from members of indigenous communities, who really owns these objects?

Responding to such questions, a number of anthropologists like Warren have modified how they do cultural research, including inviting the subjects of their research to be collaborators in all stages of the research, from the definition of the study all the way through to publication. In "Anthropologist as Problem Solver: Michael Ames and Collaborative Museum Exhibits" we explore how one anthropologist collaborated with indigenous people in the creation of museum exhibitions.

THINKING LIKE AN ANTHROPOLOGIST: CULTURE

Discuss whether people from one culture could "own" a dance—like the samba from Brazil—that originated with people from another ethnic group. Could anyone own a style of pop music?

Conclusion

At the heart of all anthropological discussions of culture is the idea that culture helps people understand and respond to a constantly changing world. As we have defined it, culture consists of the collective processes through which people construct and naturalize certain meanings and actions as appropriate and even necessary. Based on symbols and expressed through values, norms, and traditions, culture offers a relatively stable and common base of information and knowledge so that people can live together in groups. A holistic perspective on culture illustrates how different domains of a society interrelate. But culture is also dynamic, responding to innovation, creativity, and struggles over meaning.

In spite of the many difficulties involved in studying culture, it is more important than ever to understand culture, what it is, and how cultural processes work. The big and urgent matters of our time have cultural causes and consequences. These matters range from the problems posed by development and change for indigenous groups and heated conflicts about social identity over mascots and traditions on college campuses, to others like terrorism, environmental degradation and sustainability, ethnic diversity and racial conflict, religious intolerance, globalization, and health care. As you read this book, you will learn how anthropologists use cultural perspectives to understand, explain, and even contribute to resolving problems related to these matters.

KEY TERMS

Critical relativism   p. 36

Cross-cultural perspective
    p. 34

Cultural appropriation   p. 43

Cultural construction   p. 35

Cultural determinism   p. 36

Customs   p. 39

Enculturation   p. 32

Functionalism   p. 41

Holistic perspective   p. 41

Interpretive theory of
    culture   p. 33

Norm   p. 39

Social institution   p. 40

Social sanction   p. 39

Symbol   p. 32

Tradition   p. 39

Value   p. 38

Reviewing the Chapter

Chapter Section	What We Know	To Be Resolved
What is culture?	Culture is a central component of what it means to be human. Culture involves the processes through which people comprehend, shape, and act in the world around them.	Although most definitions of culture emphasize common themes, anthropologists have never agreed on a single definition of culture.
If culture is always changing, why does it feel so stable?	Cultural processes are emergent, fluid, and marked by creativity, uncertainty, differing individual meaning, and social conflict. Yet culture is also remarkably stable.	Anthropologists continue to debate which is more important—dynamism or stability—in explaining how culture works in people's lives.
How do social institutions express culture?	A holistic perspective enables anthropologists to understand how different social institutions and domains of a society are interrelated.	Anthropologists continue to debate how and why social institutions in any society change.
Can anybody own culture?	The phenomenon of cultural appropriation illustrates the tensions between cultural change and stability and raises important ethical and political questions about anthropological knowledge itself.	Anthropologists continue to debate over which research and collaborative strategies are most effective in responding to the ethical and political issues raised by the creation of anthropological knowledge about culture.

READINGS

For an overview of different theories of culture in anthropology and how and why they differ across schools of thought within the discipline, see Adam Kuper's *Culture: The Anthropologists' Account* (Cambridge, MA: Harvard University Press, 2000). In the book Kuper expresses deep skepticism about the centrality of the culture concept to anthropology and illustrates why anthropologists continue to debate what culture means.

For an intellectual history of the development of the culture concept in anthropology and its place in the discipline during the early twentieth century, the essays in George Stocking's book *Race, Culture, and Evolution: Essays in the History of Anthropology* (Chicago: University of Chicago Press, 1968) are classics and remain relevant today.

The book *Who Owns Native Culture?* by anthropologist Michael Brown (Cambridge, MA: Harvard University Press, 2003) is a highly readable account of the vexing legal, ethical, and methodological issues involved in who owns native cultural symbols and heritage.

Human Biocultural Evolution

Emergence of the Biocultural Animal

SLEEPING IS ONE of the most important aspects of human life. We spend about a third of our lives doing it, and our daily well-being is shaped by how much of it we get. Over time, regular sleep deprivation can lead to more serious maladies like memory loss, depression, chronic illness, and even death. Because our bodies need it, it is common to think of sleeping in terms of its biological functions. This view is supported by research that shows the critical role of sleeping in human cognitive development, hormonal regulation, long-term memory and learning, energy conservation, and physical restoration.

But sleep also has complex cultural and behavioral dimensions. How, when, where, and with whom people sleep are patterned by collective cultural expectations, moralities, and available paraphernalia such as bedding, head rests, and so on (Mauss 1973; Glaskin and Chenhall 2013). Because they are learned, sleep practices are a key site of enculturation in every society. Although North Americans tend to think of sleep as something to do in private, many people around the world view it as a social activity and sleep in groups. The cross-cultural diversity surrounding how people think about and engage in sleep clearly demonstrates that it is not simply a biological phenomenon.

For all of these reasons, sleep is, from a holistic anthropological perspective, a complex **biocultural** phenomenon that intertwines

---

Sleeping as a Biocultural Phenomenon.   The human behavior of sleeping is variable and plastic across our species. Because sleeping involves the complex intertwining of biological, evolutionary, and cultural processes, it is useful to approach it as a biocultural phenomenon.

● **Biocultural.** The complex intersections of biological, psychological, and cultural processes.

human biology with the processes of culture (Worthman 2012). Among hominins, sleep evolved under particular environmental and social conditions. Because it creates vulnerability to predators, social animals like primates adapted by sleeping in groups and developing a pattern of restful deep sleep interspersed with light sleep for maintaining vigilance. The evolution of hominin sleep patterns was especially affected by bipedalism (Worthman 2007). Bipedalism generated two conflicting evolutionary trends, one of structural refinements that saw the pelvis and birth canal get smaller to support bipedalism, and the other of increasing brain size to accommodate greater learning and social complexity. The adaptive compromise was the birth of neurologically immature infants for whom the majority of brain growth occurs outside the womb (McKenna 1993). This created the need for increased and sustained parental contact with infants, what biological anthropologist James McKenna refers to as a "dynamic, co-evolving interdependent system" between infant needs and parental response, which includes parents and infants sleeping together in close contact.

McKenna and his research team at the University of Notre Dame's Mother-Baby Behavioral Sleep Laboratory have studied the intricacies of that interdependent system up close. They have learned that the touch, vision, smells, vocalizations, movement cues, breathing sounds, exchange of CO_2 gas, and breast milk involved in parent-infant co-sleeping provide critical physiological and neurological conditions for infant development. These things can even reduce the risk of sudden infant death syndrome (SIDS) (Ball, Tomori, and McKenna 2019). These studies support the notion that co-sleeping, along with breastfeeding, evolved as critical elements of human infant development, and both are involved in our reproductive success as hominins.

The majority of human societies continue this close-contact sleeping with infants. One exception is postindustrial Western countries such as the United States and Canada, where cultural attitudes, supported by a century of pediatric medical and public health beliefs, emphasize that babies should sleep alone. These attitudes are based partly on fears that an adult will roll over and suffocate the baby and partly on the belief that co-sleeping will create too much emotional dependency in the individuals as they grow up. Some hospitals even disallow newly born infants to be in bed with the mother at all.

From an evolutionary perspective, these beliefs and the behaviors that stem from them put mothers and babies at odds with their bodies. They are based on often flawed or insubstantial evidence and can even be detrimental to infant development, making them urgent issues for public discussion. For anthropologists, they also raise some important issues about the relationship between human cultural processes and the evolution of our species. At the heart of this issue is the question around which this chapter is organized: *How should we make sense of the biological and cultural factors that together shape humanity's evolutionary trajectories?* We can answer this question by considering a number of related questions around which this chapter is organized:

Life changes. But what does it mean to say it evolves?

What are the actual mechanisms through which evolution occurs?

How do biocultural patterns affect evolution?

Are modern humans evolving, and where might we be headed?

Because of our capacity for particularly complex culture, many evolutionary processes humans experience differ from those of other species. It is thus necessary to bring biology and culture into the same frame—a biocultural frame—in order to understand the conditions under which human evolution occurs. But before we get there, it will be helpful to start with a basic introduction to evolution.

3.1 Life Changes. But What Does It Mean to Say It Evolves?

Populations of living things change over time because of how they interact with environments and other life forms. Think about the exotic shapes and behaviors of deep-sea fish and how these characteristics allow them to cope with the intense pressures and low light conditions of the deep ocean. The interactions the ancestral populations of fish had with their surroundings generated changes in physical form and behavior that we can observe in present populations. Understanding those changes can help us understand ourselves and other life forms. But why call these things *evolution* and not simply *change?*

We can start by clarifying that evolution is both a body of factual evidence and a theory. It is a body of factual evidence—observable and verifiable truths—because we can examine fossils (the preserved remains of past life), analyze the biochemistry of organisms, or study geological patterns, and each of these demonstrates empirically that change over time has happened. It is also a theory, that is, a set of well-supported, testable hypotheses that explain *how* such changes occur. In this sense, evolution provides an explanation and a model for how change occurs. The theory of evolution is supported today by repeated testing over the past century-and-a-half across many different domains of life, from humans to microbes. When and how did this theory emerge?

A Brief Primer on the Rise of Evolutionary Thinking

All societies give some form of classification to their worlds, explaining how things came to be and why there are similarities and differences between groups of people, animals, plants, and landscapes. Underlying these concerns is a key question: How can we explain the origins and diversity of life? Natural and social scientists, among them anthropologists, have sought to explore this question with evolutionary theory.

Until a few hundred years ago, evolutionary theory did not exist and the dominant explanation in Western culture about the origins and diversity of life was based on several key notions, including the following:

- **Essentialism.** The philosophical position that dictates that each organism has a true, ideal form, and that all living representatives of that organism are slight deviations from the ideal type.

- The ancient Greek idea of the Great Chain of Being, in which all forms of life exist in a ranked, hierarchical order (Figure 3.1).
- The concept of **essentialism**, which holds that organisms each have an ideal form, and that actually living versions of any organism are minor deviations from the ideal type.
- The Judeo-Christian creation story that God created all the world's creatures in an order that ends with a man, Adam, situated in a position of dominion over others, and everything that exists was created exactly as it is now. In 1650, the archbishop of Ireland, James Ussher, calculated that the creation occurred in 4004 BCE, meaning the earth was about 6,000 years old.

In other words, everything is ranked in a specific order, things do not change too much from their essential form, and it had all been done flawlessly by God so there is no reason to question it. This explanation for origins and diversity endured for centuries.

During the sixteenth and seventeenth centuries a new emphasis on the careful observation of nature, sensory evidence, measurement, hypothesis building, mathematical proof, and experimentation contributed to radical new ways of thinking about these old questions. Natural philosophers (who today we might call scientists) began to examine the geological history of the earth and to study and classify plants and animals on the basis of their similarities and differences, realizing that changes in life forms had occurred on the planet. Some of these individuals laid the intellectual foundations for the rise of evolutionary theory, which we review in Table 3.1.

By the mid-1800s, the table was set for a new and refined scientific theory to account for the diversity and origins of life on earth. Two naturalists, Charles Darwin and Alfred Russel Wallace (1823–1913), built on the intellectual history expressed in Table 3.1 to make this new theory.

Darwin, whose story we introduced in Chapter 1, had observed the variety of plants and animals during his travels on the HMS *Beagle* and was also a domestic-pigeon breeder (Figures 3.2, 3.3). With this background, he wondered if the variety of life forms he encountered might be the result of interactions between organisms and their environment. He proposed that if some individuals had traits that helped them acquire more food and survive better in an environment, they would leave more offspring. The offspring who inherited the traits would benefit from them as well. He suggested that variations do not arise from a will to change, as Lamarck argued, but are found in the preexisting traits of individuals within a population.

By 1844, Darwin had organized this thinking into a new theory he called "descent with modification." He did not use the term *evolution* because he felt it could imply progress, improvement, and the possibility of an ultimate and perfect creation, all of which he rejected. Darwin held off on publishing his theory, wanting to be wholly certain that the data fully supported it and concerned that it would provoke outrage in conservative 1840s England.

Figure 3.1   The Great Chain of Being. This 1579 drawing by Didacus Valades from a book called *Rhetorica Christiana* represents the ancient view of the hierarchy of all living things.

TABLE 3.1	EARLY CONTRIBUTORS TO THE FORMATION OF EVOLUTIONARY THEORY
KEY FIGURE	**MAIN IDEA**
Carl von Linnaeus (1707–1778)	Developed **taxonomy**, the system of naming and classifying organisms still (more or less) in use today. He grouped together organisms with similar anatomy, suggesting that physical similarity indicates relationship. His taxonomy placed all organisms on the same level, chipping away at the Great Chain of Being.
George-Louis Leclerc, Comte du Buffon (1707–1788)	The relationship between organisms and their environment is dynamic. Active forces of nature—not biblical creation—create ever-proliferating forms of life.
Erasmus Darwin (1731–1802)	Life arose from an original filament (God), but groups of organisms can undergo gradual changes and become different from the first group, thus producing the diversity of forms we see on the planet.
Jean Baptiste Pierre Antoine de Monet, Chevalier de Lamarck (1744–1829)	When an organism confronts a challenging environment, it can intentionally direct fluids or forces to change its body, developing, for example, new organs. These physical changes are passed to offspring, or if the new organs fall into disuse, are modified into another form or gradually disappear, all within the lifetime of a single organism. These ideas about the mechanisms for change (the organism's will to change), inheritance patterns (inheritance of acquired characteristics), and time frame (within a lifetime) were all rejected. But it was the first theory of biological evolution, and his idea that creatures make modifications in form to meet environmental challenges would endure.
James Hutton (1726–1797) and Charles Lyell (1797–1875)	Geological processes, such as the creation of mountains and erosion, occur slowly so the earth must be older than 6,000 years. They introduced the concept of "deep time" to explain that slow pace. Lyell's 1830 book, *Principles of Geology*, referred to these processes as "evolution," meaning a gradual unfolding, marking the first use of the term in scientific literature.

Sometime during that decade, he began receiving letters from Wallace, a young English naturalist and museum collector traveling around the islands of Southeast Asia. Wallace came up with ideas similar to Darwin's, based on similar experiences and by reading many of the same naturalist publications. Wallace described these ideas in letters to Darwin, and in 1858, the two of them agreed to jointly write and present a paper about their ideas—descent with modification—to the Linnaean Society of London and have the paper published in its journal. The next year, Darwin published what was to become one of the most famous books of all time, *On the Origin of Species* (1859). It refers to the concept of *evolution* only once, in the last line: "There is grandeur in this view of life, with its several powers, having been originally breathed into a few forms or into one; and that, whilst this planet has gone cycling on according to the fixed law of gravity, from so simple a beginning endless forms most beautiful and most wonderful have been, and are being, evolved" (Darwin 1859:490).

● **Taxonomy.** A system of naming and classifying organisms.

Differentiating Evolution from Simple Change

Evolutionary theory has continued to change since the nineteenth century, as we will explain in the next section. But now we have enough background to differentiate evolution from simple change. One of the key issues Darwin and Wallace had posited is that *change over time is intimately tied to variation in the present*. That is, if you observe, as Darwin did during his journey to the Galápagos Islands, that finches have variably sized and shaped beaks, evolution provides a testable, if not also reasonable, explanation for that variation. The variations between physical traits that interest us from an evolutionary point of view are the ones that occur because of particular environmental challenges.

🌱 **Figure 3.2 The Naturalists and the Theory of Selection.** Charles Darwin (*left*) and Alfred Russel Wallace (*right*). Each independently developed the idea of natural selection based on observations of a variety of animal species and similar personal and intellectual trajectories.

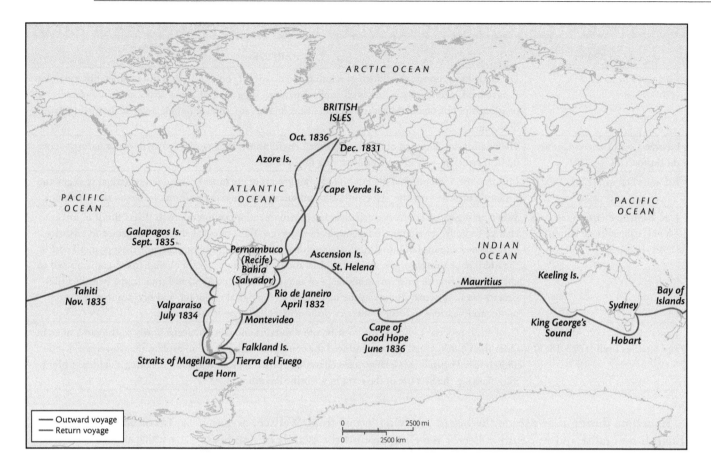

ARCTIC OCEAN

BRITISH
ISLES

Oct. 1836   Dec. 1831

Azore Is.

PACIFIC
OCEAN

ATLANTIC
OCEAN

Cape Verde Is.

PACIFIC
OCEAN

Galapagos Is.
Sept. 1835

Pernambuco
(Recife)
Bahia
(Salvador)

Ascension Is.
St. Helena

INDIAN
OCEAN

Mauritius

Keeling Is.

Bay of
Islands

Tahiti
Nov. 1835

Valparaiso
July 1834

Rio de Janeiro
April 1832

Montevideo

Cape of
Good Hope
June 1836

King George's
Sound

Sydney

Hobart

Falkland Is.

Straits of Magellan   Tierra del Fuego
Cape Horn

— Outward voyage
— Return voyage

0   2500 mi

0   2500 km

Figure 3.3   Voyage of the Beagle. In 1831, at the age of twenty-two, Darwin became the captain's companion and naturalist aboard the HMS *Beagle* during a five-year surveying voyage around South America and the Pacific. During the voyage Darwin was exposed to something that few other scientists had seen: natural diversity across a wide range of habitats, locations, and environments (Fuentes 2007:32).

• **Adaptation.** The development of a trait that plays a functional role in the ability of a life form to survive and reproduce.

So the reason for the variability in the beak size and shape of finches is closely related to the type and size of food sources available in each finch population's geographic area (Figure 3.4).

Because variations in physical traits are closely related to a life form's survival, what also interests us from an evolutionary perspective are *adaptive* changes. **Adaptation** refers to the development of a trait that plays a functional role in the ability of a life form to survive and reproduce. For Darwin (and Wallace), that mechanism of adaptation was natural selection, which is not a force or a guided process. It is a *process of selection* among traits that provide fitness in a particular environment.

Evolution is thus *non-directional*, that is, not progressive, linear, or necessarily leading toward improvement. Environmental changes can make a physical trait work against the population's survival, and not all changes are adaptive. Some changes might enable individuals or a population to survive, while others might lead to death and extinction. What counts is the extent to which any changes enable a population to survive under very specific environmental conditions.

Another key principle is that those traits that enable successful adaptations are *inherited*, that is, passed on across generations. Although Darwin and Wallace did not understand exactly how inheritance worked, scientists had long recognized that parents often passed physical traits on to their children. By 1866, the Austrian monk Gregor Mendel, an amateur scientist who doubled as his monastery's gardener, provided the first refined understanding of inheritance. He had identified seven traits in common edible peas, including a purple or white flower, tall or short stem, yellow or green pod, and so on. Based on close observations, he connected those traits to specific parents and learned that the characteristics of offspring could be controlled by selective breeding. From the theory of Mendelian inheritance we derive a general

1. Geospiza magnirostris.
2. Geospiza fortis.
3. Geospiza parvula.
4. Certhidea olivasea.

Figure 3.4 Darwin's Finches. The most important differences between the finches Darwin described in his book *On the Origin of Species* were in their beak sizes and shapes, which are adapted to specific food sources found in the environment.

understanding of the inheritance of physical traits, such as the understanding that each parent passes separate genetic material to their offspring and that dominant traits will mask recessive traits.

A final point is that evolution directs our attention to *relational* change. Changes always happen in relationship with other factors, primarily environmental conditions and what other life forms are up to, but also the specific biological and genetic factors unique to a population's common ancestry. Understanding those relationships of common ancestry is thus critical to understanding the evolution of any life form.

What It Means to Have Common Ancestry

To establish common ancestry, it is necessary to have some way of naming populations. This is where Linnaeus from Table 3.1 returns to the story. Linnaeus developed the taxonomic system we use to organize and name organisms, called **binomial nomenclature**, or a two-name naming system. It groups together those organisms with similar form into a *genus* (plural, *genera*) and those that share even more specific features into a *species*. In the Linnaean system, genera and species are the basic levels of classification, but the taxonomy also groups life forms into even higher and more general categories, as we show in Figure 3.5. Using the methods established by Linneaus, scientists are able to produce a taxonomy of all living forms on earth.

Linnaean taxonomies can imply suggestive ancestral connections, but morphological similarities alone do not provide useful information about evolutionary processes because they do not capture the dimension of time or the relationship between descendants and their ancestors. To describe those relationships, scientists create a **phylogeny**, a chart that looks somewhat like a family tree and traces the evolutionary history of a species or group, focusing specifically on points when an evolutionary event or change happens, such as the creation of a new species (Figure 3.6). Like a family tree, you read from the root of the tree to branches and tips (called lineages).

Binomial nomenclature. A taxonomic system that assigns two names to organisms.

Phylogeny. A graphic representation that traces evolutionary relationships and identifies points when an evolutionary event or change occurred, such as the creation of a new species.

Figure 3.5   Classifying Life.
The Linnean taxonomy organizes life into hierarchical groups, from the most specific, in ascending order, to the most general.

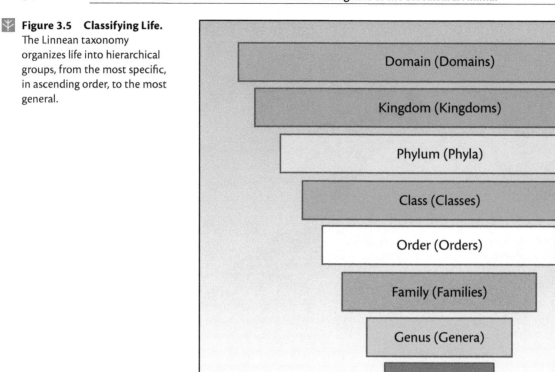

Figure 3.6   A Basic Phylogeny. Like a family tree, you read from the root of the tree to branches and tips, which are called lineages. Each branching point is where a single ancestral lineage gives rise to two or more descendant lineages.

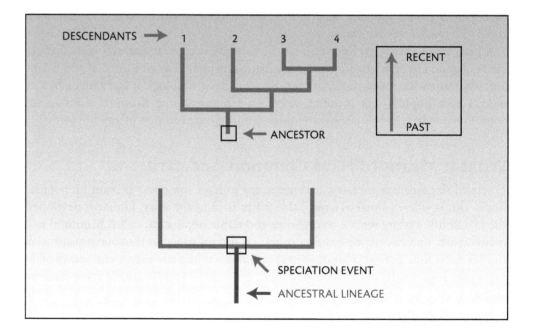

At each branching point a single ancestral lineage—the common ancestry—gives rise to two or more descendant lineages. Those lineages each have their own unique histories. Because of this fact, no organism is higher or "more evolved" than others, and life forms evolve traits unique to their lineages.

Phylogenies are constructed using morphological, molecular, and fossil data. In creating phylogenies, scientists look for three features. The first is **shared characteristics**, traits or structures that are shared by all or most species in a group because they

• **Shared characteristics.**
Traits or structures that are shared by all or most species in a group because they are inherited from a common ancestral species.

are inherited from a common ancestral species. A good example is hair among mammals. Second is **derived characteristics**, which are unique to a species. These traits evolved after two or more species who have shared a common ancestor diverged; the chin in modern humans is an example (see Chapter 8). Third is **shared derived characteristics**, which are traits that evolved after all the species being compared shared a common ancestor, but prior to some more recent speciation events, seen, for example, in the larger brains of humans and apes relative to the brains of monkeys. Understanding distinctions between traits that are ancestral, derived, or shared derived helps us understand the evolutionary relationships between species.

- **Derived characteristics.** Traits unique to a species that evolved after two or more species who have shared a common ancestor diverged.

- **Shared derived characteristics.** Traits that evolved after all the species being compared shared a common ancestor, but prior to some more recent speciation events.

Why Evolution Is Important to Anthropology . . . and Anthropology to Evolution

Evolution is important to anthropology for a number of reasons. It helps us understand our origins as a species, identify the evolutionary changes that make our species distinctive, and specify traits we share with other creatures with whom we have common ancestry. It also helps us make sense of biological and cultural variations between human populations. In "Classic Contributions: Clyde Kluckhohn and the Role of Evolution in Anthropology," we explore how one influential anthropologist understood its importance.

But the relationship between anthropology and evolution is not a one-way street. Anthropologists are at the forefront of contemporary evolutionary theory, and anthropologists bring a lot to it. Most significant is its challenge to the biological reductionism of much evolutionary theory, offering the holistic (embracive) perspective that Kluckhohn called for. As Jonathan Marks (2012:148) observes, "While it may be attractively pseudoscientific to imagine human evolution as simply biological history driven by simple biological processes, the most fundamental aspects of human evolution belie that assumption. They are not biological features with biological histories, but biocultural features with biocultural histories." What he means is that culture also plays a critical role in human evolutionary history, and that the selective processes emphasized in Darwin's approach are not the sole—or necessarily even most important—means through which human populations evolve. Before we really unpack what the implications of this point are, it is important to explain in detail how and why the processes emphasized by Darwin are not the sole means through which evolution happens. We address this matter in the next section.

THINKING LIKE AN ANTHROPOLOGIST: BIOCULTURAL EVOLUTION

A centerpiece of evolutionary theory since Darwin is that it is non-directional change, that is, it is change that could lead in a number of possible directions. Yet a misconception in popular usage is that the word "evolution" implies progress and improvement in one direction. What do you think might explain the gap in understanding? What can anthropologists do to communicate the more nuanced view that emphasizes its non-directionality?

Classic Contributions
Clyde Kluckhohn and the Role of Evolution in Anthropology

CLYDE KLUCKHOHN (1905–1960) was an important theorist of culture. At Harvard University, where he spent his career, he was a key figure in the interdisciplinary Department of Social Relations, among whose faculty and graduates have come some of the most influential social scientists of the twentieth century. In 1959, toward the end of his life, he reflected on the relationship between evolutionary theory and anthropology in the concluding chapter of a volume entitled *Evolution and Anthropology: A Centennial Appraisal*, which brought together prominent anthropologists to assess the Darwinian legacy in anthropology. In his essay, Kluckhohn asserts that neither biological nor cultural aspects of humanity can be understood as a series of separate creations but only as a continuum of small changes, often cumulative, that bear some relationship to selective pressures. In the excerpt here, Kluckhohn outlines some of his main insights, which hold as much relevance for the discipline of anthropology today as they did in 1959.

Clyde Kluckhohn.

If the future role of evolutionary thought in anthropological studies is to be an optimal one, I think the following conditions must be fulfilled:

1. *More attention to the evolution of behavior and psyche;*
2. *Still greater fusion of the biological with cultural-social-psychological dimensions [of being human];*

3. *Bold and imaginative focus upon the constant interactions between the environment (both physical and cultural) and the constitution and experience of individuals;*
4. *The creation of models that are as embracive [inclusive] as possible.* [Kluckhohn 1959:154]

Questions for Reflection

1. Kluckhohn suggests that culture influences human evolution. Can you think of a scenario in which cultural processes (like the use of e-mail or cell phones, or medical technologies, for example) might accelerate or alter the rate of evolutionary change?

2. How do you think evolutionary processes could explain human "behavior and psyche?"

3.2 What Are the Actual Mechanisms Through Which Evolution Occurs?

Knowledge about evolutionary processes has come a long way since Darwin and Wallace's time. For example, we know a lot more about the empirical relationship between evolution and genetic processes. In recent years, it has become clear that non-genetic processes are also involved in evolution. We begin by explaining the genetic mechanisms through which evolution occurs.

The Modern Synthesis

Although it was initially controversial, Darwin and Wallace's theory was widely adopted in the natural sciences and anthropology by the end of the nineteenth century for a simple reason: it offered a coherent theoretical framework with explanatory power that was, at the same time, open to empirical testing. Neither naturalist knew anything about genetics, but by the 1930s and 1940s, new scientific fields like molecular biology and population genetics had shown there was a close relationship between genetics and evolution. A growing understanding of patterns of inheritance, coupled with statistical modeling of change and populations, allowed researchers to gain insights unavailable to nineteenth-century evolutionary thinkers. The expanded description of evolution put forward by these scientists has been called the **modern synthesis**. The modern synthesis recognizes *four* processes of evolution—mutation, natural selection, gene flow, and genetic drift—whereas Darwin and Wallace primarily understood only natural selection. These four processes form the basis for a single unified theory of evolution accepted during the second half of the twentieth century.

A key feature of the modern synthesis is that evolution can only be measured across generations and within a **population**, a cluster of individuals of the same species who share a common geographical area and find their mates in their own cluster. In other words, individuals do not evolve within their own lifetimes, and evolutionary change is only observable across many generations. Importantly, this change is driven at the genetic level.

- **Modern synthesis.** The view of evolution that accepts the existence of four genetically based processes of evolution: mutation, natural selection, gene flow, and genetic drift.

- **Population.** A cluster of individuals of the same species whose members share a common geographical area and find their mates more often in their own cluster than in others.

- **Deoxyribonucleic acid (DNA).** Spiral-shaped molecule strands that contain the biological information for the cell.

Basic Sources for Biological Change: Genes, DNA, and Cells

Genes are the building blocks of our bodies, the basic units of information for living things. They provide the primary means by which individuals pass on biological information to their offspring. Genes are found in the nucleus of every cell, the main unit of construction in our bodies. Variation in genes, which is at the heart of biological variation in organisms, acts as the basic source for biological change. Traits vary from one individual to another, and these differences result partly—but not entirely—from genetic variation. Without genetic variation in a population, evolution and biological change from generation to generation are very unlikely.

Genes are segments of the filaments of **deoxyribonucleic acid** (DNA), which consists of molecules that reside in each of our cells in the form of spiral-shaped strands (Figure 3.7). DNA is inherited from our parents, and with it the genes that make up the DNA. A significant part of what DNA does is related to its physical and chemical structure. The structure of the DNA molecule is a double helix, or spiral, which allows the molecule to be easily opened into a ladder-like shape and closed. Chemically, DNA is composed of three major units: nucleotide bases, sugars, and phosphates. Usually, DNA is condensed into chromosomes, which are supercoiled masses of DNA in the nucleus of cells (Figure 3.8).

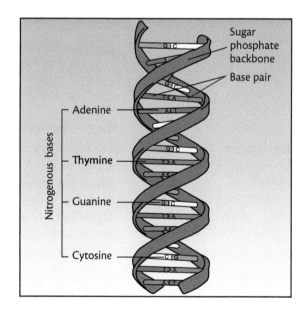

Figure 3.7   The DNA Molecule. This figure shows the molecule with its sugar-phosphate backbone. A series of sugar and phosphate groups make up the sides of the "ladder," and two nucleotide bases make up each rung. There are four nucleotide bases—adenine (A), cytosine (C), guanine (G), and thymine (T)—and each has a specific affinity, or chemical attraction, to one of the other bases. The rungs of the ladder of DNA are always composed of an A-T or C-G pair.

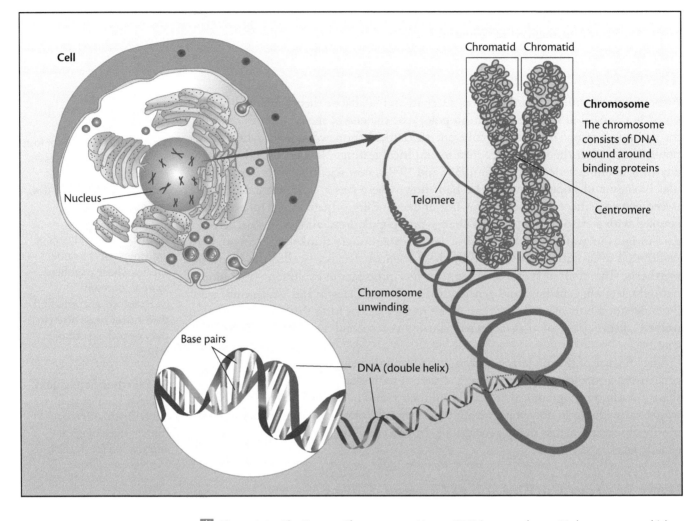

🌿 **Figure 3.8   The Human Chromosome.** Human DNA is grouped onto 46 chromosomes, which come in the form of 23 pairs. Each of us has two copies of the first 22 chromosomal pairs, which we get from our mother and father. The 23rd chromosomal pair defines the sex (two X chromosomes being a female, and an X and a Y being a male).

The Functions of DNA

- **Replication.** The process by which DNA makes copies of itself.

DNA has two main functions, replication and protein synthesis. **Replication** is the ability of DNA to copy itself. DNA's double helix structure enables it to unwind, which happens with the assistance of enzymes that respond to chemical cues. Once the ladder is opened, the chemical makeup and shape of the bases prove to be a strong allure for their complementary bases. The process of pairing up bases is repeated along the entire length of both sides of the opened ladder as shown in Figure 3.9.

- **Mitosis.** The process of cell division and replication.

- **Meiosis.** The process of gamete production.

DNA copies are necessary for two of the primary functions of cells: mitosis and meiosis. **Mitosis** is the creation of two new cells out of one cell, by a process of division. This is required for our bodies to grow and heal. We also constantly lose cells due to death or injury, and mitosis ensures their replacement. **Meiosis** is like mitosis but occurs in only one set of specialized cells that produce the gametes (sperm and eggs).

- **Protein synthesis.** How DNA assists in the creation of the molecules that make up organisms (proteins).

Protein synthesis is the other major function of DNA. The organic structures of our bodies are made up of proteins, which are strings of amino acids. By itself, a string of amino acids is called a polypeptide. To become a protein, the polypeptide changes shape and folds itself in various ways, acquiring a specific chemical signature. The DNA is the "code," or set of basic assembly information about the right sequence of amino acids to create a particular polypeptide which will serve as the basis for a protein (this "code" is, in essence, a gene).

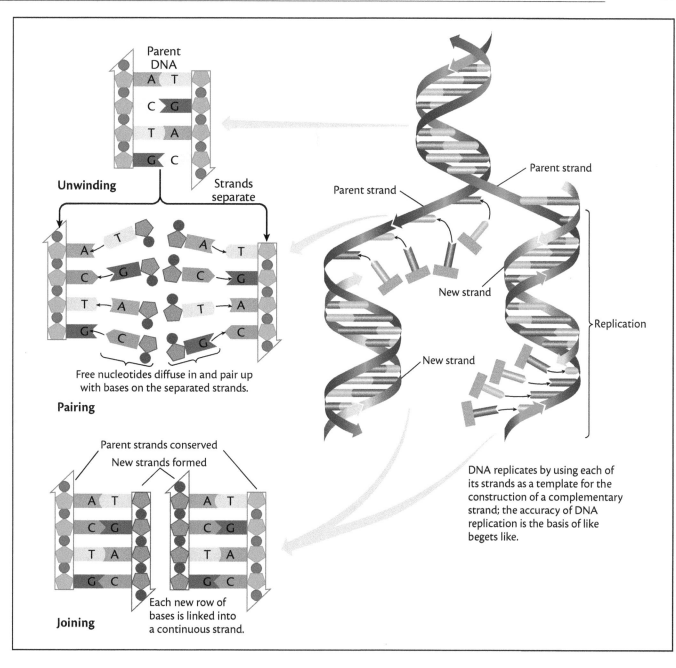

Parent DNA

Unwinding

Strands separate

Free nucleotides diffuse in and pair up with bases on the separated strands.

Pairing

Parent strands conserved

New strands formed

Each new row of bases is linked into a continuous strand.

Joining

Parent strand

Parent strand

New strand

New strand

Replication

DNA replicates by using each of its strands as a template for the construction of a complementary strand; the accuracy of DNA replication is the basis of like begets like.

Figure 3.9 Replication of the DNA Molecule. As the strands unwind, the base pairs attach to their complements. The rows of new bases are then linked into a continuous strand.

Parents pass on to their offspring DNA segments that provide the information for constructing proteins. A unit of heredity is the segments of DNA that contain messages for a protein. These segments occur in the same places in the DNA (and thus on the chromosomes) in all humans. A gene, then, can be further defined as a segment of DNA that contains the sequence, or message, for a protein. All humans have the same genes, but for most genes, a number of different nucleotide sequences make up the protein message, each producing slight variants on the same final product, which are the observable physical traits. Variations in the sequences of the same gene are called **alleles**. For example, over twenty genes with hundreds of alleles are responsible for the variation in eye color across the human species. These alleles, or genetic variations, provide the fuel for evolutionary change.

Comparing the DNA sequences of individuals, groups, or species can help us understand molecular patterns. This approach provides a method independent of

Alleles. The variants in the DNA sequences for a given gene.

morphological comparison for testing hypotheses about the taxonomic status and evolutionary histories of different species—in other words, whether creatures are connected through common ancestry.

Genetic Mechanisms of Evolution

The modern synthesis accepts that there are four major processes that contribute to biological change in groups of organisms over time. These processes are involved in the creation, movement, and shaping of alleles, as well as the shape and function of living things. At the core of these processes is genetic variation. New genetic variation arises through mutation, and three other evolutionary processes—natural selection, gene flow, and genetic drift—move genetic variation around; they do not create new genes or new traits.

Mutation

- **Mutation.** Change at the level of the DNA (deoxyribonucleic acid).

Variation initially arises with **mutation**, which is a change in a DNA sequence. The machinery of our cells normally repairs these changes, which usually have neutral or no effects anyway. Some organisms with negative mutations may not survive. But sometimes changes are not repaired, creating variation. If there were no mutations among organisms in a population, each generation could only have the exact same genetic structure as its parent generation.

One example of a mutation-related variation is sickle cell anemia in certain human populations that trace their ancestry to West Africa. DNA is involved in producing a protein important for helping red blood cells carry oxygen around the body. The blood cells typically have a circular form, but one mutation in a section of DNA that changes the resulting protein causes red blood cells to bend and curve into a sickle-like form. The sickle-shaped cells cannot carry oxygen effectively, which affects proper bodily function. Mutations do not always have negative effects, however; sickle cells also provide a resistance to malaria, a potentially deadly tropical disease.

Natural Selection

- **Reproductive success.** Measured by how many surviving offspring an organism has.

- **Natural selection.** The process through which certain heritable traits become more or less common in a population related to the reproductive success of organisms interacting with their environments.

- **Phenotype.** The observable and measurable traits of an organism.

- **Genotype.** An organism's genetic component.

Getting enough food, avoiding predators, and finding a mate for reproduction are difficult, and some individuals do better than others at these things. Biologists sometimes speak of the "survival of the fittest," but what they really mean is competition for **reproductive success**—an organism's number of surviving offspring. The greater the number of offspring that reach maturity and have offspring themselves, the better their reproductive success. If some individuals are better able to produce offspring than others, because of factors related to specific heritable traits, then over time the more successful (or "fit") genetic variants will become more common in the population. This mechanism of change is called **natural selection**.

According to natural selection, over many generations the interactions between organisms and their environment result in gradual genetic shifts within a population. We can understand these shifts as changes in **phenotype**, the observable and measurable physical traits of an organism. Phenotype, not DNA, interacts directly with the environment. The organism, or more specifically its physical traits, must successfully pass through the environmental filter by reproducing successfully so it can leave more copies of its **genotype** (the genetic component).

A classic example of natural selection is the peppered moth in England, which historically had two varieties, light and dark (Figure 3.10). The light moths were more numerous because they could hide on light-colored buildings and trees. The darker moths were more visible and thus more often eaten by birds. But during the Industrial Revolution (mid-1800s), factory pollution changed the environment by covering buildings, trees, and rocks with a dark-colored soot. The tables were turned: birds

Figure 3.10 Natural Selection of Peppered Moths. The peppered moth illustrates natural selection. Dark-colored moths were more visible to birds on light-colored bark and more often eaten until soot from factories during the Industrial Revolution made tree bark darker.

could now see the light-colored moths much more easily, and the dark moths now had the better fit. In both cases, selection was occurring.

Gene Flow

Gene flow is the movement of alleles within and between populations. Choosing a sexual partner affects the pattern and process of moving genetic variation around in two ways, through migratory movement and whom individuals choose as their mates. The migration of individuals from one population to another can alter genetic variation in all populations involved (Figure 3.11). Populations that are geographically distant from one another tend to experience less gene flow, while nearby groups usually have more. Gene flow can also occur through nonrandom mating. When individuals choose their mate, they can either stick with their group (inbreeding) or choose a mate with specific traits that are attractive to them (called assortative mating). A good example of gene flow based on nonrandom mating comes from anthropologist Michael Park's (2003) work with communities of Hutterites, a Protestant sect in Canada. The Hutterites, who resemble the Amish in the United States, live in small farming communities and follow lifestyles that date back centuries. Because of their cultural and religious beliefs, they seldom marry outside their group. Park examined over a thousand fingerprints as indicators of genetic variation from two Hutterite colonies formed when a larger founding colony split in 1958. Surprisingly, he found that these two colonies were more genetically similar to one another than either was to the founding colony. The reason is that the two new colonies were geographically

• **Gene flow.** The movement of genetic material within and between populations.

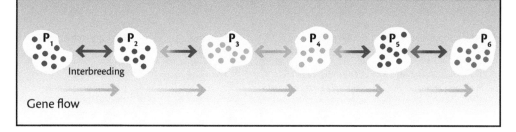

Figure 3.11 Simple Gene Flow Between Two Populations. In this graphic, P1 through P6 represent geographically localized populations of the same species. All are linked through gene flow (or interbreeding between populations), although every population doesn't interbreed with every other population.

close to one another, and individuals from each colony often found marriage partners in the other group. Gene flow had occurred between the two offshoot colonies, which reduced variation between them.

Genetic Drift

Genetic drift is a change in genetic variation from one generation to another caused by random factors, such as accidents, who gets to mate, or other events that change the makeup of a population. It is observable in small populations, because random events are more likely to have a genetic impact. A well-known example is found among the people who live on Tristan de Cunha island, a small island in the Atlantic Ocean near South Africa, settled by fewer than fifty British subjects in 1816 (Roberts 1968). For almost a century, the islanders had little contact with the rest of the world. In 1961, a storm threatened to wipe out the island's 294 residents, and they were evacuated to the United Kingdom, where everyone was examined by medical personnel. These exams found an unusually high frequency of the specific genetic variant (allele) for a serious eye disease called retinitis pigmentosa, which leads to blindness. Though it is rare in the British and South African populations from which the islanders came, a few members of the original founding population carried the genetic variation responsible for the disease, but not the disease itself. Inbreeding on the island, as well as little gene flow, resulted in the high frequency of the alleles for the disease. This situation is known as the **founder effect**, which is the loss of genetic variation when a new population is founded by a small number of individuals (Figure 3.12).

Non-Genetic Mechanisms of Evolution

The modern synthesis revolutionized evolutionary theory, but even today understanding of evolution is still changing. During the past decade, numerous scientists, among them anthropologists, have begun to argue that the primary legacy of the modern synthesis—that evolution occurs only through genetic processes—does not capture the full gamut of evolutionary processes that have been observed (Laland et al. 2014). Calling their approach the **extended evolutionary synthesis**, these scientists emphasize that a number of non-genetic processes are also involved in evolution.

The key idea behind the extended evolutionary synthesis is that organisms are not simply robots programmed by their genes but are also constructed during the developmental process of life itself. They also do not necessarily "fit" into natural environments but can shape those environments or co-evolve along with them. Not all

- **Genetic drift.** A change in genetic variation across generations due to random factors.

- **Founder effect.** A form of genetic drift that is the result of a dramatic reduction in population numbers so that descendant populations are descended from a small number of "founders."

- **Extended evolutionary synthesis.** The view of evolution that accepts the existence of not just genetically based, but also non-genetically based, processes of evolution: developmental bias, plasticity, niche construction, and extragenetic inheritance.

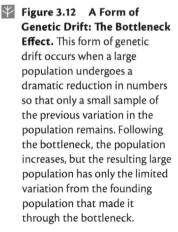

Figure 3.12   A Form of Genetic Drift: The Bottleneck Effect. This form of genetic drift occurs when a large population undergoes a dramatic reduction in numbers so that only a small sample of the previous variation in the population remains. Following the bottleneck, the population increases, but the resulting large population has only the limited variation from the founding population that made it through the bottleneck.

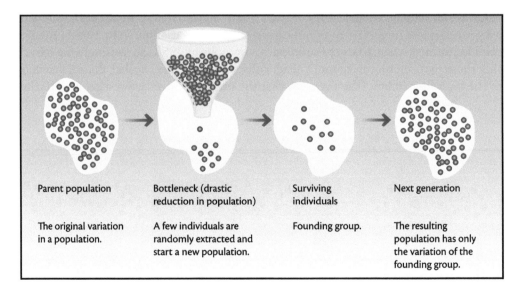

Parent population

The original variation in a population.

Bottleneck (drastic reduction in population)

A few individuals are randomly extracted and start a new population.

Surviving individuals

Founding group.

Next generation

The resulting population has only the variation of the founding group.

scientists agree with these claims, but there is increasing evidence coming from fields like our own, anthropology, and others such as developmental biology, genomics, epigenetics, and ecology that recognizing these mechanisms is changing the fabric of evolutionary theory (Laland et al. 2014).

Developmental Bias

Developmental bias refers to the idea that not all variations come about randomly, because the developmental processes that organisms undergo during their lives tend to generate certain forms more readily than others (Arthur 2004). For example, there is a group of centipedes with over 1,000 species and all of them have odd-numbered leg-bearing segments, which is closely related to how those segments develop. Developmental processes can also explain how organisms adapt to their environments and become multiple species. A compelling illustration is that African cichlids (a type of fish commonly sold in pet stores) in Lake Malawi and Lake Tanganyika have different evolutionary histories yet have developed parallel forms, including similar body shapes, facial features, and jaws (Brakefield 2006). Although this process probably works in conjunction with natural selection, it demonstrates that selection is not a completely wide-open process but follows certain physical properties and pathways (Laland et al. 2014).

- **Developmental bias.** The idea that not all variations are random but are a function of the developmental processes organisms undergo during their lives that tend to generate certain forms more readily than others.

Plasticity

Plasticity is a particular form of developmental bias in which an organism responds to its environment by changing during its lifetime, such as how tree leaves will change their shape under certain water and soil conditions. This could be a first step in adaptation, and natural selection here can also play a role if the new traits enhance the survivability of the organism. But instead of changes in the genes driving this adaptive process, the modification may happen first and then through mutation or selection the genes follow to cement the change generations later (West-Eberhard 2003).

If something about this idea seems familiar, perhaps you are thinking it is a new version of Lamarckism described in Table 3.1. It is not, however. Something more subtle is at work, which involves the interaction of development with selection. An interesting illustration of that interaction is an experiment involving dragon fish, an unusual fish with lungs and the ability to breathe air, that were raised out of water. Through plasticity the fish developed the ability to move around on dry land using their fins. The fish have the hidden capacity to build stronger limbs, but in water they don't need them so that capacity remains invisible, or "cryptic" as scientists would say. When their environment changes, the relevant trait becomes visible, which exposes that genetic variation to selection (Myers 2014).

- **Plasticity.** A particular form of developmental bias in which an organism responds to its environment by changing during its lifetime.

Niche Construction

In **niche construction** organisms play an active role in their evolution by reshaping the environment to suit their own needs, which can bias selective processes. Organisms are still influenced by environmental dynamics, but their ability to control certain environmental factors plays a role in their success. For example, termites build mounds in systematic and repeatable ways, reflecting previous selective processes, but the mounds they actually build in turn shape future selective processes.

- **Niche construction.** When organisms play an active role in their evolution by reshaping the environment to suit their own needs.

Extra-Genetic Inheritance

Extra-genetic inheritance refers to the observation that parents and social groups create environments for their offspring that can aid in their adaptive success. Socially transmitted behavior across generations is one of those inheritances. Chimpanzees, for example, teach their young to crack nuts and fashion sticks into rudimentary tools. The migratory patterns of certain fish are also transmitted across generations (Laland et al. 2014).

- **Extra-genetic inheritance.** The socially transmitted and epigenetic factors that can aid in the adaptive success of organisms.

As we will see in the next section, all of these mechanisms—both genetic and non-genetic—are relevant to the story of human biocultural evolution.

THINKING LIKE AN ANTHROPOLOGIST: BIOCULTURAL EVOLUTION

The idea of niche construction emphasizes that human evolution today is affected by new conditions that select for different traits than those our prehistoric ancestors were selected for. Can you think of a human activity today that might not have existed during prehistoric times that is affecting our current evolutionary trajectory?

3.3 How Do Biocultural Patterns Affect Evolution?

● **Constructivist approach.** A theoretical approach emphasizing that a core dynamic of human biology and culture is processes of construction: the building of meanings, social relationships, ecological niches, and developing bodies.

Building on the foundations laid by the modern synthesis and the extended evolutionary synthesis, anthropologists are at the cutting edge of examining how biology, culture, and evolution interact. In this section, we pull these threads together, offering a **constructivist approach** which emphasizes that a core dynamic of human biology and culture lies in processes of construction—the construction of meanings, of social relationships, of ecological niches, of developing bodies, and so on, all of which interact in complexly intertwined ways (see Fuentes and Weissner 2016).

Human Inheritance Involves Multiple Systems

Most explanations of human evolution have traditionally focused on only one system of inheritance, the genetic system. Observing that this approach is too narrow to appreciate human evolutionary complexity, biologists Eva Jablonka and Marion Lamb (2005) argue that three other systems of inheritance need to be considered as well (Figure 3.13). Those systems include the following:

- *The **epigenetic system of inheritance**:* The biological aspects of our bodies that work in combination with the genes and their protein products, such as the machinery of the cells, the chemical interactions between cells, and reactions between tissue and organs in the body. This system helps the information in the genes actually get expressed, which alters an individual's physical traits. Offspring may inherit those altered traits due to the past experiences of their parents.
- *The **behavioral system of inheritance**:* The patterned behaviors that parents and adults pass on to young members of their group via learning and imitation. As members of a society, we learn a wide variety of behaviors—how to get food, when and how to talk to strangers, how to act when visiting a government office, and so on—from authority figures and peers, simply by observing and being corrected in everyday life. None of this is encoded in genes.
- *The **symbolic system of inheritance**:* This idea refers to the fact that humans store and communicate their knowledge and conventional understandings through extensive use of symbols and language. As we explained in Chapter 2, the specific symbols and the meanings people attribute to them are socially constructed and are not encoded in the genes.

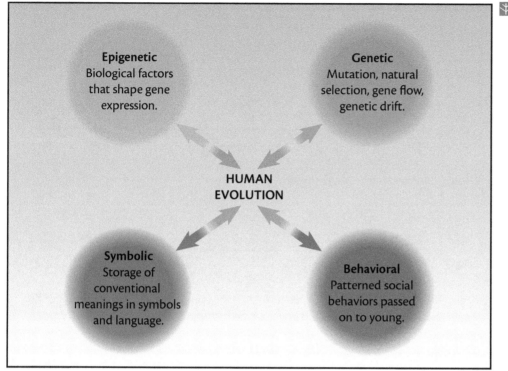

Figure 3.13 The Four Types of Inheritance.

A Fifth System? The Ecological Inheritance

As we will explore in future chapters, a critical aspect of our biocultural existence involves altering and reshaping the natural niches in which we live. All living creatures remake and reorganize their niches though their metabolism, their activities, and their behavior (Odling-Smee, Laland, and Feldman 2003). The scale of the construction and destruction of our niches can occur at the local level, as when people shape an environmental region such as a valley or body of water, or on a global scale, as the world is currently experiencing with global warming. Each of these processes can change the kinds of natural selection pressures placed on the organisms involved.

Much of what we take as "natural" in a landscape is actually an artifact of human niche construction and its effects (see Chapter 14). By 12,000 years ago, human societies covered at least three-quarters of the earth's land, engaging in ecologically transformative land use practices through burning, hunting, species propagation, and cultivation, all of which have had long-term effects on the terrestrial biosphere (Ellis et al. 2021). Even where those practices are not occurring contemporaneously, the species composition of plants and animals can be tied to previous historical human shaping of a landscape. Reflecting the view that human influence over ecosystems and Earth's surface is the defining dynamic of our world today, a number of scholars have begun referring to our current geological epoch as the **Anthropocene**.

When humans reorganize ecosystems they create the conditions for a co-evolutionary process in which humans, plants, animals, and microorganisms can mutually shape each other's evolutionary prospects. The humans born into that set of relationships inherit particular challenges and opportunities for making a living. Put in terms that Jablonka and Lamb might use, niche construction creates a kind of "ecological system of inheritance" (Figure 3.14).

• **Anthropocene.** Refers to the geological epoch defined by substantial human influence over ecosystems.

Figure 3.14   Niche Construction and the Loss of Wetlands. The conversion of wetlands illustrates the effects of environmental alteration with evolutionary dimensions. Environmental change creates new selection pressures on organisms, and those species that cannot adapt to the new conditions may go extinct, especially if there is no other environment in which they can live.

• **Developmental systems theory (DST).** An approach that combines multiple dimensions and interactants toward understanding the development of organisms and systems and their evolutionary impact.

Evolutionary Processes Are Developmentally Open-Ended

Another foundation of the biocultural perspective is the shift in thinking about evolution that came with the introduction of **developmental systems theory** (DST), which is a version of the concept of developmental bias introduced in the previous section (Oyama, Griffiths, and Gray 2001). DST rejects the idea that there is a gene "for" anything. It accepts that evolutionary processes are fundamentally open-ended involving the ongoing assembly of new biological structures interacting with non-biological structures.

In this sense, development comes from the growth and interaction of several distinct systems (Fuentes 2014a). These systems include genes and cells, muscles and bone, and the brain and nervous system, all developing over the lifetimes of individuals. From this point of view, evolution is not a matter of the environment shaping fundamentally passive organisms or populations, as suggested by natural selection theory. Rather, it consists of many other developmental systems simultaneously changing over time. In humans, evolution is thus characterized by a complex set of interactions among the various biological systems that occurs throughout an individual's lifetime, all of which interact with factors like human demography, social relationships, cultural variations, language, and environmental change. As such, these processes make it much more difficult to describe our evolution, but they recognize the actual complexity involved in how human biocultural systems work.

The Importance of Constructivist Evolutionary Approaches for Biocultural Anthropology

Genetic mechanisms are not the main or sole force in human evolution. This assertion fits well with the ways in which some researchers have long seen selection interacting with environments over the course of evolutionary time without reducing those processes to natural selection. The constructivist approach here acknowledges that biocultural dynamics are open-ended and involve interactions between diverse forces and agents. As we suggest in the Anthropological Life box, it can help us understand the relationship between human awe, imagination, and creativity. More importantly, this approach can also help us understand how humans are evolving today.

THINKING LIKE AN ANTHROPOLOGIST: BIOCULTURAL EVOLUTION

Throughout this book, not just in this section, we take a broadly constructivist view of human culture, biology, language, and prehistory. What are some of the strengths and weaknesses of the constructivist perspective? How is it possible to reconcile a constructivist definition of culture, such as that found in Chapter 2—"culture consists of the collective processes through which people in social groups construct and naturalize certain meanings and actions as normal and even necessary" (p. 36)—with the constructivist approach toward evolution presented here?

The Anthropological Life
The Biocultural Awesomeness of Awe

A few years ago, one of the co-authors of this book, Agustín Fuentes, was working with *National Geographic* to place HD cameras on barbary macaque monkeys in Gibraltar (Fuentes 2022a). Because of their placement, the cameras closely tracked what the monkeys saw from their point of view. When he looked at the recordings Agustín saw something startling and unexpected: one of the monkeys named Sylvia, sitting near the top of one of the famed rock's peaks at "golden hour" (the last hour before sunset or sunrise), fixed her gaze for a few minutes on an incredibly beautiful panorama of the Mediterranean Sea with North Africa in the hazy distance. It was an awe-inspiring vista, and clearly not just for Agustín. Scientists have documented numerous instances of animals exhibiting outward signs of awe, transfixed in wonder and fascination by some stimulus, among them wild chimpanzees who will join researchers to watch the sunset.

Given our extensive evolutionary connections that have produced similar neurobiological, visual, and emotional physiologies (see Chapter 5), it should come as no surprise that primates might experience something like what we call awe. But our own human ancestors also branched off millions of years ago, and that means we "do" awe differently because of how it is entangled with society and cultural meaning. As Agustín has written (Fuentes 2022a), among humans "awe is experienced as a feeling of reverential respect mixed with fear or wonder, or an emotion combining dread, veneration, and marvel, and humans make it a social reality."

☥ **Barbary macaque in Gibraltar.**

The distinctive thing about awe for humans is that it is not just a one-off event: we do things collectively with it that cause us to think of our world anew and shape the reality in which we will live. It stimulates religion and faith, imaginative works of art, and scientific inquiries. It can also create awe-inspiring destruction: weapons of war, the large-scale destruction of ecological systems, and so forth. It's possible that the experience of lightning pushed human imaginations beyond just using stone tools and into the desire to capture fire and use it intentionally. This last one is just speculation. But what is not is that our version of awe is a biocultural phenomenon, an entanglement of brains, bodies, and societies. Think about that next time you watch the sunset!

3.4 Are Modern Humans Evolving, and Where Might We Be Headed?

A common assumption about evolution is that "it happened in the past." Underlying this view is the belief that evolutionary processes are driving toward a goal, a plateau where the species is in tune with its environment, and a point that most species we encounter have reached. This is simply not the case. Evolution continues, unabated, until a species becomes extinct. It has no particular direction and there is no intrinsic value of one adaptation over another except survivability. As humans, we are continuing to evolve. But because we can extend the ability to survive and flourish beyond the mere genetic, human evolutionary patterns are complex, and there is a fuzzy line between biological and cultural influences.

The Impact of Disease on Evolution

We've all had colds, which are widespread in our species. Coronaviruses, a group of viruses that cause colds, do not seem to pose a great existential challenge for us. But every now and again, viral outbreaks can be deadly. The most obvious illustration is the COVID-19 outbreak that began during 2019 in Wuhan, China, in a wet market where this particular coronavirus variant was circulating among live animals and passed to humans through close contact, butchering, or undercooked meats. Human cultural behavior combined here with an evolving virus to threaten members of our species, creating a new evolutionary pressure on humans.

A major effect of human practices of niche construction is that they spark dynamic interrelationships between humans, animals, and viruses that set the stage for epidemics (Fuentes 2020). Thanks to this, human history is marked by the constant circulation of population-shaping diseases, such as bubonic plague, smallpox, cholera, and influenza, among others. Every time a major disease outbreak occurs in which members of a population die, a set of genetic complexes disappears from that population. Evolution is taking place here: when the epidemic subsides, the surviving population is genetically different from before because there has been a change in allele frequencies.

It is important to note, however, that biocultural practices strongly shape the experience and effects of disease. We explore this issue in more depth in Chapter 8, but consider the case of the human immunodeficiency virus, or HIV, which causes AIDS. If you live in North America or Europe where medicines are available, AIDS is now a manageable chronic condition. But in many less economically developed nations where those medicines are scarce or too expensive, AIDS remains a fatal disease. In sub-Saharan Africa, for example, AIDS is a disease of young adults—important years in the reproductive life of any individual—and is having important impacts on the evolutionary trajectory of that continent's populations, although it's not yet clear what those effects are. The important point is that the evolutionary pressures of diseases affect different populations differently, but not necessarily because there are any underlying genetic conditions in the populations. Rather, it is due to the differential access people have to healthcare because of broader socioeconomic and political relationships and processes.

Cultural Practices, Morphology, and Evolution

Cultural practices can alter human morphology, which refers to the shape and form of the human body, as well as the flow of genes between populations. If these practices affect human lives across generations, they can translate into long-term evolutionary change. These practices include diet, body modification, daily activity patterns, and human migration patterns.

Diet

Although all humans need certain basic nutrients and calories to survive, grow, and reproduce, different populations get those nutrients in varying quantities. Thanks to culture and important socioeconomic patterns like globalization, there are huge variations across populations in how people obtain and prepare food, and in what they eat (see Chapter 14). An individual's height and weight range are inherited, but the relative caloric, dietary fat, and carbohydrate contents of any given diet affect body shape and physiology. We can see this pattern in the development of obesity. In "Anthropologist as Problem Solver: Clarifying the Biocultural and Evolutionary Dimensions of Obesity," we examine the interactions of diet, morphology, and evolution more closely.

Body Modification

Different human populations have distinct genetically based differences in physiological and morphological patterns. For example, in many populations men have a physiological pattern that gives them facial hair, while in others (such as in Southeast Asia), men have minimal facial hair. Gene flow within and across populations probably played a role in creating these genetically inherited differences. But then, men alter these patterns through cultural behavior—it's called shaving. People usually modify their bodily appearance because of cultural beliefs about attractiveness. Around the world, these practices are quite variable: people scar their skin, get tattoos, modify their genitals, have breast enhancements or reductions, change their teeth or get a new jawline, work out at the gym to build muscles, and any number of other things (Fuentes 2018a). Do these things have evolutionary significance? Maybe, by enhancing an individual's reproductive success. But unless the practice actually affects success—for example, by creating sterility—it may not have any long-term evolutionary impact (Figure 3.15).

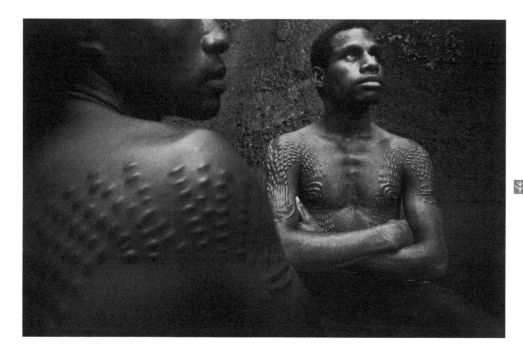

Figure 3.15 Body Modifications and Evolution. In practically every human society, people modify their bodies through practices like tattooing, piercing, scarification, and other practices. Under what conditions might these practices have evolutionary counterparts?

Anthropologist as Problem Solver
Clarifying the Biocultural and Evolutionary Dimensions of Obesity

The past sixty years have seen a dramatic global rise in obesity, which is the creation of excess body fat to the point of impairing bodily health and function, and of people being overweight, or having abnormal fat accumulation. There are now more overweight and obese people in the world than undernourished people, and several dozen countries have obesity rates exceeding 10 percent of their populations. Because these conditions can cause chronic diseases—diabetes and heart disease among them—health officials and researchers consider them to be among the most serious public health crises facing our world today. Because of our detailed knowledge of human relationships with food, morphology, and socioeconomic patterns, holistic anthropology has important contributions to make to address this crisis.

The ability to become obese is a universal human trait. But it was essentially non-existent until about 10,000 years ago (P. J. Brown 1991). Although historically obesity is associated with the wealthy, the situation is reversed in industrialized nations like the United States, where rates of obesity among the poor have far surpassed those of the wealthy. This fact has led to two explanations that have captured the public imagination and shaped national dialogue about the matter. One is that cheap, processed fast foods cause obesity, and some people simply cannot resist the temptations of food that is bad for them. In these terms, obesity is a problem of simply not having the individual willpower to control oneself in the face of tempting and inexpensive foods.

The other explanation is some version of the "thrifty gene hypothesis," which holds that certain groups of people evolved to metabolize energy efficiently, which helps them when food is scarce. But in times of abundance, these same people are predisposed to gain weight quickly because their bodies are ill-equipped to handle the extra calories (Neel 1962). Both of these explanations assume that eating "bad" foods that diverge from the normal human diet causes obesity (Leonard 2002). As appealing as these explanations may sound, however, they wrongly assume that humans have a "normal" diet, which is not the case. As omnivores, our dietary physiology evolved to be open-ended, leaving our needs to be met within the natural environments and socioeconomic and cultural contexts in which we live.

Deep in our evolutionary past, hominins evolved traits that promote the accumulation and storage of energy as adipose tissue, or fat. These traits likely developed for lean times when food was less available, but they are also linked to the demands of our developing brains, and, among females, to fertility. As a result, there are genetic dimensions to obesity (Choquet and Meyre 2011), but there is no single gene (thrifty gene) that causes individuals to gain a lot of weight, and obesity is definitely not genetically determined anyway.

From a biocultural perspective, obesity is a complex metabolic syndrome, or combination of medical conditions, that has some genetic dimensions but also non-genetic ones. Factors like maternal health and diet during pregnancy as well as local environmental conditions can influence an individual's predisposition. For example, smoking, insufficient nutrition during pregnancy, socioeconomic class, high temperatures in the natural environment, and certain environmental toxins all appear to be linked to a higher likelihood of developing obesity later in life. Cultural factors also shape access to food and how much is consumed at a meal. Furthermore, obesity is not inevitable. Although individuals may be predisposed to gain weight more easily than others, it can only develop if a person eats a lot of food while expending little energy (Ulijaszek and Lofink 2006). We now understand that it is a mix of biological and cultural factors that contributes to weight gain.

What contributions do biocultural insights have on public efforts to tackle obesity? One major point is that obesity cannot be successfully addressed as a public health issue by reducing it to a matter of an individual's willpower, "thrifty genes," and/or genetic predispositions, all of which have often led to failed diets or inappropriate medical solutions. Obesity is a complex emergent phenomenon that involves developmental processes in the body, socioeconomic networks and inequalities, and behaviors shaped by culture. Thus, as biocultural anthropologist Daniel Lende suggests (2008), it is necessary to address the broader systemic dynamics that prioritize cheap low-quality food, inactive lifestyles, and what he calls the "cultural biology system" that shapes eating patterns, body image, and expectations about exercise. Anthropologist Alexandra Brewis (2011) adds that the connection between obesity and socioeconomic disadvantage means that obesity needs to be framed as a social justice issue. In her view a fair society will do a much better job of distributing amenities—such as parks, walkable neighborhoods, and healthy food sources—in low-income areas, which would lower obesity rates. In practical terms, these anthropologists support a call to intervene in public discussions and policy debates promoting more holistic bio-cultural perspectives than currently exist.

Questions for Reflection

1. The idea that an individual can change his or her motivations through willpower is one version of a broader "self-help" culture that exists in North America. Why do you think this view is so persistent?

2. What role do you think evolutionary arguments should play in our public and policy debates over matters like obesity?

Obese Morphology.

Daily Activity Patterns

Peoples' daily activity patterns—of work, movement, and so on—can have evolutionary consequences, since they can directly affect reproductive physiology. Mass rural–urban migration, modern transportation using motorized vehicles, and other factors have changed how people use their bodies. Sitting for long periods in an office or automobile, especially when combined with longer periods of social stress and poor dietary patterns, can greatly impact individual physiology. The consequences include chronic high blood pressure, heart disease, and reduced fertility, among others.

Human Migration Patterns

Gene flow is our most easily observable evolutionary process today. High rates of transnational migration, which bring diverse populations into contact with each other, produce important changes in alleles. Cultural changes contribute to migration and the movement of alleles. These changes include improvements in travel technology; social changes promoting mobility; wars, terrorism, civil unrest, and environmental problems that drive out-migration; even government actions, such as creating resettlement programs welcoming refugees. The overall effects of such migrations for modern humans include (1) reduced differences in allele frequencies between populations; and (2) increased overall genetic variation within populations as specific, new alleles are added (Fuentes 2018a).

It is not easy to predict exactly how all of these practices actually affect the course of human evolution, although there are certain things that we should anticipate based on our knowledge of biocultural evolution. It could be that they only influence the expression of human variation, displaying our capacity as a species for behavioral and morphological diversity, without really affecting the species as a whole. Nevertheless, it does lead us to ask: Where is our species' evolution headed?

3.5 Looking to the Future

During the past 50,000 to 40,000 years, most evolutionary changes among humans have occurred through gene flow, adaptive immune responses to new diseases, and cultural changes in behavior. However, evolutionary change is a constant of nature, and looking ahead, three biocultural issues could affect our evolutionary future as a species: global population and human density; genetic manipulation; and adaptive behavioral patterns in the context of changing global climate.

Global Population and Human Density

The global human population has grown dramatically in recent decades. Only 10,000 years ago, between 5 million and 20 million humans inhabited the planet; today it is nearly 8 billion. This situation is unprecedented for our species, and we are just beginning to grapple with its evolutionary implications. This growth affects our ability to feed ourselves, although there is considerable unevenness in access to food across populations. Thanks to developments in medical technology, infant mortality rates are generally falling as life expectancy rates continue to increase. Unequal distributions of technology, wealth, and access—not genetic causes—will shape how human populations adapt to these challenges. Although it is still too early to tell what the long-term evolutionary impacts of high population densities might be, we do see changing patterns of non-infectious diseases in these areas. There are also demographic dimensions here, one aspect being that the age structure of many human societies is changing, which carries important socioeconomic implications. Against this backdrop of uncertainty, we do know that as a population grows, genetic diversity tends to increase. This has adaptive potential for the species in the long term, but only as long as individuals reach reproductive age and have children to pass on that genetic material.

Genetic Manipulation

Scientists can alter allele frequencies and even create new alleles for transgenic (across species) insertion into organisms. Transgenic and genetically modified foods, cloning, and genetic therapies are increasingly important dimensions of our evolutionary future as a species, as well as the plants and animals we interact with. In gene therapy, sequences of DNA are altered by inserting a specific sequence into a non-coding region of DNA to replace a non-functional gene. Of course, genes never operate in isolation but are always expressed in relation to developmental, environmental, and sociocultural contexts. From an evolutionary perspective, hundreds of generations will probably have to pass before we can tell if genetic manipulations have long-term effects on our species. Nevertheless, one effect of the hype around genetic manipulation is the creeping **geneticization** of health, intelligence, personality, and the like, which involves the use of genetics to explain health and social problems rather than other possible causes (Lippman 2001).

● **Geneticization.** The use of genetics to explain health and social problems rather than other possible causes.

Climate Change and Adaptive Behavioral Patterns

When a behavior emerges that gives individuals within a population some kind of reproductive advantage, it is considered adaptive. One of the big debates about adaptive processes in humans is how much of current behavioral patterns emerged during our evolutionary past and how much expresses our broad behavioral potential that is made possible by specific current environments (Fuentes 2018a). Some researchers argue that many human behavioral patterns—things like sleeping, sexual attraction, jealousy, male aggression and competition, marriage, and so forth—were adaptive responses of humans who lived as hunter-gatherers many thousands of years ago. Others (such as the authors of this book) argue that rather than reflecting specific past adaptations, most modern human behavior emerges through the life experiences of individuals and the social, political, economic, and historical contexts in which they live.

The contemporary crisis of climate change can offer useful perspective on this issue. Climate change is not new for humanity: the evolutionary origins, spread, and adaptive capacities of our ancestral hominins and early *Homo sapiens* are associated with periods of high climate and ecological variability (Potts and Faith 2015). These conditions likely contributed something to our generalized dietary, social, and mental flexibility, enabling humans to adapt to almost any imaginable weather and climate conditions in the world. What is new for humanity is our potential, through our social practices and technologies, to totally transform the environmental conditions under which we might evolve. There is thus no direct line between the ancient environments in which early humans evolved and the potential evolutionary implications of contemporary climate change, which is rooted in human industrial economic practices and advances in technology during the past 200 years. As current patterns of global warming continue to intensify, some groups will be better able to adapt to environmental changes than others and their capacity to do so will be based in cultural, social, and technological processes. It is highly likely that climatic changes will also force some groups to migrate to new areas, which could lead to gene flow. Nevertheless, whether any of these things will have any actually evolutionary effects on human bodies and reproductive success is totally unclear.

Predicting our behavioral futures is tricky, at best. One of anthropology's hallmark findings is that our behaviors are not "hardwired," that is, genetically determined and inflexible. Human biocultural dynamics are so complex that it is simply too difficult to separate biology from culture in understanding why people do the things they do. Whatever success we might have predicting our species' evolutionary futures will happen through greater commitments to anthropology's holistic and integrative potential.

THINKING LIKE AN ANTHROPOLOGIST: BIOCULTURAL EVOLUTION

During the last three centuries of industrialization, all the biocultural forces and processes we discuss here have been present since all humans were hunter-gatherers, with one exception: genetic manipulation that comes from biogenetic engineering. How is this dynamic, new factor likely to change the human evolutionary trajectory in different ways from all the other evolutionary processes?

Conclusion

Patterns of evolutionary change are complex. We can see these complex patterns in something as apparently straightforward as sleeping, the theme with which we opened this chapter. Hominin sleep evolved by favoring group sleeping, and our shift to bipedalism produced neurologically immature infants, leading to close parent-infant sleeping arrangements. Our own culture's message that babies should sleep alone is not universal among contemporary humans and pits our behavior against our deep evolutionary history. As this example shows, the intersections of biology, evolution, and culture mean that mundane behaviors, like sleeping, are not as straightforward as they seem.

Understanding human evolution through a biocultural lens is relatively new, but it builds on innovations in evolutionary theory. These new theories focus on multiple inheritances, social learning, changing relationships with the environment, and the power of human culture when asking questions about human evolution and behavior. They help us approach biocultural dynamics as open-ended, emergent, and characterized by interactions between diverse forces and agents.

Humans are still evolving and will continue to do so. We know that disease, diet, activity patterns, medical practices, and global migration impact our morphologies and physiologies in diverse ways. Whether they have evolutionary implications is in many cases still unclear because the complex intersections between culture, behavior, and biology make predictions about human evolutionary trajectories difficult. But these processes do generate important variations among contemporary human populations, a theme we will explore in a number of future chapters.

KEY TERMS

Adaptation   p. 54

Alleles   p. 61

Anthropocene   p. 67

Behavioral system of inheritance   p. 66

Binomial nomenclature   p. 55

Biocultural   p. 49

Constructivist approach   p. 66

Deoxyribonucleic acid (DNA)   p. 59

Derived characteristics   p. 57

Developmental bias   p. 65

Developmental systems theory (DST)   p. 68

Epigenetic system of inheritance   p. 66

Essentialism   p. 52

Extended evolutionary synthesis   p. 64

Extra-genetic inheritance   p. 65

Founder effect   p. 64

Gene   p. 59

Gene flow   p. 63

Genetic drift   p. 64

Geneticization   p. 74

Genotype   p. 62

Meiosis   p. 60

Mitosis   p. 60

Modern synthesis   p. 59

Mutation   p. 62

Natural selection   p. 62

Niche construction   p. 65

Phenotype   p. 62

Phylogeny   p. 55

Plasticity   p. 65

Population   p. 59

Protein synthesis   p. 60

Replication   p. 60

Reproductive success   p. 62

Shared characteristics   p. 56

Shared derived characteristics   p. 57

Symbolic system of inheritance   p. 66

Taxonomy   p. 53

Reviewing the Chapter

Chapter Section	What We Know	To Be Resolved
Life changes. But what does it mean to say it evolves?	Evolutionary thinking developed to understand the origins and diversity of life and is still changing. "Descent with modification" provided the first coherent scientific theory of evolution. Evolution differs from simple change because it is change that is adaptive, non-directional, inherited, and relational. Through the construction of phylogenies, we can understand how evolutionary change is rooted in relationships of common ancestry.	The particular meanings of evolution continue to develop as new facts are discovered and theoretical explanations and models are refined.

Chapter Section	What We Know	To Be Resolved
What are the actual mechanisms through which evolution occurs?	Through the modern synthesis, advances in genetics have been incorporated into evolutionary theory, and the extended evolutionary synthesis recognizes non-genetic dimensions of evolution. The basic building blocks of evolution are genes and DNA. Genetic variation arises through mutation. Natural selection, gene flow, and genetic drift move that variation around. Non-genetic mechanisms include developmental bias, plasticity, niche construction, and extra-genetic inheritance.	Some scientists believe that recognizing the non-genetic mechanisms of evolution undermines the coherence of evolutionary theory under the modern synthesis.
How do biocultural patterns affect evolution?	The intertwining of biology and culture in human evolution has produced biocultural dynamics that are open-ended and emergent. Key elements of these processes include multiple inheritances (genetic, epigenetic, behavioral, symbolic, and ecological), as well as developmental openness.	Although the constructivist approach presented here strives to take biology and culture equally seriously, not all biological anthropologists share that philosophical orientation to human evolution, and debates continue about the relative influences of biology and culture on human evolution.
Are modern humans evolving, and where might we be headed?	Modern humans are continuing to evolve, and they do it in biocultural contexts. Although humans can change their morphology quite readily, it is not always clear what the evolutionary implications of those actions might be. Nevertheless, migration and disease transmission have clear evolutionary impacts on contemporary humans. A focus on population growth, genetic manipulation, and dynamics of behavioral adaptation can yield insights into possible evolutionary futures.	Given the complexity and emergent qualities of biocultural processes, any predictions about our species' evolutionary trajectories are riddled with uncertainties.

READINGS

Charles Darwin's *On the Origin of Species* is still available in many reprint editions (a 150th anniversary edition was published in New York by Signet in 2003). Ernst Mayr's classic *What Evolution Is* (New York: Basic Books, 2002) offers an excellent accompaniment to Darwin's original.

Stephen Jay Gould wrote extensively on the history of evolutionary thinking and the biology of evolutionary processes, including a column for *Natural History* magazine, compiled into highly readable books of essays. A good place to start is his third volume of collected essays,

Hen's Teeth and Horse's Toes: Further Reflections on Natural History (New York: W. W. Norton, 1983), which includes his classic essay "Evolution as Fact and Theory."

The journal *Nature* hosted a debate entitled "Does Evolutionary Theory Need a Rethink?" (https://www.nature.com/articles/514161a), presenting arguments for and against the extended evolutionary synthesis (Laland et al. 2014).

In his book *Tales of the Ex-Apes: How We Think About Human Evolution* (Berkeley: University of California Press, 2015),

Jonathan Marks offers an approach to human evolution similar to the one we take in this book. He critiques biological reductionist approaches and explains how and why we are a biocultural species.

As Alexandra Brewis reports in *Obesity: Cultural and Biocultural Perspectives* (New Brunswick, NJ: Rutgers University Press, 2011), the study of the causes and consequences of obesity is a relatively new area of research for anthropologists. This book provides an overview of the issues as they relate to biocultural anthropology.

Cross-Cultural Interactions

*Understanding Culture
and Globalization*

4

BETWEEN 2013 AND 2017, a Hawai'ian sailing canoe named the Hōkūle'a made a circumnavigation of the globe, to raise awareness about global environmental sustainability and to celebrate the importance of creating new relationships across cultures. Its message: We live on a small planet and humanity's future depends on our ability to get along, across our differences, to address key global challenges.

But that same journey also says something about our past, because it was achieved with a twist that seems unimaginable in our modern technological era: the Hōkūle'a has no navigational instruments or technologies. The Hōkūle'a is a large, double-hulled Polynesian voyaging canoe capable of traveling across great ocean distances, the type of vessel that will be familiar if you have seen the Disney movie *Moana*. During the four-year voyage, a rotating crew of sailors trained in traditional Polynesian navigation knowledge and techniques directed the boat using sophisticated and subtle understanding of the sky and stars, wind and current patterns, weather systems, wildlife behavior, and other natural processes.

The Hōkūle'a was first built in the 1970s as an anthropological experiment of sorts. At the time, a predominant theory about the settlement of the Pacific held that ancestral Polynesians came from South America without navigation, sailing on rafts and canoes with the western trade winds and currents until they accidentally landed on Pacific islands. Norwegian adventurer Thor

A sailor using traditional navigation techniques on the Hōkūle'a.

Heyerdahl famously tested and found support for this theory in 1947 when he and a small crew set out from South America on a raft called the Kon-Tiki and eventually landed on an island in Tuamoto, French Polynesia (Heyerdahl 1958).

But for some native Hawai'ian activists and sailors, as well as cultural anthropologists and archaeologists, this theory was dubious because it assumed that Polynesians were so primitive that they couldn't make purposeful and accurate trips through the Pacific against those trade winds. They had a competing theory, which was that the origins of Polynesians were among Asians who traveled from east to west. But they did not understand how that happened. An organization called the Polynesian Voyaging Society was founded to test that theory, researching traditional Polynesian navigation and creating replicas of traditional voyaging boats like the Hōkūle'a to test, refine, and preserve those techniques (Finney 2004).

It was a daunting challenge, not least because much of that traditional wisdom had been lost because of rapid social change and new technologies that had swept through the Pacific islands. But the discovery of a Micronesian sailor named Mau Piailug, who was willing to train young Hawai'ians in those secretive techniques, as well as many experiments with traditional voyaging boat design, eventually culminated in a successful journey from Hawai'i to Tahiti in 1976. Since then the Hōkūle'a has made dozens of successful journeys across vast oceanic distances—the most ambitious being the recent circumnavigation of the globe—proving the sophistication and accuracy of traditional non-instrument navigation techniques.

The Pacific was long assumed to be the most isolated place on earth. But Polynesians and Micronesians weren't isolated. Every island's inhabitants had ties with other island groups, relying on those inter-island ties to engage with kin, friends, and unknown cultural groups in extensive trade networks and political activities. These ties helped islanders survive devastating typhoons, droughts, and volcanic eruptions on their home islands. Archaeologically we can trace connections though the distribution of objects of material culture found in different island groups. Biologically we can observe these commonalities in the DNA sampled from communities across the Pacific. Ethnographically, we can identify the presence of similar cultural patterns and material objects on different islands as well as from many local myths placing each community's origins on other island groups. And linguistically, we can see these linkages from the common terms for similar objects, from similar grammatical patterns, and other common traits found in different Pacific languages.

In our fast-paced world with its new technologies, means of transport, and modes of communication, it is easy to assume that the kinds of human movement, trade, and cross-cultural interactions we today call "globalization" represent a totally new phenomenon for humanity. But a key element of the human story, past and present, is the importance of cross-cultural interactions and interconnections. The question that stands at the core of these matters is this:

What do intensive cross-cultural interactions and interconnections mean for understanding cultural processes? We can answer this question by considering a number of related questions around which this chapter is organized:

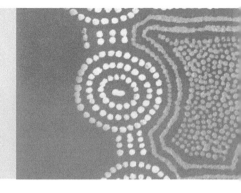

Are cross-cultural interactions all that new?

Is the contemporary world really getting smaller?

What are the outcomes of global integration?

Doesn't everyone want to be developed?

If the world is not becoming homogenized, what is actually happening?

We aim to deepen your understanding of culture as a dynamic process by showing its importance for understanding cross-cultural interactions and global processes. For anthropologists, these matters illustrate how people create and change their cultures through interconnections with others. But not everybody participates equally in these diverse kinds of cross-cultural and global interconnections, which means we also have to consider power relations and social inequality.

4.1 Are Cross-Cultural Interactions All That New?

During the past 150 years, archaeologists and cultural anthropologists have learned much about the history and extent of the cross-cultural processes of trade, migration, and inter-group conflict. One of the major conclusions is that, while certain patterns of cross-cultural interaction today are new and distinctive, for many thousands of years human groups have been interacting directly and indirectly with groups that are culturally and linguistically different from themselves (Jennings 2011).

The notion that isolated groups of people exist in the world is an idea that has long captivated Euro-American imaginations. Even today this idea periodically hits the headlines as some previously "uncontacted" society in a place like the Amazon basin or the jungles of New Guinea is encountered. But such encounters are the exception, not the rule, in human interconnectedness. The social processes and cross-cultural interactions that linked nearly all societies with their neighbors as well as more distant societies have been part of the human experience since our ancestors became human.

One recent indication of these early interactions comes from the study of DNA of ancient Neanderthal skeletons. When anthropologists analyzed that DNA they found that modern humans whose ancestors come from Europe or the Middle East tend to share a bit more than 1 percent of their DNA with the DNA of ancient Neanderthals, indicating a long history of sexual relations—perhaps even intermarriage?—between *Homo sapiens sapiens* and *Homo sapiens neanderthalensis*. In later prehistoric times, most humans (as today) intermarried with people living nearby. One pattern seems to be true across human history and prehistory—namely, that people have sex with people in their vicinity, regardless of what their ethnic identities and backgrounds may have been.

During the late nineteenth century, anthropologists generally believed that all human societies were also linked through trade, friendship, marriages, and other relationships. But in many early anthropology textbooks, one society was singled out as completely isolated. This was the relatively small group of Polar Inuit living above the Arctic Circle in the far northwest of Greenland. Many early textbooks claimed that they were entirely unaware of any other humans until European whalers and later explorers arrived. But when archaeologist James Van Stone in the 1970s examined the earliest museum collections from the Polar Inuit he found evidence in their material culture suggesting that even these remote and isolated people were not isolated from other groups (Vanstone 1972).

Nearly all people in prehistoric and early historic societies interacted with people beyond their own cultural and linguistic communities through trade and the exchange of material culture. If one group had a more effective form of weapon or a way to hunt or garden more successfully, it was borrowed, imitated, or taken by neighboring groups, including some who may from time to time fight with one's own group. If neighboring groups did not adopt the more effective tool or practice they might lose out to more successful neighbors. Anthropologist James B. Watson called this aspect of diffusion from one group to neighboring groups the "Jones Effect," because to compete successfully with their neighbors, they had to "keep up with the Joneses" in neighboring communities (Watson 1977). And in plenty of cases, where one group dominates another, these tools and procedures were not simply "borrowed" but often impressed upon the less powerful group. These dynamics have been observed by cultural anthropologists in living societies but they are also found in the archaeological records of ancient and prehistoric societies.

For example, in early archaeological sites across the Fertile Crescent (6,000–4,000 BCE) it is clear that there were mechanisms for dispersing cultural materials, food, and raw materials from one community to another within the earliest recorded states and empires. People sought access to food and other key goods, or they would push to leave the political and economic ties of their central governing authorities. In all likelihood, most ordinary people relied almost entirely on products made locally, supplemented occasionally with some exotic raw material, obtained from a distant land, that could be turned into a useful tool or ornament. As the ranks of elites began to grow, these elites seemed to have greater access to exotic goods from hundreds of miles away. Once Carbon-14 dating became available to archaeologists after World War II (see "Methods Memo: How Does Carbon-14 Dating Work?"), they were able to better understand the actual dates and sequence of activities in any particular site.

In the earliest sites there exists only limited evidence of intercultural interactions, largely restricted to a few exotic types of stone that must have been acquired from neighboring groups. The prominent early Middle Eastern site of Jarmo, 10,000 years old, has relatively few exotic materials that might not have been found in the vicinity. But by 6,000 years ago exotic items started to become more common. By the 1960s it was obvious to archaeologists that prehistoric peoples in Mesopotamia were importing obsidian from hundreds of miles away. Obsidian is much easier to source because its volcanic origins mean that it has a certain chemical signature or composition that is identifiable from an Accelerator Mass Spectrometer, often referred to as AMS (see, e.g., Beta Analytic Testing Laboratory 2018). For example, archaeologists had excavated and sourced an eight-inch obsidian bowl at the Mesopotamian site of Tepe Gawra in modern-day Turkey (Dixon, Cann, and Renfrew 1968). Using spectroscopic trace chemical analysis, they were able to determine that the obsidian came from a quarry site 400 miles away. In theory it is possible that the prehistoric people of Tepe Gawra traveled this distance to quarry the obsidian themselves; but it is much more likely that early groups living near the quarry harvested the obsidian and traded it to one of their several neighbors, probably in exchange for some other useful material. It may have been traded through several different groups until the obsidian reached Tepe Gawra. It is clear that early Middle Eastern communities relied heavily on exchanging or trading valuable raw materials, distributing these resources from a small number of quarry sites to communities across the region (Adams 1974).

Similar dynamics characterized other parts of the ancient world. On the north coast of New Guinea, for example, prehistoric people lived in small villages varying from 100 to a few hundred people, but they imported obsidian that was quarried primarily on one of two small volcanic islands in what is now Manus province, 800 miles away, much of it across the ocean. By analyzing used and discarded flakes of obsidian found along the beaches at some of these village sites around Aitape, archaeologist John Terrell and his colleagues were able to distinguish between the two important quarries in Manus from the density of the obsidian flakes. They were also able to determine that some had been quarried hundreds of years earlier than the others. Because we know the source of both kinds of obsidian and the history of these volcanoes, Terrell could determine that some deposits had been quarried before an eruption at one volcano covered up the quarry and that the other quarry was known to have been exploited at a later date (Golitko, Schauer, and Terrell 2013b; Terrell and Schecter 2011; Welsch 1996, 1999; Welsch and Terrell 1998). More recent analysis of these and other samples suggests that a small number of flakes had come from Ferguson Island, a site much farther away, about 1,500 miles by sea from where they had been deposited (Golitko et al. 2013a; see Figure 4.1).

It was also becoming clear to archaeologists that many ancient state societies, including those of Mesopotamia, Egypt, Persia, and the Greco-Roman world, were developing centralized control over food production across large geographic territories. All of these ancient empires developed extensive trading networks in which vast quantities of grain, meat, and raw materials moved from one part of the empire to another, even though the various segments of the kingdom often spoke different languages and had different cultural patterns. As each of these ancient states emerged,

Figure 4.1 Prehistoric Obsidian Sites in Papua New Guinea (from Golitko et al. 2013a).

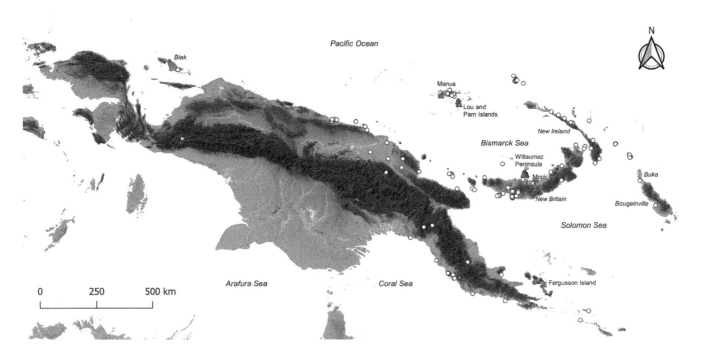

the diverse and often quite varied cultural patterns among the scattered communities that came under their control were smoothed out by being part of the same kingdom, paying taxes or tributes to the central governing authorities, and benefiting from the trade and regional commerce that helped to smooth out the cultural, ethnic, and subregional differences without eliminating them.

Archaeologists have since documented similar dynamics in non-state and non-empire societies, especially in places like the American Midwest at Cahokia and at the numerous Adena and Fort Ancient mound sites from Illinois to Indiana and Ohio (Shetrone 2004; Lepper 2005; Pauketat 2010). Such evidence from archaeologists and cultural anthropologists reinforces the view that extensive and persistent cross-cultural interactions characterize human history. And what about the present?

THINKING LIKE AN ANTHROPOLOGIST: CROSS-CULTURAL INTERACTIONS

Where do you think Euro-American fascination about isolated, undiscovered, and uncontacted peoples comes from, and how and why does it persist?

4.2 Is The Contemporary World Really Getting Smaller?

Asian hip-hop in London, American retirement-fund investments in a South Korean steel conglomerate, Indian "Bollywood" movies in Nigeria, Mexican migrants cooking Thai food in a North Carolina restaurant—each of these situations confirms our sense that the world is "getting smaller" and cultural mixing is on the rise. This sense extends to anthropologists, who recognize that the people whose lives we study are often profoundly affected by global interconnections, migratory flows, and cultural mixing. During the past several decades, understanding how those processes of global interconnection affect culture has become an important issue for all anthropologists. For a discipline that has long tried to understand the differences and similarities between human groups and cultures, the idea that the world is getting smaller might suggest that the differences are melting away. But is the world really getting smaller? To answer this question, we first need to understand what globalization is.

Defining Globalization

Defining globalization is a challenge for two reasons. First, different academic disciplines define globalization differently because they study different things. Economists focus on investment and markets, political scientists on policies and interactions of nation-states, and sociologists on non-governmental organizations (NGOs) and other international social institutions. But there is a second problem. Is globalization a general *process* or a *trend* of growing worldwide interconnectedness? Is it a *system* of investment and trade? Is it the *explicit goal* of particular governments or international trade bodies that promote free trade? Or is it, as some say, "globaloney," something that does not actually exist at all (Veseth 2005)?

Anthropologists define **globalization** as the contemporary widening scale of cross-cultural interactions owing to the rapid movement of money, people, goods,

• **Globalization.** The widening scale of cross-cultural interactions caused by the rapid movement of money, people, goods, images, and ideas within nations and across national boundaries.

images, and ideas within nations and across national boundaries (Kearney 1995; Inda and Rosaldo 2002). But, as we explained in the previous section, we also recognize that social, economic, and political interconnection and mixing are nothing new for humanity.

Early American cultural anthropologists also recognized these facts. Franz Boas and his students Alfred Kroeber and Ralph Linton developed a theory of culture that emphasized the interconnectedness of societies. The Boasians were **diffusionists**, emphasizing that cultural characteristics result from either internal historical dynamism or a spread (diffusion) of cultural attributes from one society to another (Figure 4.2). Later, beginning in the 1950s, Marxist anthropologists like Eric Wolf argued against the isolation of societies, suggesting that non-Western societies could not be understood without reference to their place within a global capitalist system.

And yet, until the 1980s, such themes of interconnectedness were generally at the margins of cultural anthropology. Mainstream anthropology was locally focused, based on research in face-to-face village settings using ethnographic methods (see "Methods Memo: Studying Culture and Social Relations Using Ethnographic Methods"). This was true even as nearly all those societies were heavily engaged with neighboring communities, either as friends, economic partners, or hostile enemies. It was, arguably, an important blind spot but one that in intellectual context makes sense: most anthropological research was focused on small-scale non-Western societies, one reason being that these were the societies the "salvage paradigm" (see Chapter 1)

Diffusionists. Early twentieth-century Boasian anthropologists who held that cultural characteristics result from either internal historical dynamism or a spread (diffusion) of cultural attributes from other societies.

Figure 4.2 A Global Ecumene. The Greeks referred to an "ecumene" as the inhabited earth, as this map shows. Much later, anthropologist Alfred Kroeber (1876–1960) used the term to describe a region of persistent cultural interaction. The term became current again in the 1980s and 1990s as anthropologists adopted it to describe interactions across the whole globe.

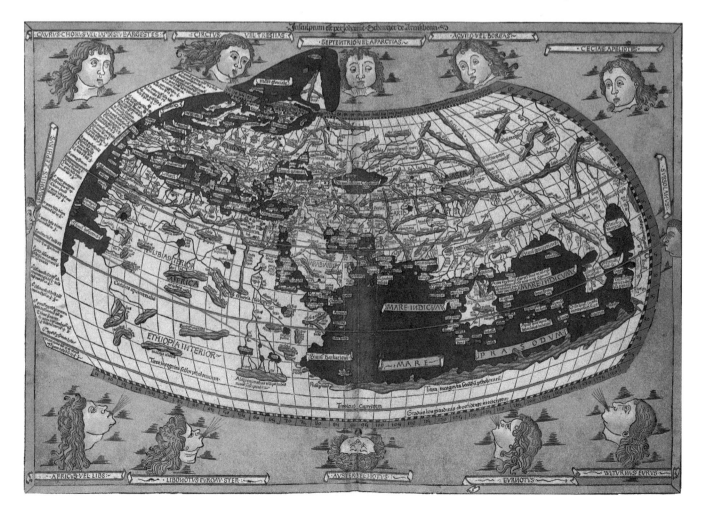

had identified as priorities to study "before they disappeared." Today, anthropologists realize that paying attention only to local settings gives an incomplete understanding of people's lives, because those same peoples didn't disappear; they adapted and changed. Anthropologists also realized local perspectives alone give an incomplete understanding of the causes of cultural differences, which often emerge not in spite of, but *because of*, cross-cultural interactions and interconnections. While not every group participates at the same level in these broad regional or global connections, most communities are more interconnected than many researchers imagined as recently as twenty or thirty years ago.

The World We Live In

How do anthropologists characterize the world in which we live today? Several factors stand out, including the scale of human interconnections and awareness of these interconnections (Nederveen Pieterse 2004). But these changes hardly mean that everybody is participating equally in the same globalizing processes. Further, the word *globalization*, unfortunately, tends to make us think of the entire globe, exaggerating the scale and expanse of financial and social interconnections, which, while great, are typically more limited and often more subtle than the word implies. Indeed some anthropologists prefer the term **transnational** in this context because it imagines relationships that extend beyond nations without assuming they cover the whole world (Basch, Schiller, and Blanc 1993). Whatever the case, it is useful to think of globalization as indicating persistent interactions across widening scales of social activity in areas such as communication, migration, and finance.

- **Transnational.** Relationships that extend beyond nation-state boundaries but do not necessarily cover the whole world.

Communication

At the heart of globalization are rapid increases in the scale and amount of communication taking place. With smartphones, the Internet, and email accessible in most parts of the world, it is clear that the scale of contact has made a quantum leap forward over the past generation. Such rapid and much more frequent communication means that people in very remote places can be in contact with others almost anywhere on the globe (Figure 4.3).

But access to these innovations is generally distributed unevenly. In 2018, for example, only about half the world's population (55 percent) used the internet. Africa is the least connected, with only about 36 percent of that continent's people being internet users. In contrast, only 85 percent of Europeans were internet users (Internet World Stats 2018). As a result, some observers, to highlight real inequalities of access, prefer to talk about the globalization of communication in terms of wealth and poverty.

- **Migrants.** People who leave their homes to work for a time in other regions or countries.

- **Immigrants.** People who enter a foreign country with no expectation of ever returning to their home country.

- **Refugees.** People who migrate because of political oppression or war, usually with legal permission to stay in a different country.

- **Exiles.** People who are expelled by the authorities of their home countries.

Migration

Another key feature of the changing scale of globalization is the mobility of people. Whether they be **migrants** (who leave their homes to live or work for a time in other regions or countries), or **immigrants** (who leave their countries with no expectation of ever returning), or **refugees** (who migrate because of political oppression or war, usually with legal permission to stay), or **exiles** (who are expelled by the authorities of their home countries) (Shorris 1992), people are on the move. According to the United Nations, the number of international migrants—people living in a country other than the one in which they were born—reached 244 million in 2015, which was a 41 percent increase from the year 2000 (United Nations 2016). Nearly two-thirds of

Figure 4.3   An Explosion in Mobile Phones. Seven billion people, or 95 percent of the world's population, now live in an area covered by a mobile network. This connectivity, which was unimaginable even a generation ago, has had important consequences for people everywhere, including these young Aboriginals of the Taroqo tribe in Taiwan.

those international migrants live in Asia or Europe, but the United States is the single country with the largest number of international migrants (47 million) (Figure 4.4). These movements of people bring larger numbers in contact with one another, offering many possibilities for intercultural contact.

Finance

In the modern era, financial globalization involving the reduction or elimination of tariffs to promote trade across borders began in the 1870s. In recent decades, finance and the rapid movement of money across national boundaries have allowed corporations to move factories from one country to another. A generation ago, US factories moved their operations to Mexico and China, but now many of these same factories have been shuttered and relocated to Honduras or Vietnam because of rising hourly labor costs in Mexico and China.

Under these conditions of globalized capital, many transnational corporations have accumulated vast assets. Currently, sixty-nine of the world's one hundred largest economic entities are corporations, and the other thirty-one are countries. Walmart, the world's largest retailer, ranks as the tenth largest economic entity in the world, just behind Canada and ahead of Spain (Global Justice Now 2016). Because powerful corporate interests often influence the policies of governments, some see in this situation a movement of power away from nation-states (Korten 1995). But this economic growth and trade are also highly uneven, which raises a key question: Who benefits from and who pays the costs of global interconnections? We turn to this important question in the next section.

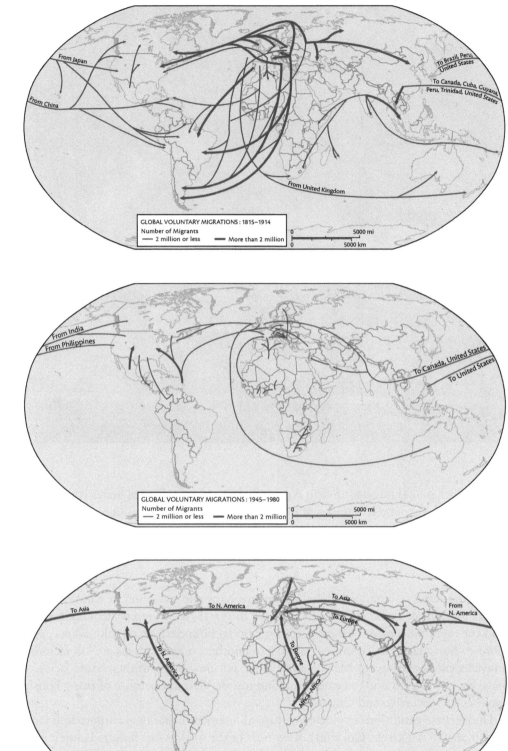

Figure 4.4 Global Voluntary Migrations. These three maps show dramatic differences in the directions of migratory flows. During the European colonial era, Europeans were motivated to migrate out of Europe because of opportunities in the colonies (*top map*). After the Second World War, decolonization saw a reversal in the flow, as non-Europeans and non-US Americans began moving into Europe and the United States in search of new opportunities for themselves (*middle map*). Today, most migrants stay within the same major region of the world in which they are born (*bottom map*).

THINKING LIKE AN ANTHROPOLOGIST: CROSS-CULTURAL INTERACTIONS

Beyond communication, migration, and finance, what are some other culturally significant forces that make the world feel smaller?

4.3 What Are the Outcomes of Global Integration?

In public debates, the most common way of framing globalization's outcomes is in terms of winners and losers. Globalization's promoters focus on winners, arguing that greater economic integration brings unprecedented prosperity to millions. They cite evidence that the more open a country is to foreign trade, the more rapidly its economy grows (Norberg 2006). Critics focus on losers, invoking images of sweatshops and poverty. They offer evidence that the gap between rich countries and poor countries has actually widened, and we are witness to a "globalization of poverty" (Chossudovsky 1997). In recent years, nationalist backlashes have emerged, evident among some political leaders in the United States, Great Britain, France, and Russia who have argued that the real "losers" in globalization are the working classes in their countries whose jobs have been shipped overseas or "taken" by newer immigrants. In the face of such arguments, it is useful to remember that all sides are often discussing fairly narrow economic policy questions related to free trade, labor conditions, outsourcing of jobs, and so on. These are important issues, but they tend to ignore the cultural nuances of global interconnections, which include inequality, confrontation, domination, accommodation, and resistance.

Colonialism and World Systems Theory

For several decades, **world systems theory** has provided the social sciences with an important theoretical lens for understanding global inequality. Developed by economic historians André Gunder Frank and Immanuel Wallerstein, world systems theory rejects the idea that global interconnections are anything new, identifying the late fifteenth century as the beginning of a new capitalist world order that connected different parts of the world in new ways. During this historical period, according to world systems theory, the expansion of overseas European colonies was enabled by and rooted in the creation of a global capitalist market. This market was based on unequal exchange between a "core" (the home countries) and a "periphery" (the rest of the world). The core (the winners) developed its economy by exploiting the periphery (the losers), whose role was to provide labor and raw materials for the core's consumption. European colonial institutions and authority secured capitalism's ability to extract labor and natural resources from the periphery. The result is the periphery's long-term poverty, underdevelopment, and dependency on the core. In relation to these conditions, anthropologists have posed a question other social scientists have not: How has this world system affected the native peoples and cultural systems of the periphery?

In his influential book *Europe and the People Without History*, anthropologist Eric Wolf took on this question. Wolf argued that long-distance trade and cultural interaction were around long before the development of capitalism but that the expansion

● **World systems theory.** The theory that capitalism has expanded on the basis of unequal exchange throughout the world, creating a global market and global division of labor, dividing the world between a dominant "core" and a dependent "periphery."

Classic Contributions
Eric Wolf, Culture, and the World System

ERIC WOLF (1923–1999) studied issues of power, inequality, and politics in Latin America. He insisted that anthropologists and other social scientists needed to discover "a history that could account for the ways in which the social system of the modern world came into being" (1984: ix). He was interested in the origin and workings of peasant and tribal societies, but always in relation to the powerful governmental and business interests that so often kept peasants poor. In this selection, Wolf presents why anthropologists should view most societies over the past 500 years as societies linked to other societies, often with tragic consequences for some of the people involved.

Eric Wolf.

While some anthropologists thus narrow their focus to the ever more intensive study of the single case, others hope to turn anthropology into a science by embarking on the statistical cross-cultural comparisons . . . drawn from large samples of ethnographically known cases. . . .

What, however, if we take cognizance of processes that transcend separable cases, moving through and beyond them and transforming them as they proceed? Such processes were, for example, the North American fur trade and the trade in native American and African slaves. What of the localized Algonkin-speaking patrilineages, for example, which in the course of the fur trade moved into large nonkin villages and became known as the ethnographic Ojibwa? What of the Chipeweyans, some of whose bands gave up hunting to become fur trappers, or "carriers," while others *continued to hunt for game as "caribou eaters," with people continuously changing from caribou eating to carrying and back? . . . What, moreover, of Africa, where the slave trade created an unlimited demand for slaves, and where quite unrelated populations met that demand by severing people from their kin groups through warfare, kidnapping, pawning, or judicial procedures, in order to have slaves to sell to the Europeans? In all such cases, to attempt to specify separate cultural wholes and distinct boundaries would create a false sample. These cases exemplify spatially and temporally shifting relationships, prompted in all instances by the effects of European expansion. If we consider, furthermore, that this expansion has for nearly 500 years affected case after case, then the search for a world sample of distinct cases is illusory.* [Wolf 1984:17–18]

Questions for Reflection

1.   What happened about 500 years ago that changed the relations between societies from what they had been?

2.   Why does Wolf feel that most societies have been in touch with Europeans and others outside of their society for the past 500 years?

3.   How would you explain to your younger brother or sister why Wolf feels anthropologists should not view societies as bounded and unconnected to other societies?

of European colonialism and capitalism drew non-European people into a global market, in which, as producers of commodities, they were to serve the cause of capital accumulation as a subordinate working class (Wolf 1984:352–53). These processes disrupted, even destroyed, many societies (Bodley 1999).

But Wolf rejected the customary divisions we make between "West" and "non-West." He insisted that people in the periphery also have helped shape the world system because they have often resisted capitalist expansion. These are the common people usually ignored by the victorious elites when they wrote their histories. Wolf argued that we need to pay close attention to the peripheral people's active role in world history. As we explore in "Classic Contributions: Eric Wolf, Culture, and the World System," Wolf's argument challenged not only popular stereotypes of indigenous people as isolated and passive but also cultural anthropology's bias toward the local—that is, the traditional ethnographic focus on villages and other small groups.

Because world systems theory focused on the rise of capitalism as a global system, this macro-level perspective did not readily lend itself to ethnographic research of smaller communities and non-global economics. But the theory helped anthropologists better explain the historical emergence and contemporary persistence of uneven development patterns around the world and has been of critical interest to scholars of **postcolonialism**, the field that studies the cultural legacies of colonialism and imperialism. It has also helped anthropologists understand the linkages between local social relations (families, kin networks, communities) and other levels of political-economic activity, like the regional, national, and transnational.

- **Postcolonialism.** The field that studies the cultural legacies of colonialism and imperialism.

Cultures of Migration

One of world systems theory's key assertions is that the same conditions that produced an unbalanced world order have also generated territorial displacement and population flows, especially to supply labor for capitalist needs. Migratory flows involve structural **push-pull factors**. These factors include poverty, violent conflict, political uncertainties, and others that "push" individuals to migrate from their home countries, and factors like economic possibilities and social and political opportunities that "pull" them to host countries (Massey et al. 1993).

- **Push-pull factors.** The social, economic, and political factors that "push" people to migrate from their homes and that "pull" them to host countries.

Anthropologists take such structural factors into account when studying migration. But detailed ethnographic studies of migrant-sending and migrant-receiving communities, as well as of migrants themselves, have revealed a greater level of complexity to these processes than a simple push-pull model allows (Brettell 2003). For example, when they migrate, individuals rarely act in social isolation. Their decision to migrate is often made by members of a household who consider its resources, the varying talents and abilities of its members, community traditions such as whether there is a history of migration, and the relative strength of opportunities in the destination (Kearney 1996; Cohen 2004). Not all individuals in a community have equal access to migration, either, because certain social groups—for example, relative economic elites or members of a certain gender or ethnic group—sometimes have greater ability to be mobile than others. This pattern is not simply a contemporary phenomenon. In his studies of Hungarian migrants to the United States during the early twentieth century, for example, George Dorsey found that most were landowners (see Chapter 1, "A World in Motion").

Moreover, migrants typically move within and between social networks, made up of kin and other social connections, that shape their choice of destination. Reconnecting with those social networks is often a high priority for involuntary migrants, especially since governments and bureaucracies that manage refugees often ignore the importance of these social ties in successful adaptation to a new place. Recognizing the simple anthropological insight that migrants want—at least initially—to

- **Transnational community.** A spatially extended social network that spans multiple countries.

- **Culture of migration.** The cultural attitudes, perceptions, and symbolic values that shape decision-making processes around, and experiences of, migration.

maintain ties with people who speak their native language and understand their background can help immigrant groups adjust to life in their new country.

In some circumstances, social networks are so spatially extended that migrants participate in a **transnational community**. Roger Rouse (1991) documented this phenomenon while studying the effects of migration on the rural Mexican village of Aguililla [ah-gee-**lee**-uh]. As a result of out-migration, Aguilillans were scattered across multiple outposts and settlements in urban Mexico and the United States. Nevertheless, community members still felt that they were members of a single social unit, and they maintained close social, kin, and economic ties through regular phone contact and movement of individuals between settlements, and by ensuring that important decisions were made collectively. Rouse found that what bound Aguilillans together, even across national boundaries, was not a nostalgic tie to their home village but a close connection to the migratory circuit itself (Figure 4.5).

Cultural attitudes, perceptions, and symbolic values also shape migration, creating what anthropologists call a **culture of migration**. Through migration, people generate new meanings about the world, their homes, and themselves. In many places where migration is prevalent, it is viewed as an important, even necessary, rite of passage into adulthood, a means to elevate or maintain social status, and an experience in which new social identities are formed (Nagengast and Kearney 1990). For example, in her fieldwork among Portuguese migrants in Portugal, Brazil, France, and North America, Caroline Brettell (2003) found that the concept of "the emigrant" holds a powerful symbolic meaning in people's ideas about what it means to be Portuguese. It shapes and reinforces Portuguese people's national constructions of themselves as tolerant and worldly people who have been proactive in shaping the conditions of the modern world, and it forms the basis of a strong ethnic identity in countries where Portuguese people have settled.

Resistance at the Periphery

The expansion of the capitalist world system has generated greater cross-border movement, but it also met with resistance from the peripheral peoples affected. Anthropologists have devoted considerable attention to this resistance, finding

Figure 4.5   Migration and Social Status. The Zapotec village of Santa Maria de Yavesia, in the southern Mexican state of Oaxaca, has experienced migration to the United States and other parts of Mexico for decades. One way migrants demonstrate their success and show new social status is by sending back money or returning home and building nice new homes painted in bright colors.

examples that range from open rebellion and mass mobilizations to more subtle forms of protest and opposition.

Many forms of resistance may not be obvious to us because they are rooted in culturally subtle forms of expression. For example, in one factory in Malaysia, spirit possession episodes have erupted, disrupting work and production goals (Ong 1988). According to the factory women of Malaysia, the facility violated two basic moral boundaries: close physical proximity of the sexes and male managers' constant monitoring of female workers. Young female workers, who as Muslims are expected to be shy and deferential, believed that these two factors forced them to violate cultural taboos that define social and bodily boundaries between men and women. They also believed that the construction of modern factories displaces and angers local spirits, who then haunt the toilets. For the women, these transgressions combine to provoke spirit possession, in which the women became violent and loud, disrupting work in the factory. Spirit possession episodes helped the women regain a sense of control over both their bodies and social relations in the factory (Ong 1988:34). Such resistance interests anthropologists because it shows how people interpret and challenge global processes through local cultural idioms and beliefs.

Globalizing and Localizing Identities

Greater global integration also opens up opportunities for the creation of new social identities. The world today is full of "cosmopolitans"—border-crossing businesspeople, backpack travelers, intellectuals, artists, and others—whose incessant movements around the globe identify them as fully modern, sophisticated, and progressive subjects. But the cosmopolitan is also an old idea that has political dimensions as well. Ancient Greek Stoic philosophy defined "cosmopolitan" as an orientation to the world in which all human beings are thought to belong to one community built on a foundation of mutual respect. In our era, this idea is often expressed through the language of "global citizenship." The identity of global citizen is a compelling one for individuals in the global North seeking ways of sharing responsibility for addressing global inequalities. Perhaps because of disciplinary concerns with these matters, anthropology can attract, guide, and inform individuals who identify with these ideas and values, as we explore in the following "Anthropological Life" box.

Globalizing processes also promote a contrasting phenomenon anthropologists call **localization**—the creation and assertion of highly particular, often place-based, identities and communities (Friedman 1994). Localization is evidenced by the recent rise of autonomy movements among Hawaiian separatists and other indigenous groups throughout the world that seek self-determination; nationalist and ethnic movements like that of the Basques in Europe; and other movements engaged in reinforcing local control—for example, by encouraging community-supported agriculture and the use of local currencies (Friedman 1994). Each of these movements seeks to recuperate and protect local identities and places in the face of greater economic and cultural integration within a nation or a transnational network.

- **Localization.** The creation and assertion of highly particular, often place-based, identities and communities.

Other evidence of localization lies in people's patterns of consumption, which is a common way that people express their local identities and ways of being. In our own society, people choose certain clothing and shoe brands because they believe it says something about them as individuals: their social status, lifestyle, and outlook on the world, in particular. People in other countries do this too, but because of local culture and history, patterns of consumption can communicate very different things.

For example, among the Bakongo in the Republic of the Congo, a former French colony in Central Africa, poor Bakongo youths in urban shantytowns of the capital city, Brazzaville, compete with each other to acquire famous French and Italian

The Anthropological Life
Coldplay and the Global Citizen Festival

The rock band Coldplay is well known for its songs about love, relationships, fear, and hope. But it has also gained a reputation for its concerns about global power imbalances, social inequality, racism, environmental degradation, and the plight of the poor. For two of its prominent members—Will Champion, who earned his degree in Social Anthropology, and Chris Martin, who studied Classical Archaeology—these themes were an important part of their undergraduate studies in anthropology at University College London.

In 2010 the band performed in the Hope For Haiti Now telethon to provide aid for the victims of the devastating earthquake. They performed at the One Love Manchester benefit concert for the victims of the 2017 Manchester Arena bombing, and at many other concerts aimed at raising funds to support victims of tragic events around the globe. In 2014 they performed at a concert to raise money for the Ebola crisis in the West African countries of Guinea, Liberia, and Sierra Leone. More recently, they performed as special guests at the "Concert for Charlottesville" in Virginia in reaction to the "Unite the Right" rally of August 2017. Their *Plastic Oceans* album was released in February 2018 at the Ocean Plastics Crisis Summit in London, wanting to make their supporters aware of the growing problem of plastics in the world's oceans. All of these efforts were aimed at specific social problems in different parts of the world.

Among the most consistent and visible of Coldplay's activities in recent years has been their sponsorship of the annual Global Citizen Festival in New York's Central Park, which was launched in September 2012. For many of their benefit concerts and activities, Coldplay has stressed causes to help people directly affected by earthquakes, storms, and the devastation caused by war. But when they organized the Global Citizen Festival, they had a deeper goal from the beginning, which was to encourage their audience to support efforts to stem extreme poverty around the globe. The Global Citizen Festival required tickets to attend, but tickets were not sold. Rather, they were acquired by showing evidence of having completed some community service.

Some critics have challenged whether Coldplay's annual concerts could "fight poverty," arguing that actions at the governmental level are necessary for real change, not just a rock concert. We would argue that recognizing and understanding the relationship between certain economic patterns and extreme poverty is critical for the general public to push policymakers to fight extreme global poverty in their own countries and in the foreign aid decisions of their own governments.

Extreme poverty globally has declined substantially since 1990, falling by a few percentage points each year (World Bank 2018). The World Bank now believes it is possible to eliminate extreme world poverty by 2030, although it also recognizes this is extremely challenging in several countries. It's simply impossible to attribute such a decline to the efforts of any rock band. But indirectly the concert and Coldplay's efforts have allowed the public to become more aware of global patterns of extreme poverty, and directly, they have raised substantial funds for disaster relief. They have urged their audiences and supporters to help by providing community service in small ways, arguing that change starts in the listener's own communities. Coldplay is, first and foremost, a group of musicians. But the fact is, they have used their anthropological, archaeological, and world history training to guide how they promote their music and how they can help shape the world.

Questions for Reflection

1. How might anthropological training have shaped Champion and Martin's efforts in promoting the international causes they have supported?

2. While concerts may raise funds from telethons and online contributions, could an annual concert act in a more subtle manner to shape the ways young people approach and think about global poverty?

3. How do you think efforts like those of Coldplay contribute to the construction of cosmopolitan social identities in the contemporary world?

Can music fight poverty?   Singer Chris Martin and his band Coldplay perform at the 2017 Global Citizen Festival in Germany.

designer clothes (Figure 4.6). Calling themselves *sapeurs* (loosely translated as "dandies"), the most ambitious and resourceful go to Europe, where they acquire fancy clothes by whatever means they can. By becoming hyper-consumers, *sapeurs* are not merely imitating prosperous Europeans. Europeans may believe that "clothes make the man," but Congolese believe that clothes reflect the degree of "life force" possessed by the wearer (Friedman 1994:106). The *sapeur*'s goal is not to live a European lifestyle; his goal is to accumulate prestige by linking himself to external forces of wealth, health, and political power. In highly ranked Congolese society, the poor Bakongo urbanite ranks lowest. By connecting to upscale European fashion trends, the *sapeur* represents an assault on the higher orders of Congolese society, who normally dismiss him as a barbarian.

People always define their identities locally. What is different today from previous generations, perhaps, is that people increasingly express their local identities through their interaction with transnational processes, such as communications, migration, global citizenship, or consumerism, and with institutions, such as transnational businesses and human rights organizations. In today's world, people participate in global processes *and* local communities simultaneously. But they rarely participate in global processes on equal footing, because of their subordinate place in the world system or in their own countries—a theme we explore in "A World in Motion: Instant Ramen Noodles Take Over the Globe." Nevertheless, many anthropologists feel that to identify them in stark terms as *either* winners *or* losers of global integration greatly simplifies the complexity of their simultaneous involvement in globalization and localization processes.

As these examples show, people can be accommodating to outside influences, even while maintaining culturally specific meanings and social relations, whether because of defiance or because they actively transform the alien into something more familiar (Piot 1999). In these circumstances, cultural differences exist not in spite of, but because of, interconnection. But it still seems difficult to deny that so many millions of people are striving to become developed and to pursue lifestyles similar to those of middle-class Americans.

Figure 4.6 Bakongo *Sapeur*. The *sapeur*'s engagement in both transnational fashion worlds and local processes of social stratification destabilizes any strong local-global dichotomy.

A World in Motion
Instant Ramen Noodles Take Over the Globe

The story of instant ramen noodles offers insight into the ways in which industrialization, global processes, and local meanings shape changing dynamics in what people eat. Invented in 1958 in postwar Japan, instant ramen is now eaten in all corners of the globe, selling over 103 billion packages and cups in 2018 (World Instant Noodles Association 2019). Industrially produced ramen begins with vitamin fortified wheat noodles that are steamed, fried in palm oil, and then infused with salt, monosodium glutamate (MSG), and artificial flavors. The result is an inexpensive product with a long shelf life that is easily prepared, palatable, and filling (Errington, Fujikura, and Gewertz 2013).

These qualities have enabled the penetration of ramen into food systems around the world, often in contexts where people are experiencing big political-economic transformations. For example, in Papua New Guinea, rapid urbanization has drawn people with dreams of economic prosperity to migrate from rural villages and settle in urban areas. These migrants often confront precarious

❦ **Varieties of instant ramen in a southeast Asian market.**

realities of underemployment, scarcity of cash, and inadequate access to food. In this context, Maggi brand instant ramen noodles (made by Nestlé, the Swiss multinational corporation, which has a factory in the country) have become a ubiquitous element of people's diets. Nestlé has set up a vendor system in which individuals with street carts prepare inexpensive ramen-based meals for sale. One effect is that instant ramen noodles have "greased the skids of capitalism" by helping Papua New Guineans reimagine themselves as "consumers" participating in the modern world through their identification with certain global brands (Errington, Fjikura, and Gewertz 2013:8). At the same time, the calories ramen provides sustain their bodies as productive labor at the lowest rungs of capitalism and the informal economy.

Another important quality of instant ramen noodles is the flexibility they allow to add ingredients and channel localized meanings. In American prisons, for example, ramen noodles are immensely popular; inmates purchase them and combine them with other commissary-bought ingredients in imaginative "spreads" to break the monotony of incarceration and prison food. On National Public Radio in the United States, middle-class Americans reflect with nostalgia on meals made with ramen during family events like camping trips. In Japan, upward of 600 varieties of ramen are introduced every year, promoted with clever advertising campaigns that draw a lot of attention. There, instant ramen noodles are positioned to appeal to any number of tastes and social identities.

Instant ramen provides hundreds of millions of people with an important part of their daily sustenance. Some multinational noodle companies claim they are giving people what they want while helping to solve the problem of world hunger. The discussion over what all this might mean for globalization's impacts on public health, agriculture, the environment, and local foodways and food cultures is really just beginning.

4.4 Doesn't Everyone Want to Be Developed?

Long before the current globalization craze, discussions about global integration were often framed as the problem of bringing "civilization" (Western, that is), and later economic development, to non-European societies. But the question we pose here—Doesn't everyone want to be developed?—has no easy answer. Ideas differ about what development is and how to achieve it, so first we must ask: What is development?

What Is Development?

In 1949, US President Harry Truman gave his inaugural address in which he defined the role of the United States in the post–World War II world, when the West confronted the communist nations. He said, "We must embark on a new program for making the benefits of our scientific advances and industrial progress available for the improvement and growth of the underdeveloped areas" (Truman 1949). He defined two-thirds of the world as "underdeveloped" and one-third as "developed." Truman believed that if poor people around the world participated in the "American dream" of a middle-class lifestyle, they would not turn toward communism (Esteva 1992).

The Cold War is over, but development is still with us. It is a worldwide enterprise that was never solely American. Many European nations give aid to their former colonies. The stated goals of this aid range from expanding capitalist markets through trade and the building of infrastructure to alleviating poverty, improving health, and conserving natural resources. Key actors include the United Nations, the government aid agencies of most industrialized countries, lending agencies like the World Bank, and non-governmental organizations (NGOs) like CARE International.

Contemporary international development still aims to bring people into the "modern" world and correct what it identifies as undesirable and undignified conditions like poverty and lack of modern conveniences. Just as in the colonial era, "advanced" capitalist countries still provide the economic and social models for development.

But there is ambiguity to the concept of development. Is it a means to a particular end? Or is it the end itself? Who defines the shape and course of development? More important for our purposes, development has an ambiguous relationship with cultural diversity. Is its goal to foster the unfolding potential and purposeful improvement of people—from their own local cultural perspective? Or is it a program of forced change that is eliminating cultural diversity to create a world ordered on the universal principles of capitalist societies?

There are two distinct anthropological approaches to development: **development anthropology** and the **anthropology of development** (Gow 1993). While development anthropologists involve themselves in the theoretical and practical aspects of shaping and implementing development projects, anthropologists of development tend to study the cultural conditions for proper development or, alternatively, the negative impacts of development projects. Often the two overlap, but at times they are in direct conflict.

- **Development anthropology.** The application of anthropological knowledge and research methods to the practical aspects of shaping and implementing development projects.

- **Anthropology of development.** The field of study within anthropology concerned with understanding the cultural conditions for proper development, or, alternatively, the negative impacts of development projects.

Development Anthropology

Development anthropology is a branch of applied anthropology. It is a response to a simple fact: many development projects have failed because planners have not taken local culture into consideration. Planners often blame project failures on local people's supposed ignorance or stubbornness (Mamdani 1972). But it is often the planners themselves who are ignorant of local issues or set in their ways. Projects are more likely to meet their goals when they are fine-tuned to local needs, capacities, perspectives, and interests.

A classic example recognized by many anthropologists is the work of Gerald Murray on deforestation in Haiti. In the 1970s and 1980s, the US Agency for International Development (USAID) invested millions of dollars in Haitian reforestation projects that consistently failed (Murray 1987). Poor farmers resisted reforestation because it encroached on valuable croplands. Worse yet, aid money directed to farmers kept disappearing in the corrupt Haitian bureaucracy. Murray saw that the planners misunderstood the attitudes and needs of local farmers, not to mention the most effective ways to get the resources to them. He suggested a different approach. Planners had conceived of this project as an environmental one. He convinced USAID instead to introduce it to farmers as planting a new cash crop and to avoid involving the Haitian bureaucracy. Farmers would plant trees along the borders of their lands, allowing crops to continue to grow (Figure 4.7). After several years, they could harvest mature trees to sell as lumber. It was a very successful project: within four years, 75,000 farmers had planted 20 million trees, and many discovered the additional benefits of having trees on their land.

Figure 4.7   Haitian Farmers Planting Saplings for Reforestation.

Development anthropologists often think of themselves as advocates for the people living at the grassroots—the poor, small farmers, women, and other marginalized people—who could be most affected, negatively or positively, by development but who lack the political influence to design and implement projects (Chambers 1997). Today, many anthropologists work in development agencies, both internationally (such as in USAID) and domestically (in community development organizations). As recently as 2019, the president of the World Bank, the world's largest development bank, was an anthropologist named Dr. Jim Yong Kim (see Chapter 13). And yet there are limits to what anthropologists can do. Policymakers and development institutions may not pay attention to their advice. Or the anthropologist may not have enough time to fully study a situation before having to make recommendations (Gow 1993).

Anthropology of Development

Other anthropologists have taken a more critical perspective. They argue that no matter how well intentioned, development is ethnocentric and paternalistic, and that the outcome of most projects is to give greater control over local people to outsiders, or to worsen existing inequalities as elites shape development projects to serve their own interests (Escobar 1991, 1995).

Anthropologist James Ferguson applied some of these perspectives in his study of the Thaba-Tseka Rural Development Project. This project was a World Bank and UN Food and Agriculture Organization (FAO) project that took place between 1975 and 1984 in the southern African country of Lesotho (J. Ferguson 1994). Its goal was to alleviate poverty and increase economic output in rural villages by building roads, providing fuel and construction materials, and improving water supply and sanitation. But the project failed to meet its goals.

Ferguson argued that intentional plans like this one never turn out the way their planners expect because project planners begin with a distinctive way of reasoning and knowing that nearly always generates the same kinds of actions. In this case, planners believed that Lesotho's problems fit a general model: its residents are poor because they are subsistence farmers living in remote and isolated mountains, but they could develop further if they had technical improvements, especially roads, water, and sanitation.

According to Ferguson, this perspective has little understanding of on-the-ground realities. He noted that people in rural Lesotho have been marketing crops and live-stock since the 1840s, so they have already been involved in a modern capitalist economy for a long time. They are also not isolated, since they send many migrants to and from South Africa for wage labor. In fact, most of the income for rural families comes from family members who have migrated to South Africa.

Ferguson argued that people in rural Lesotho are not poor because they live in a remote area and lack capitalism; they are poor because their labor is exploited in South Africa. By viewing poverty as a lack of technical improvements in the rural country-side, the project failed to address the socioeconomic inequalities and subordination that are the underlying causes of poverty in rural Lesotho. But the project did have a major unexpected consequence: the arrival of government development bureaucrats to put the development project's technologies in place undermined the power of tradi-tional village chiefs. Ferguson concluded that development exists not to alleviate pov-erty but to reinforce and expand bureaucratic state power over local communities.

Nevertheless, some anthropologists counter that we cannot sit on the sidelines of development, that we have a moral obligation to apply our knowledge to protect the interests of the communities we study. Others insist that critics ignore the struggles within development institutions that indicate that there is not simply one discourse of development but a variety of perspectives among developers (Little and Painter 1995). Still others insist that development is less paternalistic and more accountable to local communities than it has ever been (Chambers 1997).

These debates remain unresolved, but now that we have some background, we can begin to answer the bigger question: Do people really want to be developed? The answer often depends on how much control over development processes people will have.

Change on Their Own Terms

In indigenous and poor communities around the world, it is not uncommon to hear variations on the following phrase, originally attributed to Lilla Watson, an Aboriginal woman in Australia: "If you have come here to help me, you are wasting your time. But if you have come here because your liberation is bound up with mine, then let us work together." According to this perspective, outside help is not automatically virtuous, and it can undermine self-determination. Some scholars view this basic desire—to negotiate change on one's own terms—as a fundamental challenge to development's real or per-ceived paternalism and negative effects on local culture (Rahnema and Bawtree 1997).

Understandably, in the face of forced change, people want to conserve the tradi-tions and relationships that give their lives meaning. This point is one of the keys to understanding culture in the context of cross-cultural interactions and global change. Culture helps people make sense of and respond to constant changes in the world, and it is itself dynamic. But culture also has stable and conservative elements, and different societies have different levels of tolerance for change, both of which mean that cultural change is not a uniform process for every society. This situation of uneven change partly explains why we see the persistence of cultural diversity around the world in spite of predictions that it would disappear.

THINKING LIKE AN ANTHROPOLOGIST: CROSS-CULTURAL INTERACTIONS

Are anthropologists ethically obligated to help communities develop if members of the community want their help?

4.5 If the World Is Not Becoming Homogenized, What Is Actually Happening?

Like the previous question about whether everyone wants development, this one has no simple answer. Anthropologists are divided on this question. The interaction of culture with political, economic, and social processes is complex, and in many ways the world's material culture and associated technologies are becoming homogeneous. Anthropologists who study these processes pursue one or another form of cultural convergence theory. Other anthropologists see people all over the world using foreign cultural imports in their own ways and on their own terms. These scholars use an approach called hybridization theory. In this section, we examine both theories.

Cultural Convergence Theories

In the 1960s the famous media scholar Marshall McLuhan suggested that the world was becoming a "global village" in which cultural diversity was in decline. Many social scientists agreed. The British philosopher and social anthropologist Ernest Gellner, for example, believed the spread of industrial society created a common worldwide culture, based on similar conditions of work within the same industry. Making T-shirts in a factory is going to be similar whether situated in Honduras, Tanzania, or Vietnam. Gellner wrote that "the same technology canalizes people into the same type of activity and the same kinds of hierarchy, and that the same kind of leisure styles were also engendered by existing techniques and by the needs of productive life" (Gellner 1983:116–17). Gellner's view was that local distinctions and traditions will gradually fade as Western ideas replace those in non-Western communities.

One variation on this theme imagines "Coca-Colonization," alternatively called Westernization or Americanization (R. Foster 2008). This model proposes that the powerful and culturally influential nations of the West (especially the United States) impose their products and beliefs on the less powerful nations of the world, creating what is known as **cultural imperialism**, or the promotion of one culture over others, through formal policy or less formal means like the spread of technology and material culture.

The appeal of these theories is that they address the underlying causes of why the world feels smaller, as well as how rich societies systematically exploit poor societies by drawing them into a common political-economic system. They also appear to explain the appearance of a common **world culture**, based on norms and knowledge shared across national boundaries (Lechner and Boli 2005; Figure 4.8).

But many anthropologists disagree with the basic assumptions that convergence theorists make about culture, and in fact most proponents of convergence are not anthropologists. The fact that people might consume the same goods, wear the same clothes, or eat the same foods does not necessarily mean that they begin to think and behave the same ways. A major limitation of convergence theories is that they underestimate variability and plasticity as key features of human culture and evolutionary history (J. Nash 1981).

Hybridization

An alternative theory that many anthropologists prefer is **hybridization**, which refers to open-ended and ongoing cultural intermingling and fusion. While the convergence theories

- **Cultural imperialism.** The promotion of one culture over others, through formal policy or less formal means, like the spread of technology and material culture.

- **World culture.** Norms and values that extend across national boundaries.

- **Hybridization.** Persistent cultural mixing that has no predetermined direction or end-point.

◈ **Figure 4.8 World Culture and the Olympic Games.** The Olympic Games is a quintessential global event. Currently 206 countries participate in the Olympic Games, even more than are members of the United Nations. Drawing on certain core values—competitiveness, internationalism, amateurism, and so on—they foster an awareness of living in a single world culture.

imagine a world based on or moving toward cultural purities, hybridization sees a world based on promiscuous mixing, border crossing, and persistent cultural diversity (García Canclini 1995; Piot 1999; Figure 4.9). Hybridization has several aliases, including syncretism and creolization. Anthropologists have usually applied the word *syncretism* to the fusion of religious systems; *creolization* is used to mean the intermingling of languages. In both cases, we see the synthesis of distinct elements to create new and unexpected possibilities. In "Doing Fieldwork: Tracking Emergent Forms of Citizenship with Aihwa Ong" we examine how one cultural anthropologist studies these processes.

Hybridization theory does have critics. Some argue that cultural mixing is merely a superficial phenomenon, the real underlying condition being convergence. Others assert that all the talk about boundary crossing and mixture ignores the fact that boundaries—national, social, ethnic, and so on—have not disappeared (Friedman 1999), even getting stronger in recent years due to the combined effects of anti-immigrant sentiment, resurgent nationalisms, and the effects of the COVID-19 pandemic. At the heart of this criticism is the charge that hybridization theory ignores real political and economic power and inequalities. Others assert that these two approaches do not have to be mutually exclusive, but that convergence is happening in some places and hybridization is happening everywhere at the same time.

Figure 4.9　Hybridity and Warlpiri Media. Warlpiri people of northern Australia have taken to watching and producing their own films. Their cinematic productions reflect particular social dynamics and perspectives, in the process hybridizing a Western technology and its practices.

Doing Fieldwork
Tracking Emergent Forms of Citizenship with Aihwa Ong

Since the 1980s, Malaysian-born anthropologist Aihwa Ong of the University of California, Berkeley, has studied the interaction between globally circulating ideas and practices—especially transnational capitalism, industrialization, and neoliberal policies promoting free markets—and local cultures and politics in the Pacific Rim. One of her key contentions is that Asian societies' experiences of globalization are not simply reproductions of ideas and practices transplanted from the West but a complicated mixture of the local and the global in which new and emergent forms of social life and politics become possible and take shape. In order to support this contention, Ong has drawn on traditional site-based ethnographic fieldwork—such as her interviews and participant-observation research with Muslim women factory workers in Malaysia, discussed earlier in this chapter—as well as multi-sited research; that is, using a research strategy that moves across and through different social and political

spaces in order to understand large-scale linkages and processes.

One theme on which Ong has conducted multi-sited research is the changing ideas about national belonging and rights of citizenship in the Pacific Rim. These changes are subtle and complex, requiring fieldwork strategies that involve tracking and following ideas and practices related to citizenship as they circulate across and between different social settings in different countries. This style of research does not aim to study globalization or the world system in its totality, as Eric Wolf and other World Systems approaches sought to do. Rather, its goal is to identify interconnections and configurations that link geographically and socially dispersed settings in culturally meaningful ways. Ong's research strategies are multi-sited, including fieldwork following elite Chinese businesspeople as they travel back and forth between Asia and the US West Coast;

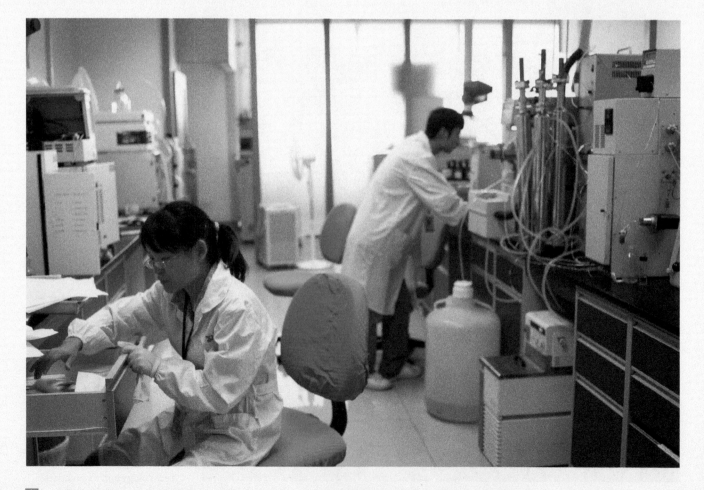

Workers in a bioscience lab in Singapore, one of the settings of Aiwha Ong's multi-sited fieldwork.

participant-observation and interviews among professional workers in Shanghai, China; fieldwork in Cambodian refugee communities in California; and participant-observation in high-technology bioscience companies in Singapore. She has also interviewed government officials, workers, business leaders, labor activists, and others who have diverse interactions with these different communities.

This transient and multi-sited method has provided important perspectives on complex changes in sociopolitical and cultural notions of citizenship. Ong argues that as states have opened their borders to attract the flow of capital, technology, investment, and workers, they have been forced to be flexible in their conceptions of territorial sovereignty, or what aspects of their national space they are willing to control and regulate. The drive to be globally competitive has led some states—such as Singapore and Malaysia—to pursue what Ong calls "graduated citizenship," which means giving different rights to different groups (Ong 2006). For example, to ensure the productivity of low-wage workers for transnational corporations, these states will encourage the importation of foreigners to work as maids or factory workers with few formal protections, create policies that weaken labor unions, and use the police or military to enforce discipline on laborers. At the same time, mobile expatriate workers in high-tech fields may receive citizen-like privileges, incentives, protections, and benefits to ensure that they bring their skills and knowledge to the economy (Ong 2006). In these circumstances, Ong suggests, the broader emphasis on skills, knowledge, and entrepreneurialism is replacing the idea of citizenship as a bundle of rights and obligations.

In addition, wealthy elites have developed their own conceptions and practices of "flexible citizenship," which involves manipulating the immigration laws of different countries to protect their wealth and security (Ong 1999). For example, Ong found that wealthy Chinese families practiced a strategy of flexible citizenship in which they might buy a house in a city like San Francisco or send their children to an elite American college, even as their businesses continue to be based in China or Southeast Asia. Their goal was not to seek citizenship in the sense of professing a national allegiance but as a way to protect their wealth and economic assets. In the United States, this attitude generated controversy among upper-middle-class whites who lived in the same neighborhoods, and Chinese business elites found themselves in an unfamiliar position of having to navigate local racial politics new to them.

In exploring these broader transformations in citizenship in the Pacific Rim, Ong has emphasized that Asian experiences of globalization are rooted in deep complexities of regional history and culture, and are not a simple matter of reacting to Western development patterns. The fact that these new forms of citizenship are emerging out of the Pacific Rim reflects Asian agency and participation in the ongoing creation of global capitalism.

Questions for Reflection

1. What would Ong have gained if she had stayed in one place to do her research on emergent forms of citizenship? What would she have lost?

2. What do you think are some of the practical problems facing an anthropologist who wants to conduct multi-sited research?

3. Do you think that multi-sited research raises any particular ethical issues?

Although these debates can be contentious, for a discipline historically accustomed to studying culture from a local vantage point (the stereotype of the anthropologist in a village), there is widespread consensus that taking on big questions like these opens up exciting new possibilities for anthropological research.

THINKING LIKE AN ANTHROPOLOGIST: CROSS-CULTURAL INTERACTIONS

Can you identify any examples of cultural hybridization in your community? How does the example you came up with connect to transnational dynamics and processes?

Conclusion

No anthropologist can claim to have easy answers to the dilemmas, dislocations, and problems raised by cross-cultural interactions and globalization. But anthropological research can provide critical perspectives on how and why people relate to large-scale social, economic, and political changes in the ways they do.

As we have established in this chapter, culture helps people make sense of and respond to constant changes in the world, which is itself dynamic. But cultural change is not a uniform process. There are many reasons for this. Different societies have differing levels of tolerance toward change, and some are more protective of their cultural traditions than others. In addition, people can be open to outside influences even while maintaining culturally specific meanings and social relations. They do this by actively transforming the alien into something more familiar. Even more important, perhaps, is that not all people participate in cross-cultural and global processes on equal terms. Their position within broader political-economic processes and regional dynamics helps shape their consciousness and their experience of global cultural integration.

During their circumnavigation of the globe, the Hawai'ian sailors on the Hōkūle'a communicated a valuable and powerful message: We face many global challenges and our future depends on our ability to get along across our cultural differences. If anybody understands the importance and persistence of culture, it is these sailors who are part of an ongoing effort to protect and revitalize Polynesian cultural knowledge and practices. Socioeconomic and political inequalities associated with globalization are one reason that cultural diversity continues to exist in the world. But there is another key reason. It is that cultures are created in connection with other cultures, not in isolation, as many anthropologists had once thought. This is not to say that there are not certain elements that make the world feel smaller, including empirical changes in communications, migration, and finances. If we do live in a global village, as Marshall McLuhan once asserted, we should understand that diversity, and not uniformity, is the defining feature of that village.

KEY TERMS

Anthropology of
    development   p. 97

Cultural imperialism   p. 100

Culture of migration   p. 92

Development anthropology
    p. 97

Diffusionists   p. 85

Exiles   p. 86

Globalization   p. 84

Hybridization   p. 100

Immigrants   p. 86

Localization   p. 93

Migrants   p. 86

Postcolonialism   p. 91

Push-pull factors   p. 91

Refugees   p. 86

Transnational   p. 86

Transnational community
    p. 92

World culture   p. 100

World systems theory   p. 89

Reviewing the Chapter

Chapter Section	What We Know	To Be Resolved
Are cross-cultural interactions all that new?	Archaeological and historical records show that humans have always moved around, establishing contacts and relationships with other cultures; and that sharing or exchanging things, individuals, and ideas is deeply rooted in human evolutionary history.	Very little is still understood about cross-cultural interactions that occurred between the earliest humans, such as the earliest modern humans and Neanderthals.
Is the contemporary world really getting smaller?	It is impossible to make sense of local cultural realities without some understanding of the broader political, economic, and social conditions that also shape people's lives.	Anthropologists do not have easy answers for the cultural, economic, and political dilemmas raised by globalization.
What are the outcomes of global integration?	Not everybody participates equally in the diverse kinds of interconnections that make up globalization, and taking globalization seriously means taking power relationships and social inequality seriously.	While some anthropologists emphasize the destructive and dominating effects of global capitalism's spread for many non-Western societies, others have argued that expressions of resistance, creative localization, and migration are meaningful and important responses.
Doesn't everyone want to be developed?	Development raises complex and politically charged issues about socioeconomic and cultural change for anthropologists and the indigenous and poor communities that are the target of development initiatives.	Anthropologists are deeply divided over the positive and negative impacts of development, and they continue to debate the merits and drawbacks of anthropological involvement in development and other projects that promote globalization.
If the world is not becoming homogenized, what is actually happening?	Globalization is a complicated matter that illustrates how people create and change their cultures not in isolation but through connections with others.	Although many anthropologists accept that globalization is a process primarily of hybridization, others argue that it is a process of cultural convergence.

READINGS

Globalizations and the Ancient World, by Justin Jennings (Cambridge: Cambridge University Press, 2011), interprets archaeological evidence through a World Systems Theory framework to conclude that the phenomenon of globalization is a variable process that has occurred numerous times throughout prehistoric and historic times.

The Anthropology of Globalization: A Reader, 2nd ed., edited by Jonathan Xavier Inda and Renato Rosaldo (Malden, MA: Blackwell, 2007), offers a broad overview of the history, topics, and debates in the anthropological study of globalization, including essays on themes such as migration, the creation of transnational identities, and the movement of goods and capitalist economic structures across political, economic, and cultural boundaries. For a more specific discussion of anthropological approaches to migration, see Caroline Brettell's *Anthropology and Migration: Essays on Transnationalism, Ethnicity, and Identity* (Walnut Creek, CA: Altamira Press, 2003).

Although he is not an anthropologist, Pico Iyer has written a book—*The Global Soul: Jet Lag, Shopping Malls, and the Search for Home* (New York: Vintage, 2001)—that offers a fine-grained description of many of the cultural dilemmas and situations that draw anthropological attention about global processes. Anthropologist Michael Jackson's book *At Home in the World* (Durham, NC: Duke University Press, 1995) offers an ethnographic and philosophical counterpart to Iyer's book, juxtaposing the author's own global travels and sense of uprootedness with how Australian Warlpiri construct a concept of home as hunter-gatherers who move across large geographic distances.

....

Many anthropologists have written noteworthy ethnographic monographs exploring the intersections of culture and globalization. Among the more thought-provoking are Anna Lowenhaupt Tsing's book *Friction: An Ethnography of Global Connection* (Princeton, NJ: Princeton University Press, 2005), which examines how global institutions and interactions shape the problems facing Indonesian rain forests and indigenous peoples; Charles Piot's *Remotely Global: Village Modernity in West Africa* (Chicago, IL: University of Chicago Press, 1999), which explores how village life among the Kabre of Togo is shaped by a complex mixture of local traditions and colonial and postcolonial histories; and Aihwa Ong's *Neoliberalism as Exception: Mutations in Citizenship and Sovereignty* (Durham, NC: Duke University Press, 2006), which is described in the "Doing Fieldwork" feature in this chapter.

....

PART II

Becoming Human

One of anthropology's principal tasks is figuring out when, how, and under what conditions our earliest ancestors evolved and became "human," and how our humanity differentiates us from other species. Thanks to new field discoveries, technological progress in studying ancient fossils, and theoretical advances, our knowledge of human origins has grown by leaps and bounds in recent years. They all point to one critical finding: that the material and symbolic cultures our ancestors created over time had—and continue to have—an influence over our evolution as a species. A new biocultural paradigm is reshaping not only our understanding of humanity's evolutionary past, but also how we approach contemporary human behavior, biological variations among human populations, and people's ideas and experiences of bodily health and illness.

This part opens with the first of our Methods Memos, which are short essays throughout the book that examine specific anthropological methods. In this opening memo we explore how biological anthropologists study human and primate bodies. It is followed by a chapter that examines why and how anthropologists study non-human primates, a central goal being to identify what in human behavior is general to primates, what is restricted to a few kinds of primates and humans, and what is uniquely human. We then present another Methods Memo on how paleoanthropologists study ancient humans and primates, followed by a chapter describing the latest paleoanthropological findings and theories about the human family tree and the lives of the first humans. The next chapter takes stock of contemporary human biodiversity, offering a biocultural perspective on how and why human populations vary in physiology, immunity, and body type. In that chapter, we also examine the biological fallacies and embodied consequences of race and racism. The final chapter examines complicated linkages between culture, biology, and human health and illness from the perspective of one of our discipline's most dynamic branches, medical anthropology.

METHODS MEMO

How Do Anthropologists Study Human and Primate Biological Processes?

The discipline of anthropology brings holistic and integrative perspectives to bear on the study of human and primate biological processes. These perspectives are most clear in the subfield of biological anthropology, where the goal is to understand these matters in the context of culture and social relations. Biological anthropologists thus straddle the natural and social sciences, collecting data to address a wide variety of questions related to human evolution and biocultural variation. The foundation of biological anthropological research is the scientific method. As we described in Chapter 1, this method entails a circular process of observation, the development of a testable explanation in the form of a hypothesis, tests or experiments to disprove or support the hypothesis, and the interpretation of those results.

Although research often takes place in controlled settings like a scientific lab or a zoo, biological anthropology is first and foremost a field-based science. Depending on one's specialty, fieldwork can involve two themes we examine in this memo: the observation and recording of primate behavior to explore what is general to all primates or unique to humans, or the collection of data to understand the genetic, nutritional, health, reproductive, and disease characteristics and experiences of a particular group of people. Some biological anthropologists use methods for the excavation and analysis of human and primate fossils to understand human origins, which we examine in a future Methods Memo. The wide variety of methodological techniques involved in each of these specialties reflects the great diversity of questions and problems studied by biological anthropologists.

METHODS FOR STUDYING PRIMATE BIOLOGY AND BEHAVIOR

Biological anthropologists study living primates as a window into what it means to be a primate and, more importantly, what it means to be a specific kind of primate: a human. Studies are divided between those focusing on captive animals living in a zoo or laboratory, and field studies in diverse habitats, ranging from savannahs and jungles to swamps, temple forests, and cities across the globe. In all of these settings, an anthropological primatologist studies the behaviors, activities, social interactions, health conditions, and so forth that are appropriate for answering their research questions. But each context lends itself to certain kinds of studies. For example, in a controlled environment like a lab, a researcher can teach a primate to perform certain tasks or skills with the goal of exploring that primate's behaviors or capacities on specific pre-determined tasks. In contrast, if the goal is to study questions like "How do primates move around and use their ranges, gather food, vocalize, and so on?" a field habitat would be more appropriate. There are many physical and logistical challenges to studying primates in these settings, however. In addition to observational methods that can involve tramping through difficult territory, primatologists might have to capture animals to collect fecal, blood, or hair samples to send to a lab to test for genetic relationships or disease (releasing them, safely, afterward).

Whatever the setting, anthropological primatologists need to decide whether they will use qualitative or quantitative methods, or both. Qualitative data could include the observation and description of primate qualities (appearance, smell, behavior, etc.) and contextual factors like landscape features. Quantitative data involve gathering measurable data, such as recording the number of times a primate engages in a particular behavior. Another important decision is whether to focus on a group or an individual, as each will yield distinctive kinds of data and contextual information.

A lot of these methods are the same as those used to study primates in disciplines like ecology and psychology. But their anthropological training means that anthropological primatologists are especially attuned to human influences over primate environments, as well as primate–human interactions. One area of research, ethnoprimatology (see Chapter 5), can even involve ethnographic observations and interviews with people about their attitudes toward and everyday interactions with primates.

METHODS FOR STUDYING LIVING HUMAN BIOLOGICAL PROCESSES

Biological anthropologists who study the bodies and biological processes of living humans can also utilize qualitative ethnographic methods such as observations and interviews, especially if their research involves efforts to understand how people make meaning of their biological selves, illnesses, and so on. But they also draw, often more heavily, on a distinctive and varied set of quantitative and scientific methods. Depending on their research questions, their studies might require methods for documenting aspects of human nutrition, the effects of chromosomal mutations in a community, processes of childhood growth, the transmission and prevention of disease, how bodies adapt to particular environmental conditions, or even the identification of dead people in a forensic investigation of a murder or mass killing.

Biological anthropologists have a detailed understanding of human skeletal anatomy, osteology, genetic processes, and body chemistry and physiology. They are also knowledgeable about how to collect anthropometric data, which involves systematic measurements of bodily parameters and proportions. Researchers working in forensic or archaeological settings may have limited material to work with—such as bones and teeth, or fragments of these things. They carefully measure the size and shape of these specimens, using microscopes to study patterns of use or wear, and preparing samples to be tested with instruments that can analyze chemical and cellular details. These methods can help them understand factors like the age, sex, diet, and ancestry of individuals. Researchers whose work focuses on epidemiological issues—the incidence and distribution of disease—or population-level genetic studies might take blood, saliva, hair, and tissue samples of living humans for laboratory analysis. These kinds of studies often require techniques and advanced laboratory equipment for studying DNA, chromosomes, and cellular function. With the data that these techniques generate, scholars can understand the genetic patterns and characteristics of populations, address questions about biocultural evolutionary processes, and identify genetic predispositions that certain groups of people have for certain diseases.

Thinking Critically About Biological Anthropology Methods

- Some viruses and diseases can be transmitted back and forth between human communities and chimpanzees, gorillas, macaques, and other primates. How do you think an anthropological primatologist could study those processes of disease transmission?

- Collecting human tissues, blood, and other samples can be very sensitive matters for the people providing these things to biological anthropologists. Why do you think so? What can biological anthropologists do to protect those samples and the rights and interests of those who provide them?

- What research methods might a biological anthropologist use to study the gene flow that occurs between human populations because of migration?

Living Primates

Comparing Monkeys, Apes, and Humans

5

DURING 2021, several prominent zoos around the United States reported that some of their gorillas had tested positive for COVID-19. During the pandemic, scientists learned that the novel coronavirus that originated with bats can infect a variety of animals, including dogs, cats, ferrets, minks, tigers, otters, and white-tailed deer, among others. With knowledge about how COVID-19 is transmitted across the species barrier still sparse, authorities acted quickly to control areas of concern, such as mink farms, and to reassure millions of pet owners that the risks of getting sick from the family dog or cat were low.

But the news that great apes were infected raised special alarm bells. At the time, zoos were largely closed for public health reasons. Knowing that great apes and humans share and transmit a number of diseases between us—from the common cold to polio—staff had taken precautions to avoid transmitting COVID to the apes, including testing, using personal protective equipment, social distancing, etc. It was likely the case that asymptomatic caretakers unknowingly transmitted the virus to the apes during a routine visit to the enclosure. Because gorillas live in tight family groups, the fear was that it could spread quickly and lead to high mortality rates. Fortunately, the cases were mild ones, mostly coughing and congestion, and the gorillas in the various zoos recovered. Nevertheless, imagining a nightmare scenario—that a charismatic and human-like creature, beloved by millions, might die because of human irresponsibility in an institution dedicated

Covid-19 and Great Apes. Because of our close evolutionary histories, great apes, like the gorilla pictured here, are susceptible to many infectious diseases that also affect humans, including Covid-19. During the pandemic, zoo workers scrambled to inoculate their apes to protect them.

to animal protection—zoo officials across the country raced to inoculate their apes with a newly developed experimental vaccine.

Beyond the headlines, scientists and conservationists who work with chimpanzees, gorillas, and orangutans have also been raising the alarm about the potential effects of COVID on wild ape populations, expressing concern about transmission by visiting researchers, selfie-taking tourists, or people from local communities. They feared it would be impossible to contain an outbreak, and one could compound an already dire situation for great apes suffering from the effects of habitat destruction, armed conflict, hunting for bushmeat, and outbreaks of Ebola virus— the same virus that affects humans, but with a higher mortality rate among apes. With a sense of urgency, a group of influential researchers called the Great Ape Consortium published an appeal in the scientific journal *Nature*, writing, "As leading experts in the conservation and health of these animals, we urge governments, conservation practitioners, researchers, tourism professionals and funding agencies to reduce the risk of introducing the virus into these endangered apes" (Gillespie and Leendertz 2020). Among their recommendations was the suspension of ape tourism, health monitoring, and disease control efforts that could, in theory, mean initiatives to vaccinate apes in the wild.

The immunological connections and similarities between humans and great apes are but one example of the close relationships between our species, which exist because of the extensive evolutionary history we share as primates. These connections and similarities interest biological anthropologists, who study human biological adaptations, variability, and evolution in the context of human culture and behavior. Biological anthropology encompasses the study of primates with a goal of identifying what in human behavior is general to primates, what is restricted to a few kinds of primates and humans, and what is uniquely human.

Central to biological anthropology's interest in living primates is the question: *What can studying other living primates tell us about what it means to be human?* We can answer this question by considering a number of related questions around which this chapter is organized:

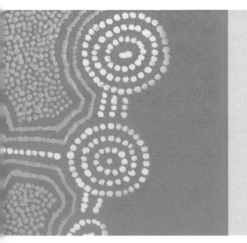

What does it mean to be a primate, and why does it matter to anthropology?

What are the basic patterns of primate behavioral diversity, and under what conditions did they develop?

How do behavior patterns among monkeys and apes compare with humans?

What can studying monkeys and apes really illustrate about human distinctiveness?

Primates are of importance to anthropology because they provide us with a comparative baseline for understanding ourselves as humans. And yet, due to our distinctive evolutionary trajectories, there is a wide array of possibilities involved in being a primate, and no single primate provides a totally adequate model for human evolution or behavior.

5.1 What Does It Mean to Be a Primate, and Why Does It Matter to Anthropology?

Throughout history and across cultures, the similarities between monkeys, apes, and humans have been recognized, celebrated, condemned, and puzzled over. It was Carolus Linnaeus (see Chapter 3) who formalized those similarities for science by classifying humans along with other apes and monkeys. In his taxonomy, he placed humans within the genus *Homo*, as well as chimpanzees and orangutans, the only other large apes known to European scientists at the time. He placed *Homo* in a family he called Primates, including in that family two other genera he called Simians and Lemurs. Later scientists would discover new species and refine the taxonomy, but the fact that Linnaeus slotted humans into his system was—and continues to be—important, and for some, controversial. Darwin faced that controversy when critics charged that his theory of natural selection communicated that humans evolved from monkeys (Figure 5.1). Humans are not monkeys, nor did we evolve from them. But monkeys and humans are both primates, and we explore what that means here.

What It Means to Be a Primate

The word *primate*, derived from the Latin word for "of the first rank," implies that these creatures are a higher order than other life forms. Linnaeus used it because as a Christian he took for granted the Great Chain of Being that placed humans and similar beings closer to the divine (see Chapter 3). From a contemporary evolutionary perspective, no creature is "more advanced" than any other. All organisms are evolving along trajectories relative to their environments and ancestries.

Primates are social mammals with grasping hands, bony and enclosed eye sockets, and relatively large brains. They share a common ancestry that split from other mammals some 65 million years ago, and live in mostly tropical and subtropical areas of the Americas, Africa, and Asia (Figure 5.2). The number of living non-human primate species is not certain: new discoveries are still being made (124 between 1990 and 2021), many species are endangered and on the verge of extinction, and taxonomists still disagree over relations between primates. For some researchers, a good working number ranges between 250 and 300 species, while the International Union for the Conservation of Nature recognizes 612 species and subspecies (Rowe 2015). What does it actually mean to be a primate?

Perhaps two of the most important things are manual dexterity and visual acuity. Being a primate means being adept and skillful with the hands, and in many cases, feet. Having five individually movable fingers involving an opposable thumb, as well as large toes, allows for fine movements—peeling, grooming, manipulating things— that having paws or fixed claws does not provide. Primates are generalists, which means they are able to live in a wide variety of environments and make use of many

Figure 5.1 Questioning Darwin. After he published his book *The Descent of Man* in 1871, which explains human origins in terms of natural selection, the satirical magazine *The Hornet* published this caricature called "A Venerable Orang-outang." Darwin's evolutionary theory, and especially his book, insisted that humans and apes had common ancestors, which provoked widespread social outrage.

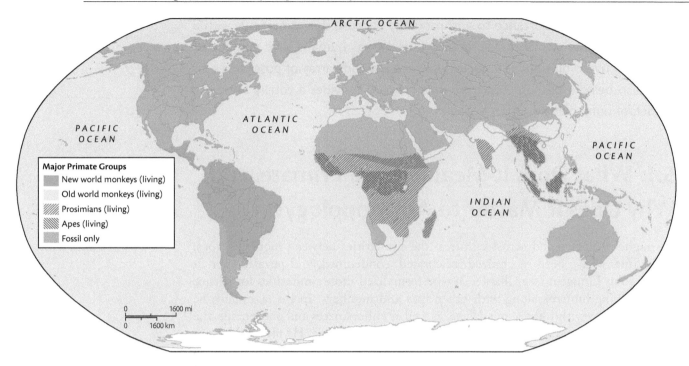

Figure 5.2   Geographic Distribution of the Living Primates. Except for a few species of Old World monkeys and humans, primates live in tropical regions.

different resources, which manual dexterity supports. Primates also have excellent vision, not relying as much on smell as other animals. Their eyes face forward and are close together, and though each eye captures its own information, together they create stereoscopic vision, or three-dimensional vision with depth perception. Stereoscopic vision has many advantages, especially helping primates to know with precision where objects such as food or predators are in relation to themselves, and for moving around in their environments effectively. Unlike other animals, the eyes are protected by either being fully enclosed by bone (picture a human skull) or with a postorbital bar, which is a ring of bone that surrounds the eyeball and protects it from being jostled by chewing.

There are several other shared characteristics: general intelligence, related to a larger brain size than similarly sized creatures; locomotive flexibility and a collar bone at the shoulders, both of which provide greater mobility—running, climbing, jumping, walking, and so on—than creatures that have to walk on all four legs; and longer gestation times and childhoods, the second of which in numerous primate species involves training to live in complex social groups.

These characteristics are still quite general, and primates vary among themselves, sometimes greatly. To get at that variation and the multiple possibilities involved in being a primate, it is helpful to break down the distinctions between the different groups of primates and to describe their characteristics in more detail.

The Distinctions Between Strepsirrhini and Haplorrhini

Taxonomists identify two suborders in the order Primates, which are the **Strepsirrhini** [strepp-**sur**-en-eye], consisting of prosimians, and the **Haplorrhini** [hap-**plor**-en-eye], which includes all species of tarsiers, monkeys, apes, and humans. Here we identify briefly the distinctions between these suborders, as well as the general characteristics of the primates that fall within them.

• **Strepsirrhini.** The infraorder of primates including lemurs, galagos, and lorises.

• **Haplorrhini.** The infraorder of primates including monkeys, apes, and humans.

(a)   (b)   (c)   (d)

🌱 **Figure 5.3 Strepsirrhines.** Shown are slender loris (a); indri with young (b); adult male crowned lemur (c); ringtailed lemurs (d).

The Strepsirrhini

There are two groups of Strepsirrhini, or prosimians: the lemurs and a group that includes the lorises and galagos. Strepsirrhines have smaller body sizes than other primates, a smaller brain-to-body-size ratio (but a larger one than most other mammals), and a keener sense of smell (olfaction) than other primates. A large portion of their brain is devoted to smell and they have a rhinarium, or wet nose, enhancing their ability for receiving chemical particles associated with scents. Most Strepsirrhines are **arboreal** (tree-dwelling), and many are **nocturnal** (active at night), with large eyes and excellent night vision (Figure 5.3).

Lemurs live exclusively on the island of Madagascar, off the southeastern coast of Africa, where they arrived approximately 40–50 million years ago. Like most Strepsirrhines, they have a grooming claw (a special nail on their feet) and a tooth comb (lower incisors) used for cleaning their own and others' fur. Because there were no other primates on Madagascar until the arrival of humans, lemurs spread out, adapting to different food sources and habitat types. Today forest destruction has caused the extinction of many lemur species and threats to others.

Galagos are a group of small, nocturnal Strepsirrhines found across forests in central Africa. They have specialized arms and legs that provide great leaping ability. They mostly eat fruit and insects, spending their time in vocal and olfactory communication. The range and diversity of their vocalizations are so important that differentiating species might be based on vocal structure, and small genetic differences, and not overt physical features, because they look so much alike (Nekaris and Bearder 2011).

Lorises consist of the Asian lorises and the African pottos. They are mostly nocturnal and fully arboreal, eating insects and other small animals. The lorises do not leap in the trees but move slowly through them, using all four limbs to grasp branches.

The Haplorrhini

There are two infraorders (groupings below the level of the order) of Haplorrhini, these being the Tarsiiformes and the Simiiformes. The Tarsiiformes include the tarsiers (family Tarsiidae). The Simiiformes include three superfamilies: Ceboidea, or monkeys of the Americas; Cercopithecoidea, or Asian and African monkeys; and Hominoidea, or apes and humans. In this book, we use two specialized terms to refer

- **Arboreal.** Living in the trees.

- **Nocturnal.** Active during the nighttime.

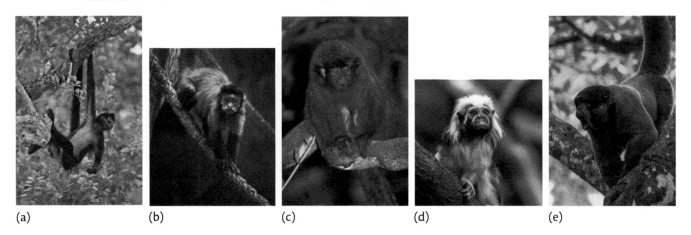

(a)   (b)   (c)   (d)   (e)

Figure 5.4   New World Monkeys, or Ceboidea. Shown here: spider monkey (a); capuchin monkey (b); titi monkey (c); cotton-top tamarin (d); and wooly monkey ©.

- **Anthropoid.** A primate superfamily that includes monkeys, apes, and humans.

- **Hominoid.** The primate superfamily Hominoidea that includes all the apes and the humans.

- **Hominine.** The division (called a tribe) in the superfamily Hominoidea that includes humans and our recent ancestors.

- **Prehensile.** The ability to grasp things, usually referring to hands or tails.

- **Terrestrial.** Living on the ground.

to the Simiiformes: **anthropoid** is a term referring to all monkeys, apes, and humans, and **hominoid** refers only to apes and humans. The term **hominine** applies to *Homo sapiens*, our own species.

The Haplorrhines have larger bodies and larger brain-to-body-size ratios than Strepsirrhines. They lack a wet nose and have more brain devoted to vision than olfaction. They show greater diversity in lifeways (tree-living, ground-living, and a mix of both), so their skeletons are more varied.

Tarsiers and Monkeys

The tarsiers of Southeast Asia are small-bodied and nocturnal. Their elongated tarsal bones (ankles) endow them with extreme leaping abilities and gives them their name. They spend their lives in small groups, typically two adults with their young. With their large eyes (whose combined weight is larger than their brain!), the tarsiers move about in dense tropical forests at night.

The Ceboidea, or Monkeys of the Americas, are widely dispersed from Southern Mexico to Southern Argentina. Though there is a lot of diversity among them, the majority are arboreal and relatively smaller than anthropoids found in Africa and Asia. They differ from other anthropoids in other ways, including having certain dental and other anatomical characteristics (three premolars, for example) (Figure 5.4). An important skeletal adaptation for life in the trees is the **prehensile** tail, which is present in a few of the Ceboidea. This tail grasps and clings to branches and foliage. A fleshy pad at the tip of the tails even has its own "fingerprint."

The Cercopithecoidea, or Old World monkeys, are found in Asia and Africa (Figure 5.5). There are two subfamilies, the cercopithecinae and the colobinae. Baboons and macaques are cercopithecinae, and are each active in the daytime in both **terrestrial** (ground-living) and arboreal contexts. The cercopithecinae also have small pockets inside their cheeks for food storage, and so they are sometimes called "cheek pouch" monkeys. The other group, the colobines, do not have cheek pouches and are typically more arboreal. Known as "leaf monkeys," they carry special bacteria in large stomachs with multiple internal folds that help them digest plant matter that other primates can't digest.

Apes and Humans

African apes (gorillas and chimpanzees), Asian apes (orangutans and gibbons), and humans are all members of Hominodiea. Hominoids generally have large bodies and brains, with gibbons being on the smaller end. The apes and humans don't have tails

(a)

(b)

(c)

Figure 5.5 Old World Monkeys, or Cercopithecoidea. Shown here: black and white colobus (a); olive baboons (b); and hanuman langurs (c).

and carry various adaptations in the upper body permitting full rotation of the arm and greater hand movement, which allow them to hang and swing among branches. The initial adaptation for swinging from limb to limb (so-called brachiation) laid the groundwork for changes that eventually led to bipedal walking, which is unique to the human lineage. Hominoids split from other anthropoids in the early Miocene, around 22 million years ago. By the late Miocene, around 8 million to 10 million years ago, we see the beginnings of a split among hominoids that led to the eventual emergence of human lineages.

In Figure 5.6 we present a primate phylogeny, which uses a combination of morphological, fossil, and genetic evidence to show what scientists traditionally accept as the evolutionary relationships between primates. Throughout this evolutionary history, a key characteristic of the primate taxonomic order is high levels of sociality and living in groups. A selective force on primate evolution has always been the local ecology, but those social contexts, along with behavioral plasticity and complexity, extragenetic learning, and some level of niche construction, have also acted as selective forces, contributing to the specific evolutionary trajectories of the individual primate species.

Primatology as Anthropology

Why do all these details about primate suborders and creatures like lemurs and tarsiers matter to anthropology? Anthropologists who study primates often have to address this question, explaining why their studies of primates do not belong in other fields that also study primates, including biology, zoology, ecology, and psychology.

Primate studies within anthropology began in the 1950s, thanks to the efforts of physical anthropologist Sherwood Washburn, who asserted, "Since [hu]man is a primate who developed from among the Old World simian stock, his[their] social behavior must have also evolved from that of this mammalian group. Thus the investigation of [hu]man's behavior is dependent on what we know of the behavior of monkeys and apes" (1961, quoted in Sussman 2014:41). Since the 1960s when it became a field science—rather than simply a lab science studying bones and fossils—biological anthropologists have been key players in the creation of primatology as an interdisciplinary field, identifying and describing new species, standardizing methods, and performing long-term studies (Sussman 2011).

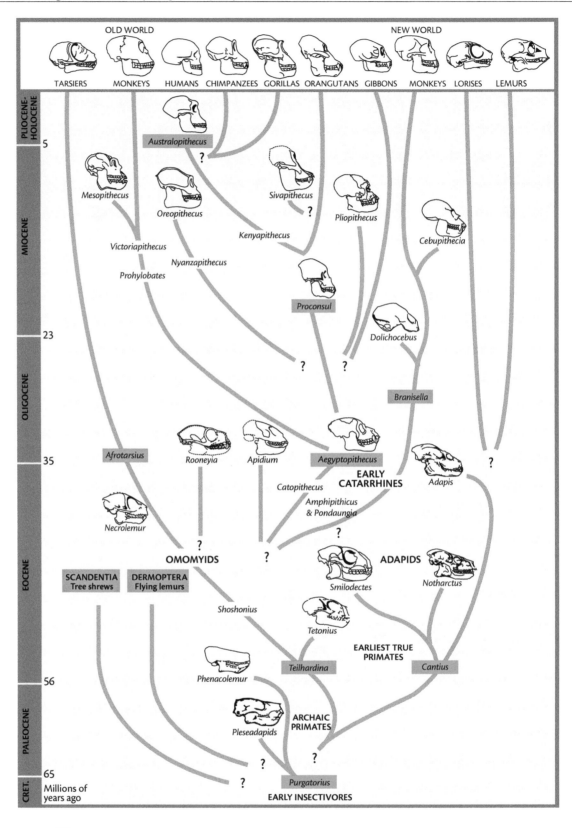

🌱 **Figure 5.6   Evolutionary Relationships in the Primate Order.** There is still debate over specific evolutionary relationships among primate taxa across some time periods, but this phylogeny gives a traditional overview.

Several features distinguish anthropologically specific approaches to primates. One is that anthropologists have often approached the study of living primates as a window into the evolution of social behaviors among humans, much as Washburn suggested. Prior to World War II, physical anthropology was closely associated with efforts to measure and categorize different human races, which anthropologists had come to disavow as racist (see Chapter 7). For Washburn and his students, those older approaches were disconnected from the exciting findings of the modern synthesis in evolutionary thought (Chapter 3), and studying the behaviors of living primates could support the creation of hypotheses about human evolution (Haraway 1989).

Anthropologists also bring holistic, comparative, and cross-cultural perspectives to the study of primates. Instead of viewing primates as programmed by their biology and evolution, anthropologists are attuned to the flexibility and plasticity of primate behaviors, which are rooted in cognitive and social complexity (Strier 2003; Ellwanger 2011). Anthropologists often document the social coordination and individual choices involved in primate group membership, which are variable not just across different primate species but also within a single species. As we explore in "The Anthropological Life," these foci provide excellent background for those who might want to work with primates as a career.

Finally, anthropological studies of primates recognize that humans and primates share historically deep and complicated relationships with each other. Our species compete with each other for food and space, and have shaped each other's ecologies, health, and evolutionary histories (Fuentes 2014b). One clear example is the exchange of infectious diseases described earlier, where the destinies of human and ape communities are intertwined through the transmission of infectious disease, hunting, and habitat destruction.

An emerging approach to primate studies called **ethnoprimatology**, which comes out of anthropology, focuses on the interface between human and ape communities, envisioning human and non-human primates as members of a dynamic ecosystem (Riley, Wolfe, and Fuentes 2011). Ethnoprimatology recognizes that many cultures around the world have strong and variable connections to primates—expressed in religious beliefs, local attitudes, and informal, everyday interactions—that are not merely competitive but also based on building intricate relationships. In numerous societies, primates have sacred status and live in religious temples, live as pets in homes, participate in tourism economies by interacting with tourists, and are hunted by humans. Not all people place primates in "nature," as Western culture and sciences do; some see primate communities as extensions of the social worlds in which they participate as humans (Haraway 1989; Fuentes 2012; Malone 2021).

From an ethnoprimatological perspective, studying the coexistence of primate species with humans is thus as much about studying primate behaviors as it is about understanding how humans think about them and under what conditions the different species come into contact with each other. In methodological terms, ethnoprimatologists are as likely to document quantitative details of primate behavior through field observations and genetic analyses as they are to document qualitative perspectives through interviews and participant observation with people (Dore, Riley, and Fuentes 2017; Haraway 1989; Fuentes 2012).

Ethnoprimatologists also produce important practical insights for the conservation of primates. Today around 75 percent of primate populations are declining and roughly 60 percent of primate species are threatened with extinction. This reality is

• **Ethnoprimatology.** The study of the interface between human and ape communities.

The Anthropological Life
So You Want to Work With Primates?

For some people, working with primates is a lifelong dream, sparked by a childhood visit to a zoo or some other highly impressionable experience. For others, they don't realize it until their undergraduate years, when an ecology or anthropology course on primates or internship at a local zoo sparks curiosity and fascination. Whatever your motivations, an undergraduate background in anthropology can provide an excellent preparation to embark on a career working with primates.

According to ethnoprimatologist Nick Malone, working with primates raises hard questions for which anthropologists are well-prepared:

> *"Is it right to habituate wild apes for scientific research purposes? Is it ethical to keep apes in captivity? Should we prioritize the health and welfare of ape populations over those of marginalised human communities? In both theory and method, divisions between scientific and humanistic epistemologies are porous; and independently they are untenable as discreet modes of primatological enquiry. Finding answers to these complex questions will require the full breadth of the anthropological toolkit"* (Malone 2021:2).

In other words, anthropology's comparative, holistic, and contextual perspectives enable deep appreciation of the cognitive plasticity and social complexity of primates, and the discipline's sophistication in studying people provides tools for understanding the complexities of human–primate interactions in the world.

There is no predetermined career path here. Veterinary medicine, medical research, and training adaptive animals can provide opportunities to work with monkeys and apes. So can gaining an internship or job in a zoo. For those drawn to the demanding conditions of field-based work in the wild, university-based research jobs exist, of course, although these jobs—which also typically require teaching—can be difficult to come by due to the competition for them. Many individuals drawn to fieldwork end up working with conservation organizations, as wildlife specialists with forestry companies, or as independent researchers or research assistants living near the landscapes where primates live. For many of these positions, an advanced degree is necessary. What draws people to work with primates is not a defined career pathway or great financial rewards. Rather, it is usually some combination of passion for a certain species, curiosity about primate lives and similarities and differences between our species, a commitment to wildlife conservation, and a desire for a life filled with adventure.

nearly entirely due to anthropogenic (human-induced) pressures on primates and their habitats, largely from global and local market demands, that are contributing to extensive habitat loss. Human political and economic realities lead to increased bushmeat hunting and the illegal trade of primates as pets and as research subjects. Given that the other primates overlap so extensively with large, and rapidly growing, human populations characterized by high levels of poverty, ethnoprimatological study is critical if we have any hope of addressing the massive risk of primate extinctions (Estrada et al. 2017, 2018). With an approach firmly grounded in anthropology, ethnoprimatologists also emphasize that successful conservation initiatives require collaboration and involvement of local communities, the very same ones that ethnoprimatologists typically make great efforts to understand and build relationships with (Malone 2021).

Now that we have considered what primates are and why anthropologists are concerned with them, we can turn our attention to how they actually behave. In the next section we consider the diversity of basic primate behavior patterns.

5.2 What Are the Basic Patterns of Primate Behavioral Diversity, and Under What Conditions Did They Develop?

In creating a comparative baseline for understanding humans, anthropologists look for three kinds of behavioral patterns in primates: primate-wide trends, hominoid-wide trends, and unique human characteristics. Explaining the patterns of primate behavioral diversity and the conditions under which behavioral diversity emerges can help us begin to move toward what might be unique to apes and ultimately to humans.

Common Behavior Patterns Among Primates

Primates share a number of common behavioral patterns, all of which are connected to the requirements of living in groups and negotiating social relationships. There is likely some genetic basis to these shared patterns (Figure 5.7), which include the following.

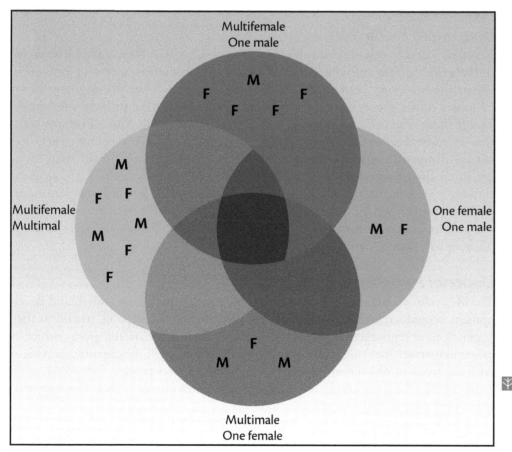

Figure 5.7   Basic Primate Grouping Patterns. Many of the primate behaviors observed are closely related to the demands of living in groups.

🔻 **Figure 5.8   Grooming Macaques.** Macaques, such as this adult, seen here grooming an immature macaque, engage in grooming behaviors to build and maintain social relations.

Mother–Infant Bond

Primates have a long period of infant dependency. The infant relies totally on others for its nutrition, movement, regulation of body temperature, and protection from predators. Mothers and other relatives have a clear evolutionary interest in ensuring that the offspring will reach maturity. In primates, this interest creates intensive caregiving behaviors called the mother–infant bond (although this doesn't mean males can't also be caregivers). Through this relationship, the infant is in frequent physical and vocal contact and is exposed to the mother's behavior and relationships. In this way, infants learn crucial information about other group members, foods, and appropriate behaviors. Caregiving is a learned behavior, gained through individual experience and observations of how other group members handle infants.

Affiliation and Grooming

- **Affiliation.** A relationship between individuals who are frequently in close association based on tolerance, even friendliness.

The ability to get along with others is critical for primates, given that they live in social groups. Individuals in frequent contact with each other usually have a tolerant, even friendly, relationship called **affiliation**. In contrast, an agonistic relationship exists where individuals are in conflict with each other. Primates create affiliations and avoid agonism through **grooming**, or moving their hands or licking the fur to remove dirt, insects, and so on. There is a hygienic dimension here, but they do it more than is necessary. When conflicts erupt, primates engage in grooming to reduce stress. Grooming relationships closely follow affiliations; in other words, grooming takes place among animals who want to associate, and agonism where they refuse to groom (Figure 5.8).

- **Grooming.** Touching another individual to remove dirt, insects, and debris, usually as a way for individuals to bond.

Dominance Hierarchies

- **Dominance hierarchy.** The ranking of access to desired resources by different individuals relative to one another.

Unequal access to resources is typical in primate groups. A **dominance hierarchy** is the ranking that individuals have relative to others for access to resources. Often the hierarchy is obvious, and an "alpha animal" has priority over other members of the group. In these situations, individuals have priority over others except those who outrank them. Dominance is a social role, not an inborn trait, that an individual occupies for a period in their life. In many primate societies, **sexual dimorphism**—where males are larger than females—means that males are often dominant over females (Figure 5.9). Nevertheless, there are circumstances in which, due to environmental circumstances, females are dominant, males and females are co-dominant, or individuals do not compete openly with one another and so dominance is not clear. Dominance hierarchies are also complicated by collective alliances.

- **Sexual dimorphism.** A difference between the sexes of a species in body size or shape.

Dispersal Patterns

- **Dispersal.** A pattern of one sex leaving the group they were born into at about the time of reproductive maturity.

The life cycle of a primate involves several main stages, including growth and development, reproductive maturity, and old age and death. At some point, usually as they begin to enter reproductive maturity, members of one sex leave the group, which is called **dispersal**. They might join other groups, while those of the opposite sex remain with the group in which they were born. Dispersal is a risky process: individuals must create relationships with non-kin, and moving between groups makes them susceptible to predation or inability to access food.

Cooperation and Conflict

It is rare for primates to spend much time alone, and they maintain social relationships through acts of cooperation. Dominance relationships tend to maintain social order, and serious fighting for resources is rare (Garber and Sussman 2011). Conflicts, of course, do occur, damaging alliances that must subsequently be repaired. Reconciliation is achieved by behaviors such as sharing, embracing, or other forms of postconflict physical contact (K. Arnold and Aureli 2007).

The Emergence of Primate Behavioral Diversity

These basic common patterns evolved over millions of years and are shared by all primates. They do not mean any of us behaves as a prosimian, like a galago does, and there are, obviously, important differences in behavior among primates. But if primates have a set of common behavioral patterns, it leads us to ask: How and why do *differences* in behavior emerge out of those basic common patterns?

Primate behaviors involve complex interactions between morphology (physical characteristics of the body), learning and experience, environmental circumstances, and chance occurrences. **Behavioral ecology** is a branch of ecology that studies how ecological conditions challenge organisms and how those organisms deal with environmental pressures through behavioral evolution. It offers useful tools for understanding how, why, and under what circumstances certain behaviors emerge. Behavioral ecologists typically look at two general kinds of pressures: socioecological pressures and energy costs and benefits.

Figure 5.9   Sexual Dimorphism. Male and female macaques exhibit important differences in size.

● **Behavioral ecology.** The study of behavior from ecological and evolutionary perspectives.

Socioecological Pressures

Socioecological pressures on primates come in four primary forms:

1. *Nutrition*, or the necessity of procuring sufficient food and water. The pressure to obtain key dietary items—fruits, leaves, insects, or other mammals—affects how and where a primate will find its food, as well as how it will capture and process it.
2. *Locomotion*, or the necessity to move around in an environment. Primates are arboreal, terrestrial, or both; yet there is still a lot of variability between and within species in terms of locomotion. For example, imagine two different species of arboreal primates. One might move around the lower, densely foliated branches, while the other uses the upper levels, moving around the smaller terminal branches. Pressures on their bodies and behaviors are quite different.
3. *Predation*, especially the necessity to avoid predators. Avoiding predators is probably one of the reasons for group living. The higher the number of individuals in a group, the lesser the odds of being eaten. Predator detection also increases.
4. *Competition*, or the necessity to gain access to resources in a context in which members of the same species (intraspecific competition), or other species (interspecific competition), compete for the same resources. Imagine, for example, monkeys and birds wanting the same fruit source (van Schaik 1989).

Sometimes these socioecological pressures act individually on an organism, but more often than not, particularities in that organism's environment intersect in unique ways to present individuals with a range of challenges. Differences in behavior emerge out of the ways organisms respond to those particularities.

Behavioral Costs and Benefits

- **Costs and benefits.** An analytical approach that considers the caloric cost of obtaining food and the calories obtained.

Within behavioral ecology, understanding an organism's response to socioecological pressures also involves the concept of **costs and benefits**. It is a basic economic model (cash in and out) for measuring energy expenditure. It strives to determine whether a certain behavior gives back to the organism what it expended; if the organism loses energy because of the behavior, thus incurring a net loss of energy; or if it gains energy, thus benefiting from the behavior. Behavioral ecologists typically assume that it is in the interest of organisms to maximize their net energy gains and minimize their costs. In theory, this should support their reproductive success. Patterned behaviors that become common within a population are known as a **strategy**.

- **Strategy.** A set of behaviors that has become prominent in a population as a result of natural selection.

One of behavioral ecology's goals is to predict how animals should behave if the patterns of behavior benefit the primates (Hamilton 1964). An important aspect of behavioral ecology is **kin selection**, which consists of favoring one's close genetic relatives over more distant relatives or non-relatives. This idea was proposed to explain **altruism**, or seemingly "selfless" acts. In evolutionary terms it doesn't make sense to maximize the fitness of other individuals, because it reduces the energy available to an individual. But kin selection offers a simple way of predicting when an individual organism behaves in a way that looks altruistic. If an individual receiving a benefit from another individual is related, then their shared genotype benefits (depending on the degree of relatedness). It amounts to a simple equation. Close relatives, which include parents, offspring, siblings, and even first cousins, share much of their genotype, so aiding each other makes genetic sense. The most obvious examples of this pattern are when parents assist their offspring or when siblings collaborate and help one another.

- **Kin selection.** The behavioral favoring of your close genetic relatives.

- **Altruism.** Seemingly "selfless" acts that have a net loss of energy to the actor but a net gain in energy to the receiver.

The Limitations of Cost–Benefit Analyses

One of the limitations of cost-benefit analyses is their inability to deal with great complexity. One complication is the fact that organisms develop different kinds of traits that are subject to different kinds of pressures. For example, certain primates use both arboreal and terrestrial environments. Being in the trees tends to favor the evolution of curved fingers for grasping, while being on the ground favors straighter fingers (or at least toes) for more efficient walking. Cost-benefit analysis would have a hard time explaining this situation. And behavioral evolution is even more complicated.

As we explained in Chapter 3, it is extremely difficult to identify direct causal links between genes and behavior. Ecological conditions create a range of selection pressures for which certain behavioral responses might be appropriate, but some behaviors will be more successful than others. Those possible behaviors exist along a spectrum. Factors like natural selection (fitness costs/benefits) and morphology (body size and shape) establish the ends of the spectrum for what might be practical behaviors. But the spectrum itself merely establishes the *potential* for a trait or behavior. The actual expression of the trait or behavior is its *performance*. The mere presence of potential doesn't generate performance. As a simple example, think about how people express physical aggression for which everyone has the potential. Factors like an individual's body size, muscle density, and health might set the range of possible aggressive acts. But other factors, such as cultural ideologies about appropriate conditions for violence (see Chapter 15) may prevent, limit, or shape its actual performance.

Moreover, potential and performance are complexly intertwined. For example, if a friend or foe sneaks up on you and scares you, your heart pumps faster, your stomach feels queasy, and you may yell or jump. A whole genre of movies (suspense/slasher movies) relies on this startle response. The fight/flight/startle physiological pattern and its generalized behavioral response are very old and found in most animals. So it stands to reason that those individuals who did not respond to predators in this way did not do so well in their overall evolutionary success. But in primates, in contrast with, say, zebras, social learning and even culture play a critical role in how primates evaluate and respond to pressures and threats.

When it comes to primates, we need to appreciate the fundamental complexity of behavior. It is also important to remember a key tenet of evolutionary thinking: our focus should not be simply on individual behaviors or traits but on how a whole population of organisms deals with environmental challenges in patterns over a lifetime. The reproductive success of those organisms as a group will affect succeeding generations. Models of energy cost and benefit tend to oversimplify these population-level dynamics, as well as lifetime patterns.

With this background, we can move to biological anthropology's interest in developing a comparative baseline for understanding humans. In the next section we examine the behavior patterns of primate relatives nearer to us in evolutionary terms and offer some comparisons with humans.

THINKING LIKE AN ANTHROPOLOGIST: LIVING PRIMATES

Factors other than natural selection affect behavioral evolution. Chance events, such as those involved in genetic drift, can influence an individual's life in ways not predictable from energy models, giving rise to new behaviors. Can you think of any other factors that might give rise to new behaviors among primates?

5.3 How Do Behavior Patterns Among Monkeys and Apes Compare with Humans?

As we said before, humans are not monkeys, and we did not evolve from them. The same is true of apes like chimpanzees, gorillas, or orangutans. Even while there are certain behavioral commonalities across all primates, monkey behavior patterns and morphology differ in key respects from hominoid (ape and human) patterns. The same is true about the behavior patterns of hominines (humans) and apes. While behavioral ecology attempts to offer theoretical explanations for *why* these patterns vary, we will use the comparative approach to show *how* these patterns vary among actual primates. Here we examine a kind of monkey called a macaque and a kind of ape called a chimpanzee and then reflect on how the behavior patterns of each compare with our own behavior as humans.

The Lives of Macaques

Macaque monkeys (members of the genus *Macaca*) are among the most widely dispersed of all primates, being found in Asia, central Eurasia, and northern Africa. The spread of the genus about 2 million years ago was similar to that of our own genus,

• *Macaca.* The genus of macaque monkeys.

Homo, at the same time, although we are currently more widespread. But among the non-human primates, macaques have adapted to the widest and most diverse environmental conditions.

Macaque Social Life

The feeding pattern of macaques is a generalist one. They prefer fruit but will eat a wide variety of other foodstuffs, including leaves, insects, and occasionally even vertebrates. They spend most of their time in the trees, but most species also move along the ground.

Most macaques live in groups with adult males and adult females, commonly between twenty and fifty individuals, but sometimes as few as ten or as many as one hundred. These groups usually have more adult females than males, and the social life of these groups is focused around related females (Thierry 2007). Males leave their birth groups and join other groups, while females stay throughout their lives with their female relatives (sisters, cousins, aunts, mother, grandmother, and so on). These clusters of related females and young are called **matrifocal units** (Wheatley 1999) (Figure 5.10). Most males are relatively solitary, only occasionally interacting with females and other males, and living just beyond matrifocal units.

- **Matrifocal unit.** A cluster of individuals generally made up of related females.

Dominance Relationships

Dominance relationships among macaques are closely aligned with sex. Between matrifocal units, more dominant units tend to push others from the best sources of food. Larger groups are typically dominant over smaller groups, although members of a subordinate cluster can usually dominate a lone female that has strayed from her unit. Macaques have a unique ranking system among primates, in which a mother's rank is passed to her youngest daughter. Because of this situation, a younger female who is the daughter of a high-ranking female can take resources from older, lower ranked females.

Figure 5.10   A Macaque Matrifocal Unit. Much of the life of a female macaque is spent interacting with maternal kin.

Male macaques also have relationships involving dominance of one individual over another, but these change frequently within any particular group or cluster. Since males leave their birth groups, they have to form associations with other individuals to help them resolve and negotiate disputes. Higher ranked males can act aggressively toward some individuals in the group while simultaneously building bonds with other males through grooming. Often males of lower rank will create coalitions to defend their position in the group or gain access to preferred food resources. Because males move between groups, their rank is always fragile compared with that of females. That movement exposes them to risk, which may explain why most groups of macaques have more adult females than males.

Sexual Behavior

Sexual behavior in macaques varies a great deal. Nevertheless, most females mate with more than one adult male, and they sometimes mate with all the males in a group. Many macaques are seasonal breeders, which means they are receptive only at certain times of the year. At these times, females often seek out and solicit sex from males. In some groups a high-ranking male can restrict access to females though a process described as "mate guarding," which involves sticking closely to the females whose sexual access they want to restrict. In slightly more than half the macaque groups where researchers have been able to determine genetic relationships among members, high-ranking males fathered the majority of infants born while they were dominant.

The Lives of Chimpanzees and Bonobos

Since Jane Goodall's groundbreaking research at Gombe in Tanzania (1971, 1986), which focused the world's attention on behavior patterns among chimpanzees and how similar they appear to human patterns of behavior, researchers have asked comparative questions about primates and the evolution of human behavior. The primate they focus on most often is the chimpanzee (genus *Pan*). Together with the gorilla, the chimpanzee is, evolutionarily speaking, our closest relative. Chimpanzees therefore share many primate-wide behavioral traits as well as shared-derived (hominoid and hominine) morphological and behavioral traits with humans. As we explore in "Doing Fieldwork: The Ethics of Fieldwork with Great Apes," some of those behavioral similarities with humans, as well as the survival challenges facing chimpanzees and other great apes, raise pressing ethical questions.

• *Pan.* The genus of chimpanzees.

There are two species of chimpanzee: the common chimpanzee is *Pan troglodytes*, and the bonobo is known as *Pan paniscus*. Both species are found across Central Africa. Chimpanzees are large and weigh 35–50 kilograms (75–130 pounds), while their smaller cousins, *P. paniscus*, weigh 32–40 kilograms (70–90 pounds). All members of the genus are primarily fruit eaters, and as a result their lives and behaviors are oriented toward the seasons and the times when particular fruits are available (Figure 5.11).

Chimpanzee and Bonobo Social Lives

Both species live in communities consisting of many adult males and females. These range from 20 to about 150 individuals. But even though we may think of these communities as a group, they are only rarely all in the same place at the same time. Most individuals spend the majority of their time in subgroups characterized by a mix of ages and sexes. Groups tend to be larger when fruit is plentiful and to disperse when fruit is scarce. Females from both species typically leave their birth group when they become adults and disperse to other groups (Stumpf 2011). Both species exhibit a

Doing Fieldwork
The Ethics of Working with Great Apes

Because of the great apes' human-like characteristics and capacities, many scientists consider them to be an excellent substitute for humans in medical experimentation and for research on human evolution. But those similarities also lead to great apes receiving higher levels of attention from the media, animal rights activists, and the public at large than other species (Fedigan 2010). This attention can produce controversy about how those apes are treated in research, resulting in calls for the extension of basic human rights to apes and, in some jurisdictions, restrictions on certain kinds of research on them. For a number of decades now, universities and research institutions have maintained animal protection review committees that vet research proposals involving primates and other animals according to three key ethical principles: that alternatives to live animals were considered, that the number of animal subjects is minimized, and that the animals will not experience undue pain and distress (Fedigan 2010). Projects involving great apes often receive special scrutiny.

But there are important practical and ethical distinctions between research in a laboratory with captive apes and in the wild among non-domesticated apes. For example, when a fieldworker is conducting observational research in the wild, it makes little sense to consider alternatives and it is often impractical and even scientifically counterproductive to reduce the number of animals under observation. Field research projects involving great apes pose unique risks for their well-being and thus raise a number of distinct ethical dilemmas and considerations for fieldworkers. These dilemmas are especially acute because of the critical endangerment of many great ape populations due to hunting and habitat loss (Gruen, Fultz, and Pruetz 2013). While doing no harm is a major ethical principle for *all* anthropological research (see p. xxx), no researcher wants to harm the well-being of animals they are passionate about, especially when they are on the verge of extinction.

Observing Chimpanzees in the Wild.

A chief ethical concern is the potential harm that the very presence of humans in the field may cause to the apes. Because of the close immunological connections between great apes and humans, fieldworkers must take all precautions to prevent disease transmission and to remove refuse and human waste from the field site. While these situations can be managed (at least in theory), a more difficult moral dilemma is whether or not to intervene when a fieldworker witnesses life-threatening harm done to an ape by an accident or by another ape or human. Because of extinction threats, if not also emotional connections, many researchers consider intervention to save an animal a morally *necessary* act. Taking this even further, some researchers become environmental activists as well, considering interventions like ape vaccination and the creation of protected areas and reserves especially important for apes threatened by extinction.

The actual research techniques fieldworkers use also raise concerns about potential harm. Long periods spent observing apes, even if it is at a distance, can cause stress to the apes and affect their reproductive rates. It can also habituate them to humans, with potentially tragic consequences when they encounter humans with less benign intentions. Putting out food to attract apes can cause similar harm, although that is less common than it once was. Catch-and-release techniques, which are used for acquiring blood, saliva, hair, skin biopsies, and other biological materials for genetic testing, are especially invasive and can cause stress and injury. Researchers often have to give great consideration to whether these actions are really necessary and under what conditions they might or might not be so, and to weigh the costs and benefits of doing these things.

Anthropological primatologists also interact with human communities, of course. They do it for practical purposes, such as hiring locals to act as guides or research assistants, and if the project is ethnoprimatologically focused, studying human-ape interactions. These interactions can raise numerous ethical issues and dilemmas, especially when a researcher witnesses illegal activities at the field site, including hunting, poaching, or harassment by local people or tourists. Foreign fieldworkers also have myriad impacts on the economies, social dynamics, and politics of the communities near a field site; in this regard, they confront ethical concerns similar to those any cultural anthropologist in a remote community would face. But often the social tensions are very high in these communities because of histories of war, or the international conservation and media interest in the survival of great apes (Malone 2021; also see Chapter 14 for an overview of issues around environmental conservation, as cultural anthropologists have studied them).

None of the issues raised here—as well as the myriad other issues primatological research raises not considered here—are simple to resolve, and they continue to provoke debate. For most researchers, as long as the scientific or conservation benefits of their research outweigh the risks, the research is justified. At the same time, it is important to recognize that all research projects need to be guided by awareness of ethical principles.

Questions for Reflection

1. What kinds of ethical considerations or concerns should prevent a prospective research project from taking place, or stop an ongoing one?

2. Review the Principles of Professional Responsibility table on the inside front cover of this book. Which principles, beyond "do no harm," might apply to research on great apes, and why? Which ones do not, and why?

number of behavioral patterns remarkable among non-human primates, including what we may think of as empathy and fairness (de Waal 2013).

Dominance Relationships

Males are more often dominant over females among common chimpanzees, but both males and females typically establish dominance relationships within their sex. These hierarchies affect access to preferred foods as well as sexual partners (Stumpf 2011). Males generally attain high rank from the alliances they form with other males (usually males of a similar age). They also employ a strategy of using spectacular displays, such as hooting while jumping vigorously through trees or by dragging large branches across the ground, apparently to get attention. Such tactics seem to intimidate other males and help them gain access to preferred resources. Male competition does sometimes cause serious injuries and even occasionally death (Figure 5.12).

Among females, high rank often results in improved access to food sources. In East African populations it is associated with higher rates of infant survivorship. Females with high rank tend to have a larger number of offspring, and mothers often use these strong mother-daughter bonds to achieve or maintain high rank, by acting cooperatively. Females can also achieve dominance via aggressive displays, but these behaviors are less frequently observed than among males.

Bonobo behavioral patterns involving dominance are somewhat different from those of common chimpanzees. Female bonobos are generally dominant over males, and among bonobos it is females who typically display their dominance by dragging objects like tree branches to get the attention of others. However, dominance interactions rarely lead to serious fighting. Instead, conflicts are resolved via genital-genital

(a)   (b)

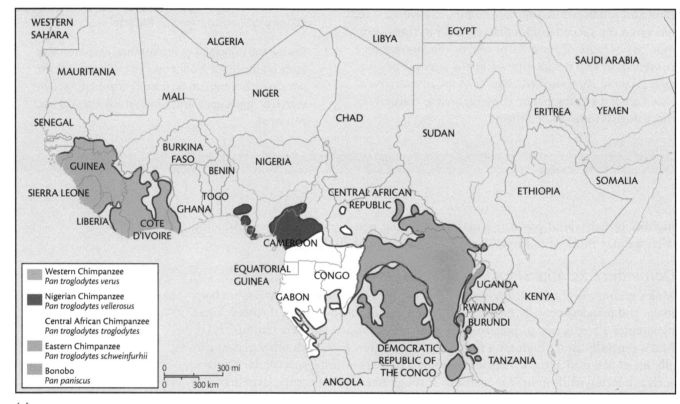

(c)

Western Chimpanzee
Pan troglodytes verus

Nigerian Chimpanzee
Pan troglodytes vellerosus

Central African Chimpanzee
Pan troglodytes troglodytes

Eastern Chimpanzee
Pan troglodytes schweinfurhii

Bonobo
Pan paniscus

Figure 5.11   The Two Chimpanzee Species. *Pan troglodytes*, or common chimpanzees (a); and *Pan paniscus*, or bonobos (b); and their distribution (c).

rubbing and other kinds of non-reproductive sexual behavior. Among male bonobos, dominance hierarchies do exist, but most commonly a male's rank is linked to the rank of his mother. Males can compete aggressively, but the overall rates of bonobo aggression are substantially lower than those of common chimpanzees.

Sexual Behavior

Females in both species show observable signs of fertility. During periods of sexual receptivity their anogenital region becomes filled with fluid, provoking interest from other members of the community. During these times, females can be observed soliciting copulation, often with several males. Primatologists observing common chimpanzee males in natural settings have reported high rates of aggression toward

Figure 5.12   Chimpanzees and Aggression. Common chimpanzees will gain dominance over others by engaging in aggression.

females, which may be a coercive strategy intended to get females to mate with them. This strategy is not, however, present among bonobos. Female choice in sexual partners plays an important role in both species, yet there is little evidence that bonobo males can effectively restrict female mating choices, since the females are usually dominant over males.

Most copulation occurs during the female's swelling periods, but most individuals in both species engage in sexual activity at other times, most notably bonobos. Bonobo males and females engage in frequent genital contact and stimulation as a common means of social interaction. This is especially the case when conflicts among females occur.

Group Aggression

Because it superficially resembles human patterns of fighting, chimpanzee and bonobo incidents of intergroup fighting have received a great deal of attention in the popular press (see, e.g., Wrangham and Peterson 1996). Among common chimpanzee populations, researchers have reported incidents of intercommunity conflict that end with some deaths. "Border patrols," or groups of males circulating around the community's geographic perimeters, have been seen in most populations. Occasionally, when these groups encounter individuals from another community, they attack as a mob, sometimes resulting in the death of the attacked individual(s) (Stumpf 2011). But the pattern of chimpanzee and bonobos patrolling their perimeters seems quite different from the broader patterns of aggression and violence found in many human communities, and violent incidents seem much less significant among both *Pan* species than in our own (Fuentes 2018b).

Social Traditions and Using Tools

In the 1950s and 1960s tool use was thought to be a hallmark of humanity (see, e.g., Oakley 1956), but we now know that many organisms use objects aside from their limbs or mouths to get food. Both chimpanzee species exhibit a wide variety of tool modification and use. They use stone hammers and anvils for cracking nuts, carefully selected sticks and blades of grass for extracting termites from mounds, pointed sticks (like spears) for stabbing and catching small mammals, and forked branches for skimming moss off the top of ponds. Although all chimpanzee and bonobo populations use tools, different groups have different ways of using similar tools, and some don't use certain tools at all. Both male and female chimpanzees use tools, but females appear to be the more prolific tool users. Tool use is a learned behavior that, in some cases, takes years to acquire (Figure 5.13).

So How Do They Compare With Us?

Being a human, you already have a pretty good sense of our general behavior patterns. As you read about the lives of these other primates, it is possible that you began to identify some of the ways our behaviors are similar to or different from theirs. But now let's get more systematic about the comparison.

First, consider macaques. Humans and macaques do share some general characteristics, such as the existence of mixed groups of males and females, social interactions around kin relations, and widespread dispersal based on remarkable adaptability. Our dominance hierarchies have certain similarities, including how we establish and maintain them. Both of our species are able to survive in diverse habitats, which is rooted in our foraging and behavioral flexibility.

But there are critical differences as well. These differences include our body morphologies, how we move around through locomotion, the size of our brains, and, most notably, the scale and complexity of social organization. There are also significant differences between male and female life patterns, which most human societies don't have, except in extreme cases.

Chimpanzees and bonobos present a more interesting, if more complicated, comparison. Obviously we have more in common with them than we do with macaques. One commonality is living in a community. The ways we divide into subgroups and the types of relationships that occur between individuals in communities have elements of similarity.

Other behavioral patterns bear resemblance to our own. Male-to-male bonding in the context of aggression is one similarity, as is the social use of sex. Another is the hunting of meat and other foods among certain group members.

Sexual aggression, mate guarding, and aggression between communities might superficially seem like rape, marriage laws, and war in humans. But debate continues over whether human and chimpanzee social patterns are **analogous** (similar in appearance but not because of shared ancestry), **homologous** (similar because of a shared ancestry), or not comparable because they are totally distinct behaviors.

An important issue, as we noted earlier, is that the two chimpanzee species exhibit behavioral diversity, both within their species and between them, which muddies comparisons with humans. Furthermore, for more than 6 million years, humans and chimpanzees have been on different evolutionary paths, and the chimpanzee species and subspecies are more evolutionarily similar to one another than they are to any humans. More important, perhaps, is that humans have dispersed more widely, adapting to many more environments on the basis of adaptations that are not genetically rooted but culturally mediated.

- **Analogous.** Similar in appearance or function, not the same due to shared ancestry.

- **Homologous.** The characteristic of being similar due to shared ancestry.

Figure 5.13   Tool Use Among Chimpanzees.
Chimpanzee tool use is learned, not inborn. Here common chimpanzees who are using specially prepared twigs to fish for termites from a termite mound.

So what does this all add up to? Can we really understand what it means to be human by turning to primates, and what do we learn about ourselves when we do? The last section takes up these issues.

THINKING LIKE AN ANTHROPOLOGIST: LIVING PRIMATES

Do you see advantages or limits in comparing monkeys, apes, and humans solely in terms of their behaviors? What are those advantages or limits?

5.4 What Does Studying Monkeys and Apes Illustrate About Human Distinctiveness?

During the past few decades, claims about how humans and primates overlap in morphological, genetic, and especially behavioral terms have proliferated and become more refined. Putting these claims simply, primatologist Frans de Waal (2013:16) has observed, "Just like us, monkeys and apes strive for power, enjoy sex, want security and affection, kill over territory, and value trust and cooperation." Certain apes, like gorillas and chimpanzees, can recognize themselves in mirrors, use sign language to create new words (see Chapter 12 on language), and use sophisticated problem-solving skills to escape enclosures.

Where does this leave us in terms of understanding human distinctiveness? The different natural and social scientific disciplines that conduct primatological studies are likely to answer this question somewhat differently, resulting from distinct theoretical and methodological trajectories. Most anthropologists would argue that this is not simply a descriptive problem—that is, it is not just a matter of simply listing the behavioral characteristics of primates and humans and checking off those that appear similar and crossing off others that do not. Rather, it is necessary to take a holistic and comparative approach that brings biological *and* anthropological data and theories into synergistic communication with each other. As we explore in "Classic Contributions: Sherwood Washburn and the New (Integrative) Physical Anthropology," Washburn signaled the importance of an integrative approach decades ago.

Primate Social Organization and Human Behavior

What does the integration of biology and anthropology tell us about human distinctiveness vis-à-vis monkeys and apes? In general terms it concludes that we are distinctive but not unique, linking our distinctiveness to the characteristics of the social behaviors and organization we have developed that enable us to deal with evolutionary processes differently than other primates (Fuentes 2018b). Most of human evolutionary history has involved humans living in small groups of mostly genetically related individuals, cooperating together in foraging, defense, and raising the young. Some 2 million years ago or so, these early humans began moving out of Africa and encountered new environmental challenges. To meet those challenges, those humans relied on tools and basic forms of social cooperation and alliances (a theme discussed in more detail in Chapter 6).

When anatomically modern *Homo sapiens* appears, social behavior changes quite radically. Human social groups grow and tend to become more sedentary (staying in the same place). They also seem to develop divisions of labor within the group and create new social roles. Sometime between 20,000 and 40,000 years ago, permanent settlements appear. The practice of agriculture enables population growth, environments begin to change, and cultural differences between groups grows (see Chapters 10 and 11).

What this all says is that, when compared with other primates, humans have certain distinctive qualities. We live in groups of mixed adult males and females, organizing ourselves into subgroups and a division of labor. Although much depends on demographic factors and cultural specificities, both males and females tend to stay with their birth groups. Most of us (but not all) live in permanent settlements, eating both plant and animal food, much of which we now grow or raise, or have these things done by others. Our bonds, both moral and social, with kin are strong, but we can also develop deep relationships with non-kin. These bonds are sometimes about mating, but often not. Because of culture, there is great variation in our mating patterns, but in general we will mate with multiple individuals through our lives, and choice can play a big role in that decision. Although certain elements of all this resemble what we see in primates, no single primate exhibits them all. There is also no primate species that mediates these relationships and behaviors so thoroughly through culture.

We Have Culture. Do They Too?

During the past several decades, the idea that non-human primates have "culture" has become more popular. Certain macaques, and especially gorillas, orangutans, and chimpanzees, do exhibit patterns of behavioral variation across groups, based on specific behaviors that are shared, learned, and maintained on a group-by-group basis. Among chimpanzees, for example, primatologists have observed several dozen behavior patterns—from tool use to grooming and courtship practices—that are customary or habitual in a particular community but not others. These observations suggest that these behavioral patterns are not reducible either to genetic or to ecological factors (Whiten et al. 1999; Whiten 2021). If these particular behaviors observed in one community but not others are not driven either by genetics or by the local ecology, then could they be a simple form of culture?

The use of the term *culture* to describe these behavior patterns has been controversial, not unexpectedly among social and humanistic scholars, but also among scientists who study other non-primate animals. Part of the problem is an empirical one, which is whether there are enough reliable data, or data of the right kind, to declare that non-human primates have culture. What is the threshold to decide that enough behaviors are "cultural" to declare that the species as a whole exhibits culture?

Another problem has been the tendency to reduce culture to socially transmitted learning. Such learning is not unique to primates; Norway rats and Japanese quail (among others) also exhibit social learning (Grant 2007; Fuentes 2018b). Primatologists have countered that in those species social learning relates to only single behaviors, while in chimpanzees and bonobos, the social transmission of behaviors is more complex and extensive. Of course, given their brain sizes and complexity relative to these other animals, it should be not surprising that chimpanzee social learning is more extensive.

But from an anthropological perspective, reducing culture to the social transmission of behaviors and variation across groups involves a vast oversimplification of how much language and symbolic abstraction lie at the heart of what culture is and how it works,

Classic Contributions
Sherwood Washburn and the New (Integrative) Physical Anthropology

IN 1951 SHERWOOD WASHBURN, then at the University of Chicago and later at the University of California at Berkeley, published a short but visionary article entitled "The New Physical Anthropology." In it he set forth a view that began integrating primatology and anthropology, clarifying the core role of evolutionary theory for anthropology generally at a time when the modern synthesis was generating excitement. Washburn's primary goal in this essay was to move physical anthropology away from the purely descriptive approaches and measurements of individual anatomical traits (such as skull features) that characterized the field from the mid-1800s though the mid-1900s. He realized that integrating evolutionary theory and the study of primates with the (then) new theory and practice of genetics would create an entirely new framework for physical anthropology. Washburn saw the value of integrating these different perspectives and envisioning humans (and other primates) both as the products of an evolutionary history and as currently evolving beings. In this excerpt from his conclusion, he emphasizes the fundamentally integrative motivations of the new physical anthropology.

🌱 **Sherwood Washburn.**

The purpose of this paper has been to call attention to the changes which are taking place in physical anthropology. Under the influence of modern genetic theory, the field is changing from the form it assumed in the latter part of the nineteenth century into a part of modern science. The change is essentially one of emphasis. If traditional physical anthropology was 80 per cent measurement and 20 per cent concerned with heredity, process, and anatomy, in the new physical anthropology the proportions may be approximately reversed. I have stressed the impact of genetics on anthropology, but the process need not be all one way. If the form of the human face can be thoroughly analyzed, this will open the way to the understanding of its development and the interpretation of abnormalities and malocclusion, and may lead to advances in genetics, anatomy, and medicine.

Although evolution is fascinating in itself, the understanding of the functional anatomy which may be gained from it is of more than philosophical importance. The kind of systemic anatomy in which bones, muscles, ligaments, etc. are treated separately became obsolete with the publication of the "Origin of Species" in 1859. The anatomy of life, of integrated function, does not know the artificial boundaries which still govern the dissection of a corpse. The new physical anthropology has much to offer to anyone interested in the structure or evolution of man, but this is only the beginning. To build it, we must collaborate with social scientists, geneticists, anatomists, and paleontologists. We need new ideas, new methods, and new workers. There is nothing new we do today that will not be done better tomorrow. [Washburn 1951:303–4]

Questions for Reflection

1. What are the different intellectual threads that Washburn is saying need to be integrated?

2. Washburn refers to the "integrated function" involved in the "anatomy of life." What do you think he means, and how will the new physical anthropology study it?

a theme we explore in Chapters 2 and 12. Symbolization, personification, metaphorization, abstraction, all of these things are mediated through culture and provide humans with a capacity not simply to interact with actual worlds but to imagine and then construct other worlds, or, for that matter, hold two competing thoughts simultaneously. We can change the shape of ecosystems and ourselves through creative and collaborative effort (Fuentes 2018b). The fact that humans do these things with such diversity across cultures suggests that studying behavior alone is not sufficient to understand culture; we also need to understand and interpret how people think and how those thoughts inform and guide their actions. The tremendous variability and flexibility of ways of thinking and living across our species as documented by sociocultural anthropologists calls into question whether there is a universal human or human behavior against which we can compare any other primate (Haraway 1989).

None of this is meant to deny that non-human primates like chimpanzees exhibit remarkable behavioral flexibility and plasticity, or that they can use a version of human sign language in limited ways, both of which are rooted in cognitive and social complexity relative to other primates and mammals. But anthropologists insist that culture and language enable humans to communicate content not accessible to other organisms and, combined with our use of symbolic representation, allows us to acquire, manipulate, and disseminate knowledge—and alter our environments through niche construction—more extensively than any primate species.

The evolutionary changes that define us as human arose over time and continue to arise. So watching a chimpanzee or a macaque can tell us a great deal about what it takes to be a successful chimpanzee or macaque, but rather little about what it means to be a human. In the same way, watching humans can tell us rather little about being a macaque or chimpanzee. Quite simply, all three primates have distinct bodies and minds that are the result of separate evolutionary trajectories.

THINKING LIKE AN ANTHROPOLOGIST: LIVING PRIMATES

If, as anthropologists argue, *culture* is ultimately not applicable to describing non-human primate behaviors, are there other terms you could think of that might work, such as *tradition*? What would be the advantages and disadvantages of the other term(s)?

Conclusion

Humans are primates. Understanding what we have in common with the other living primate species provides an important comparative baseline for understanding ourselves and what we have inherited biologically as a species. As we explored in this chapter, there are certain primate-wide physical traits—excellent vision, grasping hands, relatively large brains, for example—as well as behavioral trends, including caregiver–infant bonds, grooming, dominance hierarchies, dispersal patterns, and conflict and cooperation. Using the information generated by studying non-human primates, anthropology is in a better position to reconstruct aspects of human evolution, to better understand what is general to primates, what is restricted to a few kinds of primates and humans, and what is uniquely human.

But anthropology's interest in primates does not stop there. We are also interested in the interface between primates and humans. In the interdisciplinary spirit of integration, Washburn had once called for framing a "new physical anthropology." Ethnoprimatologists, for example, do this by drawing on cultural and primatological research methods to better understand these interfaces. As the movement of infectious diseases, such as COVID-19, between human and ape populations demonstrates, understanding those interfaces has important practical and public health dimensions.

The findings of biological anthropology tell us that as compelling as it may be to look at primates and want to see reflections of ourselves, no other primate is a perfect model for human evolution because even our closest relatives, the chimpanzees, have experienced millions of years of separate evolution. Humans are similar to other primates in a number of ways, yet specific aspects of our evolutionary history have resulted in a distinct trajectory of biocultural adaptation. In the next chapter, we begin telling that story of human evolution in more detail.

KEY TERMS

Affiliation p. 122	Ethnoprimatology p. 119	Nocturnal p. 115
Altruism p. 124	Grooming p. 122	*Pan* p. 127
Analogous p. 132	Haplorrhini p. 114	Prehensile p. 116
Anthropoid p. 116	Hominine p. 116	Sexual dimorphism p. 122
Arboreal p. 115	Hominoid p. 116	Strategy p. 124
Behavioral ecology p. 123	Homologous p. 132	Strepsirrhini p. 114
Costs and benefits p. 124	Kin selection p. 124	Terrestrial p. 116
Dispersal p. 122	*Macaca* p. 125	
Dominance hierarchy p. 122	Matrifocal unit p. 126	

Reviewing the Chapter

Chapter Section	What We Know	To Be Resolved
What does it mean to be a primate, and why does it matter to anthropology?	Primates are social animals with excellent stereoscopic vision, grasping hands, and relatively large brains. The two suborders of primates—the Strepsirrhini and Haplorrhini—differ from each other in relative body and brain-to-body sizes, and greater relative emphasis on smell or vision.	Anthropologists have long approached the study of living primates as a window into the evolution of our species, but new areas like ethnoprimatology, which studies the human–primate interface, have created promising new research directions that integrate primatological and sociocultural perspectives.
What are the basic patterns of primate behavioral diversity, and how did they develop?	All primates share certain common behavior patterns, including mother–infant bonding, affiliation and grooming, dominance hierarchies, dispersal, and cooperation and conflict. From those basic patterns, differences in behavior have probably emerged in response to certain socioecological pressures and the energetic costs and benefits of a behavior.	Cost–benefit analyses within behavioral ecology have been dominant for several decades, but they can oversimplify the complexity of behavior. More nuanced approaches are emerging that seek to understand the complicated relationship between the potential for a behavior and its actual performance.

Chapter Section	What We Know	To Be Resolved
How do behavior patterns among monkeys and apes compare with humans?	A comparison between macaques, chimpanzees, and humans can identify certain general commonalities between humans and macaques, and a more specific set of commonalities between humans and chimpanzees.	Primatologists and anthropologists continue to debate whether human and chimpanzee behaviors are analogous (similar in appearance or function, but independent of shared ancestry) or homologous (similar because of shared ancestry).
What does studying monkeys and apes illustrate about human uniqueness?	The uniqueness of humans vis-à-vis other primates has to do with the relative complexity, flexibility, and variability of our social behaviors and relationships, as well as the formation and expression of human thought and action through language and culture.	The debate over primate "culture" has not been resolved, and it seems likely to continue as more primatological experiments and field studies are conducted on the subject.

READINGS

The book *Primates in Perspective*, 2nd ed. (New York: Oxford University Press, 2011), edited by a team of top primate researchers (Campbell et al.), provides a comprehensive overview of all areas of contemporary primatology.

....

A useful and readable introduction to primatological methodology is Karen B. Strier's book *Primate Ethnographies* (Boston: Pearson, 2014) which has short essays by prominent anthropologists and primatologists reflecting on their research on monkeys and apes.

....

The website "All the World's Primates" (https://alltheworldsprimates.org/Home.aspx) is a comprehensive and up-to-date resource on primate information.

....

Nicolas Malone's 2021 book *The Dialectical Primatologist: The Past, Present, and Future of Life in the Hominoid Niche* (New York: Routledge) draws on sophistication in both primatological and cultural anthropologies to explore themes of human-primate coexistence and culturally informed conservation strategies.

....

Frans de Waal is one of the most recognizable names in primatology, and his book *The Ape and the Sushi Master: Cultural Reflections of a Primatologist* (New York: Basic Books, 2001) explores his perspectives on primate "culture."

....

METHODS MEMO

How Do Anthropologists Study Ancient Primates and Human Origins?

Paleoanthropology is the branch of biological anthropology that studies ancestral primates and humans to understand how, when, and where the human lineage originated and evolved. The primary line of evidence in this endeavor comes from fossilized bones, stone tools, and other signs of our ancient ancestors, which are difficult to find and limited in number. They are also often broken into many fragments, like so many puzzle pieces. Paleoanthropologists have developed effective scientific research strategies for uncovering, dating, and analyzing these fossils and stone tools, which are useful for prehistoric archaeologists as well. Thanks to technological advances in studying human genetics, paleoanthropologists also have new tools for studying the genetic composition of bones that are not fully fossilized, which creates the potential of linking ancient and contemporary human populations.

WHAT CAN FOSSILS TELL US?

Fossils are mute, of course, and cannot "tell" us anything. But drawing on a number of methods and techniques from such disciplines as archaeology, geology, and anatomy, paleoanthropologists can use fossils to develop clues and hypotheses about the lives of ancient primates and humans. It is not, however, easy to find useful fossils.

Under special environmental conditions, hard tissues like bone and teeth can slowly turn to stone in a process called **fossilization** (Figure MM2.1). When the body of an animal becomes buried in mud or another oxygen-free sediment that prevents decay, over tens of thousands of years minerals in the animal's bone can be replaced by rock crystals. Soft tissues such as organs, skin, and feathers do not fossilize but may leave impressions, or traces, providing clues to their physical characteristics or activities. These types of specimens are called **trace fossils**.

Given the odds, discovering an ancient primate or human fossil is highly improbable. The conditions that produce fossilization are unusual, so only a very small percentage of anything that has ever lived will become a fossil. Most dead animals will decay or be eaten. Also improbable is that the fossil will be eventually exposed by erosion or some other geologic event. Most improbable of all, perhaps, is that the fossil will be found by a paleoanthropologist who can collect critical contextual data about it to apply to an understanding of the human past.

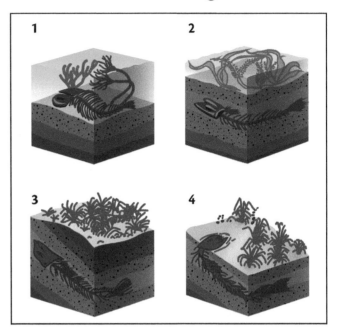

Figure MM2.1 **The Fossilization Process.** Once an animal dies (*1*), its body is buried in low-oxygen sediment such as mud (*2*), then geological processes create a dry environment (*3*), and because of erosion the fossilized remains are exposed to the surface (*4*).

Because of the rarity of fossils, our understanding of the evolutionary lineage of humans is necessarily and always based on the best fossil evidence to date, a situation that can change as more fossils are found. And yet the fossilized fragments of over 6,000 individual ancient primates and humans—not always complete skeletons—have been found. One way field researchers ensure they are prepared

- **Fossilization.** The process by which hard tissues like bone and teeth slowly turn to stone as molecule by molecule the hard tissues become rock, keeping the shape of the original bone.

- **Trace fossils.** Soft tissues such as organs, skin, and feathers that do not fossilize but sometimes leave impressions, or traces, on the sedimentary rock that forms around them.

for such discoveries is by reviewing geological, aerial, and satellite imagery surveys and talking to local miners and quarry workers so they can concentrate their efforts in areas with good fossil-bearing sediments or that have yielded fossils before.

When a potential site of interest is identified, researchers conduct a survey of the area, collecting any material evidence on the surface that might give clues that ancient humans lived there, such as animal bone fossils, or stones that are either modified for apparent tool use or laid in some kind of pattern that suggests human activity. Researchers dig a **test pit** (1m × 1m squares) that can reveal information about the depth, contents, and stratigraphy (soil layers) of the site, recording the locational details of any artifacts or biological materials they find. Researchers will also typically create multidimensional virtual maps where they can plot their finds and layer the map with other information, including landscape features, types of sediments, and so on to help them identify any patterns that might yield insights into ancient primate or human activity or point to further fossil discoveries. Prehistoric archaeologists also utilize these techniques in their own field research.

The type of excavation employed depends on the type of sediment in which the fossils are encased. A range of tools—from jackhammers, crowbars, and sledgehammers to sensitive drills—are used to release fossils. Where fossil beds exist, researchers might cut blocks of **breccia**, a rock composed of broken fragments or minerals cemented together by a fine-grained matrix, which are taken to the laboratory to be dissolved in baths of weak acid, or worked at with hammers and chisels, to release fossilized remains. These techniques are highly destructive, and excavations can often destroy the very evidence being recorded, leaving nothing but written testimony to back up key assertions.

In the laboratory, researchers glean useful information using various kinds of powerful microscopes, X-rays, and three-dimensional scanners to study the fossils up close. Knowing the physical characteristics of skulls, teeth, and bones allows scholars to infer an individual's growth, age, injury, disease, cause of death, environmental conditions, and even signs of brain size and complexity, which may offer insight into past behavior and cognitive capacities.

HOW IS THE AGE OF A FOSSIL OR ARCHAEOLOGICAL SITE DETERMINED?

How do paleoanthropologists and archaeologists establish the age of fossils or other artifacts? Both draw on multiple methods, but a primary consideration involves the object's provenance, or precise location and context in which a specimen is found. We are not talking about a location like a shelf in a museum storage facility or a rock shop, which have probably lost key contextual data. These contextual data include what type of rock it is found in, the layers or strata of rock above and below the fossil or artifact, and other fossil and non-fossil items surrounding it. If the exact location of a fossil or artifact find is not known, it is difficult—perhaps impossible—to determine its age.

There are two general methods for determining how old a fossil or an artifact is: **relative dating** and **absolute** or **chronometric dating** (Table MM2.1). Relative dating techniques provide us with rough assessments of a fossil's or artifact's age relative to other fossils, rocks, or features. Chronometric dating techniques give us a specific age for a fossil or piece of organic material, based on analysis either of a piece of the fossil or sample, or of the rocks surrounding the fossil or artifact. Many objects contain radioactive components that slowly decay into another element at a constant rate over time, such as bone, which has carbon, and volcanic rocks, which have potassium or argon. Measuring the rate of decay in an element can yield a numerical value, which is the age of the object.

STUDYING ANCIENT DNA

In addition to the formal dating methods outlined in Table MM2.1, genetic data can sometimes document the age of a sample by estimating the rate of mutation in

---

- **Test pit.** A preliminary excavation, usually of a single 1 m × 1 m square (or a half meter square) to see if artifactual material exists at the site and to assess the character of the stratigraphy.

- **Breccia.** A rock composed of broken fragments or minerals cemented together by a fine-grained matrix.

- **Relative dating.** Any dating technique that provides a rough assessment of the age of a fossil, artifact, or archaeological feature relative to other fossils, rocks, artifacts, or features.

- **Absolute dating (or chronometric dating).** Any dating method that determines an age of a fossil, rock, artifact, or archaeological feature on some specified time scale.

TABLE MM2.1 BASIC DATING TECHNIQUES FOR FOSSILS, FOSSIL SITES, ARCHAEOLOGICAL SITES, AND ANCIENT MONUMENTS

	NAME OF METHOD	DESCRIPTION	PRACTICAL USE
RELATIVE DATING	Stratigraphy	Examines the layers of sedimentary or intrusive volcanic rock to establish correlation with geological events and processes.	Nearly all paleoanthropologists and archaeologists begin with a stratigraphic analysis. It is often used with various chronometric dating techniques. One of the earliest stratigraphic analyses was William Flinders Petrie's (1891) excavation of an ancient village site known as a *tell* or mound in the desert.
	Seriation	Documents changes over time in styles of pottery, flint knapping, carving, etc.	Useful for dating archaeological sites, but rarely for fossil sites. It is especially useful for "horizontal" stratigraphy, such as when different sites were occupied at a variety of different, but slightly overlapping, times. Flinders Petrie (1899) first described this methodology for dating ancient graves in a cemetery in the Nile Delta. It has also proved useful for dating Pueblo Pottery in the New Mexico region in what has been called the Pecos Classification proposed at the Pecos Conference in 1927 by Alfred Kidder (1927, 1931).
	Faunal Correlation	Correlates a new fossil with another of a known age (Oakley 1964:33–40).	Based on the presence of certain animal bones known to be living in a region at a certain time. For example, the presence of a wooly mammoth bone places it at a certain period before these creatures went extinct, but it cannot tell us exactly when the artifact was used.
	Fluorine Absorption	Measures the relative amount of fluorine in a bone that is absorbed from groundwater.	Can only be expressed as younger or older than something of known age (Taylor 1975).
CHRONOMETRIC DATING	Carbon-14 (14C) Dating	Measures half-life of decaying Carbon-14 in artifacts of biological origin (5,730 years).	Useful for dating artifacts up to 60,000 years old, which makes it especially important for prehistoric archaeologists. See the Methods Memo "Why Is Carbon-14 So Important to Archaeologists?" in Part III, pages 275–77.
	Potassium-Argon (40K/40Ar) Dating	Measures decay of an isotope of potassium into argon.	Useful for dating minerals, clays, and sediments over 100,000 years old. Often used for dating fossils and very early stone tools, by dating a higher layer of igneous rock that was laid down as volcanic ash (Curtis 1975).
	Fission-track	Measures damage trails, or fission tracks, left by fission fragments in uranium-bearing minerals.	Can distinguish young from older and very old rocks (especially useful for very old fossils); see G. Wagner and Van den Haute (1992).
	Thermo-luminescence (TL)	Measures time elapsed since crystalline material was heated.	Useful for dating more recent archaeological items like clay fired as pottery or exposed to fire in a hearth (Aitken 1985; Renfrew and Bahn 2004:154–56), or for much older items exposed to various forms of heat like volcanic activity.

	NAME OF METHOD	DESCRIPTION	PRACTICAL USE
	Optical Stimulated Luminescence (OSL)	Measures the number of electrons trapped within the crystalline structure of minerals like quartz and feldspar after being buried in the earth for long periods. Crystals absorb energy from trace amounts of radioactive material in the soil and rock. When exposed to light the electrons are released and can be measured to estimate the date they were buried (Ahr, Nordt, and Forman 2013).	Useful for dating geological sediments and sometimes fired pottery and bricks.
	Dendrochronology (Tree Ring Dating)	Counts tree rings, each of which represents a year.	Useful in very dry regions where trees are preserved, such as the American Southwest over the past 12,000 years. In some cases it has been used for much earlier samples (A. Douglas 1919; Bannister and Robinson 1975).
	Electron Spin Resonance	Measures the buildup of electrons trapped inside crystals after they were formed.	Commonly applied to tooth enamel several thousand to several million years old (Grün 2008).
	Textual Evidence	Deciphering and analyzing writing systems such as hieroglyphs.	Egyptian hieroglyphics, Mesopotamian cuneiform, and Mayan glyphs, as well as some early writing systems in China, often appear on ancient monuments, clay tablets, stelae, papyrus, and other surfaces discussing the heroic deeds of leaders. Where translations are possible, written evidence often provides more or less precise dates for events, buildings, and documents of financial transactions.

DNA molecules. This method assumes that mutations have occurred at stable rates over long periods of time. Genetics also makes it possible to link living populations with ancient ones, as long as we can recover DNA samples from fossils. These genetic samples from fossils are even more uncommon and rare than the fossils themselves, because over time they degrade significantly. They are also easily contaminated by biological traces left by other living beings they have come into contact with, including scientists themselves. But modern advances in genomic science have enabled the recovery of DNA samples from partly fossilized bones. In practice today, paleoanthropologists and archaeologists are increasingly using several methodologies simultaneously for discerning how any new set of fossils or human skeletal remains relates to modern human groups.

Thinking Critically About Paleoanthropological Methods

- Given the limitations and fragmentary nature of the fossil record, paleoanthropologists can never provide a picture of the ancient primate and human past with complete certainty or precision. In addition to the methods described here, how do you think they build confidence in the validity of their insights?

- Imagine you are working on a paleoanthropological excavation in Ethiopia, near where several discoveries of 2- to 3-million-year-old hominins have been made. You have uncovered what appear to be a very old hominin tooth and a stone tool. What chronometric (or absolute) dating methods would you use to determine how old they actually are? What relative dating methods might you use?

- Some ancient bones and skulls are found in locations of extremely difficult access, such as deep in caves and under water. Moving them can be very disruptive and might destroy them. How do you think paleoanthropologists deal with this kind of situation? What are the possible advantages and disadvantages of studying these things in place, as opposed to moving them to a laboratory?

Ancestral Humans

6

Understanding the Human Family Tree

THE LARGEST known concentration in the world of hominin fossils lies in an area some 30 or so miles outside of Johannesburg, South Africa. It is a rugged and pocked landscape punctuated by intricate limestone cave systems that wind deep below Earth's surface. Since the 1930s, discoveries of such significance—including previously unknown species of early humans and human relatives—have been made there that it was declared an UNESCO World Heritage Site carrying the name "The Cradle of Humankind." Although sites in East Africa have also yielded important findings, research performed in this South African location has long played a major role in what Anthropology knows about our family tree and its evolutionary story.

Thanks to the recent discovery there of two new species—*Australopithecus sediba* in 2009 and *Homo naledi* in 2013—that knowledge continues to expand. Excavations, made by paleoanthropologist and National Geographic Explorer Lee Berger and colleagues from the University of Witswatersrand, University of Johannesburg, University of Wisconsin, Madison, and others, have yielded thousands of fossils of these two early human relatives. This is especially true of *H. naledi*, which has some of the most complete fossil hominin skeletons on record. Important details about these human relatives remain ambiguous, including their geographic range, their relationship with each other, and how they might relate to us. But

New Finds in "The Cradle of Humankind."   Since 2008, paleoanthropologists have discovered two new previously unknown hominins in the famed South African site. In this picture, researchers work with fossilized remains of one of them, *Australopithecus sediba*. These discoveries have created exciting new possibilities for understanding human origins.

each exhibit a mix of old and new physical traits with similarities to *Australopithecus* and *Homo*, two hominin genera and likely human ancestors. *A. sediba* lived some 1.7 to 1.9 million years ago, and like other members of its genus had some ape-like qualities and were at least partly arboreal, but like members of the genus *Homo*, they also had the ability to walk upright and had human-like hands (Berger et. al. 2010). *H. naledi* has been dated to between 236,000 and 335,000 years ago, and like us was a full-time upright walker with hands very similar to our own, though its skull was quite small compared to humans today (600cc vs 1400cc; Berger et. al. 2015; Dirks et al. 2017). Intriguingly, *H. naledi* would not have been the only species of *Homo* on the planet at that time; our own species, *Homo sapiens*, was another one, and possibly existed in some proximity to *H. naledi*.

The Rising Star cave system, where the *H. naledi* remains have been discovered, has attracted ongoing attention by Berger and his collaborators, a group that now includes this book's co-author Agustín Fuentes. Deep in that cave system, in areas that are exceedingly difficult to access, the team recently found some puzzling evidence (Berger et. al. 2023). *H. naledi* skeletal remains were laid as if they were deliberately placed there, some of them in pits that appear to have been dug. Near the locations of these bodies are engravings on the rock wall and a stone object that may have been an engraving tool. These activities would have required a light source, namely fire. Is this some kind of mortuary? Was *H. naledi* capable of symbolic thought? How and when did they begin to use fire? The debate over the meaning of these unexpected findings is just beginning as the scientific peer review process unfolds (Wong 2023). But to find these activities in a part of the cave that is so hard to get to even for contemporary humans with powerful lights, GPS units, climbing ropes, and so on, would suggest that *H. naledi* engaged in the kind of considerable social collaboration, coordination, and planning previously associated only with larger-brained humans (Fuentes et. al. 2023).

- **Paleoanthropologists.** Physical anthropologists and archaeologists who study the fossilized remains of ancient primates and humans to understand their biological and behavioral evolution.

These are exciting times for **paleoanthropologists**, those physical anthropologists and archaeologists who study the fossilized remains of ancient primates and humans to understand their biological and behavioral evolution. Thanks to new discoveries and improved field excavation techniques—many of which have garnered significant media attention—the field has been booming in recent years (Zimmer 2015). Advancements in genomic science and technology, including the use of ancient DNA evidence recovered from fossils found mostly in Eurasia, have also had a major influence on the field (Hawks 2013). Such technology was a key element in the discovery of a new group of 40,000-year-old humans called the Denisovans, as well as the announcement in 2013 that a transnational scientific initiative called the Neanderthal Genome Project had completed mapping the **genome** (the complete set of an organism's DNA) of the Neanderthals. One momentous discovery in all this is that contemporary humans share some genetic ancestry with Neanderthals and Denisovans, pointing to some level of interbreeding.

- **Genome.** The complete set of an organism's DNA.

At the heart of Anthropology's interest in human ancestors is the question around which this chapter is organized: *When, where, and how did our human ancestors emerge, and under what conditions did contemporary humans evolve?* We can answer this question by considering a number of related questions around which this chapter is organized:

Who are our earliest possible ancestors?

What did walking on two legs and having big brains mean for the early humans?

Who were the first humans, and where did they live?

How do we know if the first humans were cultural beings, and what role did culture play in their evolution?

In this chapter we meet our immediate evolutionary family. The fossil record shows that the genus to which we belong, *Homo*, emerged just over 2 million years ago and began to diversify between 1.8 million and 300,000 years ago, exhibiting a growing "humanness" in our ancestors. Although many details and connections between ancestral humans remain fuzzy, this story shows that our earliest ancestors emerged out of a period of tremendous diversity of ape species in Africa, and that until fairly recently there were several very human-like species coexisting on the planet and even interbreeding with each other. It also shows the growing role of culture in shaping the evolution of our own ancestral lineage, making us what we are today. We begin with a look at what is known about our very earliest ancestors.

6.1 Who Are Our Earliest Possible Ancestors?

In order to answer this question, it is necessary to address two issues: our evolutionary relationship to the other apes, and how that relationship affects how we view and name certain fossils found from 6 to 1 million years ago (**mya**). In other words, we have to figure out where humans sit in the family tree of the apes. The current view is that we are hominins, a small branch that is part of the larger African branch that includes the gorilla and the chimpanzee.

- **mya.** Million years ago.

Our Earliest Ancestors Were Hominins

Current knowledge of both morphological (e.g., structural) and molecular (genetic) relationships among the living apes and humans indicates that chimpanzees, gorillas, and humans are actually more similar to one another—and thus more closely related—than any of them is to the orangutan (Begun 1999; Wood 2010). This knowledge affects how paleoanthropologists reconstruct the evolutionary trajectory of our early human ancestors.

- **Hominidae.** A family of primates that includes the Hominids, namely, humans and their ancestors.

- **Homininae.** The African subfamily of the Family Hominidae, which includes humans, chimpanzees, and gorillas.

- **Ponginae.** The Asian derived subfamily of Hominidae to which the Orangutan belongs

- **Hominini.** The tribe to which humans and our direct human ancestors belong, who are referred to as hominins.

- **Bipedal locomotion.** The use of two legs rather than four for movement.

- **Foramen magnum.** The opening at the base of the skull (cranium) where the spinal cord enters and connects to the brain

- **Canine/Premolar-3 shearing complex.** A condition in which the lower first premolar tooth is somewhat sharpened or flattened from rubbing against the upper canine as the mouth closes.

All great apes and humans are placed together in the family **Hominidae**. Within the Hominidae, chimpanzees, gorillas, and humans belong in the subfamily **Homininae** (an African-derived branch of Hominidae), and orangutans are placed by themselves as the subfamily **Ponginae** (an Asian-derived branch of Hominidae). See this illustrated in Figure 6.1. The distinction between the hominines, or chimpanzees, gorillas, and humans, is placed at the taxonomic level below "Subfamily" and just above "Genus." Humans and our direct human ancestors are then classed as representatives of the tribe **Hominini** and referred to as *hominins*. In this classification, all hominins are hominines, but the reverse is not true: only some hominines are hominins, these being humans and our direct lineage.

The hominins share several unique traits in common (Figure 6.2). These include the following:

- Modifications in the lower body, the upper arms, and the backbone that make them capable of **bipedal locomotion** (walking on two legs)
- Smaller canine teeth than other members of the Hominidae family
- A forward-placed **foramen magnum**, the hole in the base of the skull where the spinal cord enters, which supports bipedalism.
- A reduced **Canine/Premolar-3 shearing complex**, in which the lower first premolar tooth rubs against the upper canine as the mouth closes, which sharpens or flattens the tooth

Thus you, the reader, and we, the authors, are hominins, and the fossils that show many or all of these traits are considered hominin as well.

The Fossil Record of Hominins in Africa

Fossil evidence of ancestral hominins comes from Africa. During the end of the Miocene epoch (22 to 5.3 mya), we find a great diversity of hominin-like apes thriving in East Africa, with a few in the Mediterranean region near North Africa. This pattern suggests that the transition by one or more hominoid lineages toward a hominin form took place in these two areas (Benefit and McCrossin 1995). Although new ancient ape species are still being discovered (Nengo 2018), three of the most important fossils are summarized in "The Evolution of Humans 6.1" (see pp. 150–151). Debate persists as to whether these fossils are undoubtedly hominin. One of the reasons is that when paleoanthropologists study morphological differences in fossils, they often translate these differences into taxonomic designations. But it is not unusual among living ape species for them to exhibit peculiar anatomical quirks, which are simply normal variations within a species, and this sparks

Figure 6.1   The Family Hominidae. In this classification, great apes and humans are placed in the same family.

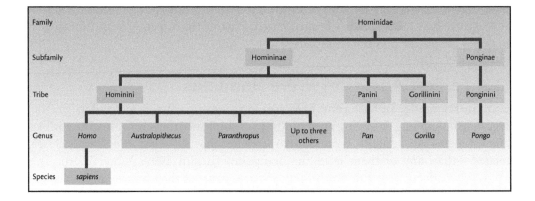

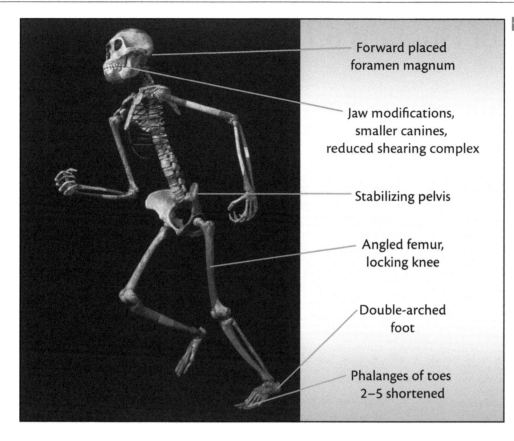

Forward placed
foramen magnum

Jaw modifications,
smaller canines,
reduced shearing complex

Stabilizing pelvis

Angled femur,
locking knee

Double-arched
foot

Phalanges of toes
2–5 shortened

Figure 6.2   General Characteristics of Hominins. Hominins have various modifications in the skull, pelvis, legs, and feet that support bipedalism, as well as modifications to their jaws and teeth that differentiate them from their evolutionary relatives.

debate about whether morphological differences are as meaningful as they seem (Zimmer 2015). Indeed, this point is an important one to keep in mind as we examine all the examples of human ancestors, because it is not only unique to these transitionary hominines but to later hominins as well.

The Three Hominin Genera

Numerous identifiable hominins emerged during the Pliocene epoch (5.3–2.5 mya) and the Pleistocene (2.5 mya to 11,500 years ago). The evolutionary relationships between these and earlier Miocene hominoids remain unclear. During the Pliocene, Africa collided with Europe, creating the Mediterranean Sea, and North America became linked to South America through the Isthmus of Panama. Though the Pleistocene didn't see such great continental movements, it did see significant periods of glaciation with cooling effects on global temperatures. The Plio-Pleistocene hominins are divided into three genera: *Australopithecus*, *Paranthropus*, and *Homo*. Numerous species of these genera overlapped in time, and in some cases geography, suggesting that there were multiple forms of coexisting hominins, and that the human family tree during this period was "bristling with new branches" (Zimmer 2015). Here we summarize the general characteristics of each genus and in "The Evolution of Humans 6.2" (see pages 154–159) we examine the individual species in more detail.

Genus Australopithecus

Of all the hominins, the genus *Australopithecus* ("Southern Ape," as many have been found in South Africa) has the longest presence in the fossil record, a span of over 2 million years. Originally discovered in the 1920s and found distributed widely throughout Eastern and Southern Africa, we have more information about these

The Evolution of Humans 6.1

The Late Miocene Transitionary Hominines, 7 to 4 MYA

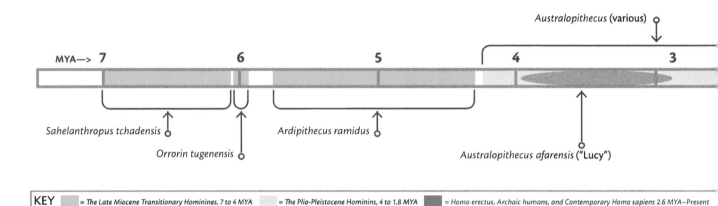

Australopithecus (various)

MYA—> 7   6   5   4   3

Sahelanthropus tchadensis

Orrorin tugenensis

Ardipithecus ramidus

Australopithecus afarensis ("Lucy")

KEY   = The Late Miocene Transitionary Hominines, 7 to 4 MYA   = The Plio-Pleistocene Hominins, 4 to 1.8 MYA   = Homo erectus, Archaic humans, and Contemporary Homo sapiens 2.6 MYA–Present

	SPECIES	DISCOVERY	RANGE
1	**Sahelanthropus tchadensis** Name means "Sahel man from Chad"	Discovered in Chad in 2001 by French-Chadian team led by Brunet (Brunet et al. 2002)	West-Central Africa
2	**Orrorin tugenensis** "Orrorin" means "original man" in Tugen language of Kenya	Discovered in 2000 in Kenya by French team led by Senut and Pickford (Senut et al. 2001)	E. Africa
3	**Ardipithecus ramidus** "Ramid" means "root" in Afar language of Ethiopia	Discovered in 1992 in Aramis site, Awash River, northern Ethiopia by Ethiopian team led by Y. Haile-Selassi (Haile-Selassie 2001)	E. Africa

1
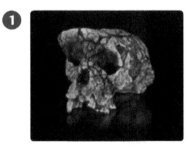

2
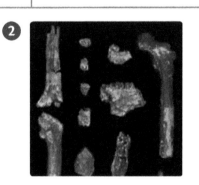

3
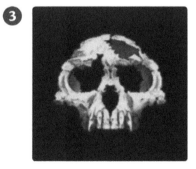

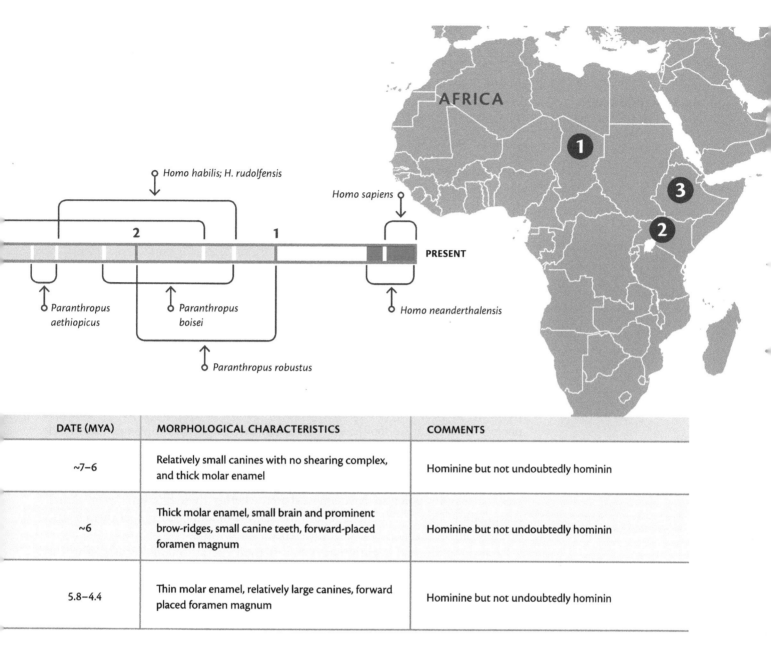

DATE (MYA)	MORPHOLOGICAL CHARACTERISTICS	COMMENTS
~7–6	Relatively small canines with no shearing complex, and thick molar enamel	Hominine but not undoubtedly hominin
~6	Thick molar enamel, small brain and prominent brow-ridges, small canine teeth, forward-placed foramen magnum	Hominine but not undoubtedly hominin
5.8–4.4	Thin molar enamel, relatively large canines, forward placed foramen magnum	Hominine but not undoubtedly hominin

- **Australopithecines.**
A word that refers to the
genus *Australopithecus*.

- **Gracile.** A body of slender
build.

ancient hominins than we have about any other early hominin. Most researchers hypothesize that the human lineage emerged from the **australopithecines** (a word that refers to the genus *Australopithecus*).

Australopithecines were **gracile** (a paleoanthropological term referring to a slender build), between 1.2 m and 1.4 m (3 ft. 11 in. to 4 ft. 7 in.) tall, and exhibited a fairly high degree of sexual dimorphism, with males larger than females. Their relatively large brain sizes, while still only 35 percent of the brain size of contemporary humans, distinguish them from their other primate ancestors. They also had a gripping hand. The discovery at several australopithecine fossil sites of stone flakes and mammalian bones with cut marks on them suggests that at least several members of this genus put their brain and hand power to processing food, perhaps as early as 3.3 mya (Harmand et al. 2015).

Like their primate ancestors, their arm length suggests at least a partially arboreal existence, although they also had bipedal stature that allowed them to walk on two legs. We do not know how much time they lived on the ground or in trees, but fossilized bipedal footprints found in Tanzania—the famed Laetoli footprints—have been attributed to one of the best known australopithecines, *Australopithecus afarensis*.

Genus Paranthropus

Between ~2.7 and 1 mya, we find a cluster of hominin fossils that differ in some morphology from the australopithecines, primarily their larger chewing bones and muscle. However, from the neck down they are very similar to the Australopithecines. There are three known species in this genus, *Paranthropus*, which means "beside" or "near" humans. Discovered originally in 1938 in South Africa and found in East Africa as well, paleoanthropologists have long debated whether these hominins were actually australopithecines or a different genus. The latest taxonomic orders split them because of a few important morphological differences.

- **Sagittal crest.** A ridge
running along the top of the
cranium, usually representing
increased bone area for the
attachment of chewing
muscles.

- **Megadontia.** The
characteristic of having large
molar teeth relative to body
size.

Paranthropines had slightly larger brains than the australopithecines. They had broad, "dish-shaped" faces, almost small foreheads, widely flared cheekbones, a pronounced **sagittal crest** (ridge in the center of the skull related to a chewing muscle attachment), and a forward-jutting jaw. They exhibit **megadontia**, or larger postcanine teeth (molars and premolars) than would be expected for the size of their bodies. Given the grinding structure of their teeth and studies of their tooth enamel, researchers initially thought that they may have relied more heavily on plant foods than australopithecines, but now we know that they simply had a broader dietary breadth. Standing 1.3 m to 1.4 m (4 ft. 3 in. to 4 ft. 7 in.) tall, all three species were bipedal, and they probably lived in open woodland or savannah landscapes. They were almost certainly tool users.

Genus Homo

The genus *Homo* emerged out of one of the australopithecine lineages sometime between 3 and 2 mya. When Linnaeus originally designated the genus *Homo* in 1758, our own species *Homo sapiens* ("wise ones") was the only species in the genus. As increasing numbers of hominin fossils have been found and studied during the past fifty years, paleoanthropologists continue to add more species to the genus, as we saw in the introduction to this chapter. Most hominin fossils found in Africa and Asia dating to younger than about 1.8 mya are generally considered members of the genus. But disagreement persists about how many species they represent, and even in some cases whether the earliest ones should be assigned to the genus *Homo* or the genus *Australopithecus* (Wood and Boyle 2016).

To be placed definitively in the genus *Homo*, fossils must display certain characteristics. One of those features used to be a large brain, but now we know that the two earliest proposed species of *Homo*—*H. habilis* and *H. rudolfensis*—have brain cavities about half the size of a contemporary human, and two later Pleistocene fossils in the genus (*H. naledi* and *H. floresiensis*) also have very small brains. Current research suggests that it might not only be brain size that is important but also changing patterns of connections and structures in the brain as well. Intriguingly, the part of the human brain associated with speech in contemporary humans appears to be present in one of the species, *H. habilis*. Early members of *Homo* were also competent bipeds, who probably lived in mixed savannah-woodlands landscapes. In addition, their fingers are slightly curved and strongly built, and their hands suggest the ability to use a precision grip, an important requirement for making tools. They made and used stone tools, called **Olduwan tools** (edged choppers named after their initial discovery in the Olduvai Gorge of Tanzania) (Figure 6.3).

Both species of early *Homo* display a mix of ancestral and derived (unique) characteristics, and these are expressed differently in each species. For example, *H. habilis* displays no sagittal crest and has large incisors, smaller postcanine teeth, and a narrower tooth row than is seen in the australopithecines (Conroy 1997; McHenry and Coffing 2000). The face of *H. rudolfensis* is broad and flat, and the cranium has no distinct brow ridge, but it does have a sagittal crest. The postcanine teeth exhibit megadontia and are absolutely larger than those of *H. habilis*, but because of the larger body size of *H. rudolfensis*, the premolars and molars are relatively smaller (McHenry and Coffing 2000).

Figure 6.3 Olduwan Tools. Named after Olduvai Gorge in Tanzania where this type of stone tool was discovered, Olduwan tools were made by striking the edge of a stone with a hammerstone, producing the kinds of hammering stones shown here, as well as sharp flakes useful for cutting food and other objects.

● **Olduwan tools.** Rocks that were modified to produce sharp flakes and edged choppers.

Who Is Our Most Direct Ancestor?

To recap, our very earliest ancestors were bipedal hominins who lived in Eastern and Southern Africa at least 4 mya and probably earlier. They did not yet have the big brain that characterizes contemporary humans, but what we do see aligns with what we would expect our early ancestors would look like. From this assortment of forms arise our direct ancestors.

But which one is most directly related to us? Is it the "missing link?" The notion that there is a "missing link" out there awaiting discovery has long captured popular imagination, suggesting that once we identify that link a lot of uncertainties about our past will fall into place. Yet, while paleoanthropologists agree that we do have a common ancestor, deciding which one is a major challenge, if not impossible, because the fossil record is still so incomplete. Furthermore, evolutionary theory rejects the possibility of a "link" because that metaphor assumes a straight and linear series of relationships—a chain—which is not really how species evolve (Chapter 3). A missing link will thus never be found. What we have instead are many "missing links," and what paleoanthropologists are looking for are further linkages (evolutionary relationships) between the hominins we have identified.

We can be reasonably certain that by 2 mya our own lineage had arisen. Because the members of the genus *Australopithecus* mostly predate members of our own genus in Eastern and Southern Africa, and because of similarities in anatomy, our genus *Homo* probably emerged from *Australopithecus* lineage. Strong similarities in anatomy indicate that most, if not all, hominins from ~3 mya on are derived from the *A. afarensis* lineage. But dating issues with *A. africanus* as well as the existence and classification of *Kenyanthropus* and *A. deyiremeda* do pose some problems for seeing *A. afarensis* as our direct ancestor.

What about the genus *Paranthropus*? This group had slightly larger brains than earlier forms and seemed capable of making stone tools. But their massive chewing

The Evolution of Humans 6.2
The Plio-Pleistocene Hominins, 4 to 1.8 MYA

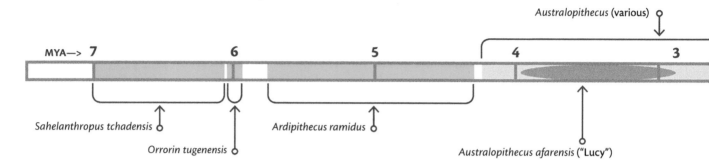

Australopithecus (various)

MYA—> 7 6 5 4 3

Sahelanthropus tchadensis

Orrorin tugenensis

Ardipithecus ramidus

Australopithecus afarensis ("Lucy")

KEY ▮ = *The Late Miocene Transitionary Hominines, 7 to 4 MYA* ▮ = *The Plio-Pleistocene Hominins, 4 to 1.8 MYA* ▮ = *Homo erectus, Archaic humans, and Contemporary Homo sapiens 2.6 MYA–Presen*

	SPECIES	DISCOVERY	RANGE
1	***Australopithecus anamensis*** "Anamensis" means "of the lake" in the Turkana language	Discovered in in 1995 near Lake Turkana in northern Kenya by team led by M. Leakey (Leakey et al. 1995, 1998; Ward, Leaky, and Walker 2001)	E. Africa
2	***Australopithecus afarensis*** "Afarensis" means "from Afar" (a region in Ethiopia)	Discovered in 1974 near Hadar, Ethiopia by American team led by T. Gray and D. Johanson. Some remains found as early as 1930 added to this species	E. Africa
3	***Australopithecus deyiremeda*** "Deyiremeda" means "close relative" in language of Afar people	Discovered in 2011 in Afar region of Ethiopia by an Ethiopian team led by Y. Haile-Selassie (Haile-Selassie et al. 2015)	E. Africa
4	***Australopithecus bahrelghazali*** "Bahrelghazali" refers to "Bar El Ghazal" (a region in Chad)	Discovered in 1995 in by M. Brunet	N. Central Africa

1

2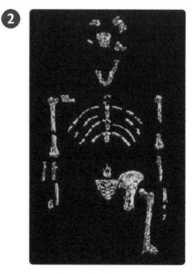

3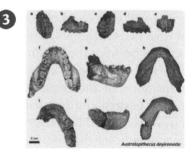

154

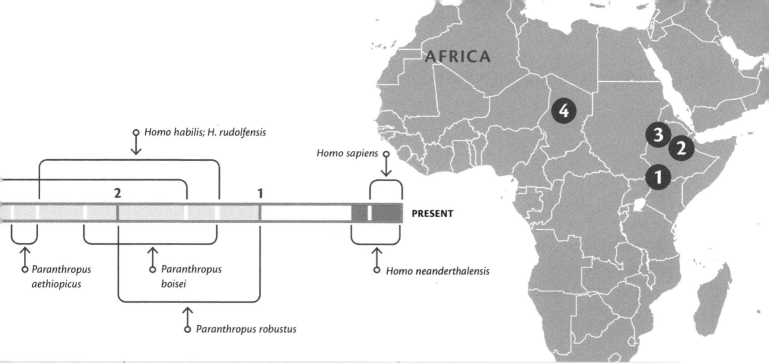

Homo habilis; H. rudolfensis

Homo sapiens

2   1

PRESENT

Paranthropus
aethiopicus

Paranthropus
boisei

Homo neanderthalensis

Paranthropus robustus

DATE (MYA)	MORPHOLOGICAL CHARACTERISTICS	COMMENTS
4.2–3.9	Large molars with thick enamel, relatively large canines, likely biped, long arms	In 2006, new 4.2 mya finds were made several km from where *Ardipithecus ramidus* (4.4 mya) was found in Ethiopia, raising questions about the relationships between them.
3.9–3.0	Large molars with thick enamel, relatively large canines, gracile, bipedal anatomy, long arms so probably partly arboreal	One of best known fossils (over 300 found in numerous sites). Team of D. Johanson discovered one in 1974 and nicknamed it "Lucy," after the Beatles song playing at the camp. Laetoli footprints in Tanzania attributed to *A. afarensis* (Conroy 1997; Stern 2000; Simpson 2002).
3.5–3.3	Similar in respects to *A. afarensis*, but its teeth are smaller, the cheekbones are more forward-facing, the lower jaw is larger, and some teeth have thicker outer enamel.	Possibly a descendent of *A. afarensis*, but fossil evidence is fragmentary and some have argued that it is not a new species at all but an illustration of diversity within *A. afarensis*.
3.3	No clear characteristic	Only a mandible fragment has been found. Some argue it may not be another species but member of *A. afarensis*.

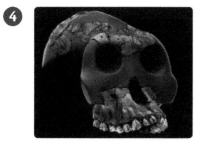

The Evolution of Humans 6.2 *continued*

The Plio-Pleistocene Hominins, 4 to 1.8 MYA

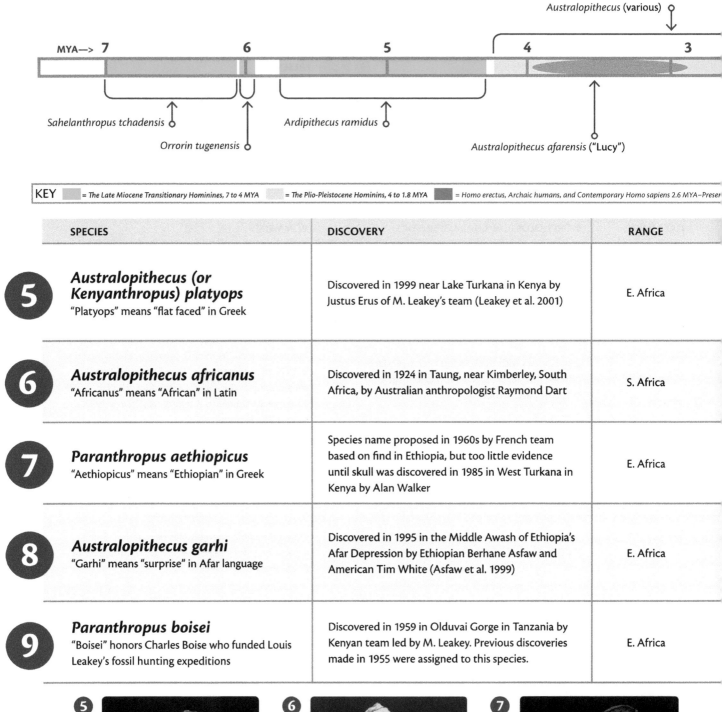

Australopithecus (**various**)

MYA—> 7   6   5   4   3

Sahelanthropus tchadensis

Orrorin tugenensis

Ardipithecus ramidus

Australopithecus afarensis ("Lucy")

KEY ▨ = *The Late Miocene Transitionary Hominines, 7 to 4 MYA*   ▨ = *The Plio-Pleistocene Hominins, 4 to 1.8 MYA*   ▨ = *Homo erectus, Archaic humans, and Contemporary Homo sapiens 2.6 MYA–Preser*

	SPECIES	DISCOVERY	RANGE
5	***Australopithecus (or Kenyanthropus) platyops*** "Platyops" means "flat faced" in Greek	Discovered in 1999 near Lake Turkana in Kenya by Justus Erus of M. Leakey's team (Leakey et al. 2001)	E. Africa
6	***Australopithecus africanus*** "Africanus" means "African" in Latin	Discovered in 1924 in Taung, near Kimberley, South Africa, by Australian anthropologist Raymond Dart	S. Africa
7	***Paranthropus aethiopicus*** "Aethiopicus" means "Ethiopian" in Greek	Species name proposed in 1960s by French team based on find in Ethiopia, but too little evidence until skull was discovered in 1985 in West Turkana in Kenya by Alan Walker	E. Africa
8	***Australopithecus garhi*** "Garhi" means "surprise" in Afar language	Discovered in 1995 in the Middle Awash of Ethiopia's Afar Depression by Ethiopian Berhane Asfaw and American Tim White (Asfaw et al. 1999)	E. Africa
9	***Paranthropus boisei*** "Boisei" honors Charles Boise who funded Louis Leakey's fossil hunting expeditions	Discovered in 1959 in Olduvai Gorge in Tanzania by Kenyan team led by M. Leakey. Previous discoveries made in 1955 were assigned to this species.	E. Africa

5

6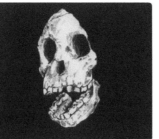

7

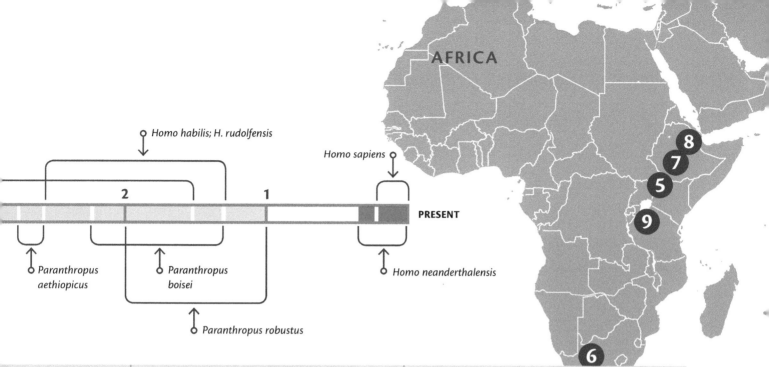

DATE (MYA)	MORPHOLOGICAL CHARACTERISTICS	COMMENTS
3.2–3.5	Only known from a single cranium, relatively small teeth, thick molar enamel	Debate continues over whether it is australopithecine or new genus, *Kenyathropus*. Recently researchers have discovered simple flakes dated to 3.3 mya that might have been used as stone tools, making these the oldest stone tools yet discovered (Balter 2014b).
3.3–2.1	Gracile build, sloping face with slightly jutting jaw, arms slightly longer than legs with hand adapted for climbing. Pelvis better for bipedalism than *A. afarensis*. Pronounced sexual dimorphism.	Also known as "Taung Child." Found at only four sites in South Africa. Possible contemporary of *A. afarensis*.
2.6	Hyper-robust, megadontia, powerful jaw, well-developed saggital crest	Primary specimen is a skull, known as "Black Skull" due to coloration of rock in which it was found.
2.5	Not very well known (only cranial and dental fragments have been found). Extremely large premolars and molars and the shape of and patterns in the teeth.	It is thought that *A. garhi* made use of stone tools for meat eating, based on the discovery of mammalian bones with cut marks clearly made by stone tools in rocks of roughly the same age as the *A. garhi* finds (de Heinzelin et al. 1999).
2.3–1.2	Robust, canines that appear like incisors. Sometimes known as "Nutcracker Man" due to flattest cheek teeth and thickest tooth enamel among hominins. Pronounced sexual dimorphism.	One of the best known early hominins. Probably made some very rudimentary stone tools, which were found in the same area.

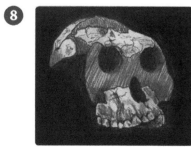

The Plio-Pleistocene Hominins, 4 to 1.8 MYA

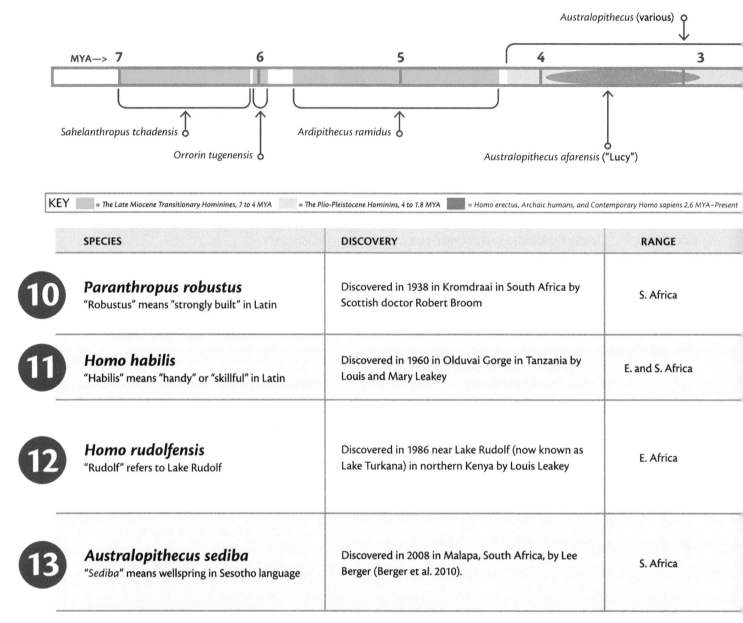

Australopithecus (various)

MYA—> 7   6   5   4   3

Sahelanthropus tchadensis

Orrorin tugenensis

Ardipithecus ramidus

Australopithecus afarensis ("Lucy")

KEY   = *The Late Miocene Transitionary Hominines, 7 to 4 MYA*   = *The Plio-Pleistocene Hominins, 4 to 1.8 MYA*   = *Homo erectus, Archaic humans, and Contemporary Homo sapiens 2.6 MYA–Present*

SPECIES	DISCOVERY	RANGE
10 ***Paranthropus robustus*** "Robustus" means "strongly built" in Latin	Discovered in 1938 in Kromdraai in South Africa by Scottish doctor Robert Broom	S. Africa
11 ***Homo habilis*** "Habilis" means "handy" or "skillful" in Latin	Discovered in 1960 in Olduvai Gorge in Tanzania by Louis and Mary Leakey	E. and S. Africa
12 ***Homo rudolfensis*** "Rudolf" refers to Lake Rudolf	Discovered in 1986 near Lake Rudolf (now known as Lake Turkana) in northern Kenya by Louis Leakey	E. Africa
13 ***Australopithecus sediba*** "Sediba" means wellspring in Sesotho language	Discovered in 2008 in Malapa, South Africa, by Lee Berger (Berger et al. 2010).	S. Africa

10
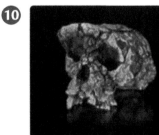

11

12
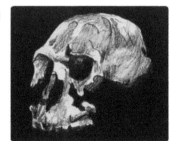

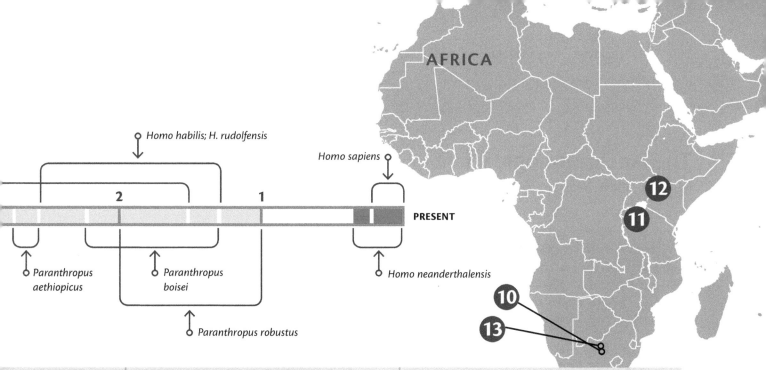

Homo habilis; H. rudolfensis

Homo sapiens

2   1

PRESENT

Paranthropus aethiopicus

Paranthropus boisei

Homo neanderthalensis

Paranthropus robustus

AFRICA

DATE (MYA)	MORPHOLOGICAL CHARACTERISTICS	COMMENTS
2–1	Robust, fairly large brain, large chewing muscles, large molars. Arms were longer than the legs, but feet and hands displayed remarkable similarities to those of later hominins.	Given its precision gripping hands, it may have been a tool user. Some bone tools have been found at *P. robustus* sites.
2.4–1.4	Large incisors, larger brain than australopithecines and paranthropines, moderately prognathic face, gripping hand for tool use	Was long considered to be first hominin to use tools, though recent evidence suggests hominin tool use was earlier.
2.4–1.6	Larger than *H. habilis* in body size, brain case, and molars, as well as a longer face	The majority of *H. rudolfensis* material comes from about twelve fossils, with very little postcranial material, and researchers are still debating whether the postcranial material that does exist belongs to this species or to *Paranthropus* (Wood and Collard 1999; McHenry and Coffing 2000).
1.9–1.7	Larger cranial capacity than other australopithecines, similar to *Homo* in tooth and jaw size, grasping hand suggests possible tool use, longer arms suggest partly arboreal existence, bipedal capacity	Example of mosaic evolution, having characteristics of both *Australopithecus* and *Homo*.

The Anthropological Life
Q & A with Briana Pobiner, Paleoanthropologist

Briana Pobiner is a highly regarded paleoanthropologist who works in the Human Origins Program at the Smithsonian Institution's National Museum of Natural History in Washington, DC. She graduated from Bryn Mawr College in 1997, and received a PhD in Anthropology from Rutgers University in 2007. We sat down with Briana to find out about her life as a paleoanthropologist.

WHAT IS IT LIKE BEING A PALEOANTHROPOLOGIST?

It's all about learning more about humanity. We try to make sense of the lives ancient people lived. The cool thing is that it's an interdisciplinary science. We bring different methods to the table, and our projects are often collaborative. It's

▼ **Briana Pobiner studies carnivore chewing damage on modern animal bones at Ol Pejeta Conservancy in Kenya while pregnant** (photo credit: Nick Walton).

challenging to figure out what happened a long time ago. For me it's about solving mysteries.

PEOPLE USUALLY HAVE NO IDEA WHAT PALEOANTHROPOLOGISTS DO, THINKING THAT MAYBE YOU GO OUT TO LOOK FOR DINOSAURS. WHAT DO YOU ACTUALLY DO?

I study the evolution of human diets. I'm interested in what people ate a long time ago. For example, I study animal fossils from archaeological sites where we know people were eating animals, and I'm trying to figure out what parts were they eating? How are they getting those animals? How important was this in their diets overall? So my fieldwork involves excavating animal fossils butchered by humans or animals that died naturally, which can tell us about the environment. I also look for tools ancient humans made. I really enjoy being outside, digging in the dirt and discovering things people haven't seen for 1 or 2 million years. The other fieldwork I do is a little less common in some ways. It's paleoanthropology, but I'm interested in what happens when predators chew on bones so I can understand chewing patterns past predators left on fossils. So I go out in modern African environments to look for bones from animals that have died recently. I love that, too, because I get to be in wildlife areas with lots of animals around.

WHAT MADE YOU CHOOSE TO GO INTO THIS FIELD?

The basic answer is a really inspiring college professor. I thought I wanted to be an English major, maybe a writer. I was not particularly science-inclined but I took an Introduction to Physical Anthropology and Archaeology class. I was looking for a fourth class for my first semester and the dean who was advising me said, "Why don't you take anthropology?" I'd never heard of it. That was the first time science was presented to me as an enterprise with unanswered questions I could participate in. And I was like, "Wait, we don't know this? And we don't know that?" That was really exciting. There will always be unanswered questions, but there were also unanswered questions where I could pose a question, construct a hypothesis, and figure out how to collect data to answer it. This was a revelation—that science didn't work in the formulaic way my lab classes in high school did, where you did an experiment and you either got the right answer or you messed something up. I loved it.

HOW WOULD YOU DESCRIBE YOUR JOB RIGHT NOW?

I have a pretty unique job within both the Smithsonian and the Natural History Museum. It includes primary research on whatever research questions I want to ask. But I also do a lot of public engagement. I help do volunteer training. I run social media accounts. I help keep our website up to date. And I facilitate public programs. While my job is in the Anthropology Department, I also work with the Office of Education, so I'm involved in larger education teams and initiatives across the Smithsonian. I really like being able to do a variety of things. One of my voluntary initiatives is research on teaching and learning about human evolution in high school classrooms. We've developed some curricular material for high school classrooms in Alabama to get a sense of how it engages students, how it helps them learn about evolution, especially in communities where learning about evolution might be uncomfortable. I also helped put together the Hall of Human Origins at the Natural History Museum. So a lot of my job involves using human evolution as a launching pad for public engagement with science more broadly.

anatomy seems to be very specialized relative to more recent members of the genus *Homo*, making it unlikely that they are our ancestors. *Paranthropus* was perhaps a sister genus that coexisted with our own for almost 1.5 million years. They might have even competed for similar resources, and predators saw both genera, at least early on, as targets (Hart and Sussman 2005). If we could understand why *Homo* flourished as *Paranthropus* went extinct, we might gain a valuable insight into what it means to be human. One attempt to model this process emphasizes that *Homo* might have gained selective advantage over *Paranthropus* through increasingly complex patterns of cooperation and niche construction (Fuentes, Wyczalkowski, and MacKinnon 2010).

At the same time, we still do not know which of the early members of the genus *Homo* is our most direct ancestor. *Homo habilis* has the right head (smaller teeth and a large brain) but the wrong body (smaller body size, pelvic and limb anatomy, and the relatively flexible feet of the australopithecines). *Homo rudolfensis* has the wrong head (megadontia similar to *Paranthropus*, but relatively smaller teeth owing to its larger body size and an absolutely larger but relatively similar brain) but the right body, including pelvic anatomy more like that of later humans than that of the australopithecines.

THINKING LIKE AN ANTHROPOLOGIST: ANCESTRAL HUMANS

The current picture of our family tree suggests that multiple hominins of the different genera—Australopithecus, Paranthropus, and Homo—had periods of overlap in their existence, but only one genus exists today. In evolutionary terms, what are the different possible things that could have happened to the others?

6.2 What Did Walking on Two Legs and Having Big Brains Mean for the Early Hominins?

Bipedalism is a major component of being human. It is one of the determining traits of the hominins and is directly linked with our emergence and our separation from the apes. Increased brain size and neurobiological complexity is also significant, as it has enabled us to acquire a degree of social complexity and tool use not seen in other apes. In this section, we explore why and how these changes occurred and their consequential effects on the evolution and behavior of early hominins.

The Benefits of Upright Movement

Most of the australopithecines and *Homo habilis* have longer arms than current humans. This feature would have allowed these forms to move effectively through the trees as well as bipedally on the ground. But there is a difference between a bipedal-*allowing* anatomy that still enables the use of four limbs for movement and climbing and a bipedal-*enforcing* anatomy, as contemporary humans have. The big question is why this shift took place; in other words, how and why did full-time bipedalism evolve? The latest thinking is that bipedalism is a consequence of multiple, independent selections that have some relation to the following points paleoanthropologists have considered (modified from Fuentes 2018):

- *It aids carrying objects.* Because it frees the arms, objects like food, tools, and infants can be carried, although these benefits would only be realized after bipedalism evolved. So it can't be the reason it arose.
- *It benefits hunting.* It is efficient for long-distance locomotion and enables weapon carrying. Unfortunately, the archaeological evidence for hunting comes later than the development of bipedalism.
- *It favors upright reaching.* Changes in the upper and lower body enabling bipedalism enhanced the ability to reach for hanging fruit and plants. But erect posture benefits both arboreal and terrestrial forms, so again, it doesn't explain why it arose.
- *It aids vigilance and visual surveillance.* The ability to stand on two legs gives a better view of potential predators, especially in savannas where early hominins lived. Because it aids predator avoidance, natural selection might be at work.
- *It aids long-distance walking and running.* Although early hominins didn't move bipedally as effectively or efficiently as we do, it would nevertheless have made the search for food or mates over large areas easier. In "Anthropologist as Problem Solver: Were We Born to Run?" we explore the relationship between walking, running, and evolution further.
- *It aids heat regulation.* It minimizes the amount of skin exposed to the sun and it could increase heat loss, especially in the challenging sunlight conditions of open savannas. However, the earliest hominins appear to have lived in forested or mixed forest-savanna settings, so it doesn't explain why it arose.

By itself, no single explanation is entirely satisfactory, probably because, as we explained in Chapter 3, evolutionary processes have overlapping dimensions and complex effects on any species. Whatever the case, what we do know is that as the end of the Pliocene and the beginning of the Pleistocene epoch approached, hominins became progressively better at walking on two legs.

The Effects of Big Brains on Early Hominin Behavior

The growth of cranial capacity in hominins over several million years gave them greater brain power. Yet hominin brains did not enlarge uniformly. In *Homo*, for example, the frontal lobe (which plays a critical role in emotional, social, motivational, and perceptual processes, as well as decision-making, attention, and working memory) expanded and elaborated at increased rates than other parts of our brains. The cerebellum, which is involved with social sensory-motor skills, imitation, and complex sequences of behavior, also experienced dramatic growth. These structural changes likely helped *Homo* over time generate more effective and expansive mental representations (Fuentes 2019).

But big brains also require a lot of energy (upward of 20 percent of the entire energy intake in contemporary humans), so the metabolic costs (in calories) for keeping the body operating also increased. If this began with *H. habilis* and *H. rudolfensis*, we would expect to see dietary changes toward more energy-dense foods. All the species of *Homo*, including us, are omnivores, but it is likely that expanding the amount of meat consumed in the diet could have helped meet the added energy expenditures of having larger brains. Roots and tubers high in carbohydrates also would have helped increase the amount of energy ingested by these hominins. The consumption of meat is supported by findings in fossil sites where processed remains of antelopes and antelope-like mammals exist alongside tools probably made by these early hominins.

Still, paleoanthropologists believe that meat remained a small portion of the diet for our early omnivorous ancestors, including *Homo*, and current evidence demonstrates that there was not a major increase in meat eating as a percentage of the diet until much later in human evolution (Barr et al. 2022). Because of their abundance and the relative ease of gathering them, roots, tubers, nuts, and fatty fruits—all sources of high-quality nutrition—were probably staple elements of their diets. We are still not certain what their foraging patterns looked like, but they probably revisited food-rich sites, scavenged meat and did some hunting, and used their growing brain power to develop tools to support their ability to gain access to and process nutritious foods.

Increasing brain power likely also supported cooperative social behaviors and group action, because it bolstered greater capacity for communication among individuals. For example, we know from the fossil sites of *A. afarensis* found at the AL-333 site at Hadar, Ethiopia, and those of *A. sediba* and *H. naledi* in South Africa, that these groups consisted of several adults, children, and infants. These hominins probably moved as groups and interacted with each other through grooming and various kinds of communicative acts, such as gestures and vocal utterances. With new evidence suggesting that *H. naledi*, a very small-brained hominin, buried some of its dead deep in caves, it is clear that intensive social cooperation and robust relationships do not wholly rely on increased encephalization (Fuentes, et. al. 2023). As we explore in "Classic Contributions: Sarah Blaffer Hrdy, Helpless Babies, and the Evolution of Human Cooperation," it also likely that early hominins developed enhanced cooperative behaviors and distinctive empathic and collaborative relationships around childrearing. Because predators such as giant leopards and hyenas roamed the savannas and foraged in the trees, they probably also figured out ways to deal with predators, perhaps by running away or organizing cooperative defense. Either way, avoiding predation was an essential behavior in the life of these australopithecines and continued with *Homo* (Hart and Sussman 2005).

Paleoanthropologists hypothesize that among the early hominins, bipedalism and increasing brain power, with associated changes in diet, tool use, and social relations, contributed to evolutionary changes that led to the later forms of *Homo* (Tattersall 2012).

Anthropologist as Problem Solver
Were We "Born to Run"?

If you haven't caught on to the "barefoot running" craze in recent years, it could be that you are not one of the estimated 65 million Americans who jog at least once a year. If you are a serious runner, perhaps you have even tried it out. This fad took off after the publication of the popular 2011 book *Born to Run*, by journalist and endurance runner Christopher McDougall. In the book he describes what seem like superhuman feats of long-distance endurance running involving hundreds of miles by Mexican Tarahumara Indians. Incredibly, the Tarahumara run barefoot or with simple leather sandals, report few injuries, and run throughout their lives into old age (McDougall 2011). These facts do not seem to square with the constant reports of chronic pain and injuries in the knees, hamstrings, heels, and feet of American runners, who run many fewer miles.

The book draws on the research of paleoanthropologist Daniel Lieberman at Harvard and his colleague biologist Dennis Bramble from the University of Utah to argue that thanks to our evolutionary history, humans are natural endurance runners. Their research suggests that adaptations for endurance running are derived capabilities of our genus that originated about 2 mya with *Homo erectus* (Bramble and Lieberman 2004; Lieberman 2020). Among these evolutionary adaptations are skeletal and muscular changes that differ from the requirements of walking, especially those that allow for greater spring, reduce the impact of running on the joints, and provide stability. These adaptations include the arch of the foot and our big knee joints; the development of springlike tendons in the legs and heel (such as the Achilles heel) that generate force economically; sweat glands that help our overheated bodies cool down; and large muscles in the gluteus maximus and upper shoulders that help stabilize us. Working together, these things allow *Homo* (and us as its sole modern representative) an unusual ability to run for longer distances and more sustained time periods than any other animal.

Walking is still more efficient than running, but there are multiple theories as to why these adaptations may have evolved (Bramble and Lieberman 2004; Lieberman 2020). One of these is that as scavengers, early *Homo* may have

Born to Run?

gained selective advantage in the search for resources by being able to cover large distances quickly and economically. Another suggests that before the development of hunting technologies like bows and arrows, *Homo* practiced persistence hunting, which means forcing a quadrupedal animal to run until it either dies from heat exhaustion or slows to the point where humans could easily kill it. Few four-legged animals have the ability to sweat and will overheat if they do not slow down to pant. Humans, on the other hand, do sweat and we carry water, and we could literally run an animal to death by forcing it to keep running. Some contemporary hunter-gatherer groups have been observed conducting persistence hunts.

The fact that the genus *Homo* did not evolve to do these things with modern running shoes on its feet amplifies one argument for barefoot running. Lieberman and Bramble's biomechanical research on the running bodies of contemporary individuals shows that modern running shoes with thick heel pads encourage heel strike first instead of engaging our complex and springy foot arch, which does a better job than the heel does in absorbing and distributing impact. One possible implication (drawn out explicitly in McDougall's book) is that the high rates of knee and other injuries seen among habitual American runners may be at least partly due to the interference of running shoes in engaging that evolved system.

Naturally, this claim has not gone over well with athletic shoe companies. A number of medical doctors have also spoken out against it; they have been treating injured runners who decided to try barefoot running and hurt themselves, a not very surprising situation since most of us who have worn shoes our whole lives have not developed the techniques and musculature for barefoot running, which involves rotating foot strikes on the front and middle edge of the foot, not the heel. Lieberman—himself a barefoot runner—and his collaborators at Harvard have taken an official position that more research is necessary on these issues, announcing, "Please note that we present no data on how people should run, whether shoes cause some injuries, or whether barefoot running causes other kinds of injuries. We believe there is a strong need for controlled, prospective studies on these issues" (Harvard University Skeletal Biology Lab 2015). Whatever the outcomes of these debates, it is clear that paleoanthropological research is relevant to the discussion about contemporary human athletic abilities and injuries.

Questions for Reflection

1. Other than the selective advantages discussed here, can you think of other evolutionary processes that could have played a role in the evolution of endurance running capacity in the genus *Homo*?

2. What do you think are the limits of using paleoanthropological evidence to address contemporary human problems?

If true, this hypothesis points to something quite powerful and new: the interaction of biology and culture through biocultural evolution to meet selective challenges. In the next sections, we examine these later forms of *Homo*—among whom we can identify the first humans—where that interaction is quite important.

THINKING LIKE AN ANTHROPOLOGIST: ANCESTRAL HUMANS

Scholars are still working through the actual sequence of evolutionary changes in hominins that led to the development of bipedalism, large brains, social complexity, and tool-making abilities. Knowing what you now know about early hominins and how evolutionary processes work, can you theorize a possible sequence of evolutionary changes?

Classic Contributions
Sarah Blaffer Hrdy, Helpless Babies, and the Evolution of Human Cooperation

SARAH BLAFFER HRDY (b. 1946) is an American anthropologist, primatologist, and pioneer in researching the evolutionary dimensions of female behavior and mother-infant dependence. Since the beginning of her career, she has been a prominent proponent of sociobiology, a theoretical approach that asserts that natural selection did not just favor the evolution of advantageous physical traits, but also of behavioral traits that increase the likelihood of reproduction. This approach has sparked controversy throughout anthropology as being too heavily reliant on genetic determinism and dismissive of more complex models of evolution (see Chapter 3). But Hrdy's work challenged both sociobiology's critics and proponents in important ways, for example by emphasizing that a broader, and more female inclusive, sociobiology could incorporate more complex views of evolution, including emphasizing the role of developmental processes in evolutionary adaptability. She also challenged the male bias in sociobiology and its close cousin evolutionary psychology, questioning the emphasis in both fields on the evolutionary importance of male aggression and dominance, which she argued ignored humanity's unusual capacity for cooperation. The selection below comes from her work *Mothers and Others: The Evolutionary Origins of Mutual Understanding,* a book in which she explores how the evolutionary changes that produced a longer infancy in hominins required changes in group behavior to ensure that those infants survived. Referring to this practice as "cooperative breeding," Hrdy emphasizes that the emergence of shared childcare supported growing cranial capacity among early hominins—especially *Homo erectus*—and the eventual rise of intersubjective understanding, the ability to read the intentions of others, and other cognitive and emotional changes that support human cooperation.

Sarah Blaffer Hrdy.

I will propose that a long, long time ago, at some unknown point in our evolutionary history but before the evolution of our 1,350cc sapient brains ... and before such distinctly human traits as language ... there emerged in Africa a line of apes that began to be interested in the mental and subjective lives—the thoughts and feelings—of others, interested in understanding them. These apes were markedly different from the common ancestors they shared with chimpanzees, and in this respect they were already emotionally modern.

As in all apes, the successful rearing of their young was a challenge. Mortality rates from predation, accidents, disease, and starvation were staggeringly high and weighed most heavily on the young, especially children after weaning. Of the five or so offspring a woman might bear in her lifetime, more than half—and sometimes all—were likely to die before puberty. Unlike mothers among other African apes,

who nurtured infants of their own, these early hominin mothers relied on groupmates to help protect, care for, and provision their unusually slow-maturing children and keep them on the survivable side of starvation.

Cooperative breeding does not mean that group members are necessarily or always cooperative. Indeed ... competition and coercion can be rampant. But in the case of early hominins, alloparental care and provisioning set the stage for infants to develop in new ways. They were born into the world on vastly different terms from other apes. It takes on the order of 13 million calories to rear a modern human from birth to maturity, and the young of these early hominins would also have been very costly. Unlike other ape youngsters, they would have depended on nutritional subsidies from caregivers long after they were weaned. [Hrdy 2009, 30–31]

6.3 Who Were the First Humans, and Where Did They Live?

Throughout the Pleistocene epoch, we see increasing qualities of "humanness" in our lineage, ranging from upright, large-brained physical qualities to, eventually, the modern body type we have today, sophisticated language, complex social formations, and aesthetic imaginations. Our lineage also begins to spread out of Africa, probably following broader climatic and ecological changes that induced them to move into new habitats and populate other corners of the earth. In this section we review who these first humans were, with greater species detail in "The Evolution of Humans 6.3" (see pp. 174–179).

Introducing *Homo erectus*

Originally, it was thought that humans came out of Asia, not Africa, as is now known. In 1891, a Dutch military surgeon named Eugène Dubois excavated ancient hominoid skeletal remains near a river bank on the Indonesian island of Java. Estimated to be 700,000 to 1 million years old, the presence of thigh bones much like our own indicate that this figure walked upright. Dubois dubbed it an evolutionary "missing link" between humans and apes. It was quite an international sensation, especially since Darwin's new theory of evolution was still fresh in people's minds. Dubois gave it the name *Pithecanthropus erectus* ("upright ape-human"), though it was known popularly as "Java Man." During the next half-century, the "missing link" theory was discredited and similar finds elsewhere precipitated a taxonomic reordering. In 1950, the species were placed in the genus *Homo*, directly within our own evolutionary lineage, and became known as *Homo erectus*.

Thanks to 150 years of excavations that have yielded hundreds of useful fossils, paleoanthropologists have learned a lot about *H. erectus*. They appeared about 1.8 mya, lived in numerous locations around the globe, and became extinct as recently as 108,000 (or, as some evidence suggests, 30,000) years ago. By the yardstick of longevity, they are the most successful species of *Homo* yet. They had human-like body proportions and height, lived their lives on the ground as obligatory bipeds, were probably good runners, appear to have cared for their young and the weak, likely had some form of proto-language, made and used stone tools, and controlled fire.

All of these qualities make *H. erectus* appear human. Of course, you would immediately notice obvious differences if one were to walk down the street. Their bones were thicker and the skeleton more robust. Their heads were different too: the shape of the cranium was long and low, with a massive brow ridge. Some of the fossils also have a **sagittal keel**, a raised area in the mid-cranium, and most have a pronounced ridge at the base of the skull. Their jaws were robust compared to those of contemporary humans, and they had no chin.

H. erectus fossils have been found throughout Africa, Europe, India, Indonesia, and China. It was long assumed that *H. erectus* evolved out of *H. habilis*, but recent finds in Kenya increasing *H. habilis*'s temporal range suggest that the two may have coexisted. As *H. erectus* spread geographically, cranial differences emerged, and paleoanthropologists distinguish between African and Eurasian forms. Some scholars argue that Asian forms, for example, have larger teeth, sagittal keels, and neurocrania (part of the skull that protects the brain and face) than African forms. These scholars have used the name *Homo ergaster* for African forms to formalize that distinction. Not all scholars accept the distinction, though, and the exact taxonomic ordering of *H. erectus* has never been totally resolved. There are three main hypotheses in the debate that

• **Sagittal keel.** A raised area in the mid-cranium.

TABLE 6.1 THREE HYPOTHESES ON THE TAXONOMIC ORDER OF *H. ERECTUS*	
Hypothesis #1	*H. erectus* was a single species that dispersed out of Africa between 1.8 mya and 300,000 years ago. Variations between Asian and African varieties are a result of genetic drift within the species. All are ancestral to contemporary humans.
Hypothesis #2	Genus *Homo* had three or four species between 1.8 mya and 300,000 years ago that moved out of Africa in waves. African *H. ergaster* and *H. erectus* are ancestral to contemporary humans, and Asian forms are not.
Hypothesis #3	All members of *Homo* after 1.8 mya are *H. sapiens*, exhibiting variations over time. Current humans are a subspecies known as *H. sapiens sapiens*.

continues today as we write this (modified from Fuentes 2018); see Table 6.1. Although the current evidence appears to support the first position, the sparse nature of the fossil record and the fact that new findings and evidence can challenge existing interpretations continue to fuel the debate.

Homo erectus *and Changing Environments and Climates*

The first hominins to expand out of the African continent were most likely early members of *H. erectus* or its immediate ancestor. As they moved around Eurasia and into Eastern and Southeastern Asia they encountered a world of new landscapes, creatures, and climates that were themselves dynamic and changing. To understand how and when hominin species dispersed and moved through habitats, paleoanthropologists have traditionally used fossil, archaeological, and genetic evidence. But new techniques for reconstructing ancient environments, details about how shifts in the earth's orbit and axis affect weather and climate, and increasingly sophisticated paleoclimate models—similar to those used in contemporary climate change research—demonstrate that the conditions under which human origins and evolution occurred coincide with periods of cooling, drying, and unusual climate variability (Potts and Faith 2015). One remarkable aspect of early hominins, even those who emerged before *H. erectus*, is their adaptability to these variable conditions—surely related to the factors we discussed above like cranial capacity, tool use, dietary flexibility, social cooperation, etc.—which translated over time into an ability to tolerate a wide variety of distinct environments.

Homo erectus appears to have been especially adaptable, capable of thriving not just in grasslands where many of its ancestors lived, but also in forested environments of what is now the Middle East and humid tropical environments of Southeast Asia (Glauziusz 2021). Paleoclimate models suggest that swings in climate correlate with evidence of *H. erectus*'s dispersal out of Africa and into new regions of Eurasia using their capabilities to adapt to environmental change and unfamiliar ecological niches (deMenocal and Stringer 2016). The disappearance of *H. erectus* also appears to correlate with climate change, including a sudden shift to more rain and cold in large areas of its habitat that led to the loss of up to half of the niches upon which they relied (Glauziusz 2021).

The Emergence of Archaic Humans

Around 500,000 to 300,000 years ago, changes in both morphology and material culture suggest that one or more new varieties of *Homo* had emerged; supporters of Hypotheses #1 and #2 (Table 6.1) see this as the emergence of a new species, while proponents of Hypothesis #3 suggest it was simply another variation of the same species. The classic *H. erectus* traits of robustness decreased and cranial capacity increased

(Figure 6.4). Over the next several hundred thousand years, the brow ridges of these humans became smaller and more separated, and the **postorbital constriction** (indention of sides of the cranium behind the eyes) reduced in size. The face became less prognathic, or forward-projecting. These humans were also known for making tools that were more refined and specialized than previous tools. We refer to individuals with these traits as archaic humans.

Anthropologists classify archaic humans in one of two ways. The first is to lump them all into one category of archaic *Homo sapiens*, a broad category that assumes that we evolved directly out of this group. Another is to separate them into two different species, *Homo heidelbergensis* and *Homo neanderthalensis*, both of which were originally discovered in Germany during the 1800s. Regardless of their taxonomic status, archaic humans are almost—but still not quite—us (Conroy 1997).

The oldest archaic human specimens are found in Africa. In 2017 a research team announced that they had dated the oldest *Homo sapiens* fossils ever found, which were excavated in Morocco, as between 280,000 and 300,000 years old. The humans there had both contemporary and archaic characteristics (Pobiner 2017). The geographic spread of archaic humans includes the Middle East, Mediterranean, East Asia, Siberia, and Eastern and Western Europe. The Spanish site of Atapuerca has abundant archaic human finds, representing thirty-two individuals who lived between 200,000 and 400,000 years ago. Some paleoanthropologists argue that these fossils represent a distinct species (*Homo antecessor*) and that they were the ancestors of the Neanderthals (archaic humans found across Western Eurasia), contemporary humans, or perhaps both (Arsuaga, Bermudez de Castro, and Carbonell 1997; Bermudez de Castro et al. 1997). And a curious find on the Eastern Indonesian island of Flores generated some surprises about the diversity of archaic humans. In 2004, a short, *erectus*-like hominin was discovered that dates somewhere between 95,000 and 12,000 years ago. These unusual hominins, which their discoverers named *Homo floresiensis* (P. T. Brown et al. 2004) and popularly referred to as "hobbits," are approximately three feet tall with a very small cranium. Most recently, some finger bones and teeth that bear similarities to the Flores finds were discovered in the Philippines and are currently being classified as another new species, *H. luzonensis* (Hawks 2019).

Figure 6.4 Two Archaic Human Crania. When compared, these show the differences in robustness. The Bodo cranium (above) dates to approximately 600,000 years ago; the Kabwe cranium (below) dates to approximately 300,000–30,000 years ago.

- **Postorbital constriction.** An indentation of the sides of the cranium behind the eyes.

Who Were the Neanderthals and Denisovans?

Few issues in human evolution have sparked as much attention and debate as the fossils of *Homo neanderthalensis* that occur in many parts of Europe and the Middle East dating from about 300,000 to ~30,000 years ago. The surprising discovery between 2008 and 2010 of a coeval archaic human dating to 41,000 years in Denisova Cave in the Altai Mountains of Siberia has added new evidence and interest in the ongoing debate.

The Neanderthals were stockier than contemporary humans, but in our same range of height and weight. The Denisovans may have been similarly robust, but the sparseness of skeletal evidence (a finger bone and two teeth) has prevented any morphological description, and most of what we know about them comes from analyzing their mitochondrial DNA. The Neanderthals' large noses and husky features were probably adaptations to the harsh cold of the Pleistocene era when glaciers were extensive throughout the northern latitudes where many Neanderthal remains are found.

There is strong fossil evidence that Neanderthals, Denisovans, and contemporary humans overlapped during a period of 10,000 years or more, across the Middle East and some parts of Eurasia as well as the cave in Denisova, Siberia, which shows remains of all three groups though not necessarily at the same time. Some sites in Europe and the Middle East have even yielded evidence of Neanderthals using modern human-like tool kits and contemporary humans using Neanderthal-like tool kits.

A World in Motion
Rethinking the Peopling of the Americas

For decades, the scientific consensus on the peopling of the Americas has gone something like this: about 13,000 or so years ago, as the Last Glacial Maximum was ending and low sea levels had exposed a land bridge across the Bering Strait, small groups of modern *Homo sapiens* from Northeast Asia walked over it into what is now Alaska. Their descendants headed south, probably along the coast, and eventually east. They moved at a fairly rapid pace, and within a few thousand years humans had occupied much of the Americas. The primary evidence for this view is the proliferation of human habitation sites characterized by the presence of so-called Clovis stone tools (named for a site in New Mexico) that were dated to this period. Various challenges were made to this view—most notably among many Native American groups whose oral traditions and origin stories often emphasize much longer histories, as well as archaeologists who have found "pre-Clovis" sites, dating to 15,000 or more years ago—but none of these were enough to fully unsettle that consensus view.

Enter recent technical advances in genetic anthropology, including the recovery and analysis of ancient mitochondrial DNA and the completion of some Native American genomes. By themselves, genetic data give an incomplete picture of human societies and their movements (see Chapter 7), but when tested against linguistic, environmental, and archaeological data, they can create a composite picture that complicates and enriches our understanding of the human past. In her recent book *Origin: A Genetic History of the Americas* (2022), anthropologist Jennifer Raff of the University of Kansas describes how all of this applies to our understanding of the peopling of the Americas.

The new version she reports goes something like this: Around 36,000 years ago a small group of East Asians began to split from its ancestral population, pushing northward into northeastern Asia. Eleven thousand or so years after that, that group itself split in two genetic groups: ancient Paleo-Siberians, and a group that would eventually become the first Native Americans. These genetic groups were mixing with another group already in the area, the ancient Northern Siberians. Members of all of these groups likely settled in "Beringia," which, although it is under water

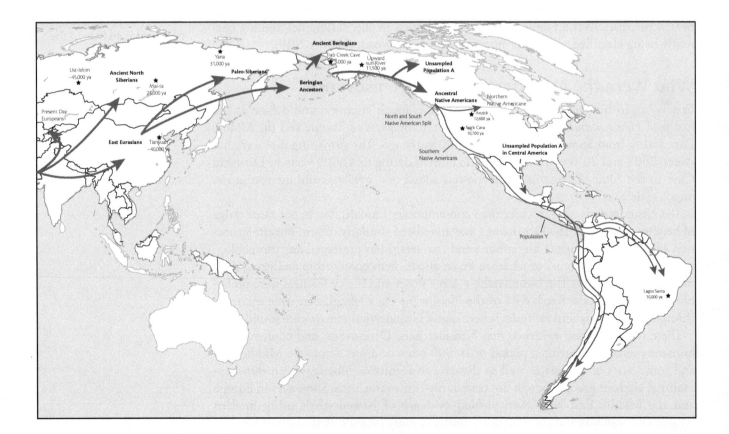

today, was not so much a "land bridge" between the Asian and American continents (it was the size of Texas) but a homeland where people lived for thousands of years. Around 17,000 years ago, the Ancestral Native Americans headed south as ice sheets began to melt in what is now coastal Alaska, and the Paleo-Siberians would remain in Asia. That doesn't mean the ice was fully melted; in fact, it is quite possible these people travelled by boat to points south. As they made it farther south of the ice, the groups split in two, one becoming ancestral to North American native peoples, the other ancestral to Central and South American native peoples. Without competition from other humans and the availability of vast resources, both genetic groups grew and spread out rapidly, their populations expanding over sixtyfold between 16,000 and 13,000 years ago. And even though many groups settled, large-scale migrations would not end; 9,000 years ago, for example, a group from Central America migrated to South America and mixed with groups there.

For Raff, there is an incredible story here about how the ancestors of the Native Americans survived the severe cold of the Ice Age, established a homeland, and eventually saw their descendants venture off to explore new lands. But she also cautions us that many questions remain unanswered and that the scientific details are still unsettled and subject to change. She also observes that this explanation has yet to fully account for Native American oral traditions, which she asserts are equally valid and demand scientific humility and respect. She suggests this version is something like the story one might construct about a person's life by piecing together the photos they posted on Instagram: not inaccurate, but also incomplete.

The story of the relationships among these varieties of *Homo* has grown more complicated and intriguing as ancient human genomics has exploded during the past twenty years, thanks to technological innovations in sequencing, informatics, and improved recovery of mitochondrial DNA from fossilized bones less than 100,000 years old (Hawks 2013). Most startling of all is that there is even sufficient DNA from the few Denisovan bones uncovered in Siberia to reconstruct their genome. Ancient human genomics is still a new science and old DNA is often terribly degraded, but the latest findings point to some level of interbreeding and gene flow between Neanderthals, Denisovans, and contemporary humans, suggesting perhaps that the Neanderthals and Denisovans never completely disappeared because they shared genetic material with contemporary humans (Sankararaman et al. 2012). Puzzling through the genetic relationships between these groups is currently one of the most dynamic areas of paleoanthropology. As we examine in "A World in Motion: Rethinking the Peopling of the Americas," genetic evidence is also shaking up our basic notions of how long ago humans migrated to the Americas.

Contemporary Humans Hit the Scene

Sometime between 300,000 and 25,000 years ago, the archaic features in the fossil record begin to change, and we see the emergence of features identified with contemporary humans (Figure 6.5). We see further changes in morphology (a high, rounded cranium; relatively slender skeletal structure; and the appearance of a chin) and dramatic changes in the types and complexity of tools and other aspects of material culture and behavior. Language as we know it probably appeared with contemporary humans (Berwick et al. 2013). Paleoanthropologists continue to debate whether these changes represent the emergence of a new species or if archaic humans were essentially *Homo sapiens*. As recently as 35,000 to 12,000 years ago, there may have been at least two, if not more, species or subspecies of humans on the planet. However, today all anthropologists agree that only one human species remains, and all humans today belong to the same species of *Homo*.

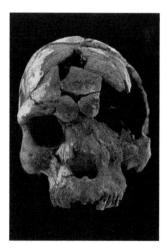

Figure 6.5 Anatomically Contemporary Human Cranium. This cranium is one of the oldest found that is considered to be anatomically contemporary. Dating from 160,000 years ago, it was found with other fossils in the Herto and Bouri region of eastern Africa.

- **Recent African origin model (RAO).** Modern humans arose as a new species in Africa about 150,000 years ago, during the late Pleistocene.

- **Multiple dispersals model (MD).** Incorporates complexities in genetic datasets to argue that humans left Africa in multiple waves.

- **Multiregional evolution model (MRE).** Modern humans are only the most recent version of a single species, *Homo sapiens*, that had been in Africa, Asia, and Europe for nearly 2 million years.

Where and when did these humans—us?—actually originate? Anthropologists have long debated this question. There are three prominent theories about the origins and dispersals of contemporary humans. The **Recent African origin model** proposes that contemporary humans arose as a new species in Africa between 200,000 and 180,000 years ago, during the late Pleistocene (Cann, Stoneking, and Wilson 1987). The **Multiregional evolution model** proposes that contemporary humans are only the most recent version of a single species, *Homo sapiens*, that had been in Africa, Asia, and Europe for nearly 2 million years (Thorne and Wolpoff 1992). Both have lines of evidence to support them. But a third model, **Multiple dispersals model** (MD) (Templeton 2002), which argues that contemporary humans left Africa in multiple waves, edges out the others given the current fossil and DNA evidence. In this model the initial movement out of Africa occurs approximately 1.8 mya. *Homo* spread around western, central, and southern Eurasia, with back-and-forth gene flow across these regions as well as with Africa, and possibly with some isolation of peripheral populations. Other dispersals include (adapted from Fuentes 2007):

- 800,000 to 400,000 years ago, influencing Eurasian populations through interbreeding, and affecting genetic patterns in the genus *Homo*.
- 150,000 to 80,000 years ago, also affecting genetic patterns throughout the genus *Homo*.
- ~50–70,000 years ago, influencing the genetic patterns of central Eurasian and African populations. This event is also followed by back-and-forth gene flow as well as isolation by distance. Populations move into northern Eurasia, Australia, the Pacific Islands, and eventually the Americas (~17,000 years ago) via migration.

This model predicts that African populations would have had forceful and recurrent effects on the genetic characteristics of humans over the past 1.7 million years. It also predicts that gene flow would be an important recurrent dynamic, with groups living closer to each other most affected by that flow.

It is admittedly difficult to pinpoint an exact dividing line between humans that are contemporary (previously called "anatomically modern") and archaic humans. There is also no evidence that identifies a single "original" human, or moment of speciation (when we became a species), in either time or space (S.-H. Lee 2018). From an evolutionary point of view, changes in complex organisms like humans are messy and fuzzy, taking hundreds or thousands of *generations* to occur (S.-H. Lee 2018). Closely aligned species can reproduce and pass genetic material between one another, as appears to have happened between contemporary humans, Neanderthals, and Denisovans. Working with ancient genomes has already begun to help clarify the genetic relatedness and biological variability of these human populations, and it promises to do more as DNA sequencing technologies advance. But genetics and morphology alone will never give us a holistic picture of the first humans, because we also know that culture played a critical role in their evolution. In the next section, we explore how we know that.

THINKING LIKE AN ANTHROPOLOGIST: ANCESTRAL HUMANS

What are the pros and cons of approaching the first humans as a single species that goes way back to *H. habilis*, as some paleoanthropologists have suggested, or differentiating them into distinct species, as many other paleoanthropologists do? What kind of evidence could help support each position?

6.4 How Do We Know If the First Humans Were Cultural Beings, and What Role Did Culture Play in Their Evolution?

The answer to this question is *not* that culture suddenly appeared and transformed everything, the way turning on a light switch transforms a dark room. Such a view is based on an erroneous conception of human evolution, that it is at its roots simply a story of biological transformation, with the spark of culture being a very recent add-on to that biological foundation. In fact, the cultural capacity of hominids emerged over a long period of time and interacted with biology to meet selective demands, in a process we call **biocultural evolution** (see Chapter 3).

When **paleolithic** humans (those that existed during the long epoch of human prehistory from about 2.5 mya to 10,000 years ago) tackled the challenges of the environment with something more than their hands and teeth, real changes occurred in the way the pressures of natural selection affected them. The material and symbolic cultures that humans have invented over time have influenced—and continue to influence—our evolution. These processes are, to an important extent, a reflection of how much human biocultural evolution is a story of niche construction, that is, about how humans have changed and constructed the world around them for a long time (Fuentes et al. 2010). So what was the cultural capacity of the first humans?

The Emerging Cultural Capacity of *H. erectus*

Beginning with *H. erectus*, we see a greater capacity for culture. We know that culture played a greater role in their lives than earlier hominins because:

- *Their diets changed*. The increased brain and body size of *H. erectus* over previous *Homo* involved higher metabolic rates, requiring more and higher quality food (Aiello and Wells 2002). *H. erectus* responded to these new pressures by ratcheting up its reliance on tools and other cultural behavior to increase the quality of its diet. This dietary pattern was omnivorous, although Aiello and Wells (2002) hypothesize that *H. erectus* relied more heavily on meat and other high-energy foods. Recent work has demonstrated that it was likely a mix of higher energy foods, not a newfound reliance on meat eating, that these early members of the genus *Homo* exploited (Barr et al. 2022). It appears that as brains grew in size, the guts (digestive organs) became smaller in *H. erectus* than in the earlier *Homo* species. Smaller guts require higher energy foods which would have required more efficient food gathering and foraging.
- *Their tools changed*. When members of the genus *Homo* first spread from Africa into Eurasia and beyond, they used Olduwan tools. With these sharp flakes and stout-edged choppers, they were able to process both animal and plant matter to reduce the pressures on the teeth and jaw. About 1.6 to 1.4 mya, a new type of stone tool began to show up in the fossil record, first in East Africa and then throughout the rest of Africa, in western and central Eurasia, and in at least one location in East Asia. Known as **Acheulean tools** (named after St. Acheul in France where they were first discovered in 1847), these tools had better edges and were more varied in style. A classic example is a hand-axe with bifacial flaking, which is produced by flaking chips off each side of the base stone to produce strong, sharp edges (Figure 6.6). They were likely used to process meat and hides, and probably for modifying wood and bones. Acheulian

- **Biocultural evolution.** The interaction of cultural capacity and biology to meet selective demands.

- **Paleolithic.** Literally "old stone," refers to a long epoch in human prehistory from about 2.5 mya to 10,000 years ago, and roughly corresponds with the Pleistocene geological epoch.

- **Acheulian tools.** A more complex and diverse stone-toolkit than earlier Olduwan tools. The main characteristic was bifacial flaking, a process that produced strong, sharp edges.

Figure 6.6 The Acheulian Toolkit. Acheulian tools appeared 1.6–1.4 mya. The technique of bifacial flaking creates a sharp edge, as can be seen with this hand-axe, a versatile tool for cutting, chopping, and various other tasks.

The Evolution of Humans 6.3
Homo erectus, Archaic humans, and Contemporary *Homo sapiens*

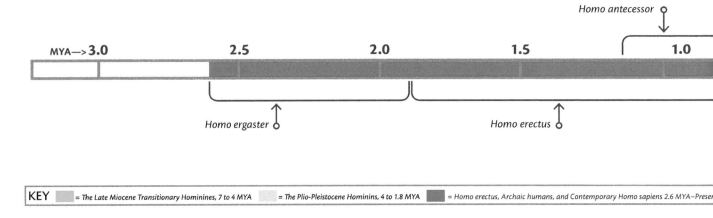

Homo antecessor

MYA—> 3.0   2.5   2.0   1.5   1.0

Homo ergaster

Homo erectus

KEY		
= The Late Miocene Transitional Hominines, 7 to 4 MYA	= The Plio-Pleistocene Hominins, 4 to 1.8 MYA	= Homo erectus, Archaic humans, and Contemporary Homo sapiens 2.6 MYA–Presen

SPECIES	DISCOVERY	RANGE
1 **Homo ergaster** "Ergaster" means "working" in Latin	New species proposed in 1975 based on analysis of already-discovered *H. erectus* jawbone	Africa
2 **Homo erectus** "Erectus" means "upright" in Latin	Discovered in 1891 in Java, Indonesia, by Dutch doctor Eugène Dubois	Northern, Eastern, and Southern Africa, Western Eurasia, and East Asia (China, Indonesia)

1    **2**

174

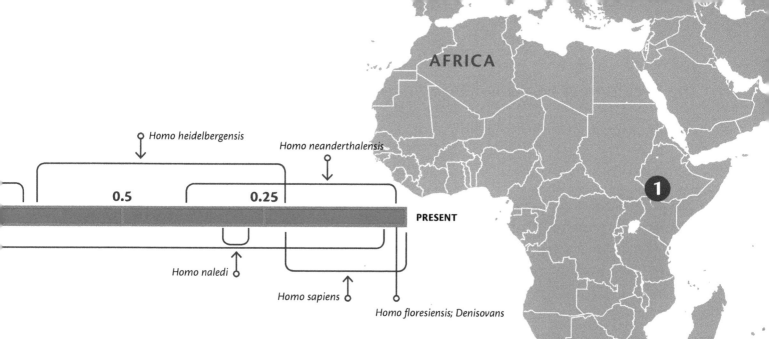

Homo heidelbergensis

Homo neanderthalensis

0.5   0.25

PRESENT

Homo naledi

Homo sapiens

Homo floresiensis; Denisovans

DATE (MYA)	MORPHOLOGICAL CHARACTERISTICS	COMMENTS
2.6–1.8 mya	Same as *Homo erectus*	Taxonomy remains unsettled. Was it a direct ancestor of *H. erectus*? So-called "Turkana Boy" discovered in 1984 is claimed to be *H. ergaster*.
1.8 mya– ~30,000?	More robust than other members of *Homo*, including *H. habilis* and *H. sapiens*. Large brains ranging from slightly smaller to about the same as modern humans, long and slender fingers like ours. Height range 4 ft. 9 in. to 6 ft. 1 in. Compared to *H. habilis*, arms were shorter relative to their legs and their legs longer relative to the body, and the size of their molar teeth was smaller. *H. erectus* fingers were long and straight like ours (Conroy 1997; McHenry and Coffing 2000).	First hominin to move out of Africa. Produced and used stone tools and used fire in controlled ways.

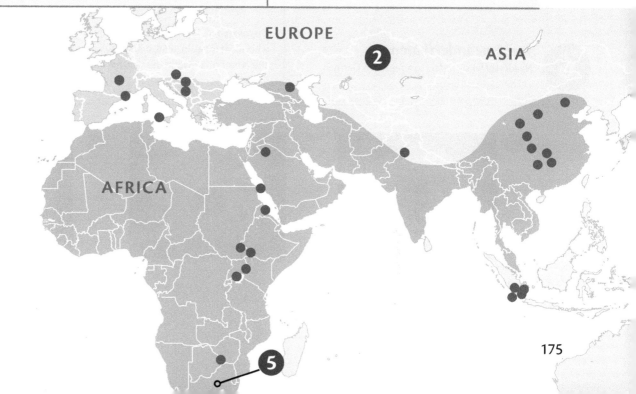

The Evolution of Humans 6.3 *continued*

Homo erectus, Archaic humans, and Contemporary *Homo sapiens*

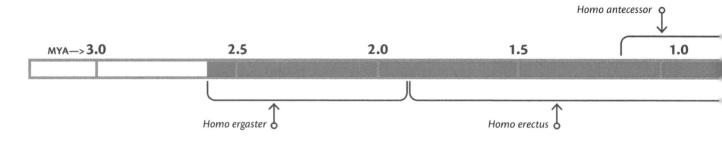

MYA—> **3.0**   2.5   2.0   1.5   1.0

Homo antecessor

Homo ergaster

Homo erectus

	SPECIES	DISCOVERY	RANGE
3	***Homo antecessor*** "Antecessor" means "explorer or pioneer" in Latin	Discovered in 1995 in Atapuerca, Spain, by Eudald Carbonell, Juan Luis Arsuaga, and J. M. Bermúdez de Castro	Europe (Spain)
	ARCHAIC HUMANS		
4	***Homo heidelbergensis*** "Heidelbergensis" refers to a city in Germany	Discovered in 1908 near Heidelberg, Germany, by a worker, and named by scientist Otto Schoentensack.	Eastern and Southern Africa, Europe, possibly Asia
5	***Homo naledi***	Discovered in 2013 in the Rising Star cave system, in Malapa Nature Reserve (see previous page, bottom)	S. Africa
6	***Homo neanderthalensis*** "Neaderthalensis" refers to a region in Germany	Discovered in 1829, although nobody knew it was a hominin fossil. In 1856, a new discovery caught the attention of German scientists who named it in 1864.	Europe, Middle East, Siberia

3
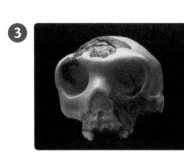

4

5
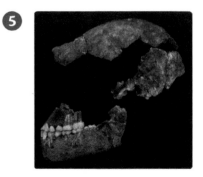

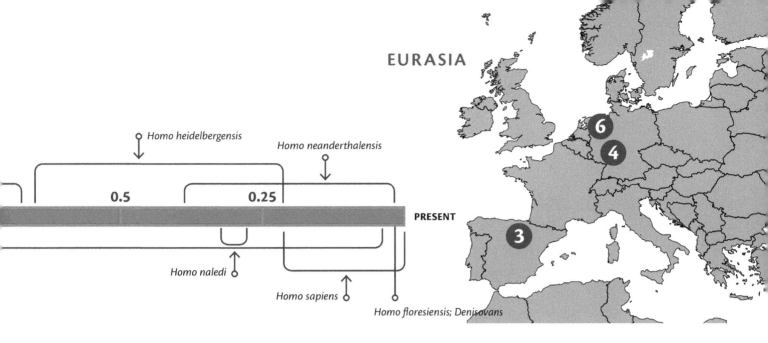

EURASIA

Homo heidelbergensis

Homo neanderthalensis

0.5   0.25

PRESENT

Homo naledi

Homo sapiens

Homo floresiensis; Denisovans

DATE (MYA)	MORPHOLOGICAL CHARACTERISTICS	COMMENTS
1.2 mya–~800,000	Same as *Homo erectus*	Taxonomy remains unsettled. Was it a direct descendent of *H. erectus*?
700,000–200,000	Brains a bit smaller than modern humans. Robust; thick cranial walls; separated brow ridges; average height of 5 ft. 9 in. (males) and 5 ft. 2 in. (females).	Appears to be the first hominin to live in colder climates and has robust adaptations probably related to the cold. Used fire, made spears and other tools, hunted large game.
226,000–335,000	Moderate body size, human-like hands and feet; body, arms, and legs have mix of *Homo* and *Australopithecus* qualities.	Taxonomic order still being determined. Current debate over how they arrived deep in the cave system: was it an accident or were they "buried" there through intentional process?
300,000–30,000	Brains slightly larger on average than modern humans. Stocky body; very large incisors, and large gap behind third molar (retromolar gap); average height 5 ft 5 in. (males) and 5 ft 1 in. (females).	Lived in cold climates, used tools similar to anatomically contemporary humans, almost certainly used language and other symbolic communication. Today most people who live outside of sub-Saharan Africa have ~1%–4% Neanderthal genetic ancestry.

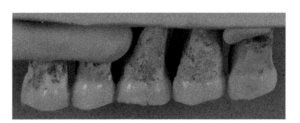

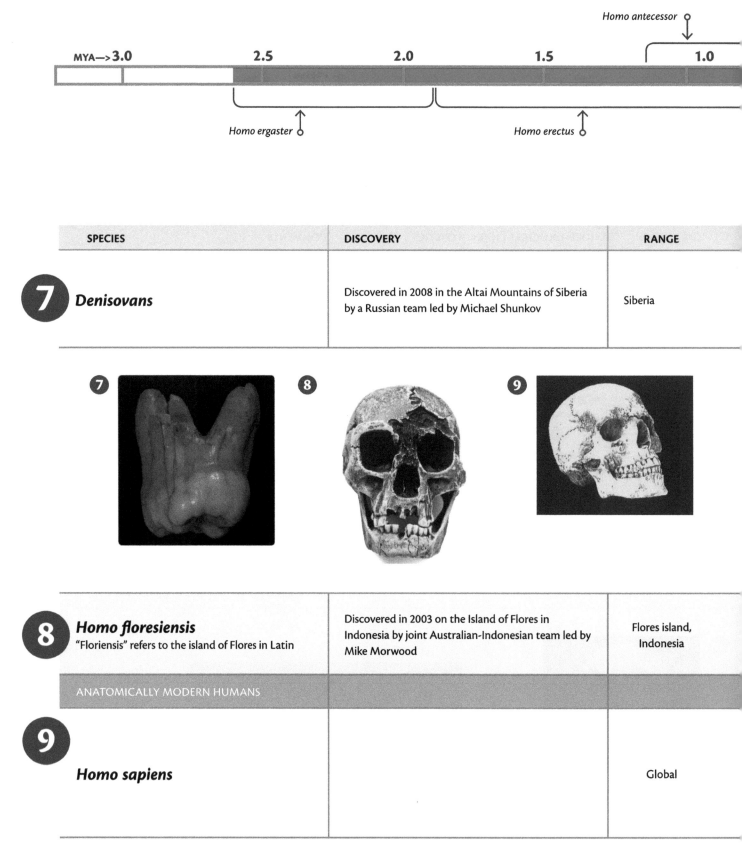

	SPECIES	DISCOVERY	RANGE
7	***Denisovans***	Discovered in 2008 in the Altai Mountains of Siberia by a Russian team led by Michael Shunkov	Siberia
8	***Homo floresiensis*** "Floriensis" refers to the island of Flores in Latin	Discovered in 2003 on the Island of Flores in Indonesia by joint Australian-Indonesian team led by Mike Morwood	Flores island, Indonesia
	ANATOMICALLY MODERN HUMANS		
9	***Homo sapiens***		Global

Timeline labels: MYA—>3.0 2.5 2.0 1.5 1.0

Homo ergaster

Homo erectus

Homo antecessor

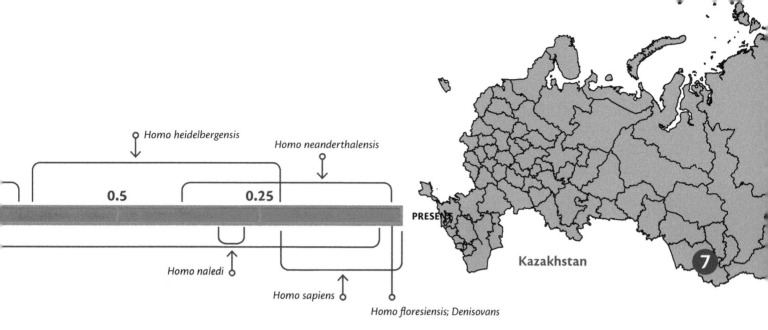

DATE (MYA)	MORPHOLOGICAL CHARACTERISTICS	COMMENTS
40,000 +/–	Physical evidence still too limited to know	Do not know if it was a distinct species. What we know at this point is based on analysis of mitochondrial DNA. Up to 6% of the genome of Melanesians, Australian Aborigines, and some East Asians derives from Denisovans.

MALAYSIA

Borneo

New Guinea

8 Flores

Australia

| 95,000–12,000 | Short bodies, very small heads, absence of a chin, different teeth form than modern humans | Some controversy has swirled over whether or not it is a distinct species; some claim it could have been modern humans with some kind of anatomical pathology. |
| ~200,000– present although recent discovery in Morocco could push it back to ~300,000 years ago | Large brain; high, rounded cranium; chin; no retromolar gap | Only living species of hominin |

tools show up in many (but not all) *H. erectus* sites as far apart as southern Africa, the British Isles, and India. But they remain extremely rare at *H. erectus* sites in East and Southeast Asia. It is possible in these places that *H. erectus* used biodegradable material such as wood, bamboo, or bone as tools, but evidence is very thin since these things don't last like stone tools do.

- *They used fire.* *H. erectus* and archaic humans created and maintained small fires. Evidence for controlled use of fire exists in France, Spain, China, and Hungary, dating to 500,000 to 300,000 years ago. We also have possible evidence—although it is still controversial—of fire use from before 1,000,000 years ago in East Africa and a little later in South Africa. However, since indications of fire use (fire pits and ashes) and fire-blackened animal bones do show up with more regularity in the archaeological record by about 400,000 years ago, it is possible that, at least in some places, *H. erectus* was using fire before then. Fire enables the consumption of a wider variety of foods and a higher energy return on foods eaten. It also marks the beginning of cooking, a process that involves a transformation of raw food that anthropologists have long considered a unique hallmark of cultural capacity (Wrangham 2009).

- *Cooperative behaviors increased.* *H. erectus* relied heavily on hunting and gathering high-quality plant material, both of which require intensive coordination and cooperation among group members. With an increase in caloric requirements, the energetic costs of reproduction, and especially breast feeding (lactation), shoot up. One group of researchers estimated that the amount of energy invested in lactation was 45 percent greater in *H. erectus* than in earlier hominins (Aiello and Wells 2002). This situation probably enhanced cooperative behaviors, as group members shared caregiving responsibilities and collaborated in foraging activities. Although we have no evidence of what their speech was like, these activities also require a level of symbolic communication beyond the limits of a simple call system typical of nonhuman animals (see Chapter 12 on language).

By themselves, none of these changes would have been sufficient to enable *H. erectus* to successfully adapt to a wide variety of landscapes across Africa and Eurasia, but together they generated an important adaptive capacity. That capacity played an even greater role in the adaptability and biology of archaic humans.

Culture Among Archaic Humans

Evidence for archaic human material culture and behavior comes from Neanderthal sites from between 300,000 and about 50,000 years ago. We see the emergence of more complex tools than the prior Acheulian style. We also see evidence of organized group hunts, such as at Atapuerca, Spain, where archaic humans forced large game animals over cliffs (Dennell 1997). The regular use of controlled fire was widespread, and we see evidence of shelters of wood and possibly hide.

By 200,000 years ago, a new tool-making technique had emerged. This new method, called the **Levallois technique**, involves flaking off pieces around the outline of a desired flake, producing higher quality blades capable of many more uses (Figure 6.7). In many Neanderthal sites, we see an even more effective method for creating tools, based on a disk-core technique, called the **Mousterian industry** (Figure 6.8). This technique requires little effort to quickly create stone flakes from a single core. These flakes have many uses and expanded opportunities for tool use. At least sixty types of Mousterian tools have been identified, hinting at regional cultural variation. Although Neanderthals never developed the technology of blade tools (a stone flake that is at least twice as long as it is wide) and therefore did not have needles for sewing, they did use clothing made of hides and probably plant materials,

- **Levallois technique.** Stone tool-making technique that involves complex preparation of the stone and provides a higher quality toolkit than previous types, with more uses.

- **Mousterian industry.** A disk-core technique of stone toolmaking that allowed the toolmakers to produce many good flakes with little effort and then turn those flakes into a wide variety of fine tools. Associated with the Neanderthals.

meaning that they were relying less on purely biological adaptations to deal with the environment and turning more and more to cultural ones.

All of these changes gave archaic humans improved access to nutrition and new pressures on the body to process the richer foods. Cooking with fire took pressure off the need for big teeth and massive chewing muscles, and we see the gradual reduction of size in both of these in the morphology of contemporary humans. The use of fire and refined tools also helped archaic humans deal with climatic challenges that exposed them to new selective pressures.

Social Cooperation and Symbolic Expression

Everything that we do as humans is based on social interdependence, imagination, and intensive cooperation. Most cooperation depends on communication well in excess of anything our chimpanzee cousins are capable of, even if we see the rudimentary beginnings of intergenerational learning and the simplest evidence of culture among some

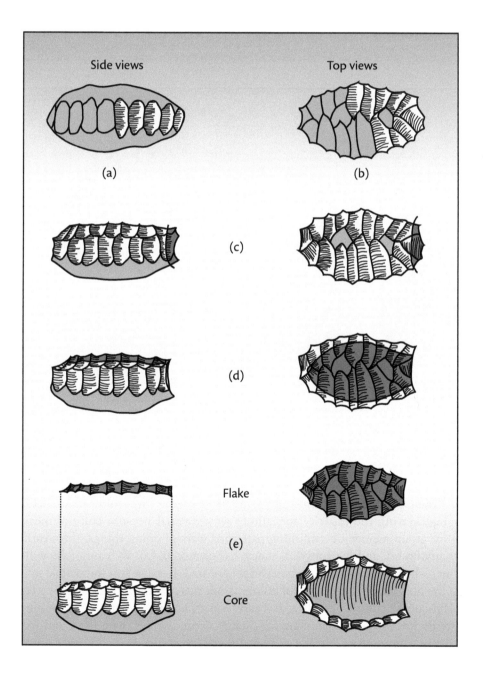

Figure 6.7 **The Levallois Technique.** This image shows the technique step-by-step. It starts by producing a margin along the edge of the core (a); shaping the surface of the core (b); preparing the striking platform (the surface to be struck) (c, d); removing the flake (e). The photo on the next page is a replica of a Levallois core and tool.

🌱 **Figure 6.7** *(Continued)*

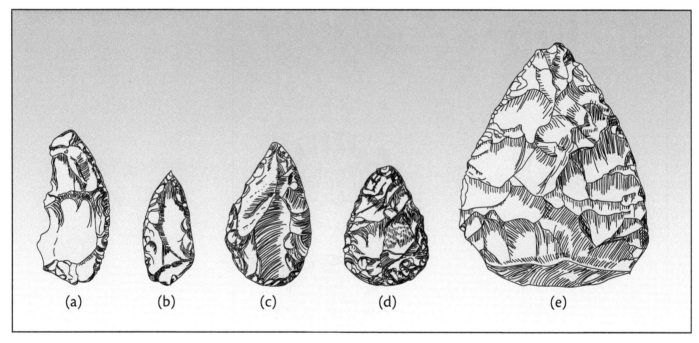

(a)   (b)   (c)   (d)   (e)

🌱 **Figure 6.8 Mousterian Tools.** Mousterian tools, which date from 600,000 to 40,000 years ago were a refinement of the Levallois technique. Pictured here are scrapers (a, c); points (b, d), and a hand-axe (e).

primates (see Chapter 5). By at least 300,000 and as many as 500,000 years ago, members of the genus *Homo* were expressing themselves creatively: engraving objects, using ochre, making beads, etc. (Kissel 2018; Fuentes 2019). It is not clear that these earliest dated examples definitively illustrate symbolic thought. But culture was definitely changing. Having the capacity for culture was essential because cultural meanings allow for group memory, establishing patterned ways of doing things, the creation of representative art, and metaphysical thought (Fuentes 2014a). We cannot say with any certainty when these specific characteristics appeared. Because it is impossible to really know the non-material processes of culture from material objects alone, many crucial details about the culture of archaic and early contemporary humans remain unknown. But we do know that archaic humans such as Neanderthals, who lived and worked together in communities, already exhibited social interdependence and even appear to have had rich symbolic lives rooted in some level of (still unknown) linguistic ability. One indication is the existence of non-functional items of personal or group jewelry, such as the 130,000-year-old modified white-tailed eagle claws found in present-day Croatia (Radovčić et al. 2015). Neanderthals possibly cared for the sick and injured, as evidenced by the high number of healed injuries and relatively aged individuals, although this interpretation of these data is disputed. The Neanderthals also treated their dead with an apparent reverence that suggests symbolic thinking and production of collective memory. Several dozen Neanderthal grave sites have been identified, many of them with "grave goods," especially stone cutting tools near the bodies and even the presence of flowers in the grave. Yet there is still far too little evidence for any viable hypotheses about their actual belief systems.

The First Humans and Artistic Expression

Although evidence for creative expression is much older, at least 65,000 years ago, humans were creating images on cave shelter walls and rocky outcrops that some scholars interpret as art. Over the next 20,000 years, art and other symbolic forms became much more common. Some of the most famous are in the caves in Altamira in Spain (18,000–14,000 years ago) and in Lascaux in southern France (17,300 years ago). Finds of 40,000-year-old cave art in Sulawesi, Indonesia, and examples of this behavior in many areas of the world show how ubiquitous this kind of meaning-making became for humans (Kissel and Fuentes 2018; Vergano 2014). The type of imagery in early visual art includes both abstract and realistic representations of bison, deer, boars, horses, birds, cats, bears, rhinoceroses, and humans. These images include etchings and elaborate paintings on cave walls, carvings on the handles of tools, and carved figurines. It is difficult to know why these things were created and if they had some intentional purpose. But they indicate that by 65,000 to 30,000 years ago, and likely well before, all humans were fully capable of symbolic thought and almost certainly language (Figure 6.9).

The cultural and symbolic capacities we take for granted as humans today emerged over a very long time. Although elements of that capacity precede *H. erectus*, it is clear that the cultural adaptations it made shaped the evolutionary possibilities and characteristics of the archaic humans who succeeded them, including Neanderthals and contemporary humans.

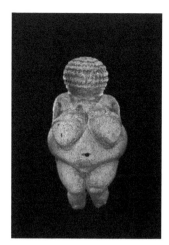

Figure 6.9   Upper Paleolithic Carved Objects. Some of these objects have a practical function and others appear to have primarily symbolic value, such as the famous "Venus of Willendorf" figurine pictured here, which is estimated to have been made 25,000–30,000 years ago.

> **THINKING LIKE AN ANTHROPOLOGIST: ANCESTRAL HUMANS**
>
> Biocultural evolution is not a "better" form of evolution, as it is clear that many hominins (especially Neanderthals) still disappeared in spite of their capacity for cultural adaptation. Yet it clearly gives certain selective advantages over the evolutionary trajectories of other non-primate animals. What do you think those selective advantages are?

Conclusion

Understanding of our human ancestors and the hominin family tree has been growing by leaps and bounds in recent decades. We have more ancient primate fossils than ever, and due to technological advancements in the lab, we also have new tools that allow researchers to access the subtle information they contain about human origins. And yet, due to the rarity of primate and hominin fossils, there is still so much to learn about the lives of those ancient creatures and their relationships to us. Set against that backdrop, it makes sense why the recent discoveries of *A. sediba* and *H. naledi* specimens in South Africa have generated so much excitement in and beyond paleo-anthropology: they have the potential to fill in critical gaps and reshape our understanding of the details of our human origins.

While we cannot yet say for certain that any specific fossil older than 2 million years represents our direct ancestral species, we do know that the human lineage arose in Africa and emerged to confront the ecological challenges of the planet in a totally new way. These hominins had certain distinctive qualities that set them apart from their own ancestral apes, especially physical changes in the lower and upper body to support bipedal locomotion, modifications to teeth and other facial structures, and increasingly larger cranial capacity. These adaptations supported and in turn influenced increasingly important cultural capacity in the first humans, including *H. erectus*, archaic humans, and our own species of contemporary humans.

While fossils, genetics, and morphology are critical elements of biological anthropology, alone they will never give us the holistic picture of humans that anthropologists strive to develop, because we also know that culture played a critical role in the evolution of the first humans. The story of biocultural evolution goes way back in time and, as we saw here, clearly shaped the social and biological lives of the first humans in complex ways. These processes continue today, resulting in a species with important patterns of biocultural similarity and difference. We examine these patterns in the next chapter.

KEY TERMS

Acheulian tools   p. 173

Australopithecines   p. 152

Biocultural evolution   p. 173

Bipedal locomotion   p. 148

Canine/Premolar-3 shearing complex   p. 148

Foramen magnum   p. 148

Genome   p. 146

Gracile   p. 152

Hominidae   p. 148

Homininae   p. 148

Hominini   p. 148

Levallois technique   p. 180

Megadontia   p. 152

Mousterian industry   p. 180

Multiple dispersals model (MD)   p. 172

Multiregional evolution model (MRE)   p. 172

mya   p. 147

Olduwan tools   p. 153

Paleoanthropologist   p. 146

Paleolithic   p. 173

Ponginae   p. 148

Postorbital constriction p. 169

Recent African origin model (RAO)   p. 172

Sagittal crest   p. 152

Sagittal keel   p. 167

Reviewing the Chapter

Chapter Section	What We Know	To Be Resolved
Who are our earliest possible ancestors?	They are hominins, who began emerging in Africa 5 mya. The three relevant genera—*Australopithecus*, *Paranthropus*, and *Homo*—exhibit varying degrees of bipedal locomotion, smaller teeth than apes, and various other physical particularities. In some cases, they exhibit toolmaking and use.	Paleoanthropologists continue to debate evolutionary relationships between the different genera and their species, as well as the interpretation of individual fossil discoveries. We will never find a single "missing link" but continue to look for further linkages between the hominins already identified.

Chapter Section	What We Know	To Be Resolved
What did walking on two legs and having big brains mean for the early hominins?	The development of bipedalism conferred a number of benefits on hominins and was followed sometime after by the development of greater brain capacity. Although big brains carry certain energetic costs, they also enable more complex social organization and more sophistication in the manufacture and use of tools.	Paleoanthropologists continue to explore basic questions about the complex interrelationships between diet, environment, and the development of bipedalism and large brains in early hominins.
Who were the first humans, and where did they live?	The first humans include *H. erectus* (1.8 mya– ~30,000 years ago), the archaic humans (500,000–27,000 years ago), and contemporary humans (200,000 years–present), who all share certain common physical traits that differentiate them from earlier hominins. The origins of the first humans were in Africa, but they dispersed throughout Eurasia and eventually other locations around the globe.	There is long-standing disagreement over how many species the fossils of early *Homo* represent and how they are related to contemporary humans. The increasing use of genetic data from recovered ancient DNA promises to clarify these issues, but ancient human genomics is still a new science and old DNA is often terribly degraded.
How do we know if the first humans were cultural beings, and what role did culture play in their evolution?	Biocultural evolution is a very old phenomenon among hominins, and especially important for *H. erectus*, archaic, and contemporary humans. Material culture, social interdependence, and symbolic thinking enabled archaic and contemporary humans to survive and thrive in a wide range of environments. These cultural dynamics drove certain morphological changes seen among contemporary humans.	Paleoanthropologists are still working through the fossil evidence to identify the complex ways culture interacted with biology, as well as the particularities of cultural capacity among the first humans. Largely because it is impossible to really know the non-material processes of culture through material objects alone, many crucial details remain unknown. New insights may come from discoveries of new physical evidence or by reinterpreting existing evidence, but some argue that challenging our own cultural stereotypes about the first humans is also necessary.

READINGS

The book *Human Evolution: A Very Short Introduction*, 2nd ed., by evolutionary scholar Bernard Wood (New York: Oxford University Press, 2019), traces the history of paleoanthropology from the eighteenth century to recent fossil finds. A similar but more extensive treatment is Ian Tattersall's *Masters of the Planet: Seeking the Origins of Human Singularity* (New York: Palgrave Macmillan, 2012), which examines the role of bipedalism and social cooperation in the evolution of *Homo*.

The book *Man the Hunted: Primates, Predators, and Human Evolution* (New York: Basic Books, 2005) by biological anthropologists Donna Hart and Robert Sussman explores compelling evidence that humans evolved not as we tend to think—as hunters dominating over other creatures—but as the hunted, that is, the vulnerable prey of other animals that drove certain kinds of adaptations that allowed our species to survive.

British paleoanthropologist Richard Wrangham's 2009 book *Catching Fire: How Cooking Made Us Human* (New York: Basic Books, 2009) provides a compelling analysis of the profound evolutionary effects of controlled use of fire and cooking among the first humans.

The discovery of genetic connections between contemporary humans, Neanderthals, and Denisovans has been widely covered in the media. Science journalists have covered the story extensively, and non-technical writings appear in the blogs of science journals like *Nature*, *Science*, science-interest magazines like *National Geographic* and *Discovery*, and even non-science outlets like *The Atlantic* and the *New York Times*. Articles from any of these outlets are easily accessible online using key word searches.

Check out Jennifer Raff's book *Origin: A Genetic History of the Americas* (New York: Twelve Books, 2022) for more detailed perspectives on the story of the peopling of the Americas explored in the "World in Motion" box.

Human Biodiversity Today

Understanding Our Differences and Similarities

7

DURING 2018, a pair of Canadian identical twins bought DNA ancestry testing kits from five different companies, and submitted their samples for analysis. One of the sisters works for the CBC (Canadian Broadcasting Corporation) and was doing an investigation of "recreational" (over-the-counter) genetic testing, which by 2020 had reached 30 million people (Molla 2020; Agro and Denne 2019). They were curious too. Knowing they had ancestors from Sicily, Poland, and Ukraine, they wondered what else they might learn about their ancestry.

Much to their surprise, the results from the five companies gave differing, even conflicting, pictures of their ancestry (Agro and Denne 2019.). As twins, their DNA is nearly identical, as close as one can get aside from clones, so in theory all five companies should produce the same results. But the details diverged, sometimes dramatically. One company indicated the largest portion (roughly 38 percent) of their ancestry was Eastern European, while another said the largest portion (60 percent) came from the Balkans. One company said one of the twins has German and French ancestry, while the other doesn't, and another company indicated a small percentage of English ancestry in one sister but Scottish and Irish in the other. One company gave a significant percentage of Middle Eastern ancestry, which none of the other companies identified at all. These women come from the same egg and sperm. Where did things go wrong?

Does DNA Really Define Us? The proliferation of commercial DNA testing kits can reinforce the idea that our genetic material defines who we are as humans. But DNA is not who we are. What makes us human is our social complexity, our cooperative ability, and our ability to innovate and change.

This is the wrong question if it assumes there is a singular "right way" to quantify a biocultural phenomenon like ancestry, and that these tests can do it. Genetic ancestry tests involve isolating a small number of variant alleles in DNA acquired from saliva. Since human DNA is 99.9 percent identical, such variations make up less than 1% of our entire DNA. The frequency of these few variants is then compared to the frequency of those same variants in reference populations whose data exist in genetic databases (a so-called reference panel), producing statistical probabilities of relationship. Technically, this is not a direct test of genetic ancestry, but a test of "genetic similarity," identifying similar variants and assuming the likelihood of a recent common ancestor. A typical sample sent for testing has about 3 billion parts, but only 700,000 or so are tested by running a computer algorithm that compares those parts against the reference panel. Each company uses its own distinct set of reference panels and algorithms, and they don't all necessarily test the same 700,000 parts of a sample. As each company acquires more genetic data, the details of their reference panels shift, with the result that any individual's reported "ancestry" will shift as well.

These points raise questions about the validity and interpretation of these tests—which even testing company executives admit are "a kind of art and science" (Agro and Denne 2019)—but anthropological concerns go even further. We know that the presence of a variant allele is no guarantee that an individual is actually directly connected to the peoples represented in a reference panel. DNA variations are not passed on to every individual, and different populations are known to develop the same variations (Bolnick et al. 2007; Royal et al. 2010). Further, reference panels comprise a very small portion of humanity who have already had their DNA examined voluntarily, mostly derived from groups of people living in what is today Europe or are European-derived peoples in the United States and Canada, which renders invisible tens of thousands of other human populations and produces results that overestimate European ancestry (Fuentes and Rouse 2016). Relying on a continental definition of "ancestry" is also deeply problematic (Lewis et al. 2022). Not only is it often impossible to locate with certainty where anybody's ancestors actually lived; countries and continents do not have genetically discrete or isolated populations, and there is no way to prove that current reference populations are the same as they were generations ago (Bolnick et al. 2007; Benn Torres 2018). Most troubling is the use of continents as a marker for genetic variation, which is typically a proxy for race and ethnicity, such as European indicating "white" ancestry and African "black" ancestry. Race and ethnicity have nothing to do with any gene or genetic variation (Lewis et al. 2022).

This is not to say that there is no biologically relevant information in genetic ancestry tests, but these tests skew how we think about our genetic makeup. They reinforce the erroneous idea that DNA shapes who we are and that racial and ethnic differences have something to do with DNA. Our DNA indicates very little about who we will be or how we will act in the world, because humans are, as we explained in Chapter 3, the product of complicated and intertwined genetic, developmental, ecological, historical, and cultural processes. Our ancestry is no different. What makes us human is not our genes but our social complexity, our cooperative ability, and our capacity to imagine alternatives, innovate, and change (Fuentes 2017).

Nevertheless, we still know that there are important genetic and biological variations among humans, which leads us to ask the question at the heart of this chapter: *How should we understand biological and genetic diversity among contemporary human populations?* We can answer this question by considering a number of related questions around which this chapter is organized:

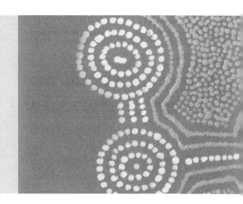

In what ways do contemporary humans vary biologically?

Why do human bodies look so different across the planet?

Are differences of race also differences of biology?

What biocultural consequences do social phenomena like

discrimination, rapid change, nurturing, and so forth have on

human bodies?

In this chapter we explore what integrative anthropology knows about contemporary **human biodiversity**, a term that refers to the similarities and differences within and across human groups that have biological and biocultural dimensions. Among other things, that knowledge challenges simplistic notions about the biological or genetic origins of racial differences. But it also demonstrates that cultural processes like racism, social stress, and nurturing can have important impacts on human biology. It is thus best to understand human biodiversity in a biocultural context. We begin by exploring the general patterns of human biological variation.

• **Human biodiversity.** The similarities and differences within and across human groups that have biological dimensions.

7.1 In What Ways Do Contemporary Humans Vary Biologically?

All humans share mostly identical genetic material—100% of the same genes and 99.9 percent of their variations—and have common physiological processes. Any differences are typically related to ancestral mutations or developmental processes that play out within an individual's lifetime. The primary interest of anthropologists is not so much concerned with individuals as it is on understanding species-wide evolutionary patterns, which means focusing on how that biological diversity works at the population level, a focus that could refer to patterns across the species as a whole, between populations of different world regions, or within specific populations in a region. If you remember from Chapter 3, a population is *a cluster of individuals of the same species who share a common geographical area and who typically find their mates in that same cluster.* In this section we examine what biological anthropologists know about four key dimensions of population-level human biodiversity: patterns of genetic variation, the role of gene flow in genetic variation, physiological differences, and immune responses to disease.

Genetic Variation Within and Between Human Populations

For most mammals, the typical pattern of genetic variation is one in which variation exists between different populations, and most individual populations are quite genetically uniform. This stands to reason: individuals mating within their population spread particular alleles around their group. Over time and depending on its size, a population can develop a specific genetic profile that differs from the profiles of other populations, as long it remains separate in space and mating likelihood, from those other populations. In humans, this situation is—uniquely—reversed. Almost all our species' genetic variations are found *within* populations, not between them. In other words, you might be Scandinavian on both sides going back as many generations as anybody can remember, but you would have the same basic genetic makeup (~99.9 percent identical) as someone who is Senegalese, Japanese, and Melanesian.

The first serious proposal that genetic variation exists between, not within, human populations came from evolutionary biologist Richard Lewontin in 1972 and was based on a statistical analysis of the appearance across human populations of certain known genes (Lewontin 1972). However, another quarter-century had to pass before more extensive empirical evidence to support this proposal could be compiled. A key contribution came from the **Human Genome Project**, an international scientific research project between 1990 and 2003 whose goal was to identify all the genetic material in humans. When the first draft of its findings were published in 1998, it established clearly that humans demonstrate relatively little genetic variation, or allele differences, between populations. Since then, whether by looking at nuclear or mitochondrial DNA, amino acid sequence variation in proteins, or non-coding regions of DNA, many research teams have repeatedly confirmed this finding (Long, Li, and Healey 2009; Kittles and Weiss 2003; Relethford 2002, 2009; Templeton 1998; Hunley, Cabana, and Long 2016; Benn Torres 2019). What this research shows is that between 83 percent and 97 percent of genetic variation is found *within* human populations, and between 3 percent and 17 percent is found *between* populations. It also shows that there is nearly twice as much genetic variation among African populations than among non-African populations, the reason for this being that the human lineage has been in Africa longer than other places on the planet.

These numbers are quite surprising for a mammal like ours that is large-bodied and well dispersed. As a simple comparison, there are greater genetic differences between white-tailed deer populations in North Carolina and Florida than between human populations from Central America, Central Asia, and Central Africa. Another way to view this is if you compare any two humans from anywhere in the world, you will find, on average, one-quarter the amount of genetic variation between them that you would if you compared any two chimpanzees, which are found in only a limited distribution in Africa (Kittles and Weiss 2003; Fuentes 2022b).

- **Human Genome Project.** An international scientific research project between 1990 and 2003 whose goal was to identify all the genetic material in humans.

Genetic Variation Is Tied to Gene Flow

One of the major reasons we find this pattern of genetic variation among humans is gene flow due to migration and mating patterns. A brief example drawn from Central America will show the important role of gene flow in producing variation within a population.

The Culí are a small population of less than 100 people who live in the Costa Rican province of Limón, a humid tropical landscape perched on the edge of the Caribbean Sea (Castrì et al. 2007). They are originally descended from indentured servants brought to the Caribbean from the Indian subcontinent to work on plantations (Figure 7.1). Historically, Limón province had a small Amerindian population. But beginning in the nineteenth century with the construction of a railroad line and the establishment of a banana industry, it attracted new settlers, among them the East Indian ancestors of the Culí, Afro-Caribbeans, Europeans, and Chinese. Though they phenotypically resist inclusion in any racial category, the Culí are a barely recognized and marginalized social community in Costa Rica.

Most anthropological fieldwork conducted among descendants of East Indians living in the Caribbean has focused on their distinctive cultural, religious, and musical practices, not their biological anthropology. Seeking to expand knowledge about the population-level dynamics of that community, in 2003 a research group headed by the University of South Florida and the Universidad de Costa Rica began collecting genetic, genealogical, and ethnographic data on the remaining Culí population (Castrì et al. 2007). The goal of the study was to understand the historic, cultural, and genetic stories of the largely overlooked population. It turns out that the Culí population has a lot of genetic variation within it due to mating patterns that permit intergroup relationships.

The researchers conducted in-depth interviews, developing a history and genealogy of the community from the perspective of its members. They also collected hair follicles and buccal (inner cheek) swab samples from forty-four Culí individuals to assess the relative degree of admixture within the population. The samples were sent to a

Figure 7.1 Labor Migration and Gene Flow in the Caribbean. The movement of indentured servants from the Indian subcontinent to the Caribbean during the nineteenth century as labor contributed new allelic variations to the ongoing mixture of populations in the region.

laboratory for DNA analysis, much as you might do with your own saliva swab, although research laboratories tend to be more cautious in their conclusions than commercial laboratories, and they utilize various other forms of data to develop a picture of genetic diversity. When the researchers compared these samples with samples from other contemporary populations, they found the Culí gene pool includes allele patterns that are typical among many populations, among them Native American, African, and Eurasian populations. In short, the Culí genotype shows a lot of mixing and a much more complex pattern than anyone would have imagined.

The researchers wrote of their results, "What is remarkable about the Culí families is that they can all be linked into one single pedigree. Our analysis of the community genealogies indicated that all living individuals descend in one way or another from a few initial founding couples, that migration continued through several generations, and that gene flow with non-Culí has been very common" (Castrì 2007:176). Complemented by ethnographic, historical, and genealogical data, this study revealed not just an interesting history of a specific population but also how and why migration and gene flow are tied to the production of genetic variation within a population.

Physiological Diversity and Blood Types

Genetic variation is not the only kind of biological variability among humans. There are also physiological variations—in blood factors, enzymes, organ functions, and so on—which powerfully shape how our bodies work. If there were any good reason to divide humans into biologically defined groups—such as efforts to divide people into biological races or ethnicities—any one of the many thousands of physiological traits could provide a more valid basis for meaningful classification than a morphological feature such as the color of one's skin (Cohen 1998). In fact, we do classify people into biologically defined groups—blood type is one example—it's just that we don't assign that trait with any racial significance.

The study of blood types offers a way to investigate human physiological diversity and can also help us understand certain human evolutionary dynamics. During the American Civil War (1861–1865) doctors began using the technique of blood transfusions to help save the lives of patients who lost a lot of blood. It became apparent that something in blood made some people's blood incompatible with the blood of some others. By 1900, these processes of blood rejection were better understood, and they could be explained by the high level of diversity in the human immune system.

Red blood cells are coated by proteins that serve a variety of functions in the human body, including delivering oxygen to tissues and producing antibodies as an immune response. We call these protein sets **blood types**. Differences between these protein sets affect our ability to exchange blood from one person to the next, since when confronted with a different blood type, those proteins produce a self-defense reaction. The ABO system, along with the Rhesus blood type (expressed as Rh+ or Rh-), are the best known. The blood type you probably identify with—for example, O- or A+—comes from this system. Scientists now know of more than fifteen blood-type systems whose alleles exist across populations and affect the transfer of blood between individuals.

The variability in blood types is likely due to mutation, natural selection, and gene flow. O is the most common blood type, probably as the original allele. That original allele mutated at some point, into A and B, which are more recent variants. This relationship is suggested by the chemical structure of A and B, which are the same as the O molecule with the addition of a terminal sugar. Significantly, the different ABO phenotypes can support disease resistance, meaning that in some environments, specific blood types may increase or decrease one's chance of surviving a pathogen attack, such as malaria. Gene flow between populations over the past 50,000 years or so have left their marks on the distribution of the ABO alleles across human populations (Figure 7.2).

- **Blood types.** Sets of proteins that coat the red blood cells, which serve a variety of functions in the human body, including delivering oxygen to tissues and producing antibodies as an immune response.

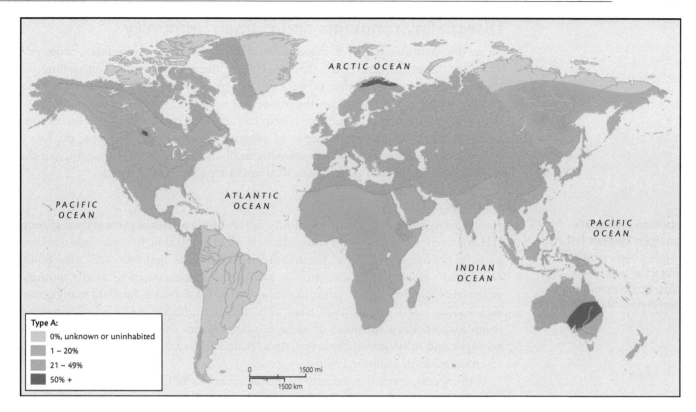

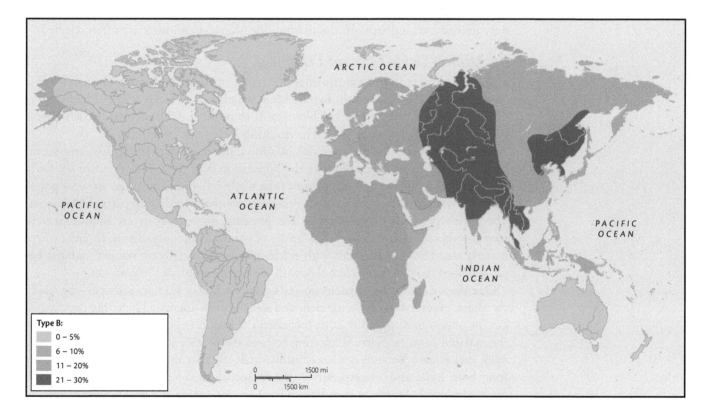

Figure 7.2   Distribution of A and B Blood Types. These maps show the distribution of blood types A and B. There is no obvious pattern to this distribution.

Disease Environments and Human Immunity

As we discussed in Chapter 3, diseases can directly shape our evolutionary trajectory. The other side of that equation is the complex adaptive response of the human immune system to disease pressures that aid survival. As a globally dispersed species, we live in a great variety of environments on the planet and encounter many pathogens, or infectious diseases. Our species' immune system has responded with both flexibility and the ability to resist. We can see evidence of adaptive responses on two levels, the first a generalized one across our species endowing flexibility to deal with pathogens, and the second providing certain populations with resistance to specific diseases.

Flexibility: The HLA System

- **Human leukocyte antigen system (HLA).** A series of proteins on the surface of white blood cells that recognize foreign particles or infectious agents.

A vital component of human immunity is the **human leukocyte antigen system (HLA)**, a series of proteins on the surface of white blood cells that recognize foreign particles or infectious agents. These proteins differentiate between "self" (the body) and "other" (outside proteins, such as pathogens), communicating to the immune system that foreign substances are in the body. The HLA system involves many genes, each having just a few to more than 100 alleles, producing many possible genetic combinations. Even members of same family may not share the exact same HLA genotype and subsequent phenotype. As a result, within any human population great variation exists in immune system response.

At the species level, this variation gives humans flexibility to handle different disease environments. Natural selection probably favored this adaptation, since the more variations we have in our immune systems, the better our chances are of fighting off any new pathogens we might encounter. The other side of the coin here is that this same variation makes organ transplants very difficult. Because of different HLA phenotypes between individuals, tissue from one human to another are often rejected.

Resistance: Sickle Cells and Malaria

Sickle cell disease is a blood disorder occurring in individuals with two copies of a recessive allele for a protein in hemoglobin, which carries oxygen in red blood cells. This protein can cause some red blood cells to become sickle-shaped, which affects their ability to transport oxygen. The resulting illness can be lethal.

Many human populations have this mutation, but because of its negative impact on fitness it tends to be selected out of the population over time. However, we see fairly high frequencies of one or more forms of the sickle cell–inducing alleles in some populations in western Africa, the Arabian Peninsula, southern India, and parts of Melanesia. The allele's persistence is related to the presence of malaria in an environment, a mosquito-borne disease caused by a family of parasitic microorganisms. In areas where malaria is endemic, individuals with sickle cell disease usually do not get malaria, because sickled red blood cells interfere with the reproduction of the parasites.

One theory about this capacity to resist malaria is that human activity—especially the alteration of habitat for settlement and agriculture—increased breeding opportunities for mosquitoes, which in turn increased the likelihood that humans will contract the malarial parasite. Natural selection favored the persistence of the alleles that cause sickle cell disease because it allowed individuals to resist malaria. Due to migrations from both India and western Africa, the frequency of the recessive sickle cell alleles present in North American populations has been increasing as a result of gene flow.

Up to this point, we have been discussing human biodiversity mostly in terms of substances and processes—proteins, genes, cells, immune responses, and so forth—that we can't see, except perhaps with the aid of powerful microscopes or laboratory tests. But what about the most obvious expressions of human biodiversity that literally stare us in the face? In the next section we examine what biological anthropologists know about how and why humans look so different across the planet.

THINKING LIKE AN ANTHROPOLOGIST: HUMAN BIODIVERSITY TODAY

Sickle cell disease offers an example in which biocultural dynamics (in this case, landscape transformation) shape the evolutionary trajectories of both humans and pathogens. Can you think of ways in which biocultural dynamics might affect one or another of the other issues we explored in this section, including genetic variation within human populations and physiological diversity?

7.2 Why Do Human Bodies Look So Different Across the Planet?

People across the planet vary, sometimes quite dramatically, in their looks. In areas of the United States where immigration levels are high—especially in large cities like New York, Los Angeles, Miami, and so on—that variability is on display every day. While some might view that display as a celebration of multicultural diversity, others see it as troubling or threatening. In our society, and indeed in many others, powerful cultural judgments and prejudices are heaped onto bodily characteristics like skin pigmentation, hair, facial features, and body type.

From the perspective of biological anthropology, these kinds of morphological variations are often overemphasized and widely misunderstood, and are, generally speaking, less significant for everyday bodily function than the kinds of genetic, physiological, and immunity issues we just discussed. Nevertheless they are important dimensions of human biodiversity. Because our bodies interact most directly with the natural environment, morphological traits can reflect evolutionary adaptations. In this section, we explain what two key morphological traits—skin pigmentation and body shape and size—can tell us about human biodiversity.

Is Skin Really Colored?

One of the most widely misunderstood aspects of skin is the feature that most of us take for granted: its "color." Skin does not have color, per se. What it does have, just under its outer layers, are cells called melanocytes that produce **melanin**, a complex polymer whose color is either black or brown. Melanin works as a pigment providing a protective tint from the rays of the sun for what lies underneath. The density and distribution of melanin, along with the thickness of the skin, blood vessels, and another orange-ish pigment called carotene, create variations in reflection and absorption of light in the skin, contributing to the perception that skin has "color" (Figure 7.3).

Melanin is a natural sunscreen that evolved through natural selection. Thanks to satellite data of the earth's climate and radiation of the earth's surface, we know that the highest levels of ultraviolet (UV) radiation from the sun are concentrated in the same equatorial latitudes where hominins evolved (Jablonski 2006; Jablonski and Chaplin 2000; Relethford 1997). UV radiation destroys DNA and undermines other bodily functions, but it also catalyzes the production of vitamin D, which supports strong bones and healthy skin. Melanin blocks the worst of the UV rays while letting in enough for vitamin D production. Through natural selection, early hominins almost certainly had high levels of melanin to regulate their UV

• **Melanin.** A complex polymer that is the main pigment in human skin, occurring in two colors: black and brown.

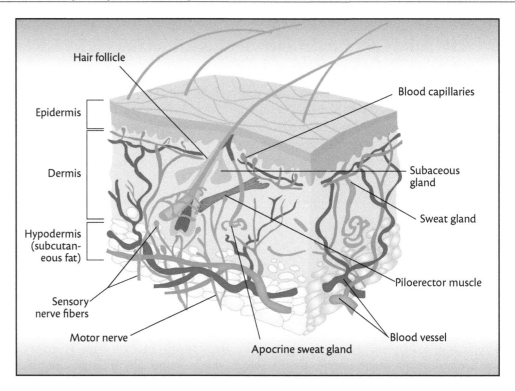

Hair follicle

Blood capillaries

Epidermis

Dermis

Subaceous gland

Sweat gland

Hypodermis (subcutan-eous fat)

Piloerector muscle

Sensory nerve fibers

Blood vessel

Motor nerve

Apocrine sweat gland

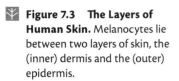

Figure 7.3   The Layers of Human Skin. Melanocytes lie between two layers of skin, the (inner) dermis and the (outer) epidermis.

exposure, and thus they had dark skin complexions. This adaptation was all the more important after humans lost their fur, which probably happened a million years ago.

The dispersal of hominins out of Africa and into northern latitudes brought new variation to skin pigmentation. Because UV concentration levels are much lower at those higher latitudes, over time northern populations (among them probably Neanderthals) lost their melanin pigmentation, and skin complexions lightened.

Of course, as anyone with light skin pigmentation who has gotten a tan can attest, short-term variations in skin pigmentation are possible. All humans have the capacity (albeit limited) to tan, which is a response to UV stress. When we tan, we temporarily increase melanin output, although that output (the actual tan we get) is affected by our age, health, and certain diseases (Jablonski 2004). While natural selection and one's ancestry sets the range of possible skin "color," what people actually look like in any given population is modified and distributed by gene flow and cultural patterns such as the use of clothing, sunblock, and artificial or natural tanning (Jablonski 2004, 2006).

The variation we see today globally in skin pigmentation can be traced to the latitude where one's ancestors spent the most time (Figure 7.4). Generally speaking, darker skinned populations either live in or can trace their ancestry to lower latitudes, including sub-Saharan Africa, South Asia, Southeast Asia, and Polynesia. Lighter skinned populations are found in higher latitudes, including the Americas, Northeast Asia, and Northern Eurasia/Europe. Of course, there are exceptions to these patterns, such as in the United States, where large, recent migrations from various regions around the planet have created many shades. As we know, human movement mixes up genetic material, producing new variations. The best we can say is only that skin pigmentation is not an accurate way to describe any population and that it only correlates in very general terms with latitude.

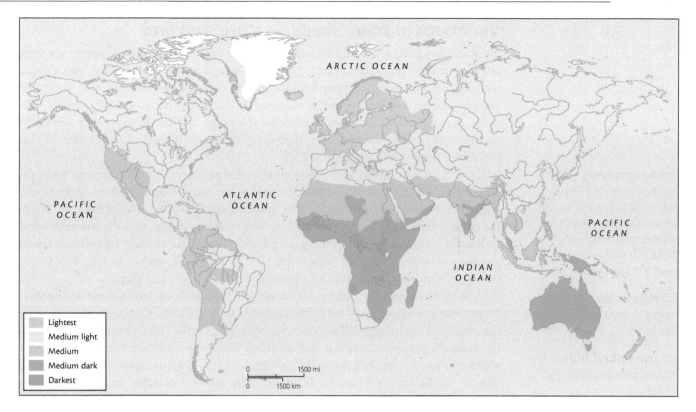

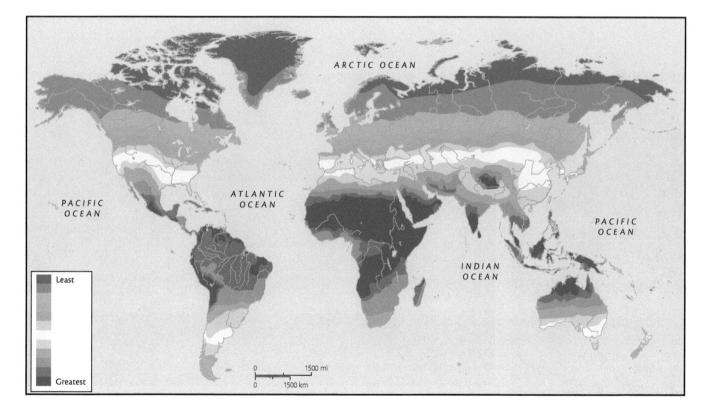

Figure 7.4   The Global Distribution of Skin Pigmentation. The top map shows general patterns in the global distribution of human skin pigmentation, based on five arbitrary categories. The bottom map shows the global distribution of UV light intensity. It is possible to see certain general patterns here, in terms of correlations between UV light intensity and skin pigmentation. What are they?

Variations in Body Shape, Stature, and Size

Humans vary greatly in body shape, stature, and size. Some groups of people are quite tall and slender, including Nilotic peoples of Sudan such as the Shilluk and Dinka, who are among the tallest people in the world. Or they can be short and somewhat stocky, such as the Baka people of Central Africa and other so-called pygmies. The differences between them, not to mention the range of other bodily types seen globally, raise questions about the adaptive significance and biological dimensions of that variability for our species (Figure 7.5).

These variations can be quantified with **anthropometry**, which measures body parameters to assess physical variation, as well as the relative contributions of particular body parts to overall body shape. These measurements take the form of indices, such as the **cormic index**, the ratio of sitting height to standing height, and the **intermembral index**, the ratio of arm length to leg length. Measurements of body fat (adipose tissue) are also common. The body mass index (BMI), a measurement of weight over height (squared), also identifies patterned variations in human size and shape.

Modern humans vary quite a bit in size and shape. That variation is as much as 50 percent in average body mass (measured as weight within each sex), meaning that the smallest humans are half as heavy as the largest. At the pelvis, human width varies by about 25 percent across our species (Ruff 2002), and average heights range from about 150 to 185 cm (just under 5 ft. to about 6 ft.). There is about 10 percent variation in height among humans, although there are also extreme ends of the height spectrum. The difference between males and females in size (sexual dimorphism), is about 15 percent, so men's bodies, on average, are typically larger than female bodies (Figure 7.6). Understanding these variations and the techniques of anthropometry, by the way, is not just of intellectual interest. It is also a critical practical issue for

- **Anthropometry.** The measurement of body parameters that assess physical variation and the relative contributions of particular body parts to overall body shape.

- **Cormic index.** Standing height divided by sitting height.

- **Intermembral index.** The ratio of arm length to leg length.

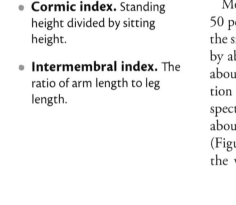

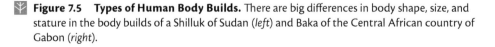

Figure 7.5   Types of Human Body Builds. There are big differences in body shape, size, and stature in the body builds of a Shilluk of Sudan (*left*) and Baka of the Central African country of Gabon (*right*).

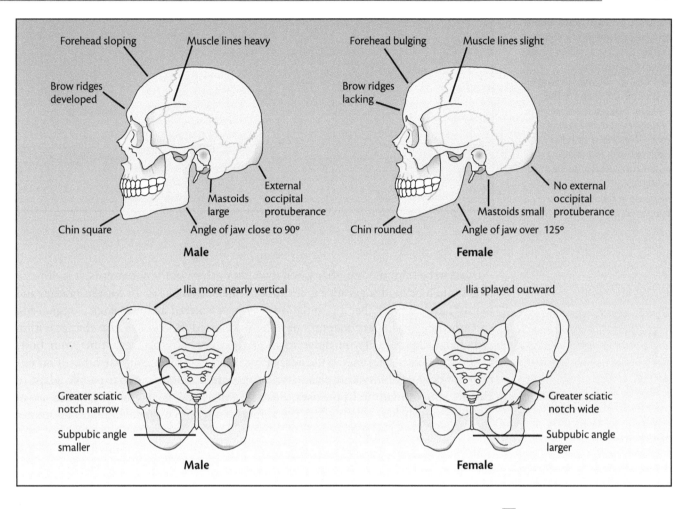

Forehead sloping
Muscle lines heavy
Brow ridges developed
Mastoids large
External occipital protuberance
Chin square
Angle of jaw close to 90°
Male

Forehead bulging
Muscle lines slight
Brow ridges lacking
Mastoids small
No external occipital protuberance
Chin rounded
Angle of jaw over 125°
Female

Ilia more nearly vertical
Greater sciatic notch narrow
Subpubic angle smaller
Male

Ilia splayed outward
Greater sciatic notch wide
Subpubic angle larger
Female

Figure 7.6   Identifying Sexual Differences in the Body. These images show distinct differences between male and female crania and pelvises. Knowing these differences helps biological anthropologists identify whether skeletal remains belong to a woman or a man.

numerous institutions, among them corporations that produce consumer goods, automobile and aerospace companies, the military, and others that make and use technologies that interact with diverse and variable human bodies.

While these contemporary variations seem important, they pale in comparison to the variability among early hominins and members of the genus *Homo* who had even greater sexual dimorphism and differences in size and mass. Those differences in sexual dimorphism reached levels we see today about 500,000 years ago. The late archaic humans (Neanderthals) had greater body mass than us, but then it started to decrease about 50,000 years ago (Ruff 2002). One reason for this is likely that humans' ability to reduce environmental stresses on the human body through culture—better access to food, protective shelter, clothing, and so on—improved. In recent decades, improvements in healthcare and the proliferation of high-calorie processed foods has reversed these trends and generated some pronounced increases in height and body mass (including historically high levels of obesity and overweight) in numerous populations (Figure 7.7).

Body size and shape have played a role in how certain populations have adapted physiologically to living in extremely cold or hot climates. People who live in the extreme North (such as Alaska) and South (such as southern Chile) tend to be stocky and have a high metabolic rate, fat insulation around vital organs, and blood-flow patterns that produce and conserve heat. Alternatively, a body shape with a large surface area such as that exhibited by the tall and slender Shilluk of Sudan enables efficient cooling in a hot climate.

Figure 7.7   The Genus *Homo* and Its Shifting Body Shape. During the past 2 million years, *Homo* has experienced decreasing robustness, changes in the size and shape of the cranium (related to increases in brain size), and decreasing tooth size. Robustness has declined even more during the past 10,000 years. Can you explain why this more recent decrease in robustness happened?

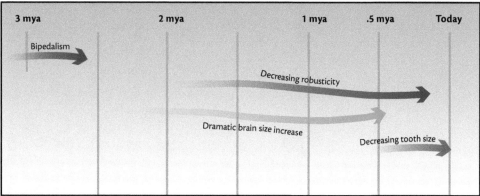

It has to be said, though, that when it comes to these kinds of patterns, it is difficult to get much beyond suggestive generalities. One reason has to do with migration and mating, and the fact that a population may have entered a climatological region too recently for evolutionary adaptations to have occurred. Bodies can also change within individual lifetimes: if you move to the Arctic, for example, over time your body would develop certain metabolic adaptations that help keep you warm based on our physiological flexibility and plasticity. Even more important is that people adapt to climate through cultural processes, including diet, activity patterns, and the use of clothing and shelter, which affect the ability to adapt to extreme climates no matter what the body shape, stature, or size.

Indeed, one of challenges of describing and explaining variations in how people look is just how much those variations can pass through and be shaped by cultural filters. And yet the idea that it is possible to organize humans into definable biological groups based on their looks is a persistent and enduring belief and is closely aligned with ideas about human races. In the next two sections, we examine the history of this idea and explore whether it has any biological significance.

THINKING LIKE AN ANTHROPOLOGIST: HUMAN BIODIVERSITY TODAY

One of the central arguments about how and why human looks vary across the planet has to do with the adaptive relevance of a physical trait. But do all traits have to serve a direct adaptive purpose? Can you think of any physical features on our bodies that may not have a direct adaptive purpose?

• **Race.** A system that organizes people into hierarchical groups based on specific physical traits that are thought to reflect fundamental and innate differences that are rooted in genetic and biological differences.

• **Scientific concept of race.** A population or group of populations within a species that has measurable, defining biological characteristics and low statistical measures of similarity.

7.3 Are Differences of Race Also Differences of Biology?

Most Americans have a worldview that assumes that **race**, which organizes people into hierarchical groups based on physical traits thought to reflect differences rooted in biological differences, is a natural and inevitable aspect of human society. Although they may feel real, powerful, and unchangeable, there is nothing fixed or inevitable—much less biological—about racial categories. The markers upon which racial distinctions are made are especially arbitrary, and they can and often do change (Figure 7.8).

In order to make critical sense of race and its relevance (or irrelevance, as the case may be) for understanding human biodiversity, we first examine how the idea has been framed scientifically and how it connects to human biological variability, showing that there are no valid biological reasons for grouping people into human races (Graves and Goodman 2021). But, as we will explore in the last section, even if race may not be "real" in the sense of having biological origins, racial discrimination and other stresses do have very real consequences on human bodies and lives.

The Biological Meanings (and Meaninglessness) of "Human Races"

Biological anthropologists work with two concepts of race. The **scientific concept of race** is one of these, referring to a population, or group of populations, within a species that has measurable, defining biological characteristics (Edgar and Hunley 2009; Kittles and Weiss 2003; Templeton 1998). In biology this is known as a **subspecies**, or a unit within a species on an evolutionary path that diverges from that of other populations within the species.

The other concept is a **culturally constructed concept of race**, in which cultural ideologies and dynamics are linked with morphological traits (things like skin pigmentation, body shape, or cranial structure) to create an artificial, "biologized" category (Marks 1995; Graves 2015). The culturally constructed conceptions of race that we take for granted today originated during the period of European colonial expansion from the fifteenth to the nineteenth centuries, with the expansion of global maritime travel and new kinds of sustained contact between geographically distant people. Europeans explained and justified their dominance and control through colonialism by developing racial classifications that evaluated non-Europeans as less human or less civilized than Europeans (see Chapter 15). Beginning in the eighteenth century, these differences were **naturalized**—made part of the natural order of things—through the production of scientific theories, schemes, and typologies about human differences. Indeed, the early years of physical anthropology (roughly 1850–1950) focused on attempts to discover the biological basis for classifying humans into races, typically through various kinds of anthropometric measurements. Although some anthropologists turned these ideas on their heads, using those same techniques to demonstrate that one could *not* classify humans into races based on morphological traits (Marks 1995), the basic notion of race in humans was adopted in mainstream scientific studies about human variation and differences.

The Problem of Categorizing Humans Racially

Scientists came up with four general approaches to categorize human races. The first approach is trait based, which isolates certain physical features, such as head size and shape, bodily structure, facial features, lip shape, eye folds, or skin pigmentation, to divide people into races according to what seems physically most typical of the group (Johnston 2004). This approach is closely associated with German taxonomist and anthropologist Johann Friedrich Blumenbach (1752–1840), who identified five racial groups: Mongoloid, Caucasoid, Negroid, Malayan, and American Indian (Figure 7.9). American folk classifications do something similar with skin color, for example, making distinctions between white, black, red, and yellow skin to denote certain racial groups. Of course, nobody's skin is really any of these colors; they are just convenient symbolic markers of much more complex patterns of difference.

Figure 7.8 "Equal Burdens." This 1874 image from the cover of *Harper's* magazine represents caricatures of a black man from the South and an Irishman from the North. Although the Irishman here is identified as "white," Irish immigrants to the United States were not really fully accepted as "white"—and shared the equal burden of racial discrimination with blacks—until the end of the nineteenth century. The rapid transformation of Irish into "white" people points to how dynamic and unstable racial identities can be.

- **Subspecies.** A population that meets the criteria defined within the scientific concept of race.

- **Culturally constructed concept of race.** A set of cultural or ethnic factors combined with easily perceived morphological traits (e.g., skin reflectance, body shape, cranial structure) in an artificial "biologized" category.

- **Naturalize.** To make part of the natural order of things through the production of scientific theories, schemes, and typologies.

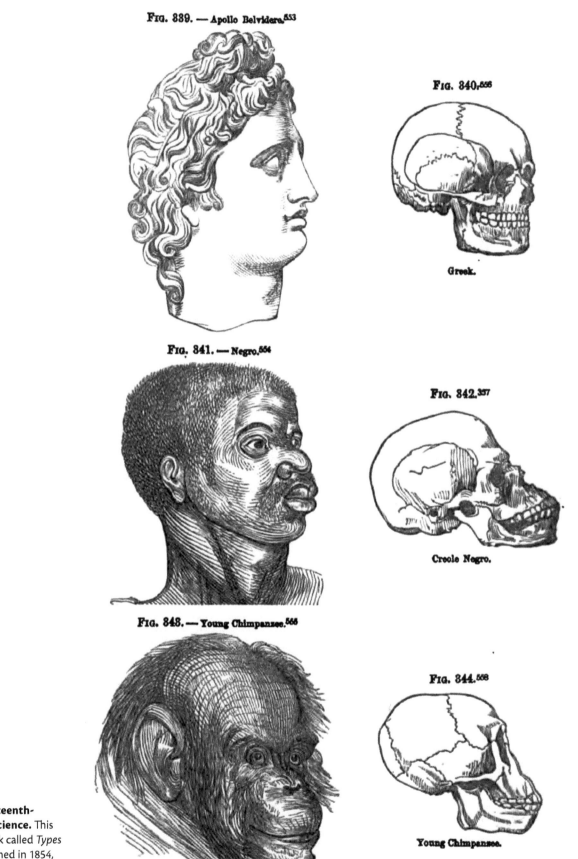

FIG. 339. — Apollo Belvidere.⁵⁵³

FIG. 340.⁵⁵⁵

Greek.

FIG. 341. — Negro.⁵⁵⁴

FIG. 342.³⁵⁷

Creole Negro.

FIG. 348. — Young Chimpanzee.⁵⁵⁵

FIG. 344.⁵⁵⁸

Young Chimpanzee.

Figure 7.9   Eighteenth-Century Racial Science. This image, from a book called *Types of Mankind* published in 1854, claims a close relationship between chimpanzees and Africans.

A second approach to categorizing races is based on geographic origins. The Swedish taxonomist Linnaeus developed such a scheme, dividing humans into four races: African, Asian, American, and European. North American racial models also reflect some elements of this approach, with our division into African Americans, Asians, Native Americans, Hawaiians/Pacific Islanders, and so forth. In recent years the US Bureau of the Census has used the racial category "Asian and Pacific Islander." The obvious weakness of this model is that political designations, such as Hawaiian and Pacific Islander, and vast continents with tremendous ethnic diversity like Asia, are made into racial groups.

Some anthropologists have refined this geographic approach into a third way of categorizing race called the adaptational approach to racial classification, which refers to the notion that people adapt to the environments in which they live and pass on those adaptations through inheritance (Coon, Garn, and Birdsell 1950). One illustration of this approach can be found in melanin's role in creating fitness and adaptability in regions of the globe with high UV concentrations. Nevertheless, as we saw, this point suggests only a very general correlation between biology and latitude and does not translate neatly to the four or five commonly defined races.

A fourth approach builds on advances in population dynamics since the 1950s and defines races as reproductively isolated breeding populations. This approach moved beyond trait-based and geography-based approaches by focusing on who mates with whom, which allows for the influence of cultural factors, such as religious affiliation or economic status, on the formation of racial groups (Garn 1961). With this approach, the number of races exploded from four to dozens, mainly because there are so many separate breeding populations in the human species. Taken to the extreme, it would also mean that every population qualifies as a race, which muddies the waters between the two concepts (Long 2003).

Each of these four approaches has its own specific limitations. But there is a common problem shared by all of them—and, for that matter, any attempt to categorize humans into natural races: these typologies rarely describe an actual individual, and they do not accurately characterize whole groups of people. What look like patently obvious "racial" differences come from a special way of sampling people. This sampling process isolates one or more arbitrarily chosen visible traits and marks the trait(s) as representative of a whole group of people. More troubling is that one trait can come to be representative of other characteristics, such as intelligence, aptitude, and personal character. Moreover, the categories themselves are just not that stable and they shift over time.

Variability in Human Populations: It's Not Race

Biological traits and genetic features never vary in neat and easily defined ways, much less in ways that correspond to the "racial" categories Americans are used to recognizing. Because of historical movement, intermingling, and gene flow, human genetic and biological variations occur in a continuous fashion. Anthropologists call such variations **clinal variations**, which means that change is gradual across groups and that traits shade and blend into each other (Marks 1995; Graves and Goodman 2021). Take any physical trait that people use to identify racial groups—facial features, skin pigmentation, body shape, and the like—and there are never clearly definable lines between any of those features in an actual population.

Clinal variation. A type of variation in which change is gradual across groups and in which traits shade and blend into each other.

Genetic and biological traits also tend to vary independently of each other. For example, there is no connection between skin pigmentation and any other supposed "racial" trait, such as certain facial features, cranial size, or body shapes. There is also absolutely no physiological parallel or relationship between these traits and the biological and social phenomena we call character and intelligence (Fuentes 2022b; Graves and Goodman 2021).

Anthropological skepticism about the utility of race for understanding human variation runs deep in the discipline's history. In "Classic Contributions: Ashley Montagu and 'Man's Most Dangerous Myth,'" we examine the perspective of one of anthropology's most prominent critics of the race concept.

But Isn't There Scientific Evidence for the Existence of Races?

So where does this all leave the scientific concept of race? To test the hypothesis that modern humans can be categorized according to the scientific concept of race, we just need to identify the biological characteristics that define a subspecies within *Homo sapiens* and then assess how those characteristics map onto human variations. If you watch television programs featuring forensic scientists and detectives, they appear to do these things all the time, such as when they announce that the skull they have discovered is that of a black male or white female. Or when you send a swab of saliva off to a genetic ancestry testing company, they send back a report that can tell you what racial or ethnic background you have. What is the actual evidence for making these claims?

Genetic Evidence

The genetic differentiation needed to classify a population or group as a subspecies in animals like birds, squirrels, or non-human primates, simply doesn't exist in humans. The variation levels are well below the statistical limits biologists use to classify subspecies or defined lineages within a species. Moreover, no single genetic marker can be used to sort people into races; that is, scientists have not found any specific Asian, Black, or white genes or alleles. Nearly all alleles are found in some members of nearly every population. Genetically speaking, humans show up as one biological race, so genetic/biological "races" do not exist (Templeton 2013; Hunley et al. 2016).

As we discussed in the chapter introduction, taken uncritically, genetic ancestry tests perpetuate the flawed notions that we can be divided into genetically distinct continental groups, and that our DNA makes us who we are. Moreover, instead of recognizing that any of us is 99.9 percent genetically similar to all other humans, test results focus on continental markers that have been used historically to racialize populations, which gives the false impression that races exist genetically. As we explore in "Anthropologist as Problem Solver: Jada Benn Torres and Reparational Genetics in the Caribbean," the proliferation of genetic ancestry testing is complicating policy debates about reparations for slavery.

Morphological Evidence

- **Forensic analysis.** The identification and description of dead people.

Forensic analysis, the identification and description of dead people, often uses cranial measurements to sort people into populations.

Forensic experts can classify a skull's race (Asian, black, or white) about 80 percent of the time. Does this mean these categories are biologically based? Not really. Health, nutrition, and evolutionary factors like gene flow create cranial variation between individuals (Smay and Armelagos 2000; Digangi and Bethard 2021). In humans, levels of cranial variations are similar to the levels of variation in our DNA (Figure 7.10). That is, about 80 percent of any variations in cranial shape would be found *within* a human population, and about 20 percent *between* populations (Relethford 2002).

Classic Contributions
Ashley Montagu and "Man's Most Dangerous Myth"

FIRST PUBLISHED IN 1942 and now in its sixth edition, Ashley Montagu's book *Man's Most Dangerous Myth: The Fallacy of Race* stands as a cornerstone in the history and practice of anthropology. Montagu (1905–1999) was an English biological anthropologist who saw the abuses and misuses of race and racism as central concerns not only for anthropology but also for humankind. Although he wasn't the first anthropologist to take a critical perspective on race—Franz Boas and his students were doing it several decades earlier—Montagu's assertions were the most direct, public, and strident. In a sense, Montagu was arguing against his own discipline, since prior to World War II, physical anthropology was closely associated with efforts to measure and categorize different human races. But he felt an obligation as a scientist, an anthropologist, and a humanist to investigate the claims that races existed, whether the people who were so categorized actually varied in biological abilities, and whether any data existed to support those assertions. He explored the vast biological and anthropological data, theories, and perspectives available to him and concluded that race not only has no biological basis but it also is a powerful myth. In the opening paragraphs of his book, reprinted here, he gets right to the point.

Ashley Montagu.

The idea of race represents one of the most dangerous myths of our time and one of the most tragic. Myths are most effective and dangerous when they remain unrecognized for what they are. Many of us are happy in the complacent belief that myths are what uncivilized people believe in, but of which we ourselves are completely free. We may realize that a myth is a faulty explanation leading to social delusion and error, but we do not necessarily realize that we ourselves share in the mythmaking faculty with all people of all times and places, or that each of us has his own store of myths derived from the traditional stock of the society in which we live, and are always in ready supply. In earlier days we believed in magic, possession, and exorcism; in good and evil supernatural powers; and until recently we believed in witchcraft. Today many of us believe in race.

Race is the witchcraft, the demonology of our time, the means by which we exorcise imagined demoniacal powers among us. It is the contemporary myth, humankind's most dangerous myth, America's Original Sin.

In our own time we have lived to see the myth of race openly adopted by governments as an expedient fiction. Myths perform the double function of both serving as models of and models for cultural attitudes and behavior. Thus myths reflect the beliefs and give sanction to the actions of society, while at the same time providing the forms upon which belief and conduct are molded. Built, as they are, into the structure of social relationships, racial myths often have a force which exceeds even that of reality itself, for such myths, in addition to the social encouragement they receive, draw upon both false biology and even worse theology for their sustenance. [Montagu 1997:41–42]

Questions for Reflection

1. Montagu understands "myth" both in its popular sense—as falsehood—and in the anthropological sense, as a powerful narrative shaping understanding of how the world works. In what senses does he believe the myth of race shapes understanding of how the world works? What evidence about race do you think supports his view?

2. If as long ago as 1942 we knew that the idea of race was based on (in Montagu's terms) "false biology," why does this misconception persist?

Anthropologist as Problem Solver
Jada Benn Torres and Reparational Genetics in the Caribbean

During the past several decades, there has been a growing worldwide surge of calls for former colonial powers to provide reparations, or compensatory payments, for past harms of enslavement and colonial exploitation. A few years ago, a handful of Caribbean nations asserted their desire to begin a conversation around reparations, arguing that European colonialism brought great harm to the basin's original indigenous inhabitants and to those who were forcibly brought to the Caribbean as slaves, producing social, economic, political, and ecological repercussions that persist today. Due to the intermixing of populations in the Caribbean, figuring out who is qualified for reparations is highly complicated and contentious. Some have expressed the potential utility of ancestry tests to help identify the descendants of those peoples to whom reparations could be directed.

In the midst of this dynamic situation, Jada Benn Torres, a genetic anthropologist at Vanderbilt University, has been conducting long-term research on genetic ancestry and population history of African and indigenous peoples in the Anglophone Caribbean. For Benn Torres, genetic ancestry is a biocultural phenomenon that varies cross-culturally, which in the Americas means it is contiguous with how people think about and experience race (Benn Torres and Torres Colón 2021). These local meanings complicate the Caribbean's politics of "reparational genetics" (Benn Torres 2018). Benn Torres is among those anthropologists who are, as we described in the chapter introduction, skeptical about limitations and implications of what she calls "recreational genetic testing" (consumer-oriented tests), especially their potential to reify biological notions of race. However, she also argues that genetic ancestry can be useful for understanding how mate choice and genetic variability in the Caribbean might have been affected by geographic barriers and social structures, especially where written and oral historical evidence might be weak. In addition, she argues that it is important to take into consideration the contemporary context of how people experience, shape, and maintain their social identities in the Caribbean, which can differ from other global regions. For example, the Caribbean historical narrative emphasizes the complete extermination of indigenous peoples. However, recent genetic data has presented evidence of the persistence and continuity of indigenous peoples, generating new solidarity movements between them across the Caribbean.

According to Benn Torres, the way forward in these ongoing debates is not through an uncritical acceptance of genetic ancestry data. Rather, it will be through sensitive contextualization of how communities with a stake in these matters define themselves, and by examining in alliance with those communities how genetic ancestry data might affect them. This is not a simple matter of conducting neutral science, but of creating ways to support marginalized communities that have endured harsh discrimination and face substantial ongoing economic and political challenges, including being erased from national histories and imaginaries. More important, she argues, the reparations issue has opened the door for some scientists and reparations critics to claim that issues like poverty, social injustice, and racial inequality are simply a reflection of the biological inferiority of the communities affected by these things, so reparations would not solve anything. Publicly challenging this kind of biological reductionism and over-simplification of what it means to be human is an especially crucial, ongoing effort on the part of anthropologists.

Questions for Reflection

1. In the United States, we also have ongoing debates over reparations for slavery, which have even made it to the court system. What role do you think genetic ancestry testing might or should play in this country's debates?

2. How do you think anthropologists should work with marginalized communities, such as those Benn Torres describes in the Caribbean, to understand how genetic ancestry data might impact them?

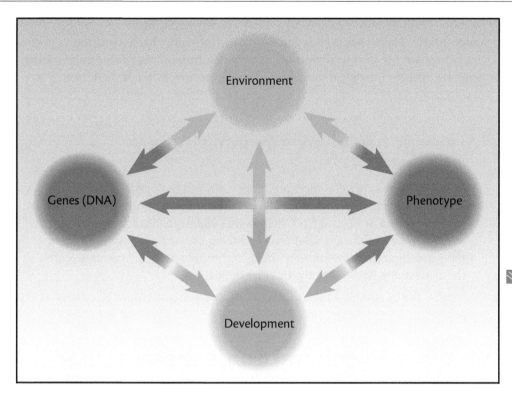

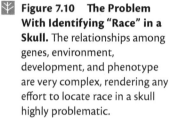

Figure 7.10   **The Problem With Identifying "Race" in a Skull.** The relationships among genes, environment, development, and phenotype are very complex, rendering any effort to locate race in a skull highly problematic.

So how do forensic scientists classify skulls into culturally constructed racial categories? The answer lies in how the crania are classified, and how many categories there are for classification. Scientists will place them in the categories that are available: the fewer the categories, the more simple it is to sort. For example, in one project forensic scientists took crania from white American males in two periods, 1979 and 1840, and easily sorted them into two groups. It was as simple as sorting the crania of modern American white and black males into separate groups (Jantz and Meadows Jantz 2000). Of course, white American males in 1979 did not belong to a different race from white American males living in 1840, but the limited number of categories scientists worked with predetermined how they would classify the skulls, and the differences seemed clear enough. But how do we explain the differences in skull measurements between the white males? The reason is that they had differences in their health and nutrition across time, as well as gene flow, especially if any of these individuals had some ancestors from other parts of the planet.

Things get even more uncertain when you look at skull measurements indicating "black" in the United States and compare them with crania from the African continent, with all its human diversity. They just don't match up. More importantly, the cranial measurements used to identify "racial" groups are not specific or unique to any of the culturally constructed racial categories. Because the cranial measurements for each group are based on averages and ranges, any specific cranium will usually diverge from the "correct" range. As a result, forensic experts can't always place crania in the "correct" category—this happens as much as one in five times. The differences here are of degree, not kind (DiGangi and Bethard 2021).

All of this evidence indicates that race is a powerful cultural *and* scientific construction, in the sense that any certainties about it have to be actively built—constructed—upon a set of assumptions that anthropology shows are flawed when applied to humans. Unfortunately, a lot of people—scientists among them—still believe that erroneous racial classifications are real, largely because they do not understand how processes of natural selection, population genetics, and human variation work

(Harrison 1998; Gould 1996; Marks 1995; Peregrine, Ember, and Ember 2003; Fuentes 2014c). Nevertheless, it is important to recognize that even if the origins of racial groups are not genetically or biologically determined, race can *become* biology, by shaping people's biological outcomes. We explore how in the final section.

THINKING LIKE AN ANTHROPOLOGIST: HUMAN BIODIVERSITY TODAY

The idea that racial differences are genetically and biologically determined is widely accepted by the US public, and the contrary and more complicated view just presented has failed to gain widespread traction even as it offers a more empirically valid understanding of the relationship between race and biology. How do you think anthropologists can communicate these ideas and findings to the broader public?

7.4 What Biocultural Consequences Do Social Phenomena Like Discrimination, Rapid Change, Nurturing, and So Forth Have on Human Bodies?

One of the criticisms of the idea that race is a myth or is culturally constructed is that it might give the impression that race is not "real" (Hartigan 2006). Race is very real because racial groupings are accompanied and supported by marginalization, exploitation, and stigma for some, and privilege for others. **Racism**, the repressive practices, structures, beliefs, and representations that uphold racial categories and social inequality, is a potent force in making race an objective reality. It works through the prejudice that people express against people who are different from them and through **discrimination**, which is negative or unfair treatment of a person because of his or her group membership or identity (Graves and Goodman 2021).

From a biocultural perspective, these processes powerfully shape a community's exposure to factors that create certain kinds of embodied health outcomes, including sickness, long-term chronic disease, stress, and suffering. Studying the ways people experience social stresses and discrimination through their bodies has become an increasingly important area of biological anthropology research because it shows how cultural processes can contribute to the production of biological variation in human populations. In this section, we examine two expressions of these concerns: eugenics and the embodied consequences of being a racialized minority.

Eugenics: A Weak Theory of Genetic Inheritance

One illustration of Ashley Montagu's concerns about the dangers of race comes from the field of **eugenics**, an early and misguided attempt at making biological anthropology an applied science whose goal was to improve human biology through selective mating. In the early 1900s, some geneticists sought to improve humanity by making it more disease resistant and smarter. They understood social, cultural, and racial

---

- **Racism.** The repressive practices, structures, beliefs, and representations that uphold racial categories and social inequality.

- **Discrimination.** Negative or unfair treatment of a person because of his or her membership in a particular social group or category.

- **Eugenics.** The study of genetics with the notion of improving human biology and biological potential; often associated with simplistic, erroneous assumptions about the relationship of behavior or cultural traits to simple genetic systems.

differences among peoples to be the result of genetic differences. Through the promotion of selective mating and sterilization programs, their intention was to protect and promote "good genes" and eliminate "bad genes" from the population.

Although at the time, these ideas were viewed as progressive and were supported by prominent social reformers, philanthropists, and government agencies, the track record of eugenics included numerous human rights abuses. It was also based on a totally incorrect way of thinking about genetics. Eugenicists believed that inheritance was a simple function of dominant and recessive genes. That is, you simply get one thing from dad and one from mom, and the one that is dominant becomes your phenotype. Using this idea—that we now know is bad science—eugenicists offered an explanation for stereotypical racial traits. For example, they argued that certain groups of social undesirables had low intelligence ("feebleminded" is the word they used) based on the belief that they inherited certain dominant traits in high frequencies.

After World War II, eugenics lost its social legitimacy when it became clear that the Nazis in Germany had used their own eugenicist ideology to identify and standardize their ideas about the superiority of Nordic and Aryan racial types. This ideology fueled the Holocaust, which took the lives of millions of Jews, Slavs, Romani (Gypsies), and homosexuals and forced the surgical sterilization of people who suffered from what Nazi doctors defined as "hereditary" illnesses—among others, epilepsy, schizophrenia, body malformations, blindness, and deafness (Lifton 1986). These actions had important individual and population-level consequences that historians, biologists, and anthropologists are still documenting and striving to understand.

Germany was not the only country where eugenics was sanctioned as official state-supported ideology. Several states in the United States developed eugenics programs, including Vermont between 1925 and 1936. In Vermont it began with a statewide survey of "bad heredity" and identification of "degenerate families"—primarily Abenaki Indians, French Canadians, and handicapped people—and culminated with the 1931 passage of "A Law for Human Betterment by Voluntary Sterilization" (Gallagher 1999). Under this law, dozens of forced, not "voluntary," sterilizations occurred. To avoid sterilization, many Abenaki abandoned any obvious signs of their Native American past, which is a key factor that currently prevents them from being recognized as a tribe by the federal government. As the example of eugenics shows, when aligned with powerful social institutions, racist ideologies can have profound biocultural consequences on ordinary people's lives.

The Embodied Consequences of Being a Racialized Minority

Another context in which we can examine these biocultural consequences is by understanding racial inequalities in health. The existence of these inequalities has become an important area of biological and cultural research among anthropologists. In challenging the notion that biologically or genetically based racial dynamics shape health conditions, anthropologists have presented an alternative picture of the relationship between race and health, by demonstrating how biocultural factors, phenotypic plasticity, and epigenetic effects shape divergent health outcomes of racialized minorities (Gravlee 2009).

Epidemiological studies in the United States indicate well-defined differences between racial groups in terms of morbidity and mortality, which refer to incidence of disease and life expectancy. One illustration of this fact is that African Americans and other minority groups like Latinos and Native Americans have higher rates of many diseases, such as hypertension, diabetes, cancer, stroke, renal failure, and cardiovascular disease, among others (Gravlee 2009). There is also a gap in black–

- **Syndemic.** A concept that refers to epidemics or adverse health events that involve the clustering of diseases, adverse interactions between these diseases, and socio-environmental conditions that exacerbate the effects of diseases or make people more vulnerable.

- **Embodiment.** A concept that refers to how people literally incorporate, biologically, the material and social worlds in which they live, from conception to death.

- **Alloparenting.** A practice in which the role of parenting is performed by individuals who are not the biological parents of children.

white life expectancy that has been recognized for many decades. Although the gap has closed, from 17.8 years in 1903 to just under 5 years today, it continues to be a problem (Gravlee 2009). When it comes to COVID-19, the prevalence of these underlying conditions within these populations has intensified the effects of the coronavirus, leading to higher rates of hospitalization and mortality than for whites (Magesh et. al. 2021). While it is common to refer to COVID-19 as a "pandemic," there is a more specific term for this particular situation: **syndemic**, a concept that refers to an epidemic or adverse health events that involve the clustering of diseases, adverse interactions between these diseases, and socio-environmental conditions that make people more vulnerable or exacerbate the effects of diseases (Singer et al. 2021). Race is not the *cause* of these health inequalities. Rather, these health inequalities are the *result* of race, or more specifically, of racism and the complex environmental influences racism creates on human biology (Gravlee 2020). One expression of racism is residential segregation by racial group, which has been shown to produce inequalities in health because it constrains opportunities such as access to education, certain occupations, and quality healthcare. It can also create social environments that influence the spread and distribution of disease, poor diets, illegal drug use, gang violence, and gunshot wounds. All of these problems are linked to poverty and social marginalization, not the biology of the populations affected. Discrimination has also been shown to have bodily consequences on individuals, producing a range of effects from high blood pressure to lower birth weights. Although they are still not understood very well, these conditions can also have epigenetic dimensions, in other words, producing lingering effects throughout childhood and well into adulthood of the next generation.

This work shifts attention toward the ways experiences of racism are embodied. **Embodiment** is a concept that refers to how people biologically incorporate "the material and social worlds in which they live," from the act of conception until death (Krieger 2005). This work also recognizes how embodied inequalities reinforce racialized understandings of human biology (Gravlee 2009). Recognizing how biological variations are produced through social processes has been a productive avenue for biocultural research beyond the study of racial inequalities. For example, rapid social change can produce stress, which has well-documented consequences like high blood pressure, reduced immune function, and depressive symptoms (Daltabuit and Leatherman 1998; McDade, Stallings, and Worthman 2000; McDade 2001; Dressler 2005; Krieger 2019).

How Do Humans Thrive?

While it is clear that some social phenomena contribute to illness, syndemics, and other challenging health conditions, biocultural anthropologists have also explored conditions under which humans can thrive. Of course, concepts like "thriving" and "well-being" are culturally relative terms, so what one group considers conditions for well-being (or even recognizes such a category, because not all do) differ from what is recognized by others (Thin 2009). Well-being is not simply the absence of physiological stressors—all humans experience these in some shape or form—but how social institutions, interpersonal relationships, enculturation, broader ecological conditions, and so forth align to cultivate and support senses of purpose, belonging, collective identity, selfhood, and moral value that have physiological consequences (Fischer 2014).

Biocultural anthropologists have documented a range of successful ways to be human across the planet and across time. But they all have one thing in common: we all do it best in community. Humans are primates, and the surest way to stress out a

The Anthropological Life
It Does, In Fact, "Take a Village": A Biocultural Perspective

☙ **Alloparenting in the Caribbean.**

Life during the COVID-19 pandemic was nothing if not socially isolating. In spite of all the digital tools for online meetings and other creative ways people found to stay in touch, long periods of solitude and loneliness have taken a heavy emotional and mental health toll on millions. For Santa Clara University biological anthropologist Robin G. Nelson, who studies the biocultural dimensions of childrearing, child development, and health outcomes, it was particularly disruptive for families and the social networks that raise children. Quoted in the *New York Times*, she observed, "People are always raised by a network of adults and support systems [including extended family, teachers, coaches, and community members...] That network of adults and caretakers is essential for every kid, everywhere" (Grose 2020). She expressed concern that the pandemic intensified distress for parents and children already suffering from a lack of social support, especially in low-income communities disconnected from the adults in schools, youth centers, and other institutions that support their healthy development.

The phenomenon that Nelson is referring to is **alloparenting**, a term that refers to parenting that is performed by individuals who are not the biological parents of children. Alloparenting is typically understood as an extension of the mother-infant dyad that evolved to meet the resource and energy needs of offspring. Most studies of alloparenting have focused on small-scale societies like foragers where these activities occur at the household level (Nelson 2020). But in a world characterized by dynamic transnational flows and labor migration, is alloparenting still relevant? Nelson's area of studies is the Caribbean where "communal parenting" has been an important biocultural adaptive system to support child growth and development among Black families. Historically, patterns of family separation due to enslavement and labor migration have created many women-headed households, male absenteeism, and extended kin groups involved in childrearing. Early social scientists—if not European attitudes more broadly—viewed this situation as pathological because it diverged from ideals of religiously ordained marriage, male dominance, and an emphasis on the nuclear family. The implication, of course, was that Black children could not thrive under these circumstances.

In her work, Nelson has rejected these ethnocentric views, offering a more complicated and dynamic picture of Black Caribbean households and social networks that flexibly adapt to provide material and emotional care for children (Nelson 2020). For example, while it is expected that the mother and her extended kin do the primary day-to-day work of raising children, fathers who may live elsewhere also contribute not-insignificant material support and affective ties. With broad economic changes, more mothers are having to work in the formal economy, even becoming migrant laborers and moving to other countries to find work and to send money home. These are risky moments for parents and children, but here is often where extended kin take over, who can benefit from having an additional helper in the home. Certainly, fostering situations provide variable levels of care, as they do anywhere, with many children experiencing appropriate psychosocial development, while others suffer from neglect and abuse. But in effect, children belong to more than one household, the advantage being that many adults are responsible for them and contribute to their economic, social, emotional, and psychological needs. As Nelson insists, situations like this expand our understanding of alloparental care and encourage us to see its evolutionary significance: that it does, in fact "take a village" to raise children, with community parenting such a flexible and adaptable phenomenon that it doesn't just extend across households but even national boundaries.

monkey or an ape is to isolate it. In isolation, without the daily social interactions with others of their group—grooming, fighting, making up, even just hanging out near each other—the body and mind of the primate weaken and it becomes susceptible to a range of infections, diseases, and other forms of ill health. This fact was on display during the extended lockdowns related to COVID-19, which led many people to new levels of stress and despair (White et al. 2022). It is not at all surprising that in 1940 the World Health Organization came up with this definition of health: "A state of complete physical, mental and social well-being and not merely the absence of disease or infirmity," and haven't changed it since (World Health Organization 2022). Human bodies and neurobiologies evolved to exist in the context of social interactions with others. Our hormone systems map to our social lives, even our brain's resting state. The neurobiological setting when we are by ourselves and not actively thinking of anything—"zoning out" you might call it—is the same as when we are in social interactions with other people. Even when we are alone our neurobiology is riffing off of, and connecting with, our social lives. Put simply, the default setting for the human mind and body *is* social. So while there are a multitude of culturally different ways to "be well," they are all connected, in one way or another, to our lives in and with communities. And nowhere is this more evident that in the raising of children. In "The Anthropological Life: It Does, In Fact, 'Take a Village': A Biocultural Perspective,'" we explore how biological anthropologist Robin G. Nelson's research on childrearing demonstrates how parenting systems can flexibly adapt to support children's growth and development.

The broader point of all this is that if we want to understand human biological variation, it is necessary to take into account the role that social relationships and cultural attitudes—such as those that produce discrimination and psychosocial stress or childrearing support—play in shaping biological processes and health outcomes. Biocultural research along these lines is still relatively young. But its importance is that it challenges reductionistic biological and genetic perspectives that reproduce the same myths of separate human races that anthropologists long ago disproved, while recognizing that race does have certain kinds of objective impacts on bodies and psychologies.

THINKING LIKE AN ANTHROPOLOGIST: HUMAN BIODIVERSITY TODAY

The approach presented here about embodiment suggests that the important thing about race is not that it is a myth but that it is deeply entrenched in social relationships and culture. Is it possible to hold both views simultaneously? Why or why not?

Conclusion

A lot of Americans believe that, thanks to the civil rights era of the 1960s and to the fact that a Black man, Barack Obama, was twice elected the country's president, race matters less in this country than it ever has. But even though segregated schooling and notorious Jim Crow laws in the South that prevented blacks from voting may have been deemed unconstitutional by the Supreme Court, race and racially based discrimination have hardly disappeared from American life. The unequal health outcomes between whites and Blacks and other racialized minorities are but one expression of the ongoing problem.

There are many reasons that racial inequalities persist, but one of the main ones is that they emerge out of a worldview that interprets visible signs of human variation as expressions of fundamental biological and genetic differences. That worldview is structured by, and infused with, racism (Graves and Goodman 2021). With knowledge of human biodiversity and history, anthropologists have demonstrated over and over again how wrong this worldview is, showing that there is much less genetic variation between populations than within them; there is no gene that codes for, or biological trait that defines, race or ethnicity. In scientific terms, humans are a single race; there are never clearly definable lines between physical traits in an actual population because variation is clinal; racial differences are culturally constructed upon arbitrary and shifting physical markers; the construction of racial typologies comes from a special way of sampling people and rarely describes an actual individual or group; morphological differences in humans are typically expressions of adaptability, not inferiority; and if there are any biologically more relevant ways to group humans, others, such as blood type or immunity, are much more consequential in terms of bodily function. The latest biocultural research adds one more element to this body of knowledge: in spite of the fact that race has no biological or genetic origins, race can *become* biology through racism and racist systems that facilitate the embodiment of inequalities, dangerously reinforcing racialized understandings of human biology.

In order to appreciate the overall pattern of human biodiversity, it is important to put human biological and genetic diversity in context. That context is biocultural. As we have shown in this chapter, human populations do exhibit certain kinds of consequential biological and genetic variations between them, but those variations are set against a backdrop of remarkable genetic uniformity across our species. To decontextualize any specific variation from the evolutionary, cultural, social, ecological, political, and economic dynamics that also shape human experience can be misleading—supporting erroneous ideas, such as the one that DNA is destiny or that race is rooted in our biology—and leads to a woefully incomplete understanding of the human species.

KEY TERMS

Reviewing the Chapter

Chapter Section	What We Know	To Be Resolved
In what ways do contemporary humans vary biologically?	There is greater genetic variation within populations than between them, which is largely a function of gene flow between populations. Humans exhibit important physiological diversity, especially in immune responses that enable flexibility and resistance to disease in variable ways.	Given how much humans move around geographically and due to the influence of cultural factors on reproduction, it can be challenging to identify and define stable human populations in a biological sense.
Why do human bodies look so different across the planet?	Because our bodies interact most directly with the natural environment, morphological traits such as skin pigmentation and body shape, size, and stature can reflect evolutionary adaptations to certain environmental pressures. They also influence biocultural outcomes for individuals and populations.	One of challenges of describing and explaining variations in how people look is contextualizing how much those variations can pass through and be shaped by cultural, not strictly biological or genetic, filters.
Are differences of race also differences of biology?	There are no valid biological justifications for dividing people into racial groups. Race is a powerful cultural *and* scientific construction, in the sense that any certainties about it have to be actively built—constructed—on a set of assumptions that anthropology shows are flawed when applied to humans.	Some scientific and medical authorities continue to produce biologized accounts of racial difference, suggesting that anthropologists still have important and unfinished work to do in challenging efforts to naturalize race.
What biocultural consequences do discrimination and stress have on human bodies?	Social relationships and cultural attitudes shape biological processes and health outcomes through embodiment. For this reason, race can become biology through the embodiment of racial discrimination, stress, and other factors.	The biocultural dynamics and consequences of embodiment represent a relatively new area of anthropological research, and the specifics of those processes are still being worked out. Anthropologists are also grappling with how dynamics of embodiment can actually reinforce racialized understandings of human biological variation.

READINGS

In 2009 the *American Journal of Physical Anthropology* published a special issue entitled "Race Reconciled: How Biological Anthropologists View Human Variation" (139, no. 1). The ten articles provide comprehensive and relatively up-to-date perspectives on current anthropological thinking about human variation.

· ·

Human Biodiversity: Genes, Race, and History (New York: Aldine de Gruyter, 1995) by Jonathan Marks offers a witty perspective on the history of thinking about human variation and race.

· ·

Genetic Ancestry: Our Stories, Our Pasts (New York: Routledge, 2021) by Jada

Benn Torres and Gabriel A. Torres Colón, offers a sophisticated and up-to-date biocultural perspective on genetic ancestry.

Nina Jablonski's book *Skin: A Natural History* (Berkeley: University of California Press, 2006) is a fascinating and masterful exploration of the 300-million-year evolution of skin, with a specific focus on its place in human biology and cultural expression.

The American Anthropological Association project "Race: Are We So Different?" is a national initiative to educate about anthropological perspectives on race. Its online portal examines the history of the race concept, race and its relationship with human variation, and the lived experience of race: http://www.understandingrace.org/.

The story of Vermont's eugenics movement is told in Nancy Gallagher's book *Breeding Better Vermonters: The Eugenics Project in the Green Mountain State* (Hanover, NH: University Press of New England, 1999). It examines the ties of eugenics with progressive social reform and the shifting scope, limits, and meanings of eugenics in America.

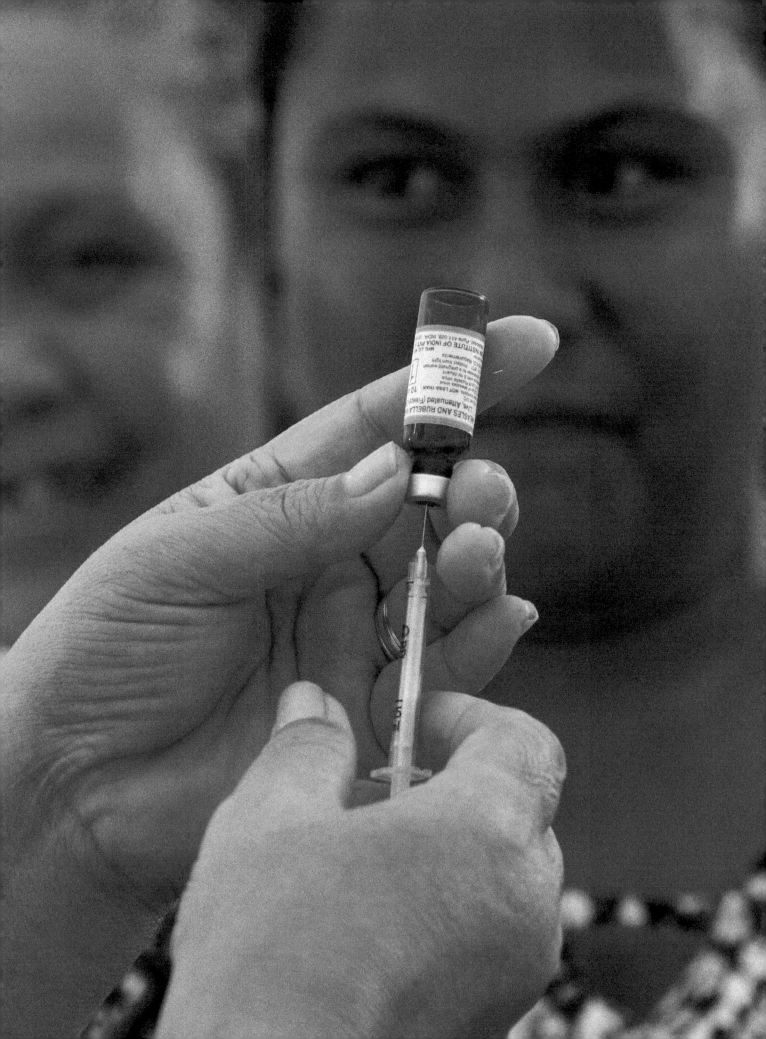

8

The Body

Biocultural Perspectives on Health and Illness

IN 2019, the central Pacific Island country of Samoa, with a population of less than 200,000 living on six relatively small islands, experienced a sudden outbreak of measles. Over 5,600 people were infected, and within six weeks more than eighty people had died, most of them children under four years old. It was an unexpectedly serious development in a country where vaccination for measles had been generally widespread.

A vaccine is a small amount of dead virus, or its antibodies, injected into the body, inducing the development of enough antibodies that they would kill the invading virus if it were encountered later. In the case of measles, one or two vaccinations are usually sufficient to train an individual's body to resist any assault from the virus, and that resistance typically lasts a lifetime. Some vaccines—influenza, for example—need an annual booster since the virus mutates quickly. But measles, smallpox, and polio vaccines typically last a lifetime and only occasionally might require a booster. If 90 to 95 percent of the population is vaccinated, those who have yet to receive the vaccine—infants and young children, in particular—are generally protected because of "herd immunity," which occurs when the virus cannot establish a foothold in the population. In the United States, measles has been considered controlled because nearly every child is vaccinated before beginning school, and the vaccine is easy to administer, has few side effects, and protects nearly everyone vaccinated.

Vaccination Worries. A Samoan nurse administers measles vaccine to local people in Apia, Samoa. One spoiled batch of vaccine led anti-vaxxers to protest, discouraging families from vaccinating their children, and resulting in the deaths of many unprotected children.

This was true as well in Samoa, which had an annual vaccination rate ranging between 60 and 70 percent. But in 2018, the rate dropped to 31 percent because several infants died after receiving incorrectly prepared measles vaccinations. Anti-vaccine groups—known as "anti-vaxxers"—picked up this story and spread it through social media to support their claims that vaccines can kill and maim. Anti-vaccination sentiments and groups have existed since inoculations were developed in the late-1700s, but in recent years a loose collection of concerned parents, celebrities, conspiracy theorists, conservative politicians, and certain religious communities have effectively used social media to spread their views. In Samoa, an individual named Edwin Tamasese was an especially vocal anti-vaxxer, publicly discouraging families from getting their children vaccinated. Tamasese was not objecting to vaccines on traditional cultural grounds but on the basis of what he had read on the internet written by other anti-vaxxers.

Many Samoans lost confidence in their healthcare system and its vaccines. In the face of a spreading public health crisis, the Samoan government declared a state of emergency. It forced the closures of schools, cancellation of public gatherings including Christmas celebrations, and the quarantine of unvaccinated households, which were required to post red flags to indicate their possible contagion. It launched a door-to-door campaign offering free vaccinations and booster shots, and arrested Tamasese, for incitement to resist its orders. Samoa has one advantage in dealing with this national emergency. As a chiefly society, the traditional authority of the chiefs now rests in the hands of the national government, which is largely managed by people from chiefly families and commoners educated principally in New Zealand. Even as activists like Tamasese may have challenged the traditional authority of the chiefs (not to mention the knowledge and education of Western-trained staff of the Samoan Department of Health), people largely began to comply in deference to that authority and within weeks a vaccination drive successfully reached 95 percent of the population (Belluz 2019; Purtill 2019).

To understand this story of a measles outbreak, anti-vaxxer reactions, and government responses as a biomedical problem is simply insufficient. This story is also a cultural one. Even as this situation carries dire consequences for many families, it shows how cultural beliefs and social relationships always shape how people think of the body and its impairment. This is true as well with other epidemics, including the COVID-19 pandemic. As we would expect, different countries have approached the problem differently, and over-reactions or under-reactions by governments and communities in East Asia, North America, and Europe have shaped the pattern of spread of the disease in different countries.

Although we still don't know the long-term consequences of the COVID-19 pandemic, one thing is clear: as of this writing almost 7 million lives have been lost to the virus globally. All of our lives have been profoundly disrupted. Many of you have lost friends or relatives to the virus. Millions of Americans lost their jobs and livelihoods as a result of the virus. Educations was disrupted in diverse ways—including those of most of you, our readers.

Even though vaccinations began to be administered in most US states in December 2020, supplies were quite limited until the newly inaugurated President Biden and his COVID-19 Response team arranged to beef up production of vaccines and to regularize supplies of them in every state. As vaccine supplies became more ample, however, anti-vaxxers began to stir up controversy even more than they had previously done, although the vaccines had proven to be effective and safe against the several variants of the virus present in the United States. By spring 2021, as the delta variant of COVID-19 began to cause sharp rises in the number of infections, hospitalizations, and deaths, attitudes around vaccination had hardened to the point that some media commentators were viewing it—and politicians exploiting it—as one more flashpoint of the so-called culture wars in the United States. Anti-vaxxers have continued to claim erroneously that there have been many side effects, but such comments are based on misunderstandings of the data provided by the Center for Disease Control (CDC) or the Food and Drug Administration (FDA), both of which publish their reports for the public to read.

These observations about disease outbreaks lead us to the question central to this chapter: *How does culture influence our experience of health and illness?* We can answer this question by considering a number of related questions around which this chapter is organized.

How do biological and cultural factors shape our bodily experiences?

What do we mean by health and illness?

How and why do doctors, healers, and other health practitioners gain social authority?

How does healing happen?

How can anthropology help us address global health problems?

The Samoan measles epidemic and the ongoing COVID-19 pandemic show how anthropology has a great deal to say about health and illness. Anthropologists have developed useful tools for understanding the links between culture, reactions to disease, and how our bodies respond to disease. This chapter explores how anthropologists put that knowledge to work in addressing real-world health crises. Let us first consider how biology and culture jointly shape the experience of our bodies.

8.1 How Do Biological and Cultural Factors Shape Our Bodily Experiences?

Since at least the 1920s, anthropologists have struggled with questions about the relative importance of our human biology as compared with the profound effects that culture has on individuals in any community around the world. In the nineteenth century anthropologists like Edward Burnett Tylor (1871) and Lewis Henry Morgan (1877) thought that biology could explain why indigenous peoples in Africa, Australia, or the Americas had such modest technologies and tools to work with when compared with those of Europeans and white Americans. Their answer: the bodies and minds of "primitive" people were not as developed as those of people from European stock. For a number of decades after 1920, it looked as if culture could shape who and what people were (e.g., Mead 1928). But in recent years, especially since the emergence of genetics and DNA research as a prominent subfield of biology, it has appeared to many Americans as if it is "all in our genes" or our biological "hardwiring." From this perspective, biology, genes, or hormones can explain sexual orientation, criminality, IQ, wealth, education, and who becomes CEO of a Fortune 500 company.

Today, as should be clear to you after reading the preceding chapters, anthropologists are deeply skeptical of grandiose claims about biological destiny. This sort of "it's-all-in-your-genes-and-hormones" thinking is a cultural idiom our society uses to understand human nature, just as other societies use other idioms and metaphors to understand their own individual and collective selves. This is not to deny that biology plays a role in who we are as individuals, but our biology works with our culture to make us who we are and to determine what we can accomplish and which maladies we will experience. As we discussed in Chapter Three, a full appreciation of the human condition requires that we avoid thinking of ourselves as *either* cultural *or* biological (natural) beings, but through a paradigm that emphasizes humans as biocultural beings in whom biological, psychological, and cultural processes interact in complex ways.

The idea of human nature and bodily experience as something fixed in our biology has been central to Western European and American ideas about humanity for more than a century. The fundamental problem with this sort of understanding is that it simply cannot account for who gets sick, who succeeds in school or business, or how many other aspects of our lives and our identities develop. We examine why in the next two sections.

Uniting Mind and Matter: A Biocultural Perspective

- **Mind.** Emergent qualities of consciousness and intellect that manifest themselves through thought, emotion, perception, will, and imagination.

One place to mend the divide between biology and culture is in the human **mind**, the emergent qualities of consciousness and intellect that manifest themselves through thought, emotion, perception, will, and imagination. There is increasing biocultural evidence indicating that even our most basic cognition does not happen separately from our bodies. The human nervous system is a complex neurological network that reads and regulates chemical and biological conditions throughout the entire body, not just our thinking brains. Human biology sets certain broad outer limits that all humans share, but the actual character of cognitive processes differs from one individual to the next and across cultures because of the influence of external factors.

These external factors include social context and culture, with which the nervous system interacts through individual cognition. For example, culture shapes some basic aspects of perception. People growing up in societies with little two-dimensional art must learn how to understand photographs after first seeing them (Shore 1996). Cultural differences in perception suggest that mental development varies with cultural practices. Research has also demonstrated that the mental stresses people experience because of rapid social and political-economic change have physical and bodily consequences, including raising blood pressure, affecting our immunity to disease, and creating symptoms of fatigue or feelings of inadequacy (Dressler 2005). These mental stresses may accompany other biological impacts, including changes in diet, nutrition, and general health (Daltabuit and Leatherman 1998). The mind manifests itself through the whole person, throughout an individual's lifetime (Toren 1996).

Culture and Mental Illness

Studies of people with psychological problems across the globe have brought into question whether the psychological dynamics observed in Western countries are universal—that is, based purely in human biology. Numerous conditions, among them schizophrenia, anxiety, depression, attention deficit disorders, and narcissistic personality disorders, vary greatly in their incidence in different cultures, suggesting that culture has a profound effect on the ways humans think about their psychology and display mental disorders. Cross-cultural differences in how people from different backgrounds express even the most basic psychological and emotional processes and conditions have an important consequence: we have to approach mental illness in a culturally relative way.

- **Culture-bound syndrome.** A mental illness unique to a culture.

Psychological abnormality is always defined culturally because what is considered abnormal is based on socially accepted norms. Not all societies define the same conditions as psychologically abnormal, nor do they necessarily share the same mental illnesses. A well-known example of a so-called **culture-bound syndrome** (a mental illness unique to a culture) is *koro*, the condition unique to Chinese and Southeast Asian cultures in which an individual believes his external genitalia—or, in a female, nipples—are shrinking and even disappearing.

Societies can even change what they consider a disorder, homosexuality being one such example. Although today few Americans view same-sex sexual attraction as an illness, until 1974 American psychiatrists classified homosexuality as a mental disorder, and until 1990 the US Immigration and Naturalization Service used the classification of homosexuality as "abnormal" as a reason for excluding gay and lesbian immigrants.

Because different societies define mental illnesses differently based on distinctive cultural understandings of individual psychology, treatments differ accordingly. For example, on the Indonesian island of Bali, persons are not conceived of as isolated or indivisible, as we conceive of them in the West. Spirits and deceased ancestors commonly reside in individuals. Madness (*buduh*) can be caused by inherited factors, congenital influences, an ancestral or divine curse, or the blessings of gods (Connor 1982). The task of the village-level healer, called the *balian*, is to identify the specific causes of madness, which are usually related to some kind of social disruption or family conflict. The *balian* then resolves the conflict or disharmony in the family or neighborhood (Connor 1982) (Figure 8.1). Western psychiatry's approach, which often

Figure 8.1 Balinese *Balians*. Balians are ritual specialists and healers who use a mix of traditional herbs, prayers, and other rituals.

🌱 **Figure 8.2   Candomblé Mediumship.** In Brazil, where some 2 million people practice Candomblé, temples where rituals are carried out are managed by women priests, known as "mothers-of-saint," often with support from men priests ("fathers-of-saint").

involves isolating the individual through institutionalization or providing pharmaceuticals, would clearly be inappropriate, if not socially disruptive, in these circumstances.

Nevertheless, as documented in Ethan Watters's book *Crazy Like Us: The Globalization of the American Psyche* (2011), Western psychological terms, notions, and illnesses have been globalizing rapidly in recent years. For example, mental illnesses such as depression, anorexia, and post-traumatic stress disorder (PTSD) seem to now exist in places that have never had them before, such as Hong Kong, Sri Lanka, and Tanzania. Watters suggests that much of this is taking place because of the increasingly global flows of Western media and psychiatric practices as well as the expansion of pharmaceutical companies into new markets throughout the globe. Watters argues that such practices, which are usually based on an assumption of "hyper-individualism," destabilize indigenous notions and ways of treating mental illness in the social context.

We can bring these insights about psychological processes and mental illness beliefs even further with a biocultural approach that combines cultural and biological insights. Rebecca Seligman has conducted research on Candomblé, a spirit-possession religion in Brazil (Figure 8.2). Seligman asked a simple question: Why do certain people become spirit mediums and others do not? Biomedicine explains mediumship as a psychological disturbance with a biological basis, but it fails to explain how and why such a disturbance might express itself specifically through mediumship. The cultural approach argues that oppressed and marginalized individuals gravitate toward mediumship, but it fails to explain why not all dispossessed people become mediums (Seligman 2005).

Seligman found that there is no single pathway to mediumship, but the interaction of biological, psychological, and cultural factors plays a crucial role. Among these are a physiological ability to achieve dissociation (trance states); conditions of poverty and oppression that cause emotional distress, which is often experienced through bodily pain; and a cultural outlet and social role that rewards people who exhibit the qualities of mediumship. Seligman concludes that without this holistic perspective on a medium's experience, we cannot appreciate the complexity of how people become mediums.

Now that we have explained how even the most basic matters of human cognition and psychology are not simply the function of our biological hardwiring, we can productively understand more broadly how *all* matters of disease, health, and illness are powerfully shaped by culture.

THINKING LIKE AN ANTHROPOLOGIST: THE BODY

If individual psychology differs from one culture to another, what might this suggest about the academic and clinical disciplines of psychology in which most psychologists treat patients who are Americans? What might these psychologists consider when dealing with recent immigrants from Africa or Asia?

8.2 What Do We Mean by Health and Illness?

At first thought, health and illness seem to be straightforward concepts. Dictionaries often define *health* as the "soundness of body and mind" or as "freedom from disease," and *illness* as being "unhealthy" or having a "disease," "malady," or "sickness." The problem is that ideas like "soundness of body" and "malady" do not suggest any objective measure of when we have health and when it has left us. For example, most people feel sore after a hard workout at the gym, and many people have mild seasonal allergies and sinus conditions that rarely impair their daily lives but can be annoying. Are these people healthy?

The borderland between health and illness is more ambiguous than we might have originally assumed. This ambiguity results from two interlaced dynamics: the "subjectivity of illness," which is how people perceive and experience their condition on a personal level, and the **sick role**," the culturally defined agreement between patients and family members to acknowledge that a patient is legitimately sick. We consider each in turn.

• **Sick role.** The culturally defined agreement between patients and family members to acknowledge that a patient is legitimately sick, which involves certain responsibilities and behaviors that caregivers expect of the sick.

These issues are at the heart of medical anthropology, which is the subfield of anthropology that tries to understand how social, cultural, biological, and linguistic factors shape the health of human beings (Society for Medical Anthropology 2014). Doctors tend to focus on treating sickness and disease in particular patients, while public health officials have traditionally focused on preventing and controlling outbreaks of disease. Medical anthropologists look at the diverse aspects of illness, its prevention, and its treatment. At its core, medical anthropology begins with the fact that, as much as we might like health and illness to be objective categories, health and illness are subjective states.

The Individual Subjectivity of Illness

Illness is a subjective experience, but it is also shaped by cultural and social expectations. This insight is credited to sociologist Earl L. Koos, who in the 1940s conducted a classic study of attitudes toward health and illness in a mainstream American community he called Regionville. In his study, he interviewed thousands of ordinary Americans about being sick. For example, he asked one working-class woman about being sick, to which she replied:

> I wish I really knew what you mean about being sick. Sometimes I've felt so bad I could curl up and die, but had to go on because the kids had to be taken care of, and besides, we didn't have the money to spend for the doctor—how could I be sick? ... How do you know when you're sick, anyway? Some people can go to bed most any time with anything, but most of us can't be sick—even when we need to be. [Koos 1954:30]

This statement demonstrates both the subjectivity of illness and how health and illness are inherently linked to social behavior, the social context of any individual's life, and their expectations, not to mention social status or social position. When our symptoms impair us so much that we cannot effectively perform the normal social and economic duties expected of us—jobs, school, and, in this case, caring for our family—we can see that our social position within our families and communities affects how we understand and define health.

To understand when a particular symptom is considered significant enough to provoke someone to seek medical care, we have to understand the ordinary expectations

Figure 8.3   Undernourished Adolescent in Mali.
In Mali, undernourishment is caused by a heavy disease load as much as by poor nutrition in the diet.

of the people involved. In the United States, these expectations are linked to issues like social class, gender, age, the kind of work the person ordinarily performs, and the person's routine lifestyle. The poor and working class routinely work more physically, eat less healthy food, and pay less attention to their health concerns than wealthier people do. It is not that lower-class people do not care about their health, of course. They simply have less time for doctors' visits, work in jobs they could lose if they miss a day, and eat the least expensive foods, which, as we discuss in Chapter 14 ("Sustainability: Environment and Foodways"), are the processed foods made available by the industrial food system. And they often have less adequate health insurance or no health insurance at all. This latter problem was what Medicare has effectively addressed for seniors since 1965, and what the Affordable Care Act of 2010 has tried to tackle for less affluent and middle-income people without health insurance.

Numerous cross-cultural anthropological studies confirm that cultural background also shapes the subjectivity of illness. For example, anthropologist Katherine Dettwyler (2013) conducted research in Mali, a West African nation at the southern edge of the Sahara. There she observed high infection rates of schistosomiasis, a liver and bladder infection caused by a parasitic worm that lives in water. This worm enters the human body through the feet and legs, causing sores on the skin and internally releasing blood into the urine. Dettwyler found this condition so common in Mali that by puberty, nearly all rural men have blood in their urine. Instead of viewing red urine as a shocking symptom, as Americans would, Malians understood it as a normal condition typical of the transition to adulthood. For these adolescents, it meant they were becoming men, not that they had an infection (Figure 8.3).

If we think about the example that opens this chapter, we can see that cultural differences led West Africans to react quite differently to the 2014 Ebola outbreak than Americans did. When the outbreak started in West Africa, it took many weeks for people to understand what was happening and even longer before they recognized how dangerous Ebola was, largely because they had never had to deal with an Ebola epidemic before. Americans hadn't seen one of these epidemics either, but the media had been circulating alarming reports about the outbreak in West Africa for some time before the virus was identified in Dallas, and it had made the prospect of a similar outbreak in America sound possible and terrifying. Undoubtedly, the absence of twenty-four-hour news media in West Africa and the presence of it in the United States contributed to the different reactions to Ebola in the two regions. In addition, many younger Americans associated a potential Ebola outbreak with the type of zombie-virus apocalypse depicted in various films that were popular in North America at the time, an association uncommon among West Africans.

The "Sick Role": The Social Expectations of Illness

In all societies around the world, when a person is ill, there are expectations of how that person, as well as friends and family, should behave. For Americans, this typically means the sick person should not go to school or work, should stay in bed and rest, should be given chicken soup, and so on. But these patterns vary cross-culturally. One of this book's authors, Robert Welsch, experienced this kind of cultural difference while conducting field research in Papua New Guinea among the Ningerum people.

One day, Welsch noticed that his body ached all over and his forehead burned with a high fever. It was malaria. At first he retired to his bed to rest, but the fever turned into chills, followed by sweats and an even worse body ache. He took anti-malarial pills and aspirin, but the headache became so bad it was unbearable to lay his head on a pillow so he was forced to sit on the floor leaning against a wall in his simple bush-materials house. Like most Americans he wanted to be by himself and endure this agony alone, and he didn't want to have to entertain villagers in this state of discomfort, situated as he was an eight-hour walk from the nearest hospital.

But Ningerum villagers did not sit idly by. As Welsch's condition worsened, more and more of his friends in the village came by the house to sit and chat and smoke. He later realized that most people in the village attributed his sudden symptoms to sorcery: someone in the area had used magic to hurt him, and people expected him to die. If it was sorcery, there was nothing anyone in the village could really do for him, but nobody wanted to be accused of having caused his death. The only sure way to avoid suspicion of being a sorcerer was to demonstrate concern. Fortunately for everybody, by the eighth day, the fever broke, and the headache and body ache subsided. The villagers who had been keeping vigil for several days went back to their normal activities.

In this instance, the anthropologist and the villagers had very different ideas of how they expect patients and caregivers to behave. Anthropologists refer to these unwritten rules as "the sick role," or the responsibilities and expected behaviors of sick people by their caregivers (Parsons 1951). To be considered legitimately sick—rather than as malingering, or faking sickness—one must accept specific responsibilities and a new social role, which exempts one from one's ordinary daily roles and responsibilities such as school or work. Two key aspects of the sick role are to want to get well, and to cooperate with medical experts.

A great example of this phenomenon comes from many of our own childhoods. During cold and flu season in the winter, many schoolchildren feel under the weather and want to stay home. When a parent agrees to let his or her child stay home, the child may decide later in the day that it would be fun to go out and play in the snow. But "Dr. Mom" steps in with her authoritative zeal to explain that if you are sick enough to stay home, you are too sick to go outside to play. Playing outside does not demonstrate that you want to get well—which is a key aspect of American ideas of the sick role—and slipping out of the house in defiance of Dr. Mom's explicit orders to stay in bed is not compliance with her medical expertise (Figure 8.4).

Both of these responsibilities, wanting to get well and cooperating to do so, may simultaneously come into play in your own college classes. For example, after being absent from a class or especially an exam, a student may need to provide a note from a doctor or a clinic to prove that he or she was legitimately sick. This note also demonstrates that the student wanted to get better and sought medical care.

Welsch found that Ningerum people had a different sick role model, believing that if patients still enjoy a minimum of physical strength, they should themselves deal with the illness. For the Ningerum patient to get help with his or her care and treatment, the patient is obliged to display to family and friends precisely how sick and disabled he or she is. Patients convey this information through their actions or visible physical signs of illness rather than through their words. Startling symptoms such as fainting, bleeding, vomiting, shrieking, and sudden weight loss call family members to action. Ningerum patients can also display the severity of their condition by using props like a walking stick to limp cautiously across the village plaza, shedding clothing, refusing to eat, or smearing their chests and legs with mud and dirt. All these actions communicate to family and friends that the patient is sick, and (silently) demand that family members show their sincere concern for the patient. Not to do so would suggest that one was not sensitive to a relative's needs—indifference that, to the Ningerum, whose culture prescribes very close kinship ties, would suggest not being fully human.

Figure 8.4   Dr. Mom.
"Dr. Mom" expects her patient to remain in bed when staying home from school.

While culture shapes a community's expectations of the sick role, our medical schools and hospitals have created a culture of medicine that often leads to tensions between the views of professionals and those of lay people. These tensions often have to do with the social authority given to doctors that makes the relationship asymmetrical, a topic we consider next.

THINKING LIKE AN ANTHROPOLOGIST: THE BODY

The "sick role" concept works well for acute diseases like measles, bad colds, and chickenpox, when patients are expected to want to get better and to help in their own care by following medical advice. To meet these expectations, patients are often considered exempt from participating in ordinary social activities, and they are generally not blamed for causing their own sickness. Compare the sick role for an acute infection with that for a chronic condition like diabetes, chronic shortness of breath, or severe arthritis.

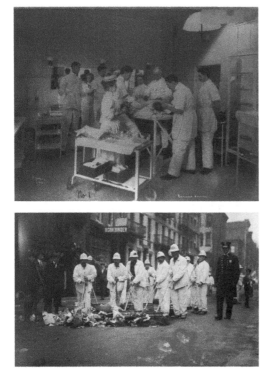

🌱 **Figure 8.5   Improvements in Public Health.** The use of antiseptics in the operating room made surgery much safer in the late nineteenth and early twentieth centuries, as suggested by this photo from 1900 (*top*). However, improvement in life expectancy came from better sanitation and hygiene across the United States, including the use of soaps to promote personal hygiene and the improvement of sewer systems. Large cities also began employing more street cleaners, such as the men shown in this photo from the 1890s (*bottom*). Note that the street cleaners wore white uniforms in an effort to convey a sense of cleanliness to the public.

8.3 How and Why Do Doctors and Other Health Practitioners Gain Social Authority?

Medical doctors in the United States have one of the most prestigious, respected, and well-paid occupations. The prestige and social authority doctors enjoy, however, are relatively new. Throughout most of the eighteenth and nineteenth centuries, American doctors had relatively low social status. Medicine was not sophisticated, and doctors often doubled as barbers. During the Civil War, surgeons were little more than butchers who amputated with large, dirty saws, using no antibiotics (the first, penicillin, was discovered in 1928), few painkillers, and no antiseptics (Starr 1982).

Many people assume that doctors gained prestige and authority because new medical discoveries and technologies improved their ability to heal people. Antibiotics like penicillin, for example, have made a huge difference in treating disease. But the major advances in health we take for granted today were mostly improvements in preventing diseases rather than curing them. Clean water, sanitation, and other public hygiene programs have saved more lives than doctors' treatments have (Figure 8.5). So how do we explain the social authority of doctors? Medical anthropologists have studied the social authority of healers in many societies. They identify several processes at work, the most important being the social processes that privilege the healers' perspectives over those of their patients, and the designation of otherwise normal conditions as health problems.

The sociologist Eliot Freidson (1970) was among the first to identify the professionalization of the field of medicine as responsible for giving the doctor's perspective privilege over the understandings of ordinary people. It is not that doctors necessarily knew more about what the patient experiences during an illness, but doctors had been trained to treat a wide variety of diseases. Subsequently, medical sociologist Paul Starr (1982) argued that during the twentieth century, medical doctors in the United States had used their professional status to increase their incomes, the level of respect they received from the public, and the exclusive right to determine the course of treatment for particular patients. American physicians formed professional associations like the American Medical Association, which allowed them to control how many new doctors were being trained. But while American physicians had achieved professional privileges, great respect, and high salaries, few of these perks were enjoyed by doctors in most other countries, which highlights the fact that social position is embedded in cultural meanings across many layers of society.

The Disease–Illness Distinction: Professional and Popular Views of Sickness

Around the world, patients often view their illnesses differently from how the doctors or healers who treat them do. In the Western world, patients often feel that their doctors do not understand the intensity of their pain and other symptoms. What frequently emerges is a clash of professional and popular (or layperson's) understandings that we call the "disease–illness distinction," in which doctors focus on **disease**, the purely physiological condition, and patients focus on **illness**, their actual experience of the disease (Eisenberg 1977) (Figure 8.6).

In our culture, the doctor, not the patient, has the greater authority in identifying and defining health and illness. Sociologist Eliot Freidson (1970:205) explains this authority as the result of a social process: "In the sense that medicine has the authority to label one person's complaint an illness and another's complaint not, medicine may be said to be engaged in the creation of illness as a social state which a human being may assume." American social structure also upholds the doctor's view as the officially sanctioned one. Because of the doctor's professional training, the hospital, governments, insurance providers, and, in extreme cases, even the courts recognize the diagnosis of the physician as legitimate. At the same time, the patient who has to live with the symptoms generally lacks any ability to authorize a prescription or treatment, or even offer an official diagnosis.

Understanding the distinction between doctors' and patients' perspectives is a key approach in contemporary medical anthropology. In the 1950s and 1960s, anthropologists typically accepted Western medicine as superior and authoritative in much the same ways that Freidson suggests. Anthropologists generally assumed that health problems in developing countries were often due to ignorance of medical knowledge and technology. A breakthrough came when Arthur Kleinman, a medical anthropologist and physician who conducted research in Taiwan, argued that the key to understanding such differences in perspective is that healers and patients often have different **explanatory models of illness**, which are explanations of what is happening to the patient's body. Kleinman asserted that the goal of medical anthropology research was not to decide who was right in their explanation but to accept that different people would come to the illness with different concerns and different kinds of knowledge.

Kleinman's approach also helped medical anthropologists realize the limitations of scientific knowledge, and they began

- **Disease.** The purely physiological condition of being sick, usually determined by a physician.

- **Illness.** The psychological and social experience a patient has of a disease.

- **Explanatory model of illness.** An explanation of what is happening to a patient's body, by the patient, by his family, or by a healthcare practitioner, each of whom may have a different model of what is happening.

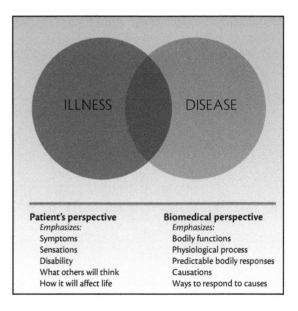

Figure 8.6 The Disease–Illness Distinction. Patients are concerned with the "illness": symptoms, how they feel, and how their activities are affected by these symptoms. Doctors tend to focus on the underlying causes of the symptoms that they speak of as "disease."

Anthropologist as Problem Solver
Heidi Larson: Vaccine Anthropologist

Medical anthropologist Heidi Larson is a professor at the Department of Health Metrics at the University of Washington. She is the founding director of the Vaccine Confidence Project (VCP), formed in 2010 to respond to increasing levels of vaccine hesitancy and outright resistance to vaccines around the world. Hosted by the London School of Tropical Medicine and Hygiene, the VCP has attempted to bring together medical anthropology and epidemiology to understand why anti-vaccine sentiments have emerged in so many parts of the world and how best to combat the widespread flow of inaccurate rumors that support the anti-vaccination movement.

Larson (2020) began her research in northern Nigeria in 2003. Here she observed that vaccine resistance was built on a collection of false rumors about the danger of taking vaccines, in spite of objective evidence of their safety. The situation in Nigeria demonstrated that once false rumors are established, government officials and healthcare workers had a hard time dispelling them, even when the rumors themselves were preposterous. For nearly two decades she observed that distrust of vaccines often emerged from people who are suspicious of many forms of authority—governments, science, and medicine—and in some cases people who are wary of past abuses by these institutions,

especially colonized peoples, minority groups, and others damaged by medical testing. But she and her research team found that in Nigeria and elsewhere, the more that civil authorities challenged these false rumors, the more they seemed to grow as people spread the untrue but scary rumors in ever widening social circles.

Larson wrote a book about this phenomenon—*Stuck: How Vaccine Rumors Start—and Why They Don't Go Away* (Larson 2020)—which went into production on January 28, 2020. Only two days later, the World Health Organization (WHO) declared that the novel coronavirus—which we all now know as COVID-19—had become a public health emergency. Although it was viewed by many as a controversial announcement, the WHO obviously made a correct determination, as the virus would go on to infect hundreds of millions around the globe and kill almost 7 million people worldwide, over 1 million of them Americans. At least 200,000 of those Americans died because of active vaccine resistance. With her book not yet published, Larson quickly shifted her attention to COVID-19, applying insights from her studies of the so-called swine flu (H1N1) vaccines in 2009 and historical accounts of a related influenza from 1918 (the "Spanish Flu" pandemic).

Larson has not solved the problem of how to stop false and harmful claims about vaccines in their tracks. But she has shown that an anthropological approach can help us understand how and why these false rumors spread, opening the door for creative solutions that involve public health officials, marketers, social media influencers, and others. The VCP's "Rumor Diagnostic Tool" built on anthropological interviews with hundreds of informants across the country and the world helps us understand this process of growing vaccine resistance, both in the case of COVID-19 and in the Samoan measles outbreak with which we began this chapter (Ofri 2021).

Questions for Reflection

1. Why do your friends tend to believe any account that supports a position or stance they have about some controversial topic?

2. Do these same friends dismiss as false any perspective that challenges these views?

3. How do these experiences help us understand why some people and groups of people have been so unwilling to get one or another of the several COVID-19 vaccines?

🔻 **Heidi Larson.**

TABLE 8.1 THE VACCINE CONFIDENCE PROJECT'S RUMOR DIAGNOSTIC TOOL		
I. Rumor Prompters (the "Triggers")	**II. Sustaining and Amplifying Factors**	**III. Outcome and Impact**
• Media and social disease reports	• Geographic spread	• Vaccine refusals (or other control measures)
• News research	• Frequency of rumor reported	• Vaccine is suspended (often more anxiety and rumors)
• New recommendation or new policy change	• Media reports	• Vaccine prevfentable disease outbreaks
• New product	• Historic bad experience that lowers public trust	
• Adverse event following immunization	• Socioeconomic marginalization	
• Political motivations	• Previous existence of self-organized community groups	
Source: National Academies of Sciences, Engineering, and Medicine 2017:48.		

to challenge whether the doctors always had such special and privileged knowledge. Perhaps the patient understood some aspects of his or her body that the physician did not, and perhaps could not, understand. We have already discussed the subjectivity of pain and other symptoms. But in addition, medical knowledge is constantly changing, so how could doctors always have all the answers for how to treat their patients?

We have seen this play out repeatedly during the COVID-19 pandemic, since medical researchers and practitioners were learning in real-time about the new virus, how to treat it, and how the vaccines responded to each new variant. People opposed to vaccine mandates and conservative politicians took advantage of this situation to challenge vaccines, mask-wearing, and other interventions made on the basis of medical authority. A growing number of medical anthropologists and biological anthropologists have offered insights into what is behind this resistance. Medical anthropologist E. J. Soba of San Diego State University challenges the notion of "vaccine hesitancy" itself. Soba suggests that the reasons why people in her community refuse to get one or another of the vaccines may not be "hesitancy" (in the sense of being motivated by political or ideological reasons to refuse the vaccine) as much as it is lack of information and resources about how to set up an appointment, where to get the vaccine in the first place, and whether it is truly safe. These reasons for hesitation tended to be found in lower-income neighborhoods, minority communities, and areas poorly served by medical facilities (Soba 2021a, 2021b).

For older people, television programs may be the most important source of information about epidemics and vaccines. For younger people (including college students), social media sources like Instagram, TikTok, and Twitter, are likely more significant sources of information. Twitter, in particular, seems to have played

Figure 8.7   Changing Views on Infant Formula and Breastfeeding. Dr. Benjamin Spock, in his time a highly respected pediatrician, published a series of books beginning in the late 1940s (*top*) that promoted giving baby formula rather than breast milk to infants. Since the 1970s, breastfeeding has had a resurgence in the United States after it became known that a mother's breast milk gives antibodies and partial immunity to infections to her baby (*bottom*).

a more important role in shaping anti-vaccine sentiments. One of the authors of this book, Agustín Fuentes and his colleague Jeffrey V. Peterson (2021), analyzed the role of Twitter in promoting vaccine misinformation and found that a small number of voices had an overwhelmingly important impact on shaping anti-vaccination sentiments. The confusion was made all the more prevalent because what we learned about COVID-19 has changed so often and in very significant ways. In the "Anthropologist as Problem Solver: Heidi Larson, Vaccine Anthropologist," we profile how one anthropologist took on the false claims and problems of misinformation swirling around vaccines.

Of course, what we have seen recently in terms of quickly changing scientific knowledge around COVID-19 does not happen in a historical vacuum. In other words, it has happened before, though in different contexts. For example, consider what the medical profession has advised about breastfeeding for infants. Breastfeeding was universal until the 1950s, when baby formula was first developed, and most American pediatricians began to promote formula as a technologically superior way to ensure the health of the baby. Many young mothers interpreted this advice to mean that their natural breast milk was inferior to mass-produced baby formula, a fact that began to be disproved by the 1970s, when new scientific analyses of the contents of breast milk indicated that breast milk contained antibodies that helped the child ward off infections. The majority of the baby boom generation were fed formula rather than breast milk, a trend that changed dramatically in the 1980s and 1990s. Rather than viewing breast milk as unsophisticated, the medical world began to see it as nature's way of protecting the child (Figure 8.7). Ironically, about the same time in many developing countries, international aid workers were promoting baby formula as a way of producing strong, healthy babies. But by the 1990s, it became clear that this practice was not ideal: babies became malnourished because their poor mothers could not afford enough formula, and where clean drinking water was scarce, mothers often had no choice but to use unsanitary water for their baby formula, resulting in much higher rates of fatal diarrhea.

With the spread of AIDS in the developing world, we now know that mothers infected with HIV can give the infection to their infants through breast milk. So, as a result, aid workers are once again, at least in communities where incidences of HIV infection are high, recommending baby formula although with greater emphasis on ensuring it is mixed with safe water. This contrasts sharply with advice to Third World mothers in the 1960s and 1970s when aid workers almost uniformly recommended baby formula, even when clean fresh water was hard to come by. Who knows where the science of breast milk will settle in another generation? As with nearly every other aspect of medicine, few scientific facts have remained, or will remain, static.

Since medical knowledge is constantly changing, it is no wonder that new diseases and drugs to treat them are constantly emerging. One way this knowledge changes is when the professional medical system casts its net of authority out farther, to cover conditions that were not previously understood as medical problems.

The Medicalization of the Non-Medical

Over the past fifty years, the healthcare industry has expanded dramatically, taking over more and more of our individual personal concerns. It has done so by redefining certain social, psychological, and moral problems as medical concerns. This process of viewing or treating as a medical concern conditions that were not previously understood as medical problems is called **medicalization**.

Alcoholism is a good example of this phenomenon. Excessive use of alcohol has been a problem throughout the history of the United States, producing opposition to it in the form of the temperance movement in the nineteenth and early twentieth centuries, and Prohibition (with the Eighteenth Amendment to the Constitution outlawing alcohol) in the 1920s. For a long time, alcoholism was seen as a moral failing that caused (usually) men to abandon their jobs and families (Figure 8.8). By the 1980s, psychiatrists, health-maintenance organizations (HMOs), and health insurance companies began to view alcoholism as a disease, defined as "recurrent substance use resulting in failure to fulfill major role obligations at work, school, home" (American Psychiatric Association 1994). Defining alcohol abuse as a disease, rather than as a crime, socially inappropriate behavior, sinful behavior, or moral failing, reclassifies it as a medical concern.

Three major reasons have been suggested for medicalizing the non-medical. The first is financial: pharmaceutical companies, hospitals, and insurance companies stand to make larger profits when they can define a new disease for which they can provide treatment, care, and coverage. A second explanation is that medicalization enhances the social authority of physicians. A third explanation concerns Americans' current preference for viewing social problems in scientific rather than moral or social terms.

Up to now, we have largely considered how people and their professional healers make sense of and diagnose illness. But a key aspect of the illness experience has to do with how the treatments we get for our illnesses actually help us heal. As with the distinction between health and illness, how the medicines and other treatments we receive help us heal is much more problematic than we might at first assume. It is to the matter of healing that we turn next.

- **Medicalization.** The process of viewing or treating as a medical concern conditions that were not previously understood as medical problems.

Figure 8.8 The Temperance Movement. Alcohol use was condemned as a moral failing by members of this early twentieth-century movement.

THINKING LIKE AN ANTHROPOLOGIST: THE BODY

Fifty years ago, alcoholism was considered a moral failing, a behavioral problem found when people have no strong moral code to live by and do bad things to their families and others. Compare this earlier understanding of alcoholism with the now-common view that alcoholism is a disease. How do you think this shift happened? What difference does this shift in thinking have on those who suffer from alcoholism?

8.4 How Does Healing Happen?

When Robert Welsch was studying healing practices among the Ningerum, one of his informants came down with malaria. Welsch offered him some antimalarial tablets, but his informant could not swallow them because they tasted bad. After several days of lying in bed, the man's nephew performed a traditional ritual, smearing clay on his uncle's painful chest, reciting magic words, and apparently removing from the sick man's chest a packet consisting of some small object wrapped in a banana leaf from the sick man's chest. Within two hours, the man was up and about with his walking stick, heading for the spring where he showered, a visible sign to everyone in the village, including the anthropologist, that he was feeling better (see Welsch 1983) (Figure 8.9).

To the Western mind, such examples of traditional healing strain credibility. But anthropologists around the world have observed similar responses to a wide variety of non-medical treatments. We do know that the human body is remarkably resilient. If we cut ourselves superficially while chopping vegetables, the wound will bleed, scab over, and gradually new skin will cover the cut. We do not fully understand how healing works, but we know that healing is more complicated than most Americans recognize. Healing is thus a complex biocultural process. Medical anthropologists generally accept that treatments help our bodies heal in four distinct therapeutic processes: (1) clinical processes, (2) symbolic processes, (3) social support, and (4) persuasion (Csordas and Kleinman 1996). We consider each of these processes next.

Figure 8.9   The Power of Non-Medical Healing. A Ningerum healer removes a magical packet from a man's leg by reciting magical words, rubbing magical leaves on the man's body, and sucking to relieve the pain in his leg.

Clinical Therapeutic Processes

Most medical professionals working with Western medicine assume that effective treatment comes from **clinical therapeutic processes**, which involve a doctor's observing a patient's symptoms and prescribing a specific treatment, such as a pill. The medicines involved in this treatment have some active ingredient that is assumed to address either the cause or the symptom of a disorder. One example is an antibiotic, which is thought to kill a type of bacterium. Another is a vaccination, which inserts a small amount of the virus or bacterium—usually already dead—into the blood, triggering the body's immune system to react by creating antibodies so the body can fight off the infection in the future.

Sometimes doctors understand how these physiological processes work, such as with vaccines; at other times they may not understand the healing process but assume that it works by some plausible but unproven process. Whatever the case, for medical anthropologists and medical researchers there is still more to understand because

• **Clinical therapeutic process.** The healing process that involves the use of medicines that have some active ingredient that is assumed to address either the cause or the symptom of a disorder.

these clinical processes do not account for healing such as in the Ningerum case presented earlier.

Symbolic Therapeutic Processes

In most tribal societies that medical anthropologists studied in the twentieth century, there were some treatments that used herbs, teas, and potions. The explanatory models used in these societies sometimes drew on clinical models, but often the herbs and potions were important not so much for their chemical properties as for their symbolic ones. Although the chemical composition of the herb or potion might help the patient heal, people were largely unaware of these properties and used them in rituals for other reasons that usually tapped into their symbolic associations.

In such cases, healing rituals act as a **symbolic therapeutic process** by virtue of their role in structuring the meanings of the symbols used. The symbolism of healing rituals comes from a number of sources, invoking our olfactory senses and our senses of taste and touch. It can also involve chanting, drumming, singing, and other sounds that create particular moods. Typically, the rituals provide a symbolic temporal progression, as in the form of a mythological story, that the affliction is supposed to follow for the patient to recover and heal.

For example, the French anthropologist Claude Lévi-Strauss (1961) documented a healing ritual among the Kuna [**koo**-nah] Indians of Panama in which, over a period of many hours, the shaman sings, produces smells, and touches a woman in the midst of a difficult birth. The ritual chanting recounts a mythological story in which a child overcomes diverse obstacles to reach its goal. These things relax the mother and her baby so the child can emerge from the womb, just as the hero of the story reaches his final goal. Medical anthropologists Thomas Csordas and Arthur Kleinman (1996) suggest that this kind of ritual is very common around the world because so many societies have found it efficacious.

> • **Symbolic therapeutic process.** A healing process that restructures the meanings of the symbols surrounding the illness, particularly during a ritual.

Social Support

The **social support therapeutic process** involves a patient's social networks, which typically surround the patient, much like Welsch's experience among the Ningerum. Although relatives and friends may perform some (usually) minor treatments on the patient, the major thrust of this therapeutic process comes from the presence of family members who provide comfort and aid to the sick person. Feeling aided and supported by his or her relatives may affect the patient's bodily functions. For example, diabetics often have better control of their blood sugars when they are with supportive family members, but poorer control when feeling isolated.

> • **Social support therapeutic process.** A healing process that involves a patient's social networks, especially close family members and friends, who typically surround the patient during an illness.

Persuasion: The Placebo Effect

Persuasion is another powerful therapeutic process. Consider the **placebo effect**, in which a patient is given a non-medicine as if it were a medicine. The classic example of a placebo is a sugar pill given instead of some prescription drug with an active pharmaceutical ingredient. What makes it a placebo is that the sugar pill has a beneficial effect, even though it has no pharmacological or clinically active component. Usually, patients are told that they will receive a powerful medication or procedure, even though they will actually receive the placebo. This strategy, however, worries many people, including doctors, because it amounts to lying to a patient; dispensing placebos challenges professional ethical codes of behavior and even some federal laws in the United States.

> • **Placebo effect.** A healing process that works by persuading a patient that he or she has been given a powerful medicine, even though the "medicine" has no active medical ingredient.

Up to now, it has been hard to explain the placebo's effect clinically, since the placebo seems to work through persuading the patient that the drug is effective. Something must be happening within the patient's body, but it seems to lie outside the bounds of ordinary medicine.

A dramatic illustration of the power of the placebo effect comes from a French study conducted in the 1990s. In this study, researchers divided a group of hospitalized cancer patients with mild to moderate cancer pain into four groups to test the effectiveness of naproxen, at the time a new painkiller that many people now know by the brand name Aleve. None of the patients experienced so much pain that they required opiates, and the study put none of the patients in significant distress. First the patients were randomly assigned to one of two groups as they came out of cancer surgery. One group was told they would be in a random trial of a powerful new pain reliever and would receive either the test drug or an inert placebo. The second group was told nothing. Members of this second group were unaware they were in a test and would assume that they were receiving standard hospital care. Half of the patients in each group were randomly given either an inert placebo or naproxen, thus creating four groups in all. Nurses, who were unaware of the details of the study, asked patients to evaluate their pain reduction hourly using a pain scale from 1 to 100 that represented the pain they experienced (Bergmann et al. 1994; Kaptchuk 2001).

All the patients given naproxen showed a reduction in pain, confirming that naproxen is an effective painkiller. But patients who were given the placebo and told they were in the study had greater pain relief than those who were given naproxen but were told nothing about their pain treatment regimen. Figure 8.10 illustrates this study's findings. Even more remarkable: this study suggests something that most researchers were not anticipating and had not appreciated. Figure 8.10 shows the large gap in experiences of pain relief between the two groups who were given naproxen. Theoretically, if

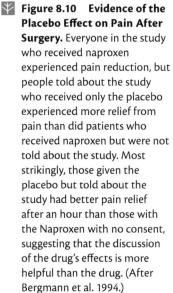

Figure 8.10 Evidence of the Placebo Effect on Pain After Surgery. Everyone in the study who received naproxen experienced pain reduction, but people told about the study who received only the placebo experienced more relief from pain than did patients who received naproxen but were not told about the study. Most strikingly, those given the placebo but told about the study had better pain relief after an hour than those with the Naproxen with no consent, suggesting that the discussion of the drug's effects is more helpful than the drug. (After Bergmann et al. 1994.)

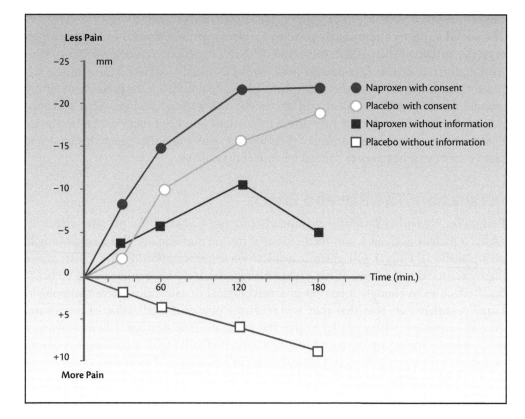

we assume that naproxen works physiologically, both groups should have experienced similar levels of pain relief. But they did not; the placebo effect enhanced the pain relief in the test group who received naproxen and were told they were in the trial. In other words, those patients in the test group knew they were in the study and expected to get good results from their painkiller. What this tells us is that the placebo effect probably enhances all clinical interventions, whether they are pharmaceuticals, surgeries, or other procedures. When patients *believe* that a pharmaceutical or medical procedure is effective, they regularly see improvements.

The insight that culture and social processes influence the healing process is a powerful insight of medical anthropology. So how do anthropologists put such insights to work? We consider this question in our last section.

THINKING LIKE AN ANTHROPOLOGIST: THE BODY

The naproxen study demonstrates the power of the placebo effect. Discuss what this study might mean for a doctor prescribing a "powerful" antibiotic or some brand-new treatment for a condition in a patient he or she sees in his or her clinic.

8.5 How Can Anthropology Help Us Address Global Health Problems?

Anthropologists have long recognized that they can contribute to alleviating global health problems by understanding the healthcare systems available to different peoples around the world, how diseases are transmitted within and between communities, and how people use the resources available to them. In recent years, anthropologists have also become more engaged and proactive in trying to improve health conditions in the communities, countries, and regions in which they work. We explore both of these themes—understanding and actively addressing global problems—below. In "A World in Motion: Medical Tourism and Yemen" we consider how the high cost of healthcare has caused problems in poor countries that are different from those in the wealthy countries but are nevertheless problems confronting people needing care.

Understanding Global Health Problems

For a number of decades now, it has been widely assumed that Western medicine will fix the world's health problems, and that any role for a discipline like anthropology in explaining different cultural systems of healthcare is largely irrelevant. After the eradication of smallpox in 1979, the World Health Organization (WHO) believed that eradication of polio and other infectious diseases was simply a matter of time. But as AIDS and other public health crises spread worldwide, and even polio proved more intractable than researchers had expected, medical anthropologists increasingly saw the need to increase their involvement in understanding what have rapidly become global health problems. We explore two issues here: medical pluralism and patterns of disease transmission.

A World In Motion
Medical Tourism and Yemen

Medical tourism is an increasingly important form of global travel. The common stereotype is of wealthy people from the global North seeking cosmetic surgery in some tropical or subtropical country with recovery at a swanky beach resort. But consider this situation, as described by anthropologist Beth Kangas (2010), about a Yemeni teacher named Aisha. At a routine medical checkup, Aisha was shocked to learn she had a cancerous tumor in her breast, as she had not felt any symptoms. Her husband worked for an oil refinery company, and at the refinery hospital a doctor decided to remove her breast immediately. But because Yemen has no radiology facilities the company sent Aisha with her husband to Jordan for chemotherapy. The suddenness of events was overwhelming and distressing, but of special concern to Aisha was that her family was poor and vulnerable—as she said, "[My husband's] income and my income, it's nothing. We just live hand to mouth" (2010:345)—and that her treatment could not be finished if the company sent them home at the end of her husband's one-month leave.

Aisha's experience captures a lot of the raw emotions, worries, and uncertainties that accompany cancer anywhere, but the fact that her country lacks advanced medical facilities to treat it—not to mention other intricate medical treatments like organ transplantations and heart surgeries—further complicates matters. What drives Americans to travel internationally for healthcare is affordability, and for Canadians and British it is access to a more timely procedure. But for people in poor countries like Yemen, who also travel internationally on medical journeys, it is to access the expertise, equipment, and procedures that Americans, Canadians, and British are bypassing in their own countries (Kangas 2010:347).

After three years conducting ethnographic research among dozens of Yemenis making international medical journeys, Kangas found that these kinds of particularities and differences are important for developing a critical understanding of this border-crossing activity. At the same time, she has also found that there were some consistent issues that drive these journeys no matter the individual and their country of origin. These include the following factors (Kangas 2010:348):

- Medical journeys involve commonplace logistics of selecting a treatment destination that is perceived as likely to be successful
- Medical travelers are motivated by a desire to alleviate the patient's suffering
- Care involves technological procedures not available locally
- Travel is necessitated by the host country's inability to provide adequate care
- These medical journeys occur within a common global arena, involving circulation of global finances, global consumerism, international transportation, and modern international communication

According to Kangas, there are a lot of labels attached to this global phenomenon—"medical tourists," "global elites," etc.—but the power of medical anthropology is to humanize the actual people, like Aisha, who are making these journeys. It also carries the potential to explain the expectations and perceptions that individuals bring with them to other countries in order to improve the care they receive.

Understanding Medical Pluralism: Comparing Different Healthcare Systems

Medical anthropologists have long recognized that there are many sophisticated non-Western systems of medicine—in places like India, China, and the Arab world—that had been effective for centuries before the medical systems of the United States and Western Europe had developed antiseptics, antibiotics, and vaccines. As India, China, and the Arab world began to establish modern industrial societies, their healthcare facilities were integrating Western medicine with traditional practices.

Medicine was not replacing these ancient traditions, but supplementing them. Nearly all other societies draw on more than one medical tradition simultaneously, a concept called **medical pluralism**, which refers to the coexistence and interpenetration of distinct medical traditions with different cultural roots.

An example of medical pluralism comes from anthropologist Carolyn Nordstrom (1988), who studied Ayurveda, a traditional medical system developed in India and Sri Lanka. Ayurvedic practitioners diagnose health problems using the classical Ayurvedic practice of reading the pulse, and they mix herbs in specified ways. But practitioners also draw upon traditional Sinhalese (referring to the people of Sri Lanka) medical ideas and practices in what Nordstrom refers to as a mediation of Ayurveda and local Sinhala medicine. She learned that practitioners often mix traditional Sinhalese herbal preparations along with those they have learned at an Ayurvedic college, and that many Ayurvedic healers frequently use stethoscopes and thermometers and dispense standard Western medicines along with their herbal preparations. She also observed that some Sinhalese Buddhist monks incorporated Ayurvedic and Buddhist principles in their therapeutic work, sometimes adding Sinhalese preparations as well (Figure 8.11).

The broader point here is that in an increasingly globalized world, medical anthropologists are learning that all medical systems are now plural systems. Successfully addressing global health problems must take this fact into account.

- **Medical pluralism.** The coexistence and interpenetration of distinct medical traditions with different cultural roots in the same cultural community.

Understanding Patterns of Disease Transmission

Medical anthropologists have also played a key role in making sense of how infectious diseases spread within a population, which is as much an anthropological or sociological task as it is a medical one. For example, anthropologists have played a key role in helping researchers understand the transmission of HIV, the virus that causes AIDS. In the United States and Europe, public health officials have promoted the use of condoms to interrupt the spread of HIV. But promoting condoms has not proved so effective in several African countries, Haiti, and certain Southeast Asian countries, each of which had very different cultures of sexuality and patterns of transmission from that in the United States (see also Chapter 16, "Kinship and Gender: Sex, Power, and Control of Men and Women"). By studying these patterns of transmission,

Figure 8.11 Medical Pluralism. Modern Ayurveda often adopts elements from biomedicine.

anthropologists played a central role in helping medical researchers understand how culture was shaping HIV transmission.

In East Africa, for example, HIV was first noticed along major highway routes where male long-haul truckers became infected through sexual contacts with infected female sex workers, taking the infection to women in the next truck stop town (Nyamwaya 1993). Truck stops produced ideal conditions for transmission of HIV because they provided a meeting place for truckers and sex workers who had connections to wide-ranging and international social networks. Anthropologist and geographer Ezekiel Kalipeni (2004) suggests that epidemiologists and medical researchers had completely missed seeing these patterns. He argues that medical researchers explained the observed distribution of cases in terms of traditional patterns of African sexuality. Traditional culture was demonized, and the appearance of modern lifestyles, population growth, social inequality, and mounting poverty that was sending villagers in many African countries to urban centers and new forms of employment all went ignored. Anthropologists provided detailed observations of people's ideas about the disease and their explanatory models as well as specific information about the sexual practices and behaviors of women and men, helping illuminate the patterns of HIV transmission (McGrath et al. 1992; Nyamwaya 1993).

Anthropological Contributions to Tackling the International HIV/AIDS Crisis

As their understanding of global health problems has become more sophisticated, anthropologists have become more assertive in putting their ideas to work. One way they do this is by working with communities to design aspects of the public health system to meet the needs, understandings, and cultural expectations of people in the community. To continue with the example of the HIV/AIDS crisis, we examine the work of Paul Farmer.

Using anthropology's holistic perspective to understand communities and their social problems, anthropologist and physician Paul Farmer (1992) began research for his dissertation in Haiti. As an undergraduate, Farmer had majored in anthropology at Duke University. In 1983, before beginning medical school at Harvard, he spent some time in Cange, a community in the mountainous central plateau of Haiti. In this extremely poor area, he could see firsthand that the social, economic, political, and health problems were interconnected. Farmer saw these connections before HIV/AIDS had been identified and before large numbers of HIV/AIDS cases had been diagnosed in Haiti. When the HIV/AIDS epidemic broke out, the connections between the health of Haitians and socioeconomic and political conditions became even more obvious.

Working with another MD-PhD student, Jim Yong Kim, who went on to head the World Bank (see Chapter 13, "Economics: Working, Sharing, and Buying"), Farmer helped found an organization in the highland district of Cange in 1987. They called this organization Partners in Health (2010) and developed a small health center. The international health community was initially focused on treating HIV/AIDS patients and on dealing with other public health concerns to slow the spread of HIV/AIDS. But Farmer and Kim had larger goals that they saw as related to health in the Haitian community. They began encouraging local people to plant trees in the once-lush forested region that had been devastated by poverty and rapid population growth, which led to deforestation as poor Haitians turned to their last resource (trees) to make into charcoal. Farmer and Kim put together an integrated program that attacked the causes of poverty and environmental degradation as a way of improving health. After twenty years of execution of this program, Farmer and Kim saw the district returned to something like its lush original environment, along with solid improvements in local health (T. Kidder 2003). In the Classic Contributions box we explore how the late Paul Farmer tried to address some of these problems in his now-classic study of AIDS in Haiti.

Classic Contributions
Paul Farmer and the Effort to Situate Global Health Problems in an Anthropology of Suffering

PAUL FARMER, WHO died suddenly of a heart attack in March 2022, while treating patients at his health center in Rwanda, was both a physician and a medical anthropologist best known for his pioneering research on AIDS in Haiti and for co-founding Partners in Health. Along with another co-founder, Jim Yong Kim, who was also a getting his MD-PhD at Harvard (see Chapter 13), Farmer was a student of Arthur M. Kleinman, who had modernized medical anthropology in the late 1970s by emphasizing the role that patients' understandings of their bodies play in shaping their response to symptoms. Farmer's medical anthropology is noteworthy in that it situated these understandings of illness that Kleinman had called "explanatory models" of an illness, in the context of a community, its expectations of health and health outcomes, and the difficult experiences of suffering shared by large parts of these underserved communities. We get an early view of Farmer's position from his best-known book on the HIV pandemic in rural Haiti, *AIDS and Accusation: Haiti and the Geography of Blame* (1992:xi–xii, 253). Although HIV/AIDS is no longer the scourge it was when Farmer wrote these words, this passage seems as relevant to the Ebola epidemic of the early twenty-first century in West Africa and the global pandemic of COVID-19 today. Our ability to confront novel health crises depends on social, economic, and healthcare systems that were not originally designed to provide appropriate care to everyone in a community.

Paul Farmer.

A central thesis of this book is that the world pandemic of AIDS and social responses to it have been patterned by the social arrangements described in the historical chapters [of this book]. ... If there has been, among my informants, any consensus about the meaning of AIDS, it has been that the biological and social effects of this new scourge have to be examined in the light of past misfortunes. ...

Indeed, poverty is the central fact of life for most rural Haitians. To live in a village is to witness the struggles of the poor as they confront the deepening economic crisis that currently grips Haiti. Anthropological research conducted there is inevitably mired in a world of want, and ethnographic texts should reflect the hunger and fear and sickness that are the lot of most Haitians. But describing suffering, no matter how touchingly, is not a sufficient scholarly response to the explanatory challenges posed by the world pandemic of HIV disease. AIDS in Haiti fits neatly into a political and economic crisis, in ways that demand explication—patterns of risk and disease distribution, social responses to AIDS, and prospectives for the near future are all illuminated by a mode of analysis that links the ethnographically observed to historically given social and economic structures. Our ability to confront and prevent HIV infection in a humane and effective manner demands a holistic understanding of this new sickness.

Anthropology is uniquely equipped to investigate a new disorder, but the anthropological study of AIDS should be more than a search for "cultural meaning," that perennial object of cognitive and symbolic inquiry. [Paul Farmer 1992:xi-xii, 253]

Questions for reflection

1. In what ways is the recent COVID-19 pandemic similar to the HIV-AIDS epidemic of the 1970s and 1980s? How is it different?

2. In the United States some communities have objected to mask mandates and vaccine mandates as ways of fighting this novel corona virus. How might these responses be understood in terms of Farmer's quest for a holistic understanding of both the disease and the social and cultural context in with it emerges?

THINKING LIKE AN ANTHROPOLOGIST: THE BODY

Medical anthropologists have traditionally been involved in public health efforts to vaccinate children, to provide clean drinking water, and more recently to assist with combating pandemics. Why would such public health efforts be a natural role for anthropologists, rather than involvement in clinical settings that include physicians and their patients in modern urban settings?

Conclusion

This chapter's focus on issues of our bodies reflects what most of us feel, implicitly, is the most natural part of our beings. But how we understand our bodies and minds and how we make sense of impairments to them are inevitably shaped by the culture we have grown up in and by the concerns and preoccupations people around us have. Whether we are considering chronic pain, psychological issues like PTSD, or infectious diseases like Ebola or HIV, the cultural expectations of the community always shape people's responses to any illness condition.

As we saw with the 2019 outbreak of measles in Samoa, discussed in the chapter opener, people living in different cultures, with varying views and cultural expectations, react differently to essentially the same set of facts. In an effort to protect their citizens, different national leaders approach problems of health and epidemics somewhat differently, because in each case it is not the virus or the epidemiology but the local cultural assumptions that shape these leaders' actions. Arresting an anti-vaxxer for his anti-social behavior may seem culturally unacceptable to most Americans, whereas in Samoa it is deemed appropriate because of cultural attitudes toward traditional authorities. No matter which society we examine, when individuals become ill, the society responds in locally meaningful and appropriate ways, whatever the signs, symptoms, and implications of those illnesses may be.

Recent research even suggests that our bodies respond according to our expectations about the effectiveness of a treatment. Western physicians have dismissed such responses as merely the "placebo effect," but for millennia, societies have looked after their sick with herbs and local rituals that seem to bring relief to the sick.

The research medical anthropologists are conducting today comprises some of the most important applied projects in the discipline. But these research projects have demonstrated that global health concerns and modern epidemics are much more than medical problems. Like everything else in life, health and illness are linked to the kinds of society we live in, our biology, the historic traditions that have motivated and shaped our communities, and the meaning and significance we give to these biological and social facts. These biocultural linkages taken together are what make us human.

KEY TERMS

Clinical therapeutic process
    p. 232

Culture-bound syndrome   p. 221

Disease   p. 227

Explanatory model of illness
    p. 227

Illness   p. 227

Medical pluralism   p. 237

Medicalization   p. 231

Mind   p. 220

Placebo effect   p. 233

Sick role   p. 223

Social support therapeutic
    process   p. 233

Symbolic therapeutic process
    p. 233

Reviewing the Chapter

Chapter Section	What We Know	To Be Resolved
How do biological and cultural factors shape our bodily experiences?	Biocultural perspectives and evidence are breathing new life into classic anthropological interests in cognition, psychologies, and our bodily experiences, suggesting that "human nature" is not a singular condition.	Anthropologists continue to debate how the cultural variability around psychology, emotions, and mental states relates to biological and other psychological processes.
What do we mean by health and illness?	A person's culture shapes his or her interpretation of symptoms and understanding of the illness condition.	How people in any particular society will interpret the symptoms of illness can be determined only by detailed evidence from illness episodes in a particular society.
How and why do doctors and other health practitioners gain social authority?	By dealing with human concerns as medical or biomedical problems, our society implicitly gives power to health practitioners who can prescribe drugs and other therapies.	It is not entirely clear why some peoples around the world are so ready and willing to give authority to healers, while people in other societies are not willing.
How does healing happen?	Not all healing can be explained by the clinical processes familiar to physicians and medical students. Healing has important social and cultural dimensions.	While the power of the placebo effect is demonstrated, we still don't understand why it can work on our bodies.
How can anthropology help us address global health problems?	Clinical solutions to global health problems cannot work effectively without an understanding of the local culture of the people whose health-related behavior we want to improve, as well as the fact that, due to medical pluralism, most societies combine distinct healing systems.	Up to now, there has been no single solution to a health problem that will work in all societies; it is not clear if there are general strategies applicable to most societies.

READINGS

One of the most accessible ways that students can enter the world of medical anthropology is through Katherine Dettwyler's *Dancing Skeletons: Life and Death in West Africa*, 2nd ed. (Prospect Heights, IL: Waveland Press, 2013). Dettwyler's narrative gives students a sense of what it is like to be a medical anthropologist in a developing country. Anne Fadiman's *The Spirit Catches You and You Fall Down: A Hmong Child, Her American Doctors, and the Collision of Two Cultures* (New York: Farrar, Straus & Giroux, 1997) offers a glimpse into the tensions between American biomedical culture and an Asian immigrant medical culture, which is as religious as it is medical.

Arthur Kleinman's classic *Patients and Healers in the Context of Culture: An Exploration of the Borderland Between Anthropology, Medicine, and Psychology* (Berkeley: University of California Press, 1980) provided the first modern formulation of medical anthropology as a systematic branch of anthropology, complete with a methodology that could help us understand interactions between patients and healthcare providers, whether the latter are doctors, traditional healers, New Age consultants, or neighbors. Mary-Jo DelVecchio Good, Paul E. Brodwin, Byron J. Good, and Arthur Kleinman's edited volume *Pain as Human Experience: An Anthropological Perspective* (Berkeley: University of California Press, 1992) explores how medical anthropologists can study the problem of chronic pain using approaches previously suggested by Kleinman.

Paul Farmer's book *Pathologies of Power: Health, Human Rights, and the New War on the Poor* (Berkeley: University of California Press, 2004) offers an approach to issues of access to healthcare resources in a variety of contexts around the world, showing how access to healthcare is as important as the way patients and healers understand illness.

PART III

Humans and Their Material Worlds

Human social relations are characterized by interdependence, intensive cooperation, and sharing, all of us as individuals relying on others to meet our basic needs. Our capacity for social cooperation has undoubtedly been one of the critical reasons for the evolutionary success of the human species. That success is also the result of how we interact with and transform the material world by exploiting and reorganizing it to suit our interests and needs. Until 7,000 or so years ago, most prehistoric human groups met the challenge of living in society and nature in more or less the same ways, living in small face-to-face groups, using simple technologies and collective efforts to gather and hunt what they needed to survive. When people began to grow their own food and create more complex social formations, social relations underwent a radical shift. The formation of larger village settlements and later cities and states brought with them various forms of social inequality, and social relations between and among communities underwent significant change. Yet these processes were not uniform, and since that time, matters of feeding, provisioning, organizing, and controlling people have varied greatly across our species, each form or social arrangement bringing with it distinctive consequences for the actual lives that all individuals in the community will lead. Archaeology is the subfield of anthropology that specializes in understanding the details of how these historical processes have played out around the world.

We begin this part with a Methods Memo exploring how archaeologists excavate and identify the material objects they use to understand those historical processes. What follows is a chapter on how archaeologists think about and use material objects to study human lives, which effectively renders anthropology as not "simply" the study of people but also the intertwining of people and material objects. In preparation for the chapter that comes next, we insert another Methods Memo on a pervasive dating technique used by archaeologists, Carbon-14 analysis. The following chapter examines what archaeology has found out about why and how prehistoric humans shifted from living in small family groups based on lives of gathering and hunting to producing their own food. Another Methods Memo follows, focusing on how archaeologists analyze and interpret the material evidence they find in their excavations. This part concludes with a chapter on the story of how, why, and when larger scale social groupings emerged. In these communities social complexity—understood as inequalities of power and social hierarchy—took shape.

METHODS MEMO

What Field Methods Do Archaeologists Use to Study the Human and Environmental Past?

One of the central challenges of archaeological research is finding useful, interesting, and important sites from which to study past lives and landscapes. When archaeologists find great monuments, tombs, or the ruins of temples and palaces, it seems pretty clear where the work is going to take place. But knowing where to conduct research does not usually begin with the presence of large structures, and anyway, most interesting materials for archaeological analysis are usually hidden underground and require careful excavation. The archaeological process actually begins with the questions an archaeologist or a team of archaeologists wants to answer. Once the researchers have a clear question in mind, they seek sites that will help answer these questions. Then they develop a plan for surveying, sampling, testing, and excavating within an area or region, using techniques that were largely developed in the early 1900s. Thanks to the use of new mapping and remote sensing technologies, archaeologists have been developing new field methods that are less invasive.

HOW DO ARCHAEOLOGISTS CONDUCT FIELDWORK?

Archaeological fieldwork is intellectually and physically demanding and requires excellent recordkeeping skills. Archaeological fieldwork can involve any of the following:

- **Ground surveys**. Archaeologists often begin by walking over an area that is divided into a grid pattern, collecting any artifacts they find scattered on the ground surface. The artifacts themselves are known as **surface collections**, and they rarely have any sort of systematic pattern because they have been moved around by farmers' plows, winds, heavy rains, or other

- **Surface collection.** A collection of pottery and stone artifacts made from the surface of the soil around a possible site.

- **Habitation sites.** A place where people lived at some time in the past, perhaps repeatedly over a number of seasons

- **Test pit.** A preliminary excavation, usually of a single 1 m × 1 m square (or a half meter square) to see if artifactual material exists at the site and to assess the character of the stratigraphy.

disturbances. For years, amateur arrowhead hunters have used a strategy of walking on agricultural fields after farmers plow them, looking for whatever artifacts are exposed. Professional archaeologists might do something similar, except they simultaneously note changes in soil color or texture, which can generate insight into ancient landforms. Such ground surveys also look for landscape features that might suggest how people might have used a site and the natural resources that surround it. As they walk the ground, archaeologists keep careful records about which fields and which parts of a field yielded which sorts of artifacts, saving the surface finds in plastic bags that prevent contamination from other specimens. Each bag needs to be marked by grid location and depth, usually written on a slip of paper kept inside the bag or a tag tied around its opening. Archaeologists know that if they find larger quantities of arrowheads and potsherds on a slight rise in a field, situated not far from a stream, they have likely identified a **habitation site**, a place where people lived at some time in the past, perhaps repeatedly over a number of seasons. There may have been some resource in the area, such as certain fruit or nut trees, wild berries, or some animal burrow or nest. Surface collections only tell us about what has happened on the uppermost few inches of the soil, surfaces that are still being acted upon by plows and the environment. If sedimentation has been active over an extended period, archaeologists may not find anything since the artifacts lie deeper in the soil. For example, at an Illinois site called Kampsville, near the famous site of Cahokia, a dog burial was found. Though it was originally a shallow burial, over time it was covered with more than twenty feet of sediment, which was runoff from an adjacent hillside. Some archaeologists advocated using heavy equipment to dig down to an interesting layer, but now most archaeologists feel such clearing does irreversible damage to the site and reject this strategy. Such an example illustrates the need to determine where the original surface was and how much sediment has covered the site over time.

- **Test pits and excavation**. When a potentially interesting site has been identified due to a concentration of surface objects, a few **test pits** are dug. These are

1m × 1m squares (or even squares that are 50 cm on each side) that will offer a sense of what this part of a site was used for, how many different periods of occupation are represented, and whether it was continuously or sporadically occupied. After several test pits, the archaeologists may determine the site suitable for addressing the research questions. Whether large or small, excavations are costly, usually requiring grant funding, and they are always destructive. They require considerable time and labor, both in removing soil from a pit and recording the location and position of every artifact uncovered. As exciting as opening up a new excavation may be, digging into the soil permanently destroys that part of a site for future researchers.

- **Visual documentation**. With the rise of digital photography, archaeologists conduct a comprehensive photo-documentation of each phase of the excavation as every layer is uncovered, soil profiles are revealed, and new artifactual material is revealed. Nineteenth- and early twentieth-century archaeologists were lax about recording subtle differences in soil characteristics, particularly when moving large quantities of dirt, such as when excavating some earthen mounds. Today, the same mound would be excavated far more carefully to document changes in soil color or composition, impurities, and the like. We often think of archaeology as about digging for artifacts, but twenty-first-century archaeologists are sensitive about excavating in less destructive ways.

- **Regional, aerial, and satellite surveys**. Some research projects are focused on understanding interactions between settlements across a broad region. Regional surveys, which involve surface collecting over a broad region, are standard practice for most archaeologists in the Americas. Typically, these regional surveys were preliminary to a major excavation at one or two locales within an area. More recently, the strategy has developed from being a preliminary step in fieldwork into a field of inquiry all its own. As the costs of excavation have risen, regional surveys offer two major advantages. It is much easier and less expensive to make surface collections over a broad region than to conduct in-depth excavations. Moreover, surface collecting is less destructive to potential sites than intensive excavating. A specific type of regional survey is aerial photography, which refers to any photographic survey made from the air.

Aerial photographs can be either vertical, from directly overhead, or oblique, shot from an angle. Each has its own distinct advantages, providing either a ground plan from overhead or revealing texture in the terrain from angle shots (Reeves 1936). Aerial photographs shot in sequence allow the archaeologist to view them stereographically (using pairs of photos with slightly different angles) to reveal the three-dimensional texture of landscapes. Recently, because of the easy accessibility of satellite imagery, aerial surveys have become a standard archaeological tool. These images do not reveal archaeological sites on their own, but they do allow archaeologists to interpret the textures and features in the imagery to identify evidence that human activity has altered some aspect of the natural landscape.

- **GIS**. The use of **Geographical Information Systems** (GIS) for mapping archaeological sites and regions is widespread in contemporary archaeology. GIS brings together many different databases of geographic information. Researchers map and digitize variables, such as vegetation, rocks, or geologic formations, onto different databases, several of which are linked to a baseline map. Digital maps with a separate overlay for each variable can be viewed individually or together to analyze any combination of variables on the landscape. The main drawback of GIS is that producing digitized maps is very labor-intensive. Most paper maps need to be digitized along with information about each variable. And sometimes information about each variable needs to be collected from some sort of field survey. It only makes sense to code such detailed information when researchers want to conduct more systematic analysis of a site or a regional network of sites. Nevertheless, once physical features and other information have been digitized, GIS can identify patterns in several variables quickly and easily. For example, it may be useful to know which locations are within a certain distance of a stream, above a certain elevation, and near some possible source of flint or chert. Then, during ground reconnaissance, the researcher can investigate whether such locations are viable archaeological sites.

- **Geographical Information System (GIS).** A computerized methodology that brings together data from several sources and integrates them with a geographic reference map.

- **Remote sensing**. Archaeologists draw on remote sensing techniques, which tend to be much less destructive than an excavation, or because it can help them gain distanced and new perspectives on a landscape and its sites. Among the most productive are magnetic surveys, which allow researchers to walk systematically back and forth across open fields or other spaces with a magnetometer, the reading of which can be linked to locational data. These data produce a magnetic picture of the site, often revealing the original arrangement and structure of a site. For example, in rural southern Ohio, where so many mound complexes and earthworks were leveled in the nineteenth century, it is common for nothing to remain visible on the surface that could indicate any obvious human occupation. One such example is the Junction Works site on Paint Creek near Chillicothe, Ohio. Squier and Davis (1848) included a sketch map of the site in their survey of Ohio valley mounds and earthworks. Farmers had flattened the site for agricultural use during the twentieth century so that nothing of the original earthworks remained. In 2005 archaeologist Jarrod Burks conducted a magnetic survey of the site to reveal the underlying structure of the former site. The magnetometer reads soils under the former earthworks that were more packed down differently from areas without any additional earthworks. When these magnetic images are plotted on a mapping of the site they reveal the shapes of the original structure (Lepper 2015; Burks 2014). One of the main advantages of magnetometry is that it does not disrupt sites.

  A variety of new strategies for remote sensing have emerged thanks to advances in technology. For example, archaeologists can use aerial drones and satellites to identify landscape features that might point to indications of human habitation. One example is the work of archaeologist Jesse Casana (2020) who tapped into a Cold War–era archive of 800,000 historic satellite images of the border between Turkey and Syria to identify early sites in the region where people lived or worked, and to begin delineating rough boundaries of early prehistoric settlement areas, fields, and the like that had not been previously identified.

- **LIDAR**. Similar in concept to radar and sonar, this ground-penetrating device produces pulses of light that are reflected back, recording differences in reflection times that indicate spatial differences. Mapping these differential signals can produce a fairly accurate depiction of the existing topography from which the archaeologist can identify likely changes in the topography due to erosion or deposition. LIDAR is also useful for regional surveys, capturing the underground details over large areas that can direct archaeologists to specific locations for excavation.

STUDYING PAST ENVIRONMENTS

A critical aspect of archaeological understanding of any human group is knowledge about what past environments were like. Whether people lived in a forest or a grassland, whether temperatures were warm or cool, whether the climate was wet or dry, whether there were rivers or lakes nearby, or whether or not plant and animal resources were available, the natural environmental context makes a big difference in the possible lifeways a society may adopt. What makes this a complicated methodological problem is that natural environments are dynamic and exhibit great changes, particularly over the thousands of years humans have lived on the planet. As a result, we cannot assume that any past environment was similar to what we observe today. Archaeologists have developed methods for understanding these changing environmental conditions and the complex relationships between global and regional environments. These methods include the following:

> **Studying changing sea levels and climates.** One of the most important aspects of any prehistoric environment has to do with alternating periods of glaciation (ice ages) and warming that have occurred over the past million years. A large part of human history occurred during the Pleistocene epoch, informally known as the "Great Ice Age" (ca. 1.6 million years ago to 10,000 years ago). During the Pleistocene, global temperatures were generally much cooler than at present. But this time period was also punctuated with warm periods between the times when glacial ice reached it maximum extent, known as interglacials, causing sea levels to go up or down over time. For example, during the last glacial maximum, about 20,000 years ago, the mean sea level was about 400 feet lower than it is today. Such significant changes in sea level had large impacts on human activity, and these fluctuations may explain why it is so difficult to identify archaeological sites from the last

glacial maximum (roughly 12,000–20,000 BP, or Before the Present). Coastal populations were likely larger than populations in interior regions because of the rich sources of fish, shellfish, and other resources found along coasts. But it is nearly impossible to find evidence today because most coastal sites from 14,000 BP and earlier are now covered by 300–400 feet of saltwater (Figure MM3.1).

One important technique for studying these matters is to take core samples of bogs, swamps, lakebeds, coastal sites, and other places where ancient pollens are likely to have been deposited. Under ordinary conditions, pollen is fairly stable, particularly if the pollen deposit was covered by soil, water, or other debris. Because the cores show different layers of pollen—essentially what pollens were floating in the air at any given time—it is possible to identify vegetation and climate conditions over centuries and even millennia.

Studying changing landscape forms and features. Archaeologists often collaborate with geologists and geomorphologists, who study the origin and change of landforms to reconstruct prehistoric landscapes. They know that most landscapes are constantly undergoing processes of subsidence (sinking), uplift (the movement and colliding of geotectonic plates to create hills and mountains), erosion (when sediments from mountains and hillsides become deposited in valleys, lakebeds, and the ocean floor), and floods. In addition, rivers often change course, leaving behind rich **alluvial soil** (rich, fine-grained soils deposited by rivers and streams). Because alluvial soils are so fertile, people have often chosen such areas for their settlements. When these streams empty into shallow bays and lagoons, they often produce abundant and varied plant and animal resources. Because of environmental change, archaeologists need to be conscious of where streambeds were situated in relation to habitation sites during their occupation. The key is to sample enough of the sediments around a site to determine which are original and which have been eroded from other sites. Such patterns of deposition and erosion are critical in understanding the history of an archaeological site and how human action may have influenced these sediments. A variety of other, more specialized paleoenvironmental techniques have been developed to address particular environmental dynamics. These include ice cores in the arctic or high mountain regions, lake or sea varves (layers of silt or sand deposited by wave action), and volcanic strata in areas where volcanic activity has transformed the

- **Alluvial soil.** Rich, fine-grained soils deposited by rivers and streams.

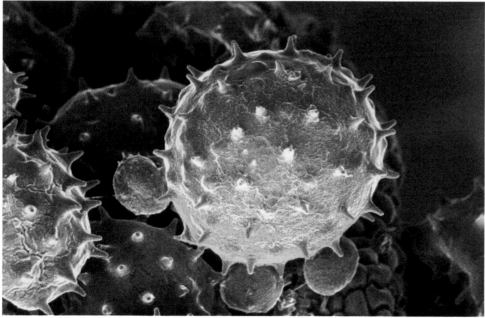

Figure MM3.1 **Pollen Under a Microscope.** High magnification shows that pollen grains are as varied as the diverse plant species they come from.

environment. An example of volcanic strata comes from obsidian samples found all along the north coast of New Guinea and the Bismarck Archipelago. Archaeologists have identified two important obsidian quarries in the Bismarck Archipelago that were the source of most of the obsidian used in this vast region for 3,500 years. After a volcanic eruption covered the first quarry under several meters of ash, all obsidian production shifted to the other quarry. Since each quarry produced obsidian with a different density, the density of obsidian flakes or fragments found in other parts of the country can now be dated roughly by determining which quarry the flake came from. The technique is simple and requires a fluid with a certain fixed density. Flakes of obsidian from one source will float on top of the fluid, while flakes from the other will sink. Thus, if the sample has one density, it is from one quarry site and we will know the period in which it was first used; if another density, we know it was obtained later and from another quarry, in this particular case many centuries later.

Studying plants, changing human diets, and climate change. Paleoethnobotany is the study of ancient plant remains to reconstruct a picture of prehistoric environments. It also focuses on human–plant interactions in archaeological settings to gain perspectives on prehistoric diets, crop production, land use, and seasonal occupation (Hastorf 1988). With growing interest and concern over global climate change, some archaeologists have drawn on techniques of paleoethnobotany to track the relationship between changing prehistoric climates and the presence and density of certain plant species, studying how changes in human diets and cultivation practices correlate with knowledge of changes in precipitation and

temperature (Langgut et al. 2021). It can involve the study of coprolites (human and animal excrement), plant impressions in clay, and plant residues in cooking vessels. Another key method, developed by Norwegian geologist Lennart von Post (1946), involves the study of ancient pollen grains.

As mentioned earlier, pollen grains preserve fairly well in acidic peat bogs and lake sediments. They have varied and distinctive shapes that allow researchers to identify the species to which a well-preserved grain belongs. Once samples of pollen from bogs or lake sediments are retrieved and their species identified, it is possible to calculate the relative proportion of grains from the identified species. Grasslands have an abundance of grasses represented, while forests have few grass pollens but large proportions of tree pollens. Rain forests typically have a wider variety of species than temperate forests. Because pollen is generally airborne and can travel several miles, a lakebed or bog some miles from an excavation can tell us what kind of vegetation was present in an area (Figure MM3.2). The most difficult challenge in pollen analysis is to make sure that the samples are from the same layer of sediment and have not been contaminated by the excavator or by some natural process.

In summary, environments in all parts of the globe have changed a great deal over the past 20,000 years, processes that have both affected and been affected by human action. To understand any changing lifeways demands understanding the changing environment and then inferring how people have adapted to these changing conditions. Most of the time we have much less evidence than we would like, but archaeology is about making sense of and drawing inferences from what disparate bits of evidence may be available.

Thinking Critically About Archaeological Field Methods

- What are the costs and benefits of excavation (as opposed to some of the other methods we've covered here)?
- The majority of field excavations conducted in the United States today take place because of some construction project, where sites will be disturbed when the highway or building is constructed. Does this

disturbance justify a more destructive excavation? Why or why not?

- Where might you look to find changes in the flora that were present in ancient environments, such as the late period of the Ice Age in more northerly regions or in tropical areas? How would the environment express these climate changes in measurable or observable ways?

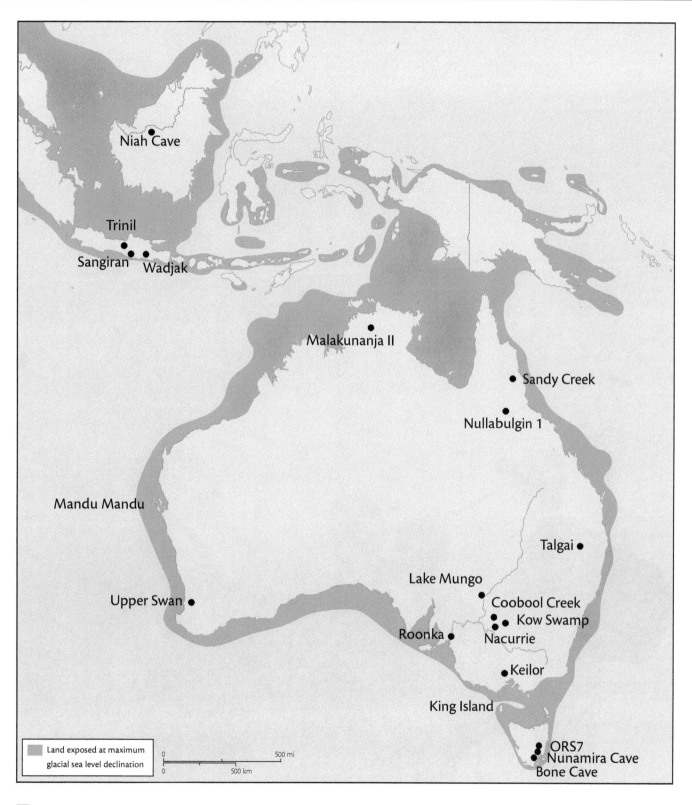

Labels on map:
Niah Cave
Trinil
Sangiran Wadjak
Malakunanja II
Sandy Creek
Nullabulgin 1
Mandu Mandu
Talgai
Lake Mungo
Cooboool Creek
Upper Swan
Kow Swamp
Roonka Nacurrie
Keilor
King Island
ORS7
Nunamira Cave
Bone Cave

Land exposed at maximum
glacial sea level declination

0   500 mi
0   500 km

Figure MM3.2   Ice Age Sea Level and Contemporary Sea Levels in Southeast Asia. Late Pleistocene sea level circa 14,000 BP and modern coastlines in the islands and mainland of Southeast Asia, New Guinea, and Australia.

Materiality

Constructing Social Relationships and Meanings from Things

MUCH OF THE US–Mexico border is fenced to prevent or dissuade immigrants from crossing into the United States. But there are plenty of places where holes exist in the fencing, or where the terrain was deemed too rough to require a physical barrier, especially in the Sonoran Desert along the Arizona and New Mexico borders. Anthropologist Jason De León, a professor at UCLA, has been studying migration across this especially difficult part of the border for a decade, documenting the lives and hardships experienced by migrants who pass through the area. His research began with interviews of migrants who had somehow or another found their way through (De León 2015). With training as an archaeologist, he also noticed that many migrants had left behind objects, things like bits of torn and tattered clothing, wrappers and containers of food, empty bottles, blankets, utensils, and the like. He knew that paying close attention to these objects offered another way to document the difficulties and hardships these migrants had endured.

He published many of these stories in his book, *The Land of Open Graves* (2015), but he wanted to find other ways to convey the harsh realities of these deadly migration experiences. Turning his attention to those who had perished during their journey northward, he plotted the many hundreds of migrant deaths in Arizona. To make his findings accessible to the general public, he turned these data into a "pop-up" exhibit that captured these tragic stories by representing each migrant's death using a colored

The Human Toll of Migration. "Toe tags" representing each of the migrant deaths reported in the Southern Arizona desert from the Hostile Terrain 94 "pop-up" exhibit touring the United States in 2019 and 2020.

toe tag—the kind that are placed on deceased peoples' toes to identify them— with some personal information and location of death inscribed on it. These toe tags were mounted on a large map of the area. "Hostile Terrain 94" as the exhibit is called, is a critically acclaimed pop-up installation that in 2019 began traveling to 150 venues, many of them college campuses.

De León's installation follows in the tradition of other temporary exhibits whose goal is to call attention to tragedies that demand public attention and remediation. The most important and famous of these was the AIDS Memorial Quilt, conceived of in 1985, which has been touring ever since and is currently the largest piece of community folk art in the world. In both cases, these temporary exhibits materialize tragic deaths, letting something tangible stand in for the human lives lost. They also illustrate what anthropologist Simon Ottenberg (1991:81) suggested some years ago, that "curating an exhibit is a political act." In this case, his words seem like an understatement. The cardboard toe tags represent the struggle, pain, and suffering of real people who died of disease, heat exhaustion, dehydration, or hunger in the Arizona desert.

• **Materiality.** Having the quality of being physical or material.

At the heart of De León's work is the theme of **materiality**, the quality of being tangible or physical. In approaching and using objects, his goal is to understand and communicate about social relationships and cultural processes that have tragic outcomes. The power of this approach raises an important question central to this chapter: *What is the role of objects and material culture in constructing social relationships and cultural meanings?* We can answer this question by considering a number of related questions around which this chapter is organized:

Why is the ownership of prehistoric artifacts and objects from other cultures such a contentious issue?

How should we look at objects anthropologically?

How and why do the meanings of things change over time?

What role does material culture play in constructing the meaning of a community's past?

• **Material culture.** The objects made and used in any society; traditionally, the term referred to technologically simple objects made in preindustrial societies, but material culture may refer to all of the objects or commodities of modern life as well.

This chapter examines **material culture**, the objects made and used in any society, which is of special interest to archaeologists and cultural anthropologists in particular. The term originally referred to technologically simple objects made in preindustrial societies, but material culture may refer to all the objects or commodities of modern life as well. It even encompasses the tangible toe tags created for De León's exhibit. When we take objects seriously, all the ways people use objects to deal with their physical needs and how the objects help us communicate with others, define themselves through objects, and control others using objects, anthropology is not "simply" about people but about the intertwining of people and material things.

9.1 Why Is the Ownership of Prehistoric Artifacts and Objects from Other Cultures Such a Contentious Issue?

In the United States, the discipline of anthropology began in museums, arising amid the scramble for collections of cultural, archaeological, linguistic, and biological data to document the human story. At first, most of the material culture was from Native Americans in the western states. From 1850 on, many of these objects were held in the Smithsonian Institution in Washington, DC.

By the time of the Chicago World's Fair of 1893, the Smithsonian's curators had assembled impressive anthropological exhibits. But rather than relying exclusively on the national collection, the Chicago organizers of the World's Fair appointed Professor Frederic Ward Putnam of Harvard's Peabody Museum of Archaeology and Ethnology (established 1866) to organize the World's Fair Committee's own anthropological exhibits. Putnam competed with the Smithsonian researchers to present exhibits about the cultures and prehistory of the New World, sending out teams of researchers to acquire new collections from dozens of Indian tribes and to excavate Indian mounds in Ohio, pueblos like Mesa Verde in the Southwest, and ancient sites in Peru. Putnam had also hired a young Franz Boas, who supervised collections from the Northwest Coast cultures on Vancouver Island in British Columbia that he had himself collected, as well as other exhibits from collectors hired by Putnam. At the end of the Fair, most of those collections were purchased for the newly formed Field Museum (Hinsley and Wilcox 2016; Figure 9.1).

After a year or so helping launch Field Museum's anthropology department, Boas left Chicago for New York and was based at the American Museum of Natural History in New York City. He would eventually start the anthropology department at Columbia University and train the first two generations of anthropology graduate students. But in these early years he focused on building up that museum's collections, organizing a series of collecting expeditions to the Northwest coast that brought back many objects for display as well as many volumes of myths and field notes about local customs to help interpret these collections. The most important of these expeditions were funded by banker and philanthropist Morris K. Jessup, chair of the American Museum's board of trustees. Named the Jessup North Pacific Expedition, it sent a dozen anthropologists, biologists, and linguists to Alaska, Canada, and eastern Russia to collect data and specimens for the American Museum.

What followed during the early twentieth century was an international scramble for collections from societies that Western scholars thought of as "primitive" (Cole 1985; Schildkrout and Keim 1998; O'Hanlon and Welsch 2000). To the peoples who had made, used, or celebrated these objects, these collections represented the stuff of life, ranging from ordinary things to the most sacred and meaningful ritual objects. For the museum-going public they were tangible evidence of how different the lives and material culture of these exotic peoples actually were from their own.

Major American museums were actively competing with one another for objects, in the process employing a lot of anthropologists. At first, nobody was concerned about who owned all of these objects, since in a legal sense they belonged to the individual museums. But in recent decades, questions of ownership and control over these objects have become a contentious issue. Shouldn't the people whose direct ancestors made or used these objects have some rights over these collections? Who has the moral right to display and interpret them? Who had the right to say what significance

Figure 9.1   Kwakiutl Indians with Totem Poles. Collected for F. W. Putnam and displayed at the World's Columbian Exposition in Chicago in 1893, now in the collections of The Field Museum. From *Vistas of the Fair in Color: A Portfolio of Familiar Views* (Chicago: Poole Brothers, 1894). © The Field Museum. #GN85650c.

they held? Do the museums who own these objects have the right to say whatever they want about another culture's objects, or should the people from whom the objects were collected have a say? These are complex questions that may be easiest to answer if we begin by asking who actually owns ethnographic objects and the archaeological and skeletal material found at any archaeological site.

Archaeological Excavation and Questions of Ownership

In the nineteenth century, rights to Indian lands were governed by treaties and later by legislation, particularly the Dawes Act of 1887, which allowed commonly held lands on Indian reservations to be surveyed and divided up into individual lots. As a result, much of the land on most reservations was able to be sold off as individually owned lots to non-Indian owners by 1950. By the mid-1960s, when civil rights legislation began to protect Black people, American Indians began pressing their claims against drilling, mining, pipelines, and agri-business farming on their reservations, issues that persist today. They also protested the ways their peoples and cultures were depicted in movies (particularly Westerns), books, and, importantly, in museums. But the claims that seemed to reach the American public's consciousness most directly were those against archaeological excavations of sacred Indian sites and cemeteries.

During the 1970s, activists associated with the **American Indian Movement (AIM)**, a prominent Native American rights group founded in 1968, began to protest the disrespectful ways national, state, and local officials treated Indian remains (Banks 2004). They also pointed to histories of forced settlement on reservations; punishment for speaking their native languages in government schools; and pressures on reservations to sell their lands to White Americans. Calls for **repatriation**, or the return of human remains and artifacts to the communities of descendants of the people to whom they originally belonged, came to stand for something much more important than the objects themselves. Repatriating human remains and artifacts became an especially important symbol of respect for American Indian identity because most Indian groups found it repugnant that academic departments and natural history museums held the skeletal remains and possessions of their ancestors. The objects in museums implicitly represented the dominant culture's control over Native Americans.

- **AIM (American Indian Movement).** The most prominent and one of the earliest Native American activist groups, founded in 1968.

- **Repatriation.** The return of human remains or cultural artifacts to the communities of descendants of the people to whom they originally belonged.

The Road to NAGPRA

An incident in Kentucky in 1987 led to new state and federal laws that make it a felony to disturb archaeological sites on both government-owned and private lands everywhere in the United States and its territories. Anthropologists and archaeologists had been aware of an important late prehistoric site on the property known as Slack Farm near Uniontown, Kentucky, that included an intact cemetery containing more than 1,000 Indian graves, plus grave goods (pots, beads, pipes, arrowheads, and ritual artifacts). The owners of the land sold rights to dig on this site for $10,000 to a group of pot hunters who dug up the site with abandon, leaving skeletal material and broken pots all over. The state police arrested and fined the looters on the misdemeanor charge of desecrating a venerated object (Fagan 1988; Arden 1989). But this incident, which became known as the "Tragedy of Slack Farm" (Fagan 1988), was so offensive to American Indian groups, anthropologists, and archaeologists that it led the Congress to pass the **Native American Graves Protection and Repatriation** Act of 1990 or **NAGPRA**.

NAGPRA requires the repatriation of human remains and artifacts found with those remains to the tribes or families of the dead individuals. The law also required all museums or other institutions that hold human remains or cultural objects from any native group covered by the act to inform tribal representatives of their holdings. If the group feels that an object is of special cultural, religious, or historic significance, it may petition the institution to return or repatriate the object. Although many museums own objects from other countries, NAGPRA covers only material from American cultural groups, including American Indians, Hawaiian Islanders, Native Alaskans, and the indigenous peoples of American Samoa and Guam.

- **NAGPRA (Native American Graves and Repatriation Act).** In the United States, the 1990 law that established the ownership of human remains, grave goods, and important cultural objects as belonging to the Native Americans, whose ancestors once owned them.

Different native groups have distinct cultural values about both skeletal material and artifacts made by their ancestors. While most tribes wanted to rebury skeletal remains, some groups wanted nothing to do with the bones of their ancestors, feeling that any contact with these remains might harm the living. Over the past quarter century most sets of human remains have been returned to various tribes, as have many objects of very special significance. Most important cultural institutions have taken advantage of NAGPRA to establish or reestablish relationships with Indian groups over repatriation concerns. These efforts have involved inviting tribal leaders to visit the museum and study what collections the museum may have from their community. Museums have learned a great deal about their collections by working closely with Indians, and tribal representatives have also learned a great deal about their past from seeing the material culture of their ancestors preserved by the museums. In the process of returning material items to their original communities, both museums and host communities add to the meaning of these objects (Figure 9.2).

Although NAGPRA has no authority over how to deal with objects collected from cultures outside the jurisdiction of the United States, many US institutions have used questions about repatriation to build relationships with native groups in other countries as well. We explore an example of this sort of relationship building below in "The Anthropological Life: Working as a Collections Manager at the Field Museum."

Protection of Historic Sites Around the World

- **World Heritage Site program.** A program that provides financial support to maintain sites deemed by the World Heritage Committee to be of cultural or natural importance to humanity.

Many countries have implemented legislation and programs of their own to recognize and protect historic sites, and most governments support UNESCO's **World Heritage Sites program**, which provides financial support to maintain sites of importance to humanity. The majority of the 814 cultural heritage sites currently recognized by UNESCO's program have played a key role in human history. Five of them are sites where early fossil hominids have been found in Africa, China, and Australia. Others are key archaeological sites such as the pyramids of Giza and the temples and palaces of Ancient Thebes in Egypt, Angkor Wat in Cambodia, Chichén Itzá in Mexico, Mesa Verde in Colorado, and the moai statues on Rapa Nui (Easter Island), all of which are typical of what we often think of as ancient historic and prehistoric sites. Many others are historic cities like Fez in Morocco.

Cultural Resource Management

- **Cultural resource management (CRM).** Research and planning aimed at identifying, interpreting, and protecting sites and artifacts of historic or prehistoric significance.

In response to the new legislation, archaeologists in the United States have taken a leading role in managing and preserving prehistoric and historic heritage. These efforts are often referred to as **cultural resource management (CRM)**, which is a form of applied archaeology. CRM's goal is to protect and manage the cultural resources of every community, especially important prehistoric sites and structures. The vast majority of archaeological work in the Americas and around the world is done by contract archaeologists, and CRM has become a major focus for those seeking careers in archaeology, including many with undergraduate degrees in anthropology. In a number of states, researchers with a bachelor's degree in archaeology or anthropology can help with an excavation, but a master's degree or PhD are required to lead an excavation in most jurisdictions. Many projects are done under the supervision of the National Park Service or state department of historic resources.

Although many Indian groups historically criticized archaeologists as doing little to help their communities and disturbing the bones of their ancestors (Deloria 1969), an increasing number of Indians have earned postgraduate degrees in archaeology and use the techniques of CRM to preserve their tribes' cultural heritage. Nearly all tribes that use CRM view heritage management differently than most federal government agencies (Anyon, Ferguson, and Welch 2000:132). One key difference is that non-Indian agencies nearly always see heritage resources as tangible places and things, and scientific study as a way of finding a middle ground between the heritage resource and some other use. Emphasizing their spiritual connections to the past, many tribes tend to prefer avoiding the disturbance of the heritage resource altogether, including scientific investigation (Dongoske et al. 1995).

🌿 **Figure 9.2   Repatriating a Chilkat Blanket to the Tlingit at a Memorial Potlatch in Sitka, Alaska, Fall 2002.** Above, Tlingit elders who organized the memorial potlatch wearing Chilkat blankets or button blankets: Edwell John (Killer Whale Clan), Joe Murray (representing Killer Whale Clan), a man from Wolf Clan (Kaagwaantaan), Dan Brown (Brown Bear or Teikweidee Clan), and Randy Gamble (Kaagwaantaan Clan). They wear headdresses from their respective clans. Below, on the right Kellen Haak (Registrar of the Hood Museum of Art at Dartmouth College) presents the Museum's Chilkat blanket being returned to the Deisheetaan Clan in the Raven Moiety. To the left is Nell Murphy (from the American Museum of Natural History in New York), anthropologist Sergei Kan (Dartmouth College) speaking for the group, and Terri Snowball (National Museum of the American Indian in Washington, DC). Tlingit leaders in this photo include Alan Zuboff (Dog Salmon Clan) and Garfield George (Deisheetaan Clan).

As this section has demonstrated, the social conflicts around objects are complex, suggesting that the meanings and uses of objects are not straightforward matters. In the next section we expand on this point by pulling back and reviewing how we can look at objects anthropologically.

The Anthropological Life
Working as an Ethnographic Collections Manager at the Field Museum

Maybe it seems obvious, but working in a museum as an ethnographic collections manager involves handling, conserving, studying, and curating objects for display. But an important part of the job description is also maintaining collaborative relationships with the communities that created the objects held in the museum collection. Take the case of Christopher Philipp, who graduated from Beloit College with a BA in Anthropology. He works as the Regenstein Collection Manager of Pacific Anthropology at the Field Museum in Chicago.

The Field Museum holds the largest collection of anthropological objects from the Pacific Islands in the mainland United States. The highest profile Pacific object in Field Museum's collections is a mid-nineteenth century Maori meeting house with elaborate carvings on most of its house boards. It was acquired from a tribal art dealer who in 1905 purchased a nearly complete Maori meeting house known as Ruatepupuke from a member of an extended family in Tokomaru Bay on the North Island of New Zealand. Like other Maori meeting houses, the carvings that make up the walls and house posts of Ruatepupuke depict the clan's ancestors as well as stories and myths that relate to the clan's history. Members of the community see these carved figures as telling their history and as living embodiments of

their ancestors. Any meeting that takes place in the house is inevitably a kind of communion with the ancestors.

In the 1990s, Field Museum curator and archaeologist John Terrell collaborated with Māori museum professionals and community members from Tokomaru Bay to restore and reassemble the house at its current location in the museum (Hakiwai and Terrell 1994). When the curators asked members of the Maori community what they should do with the house, nearly all of the elders wanted Ruatepupuke to stay in Chicago, and younger members of the community wanted the house back. In the end, the community decided that keeping it at the Field Museum was a unique opportunity to share Maori culture with the world, and it remains a kind of cultural embassy for Maori in the United States. Over the years, many Maori have traveled to Chicago to visit the house to conduct important meetings and rituals, meet with curators, and engage with museumgoers about Maori culture.

Chris Philipp got involved in these relationships and he learned a lot about centering such collaboration in the work of managing collections. Today, his job is to look after 66,000 objects in the Museum's Pacific Collections. Since the recommitment of Tokomaru Bay to help maintain Ruatepupuke as an integral part of the Field Museum and its Regenstein Halls he, along with the rest of the Regenstein curatorial team, has been responsible for hosting and facilitating the visits of Maori as well as Filipino American, Marshallese, and other Pacific Islander visitors who want to see the house and other objects in the collection, especially ones from their own communities. Chris's team has worked hard to strengthen relationships with these visitors and other Pacific Island communities represented in Field Museum's collections.

Chris has also been sent on trips to a number of Pacific Islands to establish and nurture relationships between the Museum and these host communities. Besides visiting New Zealand, the Museum has sent Chris to the Marquesas (in 2007), Tonga (2010), the Cook Islands (2010), Samoa and American Samoa (2011), Papua New Guinea (2012), Fiji (2015 and 2018), New Zealand (2018), and Majuro in the Marshall Islands (2019). On each of these trips Chris collected some contemporary objects for the museum's collection, but the real goal of the visits was to establish and

Chris Phillip, far right, showing visiting Pacific Islanders items held in the Field Museum collections. Image courtesy of Field Museum.

reaffirm relationships with cultural leaders in these islands, to honor their stake in the Field Museum's collections, to consult with them about their concerns, and to identify opportunities for engagement and collaboration. Increasingly, museums with ethnographic collections have recognized that owning and displaying objects is not the end of the story, as it was a century ago, but is the beginning of establishing a relationship between museums and the donor communities whose objects they hold. At the heart of those dynamics are museum professionals with anthropological backgrounds, like Chris, who are committed not just to the objects but to the people and societies that created them.

THINKING LIKE AN ANTHROPOLOGIST: MATERIALITY

How do the meanings of museum collections of Native American material culture change depending on who is thinking about them? How would these meanings be different if the objects were historical artifacts from a White pioneer community in the National Museum of American History?

9.2 How Should We Look at Objects Anthropologically?

Until the 1980s anthropologists tended to look at the study of objects as evidence of cultural distinctiveness. They approached cultural and artistic objects as expressions of a society's environmental adaptation, aesthetic sensibilities, or as markers of ethnic identity. Viewed in this way, arts and craftwares were considered an expression of a particular tradition, time, or place, but even more so, an expression of the individual creativity of the artist or craftperson. This way of looking at objects may seem reasonable, but in the mid-1980s anthropologists began to look at objects in a new way. In particular, they started to recognize that objects were capable of conveying meaning in many different ways simultaneously.

The Many Dimensions of Objects

The late historian of anthropology George W. Stocking Jr. edited an influential book called *Objects and Others: Essays on Museums and Material Culture* (1985). Stocking's introduction to this book explained that anthropology's history began with the study of objects in museums decades before anthropologists even began conducting their own field research. Using these collections, they developed crude analyses of how civilized, barbaric, or primitive a society was from the kinds of objects they had or did not have. Later, when anthropologists started conducting fieldwork, they noticed firsthand the importance of objects in rituals, social exchanges, and political activities. Anthropologists began to look at objects to understand the meanings of rituals, the interconnections between people who exchanged particular objects, or the social stratification within a society that could be seen in the presence or absence of objects in a particular household or community. In its most basic sense, this approach has endured until the present. Most museums have a complex group of curators, collections managers, and conservators who look after, interpret, and make sense of their collections for the public.

But the importance of Stocking's work is his argument that objects are multidimensional, and if we really want to understand them, we have to recognize and try to understand not just their three basic physical dimensions—height, width, depth—but four others as well, among them time (history), power, wealth, and aesthetics, making a total of seven dimensions that he recognized.

The dimension of *time* or *history* refers to the fact that objects in museums came from somewhere and each had an individual history. In part this asks when, by whom, and how were they produced; how did they get to the museum or their current location; and how have interpretations of the object changed over time? The dimension of *power* reveals the relations of inequality reflected in objects, especially why the objects of non-Western people sit in ethnographic museums, while very few non-Western peoples have museums or repositories where local people can view Western objects. During the heyday of colonialism, European and American anthropologists collected thousands of objects from the peoples they studied. Rarely could a community know enough about how these objects might be displayed or studied to be able to give informed consent. *Wealth* reflects the fact that people use objects to establish and demonstrate who has wealth and social status. We have seen how the American museum directors saw showy and impressive objects as being quite valuable for their museums and the museums' reputations. The dimension of *aesthetics* is reflected in the fact that each culture brings with it its own system or patterns of recognizing what is pleasing or attractive, which configurations of colors and textures are appealing, and which are not.

What intrigued Stocking most about objects, especially those now found in museums, was that these things were a historical archive in multiple dimensions that can tell us a great deal about the cultures that made and used these objects as well as the relationships between the collectors' societies and the communities who originally used them. Furthermore, objects could offer a window for understanding local symbolic systems of meaning. This point was more expansive than just being focused on the objects found in art and ethnographic museums. His insights can actually be applied to any everyday object. Consider, for example, a shiny new bicycle.

A Shiny New Bicycle in Multiple Dimensions

Picture a shiny new bicycle chained to a bicycle rack on your campus (Figure 9.3). Made of a strong yet lightweight alloy, it is fast, sleek, and an exquisite example of modern technology applied to an object that has been around for more than a century. Like all objects, this bicycle has the physical properties of height, length, and width, dimensions that are quite important for any individual mounting one: think of how difficult it is to ride a bicycle that is too big or too small.

Objects are defined by more than their physical traits, however. Objects also embody a temporal dimension of having a past, present, and future. The shape and form of this particular object have emerged from improvements on the workings of generations of bicycles, used by generations of cyclists as a childhood toy, as an inexpensive mode of transport, for racing, or for casual weekend riding. If we think of a bicycle in the abstract, we can choose from among all of these meanings and uses of a bicycle. The particular owner of this bicycle has certain associations that come to mind when he or she thinks of a bicycle, and these associations may be quite different from cyclists who race, from mothers who pedal around the neighborhood with their children, or from the bike messenger cycling through busy urban traffic. The owner's

Figure 9.3   The bicycle, like anything, is a multidimensional object.

view of his or her bicycle may be shaped by previous bicycles he or she may have owned; it may be influenced by feelings that the owner is being ecologically "green," using a mode of transportation that is better for the environment than other ways of getting around campus or the city. And such images shape how the owner views themselves today or how he or she imagines the future (Vivanco 2013).

This bicycle—like practically every other object North American consumers purchase—is also a commodity that—as parts and as a finished product—has circulated through a complex economic system, supported by an equally complex set of regulatory rules. As deeply personal as the selection and purchase of an object like a bicycle may be for us as individuals, it was made on an assembly line by dozens of workers, each contributing a small part to the finished effort. This happened overseas, and the bicycle has traveled through a worldwide network of economic linkages, warehouses, and shippers to reach its current owner.

In that process, the manufacturer and the mainstream culture generally have carefully cultivated the current owner's desire to own and use this object. The owner has purchased this particular bicycle and not a more expensive one and not a beaten-up secondhand one. The owner may even have replaced an older bike with this newer and more efficient one, imagining himself as more of a racer than he really is, or thinking of herself as more environmentally conscious than she might actually be. And our impressions of particular bicycles may be shaped by the images we have seen of them in films, TV programs, ads, and shiny brochures advertising one brand of bicycle (Vivanco 2013).

Finally, this bicycle, like every other object we own, is a useful object, not only for where or how far it can take us, not just in how much it can help keep us healthy because of the exercise it provides, and not simply from the fuel it saves us, but also from the impressions of us that it creates in others as they see us ride.

The point of our bicycle example is that *any* mundane object can help us imagine ourselves, our past, and where we are headed. Although Stocking's seven dimensions do not cover all the aspects or dimensions suggested about the shiny bicycle, they do offer a simple first glance at how we feel we should look at objects anthropologically and archaeologically.

The Power of Symbols

Now that we have you thinking about objects in multiple dimensions, we can turn to the aesthetic. By studying the art traditions and objects of non-Western peoples, anthropologists have learned that the complex ideas and understandings about the gods, ghosts, spirits, and other supernatural beings who inhabit their cosmologies are embodied in the physical representations—for example, in carved objects that they make (Figure 9.4).

There is every reason to believe that carvers and other people alike could imagine that their spirits and demons looked like the carvings. But when one grows up and the only depiction of a particular spirit is the mask or carving that represents the spirit, one will likely understand the spirit to look just like the carvings. Similarly, although nobody knows what the ancient Hebrew prophet Moses may have looked like, when we hear a discussion of Moses, most of us will immediately imagine Charlton Heston, who starred as Moses in the classic 1956 film *The Ten Commandments* (de Mille 1956), because this is the way Moses appears in nearly all popular images of this ancient figure.

Figure 9.4 Rethinking African Art. [Antelope mask from the Hood Museum]

The Symbols of Power

Just as the aesthetic dimensions of objects shape an object's meaning, powerful people use aesthetics in ways to demonstrate and legitimate their social, political, or religious power. In many traditional African kingdoms, such as those whose artworks now get displayed in museums in places like New York, the kings and chiefs who ruled these communities distinguished themselves from ordinary people with symbols of rank and authority—staffs, chairs, thrones, clothing, and so forth—artfully carved or woven in a particular local style or aesthetic. Similarly, in many religions, authorities employ aesthetics to indicate that the holder of an item possesses divine power as well as power here on earth.

What sets these objects of power apart is, in part, their aesthetic style that establishes the objects, and by extension their owners, as important and special. But it is also true that the aesthetic settings and ways in which such objects are used and displayed can also symbolically communicate the power of their owners. An interesting illustration comes from the island of Walis along the north coast of Papua New Guinea, as witnessed by Rob Welsch, one of the authors of this textbook, in 1993. A century earlier, a religious leader named Barjani had foretold the coming of Europeans and was believed to be a prophet. After his death, his family's clansmen had erected a shrine to him, where people in need of supernatural assistance could leave a small amount of money or tobacco to ensure Barjani's assistance. When Welsch and his colleague, John Terrell, went to see the shrine, they were mostly interested in the building's historically important architectural style.

But the real surprise came when they climbed the small ladder to peer into Barjani's shrine. The interior of the small shrine held a single object in a place of honor on a simple but small platform of palm leaves: an old and well-worn bowler hat, much like the one Charlie Chaplin wore in some of his movies. This was Barjani's hat, an object that possessed its power from Barjani's having worn it but also from being the only object in the shrine. The meaning of this hat, standing out starkly in such an unexpected place, came partly from its association with Barjani and partly from his association with the foreigners he had predicted would come. In addition, the fact that it was a foreign object that few if any other Walis Islanders could have owned must have made it both exotic and valuable as a relic of this local prophet (Figure 9.5).

Although Barjani's hat for Walis Islanders is a statement about relations between themselves and powerful outsiders, it is also a window into the historical context of both their society and the changing meaning that this bowler hat has had over its century of existence. To pursue this issue further, let us consider the next question around which this chapter is organized, which is why objects change meaning over time.

🌱 Figure 9.5   Barjani's Shrine on Walis Island in Papua New Guinea. Inside, the room was empty except for Barjani's bowler hat and offerings or gifts that had been left in exchange for Barjani's help.

Constructing the Meaning of an Archaeological Artifact

Archaeological objects and artifacts also have many dimensions, just like any other object. We should look at these objects in much the same way that we look at any other. The only difference is that archaeological objects typically come from excavations, and our research goal requires making sense of all of the artifacts, including how they were situated in the excavation site, particularly in relation to other objects. Although most excavations of American sites rarely produce more than the very occasional whole pot, even a small potsherd can be identified as belonging to a particular class of pots produced over a certain period of time and give us a rough date if similar pots have been dated for other sites. Such rough dating is particularly important when we have better dates from other sites for particular local styles.

Similarly, an arrow point, a spear point, or a scraper used to clean hides can each hint at how the object was used, how it was hafted, and how it was made. For several decades, archaeologists have used several experimental techniques to replicate how most archaeological specimens could be made. Recent techniques in residue analysis may even be able to determine what foods a stone tool or pot was used with. Experimental techniques and analyses have made these conclusions much more reliable today than they were thirty or forty years ago. The key point is that each excavated artifact needs to be examined at the microscopic level, in the context of a particular test pit, as part of a site, and in the context of similar sites across a region. Put all of these perspectives together and we begin to understand the artifact's context.

The context here should be understood as the several dimensions or aspects of any object found in an excavation or on a site, including the geographic location, the nature of the object found in the site, and its spatial relation with respect to other parts of the site, including what was deposited near it, above it, and below it. These locational factors in three dimensions relate to all four of Stocking's first four dimensions—the length, width, and depth of the object in a site together with time, which often comes from the stratigraphy and perhaps carbon dating. Archaeologists typically pay close attention to how these locational factors relate to major site features, a **feature** referring to an attribute found in an excavation, such as a pit, a crude fireplace, or a wall, that was formed, created, or modified by humans.

Just like any other object, artifacts excavated from a test pit were once enmeshed in a web of social, political, and economic relationships during their useful lives, and it is the archaeologist's task to figure out from this very fragmentary evidence what these economic, political, and social relationships may have been. For example, at a late Pleistocene or early Holocene site at Tenant Swamp near Keene, New Hampshire, anthropologist Robert Goodby and his team of researchers were able to interpret the distribution of flint flakes as having been the result of sharpening some stone tools with retouched flaking. It appears that the small flakes came from retouching spear points or other tools and were apparently made while sitting inside a hide tent, as the site also contained several rocks that seem to have been used as weights holding down the sides of a tent. The hide walls of the tent seem to have kept all of the flakes within the tent rather than being more randomly distributed over the broader site (Goodby et al. 2014).

By themselves, each small flake suggests only that someone had been knapping flint at this site, perhaps retouching one surface or another. But it appears that nearly all of the flakes were contained within a relatively small circular space; by documenting the location of each flake of flint across the site, the archaeologists were able to develop a more complete story. This site is an example of archaeologists using whatever artifactual material was found at the site to reconstruct the context of how the flakes were likely deposited in a site that may have been occupied for only a few weeks more than 12,000 years ago, very soon after the glaciers that once covered New Hampshire had retreated.

• **Feature.** An attribute found in an excavation, such as a pit, a crude fireplace, or a wall, that was formed, created, or modified by humans.

THINKING LIKE AN ANTHROPOLOGIST: MATERIALITY

Most people take the objects around them at face value, but anthropologists think about things in more multidimensional ways. Consider some object, statue, artwork, building, or other physical feature on your campus and outline its different dimensions as an anthropologist might. What new insights about your campus, your school's history, or the school's distinctive local culture do you get from this analysis?

9.3 How and Why Do the Meanings of Things Change Over Time?

Anthropologists today study some of the very same museum collections that anthropologists studied over a century ago, but they interpret them differently. This is a key aspect of what Stocking was getting at when he indicated that objects have a temporal dimension: all objects change over time, *if not in their physical characteristics, then in the significance we give to them.*

Around the same time that Stocking was laying out his framework for understanding objects in seven dimensions, another group of anthropologists was developing a set of complementary theories and techniques for analyzing in depth this issue of how objects change over time. Declaring that "things have social lives," they published a book called *The Social Life of Things: Commodities in Cultural Perspective* (Appadurai 1986) in which they laid out some useful concepts and approaches for thinking anthropologically about objects. So how can an *inanimate* object have a *social* life?

The Social Life of Things

The idea that inanimate things have social lives is based on the assumption that things have forms, uses, and trajectories that are intertwined in complex ways with people's lives. Just as people pass through different socially recognized phases of life, objects have "careers" (in the sense of course or progression) with recognizable phases, from their creation, exchange, and uses, to their eventual discard. Along the way, it is possible to identify social relationships and cultural ideologies that influence each period in this career. Across cultures, these relationships and ideologies can vary drastically.

Consider a pair of running sneakers sold at a mall. This pair of sneakers may start as cotton fabric and rubber in a Chinese factory. But the shoes mean something quite different there from what they will mean to the mall salesperson, or from what they will mean to you when you first wear them to some social event. The shoes may have aged only a few weeks from the time they were made until you wear them; the change in significance comes not from aging but from moving from one person to another. That pair of shoes has a complicated life, taking on meanings from the contexts it passes through and, to the sensitive observer, revealing a whole range of complex social relations in the process. And through it all, the same pair of shoes has changed.

Three Ways Objects Change Over Time

All objects change over time, but they can do so in different ways. Most objects age and weather with time, of course, usually becoming less significant because they get old and worn out. But for the purposes of understanding the social life of things, there are three major ways that objects change over time:

1. The form, shape, color, material, and use may change from generation to generation.
2. An object changes significance and meaning as its social and physical contexts change.
3. A single object changes significance and meaning as it changes hands.

Let us consider a few examples of each of these kinds of changes to illustrate how the social meanings of an object can change over time.

Changing Form From Generation to Generation

Nearly every manufactured product has changed over time as styles and social preferences have changed. While we usually understand these changes as gradual improvements in form or technology, they are just as often due to introducing innovations or differences in style, simply to be different. One of the best examples came from an anthropological study of ladies' fashion.

Just before World War II, anthropologists Jane Richardson and Alfred Kroeber published an analysis of skirt length in women's dresses over the previous 300 years (Richardson and Kroeber 1940) (Figure 9.6). Studying all sorts of pattern books, sketches, and photographs of women's dresses, they documented how styles of dresses had changed over this period. They found that skirt length had risen and fallen in ways that most women were unaware of. Subsequent studies since 1940 have suggested that this cycle has now shortened to about twenty or twenty-five years (Bernard 2011:355).

What causes these cyclical changes? One is that fashionable women want to wear the latest fashion, and this desire encourages many others to follow their lead. Second, the factories and seamstresses have a vested interest in these objects changing. They want to sell new dresses, and the best way to sell new dresses is if the styles change so much that everyone's closet is filled with "old-fashioned" dresses. But there is more to it than simply encouraging new sales, because the symbolism of being fashionable relies on constantly changing preferences. All of this activity involves many thousands of people in the fashion industry as a whole, from the high-end designers to the most inexpensive stores and even the consignment shops, which all rely on—and help produce—those changing preferences.

Changing Meaning With Changing Contexts

Contexts often change as environments and technologies change as well. Tahitians, like other Polynesians, had no knowledge of iron until Europeans first visited their islands (Figure 9.7). On June 18, 1767, the British captain Samuel Wallis was the first Westerner to reach Tahiti, and that day Tahitians were introduced to the powerful abilities of iron tools for cutting, chopping, and carving. They quickly sought ways to

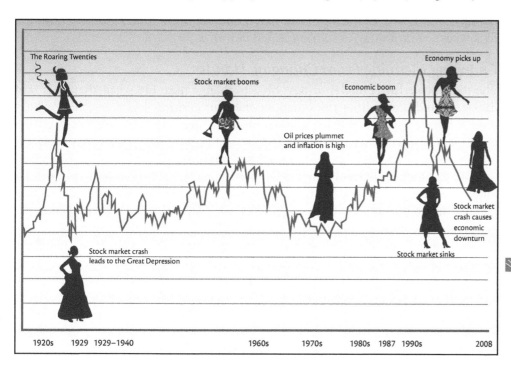

The Roaring Twenties

Stock market booms

Economic boom

Economy picks up

Oil prices plummet and inflation is high

Stock market crash causes economic downturn

Stock market sinks

Stock market crash leads to the Great Depression

1920s   1929   1929–1940   1960s   1970s   1980s   1987   1990s   2008

Figure 9.6 Shifting Dress Styles. Although dress styles in Europe and America have changed in many ways from period to period, they reflect cyclical trends and stylistic and aesthetic innovations.

Figure 9.7   Queen Oberea Welcomes Capt. Samuel Wallis at Tahiti. The queen and the captain exchanged gifts that included some small iron-cutting tools that transformed Tahitian society almost immediately.

acquire it. Although Tahitian society was traditionally sexually restrained, women discovered that sailors were very willing to trade iron knives, axes, and nails—often against their officers' orders—in exchange for sexual favors. The following year, the French captain Louis-Antoine de Bougainville arrived at Tahiti, and a year later British captain James Cook reached Tahitian shores, the latter carrying along quantities of nails and hoop iron to satisfy local demand for iron. But both voyagers and their crews were already carrying with them stereotypes of Tahitian women as lascivious. What they misunderstood was just how much it was their own sexual motivations, and Tahitian motivation to acquire iron, that had contributed to a new tolerance for sexual license in Tahitian society (Howe 1984; Salmond 2010; Gilfoyle 2020). As this example shows, new technologies can have profound impacts on local communities, in this case, contributing to shifting sexual norms.

Changing Meaning From Changing Hands

The most powerful examples of how objects change meaning when they pass into different hands come from the situation where an anthropologist or collector buys objects from exotic villagers for a museum. Until steel axes replace stone axes, the collector is buying objects that people feel are useful. But for the collector, the objects are not going to be used except as examples of a traditional society's technology and way of life. Once the object reaches a museum its meaning changes profoundly; it no longer has a useful function but becomes a rare example of something from a culture far away in time and space. Of course, being in a museum is not the only force that can change the meaning of an object with the changing of hands.

Geographical movements of objects mean that objects also move across differences in both cultural and individual perspective. Commodities, as we suggested previously, are examples of the changing significance of objects as these objects change hands. This changing of hands can carry important transnational dimensions, as we explore in "A World in Motion: The Movement of Art *In and Out of Africa*." But rather than focus too directly on how commodities create meaning, let us consider how objects represent and even help us create who we are.

A World in Motion
The Movement of Art In and Out of Africa

During the nineteenth and twentieth centuries, art collectors and museums in Europe and the United States began to pay attention to objects created in Africa—especially carved wooden statuettes, figurines, headrests, staffs, ritual objects, and the like. Reflecting their presumptions of racial superiority and unequal colonial power relations, European and American collectors initially viewed these objects in a simplistic and ethnocentric fashion, as the products of primitive minds and skills. But over time—in no small part thanks to anthropologists who helped communicate their meanings and contexts of production—those collectors and museums came to recognize the sophisticated aesthetics, symbolic complexity, and masterful workmanship that characterize certain objects, just as they should any great works of human creativity. For several decades, this growing respect has fueled a vigorous international flow of African art objects between several West African countries and cities like Paris, London, New York, and Washington, DC.

Anthropologist Christopher B. Steiner set out to study the flow of these objects, producing a book about it (Steiner 1994) and, together with ethnographic filmmakers Ilisa Barbash and Lucien Taylor, a film called *In and Out of Africa* (1992). The film emphasizes that to understand what is happening in the contemporary African art markets one cannot just visit the artists and artisans in Africa but must follow the ways these objects change hands (Nichols 1997). The film depicts the diverse actors and communities involved in the creation and trade of these objects, as well as the various meanings they make of their involvement in it. For the rural villagers who create carvings that are artificially aged in very subtle and clever ways because they know

Westerners want objects that appear old and "authentic," it is a key opportunity to participate in global markets and bring cash into their communities. For the Muslim traders who purchase them from villagers, the objects are sacrilegious because they consider them idols. They gain moral distance from the objects by referring to them simply as "wood" and justifying their willingness to trade because it enables them to support large polygamous families. For the expatriate Africans living in cities like New York who welcome and aid the Muslim traders who travel to make sales, their local connections, savvy, and logistical support make them key players. And for the white art dealers who sell the goods in upscale art galleries, they are wary and suspicious of being sold "fakes," demanding unique and authentic-seeming objects—even better if they were used in a ritual or owned by local royalty—that no other art gallery possesses so they can charge top dollar. All of these actors are looking to make a profit here in a commodity art market, but as the objects flow between them and across geographic and cultural contexts, one can see how much the meanings and uses can shift.

Since Steiner's original research, the changing meanings and significance of objects as they move from maker to vendor to trader to collector to museum has become a major theme in the study of objects from an anthropological point of view. Nowadays, if objects are seen as denoting anything, it is the often transnational linkages between distinct geographic places that are rooted in histories of collecting, the movements of exhibitions from one museum to another, and how new museum collections are assembled.

How Archaeological Specimens Change Meaning Over Time

Archaeological specimens excavated from a prehistoric site change meaning over time just as any other object does. This fact, which archaeologists have routinely observed for decades, is one reason why museums house and care for artifacts in their storerooms. What may at first seem unique as an artifact may actually be much more commonplace once archaeologists start looking for them in their excavations. Decades earlier, casual collectors may have found many examples in surface collections that can make sense of some set of artifacts identified in an excavation later. Only by examining a large number of earlier finds made over many decades does the pattern of how these artifacts have changed appear. Some of these diagnostic specimens may now be housed in museums, others in private collections. Alternatively, new information may come to light, such as a Carbon-14 date or some other association that gives the specimen new significance as part of a regional trend or a pattern of change over time.

The realization by archaeologists during the 1990s that potsherds buried for centuries can still contain grains of starch or residues of blood or food that prehistoric people consumed has transformed the significance of seemingly unimportant pieces of broken pottery. For well over a century, archaeologists have studied and documented changes in potsherds, the composition of their clays, the tempers used to bind the clay, and similar features to understand changing conditions of the communities who made and used them. None of these individual characteristics of a potsherd can tell us much by itself; they need to be analyzed together with potsherds from many sites, often deposited at different times and over a broader region of several counties or two or three states for the underlying regional and temporal patterns to emerge.

THINKING LIKE AN ANTHROPOLOGIST: MATERIALITY

The meaning of an object clearly depends on the context from which its owner views it. Over centuries the change in meaning is often obvious, but what about changes in meaning over a single lifetime? Consider some possession that excited you some years ago when you bought it or received it as a gift. How do you think about this object today? What has changed to make it more or less valuable? Is it valuable in a different way today, or has it lost its value altogether?

9.4 What Role Does Material Culture Play in Constructing the Meaning of a Community's Past?

The objects found in archaeological sites are not just data for scientific analysis; they contribute to public discourse on social and political issues relevant to our present-day concerns, especially how people view their own past. The fact is that no one can own the past, but many will claim it because it fits their ideas of what the past was supposed to be like. The effect for archaeologists is that their interpretations of the past may provoke public controversy, thus drawing them into political battles, many of which are not of their own making, although some are. In this final section, we examine the complicated politics of contemporary archaeological research.

Claiming the Past

Archaeologists encounter situations that challenge the images we have come to accept about strands in our nation's history. One of these challenges came in 1991 during the construction of a new federal office building in lower Manhattan in New York City. An archaeological assessment of the site using test pits revealed human skeletal remains; they uncovered a long-forgotten burial ground for enslaved African people used from the late 1600s until 1796 (Blakey 1998). Now known as the African Burial Ground, eventually more than 400 sets of remains—many of them children—were uncovered, showing evidence of harsh conditions, beatings, and other brutal treatment (Blakey 1998; NPR 2007) (Figures 9.8 and 9.9).

Construction teams pressured the archaeologists to excavate the graves as quickly as possible so they could complete the office building on time and within budget. Because of the forced rapid excavation, archaeologists lost considerable contextual data. Outrage arose in the African American community, and by 1992 community leaders were demanding that the remains be reinterred and a landmark established.

African Americans also wanted some control over how the site was interpreted and the kind of history it told. New Yorkers had long liked to think of their city and state as free from the evils of slavery. In fact, in the 1700s, New York was the state with the second-largest number of slaves and important slave rebellions took place there with brutal consequences for the enslaved people (NPR 2007). Black leaders wanted to use such facts—as well as this physical site—to help Americans understand the experience of their African slave ancestors and to publicize the contributions of Africans to the city and its history (Katz 2006). Based on their pressure, in 2003 the remains were reburied at one end of the site, and in 2007 President George W. Bush established the African Burial Ground National Monument.

As this situation demonstrates, uncovering the past can challenge our understandings of the world in unexpected ways and provoke social controversy in which different groups lay claim to the past.

Figure 9.8   Biological Anthropologist Michael Blakey. Dr. Blakey, of the College of William and Mary, supervised analysis of skeletal remains from the African Burial Ground.

The Politics of Archaeology

Archaeology plays a role in politics, and politics play a role in archaeology. We may want to think of archaeology as just about the facts, and nothing but the facts, but what is considered a fact has to do with the concerns and agendas of the times in which we live. Ultimately these factors affect the conditions under which archaeological knowledge about the past is produced—a point that Margaret Conkey made

Figure 9.9   Dedication of the African Burial Ground National Monument. In 2003, New York City officials stand behind four coffins containing the remains of free and enslaved African Americans. The remains were reburied in a ceremony at a site known as the African Burial Ground Memorial some 300 years after they were first laid to rest.

several decades ago about the gender biases implicit in archaeological understandings (see "Classic Contributions"). Another kind of illustration of the politics of archaeology can be found in the World Heritage Site of the ancient Maya city of Chichén Itzá.

The ruins of Chichén Itzá are situated halfway between Cancún and Mérida on the Yucatán Peninsula of southern Mexico. The city, which was originally established as early as 415–455 CE and built up over the next several centuries, has a number of dramatic pyramids, temples, and a ball court, all in the Maya-Yucatec architectural style (ICOMOS 1987).

American cultural anthropologist Quetzil Castañeda has studied how diverse interested parties—explorers, archaeologists, tourists, New Age pilgrims, and government officials—have used this archaeological site to construct various images of the ancient Maya, each supporting a particular political, economic, and cultural agenda. The story begins in the 1840s, when a US diplomat named John Lloyd Stephens (1843) "rediscovered" the ruins of Chichén Itzá, setting into motion the first of many reinterpretations of these monuments and the people who made them. Stephens's book, *Incidents of Travel in Yucatan*, provides a romanticized vision of Chichén Itzá as a "lost city" for American readers (Castañeda 1996).

But Castañeda notes that it was not just Americans who warmed to these images. Yucatec intellectuals also used them to establish a Mayan cultural heritage "that would legitimize the goal of a politically independent state" (1996:5). The Yucatán of the mid-nineteenth century declared its independence from Mexico. For such nationalist purposes, imposing ruins and monuments from an indigenous past have important symbolic power.

In 1923, the Carnegie Institution of Washington organized a long-term multidisciplinary study of the Maya. With huge financial investments from both the Carnegie Institution and the Mexican government, American researchers transformed Chichén Itzá from an archaeological site to a factory of knowledge. That research strengthened Mexico's legitimacy as a country with an ancient heritage. At the same time, this knowledge became the basis for transforming the site into a tourist attraction that could support both the project and the local Maya people. As a tourist attraction the site had two goals: (1) to showcase—and help create—an indigenous Maya ethnic consciousness, and (2) to showcase the modern science of archaeology (Figure 9.10).

Figure 9.10   Chichén Itzá.
New Age pilgrims visiting at the time of the vernal equinox in March.

Classic Contributions
Margaret Conkey and the Gender Politics of Understanding Past Lives

WHEN IT WAS established in the nineteenth century, American archaeology was largely practiced by men. For many decades into the twentieth century, not much had changed. Margaret Conkey (b. 1943) was one of the pioneering women who pursued a career in archaeology. Conkey, whose research focuses on the Upper Paleolithic period in the French Pyrénées, was long interested in how archaeologists should understand gender in their excavations. She argued that male-centered perspectives had kept many American archaeologists from accurately understanding the role of women in prehistoric societies.

Conkey's work raised questions about gender bias in archaeological research, particularly focusing on how these biases shaped the ways archaeologists interpreted their data. Such misinterpretations misconstrued, in her view, the role of women and men in ancient societies. In a classic 1984 essay she wrote together with Janet D. Spector, Conkey explains how archaeologists had addressed gender issues and how they needed a new approach to deal with the male gender bias that had emerged, perhaps unintentionally, from the fact that most archaeologists were men.

🌱 **Margaret Conkey.**

A serious challenge to the function of archaeology in contemporary society has been raised with the assertion that a largely unrecognized rationale for archaeology is the empirical substantiation of national mythology (Leone 1973:129). This use of archaeology reinforces values of which we are not always aware. As archaeologists, we "can properly be accused of being acolytes . . . to our culture," unaware of what we have been doing, and whom we serve (Leone 1973:132). Although Leone has offered a fundamental insight with respect to the relationship of archaeology to a national mythology, we show how archaeology similarly provides substantiation for a particular gender mythology. . . . [Our] review of archaeology and the study of gender should make it clear how archaeology has substantiated a set of culture-specific beliefs about the meaning of masculine and feminine, about the capabilities of men and women, about their power relations, and about their appropriate roles in society.

We argue that archaeology, like other traditional disciplines viewed through the lens of feminist criticism, has been neither objective nor inclusive on the subject of gender. Furthermore, because archaeologists lack an explicit framework for conceptualizing and researching gender and—more widely—social roles, we have drawn upon a framework that is implicit and rooted in our own contemporary experience. Thus, we must formulate not only an explicit theory of human social action (see Hodder 1982a, 1982b, 1982c) but also as part of this, an explicit framework for the archaeological study of gender. This framework must begin with theories and terms, given that our intellectual tradition is based on a fundamental and conceptual error. Man and mankind are not general, but exclusive; they are partial, and so is the scholarship about man and mankind (Minnich 1982:7). [Conkey and Spector 1984:1–2]

Questions for Reflection

1. In what ways might a male bias lead to inaccurate conclusions about the respective roles of men and women in prehistoric societies?

2. Why do you think most archaeologists were men in the years before 1970? Why didn't more women seek careers in archaeology before the 1970s?

3. What could archaeologists do to overcome these biases?

Since then, Chichén Itzá has become one of the most important tourist attractions in the Yucatán, listed as a World Heritage Site in 1988. In addition to Americans and Europeans, who visit the site while vacationing in Cancún, New Age pilgrims go there to celebrate the spring equinox (Castañeda 1996; Himpele and Castañeda 2004). Many of these New Age pilgrims have read archaeological accounts but interpret the site in their own, sometime idiosyncratic, theological terms.

Since Chichén Itzá's "rediscovery," archaeologists have played a central role in explaining its ancient past and using the site to promote their scientific credentials. But this work has always existed alongside and been influenced by others using Chichén Itzá to legitimize their own national and ethnic identities, economic interests, and religious perspectives. The important point here is that all anthropologists—not just those working over the years in Chichén Itzá—are immersed in such political and social realities.

THINKING LIKE AN ANTHROPOLOGIST: MATERIALITY

What are the ways that activists or even archaeologists and historians can try to shape the meaning of an artifact, a historic site, or even some other unique object for others?

Conclusion

Understanding how objects are given meaning by their social context is central to appreciating how people make sense of their worlds in all societies around the globe. An important point to keep in mind is that, for the most part, meaning is not necessarily intentionally constructed or interpreted; rather, it flows naturally from social patterns that make certain interpretations seem obvious and logical, and others seem foolish, implausible, or simply wrong. It is not that meanings of objects cannot be unambiguously intentional and self-conscious—think of De León's use of toe tags to represent the lives of migrants who died crossing the border. In a similar way, television commercials also intentionally construct meaning by bringing together symbols self-consciously to construct meaning, usually intending for the viewing public not to immediately recognize this construction. But as with most cultural patterns, people will recognize the meaning of these symbols because the patterns are deeply embedded in their basic expectations of the world.

The issues raised by the materiality of simple objects—whether a piece of clothing, an art object, a photograph, a bicycle, a historic building, or a commonplace object we use in daily life—highlight a broader dynamic that affects the social and cultural construction of meaning in every culture across the globe. The meanings of objects change over time, and the meaning of the past itself changes as social contexts change. Control over the meaning of basic cultural assumptions is often a highly contentious issue, with different positions put forward by different interests within the community. But control of the meaning of objects, even the significance of something as mundane as a smartphone, is equally contentious because people use them in distinct ways due to distinctions in factors like gender, age, class, race, and so on.

This dynamic has two dimensions. One lies in who has control over access to the resources, both historical, archaeological, and cultural, from which we can document and uncover the story of how things came to be. The other is that interpretations of the material world, whether from the past or the present, differ according to social interests. So the interpretation of objects, artifacts, archaeological sites, and human remains always has a wide variety of legal, moral, and political implications. These implications are constructed by many different people, each with a different set of personal and social agendas. We call this the cultural construction of meaning, whether applied to objects, bodies, practices, or human experiences, and it is this that shows us what anthropology is all about.

KEY TERMS

AIM (American Indian Movement)   p. 255

Cultural resource management (CRM)   p. 256

Feature   p. 263

Material culture   p. 252

Materiality   p. 252

NAGPRA (Native American Graves and Repatriation Act)   p. 255

Repatriation   p. 255

World Heritage Site program   p. 256

Reviewing the Chapter

Chapter Section	What We Know	To Be Resolved
Why is the ownership of prehistoric artifacts such a contentious issue?	Ownership of artifacts raises difficult moral, social, and political questions about who has the right to control, display, and interpret objects. In the United States, NAGPRA legislation has clarified who should control the bones and artifacts of Indians that archaeologists uncover in their excavations.	NAGPRA does not completely resolve conflicts over who should control archaeological objects. Some museum skeletal collections are poorly documented, so nobody now knows which tribe the remains or important cultural objects may have belonged to originally. Archaeologists, museums, and American Indians continue to have to negotiate what happens to such objects.
How should we look at objects anthropologically?	All objects, old and new, from the most special to the most mundane, have multiple dimensions.	Stocking's original notion of seven dimensions attached to objects is a useful starting point for analyzing objects. But there is debate over whether these are always the most useful dimensions for analyzing all objects, as well as which dimensions Stocking may have missed.
How and why do the meanings of things change over time?	All objects change over time, if not in their physical characteristics, then in the significance people give to them. Meanings change because of generational change, changes in social and technological context, and as objects change hands.	Anthropologists have not yet systematically explored whether the importance of objects changes and has always changed in the same ways, or if different kinds of societies (literate vs. preliterate; stratified vs. egalitarian, etc.) change the meanings of things in precisely the same ways.
What role does material culture play in constructing the meaning of a community's past?	No community can truly "own its past," but all interpretations can be understood as cultural constructions and these are subject to biases that come from factors such as that dominant social groups have more control on how to interpret everyone's past.	While nobody owns their own past, anthropologists are still debating how to interpret the objects in ways that simultaneously reflect the empirical evidence and the interests and concerns of both dominant and minority communities.

READINGS

Two solid histories of archaeology are Brian M. Fagan's *A Brief History of Archaeology: Classical Times to the Twenty-First Century* (Upper Saddle River, NJ: Pearson Prentice Hall, 2005) and Bruce G. Trigger's *A History of Archaeological Thought*, 2nd ed. (Cambridge: Cambridge University Press, 2006). For an account focused more specifically on American archaeology, one should see Gordon R. Willey and Jeremy A. Sabaloff's *A History of American Archaeology*, 3rd ed. (New York: W. H. Freeman, 1993). Joan Gero and Margaret Conkey's edited volume *Engendering Archaeology: Women and Prehistory* (Oxford: Blackwell, 1991) explores the increasingly important role of women in archaeology.

Regna Darnell's *And Along Came Boas: Continuity and Revolution in Americanist Anthropology* (Amsterdam: John Benjamins, 2000) offers an overview of the early development of anthropology in museums. Stocking's *Objects and Others* (Madison: University of Wisconsin Press, 1985) remains a classic on the topic. David J. Meltzer's 1985 essay "North American Archaeology and Archaeologists, 1879–1934" (*American Antiquity* 50, no. 2:249–60) offers a complementary view from an archaeological perspective.

For a general survey of NAGPRA and its wider implications, see the volume, edited by Devon A. Mihesuah, *Repatriation Reader: Who Owns American Indian Remains* (Lincoln: University of Nebraska Press, 2000). David Hurst Thomas's *The Skull Wars: Kennewick Man, Archaeology, and the Battle for Native American Identity* (New York: Basic Books, 2000) offers a case study of a particularly controversial set of remains from Kennewick, Washington. For a more general view of CRM, see F. O. McManamon and A. Hatton, eds., *Cultural Resource Management in Contemporary Society: Perspectives on Managing and Presenting the Past* (London: Routledge, 2000).

For treatment of objects in cultural anthropology, see Arjun Appadurai's collection of essays *The Social Life of Things: Commodities in Cultural Perspective* (Cambridge: Cambridge University Press, 1986) and Daniel Miller's *Material Cultures: Why Some Things Matter* (Chicago: University of Chicago Press, 1998). Luis Vivanco, a coauthor of this book, has applied the social-life-of-things approach to the bicycle in his 2013 book *Reconsidering the Bicycle: An Anthropological Perspective on a New (Old) Thing* (New York: Routledge).

Why Is Carbon-14 So Important to Archaeologists?

IN A PREVIOUS Methods Memo—"How Do Anthropologists Study Ancient Primates and Human Origins" (in Part II)— we explained that anthropologists who study fossils and archaeological sites use a variety of relative and absolute dating methods to determine the age of what they find. Stratigraphy commonly provides archaeologists with a relative timeline for a given site, helping to identify when some activity or use happened in relation to other sites. But archaeologists often want to know exactly when a site was occupied or used or, perhaps, when sediments were deposited on top of some human activity. In these situations, they turn to absolute dating methods, the most common of which is radiocarbon dating, also known as **Carbon-14 dating**, which is useful for dating organic materials up to 60,000 years old. Developed in the late 1940s by the chemist Willard Libby (1960), today it is a pervasive technique in archaeology because of its reliability and affordability. But how does it actually work?

WHAT IS CARBON-14 AND WHY IS IT IMPORTANT TO ARCHAEOLOGISTS?

All carbon atoms contain six protons in their nucleus and the vast majority of carbon atoms also contain six neutrons, giving them an atomic weight of 12 (six protons and six neutrons). About 1% of all carbon atoms have seven neutrons, producing a stable atomic weight of 13, which is called C-13 (six protons and seven neutrons). In the upper atmosphere, when cosmic rays bombard nitrogen atoms they create a third form of carbon, Carbon-14, which is radioactive. This atom is fundamentally unstable and half of the C-14 atoms will become stable Nitrogen-14 atoms releasing a high-energy particle called an antineutrino.

For archaeologists, the key feature of Carbon-14 dating is that radioactive carbon (C-14) is created by cosmic rays at a regular rate in the upper atmosphere so that when plants breathe in carbon dioxide, they will continuously take in C-14 molecules at a low but stable rate. But when a living plant or animal dies, it no longer refreshes its C-14, so the remaining carbon atoms gradually break down at a steady and predictable rate. Animals that eat plants, and the animals that eat these animals and breathe in carbon dioxide (CO_2), will always have a stable amount of C-14 in their bodies because the cosmic rays hitting nitrogen in the upper atmosphere continually replenish the amount of C-14 in the air.

With a half-life of 5,730 years, the amount of radioactive carbon in a piece of wood will disintegrate at a stable rate. Half of the C-14 atoms will be lost over the first half-life (5,730 years) and half of the remaining will be lost over the next half-life (after 11,460 years), and so on. So, if we can determine the relative percentages of C-12 (stable) and C-14 (unstable and radioactive) in the sample, researchers can calculate the age required for enough C-14 molecules to decompose to produce the observed proportion of C-14 remaining in the test sample. The age of the sample can be determined from the percentage of carbon that is composed of the radioactive isotope (C-14) rather than the stable isotopes (C-12 and C-13). The amount of C-14 always declines over time, and always at the same rate.

HOW IS CARBON-14 MEASURED AND HOW DO ARCHAEOLOGISTS OBTAIN IT?

Accelerator mass spectrometers (AMS) measure the percentages of each of the three carbon isotopes, allowing researchers to calculate an approximate date for when the living plant or animal died. The technology has improved considerably over the past half-century, making it much less costly and much faster than it was even twenty or thirty years ago (Figure MM3.3).

In principle, nearly any organic material can be dated with AMS. Anything made of wood might be a suitable substance to test, but in archaeological sites most wood rots and completely decomposes after a century or two. Most researchers prefer to use charcoal samples or bone fragments, both of which decompose at a much slower rate than other organic substances, such as wood, leather, hide, or flesh. Charcoal from cooking fires is the most common organic sample tested from any excavation, although bone will usually suffice if charcoal is not present. The only problem for archaeologists is finding enough charcoal or bone in a clear and identifiable context: (1) in a plain, obvious, and undisrupted stratum and (2) without evidence of contamination. Charcoal is usually stable over many centuries and produces the best C-14 results.

- **Carbon-14 dating.** A dating method that establishes the date or period of an organic artifact or feature from the relative proportions of radioactive carbon to non-radioactive isotopes.

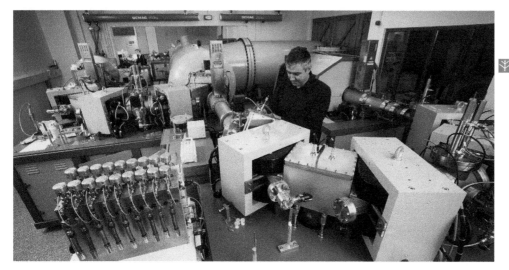

Figure MM3.1   Using an Accelerator Mass Spectrometer to identify the composition of an archaeological or paleontological sample. Recent technological advances and new digital-imaging techniques have allowed researchers more nuanced insights to all of these matters and have been used to extract additional evidence from the existing fossil record.

Sea shells also contain carbon in the carbonate that forms the shell, and such samples can also be tested for C-14. The difficulty in testing shells comes from the fact that C-14 levels in ocean water are not nearly as stable or consistent as atmospheric carbon, and thus the dating can be easily distorted. Because of the high content of carbon in wood, charcoal is always preferred over shells because carbonates from the ocean seem to be much more sensitive to seasonal and atmospheric changes than the carbon in plants seems to be.

The only other significant weakness in Carbon-14 dating concerns whether a sample or the area from which a sample of charcoal is collected has been contaminated by intrusions over the centuries after the sample was deposited. Tree roots with modern Carbon-14, rodent burrows, and the erosion of older or younger carbon onto a carbon sample can all contaminate the sample, producing either a much too early or much too recent date. For this reason, selecting an uncontaminated sample and preventing contamination after collecting are still major problems that all archaeologists confront.

A second problem with radiocarbon dating is that it is only reliable for dating carbon that is less than 50,000 or 60,000 years old. There is simply too little remaining C-14 in any sample older than that to produce a reliable date with current technology. For most archaeologists, whose field research sites range between 100 and 12,000 years old, this is not a problem. However, to overcome this limitation on sites older than 100,000 years, researchers have turned to Potassium-Argon dating, which measures the ratio of a radioactive potassium isotope (K-40) to the stable isotope of argon gas (Ar-40). The radioactive potassium isotope has a half-life of 1.248 million years. Since human and animal bodies contain far too little potassium to trace such nuclear decays, K-Ar dating is usually performed on layers of volcanic rock that was deposited by the eruption of a volcano in the region. Such K-Ar dating has been especially useful in the African Rift Valley south of Lake Victoria where early deposits are both accessible and sometimes visible following seasonal rains. This dating method has been especially useful for tracing Australopithecines and other early pre-human hominins, who lived far too early for C-14 dating to be useful.

Thinking Critically About Carbon-14 Dating

- It turns out that various geologic, atmospheric, and solar processes can affect the amount of Carbon-14 in the atmosphere, so Carbon-14 in the atmosphere is not as constant over time as we once thought it would be. One way archaeologists have been able to test the accuracy of their Carbon-14 dates is to check them against other relative and absolute dating techniques, and recalibrate the age if necessary. Can you think of another dating technique or two that might help with that calibration? Look back to the table on pages 141–42 to help you in thinking about possible answers.

- One of the biggest problems with Carbon-14 dating comes when a sample is contaminated by more recent carbon deposits or sometimes by older carbon deposits, neither of which were associated with the sample specimen we want to date. What procedures would likely prevent contamination of a sample from either older carbon or more recent carbon?

- What might cause a sample of charcoal from a fire to be contaminated even though the archaeologists have been careful not to contaminate the site during excavation?

Early Agriculture and the Neolithic Revolution

10

Modifying the Environment to Satisfy Human Demands

IN 1930 two Australian prospectors set off in search of gold in the Central Highlands of Papua New Guinea. No Westerner had been there before, and the widespread assumption was that these highland valleys were uninhabited. But the prospectors were surprised to find many hundreds of scattered individual homesteads, each surrounded by extensive gardens. Only in the eastern part of the Highlands were there what one might call villages, but it turns out that this region had over a million inhabitants, with population densities in some areas reaching as high as 1,000 people per square mile, equivalent to an American suburb.

Even more striking was the fact that these dense populations and the large herds of domesticated pigs living among them were subsisting on sweet potatoes, a crop that developed first in South America and somehow reached coastal New Guinea and from there was brought to the Highlands through gifts and interpersonal networks that stretched from the moderately populated coastal settlements across the thinly populated upland country that surrounded the Central Highlands. The unexpected dominance of sweet potatoes added a new dimension to an old debate among anthropologists about how, when, and why ancient humans, who lived by hunting and gathering, shifted to food production.

In the 1920s the Australian archaeologist V. Gordon Childe, who had studied this shift in the Middle East, described it as the **Neolithic Revolution**. The Neolithic refers to the so-called New Stone Age when humans had begun growing crops and raising

Horticulture in New Guinea. Kuk World Heritage Site in Papua New Guinea, site of the earliest known drainage ditching for draining swampy land on the island of New Guinea. Inset: Ditching used to drain fields in historic times among the Dani in the highlands in West New Guinea now a part of Indonesia.

● **Neolithic Revolution.**
The "New" Stone Age when humans began to produce their food (growing crops and raising animals) rather than relying exclusively on foraging, but using a stone-tool technology.

animals for food using stone-tool technology. According to Childe, this transformation was revolutionary because it allowed for population expansion and change in almost all aspects of society. But Childe and his successors had focused on the domestication of grains, which can be stored for long periods, and so it came as a surprise that tubers could also sustain large populations. The main problem with tubers is that, unlike grains, they tend to rot after a couple of weeks. New Guinea Highlanders did, in fact, store their tubers, but they did so in the form of animal protein, by feeding them to their large herds of pigs.

How and when did hunter-gatherers living in the Highland valleys suddenly adopt the cultivation of sweet potatoes? This is an intriguing question, but there is another element to this story that complicates the answer. In nearly every Highland community, researchers have long observed very old large stone mortars and pestles, clearly once used for grinding, mashing, or pulverizing food. Some were found in archaeological excavations, and their relative lack of portability meant that most were more or less consistently in use by New Guineans for thousands of years. These artifacts were perplexing. It was not obvious what they were used for—probably not for mashing sweet potatoes, which don't require such a tool—particularly when you consider the amount of effort required to hollow out and smooth the surface of a stone pestle a foot or two feet in diameter.

A number of archaeologists had long seen these objects as a key to understanding how New Guinea Highlanders could have so easily shifted from hunting and gathering to simple agriculture or horticulture, laying the groundwork, as it were, for the arrival and cultivation of sweet potatoes starting about 1,200 years ago. Enter archaeologist Glenn Summerhayes of New Zealand's University of Otago and his large team of research colleagues who mostly work in labs rather than in the Highland valleys of New Guinea, who have brought some new insight into this problem. One of Summerhayes's colleagues Richard Fullegar had pioneered the technique of residue analysis in the 1990s (see the Methods Memo on page 408–9), to use microscopes to determine what kinds of food were being ground up in the mortar from the grains of starch left behind. Applying this technique to those mysterious mortars and pestles, Summerhayes and his team found residues of various kinds of wild nuts that were as old as 20,000 years, a time before Highlanders were actively growing their own foods. Back then they were harvesting various kinds of wild nuts, particularly certain species of pandanus, using these mortars and pestles to break the hard shells and grind up the seeds into a mash that could be heated and cooked over a fire. Harvesting pandanus and other nuts has not traditionally been seen as a direct stage in the Neolithic revolution, but it is likely that they managed tree crops, developing a variety of new skills and technologies that eventually enabled them to subsist primarily on foods they could grow.

The assumption that New Guinea Highlanders had shifted suddenly from hunting to horticulture once sweet potatoes became available is too simplistic. It now looks as if a variety of plants were managed and at least partially cultivated for several thousand years before Highlanders began to rely totally on the cultivation of domesticated plants. These issues lead us to ask: *How did raising plants and animals change the ways people lived in their environments?* Embedded within this larger question are several smaller questions around which this chapter is organized.

How important was hunting to prehistoric peoples?

Why did people start domesticating plants and animals?

How did early humans raise their own food?

What impact did raising plants and animals have on other aspects of life?

For more than a century, archaeologists have viewed the transition from hunting and gathering to agriculture as one of the most intriguing puzzles, raising questions about how early humans learned to tend crops or how to tame wild animals to become a domestic herd. We now know that there was no single Neolithic Revolution, affecting all humanity in the same ways or at the same time. Instead, multiple transformations have played out differently in distinct times and places around the globe. The story of how and why these transitions happened must begin with how early humans got their food, and this brings us to the matter of hunting.

10.1 How Important Was Hunting to Prehistoric Peoples?

As we explained in Chapter 6 ("Ancestral Humans"), contemporary humans have been around for approximately 200,000 years. During about 95 percent of that time people ate only what they could hunt, gather, or scavenge from the natural environment. Without claws or sharp fangs like other animals, the only way early humans could hunt large game was by using tools made from sharpened wood, bone, antler, and stone. We know that small animals like possums, rodents, snakes, and lizards can be obtained by the hands alone or with the simplest of tools. People also used tools such as digging sticks and stone scrapers to hunt, gather, and prepare wild foods. But most of the time the only archaeological evidence that early humans hunted comes from their stone tools and bones with signs of cutting that they left behind. From cave art in the later Paleolithic period we have some evidence of how some groups hunted, and studies of the skeletons of ancient hunters and gatherers have offered insights into both the foods people ate and how they acquired these foods, particularly from osteology, the study of bones, and from paleopathological studies that tell us about a variety of diet-related health problems (e.g., Cohen and Crane-Kramer 2007; Eshed et al. 2010). But the information is scant, so archaeologists turned to living hunter-gatherers for ideas and insights about early practices.

Taking Stock of Living Hunter-Gatherers

When anthropology emerged in the nineteenth century, most of the world's people had been growing their own food for at least a few thousand years. It was only in the remote deserts, rain forests, and polar regions that small bands of people practiced **foraging**, or obtaining food by searching for it, as opposed to growing or raising the plants and animals people eat. For the most part, agriculture and animal husbandry had not penetrated these regions because the environment and climate were not suited to these activities. Explorers, travelers, and eventually anthropologists often described these environments as harsh, depicting their inhabitants' technologies as simple and their ways of life as crude and brutish. These were the deeply held cultural stereotypes rooted in urban European and American worldviews, and they rarely reflect the perspectives of the desert-dwelling Australian Aboriginals and the people of the Kalahari Desert, or any of the Inuit groups living in the Arctic. Most Westerners—including early anthropologists—assumed these people, who still hunted in the Arctic or the deserts, represented examples of the most primitive human societies. They must therefore, it was assumed, resemble the human ancestors of contemporary peoples living in Europe, the Middle East, India, and China who once had similar hunting practices but had evolved into more complex and sophisticated forms (Figure 10.1).

But just how difficult was it for early hunter-gatherers to get their food? How heavily did they actually rely on hunting? And just how similar were contemporary hunter-gatherers to their prehistoric ancestors? These topics and many others were at the heart of an international gathering of anthropologists and archaeologists titled "Man the Hunter."

"Man the Hunter"

In April 1966 anthropologists Richard Lee and Irven DeVore (1968:vii) hosted a conference at the University of Chicago with the title "Man the Hunter" to address the state of anthropological knowledge about hunting-and-gathering ways of life.

- **Foraging.** Obtaining food by searching for it, as opposed to growing or raising the plants and animals people eat.

Figure 10.1   Hunter-Gatherers. Some of the best-known contemporary hunter-gatherers around the world and the proportion of the family's livelihood that men and women produce in each.

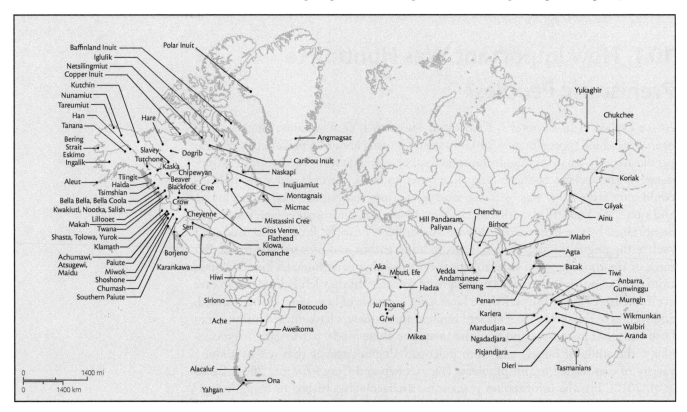

To current readers, the conference's title may sound sexist, but it was unintentionally so, because at the time the conventional term for all humans without regard to gender was "man." Yet the dominant anthropological model of these societies in the decades leading up to the conference held that hunter-gatherers live in **patrilocal bands** (small groups where men controlled resources and hunting territories). The assumptions included three key features: (1) hunting was an activity principally undertaken by men, (2) hunting was more important than gathering, and (3) men's subsistence activities were more significant than women's. Table 10.1 shows that there was, in

● **Patrilocal bands.** Small groups in which men controlled resources and hunting territories.

TABLE 10.1	THE RELATIVE IMPORTANCE OF MEN'S AND WOMEN'S CONTRIBUTIONS TO THE BASIC DIET IN CONTEMPORARY HUNTER-GATHER COMMUNITIES			
REGION	ETHNIC GROUP	EFFECTIVE TEMPERATURE(Celsius)	PERCENTAGE OF DIET PROVIDED BY MEN	POPULATION DENSITY (PER KM²)
EXTREMELY COLD CLIMATES				
Siberia	Yukaghir	8.9	90%	0.5
Alaska	Nunamiut	9.8	85%	2.0
Canada	Copper Inuit	9.1	90%	1.2
Greenland	Angmagsalik	9.0	100%	8.0
S. America	Ona (Selk'nam)	9.0	75%	
S. America	Yahgan	9.9	50%	4.6
COLD CLIMATES				
Siberia	Gilyak	10.4	70%	19.2
Alaska	Chugach Eskimo	10.5	80%	18.0
Alaska	Kaska	10.5	80%	
Alaska	Eyak	10.5	80%	
Alaska	Ingalik	10.8	80%	2.5
Alaska	Aleut	11.6	90%	65.0
NW Coast	Tlingit	10.0	90%	10–40
NW Coast	Bella Coola	10.5	80%	10
NW Coast	Tsimshian	11.1	70%	32–83
NW Coast	Quileute	11.3	70%	64.5
Canada	Chilcotin	11.2	60%	13
Canada	Chipewyan	10.3	100%	0.4
Canada	Pikangikum (Ojibwa)	11.0	90%	3.2
Canada	Sekani	11.1	95%	1.0
Canada	Beaver	11.3	68%	0.5
Canada	Saulteaux	11.7	70%	0.6
Canada	Montagnais	11.6	70%	
COOL CLIMATES				
Japan	Ainu	12.0	50%	
NW Coast	Klallam	12.3	75%	
NW Coast	Squamish	12.6	90%	
NW Coast	Nootka	12.6	65%	66–77
NW Coast	Cowichan	12.6	60%	34
Plateau	Flathead	12.1	60%	
Plateau	Gros Ventre	12.4	80%	

	TABLE 10.1 (Continued)			
Plateau	Coeur d'Alene	12.7	70%	1.5
Plateau	Kutenai	12.7	70%	2.0
Plateau	Sanpoil	12.7	58%	
California	Washo	12.3	75%	28
California	Tubatulabel	12.9	58%	30
Canada	Micmac	12.7	85%	2.3
S. America	Tehuelche	12.8	85%	
	TEMPERATE CLIMATES			
California	Achumawi	13.3	60%	17.5
California	Yurok	13.3	58%	180
California	Chimariko	13.5	80%	34.1
California	Maidu	13.5	58%	103
California	Wintu	14.6	78%	281
California	Diegueno	14.6	50%	18.1
California	S. Yokuts	14.7	73%	90
California	E. Pomo	14.7	63%	196–633
California	Wappo	14.7	63%	163
Plateau	Umatilla	13.3	70%	4.5
Plateau	Tenino	13.3	50%	
Great Basin	Tosawihi	13.0	50%	15
Great Basin	Kaibab (S. Paiute)	14.0	48%	3–4
Plains	Crow	13.0	80%	2.6
Plains	Arapaho	13.3	70%	3
Plains	Comanche	14.4	63%	5
S. America	Botocuido	14.4	78%	
	WARM CLIMATES			
Great Basin	Panamint	15.0	40%	2.1
Great Basin	Shivwits (S. Paiute)	15.1	48%	1.3
Australia	Aranda	15.9	30%	3.0
Australia	Dieri	15.9	30%	1.9
SW United States	NE Yavapai	16.0	55%	1.4–4.0
S. America	Aweikoma	16.5	70%	
Africa	Hadsa	17.7	20%	15
	HOT CLIMATES			
Africa	Ju/hoansi (Dobe)	18.8	40%	10–16
Africa	G/wi	19.3	30%	8.0
Australia	Walpiri	18.4	30%	1.0
Australia	Wikmunkan	19.6	35%	18.7
	VERY HOT AND HUMID CLIMATES			
Australia	Tiwi	22.6	38%	
Australia	Murngin	23.5	53%	5
Malaysia	Semang	23.7	80%	5–19
Africa	Mbuti	23.7	41%	17
SE Asia	Andamanese	24.4	30%	86
Source: After Kelly (1995:265).				

fact, tremendous variation from group to group in how much women contributed to the family's subsistence. In several harsh environments such as the arctic, where vegetable foods are not commonly available in winter, men's contributions in hunting are considerably more significant than women's. What this table does not reveal is that even when women collect little vegetable or plant material, this does not mean that women are not contributing to the family's survival, since they often make clothing or cook the food men bring in.

In spite of its title, what emerged from the conference was a resounding rejection of the old male-dominated model. A key revelation in toppling this old view was the consensus among participants that hunting was not *the* defining feature of these societies, as the old model held, but in fact these prehistoric societies survived because of women's subsistence activities (Table 10.1). For example, Richard Lee's (2012) research in the Kalahari Desert among contemporary !Kung San hunter-gatherers showed that women's foraging activities often provided more than 60 percent of the calories people eat. Similar findings were reported from many other living hunter-gatherer societies, where women may only rarely hunt for large game but provided the bulk of plant foods, fish, crustaceans, shellfish, and small game. Recognizing these facts, participants offered what has come to be known as the **generalized foraging model** (Kelly 2013:10). This model asserts that hunter-gatherer societies have five basic characteristics, shown in Table 10.2.

The conference also challenged the notion that hunter-gatherer lives were harsh; instead, they were examples of the "original affluent society" (Sahlins 1968, 1972). Previously, anthropologists had assumed that a hunting-gathering lifestyle was so difficult and precarious that people had to work long hours and had no time to develop elaborate cultural artifacts. But in his presentation for the conference, Marshall Sahlins rejected this image, pointing out that hunter-gatherers worked only a few hours a week. Playing on the title of economist John Kenneth Galbraith's (1958) book on US capitalism, *The Affluent Society*, Sahlins showed how ethnographic data supported the view that hunter-gatherers had more than enough food resources available to them. Further, he asserted, most people in a foraging band spent many hours each day in leisure activities, socializing, or sleeping. Their nomadic lifestyle meant that they neither needed nor desired material goods, which they would have to carry from camp to camp. Sahlins also insisted that hunter-gatherers did not view their natural environments as scarce and harsh (as we might) but as abundant and always providing for their needs, even in times of objective scarcity such as drought (Bird-David 1992).

• **Generalized foraging model.** A model that asserts that hunter-gatherer societies have five basic characteristics.

TABLE 10.2	THE GENERALIZED FORAGING MODEL: THE FIVE BASIC FEATURES OF HUNTER-GATHERERS
Egalitarianism	Mobility constrains the amount of property that can be owned and thus serves to maintain material equality.
Low population density	Population is kept below carrying capacity through intentional, conscious controls such as sexual abstention, abortion, and infanticide.
Lack of territoriality	Long-term adaptation to resource variability requires that hunter-gatherers be able to move from one region to another, so defending territories would be maladaptive.
A minimum of food storage	Since the group is nomadic and food plentiful relative to population density, food storage is unnecessary; hence the potential for food storage to create social hierarchy is thwarted
Flux in band composition	Maintaining social ties requires frequent movement and visiting among groups, which discourages violence since disputes can always be solved through groups breaking up rather than fighting.

Source: After Kelly (2013:10).

The importance of Sahlins's analysis was to insist that a different cultural logic underlies how and why foraging societies think about and relate to their natural environments. It also undermined the assumption that switching to farming and herding was necessarily an improvement in human welfare.

Recent Attempts to Understand Prehistoric Hunting Strategies

While participants in the 1966 conference dismissed the "hunter" model in favor of a generalized forager model, more recent research has shown that there is considerable variation among hunter-gatherer groups. For example, it has become clear that women often contribute a great deal to a band's subsistence needs in some places but provide much less in others (see, e.g., Peterson 2002).

For instance, in colder climates, such as among the Inuit and other Arctic groups, foraging adds little to basic subsistence since diets are based mainly on large animals, and women contribute little to food procurement. But even in these societies, women spend as much time and sometimes more time working as men do—much of their time being devoted to food and clothing preparation—so we should not imagine that Inuit women contribute little to the community's livelihood. Not surprisingly, when archaeologists first considered the role of men and women in early agricultural societies, they similarly assumed that men performed the lion's share of the work, while more recent analyses suggest that in most horticultural and agricultural societies, women's effort is typically greater than that of men.

The new view of hunter-gatherers raised an interesting question: If they could procure sufficient food with just a few hours of labor each day (as the "original affluent society" concept emphasizes), why did they not spend an extra hour each day to amass a surplus—more goods than people need—as people living in settled communities regularly do?

Anthropologists have suggested two answers to this question. The first was proposed by Lorna Marshall, a pioneer researcher among the !Kung San, whose best-known band is called the Ju/'hoansi, of the Kalahari desert region in southwestern Africa. Marshall noted that the !Kung women she observed were not lazy, but they only gathered as much as they needed for their own families because if they had more, they would be expected to share it with the entire band (Lee and DeVore 1968:94). Knowing that her labor would not help her family, most of these women intentionally avoided collecting too much. The key feature of this explanation is that among the !Kung, as in many other hunter-gatherer communities, people place great emphasis on sharing, which is viewed as a moral obligation (Marshall and Miesmer 2007). This sharing provided everyone with food whether they were successful in their gathering or not, and prevented over-harvesting of the foods that everyone ate.

The second was suggested by anthropologist Bruce Winterhalder (1993; see also Winterhalder and Smith 1981), whose research showed that even if only a few members of the band decided to harvest more than they needed on a regular basis, their actions could threaten the survival of the entire community as they depleted local resources that everyone relied upon—especially in years of environmental stress, such as drought. Winterhalder, along with Eric Smith, developed a model they called the **optimal foraging strategy**, which suggests that people capture just enough calories from the environment as they (and their families) need to survive comfortably. Any additional calories would, over time, stress the resources of the area and threaten the survival of the community.

In fact, not all societies using hunting and gathering as their subsistence strategy avoided accumulating surpluses. The best-known examples of these are the Native

● **Optimal foraging strategy.** A foraging lifestyle wherein people capture just enough calories from the environment as they (and their families) need to survive comfortably.

American communities of the Pacific Northwest that had attracted so much attention because of the early research work of Franz Boas. These groups include the Tlingit, Haida, Tsimshian, Kwakiutl, Nootka, and Coast Salish. When Europeans first visited them, all of these peoples relied primarily on fishing, especially on the annual migration of salmon returning to inland spawning grounds. Men were responsible for most of the salmon catch, but women played the largest role in cutting, cleaning, drying, and preserving it. These Indian groups—unlike nearly all other contemporary hunter-gatherers—were largely sedentary. They developed elaborate art traditions, large ceremonial houses, enormous totem poles that bore images representing their ancestors and clan affiliations, and ceremonial exchange relations involving gifts of large quantities of food and material objects.

Uniquely among hunter-gatherers, they also amassed large surpluses above their subsistence needs. Fish and other valuable objects were given away or sometimes destroyed in competitive exchanges called **potlatches**, opulent ceremonial feasts intended to display wealth and social status by giving away or destroying valuable possessions like carved copper plates, button blankets, and baskets of food (Codere 1950; Drucker and Heizer 1967; Kan 1989). Unlike exchanges in other hunter-gather societies, the goal of these gift exchanges was not to provide food or material goods to other groups but to assert political, economic, and social superiority by giving away more than the recipients could pay back at some later potlatch (Figure 10.2).

The large number of ethnographic studies of contemporary hunter-gatherers provides many insights about life under these non-agricultural conditions. But do these societies represent the actual lifestyles of our prehistoric ancestors during Palaeolithic times?

Back to the Past: Understanding Prehistoric Hunter-Gatherers

No anthropologist or archaeologist today expects contemporary hunter-gatherers to be identical to people in prehistoric communities. One key reason is that in almost every contemporary case, hunter-gatherers are linked to sedentary agricultural or industrial societies through trade and other social ties, which would obviously not have been the case before the development of agriculture. For example, the Punan, who live in the rain forests of Borneo, have been gathering forest products like rattan for the world market for perhaps a thousand years (Hoffman 1984); and Central African

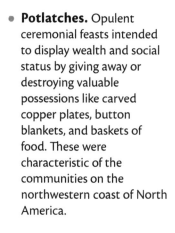

● **Potlatches.** Opulent ceremonial feasts intended to display wealth and social status by giving away or destroying valuable possessions like carved copper plates, button blankets, and baskets of food. These were characteristic of the communities on the northwestern coast of North America.

Figure 10.2 Nineteenth-Century Kwakiutl Potlatch. Note the rich material culture available to this sedentary hunting and gathering community, made possible by the harvest of migrating salmon that swim the same rivers each spring and summer. The surplus of salmon allowed competitive exchanges called potlatches between rivals.

The Anthropological Life
What Are the Responsibilities and Job Description of an Archaeologist?

In the United States, most archaeologists actually work in the field of Cultural Resource Management (CRM), with relatively fewer archaeologists teaching at universities, and fewer still working as state or county archaeologists. Most CRM firms hire field crews with some excavation experience (an undergraduate field school is usually sufficient), and nearly all of the big companies will train a young archaeologist without an advanced degree. Many of those jobs are seasonal. Nearly all year-round, career-oriented jobs in CRM require at least a master's degree with a concentration in archaeology. A bachelor's degree in anthropology or geology may be helpful on the job, but legally it is not sufficient in most jurisdictions to run a crew and supervise an excavation.

Major responsibilities of an archaeologist include these:

- Familiarity with field survey techniques that could include ground surveys, aerial surveys, and the use of remote sensing tools
- Examination, documentation, and preservation of artifacts
- Systematic recording of artifacts, soil samples, and rock samples, especially if they are not maintained in the archaeologist's own facility such as a museum, university, or private firm
- Use of standard computer applications, particularly geographical information systems (GIS), to produce maps of excavations, sites, and simulations of how sites might have looked in the past
- Producing, maintaining, and compiling written, photographic, and drawn records (sketches), as well as electronic databases for many different aspects of research in a site
- Supervising and guiding staff during surveys, excavation, and laboratory work
- Curation of specimens, particularly preserving artifacts found in excavations, inventorying these for each site, and keeping a systematic log and retrieval system
- Collecting, analyzing, and interpreting data from excavations and from data preserved from earlier excavations and museum collections

- Writing site reports, often for state officials and for public dissemination
- Presentations to the public, the media, and other archaeology professionals about significant findings
- Writing reports, papers, and other articles for publication in scholarly journals
- Preparing samples for Carbon-14 analysis
- Analyzing artifacts, features, and sites using mathematical, statistical, computational, and interpretive methods
- Familiarity with ethnographic case studies and cultural theories that can inform their interpretations
- Assessing planning applications for building developers (e.g., for presentation to planning boards, heritage commissions, etc.)
- Interacting with tribal authorities to handle NAGPRA matters
- Offering advice to local heritage commissions, planning boards, city councils, and so on about how to maintain historic and prehistoric resources
- Writing reports about particular historic or prehistoric sites for consideration as a National Register property, some sort of state register property, or local landmark site.

Although archaeological fieldwork usually takes place in teams, it is possible to work on a self-employed basis. Temporary contracts are common, but some firms hire staff on a regular basis. Your work could be based outdoors at an excavation or site, as part of an inspection team, or indoors in an office, laboratory, or museum. The most significant analyses occur at a desk with a computer, or in a lab with careful analysis of specimens excavated in the field.

RESOURCES

Texas Historical Commission. 2016. What does an Archaeologist Do? Texas Historical Commission webpage. Accessed July 14, 2023. https://www.thc.texas.gov/public/upload/archeology-what-does-archeologist-do.pdf

Target Jobs. 2022. Archaeologist: Job Description. https://targetjobs .co.uk/careers-advice/job-descriptions/archaeologist-job-description. Accessed June 3, 2022.

Work.Chron.com. 2018. Duties for an Archaeologist. https://work.chron .com/duties-archaeologist-13263.html. Accessed June 3, 2022.

pygmies were involved in trading ivory toward the coast long before Europeans reached their forests (Bahuchet 1988). Some anthropologists have even wondered whether any of the contemporary hunter-gatherer groups could actually have survived without contact with farmers and industrial societies.

Despite these concerns, some contemporary groups do have features that are important for archaeological understanding of prehistoric hunter-gatherers. First is the fact that hunting and gathering can occur in a variety of forms, with hunting and fishing making up as much as 100 percent of the diet or as little as 10 percent, while foraging makes up the rest.

The second is that our anthropological models of the typical hunter-gatherers have changed. Before the "Man the Hunter" conference, anthropologists and archaeologists saw these societies as male-dominated and focused almost solely on hunting. After the conference, anthropologists came to see them principally as egalitarian foragers, relying primarily on plant foods, where women's roles are equal or nearly equal in importance to those of men. Today, the image of hunter-gatherers is complex, emphasizing variability between groups (Kelly 2013). But for archaeologists to make sense of how heavily prehistoric peoples relied on hunting, they needed to abandon these earlier stereotypes and open themselves to possibilities not found in the ethnographic record, even when it proves difficult to find clear evidence in the archaeological record. Clearly, it is important for archaeologists to have strong familiarity with the work of cultural anthropologists in order to take on such problems. In "The Anthropological Life," we describe some of the other major things archaeologists need to know and actually spend their time doing.

In the next section, we apply these lessons to one of the biggest questions of all: What led people to shift from a foraging lifestyle in the first place?

THINKING LIKE AN ANTHROPOLOGIST: THE RISE OF AGRICULTURE

Why do you suppose that until the 1960s, anthropologists generally assumed that hunting was more important than gathering and foraging for pre-agricultural societies? Do you think this assumption is linked to American and Western European ideas about appropriate gender roles? What impact might the growing number of women professional anthropologists and archaeologists have had on how archaeologists and cultural anthropologists understood prehistoric gender roles?

10.2 Why Did People Start Domesticating Plants and Animals?

Sometime during the past 10,000 years, ancient societies developed forms of domestication more or less independently in the Middle East, China, India, Mesoamerica, and South America (Figure 10.3). One feature nearly all of these societies had in common was that at some point the people who created them abandoned their hunting-and-gathering lifestyles in favor of regular food production that involved some sort of horticulture, farming, or herding. What led them to do so?

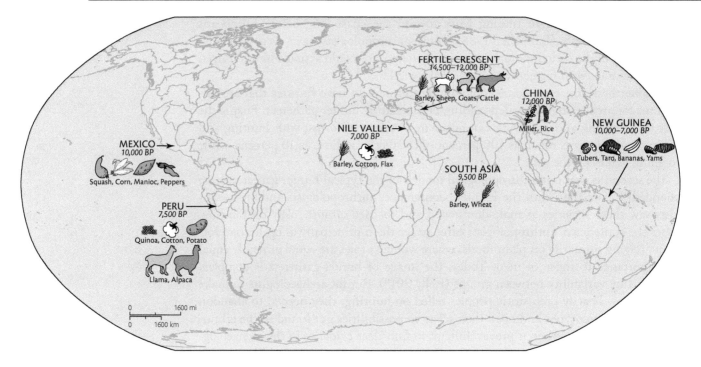

🌱 **Figure 10.3   Early Domestication.** Major areas of early plant and animal domestication, and the approximate date when widespread domestication began.

- **Maize.** The indigenous species of corn that was first domesticated in Mexico—the term is often used for any variety of corn, since all current varieties are thought to have been derived from this early version of so-called Indian corn.

- **Cultigen.** Any plant that is intentionally grown for human use.

It is not because hunter-gatherers suddenly "discovered" how to plant seeds, nor is it because they abruptly learned that by feeding certain wild animals they could control their behavior. Although it is not easy to demonstrate archaeologically, most hunter-gatherers were likely aware of several methods they could use to improve the plant and animal foods they gathered by burning, weeding, and modest tending.

One key fact is that simple agriculture emerged in the Fertile Crescent of the Middle East about 10,000 to 12,000 years ago, with similar forms emerging in the Indus valley at roughly the same period. Chinese development of simple rice agriculture emerged in the same period, almost certainly independent of the other two. In the New World, cultivation of **maize**, the plant species that evolved into modern corn, emerged somewhat later, and in the Peruvian highlands, potatoes were being cultivated since at least 8,000 years ago. The various tubers of the New Guinea Highlands, as noted, were being raised in small fields drained by ditches 10,000 years ago.

No matter what the **cultigen** (any plant that is intentionally grown for human use), humans across the globe were beginning to cultivate useful plants almost simultaneously, suggesting that a detailed knowledge of plants, as well as how they grew and developed, long preceded systematic cultivation. What seems lacking until roughly 10,000 years ago was some reason to grow one's own food.

Archaeologists have long struggled to understand the reasons hunter-gatherers shifted to agriculture. Theories range from the influence of certain geographic features to the growth of populations, which we examine in turn.

The Neolithic Revolution: The Beginnings of Food Production

Archaeologist V. Gordon Childe (1936) was the first to recognize that the shift from hunting and gathering to food production had significant consequences for the development of more sophisticated technologies, larger populations, and more complex forms of social organization—including the formation of cities, state governments, and social hierarchies. In "Classic Contributions: V. Gordon Childe on the Neolithic Revolution," we explore his thoughts on the matter.

For Childe, food production was not a single *event* but a *process* that set in motion a variety of changes, each of which encouraged other socioeconomic, political, and technological changes. Childe favored the notion that food production arose around oases in the Mesopotamian lowlands. But while Childe was correct that food production was associated with other important social changes, he did not understand what actually led hunters and gathers to begin producing their own food, and some scholars questioned whether his oasis hypothesis was correct.

The Hilly Flanks Hypothesis

In the late 1940s, the American archaeologist Robert J. Braidwood (1952) was the first to tackle this why-did-they-do-it question in a systematic way. The first evidence archaeologists had of early humans actively and intentionally planting seeds for their own food comes from excavations in the Middle East in what has come to be known as the Fertile Crescent, a curved swath of land that includes Mesopotamia; the Mediterranean coast of Syria, Lebanon, and Israel; and the Nile valley (Figure 10.4). Here we find the beginnings of sedentary lifestyles and archaeological evidence that early humans—through planting crops and domesticating animals—were transforming the foods they ate.

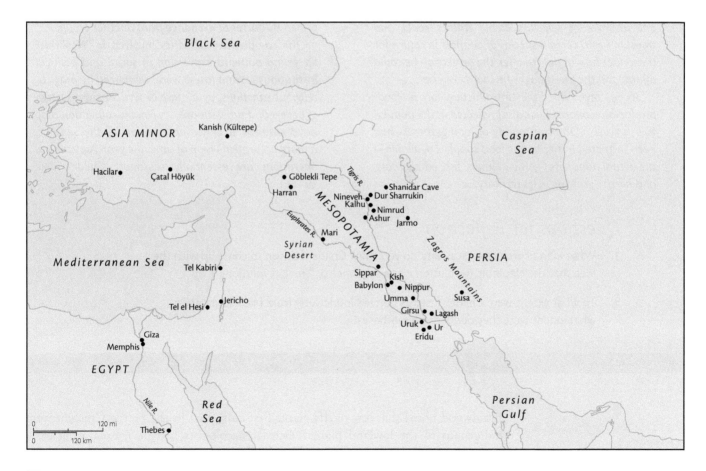

Figure 10.4 Fertile Crescent. The Fertile Crescent showing major archaeological sites providing evidence of early agriculture and later political centers.

Classic Contributions
V. Gordon Childe on the Neolithic Revolution

FROM THE 1920S until the 1950s Australian-born archaeologist V. Gordon Childe (1892–1957) was the most prominent archaeological theorist in the English-speaking world. He conducted excavations in eastern Europe and the Middle East and was the first scholar to develop a theory for understanding the shift from hunting and gathering to agriculture. In this excerpt from his book *Man Makes Himself*, Childe suggests that the shift to food production gave people control over their food supplies, removing the main barrier to population growth. Larger populations led to many other developments, all of which emerge almost as if they were a set of cascading tiles, one building off of the previous development and producing the next.

V. Gordon Childe.

The steps by which man's control was made effective have been gradual, their effects cumulative. But [some] stand out as revolutions. The first revolution that transformed human economy gave man control over his own food supply. Man began to plant, cultivate, and improve by selection edible grasses, roots, and trees ... [and] certain species of animals in return for the fodder he was able to offer, the protection he could afford, and the forethought he could exercise. ...

As a revolution the introduction of a food-producing economy [was also] reflected in the population curve. ... The community of food-gatherers had been restricted in size by the food supplies available— the actual number of game animals, fish, edible roots, and berries growing in its territory. ...

Two other aspects of the simple food-producing economy deserve attention. Firstly, [it] provides an opportunity and motive for the accumulation of a surplus. Secondly, the economy is entirely self-sufficing ... not dependent on the necessities of life on imports obtained by barter or exchange from another group. ...

The co-operative activities involved in "Neolithic" life found outward expression in social and political institutions ... and [these were] reinforced by magico-religious sanctions, by a more or less coherent system of beliefs and superstitions. ... Finally, cultivation may have required a closer observation of the seasons, a more accurate division of time, the year. Agricultural operations are essentially seasonal. [Childe 1936: 59–60]

Questions for Reflection

1. What kind of archaeological data do you think Childe drew on to come up with the idea that the Neolithic Revolution was a sequence of "small revolutions"?

2. To what extent were Childe's insights derived inductively from his field data? To what extent were they deductive hypotheses?

Braidwood noted that few of the plants first cultivated in the Fertile Crescent were indigenous to the lowland plains where archaeologists had been excavating early towns and fields. He reasoned that the upland fringes (the so-called hilly flanks in the title of the hypothesis) of the Fertile Crescent were the natural habitat of these prehistorically cultivated species. There, on the hilly flanks, not only were the necessary cultigens present but environmental conditions were conducive to cultivation because of higher rainfall than in the dry lowlands. Braidwood hypothesized that once certain plants had been domesticated in the uplands, their use as food spread to neighboring groups in the lowlands, where it enabled populations to grow, and eventually, for cities and states to emerge.

To test this hypothesis, Braidwood undertook a series of excavations across the hilly country of Iraqi Kurdistan, southern Turkey, and western Iran. He found cave sites from hunter-gatherers who may have just begun to produce some of their own food, open sites that people had used as temporary encampments with tents, and one of the earliest village sites at a place known as Jarmo. This last site produced traces of two species of wheat, one of barley, one of peas, and a certain variety of pistachios. Braidwood also argued that the domestication of sheep and goats took place here, evidenced by the large proportion of teeth found in the site from yearlings, a finding that suggested that residents were culling their herd and eating the less desirable individual animals (a process of selection, designed to improve the herd).

Braidwood's analysis suggested where people were starting to domesticate plants and animals in the Middle East, what they were domesticating, and why domestication began in these areas. But he did not explain why people started to produce their own food when they did rather than a few thousand years earlier or later. In the decades since, a number of prominent answers have been developed: the pressure of population growth, climate change, and social processes.

The Pressure of Population Growth

In the 1960s the agricultural economist Ester Boserup (1965) developed a model to explain why societies with simple economies had not taken up intensive agricultural activities, even though their neighbors had. She argued that nobody would spend a lot of time gardening and farming if they did not have to because it requires hard labor, and she focused on the issue of population growth as a possible motivator.

Using evidence from agricultural communities in Asia, Boserup examined the relationship between population growth and food production. In doing so, she challenged the assumptions of the English demographer Robert Malthus (1798), who had argued that the supply of food available to any community was inelastic—an economic term meaning it could not be increased above a certain point. For him, population growth depended on the food supply, and societies that had small populations were limited by the food available to them. Boserup turned this argument on its head, arguing instead that population growth forced people to work harder to produce more food. Her evidence came from Asian countries like India, Japan, and Indonesia, which during the nineteenth century had experienced rapid population growth at the same time they increased their food production. She argued that similar processes of population growth had triggered technological improvements and increased labor inputs throughout recorded history.

Boserup did not specifically address the rise of food production in the Middle East or other parts of the world. But her argument's relevance to the Neolithic Revolution was this: if hunter-gatherers already understood how plants grow, even a small increase in population could have been enough to encourage them to manage their food resources, at least in modest ways. Then, if incipient food production supported the existing population plus a small amount of further population growth, population pressure would encourage people to further intensify food production.

Mark Cohen (1977) built on Boserup's model, arguing that after the end of the Last Glacial Period (115,000–11,700 BPE [Before the Present Era]), environmental conditions stabilized and improved. At this point human populations were still widely scattered around the globe, as they had been for hundreds of thousands of years, but these improved environmental conditions probably allowed a small but gradual population increase. Although human populations lived in small, often scattered groups, a group of twenty-five that increased to thirty individuals—perhaps because a few more children than normal survived beyond infancy—would constitute a significant population increase of 20 percent. As human populations grew slowly over the centuries, the additional population required more food. Planting crops allowed people to control their food supply in ways that foraging and hunting could not. In this model, domestication of animals began to emerge only when populations of wild game declined.

A related model came from archaeologists Lewis Binford (1968) and Kent Flannery (1969), who suggested that in the Middle East and Mesoamerica postglacial populations increased in coastal areas that had favorable wild resources for fisher-foraging groups. Population growth, however, put pressure on some coastal residents to move away from these resource-rich coastal areas into less favorable environments. Some of these environments were situated along Braidwood's hilly flanks of the Fertile Crescent, where wild resources were less reliable. So cultivation was an obvious way to control uncertain food supplies. In Binford and Flannery's model, food production did not begin where resources were most plentiful or most scarce, but in environmental zones that were less predictable (see Bellwood 2005). Predictability of environments and resources was, thus, a central driver in this model of the origins of agriculture.

Changing Weather and Climates

Recent concerns about global warming and the increasing sophistication of computerized models of past climates have expanded archaeological interest and knowledge about the role of climate change in shaping human prehistory. There are still many questions about the scale, magnitude, timing, and frequency of past climatic changes and how societies responded to them, but it is evident that changing climates did affect foraging groups around the world and probably contributed to conditions for some of those foragers to create sedentary communities and shift to agriculture (Hassan 2009).

One intriguing case is that of the Natufians, a foraging society living in the Levant between 15,000 and 11,500 years ago. It is famous among archaeologists as the earliest society in the world to bake bread and brew beer, and one of the very first to engage in settled agriculture (Langgut et al. 2021). A group of Israeli archaeologists recently undertook a project that tracks the presence of different pollens over a 20,000 year period, looking for connections between changing distributions of plant life and Natufian food gathering and storage practices (David 2021). During the early part of that period, gradually increasing temperatures, rains, and humidity supported the growth of oak, olive, and pistachio forests. These conditions appear to have enabled the Natufians to reduce their foraging range and create semi-sedentary communities where they buried their dead and stored food. Around 13,000 years ago, a 1,000-year cold snap (the so-called Younger Dryas) occurred in Europe, moderating temperatures and affecting rainfall where the Natufians lived. Annuals grasses like wheat and barley began to grow year-round, though the end of that period brought an abrupt warming and a new pattern of seasonal rainfall, of rainy winters and dry summers. At this point it appears the Natufians began to make their settlements more permanent and grow grasses familiar to them (wheat, barley, and rye)—and to herd domesticated sheep (David 2021; Hassan 2009). Some of these villages grew and increased in social complexity (see Chapter 11), but sometime between 8,200 and 7,800 years ago, a pattern of cooler weather settles in and these settlements break up, with Levantine populations leaving for North Africa, Europe, and the Arabian Peninsula.

While there is no doubt that climate instability played a role in these events, archaeologists are careful not to reduce their complexity to climate change alone.

One reason is that similar climatic changes existed in places that did not develop agriculture, or did so with different crops, under distinct conditions and on radically different timelines (David 2021). Even in the Levant, groups closely tied to Natufians did not necessarily abandon foraging. Different groups made different decisions, responding both to ecological dynamics and the agency and capacity of groups to act collectively in ways that made sense to them at the time (Hassan 2009).

The Role of Social Processes

Another family of theories suggests that social processes were key to the beginning of food production (Bender 1978; Hayden 2003). Humans may have experienced some changes in cognitive ability that allowed them to perceive some of the longer-term advantages that came with regular food production, although what that actual cognitive shift might have been remains elusive (see, e.g., Mithen 2007). A neoevolutionary symbiosis model offered by David Rindos (1984) suggests that irrespective of why people in one region or another began cultivating plants, the people and the plants they began cultivating began to evolve together. In other words, once people started planting crops, the plants began domesticating the people.

A similar process occurs with animal husbandry; as soon as one begins to domesticate wild animals, the animals and people begin to co-evolve. Such has been most obviously the case with cattle, which have co-evolved with certain human populations, so that people's bodies gradually adapted to the lactose in the milk, and cattle have evolved to suit the needs of their human owners.

A recent discovery that might lend some support to one or another of these social explanations was found at Gobekli Tepe, in contemporary Turkey, where the community began to construct some of the earliest monumental architecture associated with complex rituals (Dietrich et al. 2012). This fact would not be surprising except that it was happening before people had actively begun food production, all of which supports some of these theories built around social elements.

Now that we have covered some of the major theories about *why* humans made the shift from foraging to agriculture, we can address the *how* of the actual transition.

THINKING LIKE AN ANTHROPOLOGIST: THE RISE OF AGRICULTURE

What evidence can you think of for why archaeologists and cultural anthropologists assume that hunter-gatherers understood that plants sprouted from seeds or from leaves, roots, or tubers? How successful would early humans have been if they were not already aware of the patterns of animal behavior and how plants grew?

10.3 How Did Early Humans Raise Their Own Food?

Hunter-gatherers and their ancestors have an extraordinary knowledge of their natural environment. They are able to eat because they know where they will find foods and at what times certain foods ripen and become edible. They understand the fact that seeds grow into mature plants and that birds and game animals deposit seeds on the soil in feces, which then sprout and grow. This information was not the result of accidental discovery but of careful observation made in their daily lives. Similarly, to be successful hunters of game, large or small, people needed to know the places animals ate or drank. They had to develop a fairly sophisticated understanding of animal behavior—ask any modern hunter, most of whom know considerably less than early humans before the Neolithic era. Given the details we discussed in Chapter 3 about human biocultural evolution and the emergence of human cognitive sophistication, it is highly likely that our human ancestors knew some or all of these things for hundreds of thousands of years, if not longer. Archaeologists have developed some plausible explanations of how people put this knowledge to work, which we review here.

Domesticating Plants

Almost immediately after humans started consciously planting wild grains from locally occurring grasses, the edible seeds became larger than their wild cousins. By tending and planting wild grass seeds, early humans were selecting the best seeds, which were also seeds from the most hardy and productive plants. These choices rapidly improved the planting stock in subsequent seasons. In fact, it is precisely these kinds of changes in indigenous grasses that allow archaeologists to trace the earliest evidence of domesticated grains and to be able to demonstrate that domestication had happened in the first place (Zohary and Hopf 2000).

In the Middle East, archaeologists have excavated sites where they found charred kernels of slender grains from wild varieties of wheat. The earliest sites date at least to 17,000 BCE. Their small size suggests that hunter-gatherers had harvested these grains from wild stands of native grasses. But by at least 7,800 BCE, charred seeds of a plumper variety from the same species appear in other sites, suggesting that humans were already selecting wheat with larger seeds. Several other wild species of wheat and barley later spread to Europe after being domesticated to become the principal cereals throughout the Middle East and Europe over the next 2,000 or 3,000 years (Figure 10.5).

To understand how these wild grains became the kinds of cereals we know today, we have to understand the role of humans in selecting for desirable traits, such as growability under certain climatic conditions, durability for storage, and other qualities like texture, flavor, and appearance. Archaeologically, these changes only emerge

EINKORN   EMMER

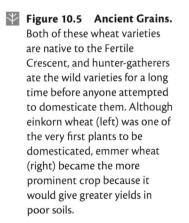

Figure 10.5 Ancient Grains. Both of these wheat varieties are native to the Fertile Crescent, and hunter-gatherers ate the wild varieties for a long time before anyone attempted to domesticate them. Although einkorn wheat (left) was one of the very first plants to be domesticated, emmer wheat (right) became the more prominent crop because it would give greater yields in poor soils.

wild   domesticated   wild   domesticated

from observing how seeds from different species of grasses changed over time as humans selected the best grains for seed, added natural fertilizers, and developed techniques for tending and storing those crops. All of this requires excavations from different periods, over a wide region or neighborhood. From these changes in the grains over several thousand years we can see that humans have left their selective imprint on nearly every cultigen.

The process by which seeds became larger through selection can also be seen in the Americas with early varieties of maize. In the early 1960s, archaeologist Richard S. MacNeish (1967) discovered a series of caves in the Tehuacán [Tay-wah-**kahn**] valley of Mexico. When he excavated these sites, he found what looked like tiny corn cobs, the size of a cigarette filter, which proved to be ancestors of the modern corn species *Zea mays*, which has been the key staple food across Mesoamerica, the subtropical and tropical regions between what is now the United States and South America. He also found evidence of squash and bottle gourds, as well as beans, tomatoes, chili peppers, and avocados. Carbon-14 dates from these caves and rock shelters convincingly documented the domestication of these important cultigens at Tehuacán at least by 7,000 years ago (Piperno and Flannery 2001), making the site one of the earliest known sources of evidence for cultivated maize in the Americas. Archaeologist Michael Blake (2015) has recently found an even earlier site in the Balsas River valley of western Mexico, where domesticated corn has been dated to 9,000 years ago from a wild grass he identifies as belonging to the grass species *Balsas teosinte* (Figure 10.6).

We have less evidence about the earliest domestication of tubers in the New Guinea Highlands. British archaeologist Jack Golson, for example, identified evidence of trenching and swamp drainage by about 9,000 BCE. Poor preservation of tubers makes it difficult to know exactly which species were cultivated in the Neolithic period. Some have suggested taro or one of several other indigenous root crops occasionally planted today. But current horticultural practices offer little help in explaining which plants were domesticated so long ago. The most common species cultivated in the same region today, for example, is the sweet potato, which originates in South

Figure 10.6 Domesticated Corn Over Time. Examples of domesticated corn from the Tehuacán valley of Mexico showing how domestication gradually produced larger and larger cobs.

America. Its introduction to the Pacific Islands is likely much earlier than James Watson (1965) and Peter White (Brookfield and White 1968) had originally assumed; it was probably introduced by some early contacts between people of the Peruvian coast and eastern Polynesia, perhaps a thousand years ago. Nevertheless, the New Guinea Highlands case demonstrates that the earliest cultigens in a region need not be grains but can be tubers or other root crops that propagate from cuttings. And as we have suggested in the opening to this chapter, trees bearing nuts could also be one of the earliest plants exploited regularly in places like the New Guinea Highlands.

James B. Watson (1977) suggested another reason that cultivation might have spread so rapidly once people started growing their own food. His argument was developed to account for the rapid spread of sweet potato growing in New Guinea, where violence and tribal fighting was quite marked (see, e.g., Gardner and Heider 1969; Gardner 2004), but his model is broadly applicable even in regions without the high levels of violence found in New Guinea. Watson called it the "Jones effect," because once a neighboring group started increasing their food supply—there in the form of potatoes and pigs—by planting sweet potatoes, there was pressure on neighbors to "keep up with the Joneses" in order to solidify alliances, better maintain friendships, and the like. The problem with this model is there is little archaeological evidence that can either support or contradict it. Of course, humans did not domesticate plants just for food; they have also domesticated plants for other uses, such as fiber-bearing plants for making baskets, string, and rope, and for other purposes. It has been important for archaeologists as well as cultural anthropologists to think about early hunter-gatherers as playing a role in the evolution of grains and other useful plants.

Domesticating Animals

Similar processes occurred with domesticated animals as they did with plants: selective breeding to favor certain qualities, such as to increase size or to favor certain other qualities and characteristics like docility, protectiveness, flavor, and appearance. But not every animal species (or plant, for that matter) can be domesticated effectively. The ancestors of modern sheep, goats, horses, and cattle were suitable for domestication because their dispositions were generally docile. For example, canines can readily bond with a dominant individual in a pack, which can be transferred to their human owners as an animal becomes tame. Other species, for reasons not well understood, like zebras, lions, tigers, and bears, have not been domesticated, partly perhaps because of their mean or unpredictable dispositions (Diamond 2002).

Domesticating animals is not necessarily an all-or-nothing proposition. We can see examples of semi-domestication in Papua New Guinea in recent times among the Ningerum people who catch feral piglets soon after they are born and keep them tied near a house while they are young. Later the pigs are released but fed every afternoon, and while they may have foraged for food during the day, they always return for food in the afternoon, where they can easily be caught when they are big enough to be part of a local pig feast. Even domesticated pigs in this community still breed in the wild because all the male piglets are gelded (castrated), so the boars in the breeding stock are all feral. But, as was likely true in prehistoric times, semi-domesticated animals do not improve as quickly from selection even though regular feeding may have a positive effect on their appearance and phenotype.

Raising animals is also an especially useful practice for people who have domesticated plants. Animal dung can be used as fertilizer to nurture the crops, and some animals, such as oxen, horses, and mules, can help till the soil. One of the most common animals domesticated very early was the dog, which was originally used for hunting but could also help with herding sheep and goats. As you can see in the great variety of dogs in existence today, the evolutionary effects of selective dog breeding is quite marked. But there is ample evidence that cattle, horses, donkeys, llamas, and even ducks and chickens have all evolved in the context of the human societies in which they were raised.

Tending Tree Crops: Recent Findings on Arboriculture

Archaeologists and anthropologists have recently begun to consider how humans may have begun manipulating their food sources in more subtle and less comprehensive ways than with wheat, barley, and maize long before these grains were domesticated. As we saw in the opening case study in this chapter with regard to pandanus nuts, trees may well have been one of the earliest groups of cultigens. For example, archaeologist Kyle Latinis (2000) suggests that arboriculture, or planting and tending tree crops whose fruits are edible, likely occurred considerably earlier than domestication of other crops in Southeast Asia. Unlike cereals and tubers, trees last a long time and can easily be tended in minor ways, such as by planting a shoot, seed, or sucker, or by weeding, pruning, and clearing vegetation so the tree gets just a little more or a little less sun. These activities take little time or energy—usually the work gets done in short bursts of effort—and yet have considerable impact on the productivity of the tree or the size of its fruit. Modest tending of sago palms, for example, can increase the amount of starch produced by the palm, doubling or even tripling the starch content as well as speeding up the maturation process.

While it is hard to find firm evidence of just when people started manipulating their tree-crop resources, in many tropical areas it was likely very early. Even today, to the casual observer, rain forests inhabited by small human populations may look like vast tracts of primary forest, when in fact they more closely resemble low-intensity orchards or tree gardens. In "Anthropologist as Problem Solver: Michael Heckenberger on the Amazon as a Culturally Managed Landscape," we consider whether the Amazon was a pristine, primeval forest or a culturally managed landscape in prehistoric times.

To return to the question of how early humans learned to grow their own food, it is likely that the earliest efforts to manipulate plants came with simple tending of useful trees. Once people began to plant seeds, roots, or cuttings, the improvements in the seeds or tubers would have been obvious because by choosing the best planting stock they would have selected for the best varieties. Such manipulations of the natural environment are often very modest at best, so modest that we may not be able to detect these manipulations in the archaeological record. But any modification in conditions should leave an impact on the productivity of the crop after a number of generations.

Other kinds of management or modification of the environment and its indigenous species can and often do have a much more significant impact on the species and on the ways that people live in their environment. More important, producing food for one's community has often meant significant changes in human lifeways, the topic we turn to next.

THINKING LIKE AN ANTHROPOLOGIST: THE RISE OF AGRICULTURE

There is a big difference between lightly tending tree crops in a rain forest and the intensive work of raising animals like horses, cattle, goats, pigs, chickens, and dogs. What was it about these domesticated animals that required a great deal of human effort once domesticated that was not present when they were wild animals?

Anthropologist as Problem Solver
Michael Heckenberger on the Amazon as a Culturally Managed Landscape

One of the enduring intellectual puzzles that archaeologists have confronted for the past century was, Just how densely populated was the New World when Columbus first reached the Americas? This question is important because for many years population estimates were drawn from early European accounts, mostly written after epidemics of European diseases had killed large sectors of the indigenous population. Clarifying this situation has major implications for how we view the history of humans in the vast and ecologically critical Amazon basin.

Archaeologists have long assumed that the rain forest in the region of the Amazon River, the largest rain forest in the world, was sparsely populated (Meggers 1971). They have recognized that rain forest dwellers in the Amazon proper and the Bolivian Amazon had been manipulating their environment for a very long time (see, e.g., Roosevelt 1999; Erickson 2000), but until fairly recently, most believed that the shift from hunting and gathering to food production had come very late, largely because the environment was not a naturally fertile region. When farmers cut down the rain forest for gardens, the heavy rainfall quickly leaches most of the nutrients out of the soil, leaving behind very little, if any, rich topsoil. As a result, anthropologists assumed that people had long been hunter-gatherers but had begun a very simple slash-and-burn farming, cutting down and burning off the forest to provide nutrients. For the most part, the region appears to be a vast pristine wilderness, a primeval forest that had supported human settlements for only the last thousand years.

University of Florida archaeologist Michael Heckenberger (2005; Heckenberger et al. 2003) addressed the question of how long people have been living in this region while working at the periphery of the Amazon in the upper reaches of the Xingu [shing-**goo**] River, one of the main southern tributaries. The Xingu is one of the least densely populated parts of the Amazon basin, and a large part of it is a Brazilian national indigenous park more than 10,000 square miles in area (about the size of Massachusetts). Drawing on more than a decade of field surveys and excavations in the region, Heckenberger asked whether the area inside Xingu Indigenous Park was a pristine natural rain forest or should best be understood as a carefully managed landscape for the last thousand years.

Heckenberger conducted extensive regional research in the Xingu from 1993 to 2002, residing at one time for eighteen months in Kuikuro village. In his excavations and regional surveys he found an unexpectedly complex pattern of regional settlement within the upper Xingu. His carbon-14 dates confirmed human settlement around 1000–1200 CE. If people had lived in the region previously, they had likely been hunter-gatherers. The archaeological sites he found were likely associated with some sort of food production. Heckenberger concludes that within a century or so the region was supporting larger populations than anybody had assumed. He found evidence of nineteen prehistoric settlements connected by paths or roads in his study area where simple slash and burn could not possibly have supported the entire population. His conclusion was that prehistoric Xingu were carefully managing their forests and agricultural lands, through the creation of a kind of soil called *terra preta* ("black earth"), which was the result of extensive composting.

Recent research in the Upper Xingu, as well as excavations in many other parts of the Amazon, seems to suggest that the rain forest supported much larger populations prehistorically than archaeologists had expected because they were managing their forests—and their topsoil—to create vast park-like gardens that we might see as essentially virgin forests. But in Xingu, by intensifying their efforts on their fields and environment, prehistoric peoples had transformed a fairly barren environment into one that could support substantial populations.

Questions for Reflection

1. What evidence would have led early archaeologists and anthropologists to conclude that when Columbus reached the New World the Amazon was sparsely populated?

2. Why might food production in the Upper Xingu area have made it possible to support larger populations than the same region with a hunting-and-gathering lifestyle?

3. In what sense might the Amazon be a thought of as a culturally managed landscape? What implications might these findings have for contemporary conservation strategies in the Xingu?

10.4 What Impact Did Raising Plants and Animals Have on Other Aspects of Life?

Knowing that the Neolithic Revolution happened over time in a series of "small revolutions"—Childe's idea that is still with us today—it is likely that the first efforts to raise food changed people relatively little. Quite likely, hunter-gatherer groups, who ranged across large territories in search of food, planted and harvested plants during the annual movements within their territory in much the same way they did with naturally occurring plants.

Herding may have brought a greater change in people's way of life, because livestock always need new food from new fields in which to graze or forage. And, as the number of livestock increased, the needs of the animals may have led some food producers to turn to **transhumance**, the practice of moving herds to different fields or pastures with the changing seasons.

- **Transhumance.** The practice of moving herds to different fields or pastures with the changing seasons.

Transhumance: Moving Herds With the Seasons

In some respects, transhumance represents a fairly simple transformation of the nomadic lifestyle of hunter-gatherers. Instead of moving from one territory to another to hunt game, a family moves itself and its livestock from one set of pastures to another to take advantage of seasonal changes. For example, the Bakhtiari people of southwestern Iran adapted their transhumant lifeways to local environments (Figure 10.7). This movement included a strenuous journey from their highland summer quarters over steep mountain passes to their lowland winter quarters (Cooper, Schoedsack, and Harrison 1999). More than 50,000 people and half a million animals crossed rivers and mountains during these semi-annual treks. Like other societies that practice **pastoralism**—the breeding, care, and use of domesticated herding animals such as cattle, camels, goats, horses, llamas, reindeer, and yaks—raising herds of livestock is a key component of such a group's subsistence economy and does not necessarily require people to settle in one place (see also Chapter 14, "Sustainability: Environment and Foodways"). But pastoralism tends to lead to larger populations and much more complex patterns of social interaction that resemble what has typically happened whenever humans become sedentary.

- **Pastoralism.** The practice of animal husbandry, which is the breeding, care, and use of domesticated herding animals such as cattle, camels, goats, horses, llamas, reindeer, and yaks.

Figure 10.7 Transhumance. Transhumance among the Bachtiari of Iran.

- **Sedentism.** Year-round settlement in a particular place.

- **Mesolithic.** The period from the end of the last ice age until the beginning of agriculture. During this period, a number of hunter-gatherer-forager groups established lakeside or seaside settlements that seem to have been year-round sites.

Sedentism and Growing Populations

Still, pastoralists are relatively few in number worldwide. Most people in the world are settled and dependent on agriculture, either directly or indirectly. Archaeologists understand that the most significant changes that accompany food production are largely the combined result of **sedentism**, or year-round settlement in a particular place, and population growth. But during the **Mesolithic**, which is the period from the end of the last ice age until the beginning of agriculture or horticulture, a number of hunter-gatherer-forager groups had established lakeside or seaside settlements that seem to have been year-round sites (J. Arnold 1996).

As we have seen, the technological shift from hunting and gathering to simple domestication of plants and animals was a fairly minor one. But once people started settling down to tend these crops, their populations grew, leading gradually to greater intensification of food production (Zvelebil and Rowley-Conwy 1984).

Larger communities required more labor inputs for food production, typically resulting in periodic shortages of food because of the growing population. These shortages, in turn, led to what we might call true agriculture, involving, for example, fertilizing with dung or mulches and the development of new technologies altogether, such as plows and the use of draft animals to pull them across a field (see also Chapter 14).

One of the most striking aspects of sedentism is that with population growth it tends to lead to permanent social inequality. But since the rise of social inequality is also one of the characteristics commonly associated with the rise of early cities and the emergence of state-like political formations, we will defer our discussion of these topics to Chapter 11, "The Rise and Decline of Cities and States," where we examine them more directly.

Dietary Consequences of Sedentism

The shift to sedentism also brought with it a change from relying on a large variety of plants and animals typical of hunting and gathering societies to relying on a small number of plant species. Indeed, the more intensive the horticulture or agriculture, the smaller the list of cultigens becomes.

For example, the few hunting-and-gathering groups in New Guinea today exploit nearly every edible plant in their environment as well as nearly all the species of birds, marsupials, bats, rodents, and insects that inhabit the rain forests. In horticultural communities, in contrast, where people typically plant mixed gardens with fifteen to thirty species of plant cultigens, most people eat fewer than a dozen species of plants on a regular basis and have access to animal protein only sporadically in spite of the fact that they have access to many of the same wild foods available to hunter-gatherers. Bolstering this food culture are complex patterns of food taboos in which individuals from various social categories, ages, and genders are prohibited from eating particular foods, while others may enjoy them. This is true even though most people have regular access to wild animal proteins from marsupials and birds they have hunted or from small fish and crayfish in the many streams.

Sedentism and Epidemic Diseases

Sedentism and population growth also have had an impact on people's health with evolutionary consequences for our species (see Chapter 3), since larger numbers of people living together allowed certain bacteria, viruses, and parasites to move from one host to another more easily. The immediate impact of these microbes was to spread quickly as epidemics throughout the population. At first such epidemics would kill off a substantial part of the population, leaving those who survived with antibodies that naturally provided an acquired or partial immunity. When the epidemic returned some years later, only young children, born since the last epidemic, were unprotected by the acquired immunity—though many of these children would have obtained partial immunity from antibodies in their mothers' breast milk.

The Fertile Crescent, where agriculture and sedentism arose earliest, was also at the crossroads of Africa, Asia, and Europe. Here, peoples from all three continents interacted through trade and marriage more often after sedentary villages had formed, and there were more people around to interact with. As a result, historian William McNeil (1976) has suggested, diseases repeatedly swept through the Fertile Crescent, and these microbial parasites left behind immunity-conferring antibodies in their surviving hosts. Such antibodies later protected the community from the most serious effects of plagues, while most populations that had not been exposed to these microbes typically suffered much more severe losses.

European colonization of the New World, where many native societies had long before become sedentary, demonstrates the effect of sedentism on epidemic diseases. These settled New World communities had experienced their own plagues and had developed some immunity to indigenous microbes such as syphilis. But they had no immunity whatsoever to common European diseases like measles and smallpox. When Europeans arrived to explore these new lands, they found large settlements along much of the coast of New England, where they stopped only briefly in the decade or so after 1600. But these early fleeting contacts were enough to pass along European microbes to the indigenous people. Diseases spread rapidly through the population, killing large numbers, perhaps as much as 90 percent of the coastal population (Loewen 1995:77ff; see also Segal and Stineback 1977:54–55). The effect of foreign plagues did not stop at the Atlantic shore but spread to inland groups who had contact with coastal peoples through trade and travel (Figure 10.8). Thus, when the Pilgrims first arrived in Plymouth in 1620, nearly the entire village had died, leaving Squanto as its sole surviving Patuxet resident. It was Squanto who assisted the Pilgrims on their arrival in 1620. While much is made by the Mayflower Society of the fifty-one Mayflower passengers who both survived the difficult passage and the

Figure 10.8 Mandan Epidemic. One of the large Mandan villages visited by the artist and explorer George Catlin in the early 1830s. A smallpox epidemic killed most of the inhabitants in 1837.

harsh first winter, it is clear that none of them could have survived without the help of the one Patuxet resident who had survived the plague initiated by the brief visit of John Smith, who later founded Jamestown in Virginia.

THINKING LIKE AN ANTHROPOLOGIST: THE RISE OF AGRICULTURE

What are some of the costs and benefits of sedentism? Why might sedentism set off a chain of both positive and negative consequences for humans living in year-round settlements that they did not experience when living a hunting-foraging life?

Conclusion

The Neolithic Revolution was not a single event occurring during a set span of years; it was many events in many parts of the world occurring at different times, each with its own unique features. In some regions, the shift to horticulture or agriculture occurred independently of similar transitions in other regions, as in the Fertile Crescent, the Highlands of New Guinea, and Mesoamerica. In other places and times, the motivation to cultivate one's food came from neighboring groups. For example, cultivation in the Indus valley of India was likely linked to what was happening in the Fertile Crescent, but the rise of rice growing in China along the Yellow River was probably independent. And cultivation of plants among the Aztecs of Central Mexico, the people of the Mississippi Valley, and those of the American Southeast were probably influenced by patterns that had emerged after domestication of corn in Mexico had spread to the Maya of Central America and southern Mexico. Even if the particular crops were quite different and growing techniques were quite independent, it was the likely the idea of active food production that allowed neighbors to innovate.

Cultivation and animal husbandry typically led to sedentism and the production of food surpluses as well as new ways of storing grains and other crops. Since people were not always on the move, they did not need to limit the food they acquired, as they did when they collected everything they ate. Growing population pressures together with the ability to amass surpluses led to radical, new ways for groups to interact. In the Fertile Crescent, intensification led to the growth of villages and towns and finally cities.

A somewhat different, but nevertheless related, pattern emerged in the New Guinea Highlands. Raising tubers began with simple cultivation plots but quickly led to draining swamps and other kinds of intensification. When the New World sweet potato reached the island, the rapid growing period of the sweet potato allowed New Guineans to expand production, providing surpluses that could support both growing human populations and increasingly large local pig herds. Soon, people began using their surplus sweet potatoes and pigs as valuables they could exchange with neighboring groups. None of these changes were possible when the ancestors of these peoples were living off the pandanus nuts they harvested and processed with stone mortars and pestles 15,000 to 20,000 years ago or perhaps more. At the same time, it is also clear that the shift to agriculture through the cultivation of sweet potatoes did not come out of nowhere but built on prior group knowledge, experience, and technologies.

Elsewhere, of course, where grains and other crops could be stored for months or years, surpluses led to other developments, most notably the rise of cities, the formation of states, and the introduction of social hierarchies with essentially permanent patterns of social inequality. In Chapter 11 we will explore these issues in some depth.

KEY TERMS

Cultigen   p. 290

Domestication   p. 282

Foraging   p. 282

Generalized foraging model
    p. 285

Maize   p. 290

Mesolithic   p. 302

Neolithic Revolution   p. 279

Optimal foraging strategy
    p. 286

Pastoralism   p. 301

Patrilocal bands   p. 283

Potlatches   p. 287

Sedentism   p. 302

Transhumance   p. 301

Reviewing the Chapter

Chapter Section	What We Know	To Be Resolved
How important was hunting to prehistoric peoples?	Early humans relied on a mix of hunting and foraging strategies, and women's contributions to the total diet from gathering were often as much as or greater than men's contributions, even though men (and many early male anthropologists) may have given more emphasis to men's hunting.	It is still unclear how closely the living conditions and knowledge of contemporary hunter-gatherers resemble those of prehistoric humans before they began to produce their own food.
Why did people start domesticating plants and animals?	Foraging is a generally reliable way to feed small populations and requires less effort and labor than agriculture. As a result, most anthropologists believe that hunter-gatherers were forced to develop more predictable ways of feeding people that agriculture enables, due to pressures of population growth. Some recent approaches have sought to connect domestication to social changes, cognitive developments, and evolutionary dynamics.	It is difficult to establish with archaeological precision the specific intentions and cognitive dynamics involved in domestication.
How did early humans raise their own food?	Hunter-gatherers knew a great deal about their environments and certainly knew that plants sprout from seeds. It was a simple matter to plant seeds. The hard part was selecting desirable traits, weeding, tending, and managing the crop.	Although we know that domesticated plants and animals evolved together with humans, there is relatively little archaeological evidence about the earliest food production.
What impact did raising plants and animals have on other aspects of life?	The Neolithic Revolution did not occur at a single moment when humans started producing food. It consisted of many small revolutions in which different societies started producing their own food at different times and in a variety of ways.	Finding archaeological evidence for the beginnings of food production is difficult and still developing. Mostly we can see evidence of food production from the gradual improvement in seeds or other characteristics of the domesticates and the social consequences of sedentism.

READINGS

For a summary of the most current thinking about the foraging activities of hunter gatherers, see Robert L. Kelly's *The Lifeways of Hunter Gatherers: The Foraging Spectrum* (Cambridge: Cambridge University Press, 2013) and Peter Bellwood's book *First Farmers: The Origins of Agricultural Societies* (Malden, MA: Blackwell, 2005).

Jane Peterson's *Sexual Revolutions: Gender and Labor at the Dawn of Agriculture* (Walnut Creek, CA: AltaMira Press, 2002) remains an important assessment of how the rise of early agriculture influenced gender relations in prehistoric societies. Another kind of change that came with the rise of agriculture was changes in people's health

resulting from changing diets. This is the subject of Mark Nathan Cohen and Gillian M. M. Crane-Kramer's *Ancient Health: Skeletal Indicators of Agricultural and Economic Intensification.* (Gainesville: University of Florida Press, 2007).

How Do Archaeologists Analyze the Objects They Find?

If your professor winces when someone expresses how much they admire the fictional film character Indiana Jones, here is a reason why: methodologically and ethically speaking, Indiana Jones was a terrible archaeologist. When Dr. Jones travels to exotic places searching for certain unique and flashy objects, he leaves behind a trail of destruction and woe, which is bad enough. But the real problem is how he regards the artifacts he is after. Dr. Jones seems to approach objects themselves as important in their own right, or because of their value to collectors and museums. This is not how actual archaeologists approach what they find in their field excavations. For them, no single artifact is typically the center of attention. Rather, their interest lies in understanding how many inconspicuous and often fragmentary objects they unearth can be used to answer questions about past social lives. The value of objects is what they tell us about the past, not their financial value to collectors. A key aspect of this work is making sure that the context in which the objects were found is accurately recorded. Often, it is the context, rather than any single object, that is the real archaeological objective. Back in their laboratories and workspaces, archaeologists then perform a very close analysis of the objects, utilizing several important techniques that we explore here: the analysis of pottery and its fragments; the analysis of subtle marks created when objects were used ("use-wear"); and the analysis of food residues that adhere to objects ("residue analysis").

ANALYZING POTTERY AND POTSHERDS

Analyzing pottery found in prehistoric sites is one of the most important aspects of archaeological practice. If a community made or used earthenware pots, potsherds—which are the fragments created when a pot breaks—can usually be found during a surface survey of the site. Because pottery leaves behind distinctive evidence of only the brief period of its active life—often only a few years before it breaks—it is typically the most important marker of when (and possibly why) a site was occupied. The key method for analyzing prehistoric pottery comes from documenting, sometimes with microscopes and varying measurement tools, the changing appearance, texture, thinness, and decorative elements of the potsherds and where they were found in order to arrange them in a local sequence.

In most communities around the globe, pottery styles change gradually over time. Archaeologists can often identify a sequence of pottery designs and styles found over a narrow region during a certain period of time. Each pot or sherd should fit into the regional sequence, offering a series of relative ages. As a dating technique, pottery sequences are not as absolute as C-14 dating is, but they have been shown to be quite reliable in every prehistoric human context where people used pottery or porcelain. It is also possible to compare potsherd designs, shapes, and styles against known examples, which can point to a period of several decades or a century when the site was occupied. When an abrupt shift in style occurs, it usually suggests that something besides the gradual change in stylistic elements may be at play, such as an interaction with another cultural group through trade or migration.

Sometimes archaeologists find trash pits containing many generations of refuse at a site. In such sites, the different layers, or strata, have been laid down over a period of many years covering up potsherds with layer after layer of soil blown by the wind. Working backward from the upper layers or strata of a test pit, the archaeologist can often construct a sequence of styles and decorative elements. Most sequences begin with potsherds found at one site or from a number of sites across a certain region. When a design or style is found in a refuse pit or in one layer in a test pit, the archaeologists can date the site either from the strata the sherd was found in or from the decorative styles of the pottery. Dating the site, whether using relative dating or absolute dating, is important because it allows the site to be placed in a much broader regional context of several or many sites.

People may have occupied a particular site routinely every year or every few years. Or they may have occupied a site just once for only a few weeks or months. In the latter situation, we can often observe different styles or design elements on potsherds from different sites, several of which can be placed in a chronological sequence, even though each site has only one decorative style. This kind of analysis is referred to as **horizontal stratigraphy**—the reconstruction of a series of time horizons from several sites, each representing a very brief human occupation or a different "layer" of time—but each "layer" is found in different sites across a narrow region. The big picture that emerges is that some sites were more permanent, while other sites were

---

- **Horizontal stratigraphy.** The study of layers of soil or rock and how they were deposited.

seasonal encampments occupied only a few times or one that was routinely visited for a short period, probably because some desired foods, water, or raw materials were accessible nearby.

USE–WEAR ANALYSIS: ANALYZING HOW A TOOL WAS USED

One of the most fascinating things archaeologists do is determining how prehistoric people used an object or tool found in an excavation. Was it for hunting big or small game? Was it used to harvest grains or to dig up root vegetables? Or perhaps it was used for crafting other tools and weapons, for tanning hides, making clothing, canoes, sails, or shields? The most important tools used by prehistoric people were blades and sharp edges that cut, pierced, and scraped. Before metal tools became available, people used wood, bone, stone, antler, and other materials for cutting, shaping, piercing, and attaching things.

The edges and cutting surfaces of each of these materials will wear differently depending on the materials they are cutting or the types of jobs to which they are put. Also, each of the materials wear somewhat differently depending on how the stone or bone tool is used. The analytical task is to work backward from the wear and tear on an artifact to determine how the object was made or how it was used. Archaeologists refer to these patterns as **use-wear**. Most use-wear analysis involves stone artifacts (called lithic analysis) because stone preserves well in almost any environment and is often the most common remaining artifactual material in an excavation. Bone tools can also be examined for use-wear, but because they can decompose, they are less often present in an excavation than stone implements. Other materials, such as hardwood, bamboo, or thorny vines, were used by prehistoric people to make cutting tools, but these materials rarely appear in archaeological sites because they tend to rot very quickly.

Use-wear analysis requires careful examination of the sharp edges that might have been used for cutting and scraping. Microscopic analysis of these surfaces (also called microwear studies) reveals minor flaking, chipping, and abrasions that cause a blade to wear down during use. Careful observations of wear can reveal which surfaces were used for cutting and which may have been used for hafting, or fastening to a handle. They can also indicate which surfaces were rubbed or polished, possibly revealing the kind of use that produced the rubbing or polishing. If we have samples of stone tools that have been used for cutting, rubbing, or scraping on various other materials, we can get a fairly

good sense of what use and with what materials the tool was used. From the nature of the chipping and abrasions on a stone tool we can learn about the manual techniques used—twisting, boring, cutting, prying, and so on—and even the movements the tool's user made with the tool and what kind of fastenings were used—all of which can help us interpret the function of the tool and how it may have been hafted to a handle.

Determining what material a tool was used to cut requires a baseline of how bone, wood, and hide respond to particular kinds of cutting tools. So archaeologists set up experiments in which newly made stone blades are used to cut a variety of materials: wood, bone, hide, meat, antler, and plants. Afterward, the blades are examined for microscopic differences in the wear each material has experienced among the different materials. The archaeologist then compares what is found on the new, experimental stone blades with the microscopic wear on actual stone artifacts.

Archaeologist Lawrence Keeley (1980) pioneered the use of the electron microscope to analyze the polish left by different materials (such things as bone, wood, hide, stone, grasses, and the like). His experimental analysis determined that different tasks, such as cutting, piercing, and scraping, produce different microscopic polishes on stone tools, which allows him to infer the materials and techniques involved in prehistoric tool use. Modern analytical techniques have improved considerably over the past quarter century and are revealing more insights all the time.

RESIDUE ANALYSIS: ANALYZING THE FOOD OR OTHER MATERIAL A CONTAINER ONCE HELD

Another kind of microscopic analysis—usually called **residue analysis**—looks at the plant or animal material left behind on the surface and edges of an artifact. For many years archaeologists assumed that wood and non-woody plant materials decomposed in archaeological sites, so they carefully scrubbed artifacts to remove all the accumulated dirt and soil. The goal was to make them look attractive and to reveal all of the surfaces, contours, and designs on the

- **Use-wear.** Patterns of wear and tear on an artifact that is presumed to be due to use.

- **Residue analysis.** Microscopic analysis of the residues of plant and animal foods, especially starches, on pottery or tools.

pottery or stone tool. We now know this practice was a mistake—washing off valuable evidence of past diets—because plant residues on a broken blades and potsherds do not, in fact, decompose entirely.

Over the past several decades the Australian archaeologist Richard Fullagar (2005) has pioneered the microscopic analysis of plant residues found on tools and pottery. Residues usually consist of microscopic grains of starch, resins, cellulose, bone, and blood. Comparisons of archaeological samples with modern plant and animal tissues—usually preserved on microscope slides—allow researchers to identify the primary foods found in prehistoric diets. Working in tropical Papua New Guinea, Fullagar began analyzing broken pottery and found starch grains clinging to the inner surfaces of the potsherds.

The most promising part of this kind of analysis has been to distinguish various preserved starch grains. Corn, rice, wheat, amaranth, sweet potato, taro, manioc, and sago—all starchy foods—have their own unique microscopic appearances. The starch cells look quite different from each other under a microscope and provide a distinctive signature for each starch. Similarly, residues of cellulose, bone, and blood are often visible under a microscope and suggest what uses were made of certain cutting edges, or in particular bowls or pots. Such identifications in recent decades have become an essential part of use-wear analysis, and in some cases the residue left on cutting or scraping surfaces can even yield microscopic evidence of materials people used the tool to work on.

Analyses of pottery, use-wear, and residues have greatly expanded the range of answers archaeologists can infer from the artifacts found in their excavations. Although they provide only partial insights into the holistic worlds of a pre-historic community, they nevertheless help archaeologists develop settlement patterns and sequences, understand what materials a tool was used with, and identify the foods a community ate at a particular moment in time.

Thinking Critically About Archaeological Methods

- Why is pottery useful for dating early settlement sites even when datable carbon samples are not preserved? What assumptions do archaeologists need to make to use pottery designs and styles as a chronological yardstick, especially if no datable charcoal or other organic material is available?

- Understanding the uses an ancient tool was put to tells us something about how it was used and perhaps the routine motions required for its use. But it is more difficult to understand the significance prehistoric users gave that tool. What, if anything, can the use of a tool tell us about the significance and meaning the people attributed to the tool or the materials it was used with?

- Knowing what foods a society ate suggests a number of features about the prehistoric society and the ways they organized their lives. Can you suggest how knowing what people cooked in their earthenware pots or what they cut with some of their blades enhances our understanding of the prehistoric society?

The Rise and Decline of Cities and States

11

Understanding Social Complexity in Prehistory

AFTER MORE THAN A CENTURY OF EXCAVATIONS, prehistoric archaeologists determined that a dramatic transformation took place in the Mississippi River bottom lands east of what is now St. Louis, beginning about 1050 CE. At a place called Cahokia, a number of loosely affiliated but egalitarian agricultural communities changed suddenly, possibly in the span of a single generation, ushering in a new hierarchical social and political order. At the top of this new order sat ruling chiefs and an elite social class who relied on other people's labor to provide food and to construct massive new earthen mounds, temples, plazas, and defensive stockades.

By 1250, Cahokia was a major urban center, with between 5,000 and 10,000 inhabitants organized into a complex social order of ranked groups. Cahokia's social, economic, and political influence spread along the Mississippi River valley from what is now Minnesota in the north to Louisiana in the south, and its economic connections reached from the Appalachian mountains to what is now Yellowstone National Park, making this city the most important center of pre-European Indian social life in what is now the United States. But by 1400, a century and a half before the first European

Cahokia Mounds. The mounds at Cahokia, just east of St. Louis, constituted the largest complex of mounds in the Ohio and Mississippi valleys. This mound complex is also the most recent, suggesting that the builders had learned things about mound construction from other groups. From their political center at Cahokia, the leaders had economic relationships with people across Indiana and Ohio for flint and pipe stone, up the Mississippi River to Lake Superior from where they received copper, along the Missouri River as far as Yellowstone from where they received agates, and down to the Gulf Coast from where they received sea shells, all exotic goods that expressed and enhanced the appearance of power of the Cahokia leadership.

explorers arrived in the area, the stratified society that was Cahokia had disappeared.

The puzzle Cahokia represents for prehistoric archaeologists is to understand how and why such social complexity emerged there when it did, and why it didn't last. This is an archaeological question because there are no written records, only prehistoric sites. One way to observe how it emerged is in the rise of status markers in material culture and changes in architecture (Pauketat 1994). In certain burial sites, for example, many exotic objects appear after 1050 marking the high status of the deceased person. These items include shell beads, war clubs, sandstone tablets, pottery, and special projectile points, many of these things made with hard-to-get exotic materials drawn from distant lands. Exotic materials include copper from Lake Superior, pipe stone from Ohio, agate from Yellowstone, and shells from the Gulf of Mexico—each decorated with special colors and designs associated with what archaeologists think were symbols of political authority and sacred powers. As the center grew, Cahokians also tore down traditional housing—tightly clustered groups of small houses built around courtyards in which family groups lived—and replaced them with large new plazas and earthen mounds, rectangular and circular buildings, and temples, all using new styles of wall construction. These reconstructions probably represent the earliest example of urban renewal in what is now the United States. Over time, elites used the center of the city—a six-square-mile area where more than 100 mounds were built—for elite residences and for religious and political purposes. Non-elites lived in settlements nearby, well outside the center of Cahokia.

Why would such a transformation take place? Why would people who governed themselves in smaller autonomous villages and communities give up their independence to be ruled by others? Based on the physical evidence, it seems likely that the new class of leaders gained authority gradually over time. They had been creating regional alliances and had exploited conflicts between political and economic factions within their community. More importantly, perhaps, they supported a new division of labor in which small numbers of craftsmen manufactured tools and peasants served as laborers. This emerging elite associated itself with certain powerful religious and ideological symbols (Pauketat 1994).

Political struggle and instability were common, a condition that likely contributed to the city's eventual disappearance. Some archaeologists also point to an environmental collapse, caused by population growth, deforestation, and the erosion of rich agricultural soils (Dalan et al. 2003). Others suggest that warfare played a role, pointing to evidence of burials with weapons, burned buildings, sacrificial victims, and defensive stockades (Chappell 2002). Still others (Pauketat 1994; Pauketat and Emerson 1997) observe that Cahokian society didn't so much "collapse" as split into different groups that moved off in different directions to take advantage of resources and opportunities elsewhere.

At the heart of prehistoric archaeology's approach to understanding the rise and decline of complex societies like Cahokia is a key question: *How and why did cities and states emerge and sometimes disappear?* Embedded in this broader question are the following problems, around which this chapter is organized:

What Does Social Complexity Mean to Archaeologists?

How Can Archaeologists Identify Social Complexity in Archaeological Sites and Artifacts?

How Can Archaeologists Explain Why Cities and States Fall Apart?

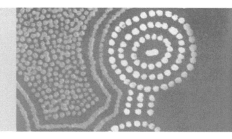

An archaeological focus on the rise of cities and states reveals much about how, why, and when humans shifted from small-scale face-to-face societies to larger-scale social groupings in which inequalities of power and social hierarchy are more common. Yet social complexity is not always associated with social inequality and hierarchy. We begin by presenting what archaeologists mean when they talk about social complexity.

11.1 What Does Social Complexity Mean to Archaeologists?

The earliest archaeologists were Europeans educated in the classic civilizations of Greece, Rome, Egypt, and Mesopotamia. Part of the fascination these ancient societies held for nineteenth-century Europeans was that they saw themselves as linked more or less directly to these older societies, which had provided the inspiration, if not the precise basis, for European legal codes, constitutions, and philosophical traditions. As the Egyptians, Mesopotamians, Greeks, and Romans were expanding their empires throughout the ancient world, however, the people of northern Europe lived in small-scale tribal groups, with none of the obvious markers of what European scholars of the time associated with high civilization, such as writing, cities, great monuments, occupational specialization, or social ranking. These early scholars wanted to know: When and where did civilization emerge? What caused these changes to occur around the Mediterranean and the Fertile Crescent?

Early archaeologists sought answers to these questions by excavating sites belonging to these ancient societies because they believed their findings would better help them understand the principles of how societies, including their own, became civilized and complex, as well as why many other small-scale societies—societies that still existed around the world during the nineteenth century—remained, in their biased view, small and "primitive."

In addition to excavating ancient sites, much of this early research focused on definitional issues, especially identifying the key traits and characteristics of civilizations. In Table 11.1 we present one influential analysis of the particular culture traits associated with the rise of complex societies produced by American anthropologist Alfred

L. Kroeber, who saw the great civilizations emerging from the accumulation of particular items of material culture. We contrast Kroeber's material culture model with that of Australian archaeologist V. Gordon Childe's view that the origins of cities and city-states was less about material things than about changes in organizational arrangements (Table 11.1).

Although Childe's work is immediately recognized among scholars as archaeological because of his many excavations, others may think of Kroeber as more of an ethnographer because of his work with a number of California Indian tribes, including his controversial relationship with Ishi, the last surviving member of the Yahi tribe in Northern California (Theodora Kroeber 1961; Sackman 2010). Although more closely identified with cultural anthropology, Kroeber was trained to approach questions in a four-fields way, as we try to do in this textbook, and he conducted his own research and published key articles in archaeology as well as in linguistic and biological anthropology. For instance, his essay on seriation as a way of dating ancient Zuñi sites in New Mexico is among the earliest examples of relative dating of sites by seriation in the New World (A. L. Kroeber 1916).

Most archaeologists recognized that there were different degrees to which specific cases fit either Kroeber's or Childe's model. But it was also clear that the social, political, and economic lives of people living in societies characterized as civilizations were very different from those of people living in small-scale societies. Nowadays, archaeologists have moved away from using words like "civilization" and "primitive" because of their ethnocentric assumptions about the superiority of our society's arrangements over other social forms. The dialogue with cultural anthropologists who

TABLE 11.1   CHARACTERISTICS OF CIVILIZATIONS ACCORDING TO A. L. KROEBER AND V. GORDON CHILDE

The American anthropologist A. L. Kroeber understood the emergence of states as a consequence of increasingly sophisticated material culture, while the Australian-born V. Gordon Childe saw urbanization as a consequence of new arrangements of how people interacted with one another, leading to social stratification (see M. Smith 2009).

A. L. Kroeber (1923)	V. Gordon Childe (1950)
Pottery and bows/arrows (Neolithic)	
Bone tools (Neolithic)	
Use of dogs (Neolithic)	
Hewn stone axes (Neolithic)	
Domesticated plants and animals (Neolithic)	
Use of metals (Bronze Age)	
Sun-burned brick	Larger population in settlements
Stone masonry	Full-time specialist craftsmen
Potter's wheel	Producers give surplus to leaders as tax to deities (via priests)
Astronomical records	Monumental public buildings
Development of iron	Priests, civil leaders, military leaders use surplus for own benefit
Writing	Writing
Elaboration of science (math, geometry, etc.)	
Conceptual and sophisticated styles of art	

also study politics and economics has also refined archaeological perspectives on these issues (see Chapters 13 and 15). Most anthropologists and archaeologists refer to the differences between these societies as differences of **social complexity**, by which they mean "the multiplicity of different parts on a social system" (Kowalewski 1990). In other words, social complexity is when people divide themselves or are divided into many separate subgroups. Some of these groups exercise power over others and control resources, while others experience inequalities relative to other groups in the society.

It is important to note that *all* societies experience some level of social complexity. No human society is "simple": even the most egalitarian face-to-face societies have ways of exercising power, controlling resources, and grouping people into smaller units for specific purposes, such as hunting parties, religious rituals, and so forth. In fact, some of the societies with the simplest technologies also have highly complex theologies and kinship systems. Anthropologists and archaeologists do not usually talk of complexity when referring to kinship terminologies or a complicated set of religious rituals, but only when the material arrangements of a society are differentiated into social or occupational classes or differences in wealth, power, and control, all of which are lacking in the egalitarian hunter-gatherer communities of Australia, the Kalahari, the Malay jungle, and the Arctic.

But not all societies with complicated social patterns are **complex societies**, that is, societies in which socioeconomic differentiation, large populations, and centralized political control are pervasive and defining features. In these societies there are many different social roles that people can play, especially in the form of specialized occupations, such as food producers, craftspeople, soldiers, leaders, and so on. Complex societies typically have political formations called **states**, which are societies with forms of centralized political and economic control over a particular territory and the inhabitants of that territory. **Cities**—relatively large and permanent settlements, usually with populations of at least several thousand inhabitants—are also characteristic of complex societies. The emergence of cities containing thousands of residents from much smaller villages and towns needed to be organized so residents were not constantly at odds with one another. Small cities did not require elaborate legal codes any more than tribes did; they already had customary ways of handling problems, disputes, and contention within the community. But as cities grew in size, one faction or another typically took control of key resources and asserted its will on the others. Thus, in most cases, like Cahokia in the New World and across Mesopotamia, these cities developed as **city-states,** autonomous political entities that consisted of a city and its surrounding countryside, with some form of centralized authority. And it was from these city-states that proper states and their larger cousins, kingdoms and empires, arose.

All of this is polite language to say that complex societies are characterized by dynamics of wealth, power, coercion, and status, in which social stratification—having elites and non-elites—ensures that the labor of the non-elites benefits the lifestyles and interests of the elites. So what led to the emergence of cities, city-states, states, and empires in the first place, and where did they begin (Figure 11.1)? Early on, archaeologists recognized that for complex societies to form, more intensive food production was necessary. It is also clear that elites began to construct a state ideology and religious ideas that explained and justified why political elites deserved the special treatment they received and groups with less power deserved fewer resources. Several other features of such societies have been suggested that we will consider here—population growth, contact with other cultures, and specialization and the differentiation of social roles—but before we do, it is important to observe that these matters of how,

- **Social complexity.** A society that has many different parts organized into a single social system.

- **Complex society.** A society in which socioeconomic differentiation, a large population, and centralized political control are pervasive and defining features.

- **State.** The most complex form of political organization, associated with societies that have intensive agriculture, high levels of social stratification, and centralized authority.

- **City.** A relatively large and permanent settlements, usually with a population of at least several thousand inhabitants.

- **City-state.** An autonomous political entity that consisted of a city and its surrounding countryside.

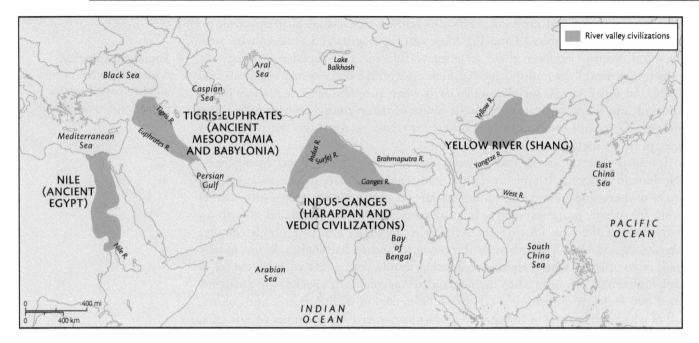

Figure 11.1 **The Four Great River Valleys That Produced the Earliest State Societies.** They largely emerged as city-states; and in the Indus and Mesopotamia regions, these states remained city-states for much of their history, only occasionally developing larger empires. By 2000 BCE, urban centers had arisen along the Tigris and Euphrates Rivers in Mesopotamia (modern Iraq and Turkey), along the Nile River (Egypt), along the Indus and Ganges Rivers in India and Pakistan, and along the Yellow River in northern China.

when, and why social complexity emerged is at the forefront of contemporary archae-ological research—and, if you pursue a field school as an undergraduate (as we discuss in "The Anthropological Life"), these themes are likely to be ones to which your labor will contribute.

Population Growth and Settlement Practices

All the complex societies that archaeologists have examined had large populations ranging from thousands to even hundreds of thousands of people. Nearly all had central locations that we could talk about as cities, even though some were much larger than others, ranging from 30,000 to 50,000 people in some ancient Egyptian cities, to perhaps as many as 65,000 in Ur at its height, to about half a million people in Rome when Augustus Caesar established the Roman Empire (27 BCE). The Greek city-states were somewhat smaller.

Large populations require a corresponding sophistication and scale of their food production, not to mention some system for distributing food to the city's inhabi-tants, which could include markets and warehouses. Importantly, societies with cities and the early hints of what would become centralized states lived side by side with small-scale and tribal societies that also produced their own food, often the same foods that were part of the diet of people in these early towns and cities. Each of these patterns of food production and food distribution gave advantages to some group or another among the elites, further enhancing their elite status. Food production to feed a growing population was thus a necessary, but not a sufficient, characteristic that led some societies to become complex.

Another way to think about population growth's relationship to complexity is that as a population grows, social conflict over essential resources such as land and water can also increase, which can trigger the rise of complexity. We consider this argument in "Classic Contributions: Robert Carneiro on the Role of Warfare in the Rise of Complex Societies."

The Anthropological Life
Archaeological Field Schools for Undergraduates

If you want to know whether becoming an archaeologist is your personal calling—or if you simply want to have an amazing educational experience—you should consider enrolling in a summer field school. These days there are many opportunities for getting training and experience in archaeological fieldwork, although not all programs are equally effective at providing a high-quality learning experience. Typically, the best field schools are those associated with universities and colleges. Many American universities have regular summer programs run by faculty or research staff (these leaders are known as the Principal Investigators, or PI's), with graduate students as crew bosses, and undergraduates learning and then performing many of the tasks involved in archaeological fieldwork, often for academic credit. The place to start figuring out which field school is the right one for you is by asking the professor teaching this course, or an archaeology professor in the anthropology department.

It is important to know at the outset that archaeological field schools can be physically and mentally demanding, often taking place under the hot summer sun in primitive outdoor conditions. A typical program, which might last between several weeks and a couple of months, begins with several days of orientation to the site and its history, as well as an introduction to archaeological methods and techniques. In addition to performing day-to-day work at a field site or excavation, field schools will often also include field trips and evening lectures with visiting archaeologists or community members. Students will often also do research projects of their own, or write up reports and submit them to the PIs. Field crews may stay in accommodations nearby or may even camp out near the site. Days are usually long: they begin early in the morning with a long work period in the field conducting surface surveys and excavations; continue in the afternoon in a lab or other facility cleaning and processing artifacts; and end with lectures and socializing in the evenings. Field schools are very social affairs—on most excavations there is a kind of supportive comradery that engulfs the whole team.

The social relationships and networks that are created in field schools can be very important if you go on in archaeology, shaping where you might decide to attend graduate school, even where you might eventually get work in the field. But even if you don't go into an archaeological career, you are likely to count field school as one of your most valuable educational experiences.

Here are some useful resources for finding field school opportunities:

- American Anthropological Association's database "Anthroguide" is searchable for field schools: https://guide.americananthro.org/24665/Practice-Settings?citcat=48_262
- Archaeological Institute of America. "Archaeological Fieldwork Opportunities Bulletin." https://www.archaeological.org/fieldwork/afob
- National Science Foundation Research Experiences for Undergraduates (REU) Program. This competitive program provides opportunities for undergraduates to receive field training opportunities, and typically provides summer stipends and travel support. https://www.nsf.gov/crssprgm/reu/reu_search.jsp

Trade and Contact with Peoples of Different Cultures

While warfare models of state formation continue to be important (e.g., Haas 1990), a second model has been proposed by a number of archaeologists. In a recent case study about the rise of civilization in the Middle East, archaeologist David Wengrow (2010) argues that it was trade between early states that brought growth and development in these societies across the Fertile Crescent. The "trade model" of state formation holds that states and complex societies have tended to form where there is interaction among groups of people of different ethnic backgrounds, especially those with access to different resources. Trade arises because people want the objects,

Classic Contributions
Robert Carneiro on the Role of Warfare in the Rise of Complex Societies

DURING THE LATE 1960s, many archaeologists began to develop models to explain social change, especially models that could explain why societies at certain times and places had shifted from tribal societies to become chiefdoms and states. One of the best examples of this trend in archaeology is the work of Robert Carneiro, who developed a model he called circumscription theory to explain what forces propelled societies to change and take on more social complexity. Carneiro (1974) turned to the problem of what happens when limited resources needed to be exploited by a growing number of people. According to Carneiro's model, as populations grew they put pressure on the land, leading to competition and warfare. The victors in these confrontations could eventually place themselves in control of more resources, allowing them to rise in status over their less successful neighbors.

The same squeeze in available arable land that led to the development of more intensive farming in certain areas of the world gave rise to another important cultural phenomenon as well: competition between one tribe and another over land.

Warfare has entirely different consequences in an area of restricted arable land and dense population than it does where land resources are extensive and population is sparse. In a circumscribed, densely settled area a defeated group could not make a strategic withdrawal. There would be no place for it to go; all of the arable land would be occupied. It would have to remain where it was and suffer the consequences. And the consequences of defeat under these conditions would generally be, first, the payment of tribute, and, at a later stage, outright incorporation into the territory of the victor. Having to pay tribute in kind, the vanquished group would have to work their lands even more intensively than before. While food production had not as a rule previously exceeded domestic consumption, a clear surplus would now have to be wrought from the soil to meet the demands of the dominant group.

The ever-increasing need for more arable land would continue to act as a stimulus to war; and warfare, through the process of conquest and amalgamation, would lead to an increase in the size of political units. At the same time it would also give rise to confederacies and alliances, as each tribe or chiefdom sought to strengthen its military position. The culmination of this process locally would be the political unification of an entire valley under the banner of its strongest chiefdom. The ultimate military and political result of the process over part or all of a continental area would be the formation of a large conquest state encompassing and controlling many valleys. [Carneiro 1974:86–87]

Questions for Reflection

1. Is it inevitable that some form of subjugation through tribute or enslavement would follow from conquest? What other ways might the victorious group respond?

2. What evidence might we look for in an archaeological site that might confirm or support Carneiro's model?

foods, or raw materials that neighboring groups produce that are not available at home. After time, some communities are able to exploit partial monopolies, exert control over access to their own or another group's resources, or take control over a busy trade route.

Similar processes have been observed and recorded in historic times, where it is possible to observe the flow of trade and the rise of political power more directly. For example, we know that some communities exploited control over different segments of the Silk Road trade route to amass great wealth. The Mongol empire of Genghis Khan used its monopoly to enhance its wealth and support its army, so the Mongols could conquer other powerful states, even the seat of government in China, already the most powerful state in Asia.

A very different pattern was seen in the fourteenth century. The entrepôt or city-state of Malacca on the Malay Peninsula (just west of modern Singapore), was tiny compared to any of the ancient Roman, Egyptian, or Persian cities, but Malacca traders were able control nearly all trade through the Strait of Malacca linking India, China, and the Indonesian islands. They did so by controlling the movement of ships through the Strait. When the Portuguese reached the Indies during the Age of Discovery they first set their eyes on control of this trade network and in 1511 conquered Malacca, which was essentially undefended. More than a hundred different languages were spoken in the city at the time, representing groups from as far away as China, India, Arabia, and New Guinea. Over the next century control over this trade made the rather small nation of Portugal a world power. In both of these historic examples—the Mongol empire and Malacca—states emerged by controlling trade. Archaeologically, these networks can be identified through multi-sited and regional strategies, including excavation of various historic sites and a review of regional museum collections to study objects found at other sites in the economic network.

Most trade models of state formation focus on the key role that a specialized class of traders plays in managing markets and marketplaces, or by providing military protection of markets and caravans, all of which they are able to do by collecting taxes or tribute. For example, as urban populations grew in Mesopotamia, the need arose for recordkeeping. It is likely that a result of this need was one of the earliest writing systems (cuneiform), which uses a writing stylus pressed into soft clay. Later, the small clay tablet can be fired in an oven, making the hardened clay nearly indestructible. The vast majority of the many thousands of these early written documents (clay tablets) in ancient Mesopotamia were records of debts owed for food, land, and other resources (see, e.g., Graeber 2011). Varying kinds of trade, differing geographies, different volumes of goods, and the like meant that the trajectory of each state's emergence was somewhat different. But in all cases archaeologists can show that having contact with diverse groups of people added to the community's social complexity by bringing new trading opportunities, technological innovations, and new social possibilities to the emerging state.

Although most trade in early societies was with neighbors within the same region, research by Kenyan-born anthropologist Chapurukha Kusimba along the east coast of Africa illustrates that inter-continental trade—which today we often refer to as "globalization"—has been much more significant over the past 2,000 years than previously suspected. We explore the findings of his research in "A World in Motion: Exploring Early Contacts between China and the East Coast of Africa."

Specialization and Production Models

Another model archaeologists have used is called the "production model" of state formation. The driving force in this model is craft specialization, which led to new social roles for food producers and craftspeople, who produced useful objects like

A World in Motion
Exploring Early Contacts Between China and the East Coast of Africa

For several decades, Kenyan-born archaeologist Chapu-rukha Kusimba, currently at the University of South Florida in Tampa-St. Petersburg, has been studying international relations between coastal East African communities and Asia in an effort to understand how these contacts influenced the rise of towns and cities along the East Coast of Africa (Kusimba 1999; Kusimba and Kusimba 2005; Kusimba 2018; Kusimba et al. 2020). One of the enduring questions for archaeologists has been to understand what role, if any, relationships with societies in various parts of Asia played in Africa's prehistoric economic, political, and social dynamics.

It has long been clear that there are deep historical ties between China, India, and the Arabian Peninsula, on the one hand, and villages, towns, and cities along nearly the entire east coast of Africa, particularly along the coastal communities of Kenya and Tanzania. Broken porcelain from East Asia could be found in almost every coastal site suggesting that Asia and Africa had been in contact for many centuries. During the nineteenth century, European travelers, colonial-era writers, and eventually archaeologies reported on the ubiquitous pieces of Asian porcelain (broken plates, bowls, and cups) strewn about many beaches and town sites.

☝ **The Gedi Ruins.** Gedi was a walled city and important Indian Ocean trading center on the Swahili Coast starting some 1200 years ago. There large quantities of Chinese porcelain have been excavated.

In the past twenty years, knowledge of trade of Arab and Chinese porcelain in East Africa has increased considerably, and a large part of these broken fragments can be identified as belonging to certain periods of about fifty years plus or minus, reaching back to at least 300 CE. Although the African trade represented a very small proportion of the porcelain production in any of these Asian communities, it is now clear that Asian contacts along the East Coast of Africa played a considerable role in the formation of powerful cities as local sites controlling those extensive trade networks. Asian porcelain is an excellent way of dating such contacts since the vast majority of porcelain tends to break and be discarded within a decade or two of use. Kusimba's research suggests that at the beginning of the second millennium CE, Eastern and Southern Africa, indeed much of Africa as a whole, had become a regular partner in the thousand-year-old long-distance exchanges that reached as far at the Arabian Peninsula, India, Sri Lanka, and China (Mitchell 2005; Pearson 2003; Walmsey 1970; Warmington 1974; Wilkinson 2003). By the 13th century there had emerged a local African urban elite along the East African seaboard. Innovations in ironworking aided agricultural intensification and specialization in hunting, fishing, and herding. These changes improved the quality of life and precipitated population growth and economic prosperity for some 200 years (Kusimba 2018:86).

By the late 1400s Europeans began to control trade in the Indian Ocean, disrupting established trade routes and relations between East Africa and Asia (see Table 11.2). Disrupting these ties with established Asian partners, replacing them with economic relations that benefited their European home countries in Portugal, France, and Great Britain benefited Europeans and ultimately laid the economic and military groundwork that brought the entire African coast under European control. Kusimba argues that all of these relationships and changes over the past 1,700 years can be read from the archaeological record, particularly from the broken pottery along the East African coast.

TABLE 11.2 DISTRIBUTION OF ARCHAEOLOGICAL REMAINS AT COASTAL SETTLEMENTS IN EAST AFRICA OVER TIME

Period	Time	Archaeological Finds	Transoceanic Trade
Period V	1750–1950 CE	Indo-Pacific beads, glass bangles, Chinese blue on white, Japanese Karatzu ware, European Floral ware Islamic monochrome pottery, iron and iron slag,	Frequent regional and international trade—Persian Gulf, India, China (decline) and Europe, Americas (expand)
Period IV	1500–1750 CE	Stylistically diverse local pottery, Indian pottery, European peasant floral wares	Regular regional and international trade–Persian Gulf, India, China, Indonesia
Period IIIb	1250–1500 CE	Stylistically diverse local pottery, spindle whorls, coins, portable stoves and lamps, chlorite schist, Islamic monochromes, Chinese Longquan and Tongan ware, Indonesian Sawankholok or Si-satchanalai jars, Indo-Pacific beads and Egyptian glass,	Regular regional and international trade with China, Southeast Asia, India, Persian Gulf
Period IIIa	1000–1250 CE	Stylistically diverse local pottery, rock crystal, spindle whorls, copper and silver coins, Islamic Sgraffiato, Chinese Qing Bai, Cizhou ware, Bronze mirrors, Indo-Pacific beads,	Regular regional and international trade with Persian Gulf, Egypt, India, and possibly China
Period IIb	600–1000 CE	Zanjian Pottery: red barnished and hagshaped cooking pots, graphite finsh and trellis patterns; Partho-Sassanian Islamic, white-glazed, Chinese green glazed stone ware, gray-green "Yue" ware, Guangdong Coastal Green, white porcelain, white stone ware, and Egyptian glass, car carnelain beads, iron and iron slag	Egypt, Persian Gulf and Indian Subcontinent
Period IIa	300–600 CE	Azanian pottery: triangular oblique, and double zigzag patterns predominate; Sassanian Islamic, glass, and carnelian beads and Roman Amphora	Some trade
Period I	100 BCE–300 CE	Local Early Iron Age pottery, iron and iron slag	No Evidence

Source: Kusimba 2018:89

stone tools and pottery. As food production and especially yields increased, the surpluses could feed the new specialist craft-producing class of non-producers. Surpluses gave rise to a military class of full-time warriors, and these warriors supported and often served a full-time class of elite leaders.

True control of production came with construction of irrigation canals and systems that developed in many early states in the Middle East. Even the Nile valley, with its seasonal floods that enriched the soil with silt, provided the basis for a network of drainage ditches that acted as an irrigation system. Control over the system gave the governing elites tremendous control over the fertility of the land and thus over the people.

• **Hydraulic despotism.**
Denotes empires built
around the control of water
resources by despotic, or
all-powerful, leaders.

The level of political and social control exerted by ancient elites lays the basis for what early archaeologists referred to as **hydraulic despotism**, which denotes empires built around the control of water resources by despotic, or all-powerful, leaders. In ancient Egypt we see in the ruins of temples, tombs, and pyramids ample evidence of what appears to have been a centralized leadership that controlled vast numbers of laborers. For years at a time these workers toiled, building extensive palaces at centers like Thebes, Luxor, and Amarna (Figure 11.2). The basis of these dynasties' control lay in their ability to control water resources.

Another model of ancient despotism is visible in the centralized empire of Ur in Mesopotamia. For much of its history Ur was a large but typical city-state rather than the powerful kingdom we think of from historical writings. But one particular phase of state formation at the city of Ur represents the flourishing of just this kind of society. Known as Ur III, because it emerged after two earlier social formations on the same site, this empire was a central state with a broad reach. From this seat of strong kings with large bureaucracies of accountants, tax collectors, and scribes, the elites at Ur III controlled the circulation of goods, services, and information (Yoffee 1995:299). The bureaucrats collected tribute and taxes from producers, arranged for the distribution and redistribution of grain and other products, sold rights to particular parcels of land, and wrote of the great accomplishments of their rulers (Kramer 1963). The need for financial recordkeeping on clay tablets or on papyrus prompted the development of writing systems, later providing a useful way of promoting the state histories and the accomplishments of increasingly powerful leaders.

These images of ancient despotism are undoubtedly reasonable at various times and places, but they are biased because there were so many Mesopotamian scribes writing about everything imaginable in cuneiform script on clay tablets that survive well in the arid lands of the Middle East (Figure 11.3). Well over 90 percent of translated cuniform relate to economic obligations, debts owed by commoners and the poor to the upper classes. Much of what we can infer about these states comes from what the rulers, their scribes, and stoneworkers left behind in the form of relief carvings, palace art, and monumental stonework engraved with cuneiform writing. Egyptian rulers and nobles left tombs carved with similar accounts in hieroglyphics, which we assume is partly the same kind of "spin" that our politicians and their supporters provide

Figure 11.2   Temples at Luxor along the Nile River. Such structures required a great deal of labor to erect the many columns, statues, and other architectural features, all of which demonstrate the pharoah's control over a large laborer class.

today to enhance their images and status, and to control how later generations will view them.

Rethinking the Scale of Mesopotamian Kingdoms

Recent archaeological findings have motivated a reinterpretation of the so-called kingdoms and empires of Bronze Age Mesopotamia. Most of these formations were rather short-lived and were really city-states rather than vast empires. The evidence suggests that most of the kingdoms were organized more like estates that served the needs of particular temples. For the period 3200–1600 BCE in Mesopotamia, for example, populations abandoned residences in the countryside near their fields in favor of the protection afforded by rapidly growing cities. It would seem that elites controlled the temples, which likely brought them an income, which they used to provide military protection from hostile neighbors. Agricultural labor was coordinated from these cities to work sets of fields near particular streams or irrigation canals, leaving other fields to lie fallow for planting in subsequent years. Such activities allowed protection for agricultural laborers, and the hydrologic system that supported agriculture was organized in the name of the divinities celebrated in the temples. In return for all this religious and military protection, farmers made payments in the form of tribute or taxes and allegiance.

Figure 11.3 **Carved Relief from the Northwest Palace of Ashurnasirpal II at Nimrud, Assyria, Dating to ca. 883–859 BCE.** Cuneiform characters are chiseled into the stone across the images of the king and other important people.

Two processes were at play in these city-states: **urbanization,** in which towns grew as residential centers, and **ruralization,** in which the countryside was configured as a contested no-man's land lying between city-states (Yoffee 1995:284). At this period, monumental architecture associated with religious shrines, temples, and leaders flourished along with the emergence of recordkeeping devices like cylinder seals and cuneiform tablets (Figure 11.4). We have much richer "historical" documentation of these

- **Urbanization.** Process by which towns grew as residential centers as opposed to being trading centers.

- **Ruralization.** Process in which the countryside was configured as a contested no-man's land lying between competing city-states.

1899.2.514

Figure 11.4 **Ancient Mesopotamian Cylinder Seal and the Impression It Leaves on a Clay Tablet.** These seals were status symbols in themselves, and they often attempted to enhance the status of their owners.

early city-states than in ancient Egypt because the latter documented the minutia of their daily lives on papyrus that does not easily survive the elements even in dry climates.

The question that arises in these ancient Middle Eastern cities, city-states, and states is why would previously independent people, working fields and herding sheep, goats, or cattle, surrender their independence to a local leader in their own community or, even more surprisingly, to a leader in a city some distance away? One likely reason is that leaders with armies and police forces at their disposal would have the power to enforce their control over farmers, whether the farmers liked it or not. But developing a warrior class of loyal men probably started off in simple ways when somewhat larger clans began coercing their less powerful neighbors. As specialization in the crafts and trades emerged, these skilled workers needed protection and willingly followed the wishes of more powerful elites who could protect them.

Does Complexity Always Imply Social Inequality?

As we have suggested, the Mesopotamian city-states were likely much smaller in their reach than the great kingdoms and empires that anthropologists and archaeologists wrote about a century ago as ancient despotism. It does not mean that these early Mesopotamian rulers were never despotic, but rather that the rise of early states seems more plausibly linked to social arrangements that allowed farmers and agricultural laborers to yield some control over their land and labor in exchange for protection from potentially hostile neighbors.

In the later Neolithic (7,000–5,000 BCE), settlements were growing in size and density, but many suggest little evidence of social inequality. The important site of Çatal Höyük in southern Turkey, for example, shows little evidence for hereditary inequality yet was a rather large settlement. This site appears quite egalitarian compared with most later Mesopotamian sites (Hodder 2006).

As more control over agricultural production was given to ruling elites and their bureaucrats, these systems might develop into despotic kingdoms. But such situations are more tenuous for ruling elites than one might suspect. For example, archaeological evidence at some of these Mesopotamian formations suggests that agricultural laborers could and perhaps often did shift their allegiances to a neighboring city-state and its leaders, when the new protection might be more secure or when they were provided other perks and benefits.

Importantly, social complexity does not always emerge from social inequality. Some societies may have social groups organized into broad regional relationships by building on individual relationships rather than relying on a central authority to organize societies. These units can coordinate their productive activities through individual arrangements, and they can even specialize in certain kinds of production. But because they view one another as social equals, these communities do not emerge as highly stratified societies. Consequently, they often lack monumental architecture, professional militaries, and writing.

One example of this kind of social complexity is found along the north coast of Papua New Guinea today. Nearly 200 politically independent communities over some 400 miles of coast have long been economically integrated through individual exchange relationships between pairs of friends. These friendships persist because they are inherited by children and sometimes other relatives. We have ethnographic, ethnohistorical, and archaeological evidence that these relationships have persisted for at least 300 years and probably much longer. In this region, each community specializes, producing fish, sago, pottery, shell ornaments, bows, arrows, nets, canoes, and a host of other products. Yet despite this specialization, everyone along the coast has essentially the same material culture and the same diet. Islanders living on islands such as Tumleo, Ali, and Seleo have no sago whatsoever, but they get sago and many vegetables from friends on the mainland where sago grows abundantly. Tumleo islanders produce pots—as they have for at least ten centuries—while the other islanders provide smoked fish and shell ornaments—as they likely have for a similar period. The pattern of specialization is quite complex, but an ideology of equality has prevailed, even when a few communities occasionally try to control a monopoly on certain products (Terrell and Welsch 1990; Welsch and Terrell 1998). The social system is too diffuse for any sort of monopoly to persist for any length of time.

Such an example challenges the idea that social complexity and specialization always take on some single universal form. But it also raises another question: How do archaeologists identify evidence of complexity in the first place?

> ### THINKING LIKE AN ANTHROPOLOGIST: THE RISE OF SOCIAL COMPLEXITY
>
> Many archaeologists have long seen the rise of cities with specialized occupations like warriors, leaders, farmers, and those who make special products as progress and advancement. But could we also see the rise of ancient cities, states, and empires as based on the rise of social inequality? How is complexity in political structure linked to inequality?

11.2 How Can Archaeologists Identify Social Complexity from Archaeological Sites and Artifacts?

Suppose a future archaeologist excavating the site of your childhood home uncovers several plastic toys, a computer chip, metal eating utensils, and assorted fragments of ceramic plates. Based on such a limited number of admittedly mundane objects, how could an archaeologist know anything about your life, much less the complexity that characterized your society? This challenge confronts *all* archaeologists interested in social complexity, not just those who might excavate centuries from now.

Archaeologists know that material objects are an expression of people's social relationships. The objects themselves also help shape social relationships, including those related to wealth, power, and status (Love 1999:129). In other words, how we use houses, jewelry, and other daily objects expresses our wealth, power, and status as individuals or as members of a group, and these objects in turn affect our daily lives in various ways. As observed by Liz Brumfiel, an archaeologist and former president of the American Anthropological Association, the power of archaeology's focus on materiality is that it can bring to light stories of ordinary people's lives in complex socieities that are otherwise lost because "dominant groups will overstate the historical importance of their own group and undervalue the contributions of others, legitimating inequalities" (Brumfiel 1992:553). But by itself, in isolation, an object recovered in an excavation cannot necessarily tell us much about the dynamics of wealth, power, and status. As we show in this section, evidence of such things usually comes from close analysis of different kinds of objects, often as an **assemblage**, or collection

- **Assemblage.** A group or collection of objects found together at a site or excavation.

of objects found together, as well as evidence of their manufacture and distribution in a site or region, and contextual clues that can connect individual artifacts to similar or related artifacts—all of which can involve various forms of archaeological, ecological, geological, and forensic expertise. Only after pulling together these different pieces of evidence and analysis does a picture of social complexity begin to emerge.

Identifying Social Complexity from Sites and Artifacts in Western Mexico

The best way to convey how archaeologists develop a picture of social complexity from handling different kinds of artifacts is to present a case study: the Tarascan empire in what is now the western Mexican state of Michoacán. It is a fresh example—only during the last few decades have archaeologists intensively studied its rise, scale, and social complexity (Figure 11.5). Beginning in the Classic Period (400 CE–900 CE) and culminating in the Post-Classic period (1000–1400s), the Tarascans organized the second-largest state in Mexico, most likely to counter the military and political pressures exerted on them by Mexico's largest empire, the Aztecs. By 1522 when the Spaniards arrived, the Tarascan king ruled a vast territory that included some 1.3 million people divided into numerous social rankings, ethnic groups, and occupational specialties, as well as a state bureaucracy that controlled the extraction of raw materials, trade, and the distribution of many goods. Evidence of the state's emergence, as well as the social distinctions and power relations within it, comes from

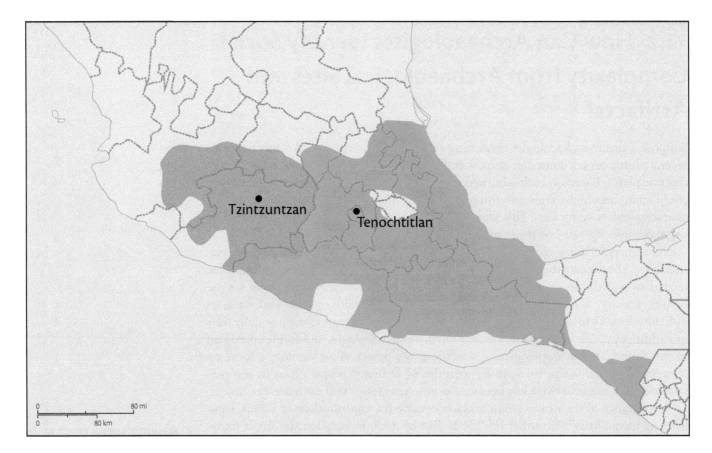

Figure 11.5   The Tarascan Empire (Green). The Tarascan state was the second largest in the New World when Spanish colonists conquered the largest, the Aztec state (orange) in 1521.

diverse archaeological sources, among them several we review here: population growth and settlement patterns; soils and land use patterns; monuments and buildings; mortuary patterns and skeletal remains; and ceramic, stone, and metal objects (Pollard 1993, 2003b).

Population Growth and Settlement Patterns

The political, economic, and social center of the Tarascan empire was in the Lake Pátzcuaro [**pahts**-quahr-oh] basin in a city called Tzintzuntzan [cheen-choon-**chahn**], whose ruins still stand today. Beginning in the period before 1000 CE, people lived on the lakeshore but eventually moved to higher ground, apparently to maximize access to agricultural land, hold a better defensive position against enemies, and gain closer access to obsidian mines for toolmaking. This move sets the stage over the next few centuries for political consolidation under single authority (Pollard 2003a:227). In the new site, an increase in the number of households and outlying settlements, as well as the construction of monuments, suggests population growth and the city's rise as the administrative and religious center.

Archaeologists also observe that over time the growing city became spatially segregated and divided into special function zones. For example, analyzing domestic trash deposits, which hold discarded foods and broken tools and pots, has revealed assemblages of finer quality objects associated with certain residences, indicating the segregation of elite and commoner residential neighborhoods (Pollard 1993). Manufacturing zones appear as well, where specific activities such as pottery-making and stone-tool manufacture were practiced in specific settlements but not others, indicating occupational specialization. Finally, carefully planned public zones were created where large monuments, plazas, and ball courts were built, and these areas were under direct control of administrative and religious authorities.

Soils and Land Use

The study of soils in and near settlements offers useful perspectives on connections between population growth, agricultural expansion, and soil degradation (Fisher et al. 2003). In recent years, a drop in lake levels has allowed archaeologists to study areas once occupied but eventually abandoned as lake levels rose. In addition, they have taken cores of lake soils in order to conduct pollen analysis, especially maize pollen, to understand the scale and location of agricultural production. By studying the mineral composition of lake soils, archaeologists have discerned that layers of sediment were released and deposited on the lake bed because of erosion of soils in higher altitude areas. All of these pieces of evidence indicate that the growth of population centers, especially Tzintzuntzan, created soil degradation. In the centuries leading up to the Spanish conquest, land managers responded to this degradation by implementing soil conservation techniques like terraces, which required abundant labor possibly controlled by elites.

Monuments and Buildings

Because they transform a landscape and require substantial engineering and collective labor, monuments and buildings are important symbols of power, wealth, and connection to the divine order. In Tzintzuntzan, specialized stone platforms consisting of rectangles with circular extensions called a *yácatas* [**yah**-kah-tahz] were constructed (Figure 11.6). The discovery of ritual paraphernalia in rooms inside these structures indicates their function as religious temples. The region also had abundant wood

Figure 11.6   Yácatas in Tzintzuntzan.

resources, and as a result many of the city's buildings were constructed of wood. Archaeologists have found elaborately carved wooden lintels, portals, and posts, as well as painted posts and walls, mainly in temples and elite residences (Pollard 2003b:85).

Mortuary Patterns and Skeletal Remains

Archaeologists have observed changes in the location and contents of Tarascan burial sites over time, including the preparation and treatment of bodies, types of burial goods, and mortuary facilities. These changes correlate with increasing population and indicate social differentiation (Pollard 2003a:236). For example, finely decorated pottery and metal ornaments in distinctive shapes and designs are common in the burial sites of elites. Burial sites are also segregated within settlements, with elites and commoners having their own mortuary zones. In burial sites of elites, skeletal remains show the modification of teeth and skull deformation, both common markers of elite identification throughout ancient Mesoamerica.

A notable shift in mortuary practices takes place with the consolidation of state power during the 1400s. Before this period, mortuary objects in elite burials, such as finished jewelry, shells, and metal objects, were imported from other distant powerful political and social centers, such as central Mexico. Later, the objects come from areas under Tarascan control. Archaeologists interpret this shift as indicating the consolidation of a distinctly Tarascan identity among elites, an identification that supported the consolidation of Tarascan state power (Pollard 2003b).

Ceramic, Stone, and Metal Objects

Changes in everyday objects—especially ceramic pottery vessels and figurines, stone tools and weapons, and metal tools, weapons, and ornaments—are also tied to increasing social complexity. By connecting these objects to their sources, archaeologists have demonstrated that expanding trade networks and administrative control brought raw materials from new and distant locales both outside and from within the growing empire. For example, before the period of state consolidation, production of ceramic pots in most parts of the prehistoric world was largely local in scale and unspecialized. With the rise of the state, full-time specialized production facilities, as well as distinctive styles and designs associated with elites, appear. Chemical analysis of clay samples in potsherds also indicates that the number and variability of clay sources increases. In one locality of Tzintzuntzan in southern Mexico, for example, the presence of large amounts of non-local ceramic ware, which is similar to materials and styles found among the Otomí ethnic group from the empire's northeast border, suggests the importance of ethnic distinctions in the city (Pollard 1993:105).

Changes in production and distribution patterns of obsidian and metals support a similar picture of the empire's social complexity. Obsidian sources increase, and greater quantities of obsidian objects appear in core administrative areas, correlating with the time period of state consolidation. Metal objects are typically associated with elite and ritual deposits. Tracking them to their sources indicates that mining, smelting, and production of metal objects was carried out by full-time specialists who worked under state control (Pollard 2003a:234).

The important point about all this evidence is that in isolation none of these findings would automatically suggest the existence of social complexity, but together they create a compelling picture that highlights the rise of state power, social divisions, and social inequality. Such a holistic approach has the potential to unlock many other rich and suggestive stories about social life in complex societies. In "Doing Fieldwork: Researching Primordial Sea Monsters and Sharks in the Mayan Jungle with Sarah Newman" we look at one especially compelling example.

Empires, cities, and states do not usually survive for more than a few centuries. So, we may ask why, after mustering the specialization and organization of production, do most complex societies not persist? We address this question in the next section.

Doing Fieldwork
Researching Primordial Sea Monsters and Sharks in the Mayan Jungle with Sarah Newman

Sea monsters and sharks do not live in jungles, of course. But for ancient Mayas who lived in jungle villages and cities a long distance from the ocean, primordial sea monsters and sharks did occupy a special place in their imaginations as unique, powerful, even divine creatures. As is the case in many complex socieities, in ancient Maya societies elite groups sought to influence and control the basic understandings and knowledge of the social, cosmological, and natural worlds. These processes shaped how Maya commoners regarded *Xook* (pronounced "shook"), or sharks.

For University of Chicago archaeologist Sarah Newman, whose research focuses on ideas about the natural world and human-animal interactions among the ancient Maya, the question was never whether the Maya were familiar with real sharks (Newman 2016). Coastal communities caught them in the Caribbean, ate them, and prepared certain medicinal treatments with them. Sharks were more than that, however, and inland people in particular experienced sharks less as actual animals and in more imaginative ways. Shark teeth have been found in excavations of

🔻 The "Signature" Glyph of Ha' K'in Xook, a Late Classic Maya Ruler (767–780 CE).

ceremonial sites; sharks were represented in iconography as sea monsters and semi-deities; and powerful rulers throughout the Maya world sought to associate themselves with sharks by incorporating the creatures in their own names. For Newman, the bigger question was what did sharks signify across the Maya world?

In order to explore this question, Newman sought to examine multiple lines of evidence—ethnohistorical accounts, an inventory of archaeological finds, and Maya iconography. In ethnohistorical accounts written during the Spanish colonial era, she found descriptions of how Maya hunted and butchered sharks, a food that Europeans considered distasteful. Across the Maya world, archaeological excavations have uncovered many shark teeth and jaws that had traveled through trading networks, ending up in artworks at temples and ceremonial sites, on portable objects like cups and bowls, and in murals among many inland Maya sites. Among the most remarkable finds are giant fossilized megalodon teeth (an enormous shark from the era of dinosaurs), which were closely associated with myths of primordial sea monsters. These remarkable objects were integrated into Maya iconography, where fantastical monsters of many kinds were often portrayed with a large single tooth. Elites who associated themselves with and controlled the cosmic representations and symbolic meanings of shark mythology and divinity used it to affirm their own connections to those divine forces.

In complex socieities, one of the ways elites established and communicated their power was to produce and control various kinds of records of their associations, relationships, and understandings of the world. Viewed from a methodological angle, Newman's ability to come to these conclusions about the real and imaginative role of sharks would not be possible by just looking carefully at the objects—shark teeth, for example—found in a single excavation. Instead, what was required was a varied and holistic strategy utilizing archaeological, historical, and interpretive techniques that tracked these objects and their representations across the ancient Maya world.

Questions for Reflection

1. A single shark's tooth in an upland Maya statue clearly meant something different from what some Maya fisherman might have caught in the sea. How should we interpret these two sets of images of sharks?

2. Why might shark's teeth be prominent in upland Maya sites, far from the sea?

3. Excavating a shark's tooth in an upland Maya site is only one artifact of many. Is Newman correct in giving these objects such prominence in her research?

THINKING LIKE AN ANTHROPOLOGIST: SOCIAL COMPLEXITY

If you were assigned to study some other ancient city or state, could you identify the kinds of archaeological evidence that might indicate greater social complexity? What evidence might suggest greater social and economic inequality?

11.3 How Do Archaeologists Explain Why Cities and States Fall Apart?

For many of us, nothing evokes romance and adventure more than the discovery of vine-draped ruins of a "lost civilization." Our fascination is fueled by a cottage industry of television documentaries, tourism promoters, literature, and films devoted to revealing the mysteries and disappearance of once-powerful and sophisticated ancient civilizations. According to this view of history and prehistory, great civilizations rose and eventually fell. But are we misinterpreting or misunderstanding the course of these ancient states (McAnany and Yoffee 2010a)?

One popular book, Jared Diamond's *Collapse: How Societies Choose to Fail or Succeed* (2005), has tapped into this fascination and attempts to clear up the mysteries with a moral message: if we understand how and why these ancient societies fell, we can learn important lessons that might prevent our own society's demise, but only if we choose to recognize the lessons and change our ways. Diamond's argument is that the root cause of societal collapse is environmental, resulting when a society overexploits its natural resource base because of population growth and overconsumption of scarce resources, or because some other factor such as climate change undermines a society's ability to feed itself through agriculture.

Picked up by media and television documentaries, it has become a popular argument. But attempts such as Diamond's to explain **collapse**—the rapid loss of a social, political, and economic order or complexity—are like viewing a low-resolution digital image: from faraway the image may seem clear, but up close it dissolves into disconnected parts (McAnany and Yoffee 2010b:5). In other words, when delving deep into the archaeological evidence, most cases offered as examples of total societal collapse

• **Collapse.** The rapid loss of a social, political, and economic order or complexity.

• **Resilience.** The ability of a social system to absorb changes and still retain certain basic cultural processes and structures, albeit in altered form.

fall apart. In fact, archaeologists mostly agree that collapse is an incredibly rare phenomenon, and that transformation and **resilience**—the ability of a social system to absorb changes and still retain certain basic cultural processes and structures, albeit in altered form—are typical for most human societies (Tainter 2006; McAnany and Yoffee 2010b).

The classic historical examples of great empires that ended, such as the Roman Empire, the Persian Empire, the empire of Alexander the Great, the early Mesopotamian states, and the many ancient Egyptian dynasties, did not generally end from collapse. Many of these met their political end from internal fragmentation, from lack of strong central institutions, or from more powerful foreign armies. For example, the Romans developed an imperial economy built on expansion and the conquest of foreign states. When the empire stopped expanding, internal dissension over two centuries led to the inability of Romans to prevent the sacking of Rome by so-called barbarian tribes. And the fall of the Eastern Roman Empire, based at Constantinople, was not a sudden collapse but a gradual decline over nearly a thousand years, as the noted historian Edward Gibbon retells in his classic *History of the Decline and Fall of the Roman Empire* (Gibbon 1784). When the barbarians captured Rome, the Western Roman Empire had been in decline for as long as the United States has been independent of England. In each of these examples, the original states disappeared or were profoundly transformed, but the people largely survived and became part of new social formations.

In the following discussion, we take two other emblematic examples of apparent collapse—the Four Corners area of the US Southwest and the Classic Maya—and demonstrate that abandoned ruins do not mean that the people themselves did not survive, although they may have undergone a substantial transformation in their social institutions and how they organize themselves.

Rethinking Abandonment in the US Southwest

During the late thirteenth century CE, the Ancestral Pueblo (Anasazi) people who lived in Mesa Verde (now in southern Colorado) and the rest of the Four Corners region picked up and moved away. They left behind well-preserved cliff-dwellings, mesa top pueblos (villages), farming terraces, towers, reservoirs, and irrigation systems (Figure 11.7). Archaeologists and others have long puzzled over why this abandonment occurred, often turning to environmental explanations, among them the "Great Drought" (1276–1299 CE) that brought erosion, soil depletion, dropping water tables, and violence (Lipe 1995; Diamond 2005; Wilcox 2010).

It is not at all clear, however, that environmental stresses are the singular cause of the Four Corners depopulation (Ahlstrom, Van West, and Dean 1995). Soil depletion, for example, is difficult to prove because of the impossibility of identifying exact locations of prehistoric agricultural fields. Furthermore, given the dry environment and the commonality of droughts, the Ancestral Pueblo had developed a wide variety of clever techniques to support dry land agriculture, among them selecting low-moisture crop seeds, farming in high water table areas or areas supplied by floodwater and snow melt, and constructing terraces and irrigation systems with small dams. They also had social networks of trade and exchange to get food and other goods, often from distant locations unaffected by local climate patterns. The likelihood that these social networks, technical adaptations, and the sophisticated knowledge that developed them all failed at once is slim, and no evidence exists to support such a failure. Furthermore, variability in climate, water levels, and water flow throughout the region mean that, even under long-term drought conditions, some localities would have remained viable.

Figure 11.7 Mesa Verde. A city of more than 600 residences.

Unsatisfied with these environmental explanations, many archaeologists have begun to view this region's prehistory through another lens. This lens views abandonment as a social strategy, not of failure but of resilience so that the people migrated to take advantage of opportunities elsewhere. In fact, the Ancestral Pueblos never "disappeared." Many Pueblo people migrated to the northern Rio Grande region, where resources were abundant. Other groups migrated to other areas in the Southwest and formed smaller, aggregated pueblo-style villages of several hundred people, a process facilitated by *kachina* (political-religious) authorities (Lekson and Cameron 1995).

These migrations created new social groups and group dynamics, processes that archaeologist Scott Van Keuren has been studying among the postmigration pueblos of east-central Arizona. His research strategy involves studying changes in ceramic production and the emergence of Fourmile style pottery as a proxy for socioeconomic interactions between groups. Van Keuren has conducted a number of excavations in different pueblos throughout the region that have yielded potsherds and whole bowls decorated in the Fourmile style (Figure 11.8).

Using these artifacts, as well as collections now in museums, Van Keuren has closely analyzed Fourmile ceramics for deeply embedded clues to social identity and experience (Van Keuren 2006). The use of sacred icons suggests that these decorations were intended to communicate religious and esoteric messages. Other messages were unintentional, however, such as those carried by the subtle ways potters painted individual vessels, especially in their paint brushstroke sequences, which Van Keuren has studied under magnification. Reconstructing brushstroke sequences involves studying overlapping strokes of paint and then reconstructing the sequence used to paint the object. Brushstroke sequences reveal consistent behaviors and techniques learned by individual potters as members of a community. In an area called Silver Creek, the specific location where the Fourmile style emerged, potters followed the same sequence, indicating that painting pottery was an activity involving certain kinds of standardized knowledge and training. Their use of religious and esoteric iconography also suggests that they were members of a particular community by way of their control of specialized bodies of knowledge.

Most important for our purpose here, the Ancestral Pueblo and their descendants (among them Hopi, Zuñi, and Rio Grande Pueblo who live in the region today) never

**Figure 11.8   Fourmile Style
Pottery.**

truly "abandoned" the Four Corners area (Cameron 1995). They continued to return to the ceremonial centers they had once occupied, viewing them as important cultural, historical, and religious centers. All of this physical movement is supported by a pervasive theme that runs throughout Pueblo legends and cultural thought, even today, which is that movement is necessary for the perpetuation of life (Naranjo 1995).

The Transformation—Not Collapse—of the Classic Maya

The Classic Maya (400–900 CE) of the Mesoamerican lowlands is *the* prototypical ancient complex state society. It was a society of extreme political centralization, rigid social hierarchy, colossal monuments, population centers housing tens of thousands of people, and a hieroglyphic script. During the Late Classic period (the eighth and ninth centuries), monumental building projects ended, royal dynasties disappeared, courts no longer functioned, and important centers were abandoned, mostly without evidence of violence—a prototypical "collapse" (Tainter 2008). Archaeologists and others have advanced dozens of explanations, the most prominent being (McAnany and Negrón 2010:145):

1. *Escalating warfare* between rulers of city-states.
2. *Out-of-control population growth* leading to environmental degradation, erosion, and soil depletion.
3. *Drought*, resulting from climate change.
4. *Inability of rulers* to adapt to changing economic conditions and social conflict.

Archaeologists continue to debate each of these theories, pulling together new and existing evidence to support their arguments. What we must keep in mind as we evaluate these archaeological arguments is that the Maya people never disappeared; the history of the Maya has been one of social change and resilience, as the existence of 7 million Maya today attests.

Escalating Warfare

Among the Maya, Late Classic period **stelae** (carved limestone slabs) that record the lives and events of Maya royalty have more accounts of warfare than other historic periods, leading some archaeologists (and Mel Gibson's 2006 movie *Apocalypto*) to argue that warfare undermined the whole civilization (Figure 11.9). While martial conflict did exist, there are several reasons to think it didn't cause collapse (McAnany and Negrón 2010). One of these is that we would expect to see widespread evidence of defensive fortifications, but their scale and distribution doesn't support a vision of extensive and constant warfare. Another reason is that Late Classic stelae also record many more accounts of royal activity of all kinds, not just warfare, indicating that more things were being recorded. Furthermore, the Late Classic hieroglyphs are more completely deciphered than those from other periods of Maya history, so we can't definitively conclude that there was more warfare during the Late Classic period than any other.

Out-of-Control Population Growth and Environmental Degradation

The theory that population growth was out of control depends on the method of estimating population density. The accepted method involves counting the number of structures per square kilometer and assuming about five people for each, then subtracting a fraction of the total for the fact that not every structure was residential. Such estimates require some level of sample surveys of the entire site, often using aerial photographs, satellite images, LIDAR, and careful analysis of Google Earth images. A high estimate for the Classic period Maya lowlands is 150 people per square kilometer, considerably lower than the population density of Los Angeles (2,700 per square mile) (McAnany and Negrón 2010:153). High population is a relative concept and one that is also related to the carrying capacity of the natural environment. Some have argued that the fragile soils of the region could not sustain large populations. Yet, recent studies of landscape modification during the Classic period indicate that Maya farmers were especially aware of this fact and practiced soil conservation techniques, such as terracing and water management using irrigation across dry slopes (Dunning and Beach 2000).

Climate Change and Drought

As climate change has become a major global concern in our own era, the question about its role in the disappearance of past societies has felt more urgent. Based on soil cores taken from the Caribbean region, scientists have argued that the climate during the eighth and ninth centuries was especially dry. Some archaeologists (e.g., Gill 2000) argue that resulting droughts and dropping water tables deprived people of food and even drinking water. There is, however, no evidence to suggest that water shortage was uniform—the Petén lakes never dried up, and a number of important centers such as Copán sat near a permanent water source. Yet Copán was one of the first cities to be abandoned (McAnany and Negrón 2010). Furthermore, cities in dry areas of the interior where there are no rivers and water is seasonally in short supply, such as Tikal, Calakmul, and Caracol, survived longer than Copán.

Figure 11.9 Maya Stelae. Much of what we know about life in the Maya lowlands of the Classic period is from stelae. The information recorded on them focused mostly on the activities of members of the royal dynasties.

• **Stelae.** Carved limestone slabs.

Ineffectiveness of Rulers to Adapt to Change

In his book, Jared Diamond (2005) argues that Maya rulers were a lot like contemporary CEOs: so focused on their own short-term interests that they ignored bigger problems, such as social unrest among peasants and ecological problems. There is no doubt that political crises and social conflict eventually rendered these leaders irrelevant, since the royal dynasties dissolved by the end of the Classic period. Economic changes, such as a shift in commercial activities and population from the interior lowlands to the coastal Yucatán peninsula, may have played a role in undermining these leaders.

So what really happened to the Classic Maya? We know that Maya farmers dispersed throughout the countryside and only occasionally congregated at the once occupied centers. Certain social and political structures persisted, including statecraft based on inherited nobility and social hierarchy (observed by the Spaniards several hundred years later). None of this suggests collapse; it does, however, suggest transformation. The important point here is that different polities experienced different histories of transformation (Webster 2002)—some held on longer than others because of their specific political, ecological, historic, and perhaps even climatic conditions. Of course, each of the factors we have considered can reinforce or mitigate the others. A degrading environment can lead to increasing conflict, which in turn can lead to the undermining of political authority, and so on. There is no uniform experience or explanation for the depopulation of a city or state.

This point has contemporary relevance as well. Climate change, environmental destruction, a pandemic, war, rising prices, and so forth have provoked intense fear among millions that humanity is on the edge of a global apocalypse. A cottage industry of films, novels, video games, comic books, and TV shows conjure images of total societal collapse, often picturing lone heroes holding out against chaos and destruction. Archaeologist Chris Begley (2021), who has studied the transformation of Classic Maya and Roman societies, observes that these images present a skewed doomsday vision and miss the lessons that a century of modern archaeology has to teach us. One of the main ones is that we tend to focus on societal collapse from our own individual perspective rather than from a societal point of view. Individuals can die from pandemics or see their homes wash away due to flood waters, and cities may fall or be bombed, as we have recently seen in Ukraine. But as cataclysmic as such things may be for anybody personally, rarely do they cause the sudden demise of whole social and economic institutions, provoking instead a gradual transformation as those institutions adjust or, sometimes, totally remake themselves to accommodate new social, environmental, political, and economic realities. Not all do, of course. But in situations where they do, social transformations are made not by those individuals who abandon society altogether to live some kind of Mad Max existence, as the movies and video games portray, but by new communities and social groupings that form in the aftermath of whatever disruptions caused it in the first place.

THINKING LIKE AN ANTHROPOLOGIST: THE RISE AND FALL OF CITIES AND STATES

We have argued that changes in early cities and states are important to understand, but we believe it is useful to think of these changes as transformations rather than collapse. What difference does it make if we think of the southwestern Pueblos at Mesa Verde as belonging to a society that collapsed because of some environmental collapse rathan than because of some more complex process of social transformation?

Conclusion

Perhaps because they left behind so many traces—monuments, temples, writing systems, irrigation canals, and burial sites full of artifacts of beauty and artistic sophistication—ancient complex societies can be easily viewed as stories of high human drama and tragedy. Our recent fascination with the idea of the collapse of great societies, cities, and states is likely because we currently face the consequences of a pandemic, war in Eastern Europe, and global warming, with prospects of sea levels rising significantly, droughts in some areas, flooding in others, intensifying storm patterns, and mass disruptions around the globe. Rigid social hierarchies, great concentrations of wealth, despotic kings, brutal authoritarian leaders, peasant rebellions, conquest and warfare between competing societies vying for access to resources or trade goods—all of this makes for rich and engaging history, allowing us to look at the past to foresee our global future.

But if we step back from the more dramatic elements of these stories, a focus on complexity is a means by which archaeologists can study the dynamics of social integration and transformation in ancient societies. It can help us focus on the conditions under which societies grew; how people reorganized their economic, political, and social patterns to accommodate such growth; and the contexts in which societies confront political, ecological, and social challenges, not by disappearing into thin air—as many narratives of collapse imply—but by transforming the social order through processes like migration or political reorganization. Viewing situations like Cahokia or the Tarascan empire from this angle, we can better appreciate these stories as human cultural processes, not as media-hyped mysteries.

Archaeologists continue to debate whether or not these processes of transformation and complexity are more or less uniform, and, thus, the expression of universal principles such as intensifying conflict and warfare or trade and production. Nevertheless, all archaeologists agree that any explanation of complexity must be rooted in and emerge from the actual evidence of artifacts and remains themselves. The closer attention we can pay to those objects and their context—whether it's knowing how a monument might have been constructed or identifying the order of brushstrokes on pottery—the greater insight we can gain into how and why states, cities, and other complex societies emerged and, in some cases, declined.

KEY TERMS

Reviewing the Chapter

Chapter Section	What We Know	To Be Resolved
What does social complexity mean to archaeologists?	Social complexity—the division of society into groups—exists in all societies. But not all societies are complex societies; that is, societies in which socioeconomic differentiation, large populations, and centralized political control are pervasive and defining features of the society.	Archaeologists continue to debate whether these processes of transformation and complexity are more or less uniform, that is, the expression of universal principles such as intensifying conflict and warfare or trade and production.
How can archaeologists identify social complexity in archaeological sites and artifacts?	Close attention to artifact assemblages, as well as the contexts of their manufacture and distribution, can yield important clues about the rise and decline of ancient cities and states, and of social complexity more generally.	The specific characteristics of states, cities, and city-states sometimes blur because these terms and their definitions do not necessarily capture the actual dynamism of human cultural processes. Sometimes different social formations can produce similar outcomes.
How do archaeologists explain why cities and Total societal collapse is extremely rare. states fall apart?	Resilience and social transformation are the rule, not the exception.	Anthropologists continue to debate the relative merits of environmental, political, economic, social, and climatic explanations for the abandonment of a city or the disappearance of a particular social or political order. But mostly these debates are specific to the causes for change at a particular site or region rather than to a single global process affecting all states and complex societies.

READINGS

Much of the literature on the rise and fall of early cities and states consists of case studies of particular ancient empires. For example, Ian Hodder's *The Leopard's Tale: Revealing the Mysteries of Çaltalhöyük* (New York: Thames and Hudson, 2006) focuses on the rise of social complexity in a very early site in southern Turkey. His research at Çaltal Höyük is one of the best documented Mesopotamian sites from a very early period.

Two studies of Cahokia along the Mississippi River are Timothy R. Pauketat and Thomas E. Emerson's *Cahokia: Domination and Ideology in the Mississippian*

World (Lincoln: University of Nebraska Press, 1997), which emphasizes the rise of social stratification at Cahokia, and Sally A. Kitt Chappell's *Cahokia: Mirror of the Cosmos* (Chicago: University of Chicago Press, 2002), which gives somewhat more emphasis on the decline of this important mound-builder site.

David Wengrow's *What Makes Civilization? The Ancient Near East and the Future of the West* (New York: Oxford University Press, 2010) offers a more general overview of the rise of early cities and states in the Fertile Crescent.

A volume edited by Patricia A. McAnany and Norman Yoffee, *Questioning Collapse: Human Resilience, Ecological Vulnerability, and the Aftermath of Empire* (Cambridge: Cambridge University Press, 2010a), challenges Jared Diamond's view that the disappearance of great societies in prehistory is generally due to environmental collapse. Archaeologist Chris Begley's 2021 book *The Next Apocalypse: The Art and Science of Survival* (Basic Books) offers lively perspectives on themes of collapse and transformation.

PART IV

Human Social Relations and Their Meanings

Throughout this book we have argued that meaning is culturally constructed by diverse social processes and relationships that touch on the political, economic, environmental, and biocultural aspects of who we are as humans. In this part we turn to how humans today actually develop and enact their social relationships to make these worlds meaningful. These topics have long been the hallmark and, for some, the special domain of linguistic and cultural anthropologies. The goal of the chapters in this last part is to examine in closer detail the complex interactions among the creation of meaning, social order, and social change.

This part opens with the acknowledgment, introduced in Parts I and II of this book, that symbolic thinking lies at the heart of what makes us human. We start with understanding language, first with a Methods Memo exploring how anthropologists study language and its relationship with culture, and then a chapter introducing the driving concerns of linguistic anthropology. Following these is this book's final Methods Memo, which focuses on ethnographic research methods. Ethnographic research is the primary method used by cultural anthropologists to study human social relations and their meanings. Following this memo, we explore several classic concerns of cultural anthropology, starting with a chapter that examines what cultural anthropologists know about human economies and the diverse ways people make, share, and buy things to create value and get what they want and need. A chapter on the closely related matter of sustainability—encompassing food production and human–nature relations— follows, exploring the diverse ways people in the contemporary world interact with their environments. After this is a chapter considering what political anthropologists know about the forms that power, politics, and social control can take in the world today. The next chapter, on kinship and gender, considers the complexities of how people think about and build social relationships around the basic facts of human reproduction. A chapter on religion closes out this section, focusing on how humans construct meaningful worlds that involve the moral, the ethical, and the philosophical. While many people assume that religion is about the supernatural, we argue that religion is about building a system of meanings that makes certain actions seem reasonable and special. This point captures the essence of the cultural construction of social relations and meaning, and indeed, lies at the heart of how cultural anthropologists understand the worlds they study.

METHODS MEMO

How Do Anthropologists Study the Relationship Between Language and Culture?

Linguistics is an interdisciplinary social scientific field whose goal is to describe and understand the structure, form, and grammatical patterns of human language. Anthropologists are active participants in this field, but in linguistic anthropology—the branch of anthropology whose primary focus is on language and its relationship with culture—there is a greater focus on the effort to understand the social and cultural dimensions of language use. This effort involves a distinctive set of methodological tools that resemble the same kinds of ethnographic research strategies cultural anthropologists use—especially immersive fieldwork and the creation of rapport with people from another culture. Nevertheless, the specific field strategy that a linguistic anthropologist adopts will depend on the kind of question he or she is asking about the use of language in another culture.

DESCRIPTIVE LINGUISTICS: A BASIC APPROACH

Descriptive linguistics is one of the basic approaches within the interdisciplinary field of linguistics in which anthropologists participate. The goal of descriptive linguistics is to identify the underlying rules of a language and determine when and how these rules should be applied. Descriptive linguistics pay close attention to issues like what are the basic rules for inflecting nouns and verbs, for placing different kinds of words together in a sentence, and how the sounds in a string of words change with their context. For example, in English the *s* sounds in *this house* [this haus] change to *z* sounds when speaking in the plural: *these houses* [theez hauzez]. These are descriptive linguistic observations made by listening to how people pronounce words in normal speech. Because the pattern is more general than just the words *this* and *house*, we can see it at work in other words or utterances, such as *this boy* [this boi] and *these boys* [theez boiz]. For other nouns, such as the pair of words *goat* and *goats*, the plural form comes from adding an *s* to make the word plural. Linguistic anthropologists have long utilized the methods of descriptive linguistics, often seeking to understand how these linguistic rules are manipulated, even when native speakers are unaware of it.

STUDYING LANGUAGE AND ITS RELATION TO CULTURE

In the early decades of the twentieth century, anthropologists saw language as central to understanding culture. Franz Boas (1911) and his team of researchers who were studying the tribes of the Pacific Northwest Coast (United States and Canada) in the late 1890s published many texts transcribed in their original Indian languages along with English translations. These studies were motivated by the "salvage paradigm" (see Chapter 1), which emphasized the importance of creating dictionaries and transcriptions of native languages threatened with extermination. These early anthropologists also assumed that the categories and concepts encoded in Native American myths and stories were distinctive to local cultural backgrounds. They pioneered a tradition—expanded by Boas's student Edward Sapir—that has come to be called **anthropological linguistics**, the branch of anthropology that studies human beings through their languages. In referring to this period, Harry Hoijer (1961:110) suggested that anthropological linguistics "is devoted in the main . . . to the languages of people who have no writing" (see also Teeter 1964; Voegelin 1965). The methods generally followed the methods of descriptive linguistics described previously and further discussed in Chapter 12.

By the 1960s and 1970s, anthropologists began to argue that it was necessary to distinguish how people *actually* speak from the ideal ways people are *supposed* to speak. Linguistic anthropologist Dell Hymes (1962, 1972, 1973) pioneered a new anthropological approach, which has been called the **ethnography of speaking** (see Bauman and Sherzer 1974), that aimed to focus on the first of these two (how people actually speak in normal conversations). This approach uses participant observation, focusing on listening to and meticulously documenting what people say, the register they say it in, the words they use, and what they are hoping to communicate intentionally as well as what they may unintentionally convey from the linguistic choices they have made.

Linguistic anthropologist Dennis Tedlock (1972, 1988, 1993) has also focused on the ethnography of speaking, but he emphasized recording precisely what an informant or research subject utters, including the pauses, the mistakes, and the specific word choices. He viewed all speech acts as performances, an approach that has come to be known as

- **Anthropological linguistics.** The branch of anthropology that studies human beings through their languages.

- **Ethnography of speaking.** An anthropological approach to language that distinguishes the ways that people actually speak from the ideal ways that people in any culture are supposed to speak.

ethnopoetics, referring to a method of recording oral poetry, stories, ritual language, and so on as verses and stanzas rather than as prose paragraphs in order to capture the format and other performative elements that might be lost in written texts. In his studies of Zuni stories and ritual texts, Tedlock (1999) pioneered ways of analyzing every pause, silence, change in volume or tone, intentional sound effects, gestures, and props. For native speakers of the language, these variables would be perceived intuitively.

Over the last several decades many linguistic anthropologists have sought to understand how people use language to mark and communicate social position. These researchers are interested in how language is gendered, how language helps establish patterns of dominance and subordination, or how one person in a community can use a language cue to influence others. Often the linguistic cues are unintentional but built into the structure of how the language is spoken rather than how the grammar puts words together. One of the first examples of this way of analyzing speech came from anthropological linguist Robin Lakoff (1975). In the early days of American feminism, female researchers began to look at how the sexual politics of the ordinary workplace was supported by the ways men and women used language. Lakoff's groundbreaking work pointed out how a whole range of linguistic markers made it clear to everyone in an office situation or classroom which gender was in control. Her point was to use the tools of descriptive linguistics, plus giving special attention to such things as tone, volume, and even more subtle aspects of intonation within a free-flowing conversation. Just like Tedlock's (1999) careful attention to pauses and raised volume or intonation, Lakoff was a pioneer in showing that American women and men used the same vocabulary and the same grammatical rules. But although they used the same grammar, the same words, and even the same rules for putting them together, American women of the 1960s used a much more deferential style when talking with men than men did when talking with either men or women, and these stylistic cues communicated a great deal about the relative social positions of women and men in these social interactions. Methodologically, Lakoff showed that using the tools one would use in studying a foreign language in its context, anthropological linguists needed to record subtle details of how language was actually being used to understand what was being communicated at the non-linguistic or non-verbal level of social interaction. It was not really the words being used, but the entire pattern of word and other linguistic choices that expressed a submissive or a superior position.

Nevertheless, as attention to how power relations are established and reproduced through language use has grown in linguistic anthropology during recent years, the limitations of descriptive linguistic approaches also became more clear. Specifically, their focus on internal structures of language tended to erase the broader colonial and postcolonial dynamics that were ordering social relations and perpetuating inequalities (Dick and Nightlinger 2020). To track these processes and how they articulate with language, many linguistic anthropologists have turned to the method of **discourse analysis**, an approach that closely analyzes the content, sociopolitical significance, and effects of semiotic practices beyond individual speech events to show how these practices are involved in and shape social processes (Wortham and Reyes 2015; Dick and Nightlinger 2020). Discourse analysis techniques include identifying speech events and narrations, documenting their immediate social contexts, and connecting these to social action, institutional dynamics, and other sociopolitical processes. It has been used in ethnographic projects such as those that study the relationship between language use and how authority and ideology are reproduced in social institutions like schools, and the co-construction of race, language, and nationalism in everyday life. But it is also useful for projects that are difficult to do in face-to-face ethnographic settings, such as the internet and social media. In fact, one of the cutting edge areas of linguistic anthropology in recent years has been using techniques of discourse analysis to understand the effects of digital technologies on social life and language.

Thinking Critically About Linguistic Anthropology Methods

- Although most linguistic anthropologists use linguistic transcription, many also incorporate various aspects of cultural analysis in their work. How might an understanding of the cultural background of greeting ritual or the expectations listeners have of song, poetry, stories, or even feature films shape the meaning these verbal performances might have for ordinary listeners?

- How can we apply some of Lakoff's findings to understand how your professors in other classes communicate?

- **Ethnopoetics.** A method of recording oral poetry, stories, ritual language, and nearly any narrative speech act as verses and stanzas rather than as prose paragraphs in order to capture the format and other performative elements that might be lost in written texts.

- **Discourse analysis.** An approach that closely analyzes the content, sociopolitical significance, and effects of semiotic practices beyond individual speech events to show how these practices are involved in and shape social processes.

12

Linguistic Anthropology

Relating Language and Culture

FEW COLLEGE STUDENTS go for long without checking their smartphones. There are any number of things about this phenomenon that might attract your professor's attention, but to the anthropologist specializing in how people use language, use of smartphones is likely to be of great interest. Digital communication such as texting, chatting, and emailing involves truncated forms of words, acronyms, and emojis. Because text messaging on mobile devices encourages simplification, common phrases are often abbreviated, as in "Where R U?" (for "Where are you?") and "LOL" (for "laughing out loud"), new terms that even penetrate offline communication. Is digital communication contributing to changes in our language? And are young people the ones actually driving linguistic change?

Scholars long assumed that educated men were driving linguistic change in the English language. But when historical linguists analyzed more than 6,000 handwritten letters from the sixteenth and seventeenth centuries, they noticed younger women were introducing new words, variations on words, and even grammatical forms into their letters, while men of all ages tended to have a more inflexible form of written English (Nevalainen and Raumolin-Brunberg 2017; McCulloch 2019:33–34). In her study of language change in contemporary American English, linguist Gretchen McCulloch (2019) found this same pattern holds. Young women's uses of language, how they text, and what conventions and abbreviations they use—"lol" being an emblematic one—have

Changing Dynamics of Language and Culture. Digital communication is contributing to broader changes in how people use language. Young people—and primarily young women—are at the forefront of these changes.

343

percolated into young men's texting, and later into that of their older peers, and ultimately into the usage of older Americans.

Anthropologists have known for some time that changes in how languages are spoken are most pronounced in cities, where the populations are denser than in rural areas (Labov et al. 2006). Young people, especially teenagers, college students, and twenty-somethings, have also long been identified as a major source of new idioms, new words, and changes in pronunciation in spoken language, often because they were seeking to differentiate themselves from the older generation or to show their belonging and status as members of an "in-group." But the fact that language change is also happening in digital settings is an important development. Even more interesting, perhaps, is the revelation that changes enter more formal language by younger women rather than from younger men or from older people of either gender, suggesting that the gender parity in some aspects of language usage has been present in American and English society, even when other rights were denied these same women.

This perspective on language leads us to ask a question at the heart of anthropology's interest in language: *How do the ways people talk reflect and create their cultural similarities, differences, and social positions?* We can answer this question by considering a number of related questions around which this chapter is organized:

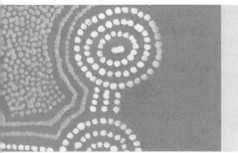

Where does language come from?

What does language actually do and how does it work?

Does language shape how we experience the world?

If language is always changing, why does it seem so stable?

How does language relate to social power and inequality?

Language is one of the most rule-bound and structured aspects of human culture. Yet, ironically, language is also one of the least consciously used and most dynamic aspects of culture. Language helps us make sense of the world around us, and our use of language both marks and reinforces social hierarchies and gender differences within a society. Before we get into these kinds of subtleties, however, it is important to understand where language comes from in the first place.

12.1 Where Does Language Come From?

• **Language.** A system of communication consisting of sounds, words, and grammar.

A **language** is a system of communication consisting of sounds, words, and grammar. This simple definition emphasizes three features: (1) language consists of sounds organized into words according to some sort of grammar, (2) language is used to communicate, and (3) language is systematic. But where does it come from? We can begin to answer this question in two ways: one is evolutionary, having to do with our biological heritage; and the other is historical, related to how languages have developed over time.

Evolutionary Perspectives on Language

The simple fact that we are able to make sounds and put them into meaningful sequences suggests two different biological abilities that both link us to and separate us from non-human animals. First is the ability to make linguistic sounds using the mouth and larynx. Second is the ability to reproduce these sounds in an infinite variety of ways to express an equally diverse range of thoughts. To what extent do we share these capabilities with other animals?

There are clearly examples in which an animal appears to talk. Animal behaviorist Irene Pepperberg worked for several decades to train her famous African Grey Parrot Alex (1976–2007) to make similar simple sentences using symbolic concepts of shape, color, and number. Alex's ability to use language was quite rudimentary compared to human speech. He was one of the few non-primates to have an obituary published in the *New York Times* (Carey 2007). But do animals really talk?

Call Systems and Gestures

Most animals cannot talk because they do not have a larynx. Yet most animals use sounds, gestures, and movements of the body intended to communicate. Anthropological linguists refer to these sounds and movements as **call systems**, which are patterned forms of communication that express meaning. But this sort of communication is not considered to be language. Why? There are four major reasons:

- **Call systems.** A manner of communication that features patterned sounds or utterances that express meaning.

1. *Animal call systems are limited in what and how much they can communicate.* Calls are restricted largely to emotions or bits of information about what is currently present in the environment, while language has few limitations in the content of what kind of information it can transmit.
2. *Call systems are stimuli dependent, which means that an animal can only communicate in response to a real-world stimulus.* In contrast, humans can talk about things that are not visible, including things and events in the past or future.
3. *Among animals, each call is distinct, and these calls are never combined to produce a call with a different meaning.* In contrast, the sounds in any language can be combined in limitless ways to produce new meaningful utterances.
4. *Animal call systems tend to be nearly the same within a species with only minor differences between call systems used in widely separated regions.* In contrast, different members of our species speak between 5,000 and 6,000 different languages, each with its own complex patterns.

Humans are evolutionarily distinct from other animals in that we developed not just the biological capacity to speak through a larynx but the brain capacity to combine sounds to create infinite symbolic meanings. Both abilities form the basis of human language.

Teaching Apes to Use Sign Language

It is clear that some apes have the ability to communicate beyond the limits of a call system, as researchers who have attempted to teach American Sign Language (ASL) to apes demonstrate. A well-known example is a chimp named Washo, who learned

Figure 12.1   Koko with Penny Patterson.

over 100 signs that had English equivalents. Even more striking, she was able to combine as many as five signs to form complete, if simple, sentences (Gardner, Gardner, and Van Cantfort 1989). Similarly, Penny Patterson (2003) worked with a female gorilla named Koko who, before her death in 2018 at age 46, learned to use more than 2,000 signs and also combined them into short sentences (Figure 12.1).

Chimpanzees and gorillas clearly have the cognitive ability to associate signs with concepts and then to combine them in original ways, comparable in some respects to the linguistic ability of a toddler. Such capabilities are not surprising among our nearest relatives in the animal kingdom, since the human capacity for language had to begin somewhere, and we would expect other advanced primates to have some limited abilities.

Several anthropologists have nevertheless challenged whether apes like Washo and Koko actually demonstrate any innate linguistic ability (Wallman 1992). These critics argue that the two apes are extremely clever and have learned to respond to the very subtle cues of their trainers, in much the way circus animals learn remarkable tricks and know when to perform them. But as linguistic anthropologist Jane Hill (1978) has noted, most of these critics have never worked with primates. Such studies of ape sign language suggest that our capacity for language may have begun to emerge with our ancestral apes. Most likely, from this rudimentary ability to associate meaning with signs and gestures, full-blown language evolved as human cognitive abilities became more complex.

Historical Linguistics: Studying Language Origins and Change

While primatologists take the evolutionary approach to the origins of language, historical linguistics focuses on how and where the languages people speak today emerged. This approach uses historical analysis of long-term language change. The approach began in the eighteenth century as **philology**, which is the comparative study of ancient texts and documents. Philologists like the German Jakob Grimm (1822), best known for his collections of fairy tales, observed that there were regular, patterned differences from one European language to another. To explain these patterns, he hypothesized that English, German, Latin, Greek, Slavic, and Sanskrit all came from a common ancestor. As speakers of languages became isolated from one another—perhaps because of migration and geographic isolation—the consonants in the original language shifted one way in Sanskrit, another way in Greek and Slavic languages, in a different direction in Germanic and English, and yet another way in Latin and the Romance languages, all of which came to be known as Grimm's Law (Figure 12.2). The supposed common ancestor language, which became extinct after these divergences took place, is called a **proto-language**.

Genetic Models of Language Change

Contemporary historical linguists call Grimm's approach "genetic," since it explores how modern languages derived from an ancestral language. To identify languages that have a common ancestry, historical linguists identify **cognate words**, which are words in two or more languages that may sound somewhat different today but would

- **Philology.** Comparative study of ancient texts and documents.

- **Proto-language.** A hypothetical common ancestral language of two or more living languages.

- **Cognate words.** Words in two languages that show the same systematic sound shifts as other words in the two languages, usually interpreted by linguists as evidence for a common linguistic ancestry.

have changed systematically from the same word (Table 12.1). As speakers became isolated from one another for geographic, political, or cultural reasons, their consonants, vowels, and pronunciation diverged until they were speaking two or more new, mutually unintelligible languages. For example, German, Dutch, and English are descended from the same proto-Germanic language, but speakers of these three languages cannot usually understand each other unless they have studied the other language.

Figure 12.2   Grimm's Law. Early Indo-European forms using *k* in Greek, Latin, and Irish shifted to *h* in the Germanic languages of English, German, Danish, and Norwegian. Many other examples include "head" and "heart."

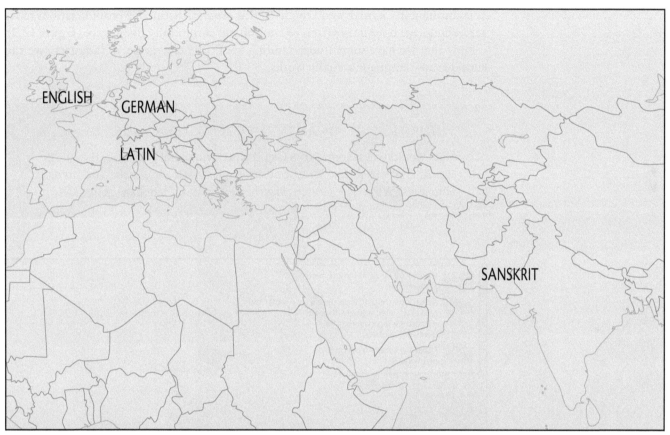

INDO-EUROPEAN INITIAL CONSONANT	ENGLISH	GERMAN	LATIN	SANSKRIT
*p	foot	Fuß	pes	pet
*p	father	Vater	pater	pita
*d	two	zwei	duo	dva
*d	tooth	zahn	dens	dan
*k	hundred	hundert	centum	satam
*k	heart	Herz	cor	
*k	hound	Hund	canis	sua

TABLE 12.1	EXAMPLES OF COGNATE WORDS IN INDO-EUROPEAN LANGUAGES							
English	Dutch	German	Norwegian	Italian	Spanish	French	Greek	Sanskrit
three	drei	drei	tre	tre	tres	trois	tri	treis
mother	moeder	mutter	mor	madre	madre	mère	meter	matar
brother	broeder	bruder	bror	fra	hermano	frère	phrater	bhrator

Non-Genetic Models of Linguistic Change: Languages in Contact

Languages also change by being in contact with another language, which is a "non-genetic" model of change. Such change generally takes place where people routinely speak more than one language. In the speech of multilingual persons, the use of one of the languages is subtly influenced by the other language's sounds, syntax, grammar, and vocabulary. Evidence of this process can be seen in the use of the flapped and trilled *r* in Europe. In southern parts of Western Europe, the trilled *r* is typical, but this pronunciation seems to have given way in the north of France to a flapped *r* as is common in German and Dutch. In this process, distinctive pronunciations move across language boundaries from community to community like a wave (Figure 12.3).

Now that we have some understanding about the emergence of language, we can consider how language actually works.

THINKING LIKE AN ANTHROPOLOGIST: LANGUAGE

How would you respond to a friend who claims that his or her dog understands English because it responds to English words in regular and predictable ways? What do examples like this tell us about language generally?

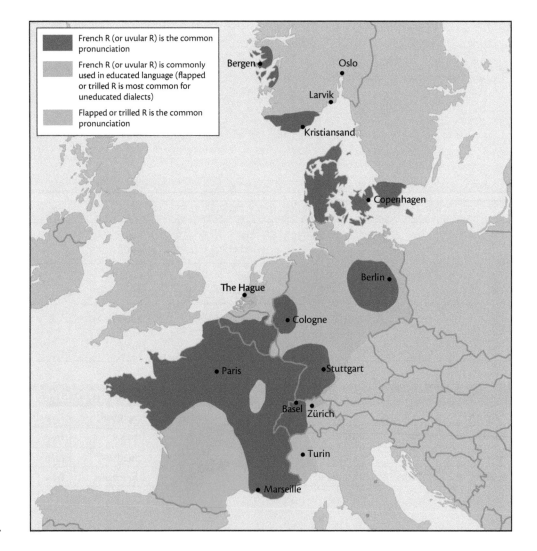

Figure 12.3   The Wave Theory of Language Change. Uvular, trilled, and flapped *r* in European languages. Note that pronunciation patterns sweep across language boundaries from French to German and even to Scandinavian languages.

12.2 What Does Language Actually Do and How Does It Work?

Over the past century, linguists and linguistic anthropologists have studied the majority of the world's languages and found that each is highly structured. From the mid-nineteenth century it was clear to linguists that peoples dismissed by ethnocentric European attitudes as "primitive" had languages that were as complex as any European language. Researchers also observed that most people are largely unaware of the structure of their language until someone makes a mistake. Even then, they do not always know what is wrong, they just know the sentence sounded wrong. As any anthropologist—and many a college student on vacation practicing their high school Spanish or French—knows, understanding the grammatical rules without understanding how people actually use the language to speak is no way to really learn a language. One has to internalize these rules to speak a language effectively.

The Russian-American linguist Roman Jakobson (1896–1982) argued that these processes are subtle, complex, and closely related to the functions of language. Of course, everyone recognized that the general purpose of language was to communicate among individuals. But Jakobson (1995), a pioneer of structural linguistics, broke down this general function into six separate components (see Table 12.2). The key feature of Jakobson's functions of language is that his approach acknowledges that language in actual use does more than just communicate facts, often using interjections, intonation, and non-verbal cues to achieve communicational intention.

Another key figure seeking to understand how language functions was the Swiss linguist Ferdinand de Saussure (1986), who suggested a distinction between the structure, or formal rules, of a language (*langue*) and the way in which people actually speak a language (*parole*). Distinguishing *langue* ("language") and *parole* ("speech") allows linguists to separate the rules and expected usage of language from what people actually say. The distinction, which has been influential among linguists and anthropologists for over a century, is useful because it helps us realize that the rules we use to produce the sounds, word formation, and grammar as native speakers of a language can differ from how we actually speak, which is as much a social and cultural phenomenon as it is a function of language's structure. Here we explore first how language is formally structured, which is the field of descriptive linguistics, and then the social contexts of language use, which is the focus of sociolinguistics.

TABLE 12.2 JAKOBSON'S SIX FUNCTIONS OF LANGUAGE (SUMMARIZED BY LOUIS HERBERT (2011)	
FUNCTION	**DESCRIPTION**
Referential function	Generally focuses on describing a situation, object, or mental state
Poetic function	Focuses on the message for its own sake and is the operative function in poetry
Emotive function	Relates to the feelings of the speaker and best illustrated by interjections, such as "wow."
Conative function	Addresses the listener directly; e.g., John, go inside and eat.
Phatic function	Language used for the purpose of interacting with another, especially for initiating or ending communication with someone else, For example, "Hello?," "Bye," "See you later."
Metalinguistic function	Using language to describe itself.

- **Descriptive linguistics.** The systematic analysis and description of a language's sound system and grammar.

- **Phonology.** The systematic pattern of sounds in a language, also known as the language's sound system.

- **Morphology.** The structure of words and word formation in a language.

- **Syntax.** Pattern of word order used to form sentences and longer utterances in a language.

- **Stops.** Sounds that are formed by closing off and reopening the oral cavity so that it stops the flow of air through the mouth, such as the consonants *p, b, t, d, k,* and *g.*

Descriptive Linguistics

The study of *langue,* or the formal structure of language, is called **descriptive linguistics**, which refers to the systematic analysis and description of a language's sound system and grammar. Linguists distinguish three types of structure in language: (1) **phonology**, the structure of speech sounds; (2) **morphology**, how words are formed into meaningful units; and (3) **syntax**, how words are strung together to form sentences and more complex utterances, such as paragraphs. (High school grammar classes mostly focus on morphology and syntax). All languages have predictable phonological, morphological, and syntactic structures.

Phonology: Sounds of Language

The sounds of language are organized by marking systematic contrasts between pairs or groups of sounds. The majority of both these sounds and the contrasts appear in many of the world's languages, and yet each language has its own unique pattern of sounds. When linguists listen to natural language, such as when people talk unselfconsciously in ordinary conversations, they identify minimal pairs, which are pairs of words that differ only in a single sound contrast.

Consider, for example, the initial sounds in the English words "pan," "ban," and "man." Three sounds, [p], [b], and [m], distinguish these three words, while the other sounds in these words are the same. The consonants *p, b,* and *m* are formed at the front of the mouth at the lips. The differences among three consonants parallel differences among the initial sounds in the words "tab," "dab," and "nab," or the final sounds in the words "pig," "pick," and "ping."

These nine contrasts distinguish three series of what linguists call **stops**, sounds that are made by an occlusion, or stopping, of the airstream though the oral cavity or mouth. But in addition, [b], [d], and [g] differ from [p], [t], and [k] in that the first group are voiced, formed by the vibration of the vocal cords (glottis), at the Adam's apple. The triplet of nasal consonants, [m], [n], and [ng], are also voiced consonants that stop the airflow through the mouth but allow the air to pass through the nasal cavity.

Mind you, these are examples of sounds that occur in English. Other languages have different sounds. One of the most distinct from our language's point of view is the click (!) sound of Southern African peoples like the !Kung (Bushmen). While most speakers of any language are not fully aware of how they form the different sounds they use when speaking, linguists recognize that sound systems are surprisingly systematic.

Dialects and Accents

Another interesting way to think about phonology is to consider accents and dialects, which are regional or social varieties of a single language. Differences in vocabulary, grammar, and pronunciation, as well as regional accents such as those found in Brooklyn or Alabama in American English, are examples of a fairly minor dialect variation. Sometimes the variation occurs between generations or among people of different social classes. Part of the difference between these forms of speech is intonation, the pattern of rising and falling pitch, but usually careful analysis of the sounds shows that they also have systematic differences in their respective sound systems.

Up to the 1970s, linguists assumed that American language was becoming increasingly homogeneous. It seemed that, owing to schools or to national broadcasts on television and radio where the accent is standardized, regional dialects would disappear. In fact, variation in sound systems seems to be greater now than ever before. The sociolinguist William Labov (1990; Labov, Ash, and Boberg 2006) observed in the 1980s that language change in the sound system of American English was concentrated in the cities. He also noted that sound change was most pronounced between generations in the same communities. Such findings suggest a much stronger role for peer groups in the transmission of linguistic forms than linguists had previously noticed.

Morphology: Grammatical Categories

The elements of grammar—tense, word order, which genders are marked, and so on—are also structured. Just like cultural patterns, grammatical patterns learned during childhood feel extremely natural to native speakers in any language, even though the same forms and structures would seem quite unnatural to speakers of most other languages. A couple of examples illustrate how varied even the most basic grammatical categories can be.

Tenses

English speakers tend to assume that there are only three natural tenses: past, present, and future. But not all languages use this same set of tenses, and some languages do not even require that tense be unambiguously marked in any particular sentence. For example, the Ningerum language of Papua New Guinea uses five tenses: present, future, today-past, yesterday-past, and a-long-time-ago-past. Events that happened earlier in the day receive a different tense marking from those that happened yesterday or the day before. Similarly, events that happened several weeks, months, or years ago take a different tense marking altogether. In contrast, Indonesian has no regular tense marking in its verbs but uses adverbs or other time references to emphasize when something has happened or will happen.

Pronouns

American English has fewer pronouns than many other languages. We distinguish between singular and plural, and among three persons (first person, second person, and third person). English also has two cases used when the pronoun is either the subject or the object. If we consider only person and number, we should have six basic pronouns, plus two extra pronouns for gender marking in the third person singular (he, she, and it)—though as we explore in "The Anthropological Life: The End of Gendered Pronouns in American English?" this may be changing. But this set of pronouns does not even begin to exhaust the possible pronoun distinctions that could be used. In French, for example, the second person singular pronoun, "you," takes two forms, *tu* and *vous* (an informal and a formal form). The Awin language of Papua New Guinea has singular, dual, and plural forms of its pronouns, meaning "you" (one person), "you two," and "you" (more than two).

These basic examples as pronouns and tenses illustrate some of the wide range of possibilities that arise in natural languages. Each configuration suggests certain distinctions that represent meaning encoded in the language's grammar. But such patterns do not alone create meaning.

Sociolinguistics

Sociolinguistics is the study of how sociocultural context and norms shape language use, the meanings of linguistic communication, and the effects of language use on society. Sociolinguists accept whatever form of language a community uses—which de Saussure referred to as *parole*—as the form of language they should study.

When one examines the actual speech (*parole*) used in any community, one often finds that different people may use the same grammar and sound system (*langue*), but the actual sentences they make (*parole*) often carry different assumptions and

- **Sociolinguistics.** The study of how sociocultural context and norms shape language use and the effects of language use on society.

The Anthropological Life
The End of Gendered Pronouns in American English?

In a range of everyday American settings, from work meetings to email signatures, it has become an increasingly common practice to announce one's pronouns. He/Him, She/Her, and They/Them are the most frequently used, although sometimes you might encounter less common ones like Ze/Hir. To many older Americans, this change in morphology has taken some getting used to—to refer to an individual as "they" or "them" can feel grammatically incorrect because of how they were educated—but younger generations have mostly adapted flexibly. Here is a clear example where something that feels so stable can change quite rapidly as social norms around language use shift.

Linguistic anthropologists have taken note. One of these is Tom Boellstorff of the University of California, Irvine (2021). He is interested in this issue, in part, because as a gay man and LGBTQ+ activist, he is deeply involved in the communities that have challenged the fact that gendered pronouns—he and she—do not reflect how many people see themselves, and exclude nonbinary and transgender individuals. Another reason is that as an anthropologist he has conducted his research in Indonesia using an "epicene" language, which is a language that uses a nongendered, common pronoun. Bahasa Indonesia, the main language of the country of Indonesia, has plenty of nouns and adjectives that can denote a person's gender, but there simply is no way to mark masculinity or femininity with a pronoun. The

standard third person singular pronoun in Indonesian is *dia*, which can mean either "he," "she," or "it" in English. It is often impossible to tell from the words themselves what the gender of the person referred to is without adding some information about the person, their clothes, their demeanor, or some other behavioral trait, all of which are heavily marked in Indonesian culture and allow anyone to discern the gender.

The fact that there are epicene languages indicates that gendered pronouns are not universal and thus they are not necessary for cognition or communication. English is already very nearly there—way moreso than languages like French and Spanish that mark gender not just on pronouns but also on many words—so Boellstorff suggests that all it needs is a concscious push to get there. He suggests we just formalize the use of "they," which he notes has been used as a substitute for he and she in everyday language and literature in English since the 1300s. Many of us regularly use "they" to denote a person without thinking twice; think of the the expression "somebody left their coat." So as a form of personal practice it should not be too jarring. Boellstorff's broader point is that if we do not tolerate gender exclusion or discrimination, we should as individuals and as members of society collectively push to eliminate gendered pronouns because—as we have been emphasizing in this chapter—language plays an important role in shaping how we see and act in the world.

Figure 12.4   One of the Most Common Signs in American Life. Even without words on it, we all know the meaning of this sign.

connotations. This is because meaning emerges from conversation and social interaction, not just the formal underlying rules of language. We can see how sociocultural context shapes meaning by looking at signs, symbols, and metaphors.

Signs

Signs are words or objects that stand for something else, usually as a kind of shorthand. They are the most basic way to convey meaning. A simple example is the ordinary traffic sign that tells motorists to stop or not to park along a certain stretch of roadway (Figures 12.4 and 12.5).

Symbols

Symbols, which we introduced in Chapter 2, are basically elaborations on signs. When a sign becomes a symbol, it usually takes on a much wider range of meanings than it

Figure 12.5   The Productive Use of Signs Around the World. This sign in front of a business in Papua New Guinea, bans the sale of betel nut. When chewing betel nut, a common practice in that island nation, one needs to spit out bright red spittle frequently.

may have had as a sign. For example, most colleges and universities in America have mascots and colors associated with their football teams. A mascot, such as a wildcat or panther, is a sign of the team, but mascots also readily become a symbol for the whole school, so that the wildcat, for example, represents all the distinctive features of the institution and its people. But note that symbols work because signs themselves are productive, capable of being combined in innovative and meaningful ways.

Anthropologist Sherry Ortner (1971) distinguished three kinds of key symbols, or culturally powerful symbols. These are summarizing symbols, elaborating symbols, and key scenarios. Summarizing symbols sum up a variety of meanings and experiences and link them to a single sign. An example would be the American flag, which many Americans see as summarizing everything good about America, especially such things as "democracy, free enterprise, hard work, competition, progress, and freedom" (Figure 12.6). Summarizing symbols are often used by political

Figure 12.6　Making Use of a Summarizing Symbol. The Marine Corps War Memorial in Arlington, Virginia, pictured here is based on the famous photograph "Raising the Flag on Iwo Jima" by Joe Rosenthal. The image of Marines raising the flag has become a symbol of the American struggle for freedom.

leaders to unify people and neutralize opposition. For example, in the 2022 Russian invasion of Ukraine, President Vladimir Putin of Russia justified the attack as an effort to "de-Nazify" Ukraine, something that confused many Americans who knew that the president of Ukraine, Volodymyr Zelenskyy, is Jewish. Among Russians the word "Nazi" does not carry anti-semitic resonances that it does among Americans, instead connoting the kind of nationalism and ethnic supremacy that motivated Nazi Germany's brutal invasion of Russia during World War II. For Russians, the symbol of the Nazi summarizes a complex history of suffering, sacrifice, heroism, and pride experienced during that war, and Putin used it as a powerful propaganda tool to communicate to Russian citizens that they are engaged in a righteous and heroic fight against evil, not an unprovoked attack on a free country as much of the rest of the world views it.

Elaborating symbols work in exactly the opposite way from summarizing symbols, by helping us sort out complex feelings and relationships. For example, the cow is an elaborating symbol among the Nuer and Dinka peoples of southern Sudan. By talking about cows, the Nuer and Dinka can talk about social relations within the community (Figure 12.7).

The key scenario differs from the other two kinds of symbols because it implies how people should act. A common American key scenario is the Horatio Alger myth. In Horatio Alger's many novels, this scenario often involves a young boy from a poor family, who works hard to become rich and powerful. It does not matter that most of us will not become these things, but the scenario does have meaning for how we feel about and evaluate hard work and persistence.

Figure 12.7　An Elaborating Symbol to Make Sense of Social Relations. Dinka cattle have various kinds of markings and colors, and the Dinka use them to make sense of social differences in their community.

Metaphors

Metaphors are implicit comparisons of words or things that emphasize the similarities between them, allowing people to make sense of complex social relations around them. For example, in our culture we metaphorize ideas as food, as in "this textbook gives you *food* for thought, and some things to *chew* over, although you probably can't *stomach* everything we tell you here." Another example is how we metaphorize love as a disease, as in "he got over her, but she's got it bad for him, and it broke her heart" (Sheridan 2006:54).

Through signs, symbols, and metaphors, language thus reinforces cultural values that are already present in the community. Simultaneously cultural norms and values reinforce the symbols that give language its power to convey meaning. Such relationships between language and culture raise a very interesting and old question: Do speakers of different languages see the world differently, just as people from different cultures might? We turn to this issue in the next section.

THINKING LIKE AN ANTHROPOLOGIST: LANGUAGE

How might paying attention to the metaphors and symbols we use in our daily language allow us to frame important issues in more or less appealing ways? Consider, as an example, the use of the term "downsizing" rather than "firing" in employment contexts.

12.3 Does Language Shape How We Experience the World?

Most Americans generally assume that the world is what it is, and our experience of it is shaped by whatever is actually happening around us. But, as we saw in Chapter 2, our culture predisposes us to presume some features of the world, while other people's culture leads them to assume something different. For many decades anthropologists and linguists have been debating a similar point in relation to language: Does the language we speak shape the way that we perceive the physical world? According to the Sapir–Whorf hypothesis, which we examine next, it does.

The Sapir–Whorf Hypothesis

In the 1920s, the linguistic anthropologist Edward Sapir (1929) urged cultural anthropologists to pay close attention to language during field research. Recognizing that most non-European languages organized tense, number, adjectives, color terms, and vocabulary in different ways from English, French, or German, he argued that a language inclines its speakers to think about the world in certain ways because of its specific grammatical categories. We explore this hypothesis further in "Classic Contributions: Edward Sapir on How Language Shapes Culture." It is anthropology's first expression of **linguistic relativity**, which is the idea that people speaking different languages perceive or interpret the world differently because of differences in their languages.

Sapir's student Benjamin Lee Whorf (Carroll 1956) expanded on this idea and pushed it further. Whorf had studied the language of the Hopi Indians and found that his knowledge of the grammars of European languages was little help in

• **Linguistic relativity.** The idea that people speaking different languages perceive or interpret the world differently because of differences in their languages.

understanding Hopi grammar. He concluded that people who speak different languages actually do—are not just "inclined to," as his teacher Sapir would have said—perceive and experience the world differently. By the 1950s, linguistic anthropologists saw the ideas of Sapir and Whorf as related and began referring to them as the "Sapir–Whorf hypothesis." Let us illustrate the hypothesis with one of Whorf's best examples, the lack of tenses in Hopi.

Hopi Notions of Time

Whorf studied Hopi language and concluded that it lacked tenses like those we have in English. Hopi uses a distinction not expressed grammatically in European languages, which he called "assertion categories." These include (1) statements that report some fact (e.g., "he is running" or "he ran"); (2) declaration of an expectation, whether current or past (e.g., "he is going to eat" or "he was going to run away"); and (3) statements of some general truth (e.g., "rain comes from the clouds" or "he drinks only iced tea"). These three assertion categories do not overlap and are mutually exclusive. When translating these Hopi concepts into English, most people will use our tenses (past, present, and future), partly because we have to express tense in English to make a sentence, and partly because this is the only convenient way to express these different types of assertions in English.

Whorf argued that the structure of the Hopi language suggested different ideas to Hopi than their translations would to English speakers. He also linked these grammatical categories to Hopi "preparing" activities that surrounded certain rituals and ceremonies, arguing that "to the Hopi, for whom time is not a motion but a 'getting later' of everything that has ever been done, unvarying repetition is not wasted but accumulated" (Carroll 1956). Americans, in contrast, might see repetitive actions before a celebration as a sapping of effort or as inefficiency (Figure 12.8).

Since Whorf's death in 1941, several linguists have challenged his interpretation of Hopi grammar. Malotki (1983), for example, argues that Hopi does, in fact, have

Figure 12.8   A Hopi Ceremony of Regeneration. Tendencies in language are reflected in and reinforced by social action, such as this ritual which emphasizes regeneration and the recycling nature of the world. Non-Hopi people are now prohibited from seeing most Hopi rituals and religious dances today; this historic image of one of these celebrations of renewal is from a century ago, when outsiders were permitted to see them.

Classic Contributions
Edward Sapir on How Language Shapes Culture

THE LINGUISTIC ANTHROPOLOGIST Edward Sapir (1884–1939) was the only professionally trained linguist among the students of Franz Boas, a founder of American anthropology. Sapir believed that language "provided the ethnographer with a terminological key to native concepts, and it suggested to its speakers the configurations of readily expressible ideas" (Darnell and Irvine 1997). In this excerpt we see Sapir's strongest statement about how language shapes the cultural expectations of the individual speaker.

🌱 **Edward Sapir**

It is an illusion to think that we can understand the significant outlines of a culture through sheer observation and without the guide of the linguistic symbolism which makes these outlines significant and intelligible to society. . . .

Language is a guide to "social reality." Though language is not ordinarily thought of as of essential interest to the students of social science, it powerfully conditions all our thinking about social problems and processes. Human beings do not live in the objective world alone, nor alone in the world of social activity as ordinarily understood, but are very much at the mercy of the particular language which has become the medium of expression for their society. It is quite an illusion to imagine that one adjusts to reality essentially without the use of language and that language is merely an incidental means of solving specific problems of communication or reflection. The fact of the matter is that the "real world" is to a large extent unconsciously built upon the language habits of the group. No two languages are ever sufficiently similar to be considered as representing the same social reality. The worlds in which different societies live are distinct worlds, not merely the same world with different labels attached. . . . We see and hear and otherwise experience very largely as we do because the language habits of our community predispose certain choices of interpretation. . . . From this standpoint we may think of language as the symbolic guide to culture. [Sapir 1929:209–10]

Questions for Reflection

1. Can you think of an example, either from your native language or another language you know, in which language predisposes you to think in certain ways?

2. How does thinking of language as a "symbolic guide to culture" impact how you think about culture?

tenses that resemble English tenses. Malotki's claims have not gone unchallenged, but if true, such a finding would call Whorf's example into question, although not necessarily his theory of the relationship between language and culture. Moreover, in the time between Whorf's and Malotki's research, Hopi have become more knowledgeable and conversant in English, suggesting that if Hopi now has tenses, these may be evidence of language change since the 1930s.

Ethnoscience and Color Terms

● **Ethnoscience.** The study of how people classify things in the world, usually by considering some range or set of meanings.

In the 1960s, anthropologists began to explore how different peoples classified the world around them, focusing on how people conceptually group species of plants and animals or other domains, such as planets or colors. The study of how people classify things in the world became known as **ethnoscience** (see also Chapter 14). These studies began with a very different set of assumptions about the relationship between language and culture from those accepted by Sapir and Whorf. These scholars assumed that the natural world was a given, and that all human beings perceived it in the same way. Differences in classification were simply different ways of mapping categories onto empirical reality.

For example, anthropologists Brent Berlin and Paul Kay (1969) analyzed the color terms of more than 100 languages and found that basic color terms are consistent across languages. For example, if a language has only two basic color terms, they are terms for dark (black) and light (white). But if a language has three terms, they are black, white, and red. The third term is never green, blue, purple, or orange. An example of a language with three basic color terms is Lamnso, spoken in the Central African country of Cameroon (see Figure 12.9). If a fourth color is present, then the terms are black, white, red, and blue/green. Some anthropologists suspect that these patterns are universal and may have to do with the way our optic nerve responds to light of different wavelengths.

This universal pattern does not disprove the Sapir–Whorf hypothesis, but it suggests that there are limits on the extent to which language shapes our experience of the world. Indeed, other studies have shown that when informants with limited numbers of basic color terms are given paint chips displaying a wide range of colors, they can distinguish among the different colors, but they classify the chips into groups that correspond to their basic color categories. Thus it seems that people who speak different languages do not actually see colors differently, they just classify them differently.

Is the Sapir–Whorf Hypothesis Correct?

By the late 1960s, ethnoscience had largely dismissed the Sapir–Whorf hypothesis as having no significance for understanding human cognition. The most powerful argument against the idea that our language shapes our thought is that we have no way of knowing for sure what cognitive processes are involved when we distinguish different sets of pronouns or have no English-style tenses. All we have is the language, which is where we started in the first place, plus the researcher's intuition (Pinker 1994).

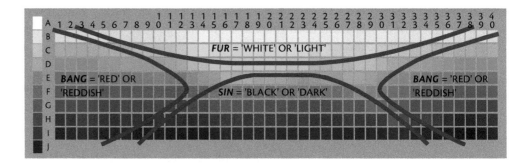

⚐ **Figure 12.9 The Munsell Color Chart.** The Cameroon language of Lamnso has three basic color terms that center on the colors called *sin, fur,* and *bang*, which we would gloss as "black" (or "dark"), "white" (or "light"), and "red" (or "reddish"), respectively. But as we can see from the plot of these three color terms on a standard Munsell color chart, our American sense of black, white, and red is not at all typical of the range of colors included in each of these Lamnso terms.

Today most anthropologists accept what has come to be called the weak or non-deterministic version of the linguistic relativity argument, which suggests (much as Sapir wrote) that the language habits of a community lead people to think about the world in certain ways and not others. Such a reading of the Sapir–Whorf hypothesis supports the idea that some ways of thinking are guided and encouraged by the language we use while others are not.

There are implications here for language change. Over the long term, such suggested ways of thinking would lead to a preference in each language for some kinds of linguistic change over others. If we take a rather static view of language, this issue might lead us to believe that languages are very stable, slow to change; and yet throughout this chapter we have suggested that language is dynamic. Let us now consider how language can constantly be changing, yet seem so stable.

> **THINKING LIKE AN ANTHROPOLOGIST: LANGUAGE**
>
> How might the coarse slang used in daily conversations by college students be interpreted differently by parents or grandparents?

12.4 If Language Is Always Changing, Why Does It Seem So Stable?

A striking paradox in linguistics is that, like culture, language constantly changes, yet most people experience their own language as stable and unchanging. We tend to notice the changes only when we hear other people in our communities using words, pronunciations, or grammatical forms that differ from our own. Usually national policies come into play to enforce or support the use and stabilization of certain linguistic forms over others, leading to language change within a strong framework of stability.

Linguistic Change, Stability, and National Policy

The increase of commerce, communication, and migration around the world over the past few centuries has produced new environments for language change. Colonial powers such as Great Britain, France, and Spain learned about new plants, peoples, and ways of living in their far-flung colonies. In the Americas, these powers also introduced enslaved people as labor from Africa, resulting in the blending of diverse African cultures, which were also blending with Native American cultures. These societies developed dynamic new languages, such as creole and pidgin languages, and implemented national language policies, in some cases to stabilize rapid linguistic change.

Creole and Pidgin Languages

In the Americas, local colonized societies developed hybrid languages that linguists call **creole languages**, languages of mixed origin that developed from a complex blending of two parent languages. A prominent example is the language commonly spoken in Haiti that combines several African languages with Spanish, Taíno (the language of Caribbean native peoples), English, and French. In "A World in Motion: The Emergence of a New Language in the Northern Territory of Australia," we examine one of the world's newest languages that involves a creole language as one of its source languages.

• **Creole language.** A language of mixed origin that has developed from a complex blending of two parent languages that exists as a mother tongue for some part of the population.

A World in Motion
The Emergence of a New Language in the Northern Territory of Australia

Colonialism, globalization, and travel have brought speakers of different languages together for millennia. For some groups, these dynamics have led a crisis of extinction such as that facing many small-scale indigenous languages in the world today, while in other cases it has led to the emergence of new languages. One scholar documenting when, why, and how new languages emerge is linguist Carmel O'Shannessy from the University of Michigan, whose research focuses on a new language that has been emerging since the 1980s in the Northern Territory of Australia among the Warlpiri people (Bakalar 2013; Khazan 2013).

Australia's Northern Territory is home to a number of distinct Aboriginal languages. After English settlers began arriving in the area during the nineteenth century, an English-based creole language, aptly named "Kriol," emerged and proved useful as a trading language and for facilitating interactions among the diverse linguistic groups in the region. In Warlpiri communities, people have maintained their traditional language, but as O'Shannessy has observed, they also regularly weave Kriol and English words and expressions into their speech in a practice known as **code-switching**, which refers to alternating between two or more different languages during a conversation. Her research on how young speakers learn and use the language revealed something important: young people do not experience this speech as three separate languages that are being actively mixed, but as one single linguistic system.

- **Code switching.** Alternating between two or more different languages during a conversation.

According to O'Shannessy, it is on this basis that young people have developed a new mixed language—she calls it "Light Warlpiri"—that draws on the three languages. In some respects, the speech of young people resembles the speech of their elders, but it also differs from it in other ways. For example, Light Warlpiri draws its nominal morphology (grouping of nouns) from Warlpiri language but its verbs and verbal morphology from English and Kriol. But what makes this situation especially unique is that Light Warlpiri has also developed some structural and semantic features that are not drawn from the source languages but appear wholly novel, suggesting the presence of an emerging new language. Because it is a small language (with approximately 350 speakers), nobody can predict its future, but as a case study it might suggest how new languages emerge, which is by mixing and innovating on already existing languages.

Australian Kriol   Sign written in Australian Kriol, a creole language that draws on both English and Indigenous Australian languages. Here the word *Kantri* on the second line derives from the English word *Country*, while the other words are derived from indigenous Australian languages.

- **Pidgin language.** A mixed language with a simplified grammar, typically borrowing its vocabulary from one language but its grammar from another.

In Asia and the Pacific, these hybrid forms have generally been called **pidgin languages**, which refers to a mixed language with a simplified grammar that people rarely use as a mother tongue but to conduct business and trade. In the independent Melanesian countries of Vanuatu, the Solomon Islands, and Papua New Guinea, for example, local forms of pidgin that combine various local languages and English have become national languages along with the colonial languages of English or French. In all three countries, the ability to speak pidgin has positive social status.

National Language Policies

Different countries have tried to control language change through the creation of national language policies. Short of making one particular regional dialect the national language, however, countries have found it nearly impossible to dictate what language or what form of the national language the public will speak. Two examples—taken from the Netherlands and Quebec (Canada)—demonstrate different approaches to controlling processes of language change.

In the Netherlands during the twentieth century, Dutch linguists recognized that pronunciation and vocabulary had changed so much that spelling no longer reflected how people pronounced words. Dutch linguists recommended that spelling be changed to keep up with changing language use, and twice in the twentieth century the ruling monarchs, Queen Wilhelmina and Queen Juliana, issued royal decrees changing the official spelling of Dutch words to parallel actual use. The Dutch approach is quite tolerant of changing language.

Figure 12.10   Defending Quebecois from Anglicization. In Quebec, on many store signs English words must by law be smaller than French ones.

French Canadians in the province of Quebec have been less tolerant of language change, successfully preserving Quebecois (the form of French spoken in Quebec) against the pressure of English-speaking Canadians, who have historically considered English to be the superior language. Although government officials throughout Canada must be bilingual in English and French, the province of Quebec conducts government business in French. To stem the tide of Anglicization (the creeping influence of English), the provincial parliament passed laws that require signs in public places to be in French. If English is also used, the English words cannot be longer than their French translations (Figure 12.10). In this case, language use coupled with nationalist control of the provincial parliament has encouraged the use of French throughout the population of Quebec.

Language Stability Parallels Cultural Stability

As the situation of language use in Quebec demonstrates, the potential loss of a native language can be a critical issue for a group of people. In such cases, people view the use of a particular language not just as a means of communication but as integral to their cultural identities and worldviews as well. As a result, the preservation of language and the preservation of culture are often seen as going hand in hand.

The connection between cultural stability and the ongoing use of language is an especially critical one for many indigenous peoples around the world, who are striving to protect their languages and distinctive ways of life in the face of rapid social change. In many cases, the cultural disruptions created by rapid social changes such as colonization and globalization have undermined the use of native languages. As a result, many indigenous groups around the world are facing what scholars call "language death," referring to the dying out of many minority languages. Some linguists argue that nearly half of the world's 5,000 or 6,000 languages are in jeopardy of dying out within a century (Hale 1992).

Many scholars believe that these dramatic losses will have considerable impact on the world's linguistic diversity, even as new languages are created all the time. And because of the close relationship between language and culture, the world's cultural diversity will suffer as well. As our discussion of the Sapir–Whorf hypothesis suggests, language is the primary medium through which people experience the richness of their culture, and loss of language suggests a genuine loss of a culture's fullness.

Doing Fieldwork
Exploring Language Endangerment with Anthropologist Bernard Perley

University of British Columbia linguistic anthropologist Bernard Perley is a member of the Tobique band of the Maliseet First Nation of New Brunswick, Canada. For several decades he has studied Maliseet language and culture and has had an interest in helping to preserve the language. Only 600 or 700 Maliseet of the approximately 7,000 registered tribal members in New Brunswick speak the language. Because of external pressures—forced residential schooling, territorial contraction, pressures to assimilate, influx of media, and lifestyle changes—most younger people no longer view the language as vital to their everyday lives or sense of Maliseet identity.

Perley (2011) set out to conduct fieldwork on the state of the language and efforts to head off what seemed like an inevitable death. The stakes of doing research on issues around language endangerment and death are high but are especially so for Perley given his personal and professional backgrounds. The stakes were high in other ways. He encountered skepticism by some members of the community and language preservation advocates who associated anthropology with colonization and state control over indigenous communities, and Perley had to show them that he was a legitimate scholar. At the same time, since he had left his community long before to live elsewhere, he had to prove that he was still native. Negotiating that insider/outsider status and a multifaceted identity made the research complicated and sensitive, raising questions about whether an anthropologist can really "return home."

But it also gave him unique insight into how people thought about their language. When he began his research he found that schools were teaching children Maliseet without textbooks or writing assignments because traditionally the language was only a spoken language. But the lack of textbooks and other written materials helped define the language as irrelevant to modern life. So, when the community adopted a formal orthography and written alphabet, it helped give the language some added power in the eyes of young people, all of whom were learning both English and French (Canada's two national languages) in school.

But the Maliseet language of Perley's youth has continued to decline largely because there were few contexts relevant to youth in the community where knowledge and ability in the traditional language was significant. Perley noticed that there were three institutions central to the maintenance of Maliseet identity and culture, each with their own philosophy, advocates, programs, and constituents. These are the local language instructor at the community school, the agent of the provincial government who oversees language instruction in the local schools, and

🌱 **Bernard Perley**

an academic in the Native Studies Department of St. Thomas University, who works with Maliseet college students. Perley found that the activities and role of each rarely coincided and often stood in opposition to the other two (Graham 2012).

Perley also observed that these efforts to maintain and revitalize the language were complicated by the fact that preserving the Maliseet language was simply not a high priority in people's busy lives. Meetings about the topic were poorly attended, and there was little interest in literacy programs among adults. In his view, this was a situation of the people themselves giving "assisted suicide" to the language. This is a provocative, even polarizing view, but instead of viewing it as blaming the victim, Perley asserts that people have made choices about their relationship with the language, choices that can also be reversed. In fact, he identified an emergent vitality of the language that helps it survive not in terms of quantitative indicators—such as how many people speak it—but through alternative vitalities like place names, lexicons, dictionaries, even local translations of popular rock-and-roll songs into Maliseet. His broader point is that understanding language vitality requires a holistic ethnographic perspective that situates language as one of several factors that continue to shape, build, and reinforce Maliseet identity.

Questions for Reflection

1. What happens to a culture if the language that once motivated it stops being spoken?

2. Is language preservation necessary for the continuation of Maliseet cultural identity?

3. How are the cultural processes Perley discusses both similar to and different from those involved in your own family's cultural and linguistic history?

In response to such concerns, many linguistic anthropologists have studied the conditions that endanger languages and the language revitalization efforts that seek to save them, a theme we examine in "Doing Fieldwork: Exploring Language Endangerment with Anthropologist Bernard Perley."

As we have seen in this section, issues of language stability and change are closely tied to questions of domination, control, and resistance, a theme we explore in more detail in our final section.

THINKING LIKE AN ANTHROPOLOGIST: LANGUAGE

What is it about our language that makes it feel so personal and so much a part of us? How is it that our language actually changes so seamlessly as we hear and adopt new words and expressions?

12.5 How Does Language Relate to Social Power and Inequality?

Anthropological linguists established long ago that language use channels and influences the cultural context and social relationships of its speakers. But in recent years, they have become especially attuned to issues of power and inequality in language use, specifically how language can become an instrument of control and domination. We explore these issues here by introducing the concept of language ideology.

Language Ideology

The concept of **language ideology** refers to the ideologies people have about the superiority of one dialect or language and the inferiority of others. A language ideology links language use with identity, morality, and aesthetics. It shapes our image of who we are as individuals, as members of social groups, and as participants in social institutions (Woolard 1998). Like all ideologies, language ideologies are deeply felt beliefs that are considered truths. In turn, these truths are reflected in social relationships, as one group's unquestioned beliefs about the superiority of itself and its language justifies the power of one group or class of people over others (Spitulnik 1998:154).

• **Language ideology.** Widespread assumptions that people make about the relative sophistication and status of particular dialects and languages.

Gendered Language Styles

Despite what your high school English teachers may have told you, there is no "proper" way to speak English or any other language. From the anthropological perspective of language ideology, there are only more and less privileged versions of language use. Language use either legitimates an individual or group as "normal," or even "upstanding," or defines that individual or group as socially inferior. Consider an example that echoes the opening story of this chapter, which are the findings of a classic study in sociolinguistics that explores how gendered expectations of the way women speak English in our culture can reflect and reinforce the idea that women are inferior to men. In her research (whose methods we introduced in the Methods Memo that precedes this chapter), Robin Lakoff describes how "talking like a lady" involved the expectation that a woman's speech patterns should include such things as tag questions ("It's three o'clock, *isn't it?*"); intensifiers ("It's a *very* lovely hat!"); hedge

("I'm *pretty* sure"); or hesitation and the repetition of expressions, all of which can communicate uncertainty and were largely absent in expectations about men's speech (R. Lakoff 1975).

Lakoff argued that the social effects of speaking in this way can marginalize women's voices in contexts like a courtroom or a workplace, where speaking in a way that implies uncertainty—even if the speaker is not intentionally expressing uncertainty—can undermine a woman's testimony (as in a court of law) or trustworthiness (as in a workplace). Such situations, she suggested, are used to justify elevating men to positions of authority over women.

Lakoff herself recognized that some men may communicate in female-preferential ways, and not all women use the patterns just described, since language ideologies are not hard and fast for every speaker. Indeed, more recent research of email communications between men and women (Thomson, Murachver, and Green 2001) suggests that men and women can be quite flexible in their use of gendered language styles, changing these depending on whom they are talking to. As a result, men may use female-preferential language when interacting with a woman, and vice versa, further suggesting that language ideologies do not always exercise total control over how people speak.

Language and the Legacy of Colonialism

In places like sub-Saharan Africa, nineteenth-century European colonial powers introduced their own language as the official language, because they viewed indigenous languages as socially inferior to their European languages. When these countries acquired independence, many of these languages became one of several national languages. As a way of building a national identity, many newly independent nations have had to make decisions about which language or languages among its many vernaculars to select as its official language. In Zambia, for example, which gained independence from Great Britain in 1964, the government recognized seven of the most important of its seventy-three local languages, plus English, as national languages, since nearly everyone in Zambia knows one or another of these languages. In theory each is equal to the others, but in practice they are not, as listening to Zambian radio broadcasts reveals (Spitulnik 1998).

Although all eight Zambian languages were given airtime, English dominated the airwaves, both in the number of hours per week and in having a more sophisticated and cosmopolitan content. Certain of the more widely spoken indigenous local languages also got more airtime than minority languages. Over the past decades, broadcasters have presented to their ethnically diverse listening public what they feel are appropriate topics in each of the different languages, such as themes related to subsistence farming for certain language groups considered less sophisticated, and themes related to business and politics for others deemed linguistically superior. These broadcasting decisions have shaped how the public evaluates each indigenous language, presenting some as more sophisticated than others, but all as less sophisticated than English. In this case, broadcasts not only become models of language hierarchy in Zambia but also reinforce these views of different languages and the ethnicities associated with them.

Language Ideologies and Contemporary Racial Justice

The Black Lives Matter movement that emerged in the wake of police and extra-judicial killings of unarmed Black men across the United States has brought substantial public attention to the role of language in upholding patterns of racial inequality and white supremacy. Linguistic anthropologists have also been tracking the ways language ideologies promote the view of white middle-class modes of speaking as an ideal norm, differentiating it from language use among ethnic immigrants, racial minorities, and poor whites. The linguistic differentiation of racialized groups, the circulation of racial categories in private and public spaces, and the invisibilization—at least to most white people—of these language ideologies themselves can support ideologies of white supremacy (Gal and Irvine 2019; Kroskrity 2021). These patterns can profoundly disrupt efforts to create dialogue and change to promote racial justice.

Most white people would deny beliefs in their racial superiority or in racial hierarchies, reserving the terminology of white supremacy for KKK and Neo-Nazi groups. But as Kroskrity (2021) argues, "covert linguistic racism," which he defines as "a complex of linguistic practices mediated by language ideologies that connect to political–economic structures," continues to operate and perpetuate tacit assumptions of white supremacy even among those who consider themselves anti-racist. A classic illustration comes from the late linguistic anthropologist and past president of the American Anthropological Association Jane Hill, who spent much of her career studying how racism was expressed though everyday language. Some of her most important research focused on what she called "Mock-Spanish"—the incorporation by mono-lingual English speakers of Spanish words and expressions like "no problemo," "numero ten-o," "comprende amigo," etc. She asserted that this usage, which was often viewed as funny, simultaneously critiques and belittles Spanish-speakers as ignorant and lacking intelligence because of their presumably poor use of English. What is so powerful about this example—and this extends to others that exhibit "covert linguistic racism"—is that it is viewed as innocent and clever, even when it is rooted in negative stereotypes about another group (Hill 2008).

Language Ideology and New Media Technologies

Language ideologies also shape debates over linguistic changes associated with texting and social media. Technology has always influenced our language by introducing new terms, new abbreviations, new ideas, and new ways of doing things. But do these modern devices "degrade" the language, as so many older Americans fear? At the heart of this debate is the idea that these changes make users seem "dumb" and incapable of using proper spelling.

While we may assume that new terms and spellings are the most important changes that new technology brings, the more significant changes are probably found in how texting and online communication change our grammar, morphology, and syntax. For example, social media sites have introduced a number of new verbs derived from nouns and nouns derived from verbs. The noun *friend* is now commonly used as a verb, as in "I *friended* you on Facebook"; with the addition of the prefix *un-*, it has also been transformed into a verb with the opposite meaning, as in "If you don't like my posts, you can *unfriend* me."

Thanks to new media technologies, syntactic changes have also become more widespread in the American language. One common example is the overcorrection of *me* to *I*, as in constructions like "he gave it to John and I" or "they showed Sarah and I around the property." (In both cases, the objective form *me* is traditionally considered to be correct.) Undoubtedly, there are multiple causes contributing to such changes, including the shift away from formal teaching of grammar in schools, and the rise of twenty-four-hour cable news programs that require hour upon hour of unscripted screen banter that would never pass muster with editors in print media like the *New York Times*. Yet new media technologies have quickened the pace at which changes to the "rules" of grammar become more acceptable.

Of course, these examples illustrate that language is dynamic, constantly responding and adapting to changing circumstances, without us ever really noticing that it is changing. But it is important to always remember that efforts to declare any use of language to be "correct" or more desirable than any other use—such as when older Americans complain about the "improper" use of language among young people—is evidence of language ideology at work.

THINKING LIKE AN ANTHROPOLOGIST: LANGUAGE

Students often feel they will never be able to participate in the professional lives of their advisors because their advisors and other professors seem to speak a language that many students do not understand. Of course, they are speaking English, but they use many complex words that few students know. How does language in this situation become a tool of control and power over students?

Conclusion

The capacity for language is one of the central features that distinguishes humans from other animals. Whatever the particular language being spoken, human languages are universally structured and rule bound, as descriptive linguistics demonstrates, and they change in fairly uniform ways, as historical linguistics tells us. But to end there—with the idea that language is something that all humans have access to and use in the same ways—misses the crucial fact that sociocultural context and norms shape language use and that the use of language has important impacts on everyday social relationships. To separate language from culture leads to an impoverished understanding of *both* language and culture.

This point, of course, is one that Sapir and Whorf made many decades ago when they advanced the idea that particular languages guide ways of thinking and acting. We can see a more updated illustration of the relationship between culture and language—and perhaps a more recognizable one to all of us—in the vignette that opens this chapter, with the ways digital communication affects language use or in the gendered styles of communication in American English. Their particular miscommunication is not the result of a universal human situation in which women and men cannot understand each other but the product of a particular culture that expects girls and women to speak in some ways, and boys and men in others.

We should not forget the social consequences of language use, especially when certain ways of talking and expression imply the correctness or superiority of one group, gender, or social class and the incorrectness or inferiority of another. The broader point here is that language has great power to shape not just our meanings and comprehension of the world but our experiences as social beings as well.

KEY TERMS

Call system   p. 345

Code-switching   p. 360

Cognate words   p. 346

Creole language   p. 359

Descriptive linguistics   p. 350

Ethnoscience   p. 358

Language   p. 344

Language ideology   p. 363

Linguistic relativity   p. 355

Morphology   p. 350

Philology   p. 346

Phonology   p. 350

Pidgin language   p. 360

Proto-language   p. 346

Sociolinguistics   p. 351

Stops   p. 350

Syntax   p. 350

Reviewing the Chapter

Chapter Section	What We Know	To Be Resolved
Where does language come from?	Animals do not have language, but some primates have a rudimentary ability to use signs, which is a necessary but not sufficient condition for language to develop.	Although most linguistic anthropologists accept both genetic and non-genetic models, the relative importance of these models remains unclear, and we currently have no unified models that draw on both.
How does language actually work?	Language is systematic, but most descriptive linguistic models are static and do not express the dynamic nature of language.	By and large, linguistic anthropologists have not found that historical models of language change fully explain why particular sound systems or grammatical patterns have taken the forms they have.
Does language shape how we experience the world?	Meaning is conveyed through symbols, but particular meanings have their roots in the social processes of daily life.	Although the structures of language vary widely in different languages, anthropologists and linguists have never reached a consensus about whether the structure of language actually shapes the ways we perceive the world.
If language is always changing, why does it seem so stable?	Languages are always changing in small ways as sound systems gradually change and as new words are borrowed from other languages or created anew.	Although anthropologists recognize that languages change as cultures change, there is no current consensus about how these changes emerge.
How does language relate to social power and inequality?	A language ideology links language use with identity, morality, and aesthetics. It helps us imagine the very notion of who we are as individuals, as members of social groups and categories, and as participants in social institutions. It also connects language use to issues like power relations and colonialsm.	Despite efforts of governments to control their populations by shaping language policies, creole and pidgin forms of languages are far more important than was thought to be the case half a century ago. Yet anthropologists do not have a full understanding of the precise conditions under which a creole or pidgin language can assert its own importance.

READINGS

William A. Foley's book *Anthropological Linguistics: An Introduction* (Malden, MA: Blackwell, 1997) provides a general introduction to linguistic anthropology. A more classical approach to the basics of language and its relation to culture was published by Edward Sapir in his 1921 book, *Language: An Introduction to the Study of Speech* (New York: Dover, 2004). Unlike most linguistics texts, because Sapir was an anthropologist as well as a talented linguist, this early work is much more sensitive to cultural factors than the books written by most linguists.

Linguistic anthropologist George Lakoff has published a number of books dealing with the symbols and metaphors that provide meaning in the words and phrases we hear. One of his classic studies is *Metaphors We Live By* (Chicago: University of Chicago Press, 1980). Several of his more recent publications pursue these ideas more fully.

A key survey of how governments create and promote nationalism through language policy can be found in Bambi B.

Shieffelin, Katharyn A. Woolard, and Paul V. Kroskrity's book *Language Ideologies: Practice and Theory* (New York: Oxford University Press, 1998).

One of the best introductions to gendered speech can be found in Deborah Tannen's *Talking From 9 to 5: How Women's and Men's Conversational Styles Affect Who Gets Hired, Who Gets Credit, and What Gets Done at Work* (New York: W. Morrow, 1994).

METHODS MEMO

How Do Anthropologists Use Ethnographic Methods to Study Culture and Social Relations?

Understanding the dynamic flow and messy ambiguities of cultural processes and social relations is challenging. For the better part of a century, cultural anthropologists have met this challenge using ethnographic methods, which have proven effective for generating the kind of data necessary to understand social change, complexity, and the inner lives of people. These methods emphasize holism, or systematic attention to all aspects of social life (economic, political, religious, etc.) simultaneously. Rather than a limited focus on a single dimension of people's lives, long-term immersion and participation in a community, habitual curiosity, and an open mind yield insights we would never achieve had we started with preconceived ideas about the relationships among social, economic, political, and religious institutions.

WHY DO ANTHROPOLOGISTS THINK OF FIELDWORK AS MAKING THE STRANGE FAMILIAR AND THE FAMILIAR STRANGE?

Long-term immersion in a community is called **fieldwork**. During fieldwork, which can last a year or longer, anthropologists become involved in people's daily lives, observe and ask questions about what they are doing, and record those observations. By participating directly in the everyday flow of community activities, we can observe what is important to the community, what community members discuss among themselves, and how these matters intertwine with social institutions. In a different culture, fieldwork can render behaviors, actions, and ideas that may initially seem strange to be quite sensible and familiar when understood in context.

The development of ethnographic methods during the early twentieth century for studying other cultures is typically credited to the pioneering Polish-British anthropologist Bronislaw Malinowski. His decision to live for a long period of time in the Trobriand Islands—which was a very unfamiliar community to Europeans—in order to observe and record culture and social relations led to profoundly new kinds of understandings of non-Western peoples. It had become clear that living in the community did not guarantee cultural relativism—that is, understanding a native culture on its own terms—nor did it promise that the researcher could overcome his or her ethnocentrism and cultural bias. But it increased the likelihood that the anthropologist could get some sense of the world in terms that local people themselves understood. Malinowski called this perspective "the native's point of view," and he and succeeding generations of anthropologists have considered ethnographic methods to be the most effective tool for understanding it and the culture and social relations that shape and support it (see also the film, *Savage Memory*, by Zachary Stuart and Kelly Thomson 2011, Alvarez Astacio 2013).

By attempting to see the world "from the native's point of view," we are not claiming that one culture's way of thinking is superior to another, that everyone in an observed society has a singular perspective on all issues, or that we can fully accept or adopt the culture's way of thinking (sometimes referred to as "going native"). Rather, we are attempting to make the strange familiar by unraveling the informal cultural logic and social relations that shape how and why people in another society talk, think, and act as they do.

Of course, anthropologists also conduct research in their own societies. Like the fish that doesn't see the water it swims in, the challenge of doing so is that we may not recognize culturally salient issues because we make the same unstated assumptions as the people whose lives we are investigating. In these circumstances, the anthropologist has to work extra hard to make the familiar strange, by asking why things we take for granted are the way they are and cultivating an openness and willingness to question our own preconceptions.

HOW IS FIELDWORK CONDUCTED?

Fieldwork is not a set of prescribed technical procedures or formulas but a range of skills and techniques an anthropologist can draw on, depending on the context. Fieldwork data is not simply gathered, but rather actively created through the **intersubjectivity** between an anthropologist

---

- **Fieldwork.** Long-term immersion in a community, normally involving firsthand research in a specific study community or research setting where people's behavior can be observed and the researcher can have conversations or interviews with members of the community.

- **Intersubjectivity.** The realization that knowledge about other people emerges out of relationships and perceptions individuals have with each other.

and the people with whom he or she interacts. The anthropologist observes things in the field setting, observes them a second or third time, and later inquires about them, gradually pulling together an enriched sense of what they have observed. Johannes Fabian (2014) was one of the first to discuss intersubjectivity as fundamental to the ethnographic approach to understand human societies, a theme he has promoted since the early 1970s. At the heart of this approach to creating data and knowledge are participant observation, interviewing and listening, and note-taking.

- **Participant observation** entails getting involved in and observing naturally occurring situations, interactions, and everyday activities in a community. It requires creating trusting relationships and rapport with people who are sometimes quite different from one-self. As an actual research technique, participant observation exists along a continuum, from fly-on-the-wall direct observation of others to fully immersive experiential participation in an activity. Most of the time, it is an improvisational and context-sensitive technique that combines various modes of watching and doing.

- **Interviews** are systematic conversations whose purpose is to collect field research data, ranging from a highly structured set of questions to the most open-ended ones. They involve asking questions to elicit information, explanations, oral histories, and other spoken data. Successful fieldwork requires habitual curiosity, active listening skills, and the ability to ask good questions. Table MM4.1 outlines the various interviewing strategies.

TABLE MM4.1	CHARACTERISTICS AND NATURE OF DIFFERENT KINDS OF INTERVIEWS		
KINDS OF INTERVIEWS	NATURE OF INTERVIEW	CLEAR FOCUS FOR INTERVIEW	KIND OF FIELD NOTES
Interview schedule	Questions are read from a printed script exactly as written. Often used for survey data collection.	Yes	Interview schedule form
Formal/structured interview	Interviewer has decided ahead of time what is important to ask and writes down the informant's answers or tape-records the interview. Often used for survey data collection.	Yes	Transcript of answers or of questions and answers.
Informal/open-ended interview	Interviewer has a general focus for the interview but may not have a clear goal of what information he or she wants. New questions emerge as the interview proceeds. A notebook may be present, but most of the time is spent in conversation rather than writing notes.	Sometimes	Preliminary notes that outline the discussion, later used to write up a full description of the context and content of the discussion.
Conversation	Resembles an ordinary conversation, and notebooks are not present. The anthropologist might ask certain questions, but the flow is very conversational. Afterward the anthropologist takes a few jot notes so he or she can remember the topics discussed or goes somewhere private to write up more detailed raw notes that can be fleshed out later.	Sometimes	Headnotes and jot notes, later used to write up a full description of the context and content of the discussion. Notes often include topics to follow up on in future interviews or conversations.
Hanging out (participant observation)	Involves spending time with members of the community in gender- and age-appropriate ways. It may involve helping with fishing, cooking, or planting; playing in some pickup sport; or hanging out in a coffee shop, diner, bar, or work environment. Anthropologists may occasionally make jot notes, but most of the time they record details in their notes later, when people are not around.	No	Headnotes and jot notes, later used to write up a full description of the context and content of the discussion. Notes often include topics to follow up on in future interviews or conversations.

- **Note-taking** involves writing down accurately what the anthropologist has seen, heard, and experienced. Much of the time in the field is spent scribbling **field notes**, or written records of information, snippets of conversation, and observations. Some of this scribbling happens in the ebb and flow of everyday life, as anthropologists jot down notes in conversation with others, or when a festival, ritual, or some other activity is taking place. Note-taking can sometimes be disruptive and even provoke suspicion, but with time and careful explanation about what the anthropologist plans to do with the information, people become accustomed to it. Anthropologists have an ethical commitment to share their reasons for doing research with their **informants** and collaborators openly, and explaining their goals often helps build rapport.

Not every ethnographer will necessarily experience and record the same things, even in the same community. Fieldworkers have differences in background, personality, social identity, theoretical inclination, and perception that affect what they will observe, how people in a community will interact with them, and how they will interpret the data they collect. Every fieldwork project is a unique and individual experience.

WHAT OTHER METHODS DO CULTURAL ANTHROPOLOGISTS USE?

Many fieldwork projects require additional strategies to understand social change, complexity, and the native's point of view. In these situations, cultural anthropologists can draw on a variety of other methods, including the following.

- **Participant-observation.** The standard research method used by sociocultural anthropologists that requires the researcher to live in the community he or she is studying to observe and participate in day-to-day activities.

- **Interviews.** Systematic conversations whose purpose is to collect field research data, ranging from a highly structured set of questions to the most open-ended ones

- **Field notes.** Any information that the anthropologist writes down or transcribes during fieldwork.

- **Informants.** People an anthropologist gets data from in the study community, especially people interviewed or who provide information about what he or she has observed or heard.

- **Comparative method.** The systematic comparison of data from two or more societies. Comparing social institutions, beliefs, or practices across cultures can help anthropologists theorize about similarities and differences between the cases, or understand how they might have been shaped by similar forces.

- **Genealogical method.** A system of notation for naming individuals in a community in relation to a key informant—such as "mother," "mother's brother," and so on. It is a key tool for understanding relationships in non-industrial societies where kinship relations are central to political and economic life.

- **Life histories.** Interviews that focus on an individual's phases of life, to understand how social patterns have changed or how age affects social position.

- **Ethnohistory.** Combining historical and ethnographic approaches to understand culture change, especially in societies with few or no written records.

- **Rapid appraisals.** Short-term and highly focused fieldwork, typical of applied anthropology projects.

- **Action research.** Fieldwork done in collaboration with a community affected by a social problem to create change or to empower the community.

- **Anthropology at a distance.** A research strategy when disruptions such as war prevent an anthropologist from doing fieldwork in a community. It relies on previously published research and interviews with individuals who have migrated out of the community.

- **Analyzing secondary materials.** Field notes are primary data because they are produced by the anthropologist. Anthropologists also use secondary data, which are published and unpublished materials produced by others, including newspaper clippings, government reports, institutional memos, and so on.

WHAT UNIQUE ETHICAL DILEMMAS DO ETHNOGRAPHERS FACE?

Whatever their fieldwork strategies and techniques, all ethnographers face certain common ethical dilemmas and concerns (see the "Ethical Principles for Anthropologists" table on page xxx). These issues often arise in relation to anthropologists' commitment to do no harm, considerations about to whom anthropologists are responsible, and questions about who should control anthropology's findings. These include:

- **Protecting informant identity.** Anthropologists protect informant identities by disguising the location of the research and/or changing personal names in field notes and published research. But, unlike journalists, anthropologists in the United States do not have constitutional protections that allow them to conceal the sources of their data if a legal authority, such as the police or courts, demands them.

- **Access to field notes.** Anthropologists work hard to protect their field notes from scrutiny by outsiders not involved in the research, such as police, government officials, or members of rival social groups, because they inevitably contain information given in confidence. Some communities insist they should have access to and control of anthropological field notes, since they helped create the data and should benefit from it. In these situations, the anthropologist must negotiate with community members what will be shared.

- **Anthropology, spying, and war.** Anthropologists seem to stick their noses into many aspects of people's lives, which has led many anthropologists to be accused of spying. Anthropological research does bear some similarities to the work of spies, since spying is often a kind of participant observation. When anthropologists conduct participant observation, however, we are ethically obligated to let our informants know from the outset that we are researchers. Anthropologists tend to reject military use of anthropology in one place because it might undermine the trust between local communities and anthropological researchers in other places, compromising the trust and rapport all anthropologists strive to create with the people with whom they work.

At the heart of ethnographic methods is building trusting relationships with people whose lives the anthropologist is interested in documenting and understanding. Those relationships strongly influence what the anthropologist will come to know about the cultural processes that shape those people's lives. Other keys to the method include a holistic perspective, habitual curiosity, direct experiential involvement in the community through participant observation, asking good questions, strong active listening skills, and a range of other useful tools, from the genealogical method to life histories. Above all, ethnographic methods are contextually sensitive, providing a flexible set of tools for studying a dynamic world and the nuances of human cultural diversity.

Thinking Critically About Ethnographic Methods

- Just spending time in a community doing fieldwork is not necessarily enough to cultivate cultural relativism. Why not? What are some other ways you can think of for an anthropologist to cultivate relativism?
- Fieldwork can be conducted in any social setting in which people are doing things and interacting with each other. Can you identify three social settings in your "backyard" (e.g., your campus or city) in which you would like to conduct fieldwork? Why do those interest you?

- In their publications, anthropologists disguise the identities of individuals (and sometimes entire communities) who participated in their research. Yet some individuals and communities object to this practice, because they feel it may disguise too much, such as things they are proud of, or because they want to publicly share all the details of some injustice that was perpetrated against them. How do you think an anthropologist should act in such a situation?

Economics

Working, Sharing, and Buying

AFTER THE DEATH of Chairman Mao Tse-tung in 1976, Chinese state leaders began to rethink their policies of collectivization and centralized allocation of resources. Calling the new approach "Socialism with Chinese Characteristics," the state made bureaucratic changes to encourage private control of capital and goods (Osburg 2013). As a result of these changes, private entrepreneurs have begun to flourish, and some of them have created fortunes in real estate, manufacturing, construction, entertainment, and services. Entrepreneurs have also gained a new social profile as sought-after marriage partners and trendsetters in fashion and consumption (Osburg 2013). At the same time, many are seen as morally suspect profiteers and beneficiaries of illicit activities and corruption because of close ties to government officials who provide them with contracts, licenses, and extra-legal protections in exchange for bribes and kickbacks.

This entrepreneurial sphere is a strongly masculine one, rooted in gendered forms of obligation and the creation of value (Osburg 2013). Well-connected male entrepreneurs spend a lot of time and money in luxurious clubs entertaining state officials, clients, and fellow businessmen through banqueting, drinking, gambling, and hiring sex workers (Osburg 2013). The goal of doing these things is to expand and strengthen *guanxi* [**gwahn**-shee], which are informal webs of social relationships individuals create and use to pursue their own ends. *Guanxi* can help get things done in the

The Key to Business Success. Luxurious nightclubs, such as this one pictured here in Beijing, are critical locations where Chinese businessmen and government officials cultivate *guanxi*, or social networks, and friendships rooted in sentimental bonds. These relationships are believed to be keys to business success.

slow-moving bureaucracy or get new government contracts. Reciprocity, especially the give-and-take of favors, is a key element of a *guanxi* network, and individuals who can use *guanxi* to benefit others can gain important power and social prestige.

But these networks also involve sentimental ties associated with *renqing* [**wren**-cheeng], or affective interpersonal relationships, such as those between kin and close friends. Spending many hours together in leisure and entertainment—creating shared experiences of intimacy, vulnerability, and transgression—is one of the ways businessmen can transform the short-term interests of *guanxi* into the long-term bonds of *renqing* (Osburg 2013). Yet spending so much time at clubs is exhausting and expensive, and it can generate feelings of being trapped in moral compromises and undesirable obligations (Osburg 2013).

Many Western observers have celebrated the rise of China's new entrepreneurial class as the vanguard of capitalist free enterprise and a liberal democratic opening. But this view misunderstands the complex mixture of capitalism and political authoritarianism that characterizes the Chinese economy and the heavy dependence of private entrepreneurs on the state. More importantly, this economy is not a simple transplant of capitalistic practices and beliefs from the West; rather, it is shaped by and embedded in particular Chinese political structures, social relationships, and culturally defined yet dynamic patterns of masculinity, desire, and morality. In fact, *all* economies are shaped by such social and cultural particularities.

At the heart of anthropology's interest in economics is the following question: *How do cultural processes shape what people want and need to live, and how do they shape the work people do to get it?* Embedded in this broader question are the following issues, around which this chapter is organized:

Is money really the measure of all things?

How does culture shape the value and meaning of money?

Why does gift exchange play such an important role in all societies?

What is the point of owning things?

Does capitalism have distinct cultures?

Anthropologists who study economies and economic activities are interested in how people satisfy their needs and why they want certain things in the first place. Although we have long debated the exact nature of the relationship between economy and culture, one cannot be fully understood without the other. We begin exploring this relationship by considering the nature of value.

13.1 Is Money Really the Measure of All Things?

Many North Americans and Europeans are accustomed, if not also deeply committed, to the idea that money is the measure of all things. We hear all the time that everything has a price and that the price of an object reflects its real value. But what would be the price in dollars of the original Declaration of Independence of the United States? A favorite blanket you have had since childhood? The Wailing Wall, Jerusalem's most sacred Jewish site? A gold wedding band that mothers have passed to their daughters for seven generations?

Somebody could try to set dollar values, or even try to buy or sell these things. Insurance policies for loss from fire or storm damage actually do set such values, though to the victims they often feel like they wildly miss the mark because they cannot account for important items given by a deceased parent or grandparent (Figure 13.1). Some objects and relationships carry such sacred or special qualities that they can never really be reduced to a monetary equivalent, even in our own society (Werner and Bell 2004). The awkwardness you might feel thinking about people doing so—as well as the controversies that erupt when someone tries to sell something like human body parts, virginity, or Holocaust memorabilia—suggests that some deep set of processes defines what is an acceptable economic transaction and how we establish monetary values for things. Those processes are cultural. Culture—the processes through which people construct and naturalize certain meanings and actions as normal and even necessary—not only shapes what is acceptable to transact, but also how and why the transaction will take place, and how the objects or services being exchanged are valued.

Culture, Economics, and Value

If money is not the measure of all things, where exactly within the processes of culture does **value**—the relative worth of an object or service—come from? **Economic anthropology**, the subdiscipline concerned with how people make, share, and buy

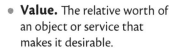

- **Value.** The relative worth of an object or service that makes it desirable.

- **Economic anthropology.** The branch of anthropology concerned with how people make, share, and buy things and services.

Figure 13.1   How Much Is Grandmother's Antique Battle-Axe Worth? In the US television show *Antiques Roadshow*, an expert evaluates the market value of household antiques. The popularity of the show, not to mention the motivation people have to go on it with their antiques, is ultimately less about the money than it is about other factors. What do you think those factors are?

things and services, has considered this question for a century. Economic anthropologists study the decisions people make about earning a living, what they do when they work, the social institutions that affect these activities, and how these three matters relate to the creation of value (Wilk and Cliggett 2007; Smith 2000).

Although both anthropologists and economists study the origins of value and how economies work, they generally have different goals. Economists typically try to understand and predict economic patterns, often with a practical goal of helping people (usually those with financial wealth) hold onto and increase their wealth. Economists study communities in terms of economic statistics, and they assume that economic transactions in one community or country are like transactions in any other.

Anthropologists, on the other hand, do not assume transactions are the same everywhere, recognizing that culture shapes the character of any transaction. Furthermore, we tend to study how people lead their day-to-day economic lives by means of direct, long-term interaction with them. As a result, we tend to focus more than economists do on understanding the world's diversity of **economic systems**—the structured patterns and relationships through which people exchange goods and services—and making sense of how the world's diverse economic systems reflect and shape particular ways of life.

Anthropologists rely on four major theoretical approaches to how economies create value (Table 13.1). Three of these (neoclassical economics, substantivism, and Marxism) are traditional approaches within the social sciences, while the fourth (cultural economics) has been developed by anthropologists. These approaches are discussed in more detail next.

● **Economic system.** The structured patterns and relationships through which people exchange goods and services.

The Neoclassical Perspective

Scottish moral philosopher Adam Smith wrote about the creation of value in his influential book *The Wealth of Nations* (1976). Smith observed that in "primitive" societies individuals did a lot of different kinds of work—growing and preparing food,

TABLE 13.1   THEORIES OF CULTURE, ECONOMY, AND VALUE

THEORETICAL APPROACH	WHAT IS THE ECONOMY?	HOW DOES THE ECONOMIC SYSTEM WORK?	HOW IS VALUE CREATED?
Neoclassical	The economy is a division of labor and the exchange of goods and services in a market.	Workers cooperate in the division of labor to produce goods. The market brings together buyers and sellers to exchange those goods.	Value and wealth are created by competition between buyers and sellers.
Substantivism	The economy is the substance of the actual transactions people engage in to get what they need and want.	Economic processes are embedded in and shaped by non-market social institutions, such as the state, religious beliefs, and kinship relations.	Value is relative, created by particular cultures and social institutions.
Marxism	Capitalism, which is a type of economic system, is a system in which private ownership of the means of production and the division of labor produce wealth for a few and inequality for the masses.	People participate in capitalism by selling their labor. That labor is appropriated by those holding the means of production.	Labor, and especially the exploitation of others' labor, is a major source of value.
Cultural Economics	The economy is a category of culture, not a special arena governed by universal economic rationality.	Economic acts are guided by local beliefs and cultural models, which are closely tied to a community's values.	Value is created by the symbolic associations people make between an activity, good, or service and a community's moral norms.

making their own clothing, building their own homes, and so forth—but in the "civilized" societies of eighteenth-century Europe, such jobs were done increasingly by "the joint labor of a great multitude of workmen" (A. Smith 1976). This change was due to the **division of labor**, the cooperative organization of work into specialized tasks and roles (A. Smith 1976). Citing the example of sewing pins, Smith marveled at how dividing the process of making a sewing pin into distinct actions performed by different specialized laborers—one laborer to draw out the wire, a second to cut it, a third to straighten it, and so on—produced exponential growth in the number of pins that could be made in a day.

> **Division of labor.** The cooperative organization of work into specialized tasks and roles.

This change was revolutionary. Before the division of labor, Smith noted that a pin would take a lot of time and effort for an individual to make, and so the value of the pin lay in the amount of labor it took to make one. But with the division of labor reducing that time and effort, the value of the pin was now established by its **exchange** (the transfer of objects and services between social actors) in a **market**, a social institution in which people come together to buy and sell goods and services.

> **Exchange.** The transfer of objects and services between social actors.
>
> **Market.** A social institution in which people come together to exchange goods and services.

For Smith and the economists who follow him, market exchange reflects a natural human propensity to (as Smith famously said) "truck, barter, and exchange." In this view, it was also the most successful mechanism for determining value and making wealth possible. Within the market, individuals pursue their own self-interest, using their capacity for reason and calculation to maximize their individual satisfaction. The world has finite resources (limited means), but everybody has unlimited desires (unlimited ends), and the result is competition among individuals. Every person's struggle to get the most value theoretically keeps prices, costs of production, profits, and interest rates low while generating great wealth (Wilk and Cliggett 2007). This theory is the foundation of **neoclassical economics**, which studies how people make decisions to allocate resources like time, labor, and money in order to maximize their personal satisfaction.

> **Neoclassical economics.** Economic theories and approaches that study how people make decisions to allocate resources like time, labor, and money in order to maximize their personal satisfaction.

Among anthropologists, this influential theory has provoked a long debate over the nature of the economy. It is, we will see, basically an unresolved debate, but exploring the positions illustrates how anthropologists interested in the relationship between culture, economics, and value have applied—and criticized—neoclassical thought.

The Substantivist–Formalist Debate

In 1944, the Hungarian-American economic historian Karl Polanyi published his book *The Great Transformation* to explain how modern **capitalism**—the economic system based on private ownership of the means of production, in which prices are set and goods distributed through a market—emerged in Europe (Polanyi 1975). Polanyi insisted that the rise of the market in Europe was not natural and inevitable but a social process that both supported and was supported by the creation of the modern state. Modern states are still very much at the heart of the social processes of capitalism, making decisions about how to regulate markets, enforcing market policies, buying goods and services from private companies to provision their citizens, and so forth.

> **Capitalism.** An economic system based on private ownership of the means of production, in which prices are set and goods distributed through a market.

In developing that argument, Polanyi proposed that studying economies involves making a distinction between "formal" and "substantive" economics. By **formal economics**, he meant the underlying (formal) logic that shapes people's actions when they participate in an economy, as we see in the apparently self-interested and rational decision-makers of neoclassical economic theory. By **substantive economics**, he referred to the daily transactions people actually engage in to get what they need or desire, or the "substance" of the economy. These transactions are embedded in and inseparable from other social institutions, such as politics, religion, and kinship.

> **Formal economics.** The branch of economics that studies the underlying logic of economic thought and action.
>
> **Substantive economics.** A branch of economics, inspired by the work of Karl Polanyi, that studies the daily transactions people engage in to get what they need or desire.

Anthropologists found this distinction useful for describing issues they were studying in other societies.

The Substantivist Position

Polanyi's approach to economics was substantivist. Its primary goal was to describe how the production and **redistribution** of goods (collection of goods in a community and then re-division of those goods among members) were embedded in and shaped by non-market social institutions, such as the state, religious beliefs, and kinship relations. Substantivism held that societies have unique social institutions and processes that influence economics like other aspects of culture. From this perspective, the value of goods in an economic system is culturally relative, rooted in particular cultures and social institutions (Wilk and Cliggett 2007).

Substantivists felt that the concept of an "economy" did not do justice to how making a livelihood is inseparably interwoven with customs and social relations in other societies. They argued that research should focus on a broad field of social relations and institutions that provided people with what they needed to live instead of any predetermined or limited notion of an economy centered on a market.

A major proponent of substantivism in anthropology was University of Chicago anthropologist Marshall Sahlins (1930–2021). In one of his most influential early papers, "On the Sociology of Primitive Exchange," Sahlins outlined what he understood as the basis of exchange in traditional societies, the sorts of non-Western societies that most anthropologists studied from the 1920s until the 1980s. Two important elements of his scheme for understanding economic relations were that (1) nearly every transaction in these societies involved an ongoing social relationship, and (2) production was organized around kin groups in what he called the "domestic mode of production." In the American context, you might think of "the family farm" as representing the domestic mode of production, though an updated view of that would need to include many local Thai, Chinese, Mexican, Japanese, or Brazillian restaurants run by family members. As Sahlins wrote,

> *The connection between material flow and social flow is reciprocal. A specific social relation may constrain a given movement of goods, but a specific transaction suggests a particular social relation. If friends make gifts, gifts make friends. A great proportion of primitive exchange, much more than our own traffic, has as its decisive function this latter, instrumental one: the material flow underwrites or initiates social relations.* [Sahlins 1965:140]

This paper set the agenda for the next generation of economic anthropologists, helping them identify how economc activity was embedded within the social patterns of everyday life. Up to then, these economic relations within families were largely ignored because they were not viewed as "economic" relationships at all. But whoever provides for children, weeds the crops, looks after a household, processes grains or sweet potatoes, and so on is also providing a significant portion of a family's subsistence, even if they do not receive a wage for these activities. The importance of these relationships has helped more than a few family businesses stay open after several years of COVID-19 restrictions, suggesting another strength of the domestic mode of production not found in larger businesses and organizations.

The Formalist Reaction

By the late 1960s, some anthropologists began to criticize substantivism's lack of attention to individual action and behavior, shifting their focus to formal economics.

- **Redistribution.** The collection of goods in a community and then the further dispersal of those goods among members.

To formalists, individuals in all societies are as rational as neoclassical economics says they are. People everywhere confront limited means and unlimited ends (wants), and therefore they make rational decisions that are appropriate to the satisfaction they desire (Smith 2000). Being anthropologists, the formalists understood that "satisfaction" could be culturally defined and variable but, they asserted, the decision-making processes people used to achieve satisfaction were basically the same everywhere (Wilk and Cliggett 2007).

By the late 1970s, the debate between substantivists and formalists had fizzled out with no clear winner. The main reason is that the two sides were essentially arguing past each other: one side was talking about societies and their institutions, while the other was talking about individuals, their rationality, and their individual transactions.

The Marxist Perspective

The substantivist–formalist debate also fizzled because a number of anthropologists had begun to adopt Marxism, the political and economic theories associated with German political economist Karl Marx (1818–1883). In his analysis of British capitalism, Marx characterized the English system as pitting the conflicting interests of a wealthy class (who owned factories) against a poorer working class (laborers in the factories) (Marx 1990). At the heart of this system, Marx argued, was a division of labor that produced inequality and conflict.

From the Marxist point of view, the substantivists and formalists had wasted their time debating the nature of exchange and redistribution, while the neoclassicists misunderstood economic activity as individual choice and decision-making. The real problem from the Marxist perspective is explaining why and how the production and trade of goods enforces and maintains the social inequality.

Marxists use the concept of **surplus value**, which is the difference between what people produce and what they need to survive, to address this problem. In a capitalist society, workers create greater output value than the amount they get paid, generating surplus value. For example, a worker in a widget factory might make $35 of widgets in an hour from $5 of materials, but gets paid only $10 per hour. What happens to the $20 of surplus value? The owner of the factory, who controls the **means of production**—the machines and infrastructure required to produce the widget— appropriates it, Marxists argue, thus exploiting the worker's productivity. This surplus value is the basis of private wealth, but it also creates permanent conflict between the worker and owner classes. The institution of private property and the state, through its social and economic policies, support this inequality.

Marxist analysis introduced issues of power, domination, and the unequal distribution of wealth into anthropology's discussions of culture and economy. But not all attempts to apply Marxist analysis to non-Western societies have been entirely satisfying, because Marxist analyses often ignore domestic modes of production, on the one hand, and on the other, the formal economic mechanisms explored by other researchers. They also rarely adequately address the culturally specific symbolic and moral dimensions of economic interaction, to which we turn next.

The Cultural Economics Perspective

The idea that symbols and morals help shape a community's economy lies at the heart of **cultural economics**. Cultural economics views the economy as a category of culture, not a special arena governed by universal utilitarian or practical reason (Sahlins 1972, 1976). The roots of this approach lie in substantivism. The cultural economist's goal is to understand, from the "native's point of view," the local beliefs and cultural models that guide and shape economic activities (Gudeman 1986).

- **Surplus value.** The difference between what people produce and what they need to survive.

- **Means of production.** The machines and infrastructure required to produce goods.

- **Cultural economics.** An anthropological approach to economics that focuses on how symbols and morals help shape a community's economy.

Figure 13.2   Members of a Cofradía in Guatemala. Cofradías, which are Catholic civil-religious associations, are a classic example of a prestige economy since members gain social prestige and authority even as they may go deeply into financial debt to participate.

Prestige economies. Economies in which people seek high social rank, prestige, and power instead of money and material wealth.

To the cultural economist, a close relationship exists between the words "value" (desirability) and "values" (moral norms). Both refer to the symbolic expression of intrinsically desirable principles or qualities. This relationship also implies that moral norms and economic activity influence each other (Sayer 2000).

Anthropologists working in this vein have been especially interested in **prestige economies**, economies in which people seek high social rank, prestige, and power instead of money and material wealth. In indigenous Maya communities of Guatemala and southern Mexico, for example, men have traditionally participated in the *Cofradía* [ko-fra-**dee**-ah] system, a hierarchical system dating from colonial times that combines civic leadership and Catholic religious authority (M. Nash 1958) (Figure 13.2). As they enter higher offices with greater responsibilities and power, these men also have the obligation to spend more of their personal wealth on community fiestas and infrastructure. Some will go broke or deep into debt doing so. Underlying this system is a moral philosophy emphasizing that the path to status and rank requires an individual to share generously with others whatever material wealth he has.

Recent studies in cultural economics have tended to focus on the dynamism of local economies, recognizing that one society may encompass several local economic models simultaneously, perhaps at different levels or among different institutions (Robben 1989; Gudeman 2001). Such a perspective can help us better understand how and why businessmen in China work so hard to build *guanxi* and *renqing* relationships with their business partners, mixing Chinese notions of appropriate and moral economic activity with capitalistic models of economic behavior.

Returning to this section's broader focus on how value is created, it should be clear that none of these theoretical approaches—neoclassical economics, formalism, substantivism, Marxism, or cultural economics—accepts that money is the measure of all things. While the specifics of these theories differ, each nevertheless accepts, at least partially, that cultural processes and social relationships play a central role in establishing value, and that culture and economics are intertwined in complex ways.

The Anthropological Life
The Economics of Anthropology

With all this writing about anthropology's perspectives on economics, it makes sense to ask, "What is the economics of anthropology?" Put in more specific terms, what economic prospects face the student who decides to major in anthropology? According to the US Bureau of Labor Statistics (2021), there are currently 8,500 jobs for anthropologists and archaeologists in the United States. During the next decade, growth in job opportunities is expected to be 7 percent, which is average growth for any occupation. Most of these jobs are in academia, government, corporations, and non-profits; they typically require a master's or doctoral degree; and the median annual salary is $62,000. If you have already decided you want one of these jobs, this is (possibly) sobering news. The situation is especially challenging for those who want to pursue careers in academia, since colleges and universities have been making cuts to faculty positions in social sciences and humanities for a number of years now.

But most students who major in anthropology in college do not go onto jobs with *that specific job title*. Like other students who pursue liberal arts degrees, they end up in all kinds of jobs and careers, bringing anthropological perspectives and skills developed as undergraduates to the work they do in fields like medicine, law, marketing, education, manufacturing, social work, and many others (see p. 23 for a list of those perspectives and skills). With this in mind, the economics of a decision to major in anthropology shifts, and any proper analysis puts anthropology majors in a pool that includes all other college graduates. It should be noted that the single most consequential impact on a salary is not *what* you major in; it is simply finishing college and getting a bachelor's degree. The average lifetime earnings of college graduate with a bachelor's degree ($1.19 million) is more than double that of the typical high school graduate and 39 percent higher than the holder of an associate degree (Hershbein and Kearney 2014). When it comes to specific salaries, anthropology majors have an average base salary of $63,000, which falls in the middle of the median salary range of all college majors (Payscale 2022). And even though they might be paid less than those with other majors, anthropology majors (like many other majors in the humanities and social sciences) report very high rates of satisfaction with their jobs (Students Review 2018; American Academy of Arts and Sciences 2018). So if making a good salary and finding meaningful work are important goals for you, you are going to do just fine if you major in anthropology.

But anthropology majors learn to take these kinds of statistics with a grain of salt—and think anthropologically about them—knowing from their studies that prospects for employment and salary are, like any social dynamic, shaped by a range of sociocultural, political, and economic factors. These factors can include possession of a graduate degree, gender, geographic location, previous work experience, economic upturns and downturns, the chosen career path and the social networks it encompasses, as well as individual imagination, flexibility, and agency.

THINKING LIKE AN ANTHROPOLOGIST: ECONOMICS

Cultural economics argues that a single society can have multiple local cultural models of appropriate economic action and behavior circulating in it. For example, in the United States, even as dominant cultural models of economic behavior resemble Adam Smith's rational economic actors, some religious communities have certain expectations about appropriate economic behavior, such as saving a certain amount of money, donating a certain percentage to the church, and so on, which make explicit connections between economic behavior and morality. Can you think of other cultural models of economic behavior in the United States?

13.2 How Does Culture Shape the Value and Meaning of Money?

- **Money.** An object or substance that serves as a payment for a good or service.

- **Commodity money.** Money that has another value beyond itself, such as gold, which can be used as jewelry.

- **Fiat money.** Money created and guaranteed by a government.

- **General purpose money.** Money that is used to buy nearly any good or service.

- **Limited purpose money.** Objects that can be exchanged only for certain things.

- **Spheres of exchange.** Bounded orders of value in which certain goods can be exchanged only for others.

- **Transactional orders.** Realms of transactions a community uses, each with its own set of symbolic meanings and moral assumptions.

If value and its meanings are created through the processes of culture, then it stands to reason that the value and meanings of **money** itself—an object or substance that serves as a payment for a good or service—are also created through culture. Money provides a standard measure of value, allowing people to compare and trade goods and services. Anything durable and scarce can serve as money. Cowrie (a type of mollusk) shells, rings made of precious metals, and even enormous stone disks have been used as money. **Commodity money** has another value beyond itself, such as gold, which can be used as jewelry. **Fiat money** is created and guaranteed by a government, such as US paper dollars. Money is not simply a medium of exchange; it has functions and implications beyond our economic lives, as we explore here.

The Types and Cultural Dimensions of Money

Across the world, money is many things to many people, and not everybody wants it for the same reasons. In market-based economies like that in the United States, people want money because it can be used to buy nearly any good or service. Anthropologists call this **general purpose money** because it is money that is used to buy almost anything. Portability and mobility are important features of general purpose money, as we see in our dollar bills, coins, credit cards, checks, college "smart" identity cards, and electronic transfers.

Another type of money is **limited purpose money**, which refers to objects that can be exchanged only for certain things. For example, the pastoral Tiv people of Nigeria traditionally could purchase cattle and pay bride price (things of value a groom gives to his bride's father) only with brass rods. The Tiv traditionally used money not for basic subsistence but primarily to gain access to goods that give social respectability and prestige, such as a marriage partner, cattle, and other livestock (Bohannon and Bohannon 1968).

For the Tiv, powerful moral rules regulated the ways in which money was used. The Tiv traditionally had three separate **spheres of exchange**, or bounded orders of value in which certain goods can be exchanged only for others: ordinary subsistence goods, prestige goods, and rights in people, especially women and enslaved people (Bohannon and Bohannon 1968). The British colonial period in Nigeria (1900–1960) undermined this traditional system, because the British introduced general purpose money. Young Tiv men working as laborers and paid in British currency began using it to pay for prestige goods like cattle for bride price. The acquisition of cash value for prestige goods, Bohannon observed, was not just an economic problem: it was a moral problem since it messed with Tiv notions about what money could be used for.

Even general purpose money, such as the use of dollars and cents, has cultural and moral dimensions beyond its function as a medium of exchange (Parry and Bloch 1989). We all know, for example, that you cannot simply walk into your university's accounting office, pay a large sum of money, and receive a diploma. Our ideas about getting an education involve a moral obligation to work hard and apply oneself. Buying a diploma could even feel "dirty," contaminating the purity and goodness we associate with the process of education. An anthropological explanation for this situation lies in the concept of **transactional orders**, or realms of transactions a community uses, each with its own set of symbolic meanings and moral assumptions (Parry and Bloch 1989). The transactions involved in getting an education, which are steeped in long-term obligations and expectations, are morally distinct from other short-term

Figure 13.3 "Dirty Money" and Transactional Orders. One of the reasons people involved in organized criminal enterprises launder money gained from illegal activities is to hide the origins of their wealth from the government. But these people are also moving this money from one symbolic realm or transactional order to another, so once it's been laundered it is symbolically "clean" and can be shared with intimates, including spouses and children who should be protected from the morally suspect activities through which it was gained. In this case, a Mexican drug cartel leader sought to launder his money through a racetrack in Oklahoma, which the FBI raided.

transactions that have no special moral obligations, such as buying a magazine at your university bookstore (Figure 13.3).

The last few decades have seen some interesting changes in the currencies people use to buy the things they need. European countries in the Common Market, for example, gave up their individual currencies to embrace a single currency, the euro, which was not simply a matter of financial policy and practice but one wrapped up in changing ideas of nationality and identity for millions of people. Something similar had happened in the United States in 1783, when thirteen previously independent states adopted a single currency, the dollar.

More recently, out of the world of high technology we have seen the emergence of so-called cryptocurrencies. These novel currencies—nearly a hundred varieties have emerged as of this writing—are "mined" by private companies that use supercomputers with extremely high processing power to solve mathematical equations and produce "blockchains" that serve as a ledger of ownership and transaction. They differ in several ways from traditional currencies, whose ownership cannot be traced or documented. These cryptocurrencies have been seen as a way of avoiding government scrutiny, such as bank reporting, and it is this feature for the moment that has made them a favorite for those engaged in illicit activities. But for the most part, the media and advertising hype around cryptocurrencies has emphasized their speculative, get-rich-quick value, not their effectiveness for everyday transactions.

The dramatic fluctuations in the value of most cryptocurrencies—in which seemingly overnight some people became billionaires and then later lost most or all of it—suggests that these currencies are not as stable as ordinary currencies. This is in spite of the fact that some countries—among them Venezuela, Nigeria, and Zimbabwe—have adopted them to combat currency volatility. In September 2021, El Salvador became the first country to make Bitcoin, the most well-established cryptocurrency, its official legal tender, and all economic agents were required to accept it for all payments (Alverez, Argente, and Van Patten 2022). The Salvadoran government developed an exclusive digital wallet for the currency. When users signed up for the wallet, they were gifted about $30 worth of free Bitcoin. But broad public skepticism, as well as infrastructure and transaction problems, plagued its use. The El

Classic Contributions
David Graeber and the Problem of Debt and Obligation in Organizing Human Societies

DAVID GRAEBER (1961–2020) was a prominent anthropologist whose books dealt directly with how capitalist economic systems created the conditions for a relatively small number of very rich individuals to control the lives of hundreds of millions of people through their control of debt. Graeber was an academic, social activist, and early supporter of the Occupy Wall Street movement opposing social and economic inequality. It is said that he was the one who created the slogan "We are the 99 percent," although Graeber himself always claimed the phrase was the product of several people working together.

▼ **David Graeber**

   At the core of Graeber's anthropology was the conclusion that "debt is the most efficient means ever created to transform social relations that are fundamentally based on violence and violent inequality and to make them seem 'right and proper'" (Graeber 2008). For him, the key to understanding debt is that by turning an obligation into some quantifiable sum of dollars or some other valuable, it changes the moral obligations we have as human beings into something without any morality aside from the obligation to repay the debt, often at high rates of interest and no way to reconfigure the obligations, the interest charged, or the term of the obligation. Today, student loans in the United States are the one form of financial obligation that by law cannot be reconfigured or refinanced. By incurring the debt in the first place, every student is constrained by its power over their lives, a power that is backed by the central government, with its military, its police, its courts and judicial system, and its system of incarceration, all of which can be put into service to guarantee repayment. No wonder many students have been clamoring for debt forgiveness in recent years!

Debt has come to be the central issue of international politics. But nobody seems to know exactly what it is, or how to think about it.

   The very fact that we don't know what debt is, the very flexibility of the concept, is the basis of its power. If history shows anything, it is that there's no better way to justify relations founded on violence, to make such relations seem moral, than by reframing them in the language of debt—above all, because it immediately makes it seem that it's the victim who's doing something wrong. Mafiosi understand this. So do the commanders of conquering armies. For thousands of years, violent men have been able to tell their victims that those victims owe them something. If nothing else, they "owe them their lives" (a telling phrase) because they haven't been killed....

   What precisely does it mean to say that our sense of morality and justice is reduced to the language of a business deal? What does it mean when we reduce moral obligations to debts? What changes when the one turns into the other? And how do we speak about them when our language has been so shaped by the market? . . . [A] debt, unlike any other form of obligation, can be precisely quantified. . . . One does not need to calculate the human effects; one need only calculate principal, balances, penalties, and rates of interest. If you end up having to abandon your home and wander in other provinces, if your daughter ends up in a mining camp working as a prostitute, well, that's unfortunate, but incidental to the creditor. Money is money, and a deal's a deal. [Graeber 2011:4–5, 13–14]

Questions for Reflection

1. What might be the difference between an obligation one might have with a friend or relative and some debt one has with a credit card company or a bank?

2. Graeber spent many chapters in his book outlining the "culture of violence." How can this culture of violence support and be supported by many forms of debt?

3. Could there possibly be a form of debt that wasn't enforced by a government with a police force, a military, a judicial system, and a prison system?

Salvador example confirms that it is too early to know if cryptocurrencies will be successful at operating in the real world of everyday transactions where coins and bills still dominate.

Money, Debt, and the Distribution of Power

Different kinds of money reflect and shape the distribution of power in distinctive ways. In his book *Debt: The First 5,000 Years*, anthropologist David Graeber (2011) explores the historical relationship between money and debt cross-culturally. He observes that when we are in debt to others we feel great moral pressure to pay it off, even if it causes sacrifice and suffering. Graeber writes that this situation began 5,000 years ago when states started creating new kinds of money to promote trade. Commodity money was historically common because it required no trust to exchange. Indebtedness and violence tend to grow with the rise of commodity money, however, because it is scarce, can be stolen, and is not easily traceable. As an alternative approach, governments have created fiat money to regulate and control the flow of money and intervene in creditor–debtor relations because political unrest grows with high levels of indebtedness. These different types of money are related to distinctive kinds of social dynamics and power relations, some of them quite violent and negative. But whatever the type of money, the broader pattern is one in which debtor–creditor relations are full of tension and conflict. In "Classic Contributions: David Graeber on the Problem of Debt and Obligation in Organizing Human Societies," we explore this idea in more detail.

Being in debt to others is not universally viewed as a moral problem or characterized by conflict. In many societies with what Graeber calls "human" (as opposed to "commercial") economies—in which people's goal is not to acquire money but to create and maintain social relationships—credit and indebtedness is a sign of trust and solidarity. Money, which may take the form of yams, pigs, stones, or other objects, is used not to acquire goods or gain material wealth but to provide a unit of account or measure for socially important things—for example, to arrange a marriage, prevent a feud, console mourners at a funeral, or seek forgiveness for a crime (Graeber 2011:130). Sometimes debts incurred in these processes remain unsettled because they are so important socially that they cannot be repaid using money. For much of history, most economies worked this way, and some still do, as we explore in the next section.

THINKING LIKE AN ANTHROPOLOGIST: ECONOMICS

Do you feel a need to protect certain relationships from money? What relationships? What is the meaning of money for you in these situations?

13.3 Why Does Gift Exchange Play Such an Important Role in All Societies?

Exchange, which anthropologists understand as the transfer of things and gifts between social actors (Carrier 1996a:218), is a universal feature of human existence and relates to all aspects of life. In many societies, the exchange of gifts is the central defining feature of its economy.

Gift Exchange and Economy: Two Classic Approaches

It may sound strange to think of a gift exchange in economic terms. We tend to think of gifts as personal expressions of **reciprocity**, the give-and-take that builds and confirms relationships. For Americans the problem here is that we distinguish the economy from gift-giving, while in the non-industrial societies that anthropologists have traditionally studied, exchanging gifts is at the heart of the local economy. So how are gifts related to economy? Two classic approaches to this question date back to the 1920s.

Malinowski and the Kula

The exchange of gifts is a central feature of life in Melanesian societies of the Southwest Pacific, a fact Malinowski discovered while he was in the Trobriand Islands. He wrote that for Trobrianders "to possess is to give. . . . A man who owns a thing is expected to share it, to distribute it, to be its trustee and dispenser" (1922:97).

He found no better illustration of this phenomenon than the *kula* [**koo**-la], an extensive inter-island system of exchange in which high-ranking men gave ornamental shell armbands (*mwali*) and necklaces (*soulava*) to lifelong exchange partners on other islands. In the highly structured *kula*, armbands traveled in one direction and necklaces in the opposite direction (Figure 13.4). For Trobriand Islanders these shell valuables were about the most valuable things one could possess, even though men typically owned them for only a few months before they gave them to other partners (anthropologists call this **delayed reciprocity**—which means a long lag time between giving and receiving). These shell valuables had no real function, as they were rarely worn, and had no other use. Their value came when they were given away because that is when they brought renown to the man who gave them away.

Malinowski did observe that when men sailed to visit their partners on another island, in addition to the armbands and necklaces, they always brought along many utilitarian goods, such as vegetables, fish, or pots to exchange on the side for things they could not get on their own island. Malinowski theorized that these ritualized *kula* exchanges functioned to enhance the status of individual men and distribute goods that people could not otherwise get on their home islands. *Kula* is such an important dimension of Trobriand society that colonialism did not undermine it. In fact, it has expanded in recent decades, involving more islands and lower-ranking individuals.

● **Reciprocity.** The give-and-take that builds and confirms relationships.

● **Delayed reciprocity.** A form of reciprocity that features a long lag time between giving and receiving.

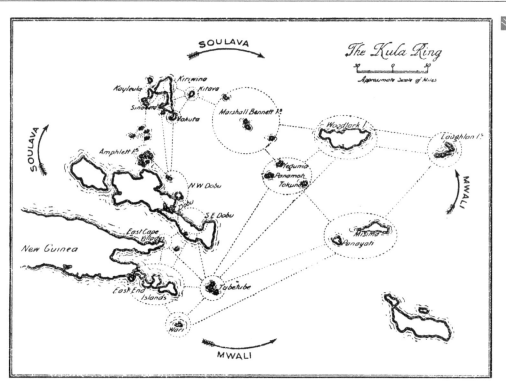

Figure 13.4 **The** *Kula* **Ring with** *Mwali* **(Armbands) and** *Soulava* **(Necklaces).**

Mauss and the Spirit of the Gift

Marcel Mauss (1872–1950), nephew and colleague of the French sociologist Emile Durkheim, was the founder of modern French anthropology. In 1924, he published his most influential work, *The Gift* (Mauss 2000), which compares gift exchange and its functions in a wide range of non-Western societies.

Unlike Malinowski, who viewed gift exchange primarily in terms of how it contributed to an individual's status and identity, Mauss viewed gift exchange in terms of how it builds group solidarity. Gift exchange, Mauss insisted, is based on obligation, which has three dimensions: (1) *the obligation to give*, which establishes the giver as generous and worthy of respect; (2) *the obligation to receive*, which shows respect to the giver; and (3) *the obligation to return the gift in appropriate ways*, which demonstrates honor. It thus creates and maintains bonds of solidarity between people who, Mauss believed, would otherwise pursue their own personal interests (Mauss 2000).

Later anthropologists have built on Mauss's insights into how gift exchange lies at the heart of human society. One of the most influential of these was Marshall Sahlins (1972), who argued that gift exchanges help manage group boundaries. Sahlins identified three types of reciprocity involved in gift exchange, each of which defines the social relationship between a giver and a receiver:

Generalized reciprocity refers to giving something without the expectation of return, at least not in the near term. It is uninhibited and generous giving, such as that which takes place between parents and children, married couples, or close-knit kin groups.

Balanced reciprocity occurs when a person gives something, expecting the receiver to return an equivalent gift or favor at some point in the future. The *kula*, *sagali*, and American birthday presents among good friends are examples.

Negative reciprocity, which economists call barter, is the attempt to get something for nothing, to haggle one's way into a favorable personal outcome. It exists between the most distant relations, such as between strangers or adversaries.

- **Generalized reciprocity.** A form of reciprocity in which gifts are given freely without the expectation of return.

- **Balanced reciprocity.** A form of reciprocity in which the giver expects a fair return at some later time.

- **Negative reciprocity.** A form of reciprocity in which the giver attempts to get something for nothing, to haggle one's way into a favorable personal outcome.

Figure 13.5   Marketing Celebrities to Sell Goods.
Retailers try to help us overcome the impersonality of commodities by creating marketing campaigns that personalize their products. One strategy is to associate a product with widely recognized celebrities, such as Beyoncé Knowles-Carter, pictured here. Celebrities can generate positive feelings about a product even if they don't actually say anything about its quality.

• **Commodities.** Mass-produced and impersonal goods with no meaning or history apart from themselves.

Sahlins's typology is useful because it suggests that social relationships shape the kinds of reciprocity people practice. But recent studies of gift-giving have focused less on the objective types of reciprocity and more on how people interpret gift exchange. For example, anthropologist Marilyn Strathern (1988) argues that certain Melanesian cultures believe that people acquire their individual identities through gift exchange. These Melanesians do not conceive of people as independent units who *enter into* gift exchange; instead, they see themselves as *made* into people by gift exchange itself. Strathern's broader point is that culturally different concepts of personhood and relationship lead to different understandings of and motivations for gift exchange.

Gift Exchange in Market-Based Economies

Although our cultural models dismiss its economic significance, gift exchange is tremendously important in American and European societies for a lot of the same reasons it is in other societies: it establishes social status, reaffirms relationships, and gives people access to the goods and sometimes the influence that they want and need. As in any society, important implicit rules guide our gift exchange.

Even the gifts we give for holidays and birthdays follow implicit rules. Gifts between siblings or friends have to be repaid in equal value every bit as much as the *kula* valuables do. Ideally, gifts should also be personal and embody the relationship between giver and receiver. Thus most Americans feel these gifts should not be cash, because it places a concrete value on the relationship. Somewhat less impersonal are **commodities** (mass-produced and impersonal goods with no meaning or history apart from themselves) bought at a mall (see Chapter 9). Yet in many ways commodities are equivalent to the money spent to buy them. One solution described by anthropologist James Carrier (1995) is to turn impersonal commodities into personal gifts, by wrapping objects as personal presents, or if they are too difficult to wrap, putting bows on them. This simple action symbolically distances the goods from an anonymous retail environment, suggesting that the giver made a greater effort than simply going to a store (Figure 13.5).

Three points stand out here: (1) gift exchanges are deeply embedded in the social relations of every society, including our own; (2) by personalization we can transform impersonal commodities into personal gifts; and (3) we, like everyone else in the world, invest tremendous symbolic meaning in the things we give, receive, and consume. This third point has significant subtleties, which we explore in more detail in the next section.

THINKING LIKE AN ANTHROPOLOGIST: ECONOMICS

According to anthropologists, "reciprocity," "exchange," and "sharing" each have different meanings. In what ways do you think these are different from each other?

13.4 What Is the Point of Owning Things?

People impose control and exclusive possession over objects, which raises the issue of ownership. As with all economic systems and transactions, questions about why and how people own things are best addressed through a cross-cultural lens.

Cross-Cultural Perspectives on Property

For anthropologists, ownership is about interactions between people. Two major issues characterize these interactions: (1) they are about the assertion and negotiation of rights in something, many of these rights being held not by individuals but by a group, and (2) they involve declarations and claims that are rooted in culturally specific forms of symbolic communication (Strang and Busse 2011:4).

For example, in societies where the kinds of gift-giving systems described in the previous section are pervasive, some objects cannot be given away. Annette Weiner (1992) calls these objects "inalienable possessions," and their inherent value transcends their exchange value. For example, the Maori "Sacred Cloak," made from the feathers of kiwis and other birds and worn traditionally by nobility, is understood to be a manifestation of a kin group's cosmological origins and historical continuity (Figure 13.6). It cannot be given away by any individual because rights in it are held by the kinship lineage.

Weiner observes that in some circumstances, inalienable possessions are transferred to others, but only as temporary loans. She contends that in an economy where the moral code is based on gift-giving, transferring such objects means that the giver/owner has rights over the receiver, thus creating status differences between people (Godelier 1999).

Appropriation and Consumption

So why do people come to want certain things in the first place? Sometimes it has to do with securing access to a critical resource, but often it also has to do with what a community considers "cool"—that is, impressive, status-giving, or trendy. But objects are not naturally "cool." Whatever symbolic distinctions or qualities they have are culturally constructed through the process of **consumption**, defined as the act of using and assigning meaning to a good, service, or relationship (see also Chapter 14). Through consumption, people make cultural meaning, build social relationships, and create identities (M. Douglas and Isherwood 1978; Appadurai 1986). Every culture distinguishes between what is appropriate and what is inappropriate to consume, providing social avenues to consuming culturally accepted goods and limiting consumption of things considered inappropriate.

Consumption begins with an act of **appropriation**, which is a process of taking possession of the object (Carrier 1996b; Miller 1987, 1995). Consider, for example, the consumption of a smartphone. The initial act of appropriation takes place as you shop for it. Shopping entails narrowing your choices on the basis of price, size, look, brand, special features, and your sense of how you want to be seen by others until you identify the one you want to buy. After paying for it, you continue the appropriation process by personalizing it—by using it in certain ways, such as programming its memory with your special apps, putting a case with special designs on it, or otherwise customizing it to reflect what you want out of a phone. These customizations, as well as how and when you use your smartphone, in turn reflect and define who you are as a person—for example, an informed techie who loves the latest gadgets or a social butterfly who is always networked—and your position in society.

- **Consumption.** The act of using and assigning meaning to a good, service, or relationship.

- **Appropriation.** The process of taking possession of an object, idea, or relationship.

Figure 13.6   Maori Sacred Cloak.

In societies where people still make many of the things they consume, people may be just as concerned with wanting cool things—things that identify the owner as worthy of respect—as many Americans are. Of course, other cultures' ideas of what "cool" is may differ greatly from ours. For instance, when people around Aitape on the North Coast of Papua New Guinea exchange food and other subsistence goods with their friends in neighboring villages, they also often give their partners hand-made netted string bags with unique designs common to their home villages. String bags are a tangible manifestation of the trader's generosity and commitment to the social and economic relationship between the two exchange partners (Figure 13.7). People are especially proud of the bags that come from very distant villages because possessing them indicates having an extensive network of friends.

Returning to the situation that opens this chapter, it is clear that a shift toward a market economy in China made it possible for Chinese people to consume things they could not during the Maoist era. Consumerism itself was not new in China; many people had long been **consumers**, people who rely on goods and services not of their own making (Humphrey 2002:40). But consciousness of consumption changed. Now that the state no longer controls the production of many consumer goods, and foreign goods pour in, Chinese people have a bewildering array of choices about how and what to consume. The consumption patterns of new rich entrepreneurs—their choices of fashion, the cars they drive, the foods they eat, and so on—have become important because they help common Chinese people navigate through that variety and shape their sense of what objects and services carry symbolic prestige. The influx of new consumer goods is the grounds for creating new cultural meanings and social relationships in Chinese society.

Consumption is a key feature of capitalism, but if consumption varies around the globe, does the capitalist system also vary?

Figure 13.7   **Prestige Goods.** Although both of these bags are considered prestige goods in their specific cultures, a vast conceptual distance exists between how and why people consume them. String bags (*top*) represent an individual's wealth in social relationships, while Gucci bags (*bottom*) represent an individual's material wealth.

> **THINKING LIKE AN ANTHROPOLOGIST: ECONOMICS**
>
> If it is true that changing consumption patterns are visible manifestations of broader cultural changes, what can the massive acquisition of cellular and smartphones by millions of people during the past decade tell us about changes in how people communicate?

13.5 Does Capitalism Have Distinct Cultures?

For the better part of the twentieth century, capitalism and socialism existed as opposed forms of economic organization, an opposition that dominated global politics during the Cold War. After the collapse of the Soviet Union and Eastern Bloc regimes in 1989 and China's shift toward "Socialism with Chinese Characteristics," many economists and political leaders, especially in the United States, asserted that "capitalism won." But under the influence of local cultures, capitalism can take more varied forms than we might assume. As defined previously, capitalism is an economic system based on private ownership of the means of production, in which prices are set and goods distributed through a market. Beyond this generally accepted definition, theoretical approaches to capitalism vary depending on the researcher's philosophical and political approach (Blim 2000). For example, followers of influential sociologist Max Weber study the distinct types of capitalism that have existed in different times and places; formalists study capitalism through the actions of individuals and institutions; and Marxists study the changing nature of industrial production, the conditions of workers, and the connection between small-scale economic activities and broader global economic trends.

In spite of theoretical orientation, however, anthropologists view capitalism as a cultural phenomenon. In fact, its deepest assumptions are cultural: capitalism assumes certain values and ideals to be natural, in the sense that this is the way things really are. It seems inevitable that well-being can be achieved through consuming material things. Anthropologists Richard Robbins and Rachel Dowty (2019) suggest that capitalist systems are culturally organized into four distinct social roles. *Capitalists* invest money in real estate, buildings, machinery, and so on to make a profit. *Laborers* work for the capitalists; their sole means of support comes from the sale of their labor. The primary role of *consumers* is to purchase and consume quantities of goods and services. Finally, the *state* institutes and enforces policies that structure the

• **Consumers.** People who rely on goods and services not produced by their own labor.

relationship between these three other actors, attempting to ensure that capitalists invest, workers work, and consumers consume. These social categories and the cultural ideals associated with them are the basic and universal elements of capitalism.

But anthropologists also recognize that the cultural contexts and meanings of capitalist activities take diverse forms. Let us compare two examples—one drawn from Wall Street, the other from Malaysia—to illustrate how capitalist activities and meanings can vary across cultures.

Culture and Social Relations on Wall Street

Investment banks on Wall Street, site of the New York Stock Exchange and America's financial capital, are popularly seen as a bastion of individual entrepreneurialism and cold rationalism in pursuit of profits (Figure 13.8). If Adam Smith were alive, he'd probably see Wall Street as the epitome of capitalism. But anthropologists have found that social relationships and cultural processes shape transactions on Wall Street in far more complex ways than our image of Wall Street may suggest.

What interests anthropologists is how people construct meanings in the context of such social relationships and how those meanings shape social action and individual conduct. For example, anthropologist Karen Ho (2009) studied investment banks and the international banking industry on Wall Street using participant observation and open-ended interviews just as an anthropologist working in a foreign village would. She reports that bankers and traders think of Wall Street as an entity that mediates vast and anonymous flows of capital throughout the world.

But Ho had conducted participant observation within these global networks as an investment banker herself. Throughout her time on Wall Street, Ho also found that strong personal relationships were essential to successful transactions, precisely because the market was so vast and because the risks and strengths of any particular global segment were so difficult to decipher with assurance. As a result, bankers who told their clients they had "global reach" and coverage "everywhere in the world"— which was a central part of the image they promoted to convince investors to do business with them—were not being entirely honest. In reality, Ho found, most firms had minimal coverage in most parts of the world, often maintaining empty or barely staffed offices where they only did occasional business. Their relationships with local banking firms and clients were nearly dormant, only being reactivated when new investment opportunities arose. Ho's point is that without the rich personal relationships and knowledge of local conditions and markets, these banks have almost no reach whatsoever, demonstrating that modern financial markets are every bit as dependent on social relationships and local knowledge as any daily transaction anthropologists might study in a rural village setting.

▼ **Figure 13.8   The New York Stock Exchange on Wall Street, the Heart of US Capitalism.**

Entrepreneurial Capitalism Among Malays

The Southeast Asian nation of Malaysia provides an example of a very different culture of capitalism. During the past several decades, Malaysia has aggressively pursued economic growth through industrialization and the creation of investment opportunities. Malaysia is an Islamic country; the majority of the people are Muslim ethnic Malays. During British colonial times (early 1800s to the mid-1900s), the nation's

Chinese minority dominated the economy and remained considerably better off than most of the Malay majority. Since the late 1960s, the Malaysian government's goal for economic growth has been to reduce economic inequality between the country's ethnic Chinese and ethnic Malays by giving Malays preferential treatment and greater control over economic resources through set-aside provisions, government subsidies, special investment programs, and preferential opportunities for university education.

Anthropologist Patricia Sloane (1999) studied the impact of these laws on the culture of Malay entrepreneurs in urban Kuala Lumpur, Malaysia's capital. Few Malay capitalists in her study were extremely wealthy but were part of the growing Malaysian middle class. These Malay capitalists' aspirations are not "global" but self-consciously local. The ideology of business was embedded in local values and committed to promoting the economic interests and growth of the Malay ethnic group.

These processes have created a new class of Malay entrepreneurs who think of themselves as the cornerstone of a new, modernized Malaysia. They accept that capitalism is a self-interested enterprise, but they also feel bound by traditional Malay values, insisting on investment and development that serve traditional obligations to family, community, and other Malays. Their idea of capitalism is one in which wealth, social balance, and even salvation are the rewards for those who abide by the moral dictates of social responsibility and obligation. At the heart of these values lie Islamic economic principles—such as the prohibition on charging interest, prohibitions on exploitive or risky activities, and the obligation to share wealth after meeting one's family needs (Sloane 1999:73).

One effect of these ideals is that few enterprises are economically successful, so business failures are common. But Malays do not view these facts with embarrassment, because for many individuals the primary business goal is not to generate huge profits but to extend and deepen their social networks and to cultivate contacts with powerful people. Entrepreneurship is thus not simply about economic action and profit accumulation; it allows people to show how they are both fully engaged in the modern world of global capitalism and respectful of traditional Islamic and Malay obligations and values.

The challenge for Malays, in other words, has been to pursue a capitalist economy that both improves their material quality of life and conforms to their local cultural values, social practices, and on-the-ground realities. This challenge is not unique to Malaysia. In "Anthropologist as Problem Solver: Jim Yong Kim's Holistic, On-the-Ground Approach to Fighting Poverty," we consider how one anthropologist has sought to create capitalist development that is sensitive to local realities.

THINKING LIKE AN ANTHROPOLOGIST: ECONOMICS

If capitalism can vary across cultures, do you think models of capitalist behavior and thought can also differ within a society? Can you think of any examples drawn from what you know about the different kinds of industries and businesses you would find in the American capitalist economic system? How can you explain the variability of capitalism within a single society?

Anthropologist as Problem Solver
Jim Yong Kim's Holistic, On-the-Ground Approach to Fighting Poverty

Between 2012 and 2019, Jim Yong Kim was president of the World Bank, which lends money to countries throughout the global South to promote capitalist economic development and fight poverty. Kim was not just the first anthropologist and physician to hold such a high position in the world's largest development agency but was also the first leader to actually have direct work experience in the field of international development. Kim, who was raised in Iowa as the child of Korean War refugees, received an MD and a PhD in medical anthropology from Harvard and is a co-founder of Partners in Health, a Massachusetts-based organization that provides high-quality healthcare for poor people in Haiti, Peru, Mexico, Russia, and parts of Africa. Within the World Bank, which had traditionally been led by economists or businessmen, there has been concern that someone whose career had focused so much on community-level health and humanitarian intervention is not an appropriate leader for an institution that lends money to Third World countries to promote capitalist economic development and fight poverty (Boseley 2012; Rice 2016).

As a medical anthropologist, Kim viewed poor health as a symptom of—and a contributor to—deeper patterns of social inequality, poverty, and lack of economic opportunity. This understanding shaped the work he had done with Partners in Health, which was the first healthcare provider in Haiti to provide HIV and tuberculosis treatment for the poor. Kim and his colleagues approached community health as not just a matter of medical treatment but as one that requires a holistic and on-the-ground approach working to remove the causes of poor health in the first place. There are many factors at work, including specific cultural patterns of disease transmission, dirty water, lack of food, political disempowerment, and weak access to jobs and economic opportunity. Partners in Health worked on all these issues, and many of them are the same ones the World Bank works on. But the World Bank addresses these things from a very different and abstract vantage point, one that involves looking at balance sheets, budget documents, and economic models and charts.

As a profit-driven development bank, the World Bank is a very different kind of institution than Partners in Health. Its lending practices and policies have long been criticized for deepening poverty and human suffering. But in the past couple of decades the World Bank has been changing—for example, by introducing social and environmental safeguards into projects it funds. Kim, who had been a staunch critic of the bank, saw an opportunity to help further its evolution.

Before his unexpected resignation in 2019, only two years into his second five-year term, Kim had instituted a number of changes at the bank, including some that were controversial and tumultuous—internal reforms in how the bank functioned primarily—and others that were widely considered to be successful, especially a new emphasis in the Bank on ending extreme poverty by 2030 and boosting the prosperity of the poorest 40 percent of the world (Edwards 2019). In this new vision, Kim emphasized greater appreciation of local development priorities, a deeper understanding of the actual impacts of

 Jim Yong Kim

economic policies on people's lives, and a stronger humanitarian orientation. As he once said, "Finance and macroeconomics are complicated, but you can actually learn them. The hardest thing to learn is mud-between-your-toes, on-the-ground development work. You can't learn that quickly. You can't learn that through trips where you're treated like a head of state. You have to have kind of done that before" (Rice 2016).

Question for Reflection

1. What differences do you think exist between economists and anthropologists in terms of how they think about economic development?

2. What do you think are the advantages and disadvantages of Kim's holistic, on-the-ground perspective for determining economic development plans?

Conclusion

Most North Americans assume that the best way to get the things we need and want is to get a job and begin earning a paycheck. But this is definitely not how people do it everywhere in the world. Whether they are Chinese businessmen gaining access to business opportunities through the cultivation of *guanxi* and *renqing*, Trobriand Islanders trading for goods on other islands, or Malaysian entrepreneurs pursuing business practices informed by Islamic values, people differ in their cultural strategies and ideas about how to conduct their economic lives. And, when we step back and look at our own economic lives in a consumer capitalist society, we can see that we too have developed distinctive strategies for exchanging goods and money, such as when we symbolically transform commodities into personalized gifts or possessions.

Economic ideas and behaviors never exist independently of culture, morality, and social relationships. Culture shapes what is acceptable to transact, how and why a transaction occurs, and how the goods and services being exchanged are valued. This point is especially important for understanding the complexities of contemporary global economic changes. In an economically interconnected world, the creation of new markets and economic relationships has an impact on whether and how people in a particular place will be able to acquire certain goods and services. But these processes never occur in a cultural and social vacuum, which is why economic processes continue to play out in distinct ways in communities around the world.

KEY TERMS

Reviewing the Chapter

Chapter Section	What We Know	To Be Resolved
Is money really the measure of all things?	Economies never exist independently of already existing social relationships and culture. Culture shapes what is acceptable to transact, how and why that transaction will take place, and how the goods or services being exchanged are valued.	Still unresolved is the issue of how to define the category "economic." Is it a particular logic and decision-making process? Or is it the substance of the economy, meaning the daily transactions of goods and services?
How does culture shape the value and meaning of money?	People's relationships and attitudes toward money depend on factors such as whether their society uses general purpose money and/or limited purpose money; whether it uses commodity money or fiat money; spheres of exchange; and cultural distinctions between transactional orders.	Anthropologists are still working through the diverse cultural meanings of money, especially the ways money circulates and shifts meanings through distinct transactional orders.
Why does gift exchange play such an important role in all societies?	The exchange of things is a universal feature of human existence. Many societies have met people's material and social necessities through highly organized and principled gift exchanges, but rich subtleties and cross-cultural variations exist in how, when, what, and why people engage in gift exchange.	Although anthropologists accept the central importance of gift exchange in all societies, they continue to embrace distinct theoretical models concerning reciprocity and gift exchange, and debates persist over whether these models adequately capture the complexity of other cultures' approaches to reciprocity.
What is the point of owning things?	Anthropologists approach ownership and property not as static legal categories but as culturally variable matters of social interaction and as bundles of rights. People often want to own things they think are "cool," but the symbolic distinctions and qualities that make objects cool and worthy of respect are always culturally constructed.	People's relationships with objects are more complicated than economic perspectives on consumption suggest. Anthropologists are still documenting and seeking to understand those complexities.
Does capitalism have distinct cultures?	Capitalism is as much an economic system as it is a cultural phenomenon, whose actual practices and cultural models vary across and within cultures.	The idea that capitalism is not a monolithic economic structure but a variable culturally diverse set of practices is not universally accepted in anthropology, especially by Marxist anthropologists.

READINGS

Since Bronislaw Malinowski's classic monograph on the *kula* exchange among the Trobriand Islanders, *Argonauts of the Western Pacific* (London: Routledge and Kegan Paul, 1922), a considerable amount of anthropological research has focused on gift-giving systems around the world. Marcel Mauss's classic 1924 essay *The Gift: The Form* *and Reason for Exchange in Archaic Societies* (New York: W. W. Norton, 2000) is a necessary starting point. Marylin Strathern's *The Gender of the Gift: Problems with Women and Problems with Society in Melanesia* (Berkeley: University of California Press, 1988) offers an excellent overview of gift-giving in Melanesia—where gift-giving plays an especially prominent role in the social lives of many societies—and how anthropologists should think of those issues.

For a useful overview of the field of economic anthropology and its primary theoretical debates and orientations, see Richard R. Wilk and Lisa C. Cliggett's book *Economies and Cultures: Foundations of Economic Anthropology* (Boulder, CO: Westview Press, 2007).

When the Soviet Union fell, anthropologists working in Russia and Eastern Europe found themselves in an interesting position trying to document and analyze the dramatic social transformations that were playing out in front of them. Two excellent books on this transformation are Caroline Humphrey's *The Unmaking of Soviet Life: Everyday Economies After Socialism* (Ithaca, NY: Cornell University Press, 2002) and Katherine Verdery's book *What Was Socialism? What Comes Next?* (Princeton, NJ: Princeton University Press, 1996).

Many people do not really understand the powerful role Wall Street plays in shaping the economic prospects of people who have nothing to do with investment banking. Karen Ho's book *Liquidated: An Ethnography of Wall Street* (Durham, NC: Duke University Press, 2009) provides an in-depth ethnographic description of how investment banking culture operates.

14

Sustainability

Environment and Foodways

GIVEN CURRENT PATTERNS of climate change, the Micronesian country of the Marshall Islands will probably be submerged by the end of this century. Consisting of five islands and twenty-nine coral atolls spread across 750,000 square miles of the western Pacific Ocean, all of the country's seventy square miles of land sit just a few feet above sea level. Consequently, rising seawaters represent an existential threat to the islands, adding another layer of woe in a region long fractured by the disruptions of European colonialism, the militarization of the Pacific during the Second World War, and US nuclear and missile testing that has caused many environmental and health problems.

The Marshallese are already feeling the effects of climate change, including intensified drought and flooding. Climate change raises many pressing questions for the country's 53,000 people, the most obvious being where they will go as their homes disappear. Under current international law, they cannot gain status as refugees because the legal category "refugee" applies only to people displaced by persecution, not to those displaced by an environmental problem like climate change.

One of the ironies of this situation, at least from a Marshallese perspective, is that the environmental problems facing them are not of their making. Since about 2,000 BCE, islanders have developed strategies for living sustainably in a challenging environment where natural resources like fresh water, arable land, and fisheries are scarce and extreme weather events such as droughts, tsunamis,

---

The Challenge of Climate Change in the Marshall Islands.   Climate change has intensified flooding in the low-lying Marshall Islands. In this instance, a king tide was energized by a storm surge, leading to the flooding of Majuro, the capital atoll.

399

earthquakes, and hurricanes are common. Marshallese food production systems take these ecological conditions into account. One traditional practice is to grow taro, an important tuber in the Marshallese diet, in "humidity pockets" (pits dug in the ground and lined with layers of plants, organic mulch, and coral rubble), which reduces consumption of fresh water and increases food production in nutrient-deficient soils (Bridges and McClatchey 2009). Another is to prohibit or limit fish and crab harvests, for example, by designating a reef or an island, or parts of one, as *mo*, which means "prohibited" or "taboo" (Tibon n.d.). To distribute the environmental risks of island living, the Marshallese have traditionally scattered food production sites and traded with other islands and atolls, using sophisticated seafaring knowledge to make long-distance voyages (Genz 2011).

But as a result of globalization processes, the Marshallese—like many other societies in the world today—do not manage their resources on their own terms. The dilemmas these processes create lead us to the question at the center of this chapter: *Why do some societies have sustainable relations with the natural world while others seem to be more destructive of their natural environments, and what sociocultural factors are driving environmental destruction in the contemporary world?* We can answer this question by considering a number of related questions around which this chapter is organized:

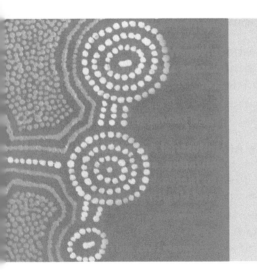

Do all people see nature in the same way?

How do people secure an adequate, meaningful, and environmentally sustainable food supply?

How does non-Western knowledge of nature and agriculture relate to science?

How are industrial agriculture, economic globalization, and climate change linked to increasing environmental and health problems?

Are industrialized Western societies the only ones to conserve nature?

Different views of the natural world are closely related to distinct environmental management and food acquisition strategies. The environmental beliefs, knowledge, and practices of different societies, as well as their foodways, have long been major concerns at the heart of cultural anthropology. These issues have traditionally been studied in the settings of small-scale, non-Western societies where beliefs, knowledge, and practices differ markedly from Western views and practices. But in recent years, as global concern with environmental degradation, climate change, the loss of biodiversity, and industrializing foodways has mushroomed, anthropologists have also been paying close attention to the effects of global economic changes on human–nature relations and what sustainability means for different people. We begin by exploring how a people's environmental values and behaviors emerge from particular ways of thinking about the natural world.

14.1 Do All People See Nature in the Same Way?

What nature means and how people see themselves in relation to it vary greatly around the world. Consider, for example, the relationships between indigenous settlement and natural ecosystems in southern Mexico and Central America (Figure 14.1). Some of these areas, such as the Yucatán Peninsula, the Petén region of Guatemala, and the Miskito Coast of Nicaragua, have been inhabited for many centuries. After the arrival of the Spanish in the 1500s they were safe areas for indigenous people

Figure 14.1 Linkages Between Biological and Cultural Diversity. This map, which is a simplified version of a map produced by the Center for the Support of Native Lands and originally published in *National Geographic*, superimposes the distribution of cultural diversity and the distribution of biological diversity in Central America and southern Mexico. The areas outlined in red mark zones where indigenous populations live and where intact biodiverse ecosystems can be found.

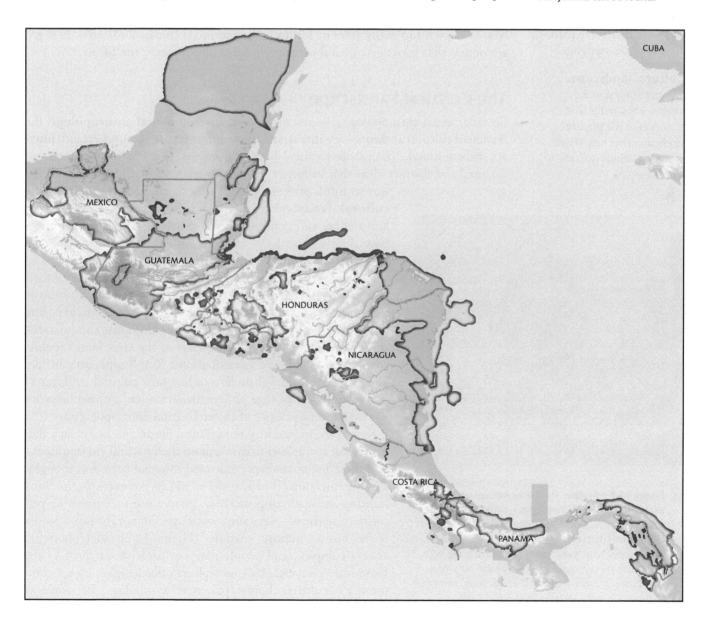

because the Spanish conquerors found the tropical heat and diseases undesirable (Lovgren 2003). Why did the indigenous people not simply cut the forest down for fields, as European settlers did in other parts of the New World?

One reason was their low population density and subsistence economies based on swidden agriculture (see the "*Horticulture*" subsection later in the chapter) in which post-harvest fields lie fallow, eventually returning to forest. But economic practices alone do not explain good stewardship; for that we need to understand the indigenous people's views of their environment. As Ken Rapp of the Center for the Support of Native Lands observed, "It's part of their belief system. They don't see a division between nature and man" (Lovgren 2003).

The Human–Nature Divide?

A good example of a group whose belief system fits with what Rapp described is the Itzaj, a Maya group that has lived in the Petén tropical lowlands of Guatemala since pre–Spanish contact times. According to Itzaj beliefs, humans and nature do not occupy separate realms; there is both real and spiritual reciprocity and communication between plants, animals, and humans. For example, forest spirits called *arux* ("masters of the wind") continually monitor people, and they play tricks on those who cut down too many trees or kill too many animals (Atran 2001:169). It is not accidental that Itzaj agricultural practices respect and preserve the forest.

The Cultural Landscape

Environmental anthropologists—practitioners of **environmental anthropology**, the branch of cultural anthropology that studies how different societies understand, interact with, and make changes to nature—have long insisted that it is important to understand the abstract ideas that influence people's interactions with landscapes. One way to think of these abstract ideas is through the concept of a **cultural landscape**, which holds that people have images, knowledge, and concepts of the physical landscape that affect how they will actually interact with it (Stoffle, Toupal, and Zedeño 2003:99). For example, the Itzaj consider nature to be an extension of their social world, full of spirits that influence their everyday lives. As a result, they are less likely to wantonly destroy the landscape in which they live because such acts would equate to hurting themselves. Different social groups can also hold distinctly different and conflicting ideas of the same landscape. As we explore in "Classic Contributions: Roy Rappaport's Insider and Outsider Models," understanding how cultural concepts of nature (referred to here as "cognized models") guide behavior has long been a priority of environmental anthropology.

Key to understanding the cultural landscape is the idea that people use metaphors to think about their natural environments, and these metaphors are connected to social behavior, thought, and organization (Bird-David 1993:112). For example, in many hunting-and-gathering societies, people use metaphors of personal relatedness—sexuality, marriage, or family ties—to describe human–nature relations (Figure 14.2). Metaphors are always complex, and people may not understand them in the same ways. Nevertheless, metaphors offer insights into a community's cultural landscapes that symbolize the society's

- **Environmental anthropology.** The branch of anthropology that studies how different societies understand, interact with, and make changes to nature and natural ecosystems.

- **Cultural landscape.** The culturally specific images, knowledge, and concepts of the physical landscape that help shape human relations with the landscape.

🌱 **Figure 14.2   Mother Nature as Metaphor.** An example of a metaphor of human–nature relatedness is "Mother Nature," a concept that is familiar in many cultures and that remains popular in North America and Europe today. It represents nature as a living force with feminine qualities of procreation and nurturing, and it is an example of an "adult–child caring" metaphor that exists in many societies (Bird-David 1993).

Classic Contributions
Roy Rappaport's Insider and Outsider Models

THE AMERICAN ANTHROPOLOGIST Roy Rappaport (1926–1997) was a major figure in the field of ecological anthropology, whose specific focus was on the relationship between humans and natural ecosystems. He was a pioneer in the use of systems theory for understanding human populations. In his landmark 1968 study *Pigs for the Ancestors: Ritual in the Ecology of a New Guinea People* (1984), Rappaport distinguished between the insider's mental models of human–nature relations, called "cognized models," and "operational models," the ecological dimensions of human–nature relations identified by the observer. He argues that the goal of the anthropologist is to figure out how cognized models guide behavior, and how that behavior helps people adapt to specific environmental conditions.

Roy Rappaport with Maring villagers in Papua New Guinea

[T]wo models of the environment are significant in ecological studies, and I have termed these "operational" and "cognized." The operational model is that which the anthropologist constructs through observation and measurement of empirical entities, events, and material relationships. He takes this model to represent, for analytic purposes, the physical world of the group he is studying. . . .

The cognized model is the model of the environment conceived by the people who act in it. The two models are overlapping, but not identical. While many components of the physical world will be represented in both, the operational model is likely to include material elements, such as disease germs and nitrogen-fixing bacteria, that affect actors but of which they may not be aware. Conversely, the cognized model may include elements that cannot be shown by empirical means to exist, such as spirits and other supernatural beings. . . . [T]he important question concerning the cognized model, since it serves as a guide to action, is not the extent to which it conforms to "reality" (i.e., is identical with or isomorphic with the operational model), but the extent to which it elicits behavior that is appropriate to the material situation of the actors, and it is against this functional and adaptive criterion that we may assess it. [Rappaport 1984:237–38; emphasis in the original]

Questions for Reflection

1. What are some reasons Rappaport might advocate a balanced approach between "cognized" and "operational" models of human–nature interactions?

2. Can you identify some elements of the insider's view or "cognized model" of our own society?

feelings and values about its environment. Whether a society has sustainable relations with nature depends on many factors beyond how they conceptualize human–nature relations, a theme we examine in the next section.

Metaphors are always complex, and different people may not understand them in the same ways. Nevertheless, metaphors offer insights into a community's cultural landscapes that symbolize the society's feelings and values about its environment. Yet, whether a society has sustainable relations with nature depends on many factors beyond how they conceptualize human–nature relations, a theme we examine in the next section.

> ### THINKING LIKE AN ANTHROPOLOGIST: SUSTAINABILITY
>
> People's images and metaphors of human–nature relatedness reflect and communicate their attitudes toward nature and act as important guides to action. Can you think of any metaphors of human–nature relatedness in our society? How do you think those metaphors relate to people's actual interactions with nature?

14.2 How Do People Secure an Adequate, Meaningful, and Environmentally Sustainable Food Supply?

How people think of their landscapes is also intertwined with how they actually get their living from it—specifically, how a community gets and thinks about its food. Anthropologists call the structured beliefs and behaviors surrounding the production, distribution, and consumption of food **foodways**. There are important cross-cultural variations in foodways, which we explore here.

Modes of Subsistence

Cultural anthropologists have long studied **modes of subsistence**, which refers to how people actually procure, produce, and distribute food. There are four major modes:

1. Foraging, or the search for edible things.
2. Horticulture, or small-scale subsistence agriculture.
3. Pastoralism, which means the raising of animal herds.
4. Intensive agriculture, or large-scale, often commercial, agriculture

For the past several thousand years, intensive agriculture has furnished most people with most of their food supplies. But foraging, horticulture, and pastoralism—which we covered in Chapter 10 on the Neolithic Revolution—are still important dimensions in many of the world's diets because societies are rarely committed to a single mode of subsistence, often combining two or more modes.

Foraging

As we explained in Chapter 10, foraging refers to searching for edible plant and animal foods without domesticating them. Hunter-gatherers, who obtain their subsistence through a combination of collecting foods and hunting prey, are foragers. Most foragers have mobile lives, traveling to where the food happens to be rather than moving the food to themselves (Bates 2005). Low population densities ensure that their impacts on the environment tend to be minimal.

A common stereotype is that foraging is a brutal struggle for existence. This stereotype is inaccurate, because in reality foragers tend to work less to procure their subsistence than people who pursue horticulture or pastoralism. For example, Richard Lee found that !Kung San (one group of which are known as Ju/'hoansi) hunter-gatherers

---

- **Foodways.** Structured beliefs and behaviors surrounding the production, distribution, and consumption of food.

- **Modes of subsistence.** The social relationships and practices necessary for procuring, producing, and distributing food.

of the Kalahari Desert in Southern Africa spent less than twenty hours per week getting food (Lee 1969). Foragers also tend to view their environments not as harsh but as giving. It is easy to view foraging communities as a survival of our Paleolithic past since humans lived this way for 99 percent of our history. But contemporary foragers tend to inhabit extreme environments where horticulture or pastoralism are not feasible, such as the desert, the Arctic tundra, or certain rain forests.

Horticulture

Horticulture is the cultivation of gardens or small fields to meet the basic needs of a household. It is sometimes referred to as subsistence agriculture, which refers to cultivation for purposes of household provisioning or small-scale trade, but not investment (Bates 2005). Horticulture emerged some 12,000 years ago with domestication, which gave humans selective control over animal and plant reproduction and increased the amount of reliable food energy (Bates 2005) (Figure 14.3).

Horticultural farmers cultivate small plots and employ relatively simple technologies (hand tools like knives, axes, and digging sticks, for example) that have low impacts on the landscape. The most common form of horticulture is **swidden agriculture**, or slash and burn agriculture, in which cutting and burning vegetation improves nutrient-poor soils. A farmer can use a plot for several years, usually planting up to two dozen different crops that mature or ripen at different times. These gardens often imitate the ecological diversity and structure of the rain forest itself, with some plants living in the understory shade, others in the partly shaded middle level, and others in the sunny top. By the time the crops are all harvested the soil is depleted, and the farmer will move to another plot to repeat the process. Old plots lie fallow, and if there are no other

- **Horticulture.** The cultivation of gardens or small fields to meet the basic needs of a household.

- **Swidden agriculture.** A farming method in tropical regions in which the farmer slashes (cuts down trees) and burns small patches of forest to release plant nutrients into the soil. As soil fertility declines, the farmer allows the plot to regenerate the forest over a period of years.

Figure 14.3 Horticulture in Papua New Guinea. Mixed garden in fence in lowland Ningerum area (*left*). Freshly planted sweet potato mounds in Highland New Guinea (*top right*). A married couple in their mature Highland sweet potato garden (*bottom right*).

pressures on them, such as population growth or new settlers coming to a rain forest area, a farmer might not return to work one of these fallow plots for several decades.

Pastoralism

- **Pastoralist society.**
A group of people who live by animal husbandry.

- **Animal husbandry.**
The breeding, care, and use of domesticated herding animals such as cattle, camels, goats, horses, llamas, reindeer, and yaks.

Pastoralist societies live by **animal husbandry**, which is the breeding, care, and use of domesticated herding animals such as cattle, camels, goats, horses, llamas, reindeer, and yaks (Bates 2005). Rather than raising animals for butchering as food, pastoralists mainly consume their milk and blood and exploit their hair, wool, fur, and the ability of animals to pull or carry heavy loads. This approach allows them to get more out of the animal in the long run. Pastoralists typically occupy arid landscapes where agriculture is difficult or impossible (Figure 14.4).

Because a livestock herd can do quick, even irreparable, damage to vegetation in arid landscapes, this mode of subsistence requires the constant movement of herds (Igoe 2004). This movement is typically coordinated among herd-owning households. At the heart of this system is common ownership of land and social institutions that ensure herders do not sacrifice the fragile environment for short-term individual gains. These social institutions include livestock exchanges to redistribute and limit herd size, punishments for individuals who diverge from planned movement patterns, and defense of rangeland boundaries to prevent invasions by neighboring pastoral groups (McCabe 1990). When these institutions work successfully, pastoralism is a sustainable mode of subsistence, providing people with a stable source of nutritious foods without irreversibly destroying the fragile landscape.

Intensive Agriculture

- **Intensification.** The use of certain preparation, management, and cultivation processes to increase yields.

While the goals of horticulture and pastoralism are to feed families, the goal of intensive agriculture is to increase yields to feed a larger community. Approaches to **intensification**, which refers to the use of certain processes to increase yields (Bates 2005), include these:

Figure 14.4   Saami Reindeer Herder. The Saami, who live in northern Scandinavia, are pastoralists who live from reindeer herding.

- *Preparing the soil*, with regular weeding, mulching, mounding, and fertilizers;
- *Using technology*, often simple, such as a harness or yoke that allows a farmer to use horses or oxen to plow a field; complex, such as a system of canals, dams, and water pumps that provide irrigation to an arid landscape; or very complex, like a combine harvester, a machine that harvests, threshes, and cleans grain plants like wheat, barley, and corn.
- *Using a larger labor force*, such as in Asian rice farming, which sustains the nutritional and energy needs of large populations and provides many people with employment (Geertz 1963).
- *Managing water resources*, which can range from the practice of adding pebbles to fields to retain soil moisture (as ancient Pueblo dwellers of North America did), to the use of large-scale irrigation and sophisticated systems implemented by modern states.
- *Modifying plants and soils*, through selective breeding of plants to produce better yields, reduce the time needed to mature, or create a more edible product, as farmers have done for major grains like maize, rice, and wheat (Bates 2005).

Intensification carries certain trade-offs. On one hand, it solves an important problem, which is how to provide food for a large number of people, including those who do not work directly in food production. It also provides a relatively steady supply of food, though famines can still happen. On the other hand, intensification can create environmental problems. By rearranging ecosystems to achieve greater control over nature, intensive agriculture is vulnerable to declining environmental conditions. For example, clearing a hillside to plant crops, build terraces, or install water works may increase productivity in the short run, but these can lead to the erosion of topsoil, lowering of water tables, concentration of salts in soils, the silting up of waterworks, and so on.

The most intensive form of agriculture is **industrial agriculture**, which applies industrial principles to farming. Key principles include specialization to produce a single crop, and the obtaining of land, labor, seeds, and water as commodities on the open market. Through the use of machines, industrial agriculture harnesses sources of energy such as steam power and petroleum, vastly increasing the scale of productivity. Technology-based farming has also redefined our notion of what agricultural work is (Figure 14.5). On some farms, such as those that produce grains like corn and wheat, farming now means tending to huge machines that provide nearly all the actual farm labor (Bates 2005). As a result of mechanization, a small rural labor force (in the United States, less than 2 percent of the total population) produces so much food that one of industrial agriculture's greatest economic problems is *over*production.

Food, Culture, and Meaning

As the variability in modes of subsistence demonstrates, the human species evolved to be adaptable to many different environments. The human diet also evolved to be flexible, and the range of things the human species can and does eat is tremendous. But our actual everyday diets usually involve a limited range of foods, determined by what is available, dietary restrictions, and by what we have learned to prefer as members of a particular social community. Foodways are always shaped by cultural beliefs and governed by systematic rules and etiquette particular to a social group. These cultural processes have implications for human sustainability because they also shape how people think about and interact with landscapes through foodways.

• **Industrial agriculture.** The application of industrial principles and methods to farming.

Figure 14.5 Factory Farms in the Twenty-First Century. In the United States, most of the farms that produce meat, eggs, and dairy products are organized on industrial principles. These farms create economies of scale to reduce costs and maximize profits.

For example, those of us who get our food from supermarkets tend to think of food as material, impersonal, and dissociated from the producer and the natural environment, reflecting a distinctly urban view of nature as separate from the human domain. In contrast, the Hua, who live in the Eastern Highlands of Papua New Guinea, believe that food possesses mystical dynamism, vitality, and danger (Meigs 1997). For the Hua, the act of eating unites them with the individual who produced or shared food with them and invigorates them with the vital essences of the organisms they are consuming. Because food is so spiritually powerful, humans are susceptible to its influences. To channel and protect these essences, the Hua have devised many rules governing who can grow, handle, share, and eat certain foods, as well as how those foods are grown.

Foodways Communicate Symbolic Meaning

In every society, food is a rich source of meaning, and people use it to communicate specific messages. Particular foods and meals can draw people together, especially when they share and consume foods that symbolize concepts like home, family, or conviviality. When you are homesick, the yearning for certain "comfort foods" is not just a desire for a familiar taste. It

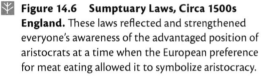

Figure 14.6   Sumptuary Laws, Circa 1500s England. These laws reflected and strengthened everyone's awareness of the advantaged position of aristocrats at a time when the European preference for meat eating allowed it to symbolize aristocracy.

is also satisfying because it ties you symbolically to home and family. But food can just as easily communicate division and unequal power relations, as with so-called sumptuary laws that limit consumption of certain items along class lines (Figure 14.6)

The use of food as a form of symbolic communication is so pervasive that some anthropologists have suggested that food operates with logic similar to that of language. English anthropologist Mary Douglas, for example, observed that an English formal dinner takes on a certain precise order, just like a sentence: appetizers, soup, fish, and so on to dessert (M. Douglas 1966; Anderson 2005:110).

Foodways Mark Social Boundaries and Identities

Food preferences, etiquette, and taboos also mark social boundaries and identities. As anthropologist Carole Counihan (1999:8) has observed, "One's place in a social system is revealed by what, how much, and with whom one eats." Eating practices might mark gender differences, as when men and women eat different foods. They might mark ethnic or regional differences, as particular groups identify themselves closely with certain foods. Or they could mark profession or class status, as certain individuals consume certain foods identified with their social station (Lentz 1999). These social markers are closely related to differing notions of **taste** that may exist between or within groups. *Taste* can refer to both the physical sensation on the tongue (as in "this crab cake tastes good") and social distinction and prestige (as in "her consumption of fine wine shows she has good taste") (Macbeth 1997).

Every society has a notion of the "perfect meal," which typically reflects people's culturally acquired tastes and is closely identified with their social identity and subsistence patterns as a group. For example, German anthropologist Gerd Spittler (1999) found that among the Kel Ewey Tuareg [kell **eh**-way **twar**-egg] nomads who live in the Sahara desert region in northern Mali, West Africa, the perfect meal is simple and is always the same for everybody, regardless of their relative wealth, involving cheese, dates, camel or goat milk, and the grain millet. Spittler theorizes that Tuareg prefer this meal because it identifies them as a people that provides a stable diet for all its

• **Taste.** A concept that refers to the sense that gives humans the ability to detect flavors; taste can also refer to the social distinction and prestige associated with certain foodstuffs.

members in a precariously dry environment. These Tuareg view variety in the diet—something that many of us take for granted—as a characteristic of people who must be so desperately poor and hungry they are forced to eat anything they can find.

Foodways Are Dynamic

Because foodways are so bound up with people's identities, it is easy to assume that people always hold on to them tightly. In some cases, foodways are remarkably persistent. For example, the diet in the southern Spanish region of Andalucía is about the same as it was during Roman times: crusty bread, olive oil, eggs, pork, wine, cabbage, herbs, onions, and garlic (Anderson 2005:163).

But foodways can also change for many reasons. Environmental changes, like over-hunting or over-fishing, alter what is available. Or people begin to identify certain foods with good health, such as the reputation beef held among North Americans during the mid-twentieth century, but which in recent decades has given way to new ideas about the healthiness of a diet based on vegetables, whole grains, and so on. Or formerly expensive foods, like white bread and processed sugar, become inexpensive because of new processing techniques. And changes in family dynamics force changes in eating habits, such as in North America, where women's increasing involvement in the workforce (leaving nobody home to cook) has helped fuel the rapid rise of convenience foods such as fast food, frozen dinners, and family restaurants (Anderson 2005:165–68).

Although foodways are dynamic, people have a pretty stable concept of an appropriate diet that reflects their understanding of proper foods, good taste, and nutritional requirements. Underlying these facts is a simple logic: if a diet works—that is, if it provides sustenance, meaning, and sustainable ecological relations—then people are unlikely to drop everything when something new comes along. People integrate new foods and cuisines into their existing dietary practices all the time, usually gradually. But since the existing logic of any local foodway is already integrated into the production, preparation, and sharing of food, dramatic change is unlikely. As we will see in the next section, the systematic ways people understand nature and sustainable management of it are also profoundly shaped by culture.

THINKING LIKE AN ANTHROPOLOGIST: SUSTAINABILITY

Even though most of us probably get our food from a supermarket, can you identify examples of other modes of subsistence in our own society? How and why do these multiple modes of subsistence persist?

14.3 How Does Non-Western Knowledge of Nature and Agriculture Relate to Science?

Anthropologists try to describe the traditional knowledge that different societies have of their natural environments, recognizing that all knowledge systems about nature, including science, are culturally based. This goal dates back to the beginnings of anthropology as a discipline. For example, during his years among the Trobriand

Islanders (1915–18), Bronislaw Malinowski was keenly interested in people's knowledge of gardening, canoe building, and navigation. From observing these activities, he concluded that "primitive humanity was aware of the scientific laws of natural process" and magical processes, and he went on to add that all people operate within the domains of magic, science, and religion (1948:196).

Do native knowledge systems have scientific validity? Malinowski reasoned that if knowledge is born of experience and reason, and if science is an activity characterized by rationality, then indigenous knowledge is part of humankind's scientific knowledge (Nader 1996:7). Since his time, anthropologists have demonstrated that scientific attitudes and methods of validation—close observation, experimentation, and analysis—are not unique to the West (Nader 1996, 8). One key difference that distinguishes many non-Western knowledge systems from Western sciences, however, is that they are not necessarily viewed as distinct realms of knowledge, but are, instead, integrated into people's spiritual beliefs and social practices, while in the West people tend to think of science as separate from all these things, as its own special domain of knowledge.

Ethnoscience

Early anthropological interest in knowledge systems of non-Western societies was called ethnoscience (see also Chapter 12). During the 1960s, when ethnoscience was at the peak of its influence, ethnoscientists aimed to describe and understand the conceptual models and rules with which a society operates, following Malinowski's call for anthropologists to see the world from the "native's point of view" (Sturtevant 1964:100). They began by comparing the systems of classification used by the different peoples they studied.

Classification systems are reference systems that group things or ideas with similar features. Examples include plant and animal taxonomies, kinship terminologies, color schemes, and medical diagnoses. Classification systems create a common intellectual framework that people use to work with the natural world, heal the sick, and communicate with each other.

- **Ethnobiology.** The branch of ethnoscience that studies how people in non-Western societies name and codify living things.

As discussed in Chapter 3, Western scientific disciplines use Linnaean taxonomy to classify all living organisms into species. Brent Berlin, who studied **ethnobiology** (indigenous ways of naming and codifying living things) of the Tzeltal Maya, has argued that the Tzeltal and most societies for whom we have data divide living things into groups based on shared morphological characteristics, as the Linnaean system does (Berlin 1973). Based on these findings, Berlin concluded that all human classification systems reflected a cognitive structure of the human brain that organizes information in systematic ways—in other words, that all human minds more or less think alike. But numerous challenges to Berlin's conclusions exist, based largely on the observation that some societies use non-morphological characteristics to classify plants and animals.

Traditional Ecological Knowledge

- **Traditional ecological knowledge.** Indigenous ecological knowledge and its relationship with resource management strategies.

These days, anthropologists interested in themes related to ethnoscience tend to focus on **traditional ecological knowledge**, which studies indigenous ecological knowledge and its relationship with resource management strategies. One of the more important findings of this field is that many ecological relations recognized by indigenous peoples are not known to Western science. One reason is that this knowledge may involve species that are endemic, which means they exist only in one place.

Another reason is that knowledge often resides in local languages, songs, or specialized ritual knowledge. Healers and shamans are important repositories of local plant knowledge and lore, and they may even keep their knowledge secret from other people in their own society. In recent years, controversy has erupted because pharmaceutical companies have been trying to gain access to the knowledge of traditional healers to identify plants that might be useful for developing new commercial drugs, sometimes without community consent (M. Brown 2003).

Because traditional ecological knowledge is customized to particular environments, it can also provide an effective basis for managing resources. For example, in the southern Mexican state of Oaxaca, Zapotec farmers have been growing maize on the same landscape for hundreds of years (Figure 14.7). Farmers have a systematic understanding of how soil qualities, weather patterns, lunar phases, plant–plant interactions, and plant–insect interactions affect maize harvests (Gonzalez 2001). Western scientists have discovered that Zapotec practices of intercropping (planting multiple crops together), building soil mounds for planting maize, letting the land lie fallow, and planting and harvesting by the phases of the moon all contribute to creating a highly productive and sustainable agricultural system (Gonzalez 2001).

Figure 14.7   Maize Biodiversity in Southern Mexico. Southern Mexico, where maize was domesticated some 8,000 years ago, has long been a hotspot of maize biodiversity. People like the Zapotec have developed tens of thousands of varieties of maize with different flavors, textures, adaptability to microclimates and soil conditions, and colors. Each variety reflects the highly specialized and customized knowledge of its farmers.

Some elements of Zapotec science do not correspond to Western science and beliefs about effective resource management, however. For example, ecological knowledge is not separate from other forms of knowledge, such as ideas about morally acceptable behavior. Zapotecs believe that cultivations, especially maize, have a soul that rewards people who share with others. They believe that the success of a harvest is directly related to the farmer's positive social relations with other members of the community.

The Zapotec case demonstrates that traditional ecological knowledge has allowed communities to thrive for a long time on a landscape without destroying it. Unlike Western sciences, which claim to have universal tools for understanding nature, the Zapotec knowledge of nature is rooted in local cultural traditions, beliefs, and landscapes. It is also not viewed as a separate domain of specialized knowledge but is integrated into people's daily lives, spiritual practices, and so on. In the contemporary world, such knowledge and practices are confronting new challenges related to the spread of industrial agriculture, economic globalization and climate change. In the next section, we examine how these challenges affect a community's environment and health.

THINKING LIKE AN ANTHROPOLOGIST: SUSTAINABILITY

The idea that traditional ecological knowledge provides an effective basis for managing natural resources is often resisted most strongly by Western agricultural scientists, who often dismiss these knowledge systems as not scientific and rigorous. How should environmental anthropologists respond to these kinds of claims?

14.4 How Are Industrial Agriculture, Economic Globalization, and Climate Change Linked to Increasing Environmental and Health Problems?

Industrial agriculture, economic globalization, and shifting climates are fueling change around the world, creating environmental problems and challenging health and sustainability. In analyzing these problems, anthropologists have found that environmental degradation results from a complex interplay of social, cultural, natural, and political-economic factors that relate to two important questions: How do people consume natural resources in their lifestyles and foodways? And who pays the cost of that consumption? In beginning to address these questions it is important to examine one of the most common—yet simplistic—explanations for environmental problems, which is population growth.

Population and Environment

Eighteenth-century theologian Thomas Malthus argued that human population grows exponentially, quickly overwhelming a limited resource base and leading to famine. Some modern environmentalists, such as Paul Ehrlich who in 1968 wrote a book with the alarming title *The Population Bomb* (Erlich 1968), have argued that the same is happening on a global scale in the world today. The problem seems self-evident: a small planet cannot indefinitely support a quickly expanding human population (now over 7 billion), and ecological ruin awaits us.

• **Carrying capacity.** The population an area can support.

There are several problems with this view. One is that social scientists have yet to identify any confirmed case of environmental and social collapse because of overpopulation or mass consumption (Tainter 2006) (see Chapter 11). Another is that humans have tended to adapt to the land's **carrying capacity**, which is the population an area can support, by developing new technologies, intensifying agriculture, or abandoning settlements and creating more simple forms of social organization, as discussed in Chapter 11. Sustainable social systems also often respond by adopting new cultural practices to cope with rapid ecological deterioration. In other words, they can be resilient, able to absorb change by changing social practices.

Anthropologists have also shown that the environmental disruptions that lead to famines are the result of a complex interplay of natural conditions and existing patterns of social inequality. For example, during the 1985 Ethiopian famine, Western aid and relief agencies like the World Food Program and the US Agency for International Development (USAID) argued that Ethiopia's population was too large, resulting in the overconsumption of natural resources, environmental collapse, and famine. Their solution was to implement programs of food relief and land reclamation projects to improve agricultural yield.

These programs failed, however, because the experts who conceived them misunderstood the complex causes of the famine. The experts based their models on exaggerated data about land degradation and ignored other data, particularly the disastrous effects of the country's civil war and socialist government, which disrupted food distribution channels. Insecure access to land also discouraged farmers from investing in traditional soil-conservation measures (Hoben 1995). This famine was not a consequence of overpopulation but the result of these other interrelated factors. No one of these factors by itself would have produced the famine and the environmental problems associated with it.

Ecological Footprint

In the Malthusian view, sustainability is a matter of controlling population where it seems to be growing most. But it does not address a simple fact: different societies, as well as people within those societies, consume differing amounts of resources. The concept of an **ecological footprint** addresses this issue by measuring what people consume and the waste they produce. It then calculates the amount of biologically productive land and water area needed to support them. As Figure 14.8 demonstrates, people in industrialized countries consume much more than people in non-industrialized countries (Wackernagel et al. 1997). Of course, these are just averages; some individuals consume more and others less, usually related to their relative wealth or poverty.

The distinction between the average Indian and the average North American as shown in the image is the latter's involvement in consumer capitalism. Consumer capitalism promotes the cultural ideal that people will never fully satisfy their needs, so they continually buy more things in their pursuit of happiness. This cultural ideal has enormous consequences for sustainability. We see these consequences in the production of goods (the extraction of non-renewable raw materials to make consumer products); the distribution of goods (the reliance on fossil fuels to transport goods to market); and the consumption of goods (the landfills that get filled with non-organic trash). As a result, while Americans make up only 5 percent of the world's population, they consume 25 percent of its resources. Most Americans do not understand the destructiveness of consumer lifestyles, although signs of it are everywhere: urban sprawl, polluted air and waterways, acid rain, unhealthy forests, climate change, and environmental health problems linked to contamination.

In most regions of the world, industrial agriculture has important impacts on a landscape. In recent decades, thanks to the **Green Revolution**—the transformation of agriculture in the developing world through agricultural research, technology transfer, and infrastructure development—rural communities throughout the world have felt pressure to shift from traditional modes of subsistence and agriculture to industrialized agriculture. Important global institutions such as the World Bank have encouraged many countries in Latin America and Africa to produce non-traditional agricultural exports, commodities like houseplants, flowers, and melons. The goal is to generate foreign revenue by exporting items that other countries do not have, so

- **Ecological footprint.** A quantitative tool that measures what people consume and the waste they produce. It also calculates the amount of biologically productive land and water area needed to support those people.

- **Green Revolution.** The transformation of agriculture in the developing world that began in the 1940s, through agricultural research, technology transfer, and infrastructure development.

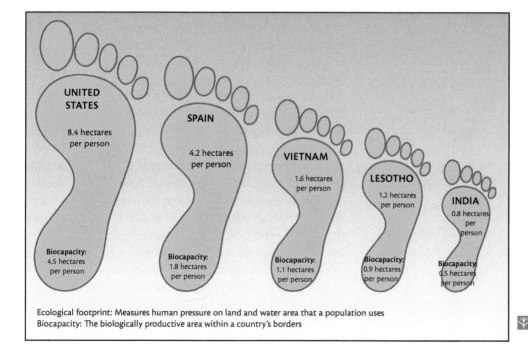

Ecological footprint: Measures human pressure on land and water area that a population uses
Biocapacity: The biologically productive area within a country's borders

Figure 14.8 The Ecological Footprints of Five Countries.

Anthropologist as Problem Solver
Urban Black Food Justice with Ashanté Reese

Across the United States, Black neighborhoods have fewer grocery stores and less access to fresh, affordable foods than white neighborhoods. Ashanté Reese, an anthropologist and assistant professor at the University of Maryland, Baltimore County, has conducted ethnographic research on how residents of the predominantly Black neighborhood of Deanwood in Washington, DC, navigate and resist the structural inequalities that create problems of food availability for them. She argues that unequal access to food is systemic, which reflects structural inequalities related to residential segregation, racism, and the practices of food retailers and corporations that shape who gets access to certain kinds of food (Reese 2019).

In the popular imagination, the terminology *food desert*—referring to a low-income place with no supermarkets or corner stores that sell little more than cigarettes, alcohol, and packaged food—is often attached to a neighborhood like Deanwood. But Reese argues that this terminology is not useful to really understand what is going on in urban Black neighborhoods. For one, *desert* connotes a barren and empty place, focusing on what is missing (supermarkets) and assuming that residents are passive and not interested in changing their situation (Reese 2019:8). Reese observed the opposite in Deanwood: aspirations and practices of individual and collective self-reliance and creative agency through which residents procure food. Residents do not let the absence of supermarkets define their foodways; they participate in communal gardening and informal exchanges in family networks, support a Black-owned community market and businesses, and shop outside the neighborhood. None of these are without struggles, tensions, and complications, but they reflect deeper histories of Black self-reliance in Deanwood that developed out of racial segregation.

Reese asserts that another problem with the desert terminology is that it tends to lead organizations to advocate for strategies of lending charitable support to treat the symptoms of hunger and poor-quality food in neighborhoods. What goes unaddressed are the patterns of spatial segregation, gentrification, crime, and poverty that affect local foodways, as well as the tendencies of chain retailers to make decisions on the basis of metrics that are tied to race, such as income, crime, concentrations of other businesses, etc. Food justice, Reese argues, is fundamentally about racial justice because race and racism shapes the everyday lives of residents and lead to the geographic, political, and economic disenfranchisement of Black communities (Reese 2019:11). The complexity of this problem is that, as she says, "food is never just about food" and it is just one concern among many facing urban Black communities (Reese 2019: 137).

Reese argues that the solutions to food insecurity for urban Black communities do not lie with what she calls the "global food regime"—the food corporations and large-scale retailers that increasingly control industrialized food systems—because it exploits and benefits from the dynamics of spatial segregation in the US food system. Neither does it lie simply in decisions of individual consumers to make changes in what or how they eat. Rather, she argues that we should look to Black communities themselves. Small-scale community-based collective action, such as the work of communal gardeners or the opening of cooperative markets, can make an important difference in people's lives by addressing multiple needs at once: providing access to

Ashanté Reese (right)

fresh and healthy foods, building institutional capacity, and creating community cohesion to confront other problems.

On a larger scale, Reese advocates for coalition and institution building between communities to share experiences, knowledge, and strategies. She points to the emergence of new alliances around race and food justice, as well as the adoption of healthy food issues by some racial justice movements, as signs that these things are beginning to take place.

Questions for Reflection

1. Reese observes that self-reliance is still often more aspiration than reality for many struggling residents of Deanwood. What kinds of pressures disrupt efforts at self-reliance?

2. What position do you think anthropologists can or should take within food justice struggles?

that the countries can make investments in domestic development and pay back loans to those international institutions.

For small-scale subsistence farmers in Honduras studied by anthropologist Susan Stonich (1993), these pressures have generated dilemmas. Since the 1950s, large commercial cotton plantations and cattle ranches have encroached on small farmers, pushing them into less productive land on mountain slopes. As commercial farms have gotten larger, the size of small farms has declined, causing many farmers to give up and migrate to the cities. Those who remain on the farm have shifted from subsistence agriculture to growing cash crops for export. The pressure to produce high yields has led them to deforest hillsides and abandon soil conservation measures that take more work because they are on steep land, both of which undermine the long-term fertility of their lands. Eventually farmers find themselves in a desperate situation in which they are aware, as the title of Stonich's book suggests, that they are "destroying the land!"

The shift from small-scale farming to producing cash crops for export can expose and deepen problems of structural vulnerability, social inequality, and insecure access to food. Increasingly, an important focus for anthropologists working in communities struggling to feed themselves is to document the power dynamics that create these conditions, as well as how those communities strive to gain control and self-determination over what they eat and grow. These studies are often in close alignment with food justice movements (Mares 2019). An illustration of this approach can be seen below in "Anthropologist as Problem Solver: Urban Black Food Justice with Ashanté Reese."

Analyses that focus on the linkages between political-economic power, social inequality, and ecological destruction are typical of the approach called **political ecology**. Many anthropologists who study environmental problems align themselves closely with political ecology, which rejects single-factor explanations, like overpopulation, ignorance, or poor land use, as explanations for environmental degradation, and focuses instead on the socio-environmental impacts of industrial economies.

- **Political ecology.** The field of study that focuses on the linkages between political-economic power, social inequality, and ecological destruction.

Industrial Foods, Sedentary Lives, and the Nutrition Transition

Even as they can provide a reliable source of food, industrialized foodways also have important consequences on people's health. One dimension of this problem is the role industrial foods have played in the dramatic global rise of people who are

- **Obesity.** Having excess body fat to the point of impairing bodily health and function.

- **Overweight.** Having an abnormally high accumulation of body fat.

- **Nutrition transition.** The combination of changes in diet toward energy-dense foods (high in calories, fat, and sugar) and declines in physical activity.

over-nourished, as reflected in growing global rates of **obesity**, which means having excess body fat to the point of impairing bodily health and function, and of **overweight**, or having abnormally high accumulation of body fat. There are now more people in the world who are suffering the effects of over-nourishment—estimated at 1 billion overweight and 475 million obese people—than people classified as undernourished, estimated at 875 million (Food and Agriculture Organization of the United Nations [FAO] 2012; International Obesity Task Force [IOTF] 2013). Because obesity and overweight can cause chronic diseases—diabetes and heart disease among them—health officials and researchers consider them to be among the most serious public health crises facing the world.

As we described in Chapter 3, obesity is a complex metabolic syndrome, or combination of medical conditions. Some individuals may be genetically predisposed to gain weight more easily than others, but obesity tends to develop in a person who eats a lot of food while expending little energy (Ulijaszek and Lofink 2006). Social factors influence how much food people eat and contribute directly to the production of obesity and overweight. These factors include the presence of other individuals at a meal, television viewing, portion size, cultural attitudes toward body fat, and learned preferences (Ulijaszek and Lofink 2006). Consider how powerful just one of these factors—television viewing—can be: in the United States during the 1990s, a child watched on average 10,000 television advertisements for food per year, with 95 percent of those foods being sugared cereal, sweets, fast food, and soft drinks, all of which are fattening (Brownell 2002).

The worldwide rise of obesity and overweight is also tied to a global **nutrition transition**, the combination of changes in diet toward energy-dense foods (high in calories, fat, and sugar) and declines in physical activity. These changes in diet are related to an abundant, secure, and inexpensive food supply, the very definition of success for industrial agriculture. But this success is double-edged, because the result is a food supply of relatively low nutritional quality, offering processed grains, fats, and refined sugars instead of fruits, vegetables, whole grains, and lean meats—the foods on which we thrive as a species. The other major change is the movement worldwide since the mid-nineteenth century of massive numbers of people away from rural areas, where they tend to lead physically active lives, to cities and suburbs, where they lead more sedentary lives and have more transportation options. For example, in 1900 only about 10 percent of the world population lived in cities. Today it is 50 percent, and rates of urbanization continue to be high around the world.

Both of these factors also explain why the problem of obesity is a problem not just in wealthy countries like the United States but also in poor countries. Because small-scale farms, which produce locally grown and nutrient-rich food, can rarely compete with the low-cost foods of transnational agribusinesses, many small-scale farms have shut down their operations. With fewer farms to support rural livelihoods, people then migrate to urban areas, where they tend to be less physically active.

Climate Change and Culture

In recent years, anthropologists have also turned their attention to climate change, offering perspectives on the nexus of nature, culture, science, politics, and belief that shapes ideas about its causes, government policies related to it, and the diverse ways people make cultural sense of it (Barnes and Dove 2015; Crate and Nuttall 2016). In the public sphere, it is common to hear that more and more local and global events—disasters, international conflicts, economic problems, and so on—are caused by climate change (Hulme 2017). But here anthropologists bring a holistic perspective to climate change, emphasizing that changing weather patterns or extreme weather

A World in Motion
Migrant Caravans, Global Warming, and Ecological Refugees

In recent years, "migrant caravans" have been departing from Central America's northern triangle—Guatemala, Honduras, and El Salvador—and heading for the northern border of Mexico in hopes of crossing into the United States. The largest of these caravans, which have included thousands of men, women, and children, have been organized by immigrant rights groups in the region. Traveling in such large groups is an innovative migratory strategy, allowing individuals to avoid the need to hire an expensive and sometimes dangerous "coyote" (smuggler) and to avoid predation by gangs or other criminals throughout Mexico (Alvarez 2019).

Conservative politicians in the United States have decried these caravans as an "invasion" of criminals, terrorists, gang members, and other undesirables. Lost in the anti-immigrant fear-mongering, however, was the fact that the vast majority of these migrants are among the region's most vulnerable people, seeking to escape threats of violence, economic stress and poverty, political instability, and the precarity of living on marginal agricultural lands. Still others are

🌱 **Migrant Caravan passing through Chiapas, Mexico, in 2018.**

ecological refugees forced to leave their rural livelihoods because of degradation of their local environments.

The environmental problems that have produced Central America's ecological refugees have been caused by economic policies and globalization processes, exacerbated by climate change, that have devastated small farmers. Central America has historically had seasonal cycles of precipitation interspersed with periods of irregular rainfall, something to which farmers have had to adapt for centuries. For example, in July and August there is a period of very little rainfall called the *canícula*. Farmers long ago figured out ways to prepare for and manage this period. But climate change has lengthened and intensified the *canícula*, creating new challenges for farmers (Miller 2017).

A bigger problem has to do with how global warming affects larger regional climate patterns. For example, every two to seven years, the cyclical El Niño Southern Oscillation occurs, which affects ocean temperatures and atmospheric patterns and leads to regional dryness, especially along Central America's Pacific side. Climate change has greatly impacted the severity of this cycle. A large El Niño between 2014 and 2016, and then another in 2018, produced unusually severe drought and widespread crop failures. At the same time, rainfall intensified in other parts of these countries, especially on the Caribbean side, causing flooding and devastating landslides.

The hardest hit by all this have typically been the most vulnerable people, chief among these being small-scale and subsistence farmers. It is many of those people whom we find in the migrant caravans. We should expect to see more of this in the coming years: as one scientist working on changing Central American climate patterns observed, "It's a paradigm of the wet gets wetter, the dry gets drier, the rich get richer, the poor get poorer. Everything gets more extreme" (Miller 2017:75).

events are but one of a number of environmental influences on people's actual lives. These patterns and events intersect in nuanced ways with local cultures and histories of colonialism, globalization, environmental risk, and vulnerability, often compounding problems but rarely being the primary cause of them (Marino 2015). Anthropologists also bring attention to the ways current patterns of industrial production and consumption related to climate change are already altering people's livelihood strategies and interactions with the economy and the environment (Crate 2008; Barnes and Dove 2015). As we explore below in "A World in Motion: Migrant Caravans, Global Warming, and Ecological Refugees," the intersection of all of these matters are related to recent Central American migrations to the United States.

Anthropologists have studied the social dynamics, cultural patterns, and institutional processes that shape how problems of climate are framed, studied, and communicated in the world of science (Crate and Nuttall 2016). Key to these social dynamics are tensions between scientific specialties that use different methods and theories, uncertainties and indeterminacies in climate modeling, and funding patterns that prioritize the reductionist perspectives of scientific authorities over the holistic perspectives of social scientists in the construction of public knowledge and policy (Lahsen 2015; Moore, Mankin, and Becker 2015).

Human societies have long dealt with climate variability, and different societies have different ways of conceptualizing that variability and adapting to it (Orlove 2005; Crate 2008). For example, as Roderick McIntosh (2015) has described, the Mande people of arid West Africa have long grappled with unpredictable and abrupt changes in precipitation and river patterns. They have developed their own climate ethnoscience in which certain individuals—"weather machines"—study their society's knowledge of long-term weather patterns and have the cultural authority to help shape community responses, which can include migration, shifts between pastoral

The Anthropological Life
Careers in Sustainability

Because of its sophisticated perspectives on the cultural dynamics that shape human–nature relations, an anthropological background is excellent preparation for careers related to sustainability, conservation, or food systems. Although some careers require more specialized education beyond the bachelor's degree, actual jobs of anthropology majors and minors have included these:

- Field researcher or policy analyst for a federal, state, or local government agency, such as the Environmental Protection Agency, Bureau of Land Management, or National Park Service

- Community liaison or organizer for a conservation, sustainable development, or social justice group

- Climate activism and advocacy, including work in alternative energy and active transportation sectors

- Field technician or project evaluator for an international development organization such as the Peace Corps, USAID, or CARE International

- Cultural resource manager for a natural area, archaeological site, or historic preservation district

- Organizational consultant for non-profits that work on sustainability issues like alternative transportation, anti-sprawl planning, or landscape protection

- Food system worker, ranging from farmer, chef/restauranteur, or food policy analyst to union organizer for farmworkers

- Public health official working at the intersections of environmental degradation and human health

- Lawyer for an environmental organization or government agency charged with environmental protection

- Environmental journalist, writer, documentary filmmaker, and/or researcher

- Environmental educator in schools or community organizations

and horticultural economies, and modifications of agricultural practices. Flexibility, resilience, and finely tuned knowledge of local ecology lie at the heart of the Mande understandings of how to deal with climate variability and change. Traditions of climate adaptability like these exist all over the world where people have lived with extreme weather patterns even before the dynamics of contemporary climate change emerged, including the Pacific Islands, the Arctic, Himalayan and Andean high mountain areas, and other regions. Nevertheless, it is important to note that these traditions have also been profoundly strained by social changes, government policies and institutions that misunderstand or dismiss those traditions, and other forces of change. All of these issues suggest broader lessons for the rest of us as we begin to better understand the effects of climate change globally.

Clearly, anthropology has a lot to offer in developing a better understanding of human–climate intersections. In fact, as we explore in the "Anthropological Life" box, anthropology has a lot to offer for individuals interested in working in practically any aspect of sustainability.

THINKING LIKE AN ANTHROPOLOGIST: SUSTAINABILITY

There is perhaps no more consequential issue for the future of human environmental and bodily health than the changing foodways in the contemporary world. What role do you think anthropologists of food should play in the issues of changing foodways? What specific kinds of knowledge or interventions do you think are most appropriate for anthropologists?

14.5 Are Industrialized Western Societies the Only Ones to Conserve Nature?

In 1872, the creation of the world's first national park, Yellowstone, ushered in a new era of modern nature conservation with global effects. Around the world today, hundreds of millions of acres of wilderness landscape and ocean are formally protected. In many cases, these efforts have stemmed the tide of near-certain destruction from extractive industries, settlement, or uncontrolled exploitation.

At the same time, the dominant cultural model for administering protected areas is based on the separation of humans and nature. It emphasizes that nature must be kept uninhabited by people, and it has led to forced evictions of indigenous peoples and generated significant social conflict (Colchester 2003; Chapin 2004). Anthropologists have studied these dynamics closely, approaching the resulting conflicts as rooted in distinct cultural approaches toward nature's protection.

In exploring whether or not non-Western societies have had similar intentions to conserve and protect nature, it is necessary to overcome a powerful stereotype that native peoples are "natural environmentalists" always in tune with the natural world (Figure 14.9). Anthropologists have documented many examples of destructive indigenous relationships with nature, among them "aboriginal overkill" that led to human-caused

Figure 14.9   Stereotypes of Green Indians. In 1971, the "Keep America Beautiful" campaign developed by the US government aired an antipollution television ad featuring an American Indian (actually an Italian American actor with the stage name of Iron Eyes Cody) who sheds a tear because of pollution. There is usually a large gap between such romantic stereotypes and the real conditions in which indigenous groups relate to their environments.

extinctions of certain animals toward the end of the Pleistocene epoch (Ice Age) (Krech 1999). The key to answering this section's question is to consider first how indigenous societies have created landscapes that either deliberately or unintentionally have the effect of protecting natural ecosystems and wildlife, and second the ways in which Western societies approach the same objective.

Anthropogenic Landscapes

- **Anthropogenic landscape.** A landscape modified by human action in the past or present.

Upon close examination, many landscapes that appear "natural" to Westerners—sometimes the very landscapes that Westerners want to conserve without people on them—are actually the result of indigenous involvement and manipulation. In other words, they are **anthropogenic landscapes**, or landscapes modified by human action in the past or present (see Chapter 3).

An important example of an anthropogenic landscape is the East African savannas of northern Tanzania and southern Kenya. The Maasai, who live there as pastoralists, have extensively modified their environment to support their cattle. They burn scrub brush to encourage the growth of nutritious pasture grass, an act that helps support wildlife biodiversity because these are the same nutritious pastures that the savanna's world-famous wildlife populations of zebras, wildebeest, and other large animals also eat (Igoe 2004). But today, some of these fragile scrublands are in crisis because of overgrazing by Maasai cattle. To understand why they now overgraze, we must look at the clash between Western and Maasai notions of managing nature.

The Culture of Modern Nature Conservation

To prevent overgrazing and to conserve resources for themselves and wildlife populations, Maasai traditionally practiced a form of pastoralism called *transhumant pastoralism*, in which they range over large territories of commonly held property on regular paths and cycles. During drought years, when pastures are most susceptible to overgrazing, the Maasai would traditionally bring cattle to swamp areas and permanent waterholes. But during the twentieth century, national parks and nature reserves were formed around these permanent wet areas (since a lot of wild animals congregate there, too), preventing Maasai access to them. Park administrators and scientists did not understand the delicate balance between people and wildlife that was sustained by the constant movement of people, their herds, and the wild animals. The result is that the Maasai were forced to overgraze areas outside the park during drought periods, creating great resentment among the Maasai, which has generated conflicts with park officials (Igoe 2004).

These park officials practice what anthropologist Dan Brockington (2002) calls "Fortress Conservation," an approach to conservation that assumes that local people threaten nature, and that for nature to be pristine the people who live there must be evicted. This approach was undergirded by the philosophical divide that Western cultures imposed between people and nature, and was enabled by European and American colonial expansion, which commonly instituted controls on native people's use of natural resources (Grove 1995).

Environmentalism's Alternative Paradigms

Anthropologists recognize that the displacement of local people for the purposes of conserving nature can be counterproductive, producing exclusion, resistance, and social tension. But we also recognize that environmentalism has multiple expressions.

During the past several decades there have been a number of experiments in "co-management" between national or international conservation groups and indigenous people. In places like Nepal, Alaska, Canada, Panama, Brazil, and Australia, indigenous people have been allowed to continue living in protected areas and have some say in park management. This collaborative approach creates new kinds of opportunities for dialogue, power sharing, and relationship building between conservationists and indigenous communities (Natcher, Hickey, and Hickey 2005). But this approach can also create new dilemmas for indigenous communities; outside conservation groups still exercise considerable control, especially over funding, and scientists often disrespect indigenous knowledge about wildlife and landscape dynamics even though they are supposed to be "co-managing" the resources with the indigenous community (Igoe 2004:158; Nadasdy 2005).

At the heart of co-management is a move toward recognizing and redressing how social inequalities and injustices affect possibilities for conservation and environmental sustainability. An even stronger approach along these lines is the **environmental justice** movement, a social movement that addresses the linkages between racial discrimination and injustice, social equity, and environmental quality (Figure 14.10).

Environmental justice is now a global movement, and unlike environmentalism oriented toward creating nature preserves that tend to focus on scenic landscapes and biodiversity, it tends to be organized around the defense of a people's livelihood and social justice concerns (Guha 2000:105). Marshall Islanders, for example, have been active in this movement, framing their situation as rooted in problems related to outsider control and domination, including nuclear fallout, sea level rise, economic underdevelopment, and poor public health, that undermine local self-determination and livelihoods.

Figure 14.10 The Birth of Environmental Justice. Environmental justice was born in the early 1980s, when a toxic waste dump was proposed in Warren County, North Carolina, the poorest county in the state and where 84 percent of residents were African American. Civil rights leaders organized a protest, arguing that these facts, not the ecological suitability of the site to store toxic waste, motivated the decision to build the waste dump in their county.

• **Environmental justice.** A social movement addressing the linkages between racial discrimination and injustice, social equity, and environmental quality.

THINKING LIKE AN ANTHROPOLOGIST: SUSTAINABILITY

Americans often assume that people interested in conserving nature tend to be middle-class people who give money to environmental groups because they have money left over after meeting their basic needs. In other words, protecting nature is a luxury that poor people cannot afford. Based on what we have discussed in this section, why is this view skewed?

Conclusion

Anthropologists agree that we must pay close attention to the social practices and structures that shape the way communities relate to their natural environments. When we do, we can see that non-industrialized people often have a deep understanding of their environments, and they routinely understand the behaviors of animals and plants as well as, if not better than, scientists from other regions. In such communities, the cultural landscape envisions nature differently than do people in the West, often using metaphors that express people's reciprocal ties to the land, or as the Marshallese case that opened this chapter demonstrates, drawing on social, political, and spiritual strategies that protect ecosystems from exploitation.

The cultural landscape of human–nature separation that we see in modern conservation initiatives has only recently begun to appreciate these facts. Historically, Western industrialized countries have designed conservation programs that expel indigenous peoples from landscapes those peoples may have lived on sustainably for many years, even living in ways that support the biodiversity of other species, as is the case of the Maasai.

Anthropologists also agree that careful use of natural resources is the basis of a sustainable society. As a result, it is important to look critically at the world's ecological crisis. But the causes of our current problems—as was the case in past ecological crises—cannot be reduced to any single source. We have to consider factors like elite mismanagement of resources, poor government policy choices, inflexible responses to change, and consumption patterns that extract key resources and create waste. We also have to consider who pays the cost of these patterns and realize that questions of unequal access to resources and social patterns of injustice are often at the heart of the world's key ecological crises.

KEY TERMS

Animal husbandry   p. 406

Anthropogenic landscape
    p. 420

Carrying capacity   p. 412

Cultural landscape   p. 402

Ecological footprint   p. 413

Environmental
    anthropology   p. 402

Environmental justice   p. 421

Ethnobiology   p. 410

Ethnoscience   p. 402

Foodways   p. 404

Green Revolution   p. 413

Horticulture   p. 405

Industrial agriculture   p. 407

Intensification   p. 406

Modes of subsistence   p. 404

Nutrition transition   p. 416

Obesity   p. 416

Overweight   p. 416

Pastoralist society   p. 406

Political ecology   p. 415

Swidden agriculture   p. 405

Taste   p. 408

Traditional ecological
    knowledge   p. 410

Reviewing the Chapter

Chapter Section	What We Know	To Be Resolved
Do all people see nature in the same way?	Different cultures have different ways of conceptualizing the boundaries between humans and the natural world. Metaphors often play a major role in these conceptualizations.	Anthropologists continue to debate the extent to which general conceptual models and metaphors, or the material forces of nature itself, shape human relations with the environment.
How do people secure an adequate, meaningful, and environmentally sustainable food supply?	Humans have developed four general modes of subsistence—foraging, horticulture, pastoralism, and intensive agriculture—each of which carries certain social and environmental trade-offs and opportunities. Cultural meanings also play a central role in shaping how people acquire, share, and consume foods.	Although they are under great pressure in a world increasingly dominated by industrial and other forms of intensive agriculture, foragers, horticulturalists, and pastoralists still persist. Anthropologists are working to understand how and why they persist, as well as the pressures on these modes of subsistence. In addition, anthropologists continue to work through how cultural attitudes and social practices surrounding food relate to social categories and dynamics such as class, race, ethnicity, and gender.

Chapter Section	What We Know	To Be Resolved
How does non-Western knowledge of nature and agriculture relate to science?	Different societies have developed highly systematic and sophisticated knowledge systems for classifying the natural world, some of which resemble closely Western science. Unlike Western science, however, which views its methods and findings as universally applicable, these knowledge systems are often highly localized and customized to particular ecosystems and rooted in local moralities.	Anthropologists are still working to understand the specific ways in which traditional ecological knowledge shapes practices of ecological and agricultural management, as well as how it is changing to adapt to new challenges, such as climate change.
How are industrial agriculture, economic globalization, and climate change linked to increasing environmental and health problems?	The ecological impact of a society depends on its ecological footprint, or the amount of natural resources people require to live their lifestyles. Industrial agriculture's rapid expansion around the globe is related closely to unequal political-economic relationships, and creates new environmental and health risks.	Anthropologists are still identifying the conditions under which social groups can adopt new cultural ideas and practices that promote resilience and sustainability. Anthropologists are also relatively new to public health policy discussions about critical issues, like food security and obesity, and have just begun to define the anthropological dimensions of these issues. One area where anthropological research has relevance is in studying how societies and social groups understand and adapt to climate change.
Are industrialized Western societies the only ones to conserve nature?	While Western conservation practice is based on the separation of humans and nature, the stewardship traditions of non-Western societies often start from principles that view humans as important actors in nature. Western nature conservation practices have often disrupted and marginalized local cultures, many of which have had highly successful adaptations to their environments.	As some conservationists have realized new opportunities of co-managing natural resources with indigenous communities, anthropologists are divided over whether these approaches actually benefit indigenous communities.

READINGS

There are several good general overviews of the field of environmental anthropology, among them Patricia Townsend's *Environmental Anthropology: From Pigs to Policies*, 2nd ed. (Long Grove, IL: Waveland Press, 2008) and Nora Haenn and Richard Wilk's edited reader *The Environment in Anthropology: A Reader in Ecology, Culture, and Sustainable Living* (New York: New York University Press, 2005).

Two books that explore dimensions of indigenous ways of knowing and interacting with natural environment include Roberto Gonzalez's study of farming in southern Mexico, *Zapotec Science: Farming and Food in the Northern Sierra of Oaxaca* (Austin: University of Texas Press, 2001), and ethnobotanist Gary Paul Nabhan's *Cultures of Habitat: On Nature, Culture, and Story* (Washington, DC: Counterpoint, 1997).

To explore how differences between insider and outsider understandings of landscapes generate conflicts over conservation, read James Fairhead and Melissa Leach's 1996 book *Misreading the African Landscape: Society and Ecology in a Forest-Savanna Mosaic* (Cambridge: Cambridge University Press, 1996) and James Igoe's book *Conservation and Globalization: A Study of National Parks and Indigenous Communities from East Africa to South Dakota* (Belmont, CA: Wadsworth, 2004).

An excellent overview of the relationship between food and culture can be found in Eugene Anderson's *Everyone Eats: Understanding Food and Culture* (New York: New York University Press, 2005). It pairs well with Raj Patel's book *Stuffed and Starved: The Hidden Battle for the World Food System* (London: Melville House Press, 2008) or Carole Counihan and Penny Van Esterik's 1997 edited volume *Food and Culture: A Reader* (New York: Routledge, 1997).

There are numerous edited volumes full of ethnographic case studies of climate change experiences around the world. Susan Crate and Mark Nuttall's *Anthropology and Climate Change: From Encounters to Actions*, 2nd ed. (New York: Routledge, 2016) is one of those worth reading.

Power

Politics and Social Control

ACCESS TO WATER is an urgent problem in many parts of the world, producing countless stories of daily suffering and struggles for something basic to life itself. One of those stories is the experience of people living in a settlement called Meghwadi, which is in Jogeshwari, a suburb of Mumbai, India. Meghwadi was established some thirty years ago by poor migrants and is classified by the state as a "recognized slum," making it eligible for municipal services such as electricity, garbage collection, and fresh water (Anand 2017). But getting water is a daily struggle: water pressure tends to be very low, complete shutdowns are common, and crumbling infrastructure creates constant leaking and clogs. Mumbai has an enormous water department but residents of poor and marginalized settlements like Meghwadi receive very little attention from it. Although Indian law provides universal equality, the government still does not quite treat such residents as citizens with full rights or equal access to public goods (Anand 2017).

Residents have largely taken matters into their own hands, seeking water connections through protests, petitions, and direct negotiations with department workers. However, any gains are unstable and temporary, so they have also employed local plumbers and drawn on their own home-grown expertise to create, repair, and maintain their own pipes and pumps that tap into and divert city water. A lot of this technical and political action is based on cooperation among neighbors. Residents use all of these

---

Water Politics and Infrastructure in Mumbai.   Access to water in Mumbai is both a technical and a political problem. For people who live in urban settlements and slums, it is an especially acute daily struggle.

water-related activities—as well the many forms, bills, and applications required when interacting with the water department—as tangible demonstrations to other branches of city government that they are good, recognized citizens (Anand 2017).

It is common to think of politics as an arena of formal constitutions and laws, legal procedures and courts, the activities of political parties and politicians, and the like. But the picture of politics here is more subtle and dynamic. The state does not have complete control or authority, and residents gain, maintain, and lose water connections through complex and ongoing social processes that move across and between formal spheres of city government and informal spaces of everyday life. In this situation, assumed dichotomies—powerful/powerless, citizen/noncitizen, legal/illegal—break down.

- **Politics.** Those relationships and processes of cooperation, conflict, and power that are fundamental aspects of human life.

To accommodate such dynamics, anthropologists take a broad view of **politics**, defining it as the relationships and processes of cooperation, conflict, social control, and power that are fundamental aspects of human life. There is considerable variety in how people think about politics and their reasons for engaging in "political" acts. It might be to enrich themselves materially or spiritually; to help their families, friends, or a social group they belong to; to pursue personal power; to resolve a conflict; or to seek dignity or freedom from oppression. It might be to produce relative order in a chaotic situation—or to produce chaos in a relatively ordered situation.

People also exert power in diverse ways. Some of these are formal and fairly stable, through institutions and procedures—government offices, armies, codified laws, rituals, or legal proceedings—that are easily identifiable elements of most societies. Others are less formal and more fleeting, such as the creation of temporary alliances, acts of protest, manipulation, accusation, sorcery, and shame. Political acts may draw attention to or disguise the true source of power. Techniques include coercion, oppression, persuasion, and influence, as well as truth-seeking, collecting and sharing information, and wanting to know intimate details about people's lives.

This approach to politics moves beyond the idea that modern states should be the sole focus of anthropological interest. Even though states are the dominant political form in our contemporary world, the actual practices of modern states are not the same everywhere. More important is the diversity in how people around the world manage power relations at all levels of social life, from the interpersonal to the national and transnational.

Thus, at the heart of anthropology's approach to politics is a key question: *How is power acquired and transmitted in a society?* We can answer this question by considering a number of related questions around which this chapter is organized:

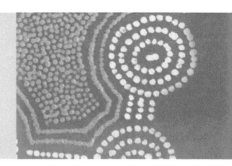

Does every society have a government?

What is political power?

How is social inequality constructed and upheld?

Why do some societies seem more violent than others?

How do people avoid aggression, brutality, and war?

For anthropologists, politics is about how people manage their everyday social relationships through force, influence, persuasion, and control over resources. We begin here by examining the opportunities and pitfalls of thinking about politics solely in terms of how formal political systems work.

15.1 Does Every Society Have a Government?

This question might seem strange because the answer seems obvious. Our society has **government** (a separate legal and constitutional domain that is the source of law, order, and legitimate force) from federal to local levels. We may assume other societies must have something similar. Otherwise, wouldn't they be in the throes of anarchy?

Not necessarily. Consider the Ju/'hoansi (one of bands of !Kung San), a hunter-gatherer society in the Kalahari Desert of southern Africa. Ju/'hoansi have historically lived in egalitarian bands of fifteen to twenty people, and are an **acephalous society**—that is, they have no governmental head or hierarchical structure. Until they were brought under the control of the Namibian and South African governments, Ju/'hoansi had no notion of a distinct political sphere, and important band decisions were made by group consensus. Leadership was informal, life was organized around sharing food, and those who did not share were taunted and shamed, even pushed out of the band (Figure 15.1). The emphasis on sharing and egalitarianism kept people more or less in line without the need for government or **laws**, or rules established by some formal authority.

If governments are not a universal feature of human existence, why do we tend to think of politics primarily in terms of how formal governments work? Part of the reason is historical, the other part philosophical.

- **Government.** A separate legal and constitutional domain that is the source of law, order, and legitimate force.

- **Acephalous society.** A society without a governing head, generally with no hierarchical leadership.

- **Laws.** Sets of rules established by some formal authority.

The Idea of "Politics" and the Problem of Order

Our modern notion of politics emerged during the Enlightenment (1650–1800), a period of social upheaval in Western Europe in which the rise of industrial capitalism and revolutionary democracies challenged the existing social and political order. Two of the major figures concerned with the problem of disorder caused by these changes were the English philosophers Thomas Hobbes (1588–1679) and John Locke (1632–1704). Hobbes believed that humans are naturally selfish, competitive, and warlike, leading to violence and a chaotic free-for-all as people pursue their own personal interests, a condition avoided only by the absolute rule of a monarch (Hobbes 1909). Locke argued that chaos was avoidable by creating a more limited government based on a "social contract" in which certain basic individual rights are recognized (Locke 2003). This is our modern idea—and justification—for democratic government, and it is what modern politicians refer to when they talk about the "rule of law."

Figure 15.1   The Power of Sharing. In many hunter-gatherer societies, such as the !Kung San pictured here, individuals are obligated to share their goods, especially food. This obligation represents a powerful force for ensuring social stability.

- **Structural-functionalism.** An anthropological theory that the different structures or institutions of a society (religion, politics, kinship, etc.) function to maintain social order and equilibrium.

- **Age-grades.** Groupings of age-mates, who are initiated into adulthood together.

- **Band.** A small, nomadic, and self-sufficient group of anywhere from 25 to 150 individuals with face-to-face social relationships, usually egalitarian.

- **Tribe.** A type of pastoral or horticultural society with populations usually numbering in the hundreds or thousands in which leadership is more stable than that of a band, but usually egalitarian, with social relations based on reciprocal exchange.

Structural-Functionalist Models of Political Stability

During the early twentieth century, the global expansion of British colonialism helped fuel the rise of anthropology in the United Kingdom. Colonial authorities often turned to anthropologists to help them make sense of the foreign societies now under British control. This situation presented British anthropologists with important opportunities for studying the maintenance of order in societies without formal governments and political leaders. The theory they developed was **structural-functionalism**, which held that the different structures of a society (such as religion, politics, kinship, etc.) functioned in an integrated way to maintain social order and control.

In Africa, structural-functionalists identified numerous ways societies maintained order and social control without formal political institutions (Radcliffe-Brown 1952). For example, kinship could work, as it did among the Nuer pastoralists of Sudan, to organize men into lineages that would normally live separately but would come together to meet external threats. The division of men from different families into associations like **age-grades**, which are groupings of age-mates who are initiated into adulthood together, such as among the Maasai of Kenya and Tanzania, could work as a rudimentary political system (Kurtz 2001). Throughout Africa, for example, beliefs in witchcraft or sorcery can also promote order. People who do not behave according to community norms are identified and punished as witches, which can maintain social conformity. Without formal courts, structural-functionalists insisted, such practices maintain social control and operate as a simple criminal justice system (Gledhill 2000).

Neo-Evolutionary Models of Political Organization: Bands, Tribes, Chiefdoms, and States

In the 1940s and 1950s, as political anthropology was taking shape in the United States, American anthropologists called *neo-evolutionists* sought to classify the world's diversity of political systems and explain how complex political systems, especially states, had evolved from simpler forms of social and political organization.

Anthropologists Marshall Sahlins and Elman Service (1960) suggested a typology of societies with different forms of political and economic organization. By considering who controls food and other resources in any given society, they defined four types of society: **bands**, **tribes**, **chiefdoms**, and **states**. Bands and tribes in this scheme were examples of **non-centralized political systems**, in which power and control over resources are dispersed among members of the society. Chiefdoms and states were examples of **centralized political systems**, in which certain individuals and institutions hold power and control over resources. Table 15.1 outlines how this classification incorporates politics, economy, size, and population density.

Challenges to Traditional Political Anthropology

Political anthropology's early focus on political systems was valuable for describing the diverse ways in which humans create and maintain social order, with or without formal governments. But reality hardly ever corresponds to simple theoretical models. A major problem, for instance, with the bands-tribes-chiefdoms-states typology is that many cases blur the boundaries between types. Societies like the Nuer and Dinka of South Sudan might have tribe-like qualities—no central authority—but because they have a population of 1.8 million people, they do not have the same kinds of social relations as a "tribe" of 500 people. For example, recent fighting between Nuer and Dinka people resembles the small-scale tribal fighting observed by anthropologist E. E. Evans-Pritchard (1940) before World War II, except that Nuer and Dinka

- **Chiefdom.** A political system with a hereditary leader who holds central authority, typically supported by a class of high-ranking elites, informal laws, and a simple judicial system. The population often numbers in the tens of thousands with the beginnings of intensive agriculture and some specialization.

- **State.** The most complex form of political organization, associated with societies that have intensive agriculture, high levels of social stratification, and centralized authority.

TABLE 15.1	A NEO-EVOLUTIONARY TYPOLOGY OF POLITICAL ORGANIZATION			
	NON-CENTRALIZED		CENTRALIZED	
	Band	**Tribe**	**Chiefdom**	**State**
Type of subsistence	Foraging	Horticulture and pastoralism	Extensive agriculture, intensive fishing	Intensive agriculture
Population density	Low	Low to medium	Medium	High
Type of economic exchange	Reciprocity	Reciprocity and trade	Redistribution through chief, reciprocity at lower levels	Markets and trade; redistribution through state, based on taxation
Social stratification	Egalitarian	Egalitarian	Ranked	Social classes
Ownership of property	Little or no sense of personal ownership	Lineage or clan ownership of land and livestock	Lineage or clan ownership of land, but with strong sense of personal ownership	Private and state ownership of land
Type of leadership	Informal and situational; headman	Charismatic headman with some authority in group decision-making	Charismatic chief with limited power, usually based on giving benefits to followers	Sovereign leader supported by aristocratic bureaucracy
Law and legitimate control of force	No formal laws or punishments; right to use force is communal	No formal laws or punishments; right to use force is held by lineage, clan, or association	May have informal laws and specified punishments; chief has limited access to coercion	Formal laws and punishments; state holds all access to use of physical force
Some examples	!Kung San (Southern Africa); Inuit (Canada, Alaska); Batek (Malaysia)	Yanomamo (South America); Nuer (Sudan); Cheyenne (United States)	Kwakiutl (Canada, Alaska); precolonial Hawai'i	Aztec (Mexico); Inca (Peru); Euro-American monarchies and representative democracies

Source: Adapted from Lewellen 1983:20–21.

- **Non-centralized political system.** A political system, such as a band or a tribe, in which power and control over resources are dispersed among members of the society.

- **Centralized political system.** A political system, such as a chiefdom or a state, in which certain individuals and institutions hold power and control over resources.

tribesmen are now using modern weapons of war with devastating results (see, e.g., Pendle 2014; Verini 2014).

The emphasis on static political systems and order came at the expense of understanding the dynamic nature of political processes, characterized by conflict, intrigue, manipulation, and other techniques. As the British anthropologist Lucy Mair (1969) pointed out, political structures only provide individuals with roles. Within a role, individuals make choices and decisions, manipulate others, and strategize, all in the pursuit of power. From this point of view, the proper focus of political anthropology is political power, an issue we turn to next.

THINKING LIKE AN ANTHROPOLOGIST: POWER

A complex institution like a college or university has many ways of governing the faculty, staff, and student body. These include formal institutions, such as a faculty senate, president's office, and disciplinary committees of various kinds, as well as less formal associations and belief structures that help maintain order. What are some of these less formal forms of governance, and how do they contribute to the maintenance of order?

15.2 What Is Political Power?

The shift from viewing politics as a problem of order to the problem of how people gain and wield power began to flourish in the 1960s and continues to the present. Power is the ability to make people think or act in certain ways, through physical coercion or through more symbolic means, such as persuasion (Kingsolver 1996). Beyond this very general definition, however, there are many nuances to political power.

Defining Political Power

Whether it is an exchange of goods, a religious ceremony, or a conversation between a man and a woman, practically all aspects of human existence are imbued with power. But not all power is *political*. For anthropologists, **political power** refers to how power is created and enacted to attain goals that are presumed to be for the good of a community, the common good (Kurtz 2001:21).

- **Political power.** The process by which people create, compete, and use power to attain goals that are presumed to be for the good of a community.

The exercise of political power requires legitimacy. Legitimacy can come from an independent source—a source outside the individuals that make up a community—such as gods or ancestors, inheritance, high office, the ability to cure an illness, or the outcome of some legal process, such as an election. Or it can come from a dependent source, that is, power given by other social actors: *granted* from one leader to another, *delegated* from a leader to a follower for a specific purpose, or *allocated* by the community to a leader (Kurtz 2001:26).

In addition, political power is tied to control over material resources (territory, money, or other culturally defined goods); human resources (willing followers and supporters); and symbolic resources (flags, uniforms, badges of rank, or other objects that give meaning to political action) (see also Chapter 11). There are other important dimensions to political power.

Political Power Is Action Oriented

People everywhere gain and manage political power through a combination of decision-making, cooperation, opportunism, compromise, collusion, charm, gamesmanship, strategic alliance, factionalism, resistance, conflict, and other processes. A focus on these processes was central to **action theory**, an approach that emerged in the 1960s. Action theorists closely followed the daily activities and decision-making processes of individual political leaders like chiefs in African villages or headmen in Amazonian settlements. They argued that politics is a dynamic and competitive field of social relations in which people are constantly managing their ability to exercise power over others (Vincent 1978). In other words, it is not enough to *be* president of the United States. One has to *act* as the president.

To follow political action, one must be familiar with a society's specific rules and codes about who gets to exercise power and under what conditions. Anthropologist F. G. Bailey (1969) compared these codes to those of playing a game. In politics, as in a game, there are *normative rules*, stable and explicit ethical norms by which players must abide, such as honesty, fairness, and so on. There are also *pragmatic rules*, which are the creative manipulations necessary to win the game itself. For example, in US politics, normative rules require political actors to be open, fair, and honest. But we know, based on reading the political news in the newspaper, that there are also the pragmatic rules of gaining and holding onto power, which often involve favoritism and even outright lying (Lewellen 2003).

With insights like this about how politics works up close, you might wonder if anthropology offers special insights for those who might want to pursue a career in politics—see "The Anthropological Life" for an answer.

- **Action theory.** An approach in the anthropological study of politics that closely follows the daily activities and decision-making processes of individual political leaders, emphasizing that politics is a dynamic and competitive field of social relations in which people are constantly managing their ability to exercise power over others.

The Anthropological Life
An Anthropological Politician?

Favoritism, lying, and scheming aside, an anthropological background can be quite advantageous for those seeking careers in politics or public office. Numerous people with anthropological backgrounds have gotten involved in the formal political sphere, including several who have served as heads of state, among them Jomo Kenyatta (president of Kenya, 1964–1978), Kwame Nkrumah (president of Ghana, 1960–1966), and Ashraf Ghani (president of Afghanistan, 2014–2021). Some people even referred to President Barack Obama as the "anthropologist-in-chief"; his mother, Ann Dunham, had a PhD in cultural anthropology, and he too was known for his sensitivity to cross-cultural perspectives (Rodman 2017).

According to Deborah Rodman, an anthropologist who served in the Virginia House of Delegates between 2018 and 2020, the study of anthropology offers excellent preparation for working in politics. The perspectives and relationships one cultivates while conducting ethnographic research is one key reason. As she explains (Rodman 2017), "While politicians base their choices on opinion polls and focus groups, we take a nonjudgmental attitude and maintain a keen interest in learning about others to develop a real understanding of people's lives and their views. We work with cultures that have very different takes on the world than we do, but we see the issues through their eyes. We do this by building trust, observing, listening, documenting patterns and connecting them to larger social, political, and historical trends." Equally important, Rodman observes, is that anthropologists can serve as neutral bridge builders between people who have different perspectives and attitudes.

Political Power Is Structural

- **Structural power.** Power that not only operates within settings but also organizes and orchestrates the settings in which social and individual actions take place.

It became clear to political anthropologists by the 1980s and 1990s that certain power relationships transcend any individual. Political anthropologists began to refer to such power as **structural power**, which is power that not only operates within settings but also organizes and orchestrates the settings in which social and individual action take place (Wolf 2001:384). "Structure" here means something very different from how the early structural-functionalists understood it. They were interested in social institutions ("structures," as a noun), while this newer perspective focuses on the processes and relationships that shape or "structure" (as a verb) social action and relationships.

In this view, power does not lie in a group or individual's exercise of will over others through domination or manipulation but is dispersed in many shapes and forms, produced and reproduced through the combined actions of social institutions, science, and other knowledge producers, and people living their everyday lives (Foucault 1978). Anthropologist David Horn (1994) used this approach to study how and why Italians of today accept state intervention in their lives. He traces their acceptance to the rise of social thought, planning, and research around the reproductive health of Italian families after World War I. During this period, the Italian government instituted a census and other programs to measure statistically the population's size, growth rate, and health conditions. Using this information, they instituted new policies of hygiene and family management, including (among others) a 1927 tax on bachelorhood and efforts to eliminate contraception and abortion. Although many of these policies failed, Horn observes that these changes had an important effect on Italians, in that they came to accept the idea that the body is not simply the domain of a private individual but a social problem that requires scientific and state intervention. As a result, they began to willingly accept that they should share intimate details about their reproductive lives with the state and that the state has the right to issue directives intended to manage citizens' lives—all of which are ideas that Italians take for granted today.

Political Power Is Gendered

During the past forty years, feminist anthropologists have observed that while men tend to dominate formal political processes in most societies, relationships between men and women intersect with political power in complex ways. In a number of societies, women exercise formal leadership and political power. In other settings, women may have very little formal power, but they can mobilize to assert power in response to events.

In many societies, women may be so disempowered that their ability to take direct action lies only in the most dramatic action of all, taking one's own life. For example, on the island of New Britain in Papua New Guinea, "revenge suicide" occurs when a woman takes her own life in response to abuse or shame by a man or his extended family (Figure 15.2). Here young women are powerless figures. But a woman's act of suicide shifts the burden of shame to her tormentor (often a husband) and can mobilize her male relatives and other community members to acknowledge the injustice and seek accountability from the offending party (Counts 1980). Although taking such actions may be difficult for many Westerners to comprehend, this situation suggests that we must consider forms of political power that are available to those we do not conventionally understand to be "powerful."

Political Power in Non-State Societies

To some extent, the exercise of political power differs between state and non-state societies. For example, in non-state societies such as tribal societies of South America and Melanesia, power tends to be temporary and episodic, emerging from personal

Figure 15.2   Revenge Suicide in New Guinea. This painting by contemporary Papua New Guinea artist Apa Hugo from 2003 illustrates how suicide can be used as a weapon of the weak. The caption in pidgin English written on the canvas means: "A man fights with his wife and the wife commits suicide. Her parents are distraught and cry in mourning" (Man krosim meri na—meri I wari na i go sua sait. Na papa mama i wari na karai i stap).

charisma, not elections or inheritance. The Amazon headman, for example, is a "first among equals." He assumes his status as leader by being able to persuade followers, not because he controls power or resources on his own. Such leaders, who are sometimes called Big Men, cannot transfer their status and power through inheritance when they die.

A Big Man cannot force others to do anything but gains influence and authority by giving away wealth and shrewdly persuading others, through a combination of smooth talk and peer pressure, to produce goods they will provide to him, which he can then redistribute. In their 1970 documentary film *The Feast*, filmmaker Timothy Asch and anthropologist Napoleon Chagnon (1997) show how a Yanomamo headman in southern Venezuela sponsors a feast aimed at building an alliance with another community with which his own community had recently been at war. As headman, he could not force anyone to help clear the plaza or cook the plantain soup that would be the centerpiece of the feast. His loud haranguing did little to motivate his fellow clan members, but he led by example and his clansmen started helping and made it a successful feast, forming a new alliance. Persuasion was his most valuable tool.

In contrast to the status leadership of a Big Man, the kind of political power your hometown mayor, especially in smaller cities, has is a quintessential expression of how political power works in a state society. Your mayor is an officeholder, a person who gets power from his or her elected or appointed office. In state societies and chiefdoms, power and authority reside in offices and institutions. Formal rules dictate who can gain an office and the conditions under which it can be gained. Officeholders usually have greater access to resources, such as money from taxes and a bureaucracy that can exercise social control over a community. Like Big Men, however, mayors and other US officials do draw on their personal connections to achieve things.

• **Nation-state.** An independent state recognized by other states, composed of people who share a single national identity.

The Political Power of the Contemporary Nation-State

Modern states are typically called **nation-states**, independent states recognized by other states and composed of people who share a single national identity. A nation is a population who thinks of itself as "a people" based on sharing—or imagining that they share—a common culture, language, heritage, identity, or commitment to particular political institutions (Robbins 2001:82). State formations have been around a long time (see Chapter 11), but the more specific political form of the nation-state, with this emphasis on the uniformity of the people, originated in Europe several hundred years ago. It has become so common that now all the world's territory falls under the control of one or another nation-state.

Contrary to Locke's idealizations of the "social contract," membership in a nation-state is not typically voluntary. For many of the world's peoples, conquest and colonialism forced them into nation-states. Leaders of nation-states exercise various forms of political power to assert coercion and social control over non-state societies and to ensure the conformity of all their citizens.

These forms of social control and coercion include promoting a sense of unity by drawing symbolic lines between those who are included—often it is some version of the "chosen people"—and those who are excluded. Excluded groups may be defined as enemies (citizens of competing nation-states, or non-state actors such as "terrorists") or as inferiors because of racial or ethnic differences. Nation-states exercise power over their citizens by creating and managing information about them using institutionalized surveillance, national identity cards, censuses, monitoring social media, wiretapping, and computer hacking. Surveillance secures and expands leaders' power and authority, by identifying potential opposition or non-conformism threatening their authority. Many nation-states also use prisons, torture, and violence against citizens who do not conform to dominant values or identities. For example, Amnesty International reports that between 2009 and 2013, it received reports of torture in 141 countries (Amnesty International 2019).

People around the world have long understood the trade-offs of living within nation-states, and, not surprisingly, many have resisted and evaded their absorption and assimilation by states. Political scientist and anthropologist James Scott (2009) has described how, for 2,000 years, disparate groups of people have been living in upland Southeast Asia in what are essentially stateless societies. The region, known as Zomia, is a rugged and remote mountainous region the size of Europe that consists of parts of seven contemporary nation-states, extending from India and Myanmar in the west through China and into Vietnam, Laos, Cambodia, and Thailand in the east. The 100 million or so people who live in this highly ethnically and linguistically diverse region have historically avoided being controlled by lowland states by living in dispersed, autonomous communities. According to Scott, over time these groups came to the highlands fleeing slavery, conscription, taxes, epidemics, and warfare in the lowlands. They have historically been mobile, avoiding persecution by pushing deeper into the highlands and developing subsistence patterns, such as foraging and shifting cultivation (see Chapter 14), that enable regular movement. Their identities are also flexible, rooted in the maintenance of oral traditions and the reinvention of kinship genealogies as groups move around from country to country. Scott suggests that this long history of autonomy may be coming to an end as contemporary nation-states have begun to assert greater control in these remote areas with the aid of what he calls "distance-demolishing" technologies, such as roads, bridges, airplanes, modern weapons systems, and global positioning systems (Scott 2009:11).

Although nation-states introduce new political dynamics—especially formalized political parties and bureaucratized elections—it is important to stress that the political mechanisms that we have explored in non-state societies can also operate in state

Anthropologist as Problem Solver
Maxwell Owusu and Democracy in Ghana

SINCE ITS INDEPENDENCE from Britain in 1957, the West African country of Ghana has alternated between civilian- and military-controlled national governments. When the most recent military government (1981–1992) allowed elections in 1992, the Fourth Republic of Ghana emerged, based on a new constitution with a foundation in democratic principles.

An influential actor in that process was Ghanaian-born political anthropologist Maxwell Owusu of the University of Michigan. Owusu served as a consulting member of the Constitutional Experts Committee, which drafted the 1992 constitution proposals. Owusu has been a staunch critic of autocratic and repressive leadership in post-independence Ghana and other African nation-states. He is an advocate of popular participatory democracy. But as an anthropologist he understood the problems of imposing foreign political models—such as Western-style democracy with competing political parties—on African societies with different histories and indigenous political traditions. As he has written (Owusu 1992:384), "African democracy may require the integration of indigenous methods of village co-operation with innovative forms of government, combining the power of universal rights with the uniqueness of each district's or nation's own customs and respected traditions."

A viable solution, Owusu insisted, is to create a decentralized state in which local authorities—primarily chiefs, headmen, and lineage heads—participate directly in state processes and decision-making. The advantage is that local leaders can better identify the needs and priorities of villagers, while being more accountable to their members and communities than are bureaucrats in a state apparatus. The 1992 constitution put this insight to work, creating "District Assemblies" as the basic unit of national government, two-thirds of which are elected and one-third appointed,

🌱 **Maxwell Owusu**

the latter being mostly traditional leaders or their representatives (Owusu 1992). Owusu observed that, far from making chiefs and other non-state political leaders obsolete, these changes have put traditional leaders at the forefront of political change in the nation-state as a whole (Owusu 1996).

Questions for Reflection

1. How does Owusu's notion of participatory democracy, which relies on decentralization of power toward local traditional leaders, differ from the way local governments at the city, town, or county level work in the United States?

2. Is it likely to be true that local traditional leaders are better able to identify local priorities than national leaders?

settings. There is no absolute separation between state and non-state political organization. One illustration is that in a number of West African countries where witchcraft beliefs are common, including Cameroon, campaigning politicians will often seek out and associate with sorcerers. While the Cameroonian government officially rejects witchcraft, some prominent politicians openly accept and perpetuate the idea that they draw on occult powers to defeat their political rivals, because it enhances their power among villagers for whom sorcery remains an important means of social control and authority (Rowlands and Warnier 1988).

Leaders of nation-states also often co-opt local political actors and their power to serve their own or the nation-state's ends. In post-independence Ghana, for example, where chiefs, headmen, and extended family lineages control village-level resources and political processes, centralized governments have co-opted traditional non-state leaders by rewarding some with high-level positions in the state bureaucracy. Such an appointment to a governmental position makes a local leader responsible for enforcing national laws and mobilizing support for state-led development programs (Owusu 1996). For several decades, anthropologist Maxwell Owusu has researched how this kind of political power works in post-independence Ghana. He has advocated formally incorporating non-state political leaders into nation-state functions. In "Anthropologist as Problem Solver: Maxwell Owusu and Democracy in Ghana," we examine how his ideas have been put to work.

We have so far discussed the exercise of political power in terms of the cultivation of relationships, persuasion, the collection of information, or the strategic manipulation of others. Political power often also involves the production and maintenance of social inequalities, a theme we examine in the next section.

> **THINKING LIKE AN ANTHROPOLOGIST: POWER**
>
> As this section shows, different anthropologists have approached political power in different ways. Do you think each of these approaches creates a fundamentally different picture of how political power works? Why or why not?

15.3 How Is Social Inequality Constructed and Upheld?

Most Americans assume that social inequalities are a natural and inevitable aspect of human society. Those social inequalities may be based on categories like race, class, ethnicity, gender, caste, and so on. Although they may feel real, powerful, and unchangeable, there is nothing fixed or inevitable about them. All social hierarchies—as well as the political power that shapes and benefits from them—appeal to a natural order to justify the rankings and categories assigned to different groups. To understand why some people are deemed inferior and others superior, we must explore how belief systems and the dynamics of political power perpetuate prejudice, discrimination, and privilege, rather than searching for any preexisting natural or moral imperatives. Here we build on our discussion in Chapter 7 to examine how the race concept organizes people into groups based on specific physical traits that are thought to reflect fundamental and innate differences—and how it reinforces widespread patterns of social inequality.

Race, Biology, and the "Natural" Order of Things

For several centuries, European and American scientists have sought to naturalize race, that is, to categorize humans into racial groups and explain why nature organizes people into those groups. But, as we covered in Chapter 7, many anthropologists have long argued that these efforts are scientifically futile. As we explained, because of historical movements and genetic intermingling, human biological variations occur in a "clinal" fashion, which means that change is gradual across groups and that traits shade and blend into each other (Marks 1995). As a result, something like skin tone can be highly variable within any human population, and there are no clear lines between actual skin tones.

We also know that there is no single gene that codes race or is unique to any group of people conventionally thought of as a race (Long 2003). Genetically speaking, humans are a homogeneous species: there is far greater variation *within* human groups than there is *between* them (Long 2003). In the face of such evidence, anthropologists argue that race is culturally constructed. But how does that happen and what does it have to do with politics?

The Cultural Construction of Race

Anthropologists, sociologists, and historians refer to the social, economic, and political processes of transforming populations into races and creating racial meanings as **racialization** (Gregory and Sanjek 1994; Omi and Winant 1996). Racialization always occurs under a particular set of cultural, political, and historical circumstances.

• **Racialization.** The social, economic, and political processes of transforming populations into races and creating racial meanings.

A powerful illustration of these processes is the creation of racial groups in colonial Virginia. After the English settled Jamestown in 1607, settlers began to raise tobacco as a cash crop. Labor shortages were a problem, so they began to bring indentured servants from England. They also began to rely on African labor. In 1619, for example, a group of enslaved Africans held on a Portuguese ship were captured by an English ship and brought to the Virginia colony as captive labor. Some English-speaking Africans living in England also began to arrive in the colony as indentured servants (Parent 2003; Smedley 2007a, 2007b). These Africans were able to work off their debts and gain freedom. Some of the men even became prosperous traders and plantation owners and gained rights to vote and serve in the Virginia Assembly, just like any other man with property. Marriages between Africans and non-Africans were not uncommon. Africans were respected because of their success at growing food in tropical conditions, their discipline and intelligence, and their ability to work cooperatively in groups (E. Morgan 1975; Smedley 2007a; L. Walsh 2013).

By the mid-1600s, the British began to rely more heavily on enslaved Africans to meet their labor needs and began to impose some restrictions on those enslaved people, among them restricted access to weapons and introduction of the practice of enslaving their children (L. Walsh 2013). At the same time, the Virginia colony was entering a period of crisis over land (Smedley 2007a). A few powerful men had taken most of the fertile land, and poor freedmen had difficulty finding any for themselves. Unhappy with their lot, in 1676, thousands of poor freedmen and indentured servants rebelled, in what is known as Bacon's Rebellion (Figure 15.3). Most were Europeans, but among them were several hundred of African origin. To prevent future unrest, the leaders began passing new laws aimed at gaining more control over laborers. A number of these laws separated out free Africans and their descendants, restricting their rights and mobility, including the ability to vote, own property, and marry Europeans (Parent 2003; Smedley 2007a). These laws took away basic rights that free African settlers had previously held. Within a few years, the colony's labor system was based completely on enslaved African labor, upheld by tight legal restrictions and physical controls over all Africans.

English colonial leaders also promoted a shift in thinking about Africans and their descendants. They began portraying Africans as uncivilized heathens, intellectually

Figure 15.3   Bacon's Rebellion, Virginia Colony, 1676.

incapable of civilization, which justified African enslavement. They also began to homogenize all Europeans, regardless of ethnicity, class, or social status. In early public records, the word "Christian" commonly appeared next to the names of Europeans but was later replaced by "white." Poor whites received land as a way to encourage their identification with the colony's elites, preventing them from siding with Africans. By the end of the seventeenth century, the terms "black" and "white" came to symbolize the differences between the two groups, and the use of this racialized language helped uphold the artificial lines of difference. Skin color became the chief way of marking status and difference; as Governor William Gooch of Virginia described it, skin color was a "perpetual Brand upon Free Negroes and Mulattos" (Allen 1997:242).

The "biologizing" of race became extreme, particularly after the Civil War. Although most African Americans are of mixed ancestry, biological traits like skin tone and ideologies like the "one-drop rule" (individuals were defined as "black" if they were believed to have just "one drop" of African blood, meaning a single African ancestor) have been used to justify oppression and inequality as the "natural" order of things (Figure 15.4). These sharp racial lines have upheld a particular social and political order and, more important, have served certain economic interests, especially of those who benefited from cheap African and African American labor.

Saying Race Is Culturally Constructed Is Not Enough

It is not enough to say that race is culturally constructed, because it might give the impression that race is not "real" (Hartigan 2006). As we also explored in Chapter 7, race is very real as a social force and by *becoming* biology, that is, by shaping people's biological outcomes due to disparities in access to certain kinds of healthcare and diets, exposure to certain kinds of diseases, and other factors that can make people either sick or healthy (Gravlee 2009).

In addition to its embodied consequences, racial discrimination is a form of social control that can express itself explicitly—through laws and bureaucracies that manage and enforce policies of institutionalized coercion and exploitation—or in disguised ways such as racial profiling. The point here is not that different racial groups cannot have differences in biology, but that these differences in biology are the product of socioeconomic, cultural, and political processes that construct and maintain racial inequalities.

Prejudice—preformed, usually unfavorable opinions that people hold about people from groups that are different from their own—also plays an important role in upholding this unequal social order. Prejudice is based on taking arbitrary features and assigning qualities of social superiority and inferiority to them. Worldwide, there is a mind-boggling variety of markers on which prejudices are based. We are most familiar with skin color and hair texture, but other markers include occupation, family lineage, religious affiliation, and gender behavior that suggests sexual orientation.

Most of us learn prejudices at a young age from people whom we regard as authorities, such as parents and other relatives, community leaders, and teachers. Anthropologist Hortense Powdermaker also wrote that prejudices are judgments about a whole group of people based on poor reasoning and insufficient evidence. In "Classic Contributions: Hortense Powdermaker on Prejudice," we examine her point in more detail.

Where they exist, prejudices may feel deep, innate, and natural, but they are not static. As attitudes toward groups change, so do accompanying prejudices. There is no better illustration of this than the fact that a majority of Americans elected an African American president in 2008, which would have been unimaginable only forty years before because of widespread anti-black prejudice. Prejudices tend to express themselves through concrete processes of social rewards and unfair treatment, but they do not always lead to discrimination. In his classic study of prejudice from the 1950s, for example, Gordon Allport (1958) observed that prejudice expresses itself in a

Figure 15.4   The One-Drop Rule. Mark Twain's classic 1894 novel *The Tragedy of Pudd'nhead Wilson* depicts the one-drop rule as a farcical tragedy. In it, Roxy (pictured here), a slave who is 1/16 black, switches her baby son, who is 1/32 black, with a white baby, knowing her son will grow up with privileges he would never enjoy if people knew he had even "one drop" of black blood.

• **Prejudice.** Preformed, usually unfavorable opinions that people hold about people from groups that are different from their own.

Classic Contributions
Hortense Powdermaker on Prejudice

ANTHROPOLOGIST HORTENSE POWDERMAKER (1896–1970) began studying race relations in Mississippi during the 1930s, making her the first professional anthropologist to conduct ethnographic research in a contemporary American setting. She had conducted traditional ethnographic research in Papua New Guinea at Lesu on New Ireland for her dissertation, becoming the first researcher to focus on women in any New Guinea society (1933). Always interested in issues of social justice (before her PhD at the London School of Economics in the 1920s she was a labor organizer), Powdermaker sought to understand how blacks and whites interacted with each other and the psychological costs of racism.

During the 1940s, she took insights gained from that research to produce the short book *Probing Our Prejudices: A Unit for High School Students*, which was required reading in New York City schools for several decades. In this excerpt from that book, Powdermaker explains how poor reasoning leads to prejudice.

Bill plays marbles with a group of boys in his neighborhood, and one of them, John, a Polish boy, cheats. Bill then concludes that all Poles cheat, and he carries this idea with him throughout his life. . . .

When he is older, Bill reads in the paper that two Italians who were drunk got into a fight and one stabbed the other. Bill has never known any Italians but he swiftly jumps to the conclusion that all Italians are drunkards and stab each other in the back.

Or he hears of a Mexican who stole some money from his boss, and so, forever after, he thinks of all Mexicans as thieves.

In all three cases Bill concluded that because one member of a group acted in a certain way, all members of that group will act the same way. This type of poor reasoning is called false generalization. To generalize is to come to a general conclusion as a result of learning particular facts or ideas. For example, if you are a member of a club that functions well at every meeting and lives up to its standards, you may justifiably say, "We have a good club." This is a true generalization based on observation. If, however, you observe another club during only one of its meetings when nothing is accomplished, and you say, "That club is no good," you are making a false generalization, because you have not based your conclusion on sufficient evidence.

We all suffer from this unfortunate habit of making false generalizations, especially about racial or religious groups or nationalities other than our own. We do not make them as frequently about our own group. If we are white Protestants and a member of our group cheats, we do not condemn all white Protestants. If we are Catholics and one of our members lies, we do not say "All Catholics are liars." In order to be clear-thinking individuals we must realize this inconsistency and avoid making false generalizations. [Powdermaker 1944:29–30]

Questions for Reflection

1. Can you think of other social or political issues beyond race and nationality where people make false generalizations?

2. Why do people accept the logical inconsistencies and poor reasoning that lead to prejudice?

continuum from avoidance and non-contact to more aggressive actions, including exclusion, physical attack, and killing. This last point raises a new question about the relationship between cultural attitudes and violence, which we explore next.

THINKING LIKE AN ANTHROPOLOGIST: POWER

Racialization is not something that happened a long time ago; it is an ongoing process that is happening in the United States today. Can you think of some examples of how it might still be taking place? Can you identify any conditions today that might shape dynamics of racialization differently from, say, during the period of the Virginia colony?

15.4 Why Do Some Societies Seem More Violent Than Others?

By the 1960s, a number of the societies that anthropologists studied were experiencing intense post-independence violence, disruption, and warfare related to the end of European colonialism. This situation prompted an urgent concern to understand the relationship between political power and violence, and why political conflicts in some societies seemed to break out in violence more than conflicts did in other societies. What might be done to end and prevent future violence?

In pursuing answers to these questions, anthropologists have learned that violence is a form of power relations rooted in cultural processes and meanings, just as other strategies of political power, such as persuasion, manipulation, and prejudice, are.

What Is Violence?

Violence is typically defined as the use of force to harm someone or something. It is a highly visible and concrete assertion of power, and a very efficient way to transform a social environment and communicate an ideological message (Riches 1986).

● **Violence.** The use of force to harm someone or something.

Yet specifying what violence consists of is not always so straightforward, because violence is different things to different people (Eller 2006). The same person might acknowledge that shoving a person into a vat of boiling water is violent, yet may not view placing a lobster, much less a handful of spinach, in that same boiling water as violent. Another factor in assessing what is violent is intention. Did the perpetrator mean to do it (violent), or was it an accident (probably not violent)? And rationality: Did the perpetrator have control over his or her actions (violent), or was it a case of "losing one's mind" (probably not violent, or at least justified)? And legitimacy: Was it a legitimate act, such as a boxer beating on another boxer (sports, not violence), or deviant, such as a man beating his wife (violent)? Even the nature of force: Was the force personal, as in one person punching another (violent), or structural, as in economic conditions depriving a child of food (open to debate)? And depending on whether you are a victim, perpetrator, or witness, you are likely to have a different perspective on whether or not an act is violent.

Even though we might all agree that violence involves some element of harm and an assertion of power over others, people nevertheless have differing opinions on what constitutes violence. To victims, violence is almost always meaningful, while it may or may not be as meaningful or obvious to the perpetrators. This distinction is partly why violence is so powerful in enforcing the rules of the powerful. Some of these opinions about violence are individually held, but some are related to differences in how we as members of a particular culture define violence and give meaning to it. Culture shapes not only how people think about violence but also how, why, and when they use it as a form of power over others.

Violence and Culture

Since Hobbes, Europeans and Americans have seen violence and warfare as a natural condition of humans. But anthropologists offer two major challenges to this view: (1) neither violence nor its opposite, non-violence, is an inevitable condition of humanity; both are learned behaviors that express themselves in particular social and historic circumstances; and (2) violence and warfare are generally not chaotic and arbitrary but tend to follow explicit cultural patterns, rules, and ethical codes.

Neither Violence nor Non-Violence Is Inevitable in Human Societies

In recent years, it has become fashionable to think of aggression and violence as genetically determined. But no animal or human carries genes for dominance, aggression, or passivity. These complex social and psychological conditions and states involve biological processes, such as the production of certain hormones, but they are not fixed properties or traits carried by genes.

So how should we deal with claims—some even made by anthropologists—that some societies are fierce and warlike and others peaceful? The answer, of course, is by demonstrating that neither violence nor non-violence is universal (Fry 2006). Two famous examples—the Yanomamo and the Semai—illustrate our point.

The Yanomamo and the Semai

Anthropologist Napoleon Chagnon (1968) described the Yanomamo Indians of southern Venezuela with whom he has worked since the early 1960s as the "fierce people." According to Chagnon, the Yanomamo have an aggressive style about nearly everything they do. They stage brutal raids against enemy settlements, and they routinely have violent responses to their fellow clansmen (Figure 15.5).

But other anthropologists, including Brian Ferguson (1995) and Jacques Lizot (1985), have seen the Yanomamo in a different light, as warm and caring people, who from time to time had to defend themselves against enemies. Ferguson's research suggests that Yanomamo "fierceness" was not the traditional behavior of these Amazonian Indians but the result of contact with foreigners: missionaries, prospectors, government officials, and anthropologists such as Chagnon, who has come under fire by Yanomami themselves for disrupting their society (Tierney 2002).

A similar point can be made about a very different case, the Semai, egalitarian swidden farmers who live in the Malaysian rain forest. Anthropologist Robert Dentan (1968) characterized the Semai as peaceful and non-violent because they committed little or no interpersonal violence during his field research. The Semai view themselves as peaceful and reject the idea that violence is a natural condition of human life. At the heart of Semai commitment to non-violence is the concept of *persusah*, referring to the value of not causing trouble for others. But the Semai are not completely non-violent either. During the communist insurrection in Malaysia from 1948 to 1960, some Semai became soldiers and a few were renowned fighters.

Figure 15.5   The "Fierce People." In the ethnographic film *The Ax Fight*, from which this image is drawn, the filmmakers represent Yanomamo lives as filled with aggression and near-constant violence. But is it really so?

Although Dentan had consistently described the ethos of the Semai as non-violent and peaceful, he quoted one former soldier who described himself and his comrades in the counterinsurgency as "drunk with blood" (1968:58–59). Robarchek and Dentan (1987) argue that the Semai are indeed socialized to be non-violent, but when they were brought into the counterinsurgency they were socialized as soldiers and were trained to kill.

The point of this example is that, as with the Yanomamo, violence and non-violence are not absolute or static conditions. They are the results of cultural attitudes and particular social and historical conditions (Fry 2006).

Explaining the Rise of Violence in Our Contemporary World

Anthropologists have long observed that violence and the threat of violence, far from implying chaos, can actually encourage social order because they reflect culturally specific patterns, rules, and ethical codes. These patterns define when and why violence is acceptable, what forms of violence are appropriate, and who can engage in violent acts.

In news reports, pundits routinely explain the rise of violence around the globe as a chaotic outburst of meaningless "tribal" and "ethnic" tensions (Whitehead 2004). Such accounts appear to offer a tidy narrative that seems to explain so much of what is going on in our contemporary world, but they are based on a fundamental misunderstanding of the relationship between violence and culture.

It Is Not Inevitable That Different Ethnic Groups Will Fight

The countries that made up the former Yugoslavia in southeastern Europe, in a region known as the Balkans, share the stereotype of ethnic and religious tribalism. We even have a word for it—"balkanization"—which refers to the fragmentation of society into hostile factions. During the Bosnian civil war in the 1990s, foreign journalists tended to describe acts of violence by Serbs, Croats, and Muslims as "ethnic violence" based on centuries-old hatred between these ethnic groups.

But this explanation ignores long histories of coexistence, cultural interchange, and peaceful relations that anthropologists had observed in the region (Lockwood 1975; Bringa 2005). A more complex understanding of the conflict sees violence as a by-product of a struggle over political power among nationalist leaders after the fall of communism. Seeking to consolidate their hold over political power and state institutions, nationalists on all sides used the media to broadcast daily doses of fear, hatred, and dehumanizing images of people from the other "ethnic" group (Bringa 2005). Their public comments asserted that one group or another had targeted violence on people of other ethnic backgrounds. The constant public discourse about ethnic violence generated fear and a sense of powerlessness among ordinary people. When nationalist leaders eventually called on people to attack their neighbors of different backgrounds, some did just that, leading to now well-known incidents of brutality and horror in places such as Srebenica, site of a mass killing of Bosnian Muslims by Bosnian Serbs (Oberschall 2000).

But while the Western media presented these divisions as age-old ethnic tensions, all three spoke the same language, Serbo-Croatian, with slight differences in dialect, and people did not initially see these labels as "ethnic" differences but more as religious ones: the Serbs were Eastern Orthodox, the Croats were Roman Catholic, and Bosnians were Muslim. For many decades these groups intermingled in the same apartment buildings and intermarried. Centuries of generally harmonious relations were on display when the Winter Olympics were held in Sarajevo (Figure 15.6).

Even during the most violent periods, many people found ways to protect their neighbors of different ethnic backgrounds from being attacked. In other words, even

Figure 15.6   A Peaceful Balkans. At the time of the 1984 Olympic Games in the Bosnian capital city of Sarajevo, commentators celebrated long-standing peaceful relations between Serbs, Croats, and Muslims in the modern city, challenging any notion of "ancient seething hatreds" portrayed in later years.

in a period of intense, artificially created ethnic conflict, not everybody participated in the violence, and many did not give in to "ethnic" hatred. Both points undermine any simplistic story of seething tribalism. Ethnic conflict is not an inevitable condition, and in this case it was manufactured to serve the political and ideological interests of certain leaders.

Violence Is a Meaningful Political Strategy

In the United States we sometimes hear in the media about events like suicide bombings in Iraqi markets and cafés; machete attacks on innocent people in Liberia, Rwanda, and Sierra Leone in Africa; or plane hijackings by some militant group. Commentators often call these shocking acts "meaningless" and "barbaric." But such acts are never meaningless. They are meaningful—to both victims and perpetrators—although the different sides interpret the violence very differently (Whitehead 2004). For one side the message is threat and hostility, and for the other it is a message of martyrdom and devotion to a cause.

When people refer to such acts as meaningless and barbaric, they interpret violence as emotional, beyond reason. In fact, violence and the threat of violence are often used as strategic tools for pursuing particular political ends. Consider, for example, the civil war in Sierra Leone (1991–2001), in which at least 50,000 people died. This conflict, waged between the government and a "people's army" called the Revolutionary United Front (RUF), gained widespread notoriety as a barbaric and brutal conflict.

According to British anthropologist Paul Richards (1996), the violence was anything but wanton and mindless. He explained that machete attacks, rape, throat slitting, and other acts of terror were "rational ways of achieving intended strategic outcomes" (Richards 1996:58). For example, during 1995, the RUF frequently cut off the hands of village women. This practice was strategically calculated to communicate a political message to the RUF's own soldiers and to prevent defections. RUF leaders reasoned that they could stop defections by stopping the harvest. To stop the harvest, they ordered the hand amputation of women who participated in harvesting grain. As news spread, the harvests stopped, and defections ended because soldiers did not want the same thing to happen to their mothers and sisters. Richards does not justify these repulsive acts. Rather, his point is that violence is not "meaningless" but is highly organized in a systematic, though brutal, fashion.

Not every conflict leads inevitably to violence. We explore this theme in more detail in our final section.

THINKING LIKE AN ANTHROPOLOGIST: POWER

Since the early years of structural-functionalism, anthropologists have recognized that violence or the threat of violence, far from implying chaos, can encourage social integration and social order. How? Why?

15.5 How Do People Avoid Aggression, Brutality, and War?

Although millions of people around the world rarely, if ever, have direct experiences of aggression, brutality, and war in their daily lives, disputes and conflicts do arise, everywhere, all the time. But, as we discussed, violence is not an inevitable human response to conflict. People always have creative and peaceful ways to manage or settle their disputes. Working out the problems that arise from those conflicting accounts inevitably touches on who has access to power and what allows them to hold it (Rasmussen 1991).

What Disputes Are "About"

Some disputes are explicitly about who can hold political power, but most disputes are also about other matters that are central to the political life of any community (Caplan 1995). Disputes are about property, who gets to make decisions, rules of social interaction, and about dividing or joining people in new ways, because when arguments happen, people take sides.

Most North Americans assume that disputes are about winning and losing. We approach a lawsuit pretty much the same way we approach a sporting event, the point being to vanquish the other side. But for many peoples around the world, disputes are not "about" winning and losing but are intended to repair a strained relationship.

When Trobriand Islanders play the game cricket, for example, the goal of the game is to end with a tie, not to win or lose (Kildea and Leach 1975). Sure, the players play hard and even get hurt in the process, but the game is really "about" reaffirming the social relationships that exist among the players and with their communities. When we look at how people manage disputes around the world, keep in mind that when presented with a dispute, most people prefer to restore harmony by settling the matter to the satisfaction of all parties.

How People Manage Disputes

Legal anthropology, the branch of political anthropology interested in such matters, has identified a number of ways that people manage disputes (Nader and Todd 1978). Some strategies are informal, including avoidance, competition, ritual, and play. Others are formal, involving specialists or specialized institutions.

One of the easiest and most informal ways that people handle their disputes is to avoid the matter altogether, which allows tensions to subside. In small-scale communities, avoiding certain subjects is often the best way of keeping the peace. People often turn to other informal strategies to handle tensions, such as telling jokes, laughter, gossip, song, duels, sporting contests and other forms of competitive play, ridicule, public humiliation, and even witchcraft accusations (Gulliver 1979; Watson-Gegeo and White 1990; Caplan 1995) (Figure 15.7).

When informal strategies do not work, people usually have more formal means of settling disputes. **Adjudication**, which is the legal process by which an individual or council with socially recognized authority intervenes in a dispute and unilaterally makes a decision, is one possibility. The image of a courtroom with a judge in a robe, a jury, and lawyers comes to mind. Not all societies do it this way, including the Kpelle [keh-**pay**-lay], rice cultivators of central Liberia. Anthropologist James Gibbs (1963) reported that while Kpelle could take their disputes to government courts, they viewed them as arbitrary and coercive (Gibbs 1963). Kpelle often turned to their own "moot courts," which are hearings presided over by respected kin, elders, and neighbors. Kpelle moot courts provided a thorough airing of grievances and a quick treatment of the problem before attitudes hardened. Instead of winner take all, their goal was to restore harmony.

In a **negotiation**, the parties themselves reach a decision jointly. British legal anthropologist Phillip Gulliver (1979) observed that in a dispute between two close neighbors over land and water rights that took place in a small district in northern Tanzania in 1957, many factors influenced the ability and willingness of each side to

- **Adjudication.** The legal process by which an individual or council with socially recognized authority intervenes in a dispute and unilaterally makes a decision.

- **Negotiation.** A form of dispute management in which parties themselves reach a decision jointly.

🌱 **Figure 15.7　Rap Battles and Social Tension.** In urban hip-hop culture, "rap battles" involve two individuals engaging in competitive rapping in front of an audience. The individual with greater lyrical prowess—the ability to rhyme, to creatively "diss" (criticize) the opponent, and so on—is the winner. Rap battles are often born from social tensions between individuals or social factions, but they can also provide a creative means to reduce tensions as problems and status differences are publicly aired.

● **Mediation.** The use of a third party who intervenes in a dispute to help the parties reach an agreement and restore harmony.

negotiate a settlement. For example, one disputant was more popular and better connected in the community, and thus had more allies to push his own agenda. But he was willing to negotiate because, like his rival, he was equally worried that the colonial court could intervene and impose a decision. He also worried that if the dispute were not settled, the other side might use witchcraft and further intensify the dispute.

Mediation entails a third party who intervenes in a dispute to aid the parties in reaching an agreement. Native Hawaiians commonly practice a kind of mediation called *ho'oponopono* (**hoh**-oh-poh-no-poh-no], or "setting to right" (Boggs and Chun 1990). This practice is intended to resolve interpersonal and family problems or to prevent them from worsening. It is based on the belief that disputes involve negative entanglements and that setting things right spiritually will lead directly to physical and interpersonal healing (Boggs and Chun 1990). *Ho'oponopono* usually begins when a leader of high status—a family elder, a leader of a community church, or a professional family therapist—intervenes in a dispute, calling the adversaries and all immediate family members to engage in the process. After opening with prayers, the leader instructs participants in the process and guides a discussion in which all participants are expected to air their grievances and feelings openly and honestly. They direct them to the leader, not to one another, to avoid possible confrontation. At the end, the leader asks all sides to offer forgiveness and release themselves and each other from the negative entanglements.

Is Restoring Harmony Always the Best Way?

It is easy to romanticize dispute settlement traditions whose goal is to restore harmony. Legal anthropologist Laura Nader (1990) observed that harmony and reconciliation are cultural ideologies, and like other ideologies they uphold a particular social order and way of doing things, usually protecting the already powerful.

Nader observed that Zapotec Indians in the southern Mexican village of Talea [tah**lay**-ah] whom she studied have a "harmony ideology." Taleans believe "a bad compromise is better than a good fight." They emphasize that people need to work hard to maintain balance and evenhandedness in their relationships with others. They go to local courts frequently, even for very minor disputes, to avoid escalation.

But peace and reconciliation have their price. Nader has seen how these ideologies can prevent a full airing of problems, can delay justice, or can be used as a form of social control. Harmony ideology sustains a particular power structure, serving the interests of some but not necessarily all.

Since the 1970s, restoring harmony has been a popular strategy in Western countries for conflict resolution studies and practice. Mediation and negotiated settlements deal with disputes from family and work-related problems to complex international clashes, including civil wars and wars between countries (Davidheiser 2007). These techniques are often called "alternative dispute management."

While some anthropologists welcome the rise of alternative dispute management (Avruch 1998), Nader (1995, 2001) questions its implicit harmony ideology. She observes that many people involved in civil wars and other large-scale conflicts do not necessarily want harmony. They want justice, fairness, and the rule of law. This is a sentiment expressed by many Mozambicans, for example, whose civil war ended in a mediated settlement in 1992. Many Mozambicans believe that the settlement, which brought with it the introduction of foreign aid institutions and International Monetary Fund stabilization policies, actually deepened their woes by generating more poverty and inequality than before the war (Hanlon 1996).

There is not necessarily a "best way" to solve a dispute. If there were, there would be no more disputes! In addition, dispute settlement is never a neutral act. In handling their disputes, people make ideological assumptions and enact social relationships that uphold particular power structures or, as Laura Nader suggests, even challenge those power structures.

THINKING LIKE AN ANTHROPOLOGIST: POWER

Think about the last time you had a non-violent dispute in your life. How did you handle it? Was one or more of the strategies we discussed—avoidance, adjudication, negotiation, or mediation—involved? How might the outcome have been different if you had pursued a different strategy than the one you did?

Conclusion

If you pay much attention to political news on television or the Internet, you may have the impression that politics is mainly about politicians and their political parties, laws, and bureaucratic institutions. This impression offers only part of the story. Politics often involves some element of state power and bureaucratic processes. Every society has individuals who act a lot like North American politicians. From status leaders such as Big Men and councils of elders who settle disputes, to leaders of armed movements organizing violent acts, leaders everywhere use strategy, manipulation, persuasion, control over resources, and sometimes violence to obtain and maintain power over others. And, as we saw in the opening of this chapter in the story about struggles over water connections in Meghwadi, these processes often move across and between formal political spheres and the social dynamics of everyday lives in subtle and complex ways.

A sophisticated perspective on politics must appreciate the diverse forms that political power takes around the world. Not all societies train their young to deal with their problems through violence, and even those that accept violence place limits on its use, encouraging more peaceful ways of handling disputes. People not considered conventionally powerful have ways of challenging the power structure in their societies.

Politics is about relationships of cooperation, conflict, social control, and power that exist in any community and at all levels of social life, from the interpersonal and community levels to the national and transnational. The reason people around the world have so many ways of managing and thinking about those relationships is the same reason that cultural diversity persists in the world today: social processes like those involved in politics are always rooted in and emerge from people's everyday social interactions, belief systems, and cultural practices.

KEY TERMS

Acephalous society   p. 427

Action theory   p. 431

Adjudication   p. 445

Age-grades   p. 428

Band   p. 429

Centralized political system   p. 429

Chiefdom   p. 429

Government   p. 427

Laws   p. 427

Mediation   p. 446

Nation-state   p. 434

Negotiation   p. 445

Non-centralized political system   p. 429

Political power   p. 430

Politics   p. 426

Prejudice   p. 439

Racialization   p. 437

State   p. 429

Structural power   p. 432

Structural-functionalism   p. 428

Tribe   p. 429

Violence   p. 441

Reviewing the Chapter

Chapter Section	What We know	To Be Resolved
Does every society have a government?	Not every society has a government as we know it or makes a distinction between those who govern and those who are governed. Some societies organize their political lives on the basis of principles such as egalitarian social relations, reciprocity, and kinship.	Although classical anthropological studies identified many political processes in non-state societies, anthropologists continue to study and debate how successful these processes have been in confronting the transnational forces that affect almost every society today.
What is political power?	Political power operates in multidimensional ways: it is action oriented, it is structural, and it is gendered. It also tends to operate in particular ways in non-state contexts and in modern nation-states.	Anthropologists debate the relative importance of political power wielded by individuals and structural power shaping fields of social action.

Chapter Section	What We know	To Be Resolved
How is social inequality constructed and upheld?	All social hierarchies appeal to a natural order to justify themselves. This natural order may feel inevitable, even morally necessary, but like all other cultural phenomena, it is constructed and dynamic. Races are socially, not biologically or genetically, determined. But due to racism, discrimination, and prejudice, race does have consequences for certain people's biological outcomes.	Anthropologists are still working to understand the ways the social dynamics of inequality, race, and racism express themselves through disparate biological outcomes.
Why do some societies seem more violent than others?	Neither violence nor non-violence is an inevitable condition. Both are learned behaviors expressed in particular social and historical circumstances.	Most peoples who have been characterized either as peaceful or violent are not uniformly peaceful or violent, yet it is not always clear what conditions might have transformed an otherwise peaceful people into a violent one or vice versa.
How do people avoid cycles of aggression, brutality, and war?	Disputes arise in all societies, but they do not necessarily result in aggression, brutality, or war because people everywhere have many peaceful strategies for settling disputes.	Anthropologists continue to debate the effectiveness of the new field of alternative dispute management, especially in cross-cultural and international settings.

READINGS

A classic approach to politics is E. E. Evans-Pritchard's 1940 ethnography, *The Nuer: A Description of the Modes of Livelihood and Political Institutions of a Nilotic People* (Oxford: Clarendon Press, 1940). John Gledhill's book *Power and Its Disguises: Anthropological Perspectives on Politics* (London: Pluto Press, 2000) offers a comprehensive overview of this history and current approaches. An excellent illustration of contemporary ethnographic approaches to politics is Nikhil Anand's 2017 book *Hydraulic City: Water and the Infrastructures of Citizenship in Mumbai* (Durham, NC: Duke University Press), on which the opening of this chapter is based.

Two books offer a useful overview of how to think anthropologically about violence, including David Riches's edited book *The Anthropology of Violence* (Oxford: Basil Blackwell, 1986) and Douglas P. Fry's book *The Human Potential for Peace: An Anthropological Challenge to Assumptions About War and Violence* (New York: Oxford University Press, 2006).

In recent years, the American Anthropological Association has encouraged national dialogue on race and racism by sharing anthropological perspectives and research on the connections between race, biology, and culture. *Race: Are We So Different?* (http://www.understandingrace.org/home.html) is a website covering the latest anthropological thinking in about race.

Understanding Disputes: The Politics of Argument (Oxford: Berg, 1995), edited by Pat Caplan, offers a useful introduction to legal anthropology and includes essays by some of the leading figures in the field.

James C. Scott has written extensively on the relationships between states and marginalized peoples within states as well those who live beyond state power. His 2009 book *The Art of Not Being Governed: An Anarchist History of Upland Southeast Asia* (New Haven, CT: Yale University Press) provides a cultural and political analysis of the Zomia region of Southeast Asia.

Kinship and Gender

Sex, Power, and Control of Men and Women

16

Soap operas are one of the world's most popular and enduring television genres. Every day, hundreds of millions of people around the globe tune into one or more of them. Although some of these American soaps have enjoyed international popularity, it is Latin American shows—produced and exported by Mexicans, Venezuelans, Argentines, and Brazilians in particular—that have ruled screens worldwide during the past two decades.

One of the most popular Latin American exports of all time is the Mexican *telenovela* [tay-**lay**-noh-**vell**-ah] *También los Ricos Lloran* (*The Rich Also Cry*). Produced in 1979, it has enjoyed popularity and rebroadcasts in dozens of countries throughout the Americas, Europe, Asia, and Africa to the present day. *Telenovelas* (as such shows are called in Spanish) usually run for only a few months and have a clear ending, unlike US soaps, which are long running and open-ended.

The basic plot of *También los Ricos Lloran*, which many subsequent *telenovelas* have imitated, is as follows. A beautiful and poor young woman named Mariana becomes a maid for a rich and powerful family. She and the youngest son in the family, Luis Alberto, have a scandalous love affair and eventually get married. She has a baby son, Beto, but in a fit of temporary madness she gives him away to an old woman on the street.

During the next eighteen years, Mariana searches desperately for Beto and miraculously finds him when he begins dating Marisabel, who is Mariana and Luis Alberto's adopted daughter (though

Kinship and the Latin American *Telenovela*.   Latin American soap operas called *telenovelas* such as the Mexican show pictured here, *Ni Contigo Ni Sin Ti* (*Neither With You Nor Without You*), have captivated global audiences for decades because of complicated, if perhaps unlikely, kin relationships they present.

she doesn't know she's adopted). Mariana tells Marisabel who Beto really is. Marisabel becomes hysterical at the thought of incest with her brother. Mariana does not, however, tell Luis Alberto, fearing he will get angry with her. He gets angry anyway because she spends so much time with Beto that Luis Alberto suspects the two are having an affair. In the final episode Luis Alberto confronts Beto and Mariana with a gun. In the program's final moments, Mariana screams "Son!" Luis Alberto goes ballistic. Beto screams, "Father, let me embrace you!" and the family is, against all odds, reunited at long last.

Dark family secrets, suspicious spouses, unruly children, irresponsible parents, and possible incest make for gripping television! But for an anthropologist—if not also for many viewers around the world—the fascination this show holds is not due simply to its unlikely storyline but rather to its presentation of the complexities of love, sex, and power that involve men, women, and children anywhere in the world.

Also noteworthy is the show's assumption that blood relations are the central defining relationships in people's lives—after all, Luis Alberto's anger disappears when he realizes Beto is his son, and Marisabel would probably not be so hysterical if she knew Beto wasn't her biological brother. For anthropologists, it is a noteworthy assumption mainly because it reflects one particular culture's way of defining family relationships. Around the world not all cultures give the same weight to biological relatedness for defining a family.

Indeed, the biological facts of procreation are only one aspect of what it means to have a family or, for that matter, to be male or female. What is more important is how these biological facts are interpreted and the special rights, obligations, and identities these facts confer on individuals. At the heart of anthropology's interest in kinship and gender is the question: *Why and how are relationships of kinship and gender more than simply a reflection of biological processes?* We can answer this question by considering a number of related questions around which this chapter is organized:

What are families, and how are they structured in different societies?

Why do people get married?

How and why do males and females differ?

What does it mean to be neither male nor female?

Is human sexuality just a matter of being straight or queer?

Family, sex, and gender are core features of people's lives and identities everywhere. The kinds of influence and control that people can exert on their relatives and individuals as men or women vary widely from one society to another. So let us begin by considering what makes a group of relatives a family.

16.1 What Are Families, and How Are They Structured in Different Societies?

Families are important in nearly every society. They give members a sense of comfort and belonging and provide them part of their identity, values, and ideals. They control wealth and the material necessities of life. And, importantly, they assign individuals with basic roles, rights, and responsibilities in relation to other relatives. **Kinship**—the social system that organizes people in families based on descent and marriage—is patterned in culturally specific and dynamic ways.

• **Kinship.** The social system that organizes people in families based on descent and marriage.

Families, Ideal and Real

In every society a gap exists between that society's ideal family and the real families that exist, because all families are dynamic. For example, as individuals grow older, they move out of their **natal family**—the family into which they were born and raised—to marry and start their own families. In addition, broader social and economic conditions change the composition, size, and character of ties between family members, as the example of the American family illustrates.

• **Natal family.** The family into which a person is born and (usually) raised.

American politicians and religious leaders frequently extol the virtues of the "traditional" family. Just what family do these people have in mind? Most likely, it is some version of the family in the television show *The Adventures of Ozzie and Harriet* (which aired from 1952 to 1966), with a working husband/father who is the head of the household, a loving stay-at-home wife/mother, and two or three children living in a spic-and-span suburban home.

This ideal is not a "traditional" family, but a new pattern—the independent American suburban family—that emerged in the 1950s and lasted for less than twenty years. During the Great Depression of the 1930s, American birth rates had fallen sharply because of limited incomes. The birth rate remained low throughout World War II. But once the millions of men serving in the military returned, they began to marry and start families. The 1950s were a time of unprecedented economic growth, and the baby boom—77 million babies in fifteen years—encouraged expansion of new subdivisions filled with these young families. By the late 1950s, around 60 percent of all Americans lived in such families.

During the late 1960s and 1970s these young postwar families had grown up, children had moved out, and some couples had divorced. Women began to join the workforce in larger numbers, lowering wages for entry-level jobs. By the 1980s it was hard for young American families to get by on one salary. Two-income households brought in more wages but put stress on couples, who still needed someone to cook their meals, clean their homes, and look after their children. Divorce became more common than ever before, and today only half of American households are headed by a married couple. When divorced couples with kids get remarried, the composition of a family (with multiple sets of step-parents and step-siblings)—and especially the obligations that individuals in the family have to each other—can get quite complicated.

Nuclear and Extended Families

Still, the **nuclear family**—the domestic family formed by a couple and their children—is the most important family structure in the United States. Ours is not the only society with nuclear families—nuclear family units occur in and are important to nearly every society around the world. Indeed, for many decades anthropologists wrote of the nuclear family as the most basic unit of kinship (Radcliffe-Brown 1941:2).

• **Nuclear family.** A domestic family group formed by a couple and their children.

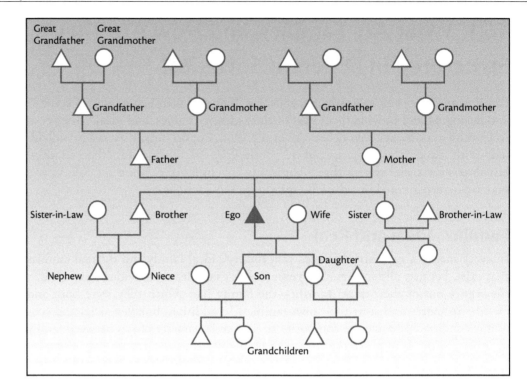

Figure 16.1   A Kinship Chart Plots All Sorts of Kin Relationships. Here the chart shows members of the extended family from a husband/father's perspective. Of course, the chart could be drawn from the wife/mother's perspective as well.

- **Kinship chart.** A visual representation of family relationships.

- **Corporate groups.** Groups of real people who work together toward common ends, much like a corporation does.

- **Extended families.** Larger groups of relatives beyond the nuclear family, often living in the same household.

- **Clan.** A group of relatives who claim to be descended from a single ancestor.

- **Exogamous.** A social pattern in which members of a clan must marry someone from another clan, which has the effect of building political, economic, and social ties with other clans.

- **Lineage.** A group composed of relatives who are directly descended from known ancestors.

Using a basic **kinship chart** (a visual representation of family relationships), we can graph a man's nuclear family easily enough, and we can add another nuclear family for his wife's natal family, and add children (Figure 16.1). Such charts only describe the biological connections, such as mother-daughter or father-daughter—without expressing the content of these different relationships. For example, when the child is young, the relationship between parent and child may involve teaching and training, while later that individual may care for the parent.

One important feature of nuclear and natal families is that they usually function as **corporate groups**, which are groups of real people who work together toward common ends, much like a corporation does. The family's goals are not just the goals of one family member but of the group as a whole. In every society around the world, families are supposed to look after the needs of all members of the family—parents, children, and any other members who happen to be in residence.

Family groups may also consist of larger groups of relatives beyond the nuclear family, which anthropologists call **extended families**. Extended families may live together and function as a corporate group, or they may merely acknowledge ties with one another. In nineteenth-century America, for example, it was common for households to include a nuclear family at its core, as well as some mix of elderly parents, a single brother or sister, the orphaned children of the wife's sister, and so on (Figure 16.2).

A **clan** is a type of extended family, a special group of relatives who are all descended from a single ancestor. In many societies, links to these ancestors can be quite vague, and in a number of societies, these ancestors are animals or humans with distinctive non-human characteristics. Clans are so important in many societies that in the 1940s French anthropologist Claude Lévi-Strauss (1969) argued that the clan, not the nuclear family, was the basic unit of kinship. Clans typically control land and other resources, as well as any individual member's access to those resources. They are also usually **exogamous**, which means that members of the clan must marry someone from another clan, effectively building political, economic, and social ties with other clans. **Lineages** are very similar to clans, but lineages tend to be composed of people who are directly descended from known ancestors, while clan membership is often vague and assumed rather than empirically known. Clans and lineages come in three types, as explored in Table 16.1.

Kinship Terminologies

Another way to think about the structure of families is to explore terms that people in different societies use to refer to their relatives. Beginning in the 1860s, with American anthropologist Lewis Henry Morgan (1871), anthropologists have collected thousands of different kinship terminologies. It happens that all of them can be grouped into six basic patterns Morgan identified long ago, as we show in Figure 16.3.

Anthropologists have also realized that kinship terminologies do not just provide descriptive names that indicate relationships between individuals but can also indicate the specific nature of the relationship, rights, and responsibilities that exist between related people. For example, in many American Indian societies, an individual will use the term *father* to refer not just to his biological father, but to his father's brothers or even other men of his father's generation with no direct biological ties. The "father" is expected to interact with his "son" in certain culturally accepted ways, such as providing food or assistance.

Kinship terminologies also help people keep track of their many relatives by assigning categorical terms. But nobody can keep track of everybody. Each society has kinspeople who are vital to keep track of, while others, usually more distant relatives, are forgotten. Anthropologists refer to this structural

Figure 16.2 Extended Families in North America. (*Top*) An Indian family from the Kainai tribe in the Canadian plains about 1900. (*Bottom*) An American extended family gathers for a reunion in Mt. Carmel, Illinois, 1904. Everyone in the photo is descended from one deceased couple, parents of seven of the senior women pictured.

TABLE 16.1	TYPES OF CLANS AND LINEAGES		
Type of Clan or Lineage	**Definition**	**Features**	**Examples**
Patrilineal	Membership based on descent from a common male ancestor.	Inheritance of property, rights, names, or titles come through an individual's father.	Omaha Indians, Nuer of South Sudan, many groups in Central Highlands of Papua New Guinea. Most Americans inherit last names patrilineally.
Matrilineal	Membership based on descent from a common female ancestor.	Every man and woman is a member of his or her mother's clan, which is also the clan of their mother's mother. It is not the same as matriarchy, in which women hold political power; it is only about identity and group membership. Land is usually owned by the clan or lineage. While women may have some say in who uses clan land, it is usually the men in the clan who have control over resources.	Trobriand Islanders
Cognatic (also known as "bilateral")	Descent comes through both mother and father.	Membership in multiple clans is possible or even typical.	Samoans of Central Polynesia

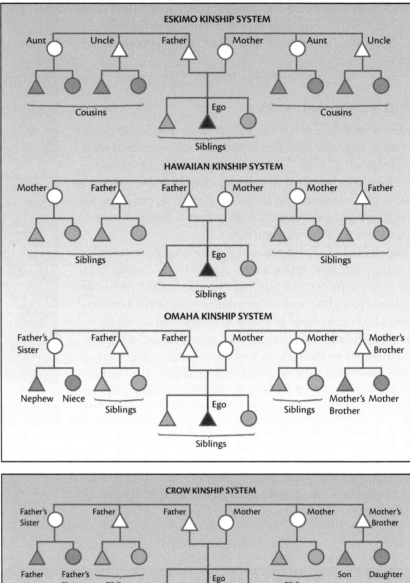

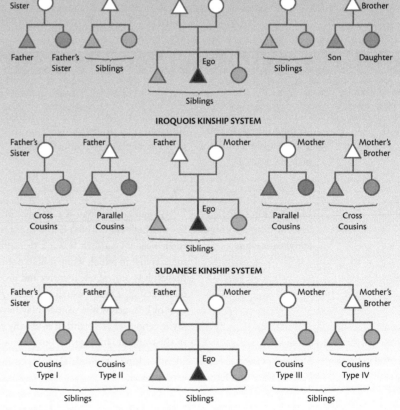

❦ **Figure 16.3   The Six Basic Systems of Kinship.** Anthropologists have identified six different basic kinship systems. The differences can be understood by how people refer to the different cousins.

process of forgetting whole groups of relatives as **genealogical amnesia**. For example, in the United States, naming practices produce a systematic pattern of genealogical amnesia as we lose track of people's surnames. One of the most obvious reasons for this is the practice of women dropping their maiden names when they marry and taking the husband's surname, which was the most typical pattern until the 1970s.

Cultural Patterns in Childrearing

Nearly a century ago, the anthropologist Margaret Mead began studying how families raised children in different cultures. Between the 1930s and the 1950s, Mead was associated with a loosely connected group of scholars known as the **culture and personality movement**, whose focus was on how patterns of childrearing, social institutions, and cultural ideologies shaped individual experience, personality characteristics, and thought patterns (Hsu 1972). They asserted that how a child is bathed, fed, and attended to in the first years of life shapes that child's approach to the world into adulthood.

In her first fieldwork project on kinship and social organization in American Samoa (Mead 1930a, 1930b), Mead observed how Samoan families were caring for their children. She wrote about these things in her popular book *Coming of Age in Samoa* (1928), where she explained that Samoan adolescent sexuality lacked a lot of the psychological distress and anxiety typical of American adolescent sexuality. The reason for this, she believed, is that Samoan approaches to childrearing involve children in work early in their lives and don't judge maturity by a child's age but according to outward physical changes, such as those associated with puberty. Today, it is clear from a variety of more recent studies by anthropologists and sociologists that parental investment of time and nurturing makes a difference in what children aspire to achieve as adolescents and adults. Understanding these matters has great practical significance, especially for those who pursue careers in social work and family law fields, as we explore in "The Anthropological Life: Family-Centered Social Work and Anthropology."

How Families Control Power and Wealth

Whatever form of family we might find in a society, one of its key functions is controlling and managing its members' wealth. The most obvious way for a family, lineage, or clan group to control its wealth is by defining rights over the productive and reproductive abilities of its women and children, as well as defining the inheritance rights of family members when someone dies. These dynamics of control involve issues like the following:

- *Claiming a Bride.* In non-industrial societies in which women provide much of the labor needed to plant, weed, and harvest food from their fields and gardens, when a young woman marries, her family loses that labor. To compensate her clan, the groom's family gives valuables to the bride's family in what has been called **bridewealth** (often known as "bride-price"). Types of valuables given can range from cattle (Zulu tribes of southern Africa) or wild game (some Amazonian communities) to pigs and shell valuables (many Papua New Guinea societies) and cash. In some societies, a young man has to work for his wife's family for a year or more, performing what can be called "bride service."
- *Recruiting the Kids.* Child price payments are another kind of payment to a woman's family, intended to buy rights in the woman's children. Such payments compensate the woman's family for a child who belongs to a different clan and allow the father to recruit the child to his clan. This sort of transaction over children is most typical in societies with patrilineal clans, rather than in those with matrilineal clans, where the children belong to their

Genealogical amnesia. Structural process of forgetting whole groups of relatives, usually because they are not currently significant in social life.

Culture and personality movement. A school of thought in early and mid-twentieth-century American anthropology that studied how patterns of childrearing, social institutions, and cultural ideologies shape individual experience, personality characteristics, and thought patterns.

Bridewealth. Exchange of gifts or money to compensate another clan or family for the loss of one of its women along with her productive and reproductive abilities in marriage. Sometimes known as "bride price."

The Anthropological Life
Family-Centered Social Work and Anthropology

Of all the subfields of cultural anthropology, the study of kinship is by far the earliest and the most fundamental in shaping how anthropologists approach what goes on in different cultural settings. Lewis Henry Morgan (1871) was the first scholar to understand the significant role that kinship systems played in shaping interaction patterns within a community. Early kinship studies allowed researchers to understand how societies were organized in the world's diverse communities. Documenting the ties between intermarried families and the competing claims placed on children and on a family's resources by a husband's and a wife's families was one of anthropology's key goals until the 1960s, when anthropologist David Schneider (1968) used basic anthropological approaches to understand American kinship patterns. Schneider was not the first to look at American kinship, of course, but his study made it clear that even in the United States, kinship and families were key building blocks in even the most "modern" society.

These are not simply abstract or theoretical matters. Understanding the kinds of details anthropologists have understood about how kinship functions in America is a critical requirement for social workers and attorneys working in family law. Social workers in particular, who are trying to assist families, encounter problems of varying kinds and they need to recognize both the broader cultural expectations and the internal social dynamics of how families work. Who has rights to visitation of children after divorce? Who should be looking after children when both parents perish in an automobile accident? If a man has been married several times, what rights do children by each of his wives have over his estate? All of these issues are questions of law that are informed by our society's customary practices of kinship. And since all American family law involving children must view the facts of any case through the lens of what is best for the children, the courts have sometimes been at odds with parents and their extended kin networks.

These are situations where some basic anthropological training can be of great benefit to attorneys, social workers, family aid groups, and the courts for sorting out in family law courts how best to look after the interests of minor children when divorce, death, or other family upheavals arise. Some years ago, anthropologist Carol Stack (1997) studied kinship in an urban Black community and found that the goal of every responsible adult in the community she was observing was to look after the children when mothers worked or had absent partners. A much wider network of individuals and alloparents filled in as "kin" (see also Chapter 7). In the community Stack studied, unmarried women having children coupled with high rates of absent fathers did not entirely deprive children of a male "father" figure in their lives, even though the biological father was often absent. Instead, other men stepped in to fill these roles. Since Stack's study more than forty years ago, we have seen much more intense social disruption in the families of the poor of all racial and ethnic groups, but the pattern of another male figure stepping into the male parent role nevertheless remains quite important almost everywhere. Understanding these patterns as an anthropologist would prevent a social worker from imposing ethnocentric assumptions and help them get at the heart of the local community's understanding of kinship and family.

mother's clan and typically live with her. In some societies, child price payments can be paid all at once, but the power of these transactions can best be understood in societies like the Daribi of the Highlands of Papua New Guinea, where payments may take place over many years. Anthropologist Roy Wagner (1967, 1969), who studied the Daribi, observed that because transactions between clans are about creating alliances, the ongoing series of payments preserve and perpetuate the relationship between the child's father and the uncle, who come from different clans.

- *Ensuring a Daughter's Welfare.* Another form of marriage payment occurs in the highly stratified communities of India. Here, high-caste families traditionally gave a **dowry** consisting of a large sum of money—or in-kind gifts of livestock, furniture, or even electronics—to a daughter to ensure her well-being in her husband's family. Sometimes the dowry was given, at least in part, to the groom as a way of attracting a prosperous and hard-working husband. The Indian government outlawed the practice of dowry in 1961, though it has continued in many parts of the country. Like many social practices that are changing, dowry can sometimes encourage poor treatment of wives and even the death of a wife as a way of gaining access to the wife's dowry, as we read periodically of dowry deaths in the news.

- **Dowry.** A large sum of money or in-kind gifts given to a daughter to ensure her well-being in her husband's family.

In any society, inheritance goes to legitimate heirs—typically the children of a socially recognized married couple. But marriage is such a complicated social institution that we should consider what motivates people to get married in the first place.

THINKING LIKE AN ANTHROPOLOGIST: KINSHIP AND GENDER

Consider the most recent wedding you may have attended, or ask a friend or relative about a wedding they attended as a guest. Who paid for different parts of the celebration (reception, officiant, wedding license, flowers, bridesmaids' dresses, groomsmen's tuxedos, gifts to bridesmaids and groomsmen, rehearsal dinner, etc.)? Who should give gifts and to whom should these gifts be given? How do the dollars and cents of a wedding outline the structure of American families and kin groups?

16.2 Why Do People Get Married?

For at least two centuries American pastors, priests, and rabbis have preached that sex is reserved for marriage; it is primarily for procreation. Yet the reality of American life is that sexual behavior is not limited to married couples, and marriage is about a lot more than sex. In this section we explain some of the reasons people have for getting married, as well as some of the diverse forms that marriage can take.

Why People Get Married

For most Americans, marriage is about love and sex, and we take for granted our individual right to choose a marriage partner. But in most societies around the world, marriage is about cultivating political and economic relations between families. In such contexts, marriage is considered too important to be left to the whims of an individual, and so family members choose an individual's marriage partner.

Marriage also provides public social recognition of the ties between the couples and their families, and social legitimacy of the children. The importance of public recognition at least partially helps explain why same-sex marriage has become a key political issue in the past two decades in many societies, including the United States, Canada, Mexico, and Argentina; it also has to do with gaining rights for couples, such as inheritance.

Forms of Marriage

- **Polygamy.** Any form of plural marriage.

- **Polygyny.** When a man is simultaneously married to more than one woman.

- **Polyandry.** When a woman has two or more husbands at one time.

- **Incest taboo.** The prohibition on sexual relations between close family members.

Just as we have seen the definition of marriage widening in some states and countries to include same-sex marriages, the tendency around the world has increasingly been to limit the number of partners to a couple. In many traditional societies in Africa, Asia, the Americas, and the Pacific, **polygamy** (or plural marriage) was far more common previously than it is today. The most common form of plural marriage was **polygyny**, in which one man is married simultaneously to two or more women. In Africa and Melanesia, for example, having more than one wife indicates an important man with wealth and high status. From a woman's point of view, being in a polygynous marriage can mean that other wives provide support in conducting household duties, such as raising children and cooking. But as these indigenous economies have been drawn into the global system, the number of men with two or more wives has declined, as it is increasingly considered too costly and too old-fashioned (Figure 16.4).

The other form of plural marriage is **polyandry**, in which one woman has two or more husbands at one time. Few societies around the world are known to have allowed polyandry. The best known are the Toda, one of the hill tribes in India (Rivers 1906; Dakowski 1990), and the Sherpas of Nepal, who formerly used polyandry to keep large estates from being divided into tiny estates (Ortner 1989). Among both the Todas and the Sherpas, a group of brothers marries the same woman, a practice known as fraternal polyandry, which limits the tensions among co-husbands.

Figure 16.4   Polygamy Is Largely in Decline Around the World. (*Top*) A polygamous family in Ramallah in the early twentieth century; today, most Palestinian men have one wife. (*Bottom*) Fundamentalist Mormons, who have broken away from the Mormon Church (formally, the Church of Jesus Christ of the Latter-day Saints) based in Salt Lake City, are the main group that still practices polygyny in the United States.

Sex, Love, and the Power of Families Over Young Couples

All societies around the world have rules about who can have sex with or get married to whom. Parents and other family members may reject certain possible partners, such as if a woman chooses a partner from the wrong socioeconomic, religious, educational, or ethnic background. There are also prohibitions against marriage with people who are too closely related.

The Incest Taboo

The prohibition on sexual relations between close family members is generally called the **incest taboo**. It is as close to a universal feature of human societies as anything. There are two well-known exceptions to the incest taboo, both of which prove its generality: in ancient Egypt, during the reigns of the pharaohs, and in Hawai'i, before Europeans encountered the islands for the first time in 1778. In both societies, ruling monarchs could engage in incest because they were considered living gods, who could only preserve the divine essence of their being by marrying a sibling.

For relationships beyond the nuclear family—such as marriage of cousins—societies vary in what they allow. In Africa, Southeast Asia, South America, Australia, and New Guinea, the incest taboo also includes prohibitions on marriage with some kinds of cousins, particularly in societies with a unilineal clan system. And in most clan-based societies the prohibition on marriage within the clan suggests that this extension of the incest taboo defines the boundaries of the clan, just as the boundaries of incest define the boundaries of the nuclear family.

Why Is There an Incest Taboo?

Social scientists have suggested two general explanations for the incest taboo. The most common is that the taboo prevents birth defects caused by inbreeding. The main problem with this explanation is that within a community as small as 300 to 500 individuals, where people are already interrelated, the odds of harmful gene combinations are effectively the same for marriage with a first cousin as for random pairings.

A second explanation, called the "Westermarck Effect," explains the incest taboo as a natural psychological revulsion toward marriage (or sex) with close relatives. Recently, evolutionary psychologists like Steven Pinker (1997) have adopted this explanation, arguing that evolution has selected genes that cause us to feel little sexual attraction for people we have grown up with. But no gene (or combination of genes) has been identified for the proposed revulsion, and the range of relatives prohibited by the incest taboo varies too widely from society to society to be explained by selection. Further, there is no reason to assume that the revulsion is the cause of the taboo, when it is equally probable that the incest taboo itself generates the psychological revulsion.

Many anthropologists reject the idea altogether that the incest taboo emerges out of biology, emphasizing its origins in culture and ordinary life. They point to the research of Melford Spiro (1958), an anthropologist who studied life in an Israeli kibbutz in the 1950s. Spiro found that the adolescents who lived together in large communal settings avoided marrying or even dating members of their communal group. There was no rule against marriage or sex within the group, but there simply was no sexual attraction because they thought of other members as siblings. This situation is not at all unlike what happens in American college coed dorms, where there is similar avoidance of sexual liaisons such as the "hallway hookup" or "floorcest" that can produce social complications for both parties (Sivo 2005).

As we have shown here, culture shapes how people handle the biological and non-biological relationships associated with kinship. In the next section, we shift gears and examine how culture also contributes to how people think about what it means to be male or female.

THINKING LIKE AN ANTHROPOLOGIST: KINSHIP AND GENDER

Americans often think that marriage is about "love," but marriage is also about economics: being married and having a family cost money. Recent studies have determined that the average age at marriage in the United States has been rising for several decades as middle-class incomes have declined. Discuss how the economics of modern American life help shape the decision to get married.

16.3 How and Why Do Males and Females Differ?

Walk into any kids' clothing store in a North American mall and the message is clear: boys and girls are fundamentally different. The boys' section is stocked with jeans, cargo pants, and blue or dark-colored T-shirts emblazoned with images of trucks, guns, or sports equipment. The girls' collection is full of frilly dresses and lace-lined

Figure 16.5   Clothing and Sexual Difference. North American ideas about gender differences are powerfully expressed through the colors and characteristics of the clothing they are assigned from the earliest ages.

- **Sex.** The reproductive forms and functions of the body.

shirts and pants in pastel colors like pink and purple, featuring images of butterflies, flowers, and so on. Judging by these articles, boys are adventuresome, active, and aggressive, while girls are nurturing, domestic, and sentimental (Figure 16.5).

These clothes convey powerful stereotypes about supposed differences in temperament and personality between males and females. In recent decades these stereotypes have become topics of intense debate in the United States as we struggle over why women are excluded from certain kinds of jobs and positions of leadership, why men dominate certain professions and positions of power, and even which washrooms transgender individuals should be required to use. The issue is not whether our culture distinguishes between males and females. The real issue is to explain why our culture constructs these differences in the specific ways it does (Brettell and Sargent 2001). What any society associates with one or another gender, how individuals fluidly enact gender, and the circumstances under which gender is important are as constructed as any of the other elements of culture we have explored in this book.

Toward a Biocultural Perspective on Male and Female Differences

The primary explanation our culture gives for differences between males and females is that they are "hardwired" differently. Differences in **sex**, the reproductive forms and functions of the body, are even thought to produce differences in attitudes, temperaments, intelligences, aptitudes, and achievements between males and females. Some studies have suggested that in all human societies boys tend to engage in more rough-and-tumble play, while girls tend to be more engaged in infant contact and care, suggesting that such behaviors are determined at a species level (Edwards 1993). Recent studies also indicate that male and female brains do in certain senses function differently: women's left-brained tendencies provide them with superior verbal skills, while men's right-brained tendencies give them superior visual and spatial skills (McIntyre and Edwards 2009).

Any conclusions about hardwired sex differences are muddied by evidence that culture also shapes male and female preferences and behaviors people associate with maleness and femaleness. For a long time, anthropologists referred to these cultural expectations of how males and females should behave as "gender." For example, the association of girls with pink and boys with blue feels natural and obvious to many Americans. However, relatively few cultures associate a color with a particular gender, and a century ago in the United States, the colors were reversed, boys wearing pink and girls blue (Kidwell and Steele 1989). American attitudes toward boys and girls did not shift; what changed was the gender association of each color, which had consequences for children's clothing preferences. Anthropologists have long argued for the importance of gender in understanding males and females, as "Classic Contributions: Margaret Mead and the Sex/Gender Distinction" explores.

The distinction Mead made between sex (biology) and gender (cultural expectations) was influential among anthropologists for decades. But in recent years it has been breaking down because it is difficult to tease apart just how much the differences in male and female behavior are caused by "sex" (that is, shaped by biology) and how much they are caused by "gender" (cultural expectations) (Collier and Yanagisako 1987). Scientists believe that sex-specific biological influences on temperament are strongest during infancy and early childhood (McIntyre and Edwards 2009). But as children get older, cultural influences on behavior become much stronger. Furthermore, "sex" is not simply a product of nature; it is also mediated and produced in the context of a specific culture. In light of this complexity, anthropologists increasingly reject an either-or perspective—that it's *either* biology *or* culture, *either* sex *or* gender—and accept that ideas and practices associated with male–female differences are shaped by a mix of biology, environmental conditions, individual choices, and sociocultural processes that construct the meanings of *male* and *female* (Worthman 1995).

Reflecting these intellectual shifts, anthropologists are changing their terminology, and commonly refer to the ideas and social patterns a society uses to organize males, females, and those who do not fit either category as **gender/sex systems** (Morris 1995; Nanda 2000). Around the world, gender/sex systems are cross-culturally variable and historically dynamic. In any particular gender/sex system a spectrum of possibilities exists for defining and expressing masculinity and femininity, as does a shared understanding of when, how, and why it is important to do so.

Gender is still a meaningful concept for anthropologists. However, rather than being viewed as a matter simply of the cultural patterning of sexual differences over a biological substrate, it now refers to the complex and fluid intersections of biological sex, internal senses of self, outward expressions of identity, and cultural expectations about how to perform that identity in appropriate ways. Gender is not an essential entity, and so it cannot be used to explain behavioral differences between males and females. Rather, gender is fluid and dynamic, and people actively construct and enact gender within a range of culturally bound possibilities, norms, and constraints (McElhinny 2003). Clearly, this view diverges from the male–female binary that dominates Western cultural thought about gender.

- **Gender/sex systems.** The ideas and social patterns a society uses to organize males, females, and those who do not fit either category.

- **Gender.** The complex and fluid intersections of biological sex, internal senses of self, outward expressions of identity, and cultural expectations about how to perform that identity in appropriate ways.

Beyond the Male–Female Dichotomy

In the idealized world of science textbooks, human beings are a sexually dimorphic species, which means that males and females have different sexual forms. You already know that, as a rule, nature divides humans into two sexes for the purposes of reproduction. You can probably name some minor exceptions to the rule—men with high voices, women with facial hair—but this is not enough to challenge certainties about the fact of male and female difference. On more systematic inspection, however, the dichotomy between males and females breaks down as variations in chromosomes, gonads, internal reproductive structures, hormones, and external genitalia become apparent (Fausto-Sterling 2000). Individuals who diverge from the male–female norm are called **intersex**, meaning they exhibit sexual organs and functions somewhere between, or including, male and female elements. Some individuals have both ovaries and testes; some have gonad development with separate but not fully developed male and female organs; and some have ovaries and testes growing in the same organ. Many intersex individuals are infertile, but not infrequently at least one of the gonads produces either sperm or eggs.

One reputable estimate puts the frequency of intersex in the United States at 1.7 percent of all live births (Fausto-Sterling 2000). At 1.7 births per 100, intersex is much more common than an unusual but highly recognizable condition like albinism, which is 1 per 20,000 births. This figure of 1.7 percent is not universal; rates of intersex vary between populations. Yup'ik Eskimos in Alaska, for example, have a higher rate of intersex births: 3.5 percent of births have congenital adrenal hyperplasia, a condition produced by a genetic mutation that produces masculine genitalia in girls.

Different societies deal with intersex differently. Many cultures do not make anatomical features, such as genitalia, the dominant factors in constructing gender identities, and some cultures recognize biological sex as a continuum. But European and North American societies have considered intersexuality abnormal, sometimes immoral, most recently turning it into a medical problem. In the United States, most intersex children are treated shortly after birth with "sex-assignment surgery," in

- **Intersex.** Individuals who exhibit sexual organs and functions somewhere between male and female elements, often including elements of both.

Classic Contributions
Margaret Mead and the Sex/Gender Distinction

SINCE THE BEGINNING of her career in the 1920s, anthropologist Margaret Mead (1901–1978) was interested in the differences between males and females, the cultural roles assigned to each, and how sexual differences shaped an individual's life experiences and personality. Mead was possibly the first social scientist to distinguish between biological sex and culturally distinct gender roles (Viswesaran 1997), which she did in her 1935 book *Sex and Temperament in Three Primitive Societies*. This book, which analyzes sex differences in three Papua New Guinea societies (the Arapesh, the Mundugumor, and the Tchambuli), ends with this influential theoretical reflection on the cultural influences on male and female difference.

▼ **Margaret Mead.**

The material suggests that we may say that many, if not all, of the personality traits which we have called masculine or feminine are as lightly linked to sex as are the clothing, manners, and the form of head-dress that a society at a given period assigns to either sex. When we consider the behavior of the typical Arapesh man or woman as contrasted with the typical Mundugumor man or woman, the evidence is overwhelmingly in favour of the strength of social conditioning. In no other way can we account for the almost complete uniformity with which Arapesh children develop into contented, passive, secure persons, while Mundugumor children develop as characteristically into violent, aggressive, insecure persons. Only to the impact of the whole of the integrated culture upon the growing child can we lay the formation of the contrasting types. There is no other explanation of race, or diet, or selection that can be adduced to explain them. We are forced to conclude that human nature is almost unbelievably malleable, responding accurately and contrastingly to contrasting cultural conditions. The differences between individuals who are members of different cultures, like the differences between individuals within a culture, are almost entirely to be laid to differences in conditioning, especially in early childhood, and the form of this conditioning is culturally determined. Standardized personality differences between sexes are of this order, cultural creations to which each generation, male and female, is trained to conform. [Mead 1963:280–81]

Questions for Reflection

1. Why would an anthropologist study three different societies in New Guinea to demonstrate that gender roles are culturally constructed rather than innately biological?

2. Some scholars have claimed that Mead's New Guinea examples are cultural stereotypes from within the three cultures she studied. If true, would these stereotypes undermine or support her claim that gender roles are cultural rather than biological?

which a doctor eliminates any genital ambiguity through surgery, and doctors counsel the parents to raise the child to correspond with that sexual assignment.

The reasons behind parents' decisions to choose sex-assignment surgery for their intersex children are rarely medical; they derive from culturally accepted notions about how a boy or girl should look. Surgeons create realistic-looking genitalia by removing body parts and using plastic surgery to construct "appropriate" genitalia. But there is no biological norm for penis or clitoris size or shape, and in fact, many boys are born with very small penises that get larger at puberty, and girls are born with much larger than average clitorises that present no clinical problems (Fausto-Sterling 2000). The goal of these surgeries is for the genitals' size and shape to convince others—parents, caretakers, other children, and future spouses—that the person is a male or a female.

Sex-assignment surgery shows that "sex" is not simply a biological phenomenon, but is—*quite literally*—constructed upon cultural assumptions of a sexual binary in humans and about what an ideal male or female should look like. These cultural assumptions stand in contrast to the evidence that human sex is not dichotomous and that natural variations occur in the shape and size of genitalia. Such surgeries seem well intentioned—to help intersex individuals avoid the emotional burdens of being different in a culture that does not accept sexual ambiguity. However, they have become highly controversial, especially among many intersex people themselves, some of whom have described it as an involuntary mutilation (Figure 16.6).

Explaining Gender/Sex Inequality

In nearly all societies with any degree of social stratification, more men are in leadership roles than women, not only in political roles, but in economic and social roles involving trade, exchange, kinship relations, ritual participation, and dispute resolution (Ortner 1996:176) (Figure 16.7). In the United States today, only 23 percent of congressional seats are held by women; in the workplace women earn on average 81 percent of what their male counterparts earn; and sex discrimination persists in social expectations, such as the notion that women should do housework. Very few of the privileges men have over women are predicated on physical strength. So why is inequality between the sexes such a common feature of many societies?

Debating "the Second Sex"

In 1949, French existentialist philosopher Simone de Beauvoir published an influential book titled *The Second Sex* in which she argued that throughout history women have been

Figure 16.6   Justice for Intersex People. During 2017, the US-based advocacy group Intersex Justice held a protest outside a Chicago hospital asking the institution to stop performing medically unnecessary surgeries on intersex children unable to give their consent.

Figure 16.7   Batek Headwoman. The few exceptions to systematic male dominance are generally found in small hunter-gatherer societies, like the Batek of the Malay Peninsula in Southeast Asia. This small community lives in bands that anthropologists Kirk and Karen Endicott (2008) report are generally egalitarian in their gender roles, to the extent that the band they lived with during their fieldwork had this woman, Tanyogn, as its headwoman (1976).

Figure 16.8   Feminism's First and Second Waves.
The first wave of feminism (late 1800s, early 1900s) in Britain and the United States focused on legal obstacles to gender/sex equality, such as laws prohibiting women from voting or owning property. The second wave (1960s and 1970s) focused on issues like unofficial inequalities and reproductive rights. Both had a major influence in anthropology.

considered "the second sex," inferior in status and subordinate to men (2010). Even before the publication of this book, during the Victorian era, a handful of women anthropologists had studied women's status and roles in other societies. A few of these anthropologists, animated by the "first-wave feminism" that was beginning to challenge male domination and win the right to vote, wanted to understand if all societies treated women as unequally as Euro-American societies did. Despite this movement, it wasn't until the mid-1950s and early 1960s that anthropologists—inspired in great part by de Beauvoir's work and the emergence of "second-wave feminism"—began to pay greater attention to the issue of gender/sex inequality (Figure 16.8).

Most feminist anthropologists rejected the idea that biological differences are the source of women's subordination. Instead, they argued that cultural ideologies and social relations impose lower status, prestige, and power on women than men. But here the agreement ends, and during the 1970s and 1980s a major debate took place over whether gender inequality is universal and what causes it.

On one side were those who argued that women's lower status is universal. Influential feminist anthropologist Sherry Ortner observed that female subordination resulted from the distinction all societies make between "nature" and "culture" (Ortner 1974). Across many cultures, women are assigned symbolically to nature because of their role in childbearing and thus are viewed as uncultured and uncivilized. Men, on the other hand, are associated symbolically with culture and thus viewed as civilized and superior.

On the other side were feminist anthropologists who argued that egalitarian male–female relations have existed throughout human history. For example, many foraging societies exhibit gender complementarity and relative equality. Where gender/sex inequality does form, they observed, it has been the result of particular historical processes, especially the imposition of European capitalism and colonization on native peoples who were once egalitarian. For example, Eleanor Leacock (1981) argued that among the Montagnais-Naskapi [mohn-tan-**yay** nahs-**kah**-pee] of the Labrador Peninsula in Canada, women enjoyed equal status with men, held formal political power, exercised spiritual leadership, and controlled important economic activities before the arrival of Europeans. By the 1700s, however, dependence on the fur trade with Europeans undercut the traditional political system and economy, and Jesuit missionaries imposed compulsory Catholic schooling, which was hostile to women's independence and power. Eventually, the Montagnais-Naskapi developed a cultural view of women as inferior and subordinate.

Taking Stock of the Debate

On all sides of the feminist anthropology debate, participants recognized that inequality between men and women is, if not universal, at least pervasive. More important, the debate brought the study of what women say and do to the mainstream of the discipline. The emergence of this so-called anthropology of women successfully challenged the discipline's historical bias toward studying males and closed a gap in the ethnographic record by producing studies of women's experiences and perspectives (Viswesaran 1997).

But the debate came to an impasse due to differences of interpretation over the evidence. Some participants shifted their positions, including Ortner, who recognized that egalitarian relations between men and women can exist although they are fragile and inconsistent (Ortner 1996). Critics of the debate, including some anthropologists, members of minority groups, and Third World academics, asserted that second-wave feminism, although well intentioned in its concern for women around the world, made ethnocentric assumptions (Mohanty 1991). They pointed out that the mostly white, middle-class feminists involved in the movement had downplayed meaningful differences between women across cultures, assuming that all women viewed the fight for political equality as a single global priority. In many other countries, women's movements are more local and oriented toward fighting militarism, challenging foreign ideals about beauty and ways of being a woman, or gaining access to local political processes or economic opportunities (Basu 2010).

Reproducing Male–Female Inequalities

The impasse in the debate also accompanied a shift in how anthropologists studied relations between men and women. A number of anthropologists began to emphasize a focus on women *and* men, especially the dynamic relationships between them in everyday life.

From this vantage point, inequality is not something static that people "possess"; it is something that they "do." For example, patterns of inequality are reproduced in basic things like everyday language. What American men and women say may include the same words but mean something different to each gender. As we explored in Chapter 12, linguistic miscommunications can happen because our culture has different expectations about how men and women should communicate.

Anthropologists also began to rethink "men." For decades anthropology involved men studying the lives of other men, but until recently very few anthropologists had examined men *as men*—that is, how men and women collectively view and shape what "being a man" means, and how men actually perform, or act out, manhood (Gutmann 1997). The anthropological study of **masculinity**, the ideas and practices of manhood, has not just opened new avenues of research for understanding how gender identities are constructed but has also generated new perspectives on the issue of male–female inequality, including the notion that ideals of masculinity are dynamic and do not in themselves necessarily assume male dominance (Figure 16.9).

By focusing on the dynamic nature of male–female inequalities, anthropologists have come to understand that male domination and female subordination are reproduced and performed in complex ways in everyday life. But anthropologists have not only studied "men" and "women"; they have also studied people who are not considered, or do not consider themselves, to be either men or women, an issue we address in the next section.

• **Masculinity.** The ideas and practices of manhood.

Figure 16.9 Masculinity in Transition. In recent years, broad social transformations—such as greater numbers of women working outside the home for money, boys and girls in schools being given equal status, and the feminist movement—have contributed to changing perceptions of manhood across the United States, including the acceptance of men's greater involvement in parenting.

THINKING LIKE AN ANTHROPOLOGIST: KINSHIP AND GENDER

Inequalities between men and women are reproduced and performed in many different ways in daily life. Can you identify examples in the following: Advertising? Sports? Language? Cooking? Shopping at a mall? At the same time, these inequalities are often challenged by both men and women. Can you find examples of such challenges in the same contexts?

16.4 What Does It Mean to Be Neither Male nor Female?

- **Gender variance.** Expressions of sex and gender that diverge from the male and female norms that dominate in most societies.

- **Sexuality.** Sexual preferences, desires, and practices.

In many societies, some people live their lives as neither male nor female. They have a culturally accepted, and in some cases prestigious, symbolic niche and social pathway that is distinct from the cultural life plan of males and females (Herdt 1994a). Anthropologists refer to this situation as **gender variance** (expressions of sex and gender that diverge from the male and female norms) or sometimes as "third gender," which recognizes the fact that many societies allow for more than two categories of gender/sex (in actuality ranging anywhere from three to five). Sometimes the terms are used interchangeably, as we do here.

Third gender has often been entangled in debates about **sexuality**, which encompasses sexual preferences, desires, and practices. It has been viewed as a form of homosexuality, since some third-gender individuals engage in what appear to be same-sex sexual activities (Herdt 1994b). But sexual preferences intersect in complex ways with gender variance. People everywhere establish their gender/sex identities, including normative categories like "man" or "woman," not by sexual practices but through social performance: wearing certain clothes, speaking and moving in certain ways, and performing certain social roles and occupations. Here we consider two examples of gender variance drawn from different cultures.

Navajo *Nádleehé*

Gender variance has been historically documented in over 150 American Indian societies, although it remains important in only a few societies. Today, where it exists, American Indian gender variance is often called "two-spirit," meaning that an individual has both male and female spirit. The phenomenon has been greatly misunderstood, largely because Western culture lacks the conceptual categories to translate the specific beliefs and customs related to gender variance in these societies (Roscoe 1994). For decades white Americans have used the term *berdache* [burr-**dash**], a derogatory Arabic term that refers to the younger partner in a male homosexual relationship, to refer to gender variance among American Indians. This term assumes that gender-variant individuals are homosexual, which is sometimes but not always the case (Figure 16.10). Western moral thought also categorized them as deviants, although in a number of Indian societies third-gender individuals are not deviant but held high social status.

The Navajo, who live in the Four Corners area of the Southwest, present an especially subtle example of gender variance. In Navajo society, *nádleehé* [nahk-**hlay**] are

Figure 16.10   Two Spirit Singers at a Gathering. Unlike traditional gender variants in American Indian societies, many contemporary two spirit individuals are gay. Due to antigay sentiment, they often experience hostility and discrimination in their home communities. They also feel alienated from white gay and lesbian society and political activism, which does not acknowledge their unique cultural heritage and the issues of poverty and racism they face as Indians.

individuals held in high esteem who combine male and female roles and characteristics. They perform both male roles (such as hauling wood and participating in hunts and warfare) and female roles (such as weaving, cooking, sheepherding, and washing clothes). Some, but not all, *nádleehé* cross-dress. Navajo families have traditionally treated *nádleehé* respectfully, even giving them control over family property. The *nádleehé* participate in important religious ceremonies, serve as spiritual healers, and act as go-betweens in arranging marriages and mediating conflicts.

Navajo recognize five genders, two of them being male and female. The term *nádleehé* (in English, "one who changes continuously") refers to intersex individuals whom they consider a third gender. The fourth and fifth genders are also called *nádleehé* but are distinct from intersex individuals. The fourth gender is the masculine-female, female-bodied individuals who do not get involved in reproduction and who work in traditional male occupations (hunting and raiding). Today they often serve as firefighters or auto mechanics. The fifth gender is the feminine-male, male-bodied individuals who participate in women's activities of cooking, tending to children, and weaving. Feminine-males may engage in sexual relations with males, although Navajo do not consider these to be same-sex relationships.

Historically, however, Christian missionaries tried to eliminate the *nádleehé*. Prominent *nádleehé* began to be more discreet about exposing their identities to the outside world, a situation that continues today (W. Thomas 1997). Although *nádleehé* continue to exist, many young Navajos, especially those raised off reservation, might not identify themselves as *nádleehé* but as "gay" or "lesbian," adopting Western forms of identification that have little to do with traditional Navajo gender notions.

Indian *Hijras*

In India, *hijras* [**hee**-drahs] are a third gender who have special social status by virtue of their devotion to Bahuchara Mata, one of many versions of the Mother Goddess worshiped throughout India (Nanda 1994). *Hijras* are defined as males who are sexually impotent, either because they were born intersex or because they underwent castration. Because they lack male genitals, *hijras* are viewed as "man minus man." They are viewed as "male plus female" because they dress and talk like women, take on women's occupations, and act like women in other ways, though in exaggerated, comic, and burlesque fashion (Figure 16.11).

Individuals from many religious backgrounds—Hindu, Christian, and Muslim—become *hijras*, but their special status emerges from the positive meanings that Hinduism attributes to individuals who embody male and female characteristics and to individuals who renounce normal social conventions. In Hindu thought, males and females exist in complementary opposition. The important Hindu deities—Shiva, Vishnu, and Krishna—have dual gender manifestations. The female principle is active, both life-giving and destructive, while the male principle is inert and latent. By becoming *hijras* men can tap into the beneficent and destructive powers of the female principle, as vehicles for the Mother Goddess. With these special powers, *hijras* provoke widespread ambivalence: on the one hand, Indians tend to view *hijras* are inauspicious and stigmatized, fearing their ability to issue curses. But at the same time, it is common to ask *hijras* to give blessings.

Hijras live in communes of up to twenty people, led by a *guru* (teacher). They live outside normal social bounds, having renounced their caste position and kinship obligations. Their primary social role is to provide blessings when a boy is born (a major cause of celebration in India) or bless a couple's fertility at a wedding. *Hijras* are typically a raucous presence at these events, making crude and inappropriate jokes, performing burlesque dances, and demanding payment for their services. Although it is stigmatized within *hijra* communities, *hijras* also work as prostitutes, engaging in sex acts with men for pay. *Hijra* prostitutes are not necessarily considered "homosexuals"; Indian society does not consider human sexuality as a dichotomy between homosexuality and heterosexuality as ours does, and *hijras* are not considered males anyway.

Although British colonialism tried to outlaw *hijras*, they continued to exist largely by conducting their initiation rites (including castration of willing males) in secret.

Figure 16.11 *Hijras* in India. The *hijras* pictured here are protesting against Indian Penal Code Section 377, which criminalizes same-sex relationships. Protestors have sought to overturn the law, alleging that the law, created during the British colonial era, is outdated and justifies daily abuse and harassment by police of members of the gay, lesbian, bisexual, and transgender communities, including *hijras*.

In recent decades they have had to adapt to a changing Indian society. Government family-planning programs have reduced birth rates, and urban families increasingly live in apartment buildings with security guards who prevent the entrance of *hijras* when they arrive to bless a baby. In response, *hijras* have exploited new economic opportunities, asking for alms from shop owners and expanding their involvement in the sex industry (Nanda 1994:415).

> **THINKING LIKE AN ANTHROPOLOGIST: KINSHIP AND GENDER**
>
> Societies in which gender variance is common tend to also be tolerant toward ambiguity and complexity in other areas of life, such as religious beliefs. How and why might a society develop an acceptance of ambiguity and complexity? Beyond gender and religious beliefs, in what other aspects of social life might one expect to see a tolerance for ambiguity?

16.5 Is Human Sexuality Just a Matter of Being Straight or Queer?

Most of us assume that sexuality (sexual preferences, desires, and practices) is an either/or issue, that people are *either* straight *or* queer. We also assume that most humans are heterosexual. The term we use to indicate heterosexuality—"straight"—implies that it is normal and morally correct, while anything else is deviant, bent, or "queer," a term that once had derogatory connotations but has been appropriated by LGBTQ communities and given a more positive connotation.

Human sexuality is far more complex and subtle, something that social scientists began to realize after Indiana University biologist Dr. Alfred Kinsey conducted a series of sexuality studies during the 1940s. Kinsey and his colleagues surveyed the sexual lives and desires of American men and women, discovering that sexuality exists along a continuum. They found, for example, that 37 percent of the male population surveyed had had some sexual experience with other men, most of which occurred during adolescence, and at least 25 percent of adult males had had more than incidental same-sex sexual experiences for at least three years of their lives (Kinsey 1948; Fausto-Sterling 1992). Many of these men did not think of themselves or lead their lives as gay; this suggests quite clearly that, in practice, people's sexuality does not fall into absolute categories. More important, Kinsey's research challenged views of same-sex sexuality that considered it a pathological and deviant condition, indicating that psychologically "normal" people may express their sexuality in many ways (Figure 16.12).

As a flexible phenomenon, human sexuality has numerous possible expressions. Some of these expressions include lesbian

Figure 16.12   Controversial Knowledge. Kinsey's work was highly controversial during a period in American history when homosexuality and heterosexual promiscuity were considered unacceptable.

sexuality (sexual attraction between women), gay sexuality (sexual attraction between men), straight sexuality (sexual attraction between men and women), asexuality (non-sexuality or lack of sexual attraction), bisexuality (sexual attraction to more than one gender), demi-sexuality (sexual attraction only to individuals with whom one has an emotional bond), and pansexuality (sexual attraction to individuals of any gender, including individuals outside the gender binary). Sexuality is not an essence buried deep in a person's psychological self or genetic makeup (Lancaster 2004), or just a matter of personal preference or individual orientation. Like other forms of social conduct, sexuality is learned, patterned, and shaped by culture and the political-economic system in which one lives (Weston 1993).

Cultural Perspectives on Same-Sex Sexuality

Anthropological attention to same-sex sexuality goes back to the discipline's early years when in the 1920s a handful of anthropologists wrote about sexual desires and practices in certain non-industrialized societies (Lyons and Lyons 2004). But it was not until the 1960s and 1970s—when a gay movement emerged in the United States—that anthropologists began paying more consistent attention to same-sex sexuality more specifically (Weston 1993). More recently the global HIV/AIDS pandemic, the visibility of openly gay celebrities, and the push for legal rights for gays have encouraged even more anthropological attention (Lewin and Leap 2009; Parker 2009). A number of ethnographers have also written about how their own experience as gay affects their work as anthropologists (Lewin and Leap 1996), a theme we explore in "Doing Fieldwork: Don Kulick and 'Coming Out' in the Field."

One of the difficulties of studying same-sex sexuality in other societies is the problem of adequately naming what is actually being studied and avoiding ethnocentrism (Weston 1993). Most North Americans hold the view that people are born straight or gay, implying a fixed and stable condition and identity. This notion originated in the late nineteenth century, when medical science and psychology turned what people had previously considered "perverse" *behaviors* into biopsychological *conditions* requiring medical intervention. In many other cultures, this idea of same-sex sexuality as a fixed and either/or condition does not exist.

One example comes from the work of anthropologist Gilbert Herdt (1981), who studied the male initiation rituals of the Sambia people of Papua New Guinea. Boys undergo six elaborate stages of initiation that involve behavior he calls "insemination." To be a strong, powerful warrior requires *jerungdu* (the essence of masculine strength), a substance a boy can only acquire from ingesting the semen of a man. Before insemination the boys must purge harmful feminine essences with a rite that mimics female menstruation: sharp grasses are shoved up the noses of the boys to make them bleed off the lingering essences of their mother's milk. Finally, they receive *jerungdu* in the form of semen directly from young married men on whom they perform fellatio. During the early stages of the initiation the boys are inseminated orally by young married men at the height of their sexual and physical powers. When the initiates reach later stages of initiation—after marriage but before they become fathers—younger initiates will perform oral sex on them. The final stage of initiation occurs after the birth of their first child. Now in their twenties or thirties, the men have sex only with women.

Herdt (1981) described these initiation activities as "ritualized homosexuality." The problem with this terminology is that Western notions of "homosexuality" imply an inborn condition or identity, yet after marriage Sambia men shift their erotic focus to

Doing Fieldwork
Don Kulick and "Coming Out" in the Field

In Brazil's third-largest city of Salvador live nearly 200 *travestis* [trah-**vest**-tees], men who cross-dress and work as prostitutes. *Travestis* adopt female names, clothing styles, hairstyles, makeup, and linguistic pronouns (like "her"). They also ingest hormones and use silicone to acquire feminine bodily features, such as breasts, wide hips, large thighs, and expansive buttocks (Kulick 1998). But *travestis* do not self-identify as women, nor do they desire to remove their penises surgically. They consider themselves men—gay men—who desire to have sex with other men—non-gay men—and fashion themselves as an object of desire for those men.

Brazilians are fascinated by *travestis*, several of whom have become national celebrities. But the reality for most *travestis* is that they are discriminated against and poor, living a hand-to-mouth existence, and often dying young from violence, drug abuse, and health problems, particularly AIDS. During the late 1990s, Swedish anthropologist Don Kulick spent a year living among Salvador's *travestis* to understand the day-to-day realities of their lives.

Kulick believes that several factors helped him gain acceptance in the insular community. One of these was that *travestis* were open to his involvement in their lives because they viewed Europeans as more liberal and cultivated than Brazilians, and he would not have the same prejudices against their lives as Brazilians would. Another is that when Kulick started his fieldwork he spoke very little Portuguese, and so could not communicate very well. *Travestis* came to see him as a non-threatening presence, someone who would not condemn them.

Kulick believes a third factor played an especially crucial role in his gaining acceptance: he is a gay man. The *travestis*

asked about his sexual orientation right away, if he was a *viado* (a "fag"). Kulick observes, "Upon receiving an affirmative answer, *travestis* often nodded and relaxed considerably. My status as a self-acknowledged *viado* implied to the *travestis* that I was, in effect, one of the girls, and that I probably was not interested in them as sexual partners. My behavior quickly confirmed that I was not, and after such preliminaries were out of the way, *travestis* realized that they could continue conversing about the topics—boyfriends, clients, big penises, hormone, and silicone—that occupy their time, without having to worry that I might find such topics uninteresting or offensive" (1998:15).

Previous research on *travestis* had been conducted by heterosexual women and a Brazilian male researcher who had presented himself as a potential client. These studies focused on their work as prostitutes, but these researchers had not gained access to the *travestis'* private worlds. Kulick believes that "coming out" to the *travestis* as an openly gay man facilitated access to confidences and discussions that may not have been granted as easily to other researchers.

Questions for Reflection

1. Kulick argues that an anthropologist's access to this community was benefited by being gay and seen as "one of them." Would this extend to other identities? For example, should women study women's lives and men study men's lives?

2. Although Kulick reports his coming out as positive, it was also risky. What kinds of risks might his coming out have had?

women. Furthermore, for the Sambia these ritual acts are not erotic per se, but intended to develop masculine strength. Herdt and others who study similar rites now refer to them as "semen transactions" or "boy-inseminating rites."

Anthropologists have also learned that concepts of same-sex sexuality differ across cultures. In Latin American countries like Mexico (Carrier 1976), Nicaragua (Lancaster 1992, 1997), and Brazil (Parker 1989, 2009), a man who engages in same-sex sexual practices is not necessarily identified as (nor would he consider himself) "gay." For example, Brazilian sexual culture distinguishes between active and passive participants in sexual intercourse, typically considering the active agent masculine and the passive agent feminine. The metaphorical language people use to describe sex acts reflects these distinctions: *dar* [darr; "to give"] is the passive role of being penetrated during intercourse, while *comer* [koh-**mehr**; "to eat"] is the action of penetration (Parker 1989). "Women" and *viados* (a colloquial term meaning "fags" or gay men) are those who "give" (receive penetration), while "men" are the active ones who "eat" (penetrate). The result is that a man who penetrates another man would not consider himself—nor would he be considered by others—to be gay, yet the man being penetrated would be considered gay.

Controlling Sexuality

Long ago, anthropologists observed that every society places limits on people's sexuality by constructing rules about who can sleep with whom. Modern governments routinely exert great control over sexuality, implementing and enforcing laws that limit the kinds of sexual relations their citizens can have. For example, in dozens of countries, and even in twenty-one US states, adultery is considered by the law to be "injurious to public morals and a mistreatment of the marriage relationship" (Adultery 2009) and is treated by authorities as a civil offense (subject to fines) or even a crime (subject to jail time). Until the US Supreme Court overturned such laws in 2003, fifteen states still outlawed "sodomy," or sex acts considered "unnatural" or "immoral" such as anal sex, oral sex, or same-sex sex acts. In our country, the most contentious public issues—including debates about abortion, gay people in the military, and the right to same-sex marriage—involve questions over whether and how the government should control the sexuality of its citizens. Family-planning programs can also be viewed as another manifestation of government control over sexuality—especially women's sexuality, since such programs tend to focus on women's bodies (Dwyer 2000).

THINKING LIKE AN ANTHROPOLOGIST: KINSHIP AND GENDER

Many queer activists in the United States and Europe have accepted and promote the idea that they were "born" with their sexual identity and that they have no choice in the matter. How do you think anthropologists, who view sexuality as culturally patterned, socially conditioned, and not inborn, should respond to this idea?

Conclusion

The concept of sexuality—who can sleep with whom and the sexual relationships and practices in which people engage—is a key dimension of the larger themes around which this chapter is organized, namely, kinship and gender. What unites all of these concepts is that they touch on an issue of central importance to human existence, which is our capacity for procreation. Yet these concepts are intertwined in complex ways, shaping the ideas and social patterns a society uses to organize and control males and females, as well as those who do not fit these categories.

It is important to remember that the ways in which we think of these matters, as natural as they feel to us, are not as universal as we may assume. Although the tendency in our own culture—if not also the Mexican *telenovela* that opens this chapter—emphasizes that kinship, family, and gender are primarily matters of blood relationships, anthropologists view the matter rather differently, having seen the great variety of ways different societies construct families and gender relations. It is also good to remember that matters of kinship and gender are not necessarily as stable as they feel to us. The ongoing transformations of the "traditional" American family and the recent normalization of same-sex marriage are two illustrations of that dynamism. The reason these things feel so stable to us in our everyday experience is that they are powerful cultural constructions reproduced and upheld in our everyday lives and most important social institutions.

KEY TERMS

Bride price   p. 457

Clan   p. 454

Corporate groups   p. 454

Culture and personality movement   p. 457

Dowry   p. 459

Exogamous   p. 454

Extended families   p. 454

Gender   p. 463

Gender variance   p. 468

Gender/sex systems   p. 463

Genealogical amnesia   p. 457

Incest taboo   p. 460

Intersex   p. 463

Kinship   p. 453

Kinship chart   p. 454

Lineage   p. 454

Masculinity   p. 467

Natal family   p. 453

Nuclear family   p. 453

Polyandry   p. 460

Polygamy   p. 460

Polygyny   p. 460

Sex   p. 462

Sexuality   p. 468

Reviewing the Chapter

Chapter Section	What We Know	To Be Resolved
What are families, and how are they structured in different societies?	Families differ in their composition and structure cross-culturally. But they are also dynamic. All societies have developed ways of ensuring that the family group has some control over collective resources or the labor of its members.	It is impossible to predict how any society's system of kinship, marriage, and the family will change without understanding the other social, economic, environmental, and political changes in that society.

Chapter Section	What We Know	To Be Resolved
Why do people get married?	Marriage can take on many diverse forms, and our own cultural model of basing marriage on love and sex is not important to all societies, especially those in which marriage is about creating social, economic, and political ties with other groups.	Although economics has an impact on who gets married and who does not, it is not clear what the long-term impact of delayed marriage or the growing number of unmarried couples with children will be.
How and why do males and females differ?	Every society makes a distinction between "male" and "female." But not all societies have the firm binary between males and females we find in Western cultures. Gender/sex systems are cross-culturally variable and dynamic, and not all attach the same meanings to biological differences, or even think differences in biology are important for explaining differences between males and females. Importantly, biological differences are not the source of women's subordination. Rather, cultural ideologies and social relations impose on women lower status, prestige, and power than men.	Anthropologists continue to work out the relative influences of biological, environmental, and cultural factors on shaping gender/sex.
What does it mean to be neither male nor female?	Many gender/sex systems around the world allow for gender variance. Gender variants generally establish their unique identities through social performance: wearing certain clothes, speaking and moving in certain ways, and performing certain social roles and occupations.	Western terminology and concepts are not always able to capture the complexity of how other cultures conceive of matters of sex, gender, and sexuality, which raises questions about how to best represent such phenomena.
Is human sexuality just a matter of being straight or queer?	Human sexuality is variable and patterned by cultural ideologies and social relations. It is also not a fixed or exclusive condition.	Anthropologists continue to work through the complex and subtle ways sexuality interacts with gender and sex, as well as other identities like class, race, and ethnicity.

READINGS

For a discussion of the origins of kinship studies in US anthropology, see Thomas Trautmann's *Lewis Henry Morgan and the Invention of Kinship* (Lincoln: University of Nebraska Press, 2008). In British anthropology, see the classic volume edited by A. R. Radcliffe-Brown and Daryl Forde, *African Systems of Kinship and Marriage* (London: Oxford University Press, 1950).

American cultural anthropology's argument that kinship is never exclusively about biology is well appreciated in two

classics: David Schneider's book *American Kinship: A Cultural Account* (Englewood Cliffs, NJ: Prentice-Hall, 1968), and Carol Stack's, *All Our Kin* (New York: Basic Books, 1997), which explores the dynamism and fluidity of "family" relations among urban African Americans.

Biologist Anne Fausto-Sterling's book *Sexing the Body: Gender Politics and the Construction of Sexuality* (New York: Basic Books, 2000) offers powerful perspectives on the construction of sex,

gender, sexuality, and intersex. Caroline Brettell and Carolyn Fishel Sargent's edited reader *Gender in Cross-Cultural Perspective*, 3rd ed. (Upper Saddle River, NJ: Prentice Hall, 2001) offers a range of anthropological arguments and case studies about these issues.

For an overview of feminist anthropology and debates over male/female inequality, see Sherry Ortner's book *Making Gender: The Politics and Erotics of Culture* (Boston: Beacon Press, 1996). Amitra Basu's 2010 edited volume *Women's Movements in the Global Era: The Power of Local Feminisms* (Boulder, CO: Westview Press, 2010) offers a recent assessment of the diversity of feminisms that exist in the world.

....

Gilbert Herdt's edited book *Third Sex, Third Gender: Beyond Sexual Dimorphism in Culture and History* (New York: Zone Books, 1994) explores gender variance across many cultures. Serena Nanda's book *Neither Man nor Woman: The Hijras of India*, 2nd ed. (Boston: Cengage, 1999) is a classic ethnographic study of gender variance in India.

....

Andrew P. and Harriet D. Lyons's book *Irregular Connections: A History of Anthropology and Sexuality* (Lincoln: University of Nebraska Press, 2004) examines anthropology's history with the study of sexuality. It pairs well with Don Kulick's ethnography of sexuality among transgender prostitutes in Brazil, *Travesti: Sex, Gender, and Culture Among Brazilian Transgendered Prostitutes* (Chicago: University of Chicago Press, 1998).

....

17

Religion

Ritual and Belief

MANY OF US think of the COVID-19 pandemic as a public health phenomenon with naturalistic causes, which is, of course, true. But pandemics are also religious phenomena, because they raise important existential questions about the fragility of life, reminding us of chaos in the world and contributing to crises of meaning, especially when a close relative or friend dies. Religious institutions and practices are often the first place people turn to make sense of such crises. But what happens when those institutions and practices are themselves disrupted by the pandemic?

This was a problem that Pakistani medical anthropologist Inayat Ali (2021a, 2021b) of Fatima Jinna Women University Rawalpindi was poised to explore during a year of fieldwork studying the impact of the COVID-19 pandemic on Pakistani lives. Almost immediately after the coronavirus arrived in Pakistan, there was a sudden rise in mortality, and health workers and government authorities found themselves struggling to manage the growing number of dead bodies. As family members began arriving to claim their relatives for burial, the authorities realized that typical funerary practices involving large numbers of people coming together in close contact with each other, with the bodies of the dead, and with Islamic religious leaders traveling between families

---

A Pandemic-Era Funeral. In Pakistan, precautions around preventing the transmission of Covid-19 disrupted traditional funerary rituals, compounding the anguish that many people experienced on the death of their loved ones.

to conduct many funerals, could become disastrous super-spreader events. So the government prohibited such funerals, in many cities burying large numbers of the dead in mass graves without any individual funeral services whatsoever. This decision likely saved hundreds of thousands of Pakistanis from dying. But it profoundly transformed Pakistani funerary practices and caused extreme anguish.

When one of anthropologist Ali's informants, a kind and gentle woman, died he witnessed firsthand how dramatically the pandemic had changed funeral practices. In pre-pandemic times, older Pakistanis had hoped to die at home with family and close friends around them. After death, family members would ritually cleanse the body, apply makeup, dress the body in a white shroud called *kafan*, and carry it on a *charpoy* (a bed made of woven ropes normally used for sleeping) on their shoulders to the cemetery, where they would participate in an Islamic funeral prayer called the *Namaz-e-Janaza* and then bury the body. This event is followed with a series of rituals and meals, each phase bringing key family, friends, and community members together, which helped support the family during their mourning. In the case of Ali's friend, none of the woman's family could be near her for fear of spreading the virus. Her death, like most pandemic deaths, took place alone in a hospital with no family present. Only her eldest daughter—wearing personal protective equipment and under strict hospital supervision—was allowed in to cleanse the body and put on the *kafan*, after which her body was put in a coffin. Like many others, the funeral was a truncated affair, a short viewing of the coffin by local family members, which was then whisked to the cemetery for burial by a few male relatives and hospital workers.

This situation was deeply unsettling to the woman's family. And of course with so many deaths, this family was not alone. This disruption in the normal ritual functions of funerals left a gap in how the families and communities rebuilt their lives. And since one COVID death in the family was often accompanied soon after by several others, the healing power of religious ritual ceased to function in its usual ways. As Ali observed, this situation has contributed to various kinds of mental health problems, particularly depression and feelings of isolation.

Funerals are just one sort of religious ritual that constructs meaning for the living by offering symbolic answers to the big questions of meaning, death, and how to live one's life, each of which defies any simple and straightforward answers. At the heart of anthropology's approach to religion is the question that animates this chapter: *How do rituals and the beliefs that support them help people construct a meaningful world in the face of so many seemingly meaningless acts?* We can answer this question by considering a number of related questions around which this chapter is organized:

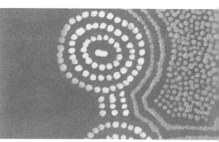

How should we understand religion and religious beliefs?

What forms does religion take?

How do rituals work?

How is religion linked to political and social action?

Religious beliefs and the rituals that support them differ strikingly in their details across the major world religions, but also among the diverse societies of Africa, Asia, Latin America, and the Pacific Islands. Common to all, however, is the fact that religious beliefs offer people a roadmap for how people should live and how they should understand other people's behaviors, actions, and ideas. They are supported by both public and private rituals that construct a meaningful and seemingly obvious and self-evident world. We begin by exploring what anthropologists think religion actually is and does.

17.1 How Should We Understand Religion and Religious Beliefs?

Western intellectuals and social scientists have historically found the subject of religion problematic. When scholars in the nineteenth century confronted peoples around the world who held mystical views, most considered these ideas to be non-scientific mumbo-jumbo, and their adherents to be people of limited intellectual capacity. But by the 1870s, when anthropology was emerging as an academic discipline, scholars began to look systematically for theories that would help them understand religious beliefs. Anthropologists came to recognize the cultural importance of religious beliefs very early in the discipline's history, although theories differed on how to make sense of them. In this section we consider four different definitions of religion that anthropologists have suggested, several of which are still commonly used today. Among these is our own approach to religion that builds on the others. In our view, the most effective way to think of **religion** is as a symbolic system that is socially enacted through rituals and other aspects of social life that relate to ultimate issues of humankind's existence.

• **Religion.** A symbolic system that is socially enacted through rituals and other aspects of social life that relate to ultimate issues of humankind's existence.

Understanding Religion, Version 1.0: Edward B. Tylor and Belief in Spirits

To make sense of the exotic religious beliefs of non-Western cultures, the British anthropologist Sir Edward B. Tylor (1871) suggested that religion had to do with belief in spiritual beings. For him, primitive religions were based on a fundamental error in thinking. He reasoned that people in all societies had dreams, but the so-called primitive peoples had misinterpreted their dreams as reality, transforming the characters in their dreams into souls or spirits. Tylor called such beliefs in spirits **animism**,

• **Animism.** The belief that inanimate objects such as trees, rocks, cliffs, hills, and rivers were animated by spiritual forces or beings.

which refers to the belief that inanimate objects such as trees, rocks, cliffs, hills, and rivers are animated by spiritual forces or beings. For him the ideas that trees and rocks might have souls and that carved images might contain spirits were just other examples of this same "primitive" misunderstanding. Tylor also reasoned that as societies evolved and became more complex, the supernatural beings they believed in gave way first to demigods and mythical heroes, then to gods and goddesses, then to a single, all-powerful God, and finally to science. Although many anthropologists later came to reject Tylor's evolutionary theories, his basic approach remained influential in anthropology for many decades.

Understanding Religion, Version 2.0: Anthony F. C. Wallace on Supernatural Beings, Powers, and Forces

By the 1950s, anthropologists in the United States had long abandoned the idea that American Indians and other non-Western peoples were "primitive." They had also come to accept, as Paul Radin argued in his influential book *Primitive Man as Philosopher* (1927), that there was nothing simple-minded in the myths, legends, and religious practices of tribal peoples. When American anthropologists began to look at how American Indian religions had changed—and continued to change—in the context of white expansion and domination, they saw systematic shifts in Indian thinking to make sense of changing times (Figure 17.1).

• **Rituals.** Stylized performances involving symbols that are associated with social, political, and religious activities.

One of the major figures of this period was Anthony F. C. Wallace, who had studied religious change among the Seneca, one of the Iroquois tribes in upstate New York (1956, 1970). For Wallace, religious change could be observed most easily in the changing religious ceremonies and **rituals** (stylized performances involving symbols that are associated with social, political, and religious activities). He recognized that these rituals made sense only in terms of religious beliefs. His definition of religion became standard in anthropology because it linked beliefs with rituals: "beliefs and rituals concerned with supernatural beings, powers, and forces" (Wallace 1966:5).

This approach to religious beliefs and behavior bounded the field of religion in ways that fit comfortably with traditional European and American views, which also emphasized the supernatural. But Wallace's definition is static, offering little or no direction for understanding how or why religious ideas and practices change. If a society practiced some tribal religion but then converted to Christianity, Islam, or Buddhism, Wallace's definition could help us document what had changed, but little else. It could not tell us what difference these changes in belief make for real people's lives. Moreover, this sense of religion tends to depict deeply religious people as intellectually limited, and it does not explain why people hold on to their religious beliefs and practices with such passion.

Figure 17.1   **The Ghost Dance.** The Ghost Dance among the Sioux in 1891 was an innovative religious movement among various tribes in the Great Plains. It was the Sioux's attempt to recover self-respect and control over traditional resources through ritual, but it led to disastrous consequences at Wounded Knee when US Army soldiers misinterpreted the ritual and killed 150 Lakota Sioux.

Understanding Religion, Version 3.0: Religion as a System of Symbols

Unsatisfied with Wallace's notion of religion as simply belief in the supernatural, the American cultural anthropologist Clifford Geertz (1966) proposed another kind of definition of religion that could help explain why beliefs are deeply held and motivational, even to the point of risking harm to oneself. Geertz argued that religion was a cultural system, or as he put it, a "system of symbols." It consisted of five elements:

> Religion is (1) a system of symbols which act to (2) establish powerful, pervasive, and long-lasting moods and motivations in men by (3) formulating conceptions of a general order of existence and (4) clothing these conceptions with such an aura of factuality that (5) the moods and motivations seem uniquely realistic (1966:4).

The most important feature of this definition is that it centers on symbols that seem intensely real and factual. For example, one of the central symbols in Christianity generally is the most improbable, the notion that after his execution Christ rose from the dead. Likely or not, hundreds of millions of people around the world accept Christ's resurrection as a historical fact.

Furthermore, the systems of meaning that these symbols generate can create a sense of moral purpose or meaning in people's lives and move them to action. These conceptualizations of the world offer a set of unquestioned assumptions about the world and how it works, called a **worldview**. The notion of culture adopted in this textbook ultimately derives from this understanding of religion as a cultural system. So when we suggest that culture is about how people naturalize certain meanings and actions as normal, we are arguing that culture consists of symbols that are created and given meaning by social life, not just in religious contexts. People's understandings of the world provided by these symbols, like Geertz's religion, seem uniquely realistic and cloaked in an aura of factuality; the world seems uniquely natural. The symbols describe a *model of* how the world is, as they simultaneously depict a *model for* how the world (morally) should be.

- **Worldview.** A general approach to or set of shared unquestioned assumptions about the world and how it works.

Most anthropologists continue to find Geertz's approach to religion useful. Following Geertz, they have tried to understand the worldview and ethos of a religion, adopting what is often called an **interpretive approach**, a style of analysis that looks at the underlying symbolic and cultural interconnections within a society. In "Classic Contributions: Clifford Geertz's Notion of Religion as a Cultural System" we explore the basis for this interpretive approach.

One problem with Geertz's approach, however, is that his definition of religion reads as if he is describing a lone believer, sitting quietly surrounded only by his own moods and thoughts as company. But a key feature of religious beliefs and behavior is that they are rooted in social behavior and social action. By acting together, the community of believers begins to accept the group's symbolic interpretations of the world as if they were tangible, authentic, and real rather than merely interpretations.

- **Interpretive approach.** A kind of analysis that interprets the underlying symbolic and cultural interconnections within a society.

Understanding Religion, Version 4.0: Religion as a System of Social Action

In July 2013, 3 million Brazilians turned out in Rio de Janeiro to celebrate mass with Pope Francis, the first Roman Catholic pope from Latin America. In this massive public ritual, we can see that religion is important for these millions of believers, and that it is an intensely exciting and social experience. It is a very different experience from a single nun on retreat praying quietly by herself for days at a time. Yet both experiences are "religious" in that they deal with worshipers' understandings of the world and how important the supernatural power of God is in people's lives. Both also get their power from their social context—whether it involves being among

Classic Contributions
Clifford Geertz's Notion of Religion as a Cultural System

CLIFFORD GEERTZ (1926–2006) was one of the most influential cultural anthropologists of the second half of the twentieth century. After serving in the US Navy during World War II, he did his PhD in anthropology at Harvard University, studying with the renowned social theorist Talcott Parsons and the cultural anthropologist Clyde Kluckhohn. Together with his first wife, Hildred Geertz, he conducted fieldwork in Central Java and then on the island of Bali (both in Indonesia), which allowed him an opportunity to study Javanese Islam (Geertz 1960) and Balinese Hinduism (Geertz 1980). The contrast in these two religious systems sharpened his focus on what was at the heart of religious beliefs and practices, and their relationship with culture. He further developed his insights after shifting his ethnographic focus from Indonesia to Islam in Morocco in North Africa (Geertz 1968).

Nowhere has Geertz's focus on religion as an anthropological topic for study been more impactful than in an essay entitled "Religion as a Cultural System," published in a short collection of papers edited by Michael Banton (1966) entitled *Anthropological Approaches to the Study of Religion.* Above in the text we referred to the five elements that make up Geertz's definition of religion, but here we add a short excerpt demonstrating Geertz's more general orientation to the anthropological study of religion.

🌱 **Clifford Geertz.**

For an anthropologist, the importance of religion lies in its capacity to serve, for an individual or for a group, as a source of general, yet distinctive conceptions of the world, the self, and the relations between them, on the one hand—its model of aspect—and of rooted, no less distinctive "mental" dispositions—its model for aspect—on the other. From these cultural functions flow, in turn, its social and psychological ones.

Religious concepts spread beyond their specifically metaphysical contexts to provide a framework of general ideas in terms of which a wide range of experience—intellectual, emotional, moral—can be given meaningful form. . . . A synopsis of cosmic order, a set of religious beliefs, is also a gloss upon the mundane world of social relationships and psychological events. It renders them graspable. . . .

In one society, the level of elaboration of symbolic formulations of ultimate actuality may reach extraordinary degrees of complexity and systematic articulation; in another, no less developed socially, such formulations may remain primitive in the true sense, hardly more than congeries of fragmentary by-beliefs and isolated images, of sacred reflexes and spiritual pictographs. . . .

The anthropological study of religion is therefore a two-stage operation: first, an analysis of the system of meaning embodied in the symbols which make up the religion proper, and, second, the relating of these systems to social-structural and psychological processes. My dissatisfaction with so much of contemporary social anthropological work in religion is not that it concerns itself with the second stage, but that it neglects the first, and in so doing takes for granted what most needs to be elucidated. . . . Only when we have a theoretical analysis of symbolic action comparable in sophistication to that we now have for social and psychological action, will we be able to cope effectively with those aspects of social and psychological life in which religion (or art, or science, or ideology) plays a determinant role. [Geertz 1966:40–42]

Questions for Reflection

1. From Geertz's point of view, what is the relationship between the symbolic and the social (or psychological)?

2. Why does Geertz focus so heavily on the meaning of religious symbols?

3. Do you think this approach to religion is relevant for all kinds of societies, i.e, small-scale indigenous societies, modern urban societies, etc.? Do you think there are differences between them in terms of how symbols construct meaning?

millions of others or by oneself—and from doing things that are so different from ordinary daily life. Indeed, the social experience of religious practice is what makes the beliefs, the organization of religion in daily life, and the religious symbols have meaning for every person present (Figure 17.2).

Thus, when we speak of religion in this book, we define it as a symbolic system that is socially enacted through rituals and other aspects of social life that relate to ultimate issues of humankind's existence. This definition implies several elements that earlier scholars have emphasized:

1. The existence of things more powerful than human beings. Although in many societies it takes the form of some supernatural force, we prefer to think of it as a worldview or cosmology that situates the place of human beings in the universe.
2. Beliefs and behaviors surround, support, and promote the acceptance of the underlying idea that things more powerful than humans actually exist.
3. Symbols that make these beliefs and behaviors seem both intense and genuine.
4. Social settings, usually involving the doing of specific things, that people share while experiencing the power of these symbols of belief.

Armed with this sense of religion, we can approach religious activities as fundamentally cultural phenomena, engaging people in meaningful symbolic and social action. This doesn't mean religions all work in the exact same way, however. As we will see in the next section, religions take very diverse forms.

Figure 17.2 Expressing Religiosity. Many religious rituals around the world are energetic and boisterous rather than somber, sedate, and pensive as Americans sometimes assume. At the top is a West African ritual performance that brings the gods into contact with the community, and on the bottom a modern megachurch in America in which participants take on a vibrant role in the service.

THINKING LIKE AN ANTHROPOLOGIST: RELIGION

Consider how each of the four definitions or understandings of religion would explain why a religious cult like the Jim Jones cult in Guyana or the early Mormons in Nauvoo, Illinois—where they were attacked by non-Mormons—emerged. Alternatively, use these four explanations or definitions to interpret local reaction in your own community toward people with widely different religions.

17.2 What Forms Does Religion Take?

Early anthropologists like Edward Burnett Tylor largely saw all "primitive" societies as having a "primitive" religion. While anthropologists today reject the notion that some peoples are more "primitive" and others more "civilized," it is clear that societies with simple technologies and small populations traditionally had very different religions from those that have formed states with centralized governments and have more sophisticated technologies. But there is no evidence that one form inevitably evolves into another, as the early anthropologists believed.

The variety of human religions that exists seems to correspond to the kinds of social orders that exist in different scales of society. Societies with small populations, for example, developed few governmental institutions larger than the family, clan, or village, and their religious institutions were typically focused on these same primary institutions.

Clan Spirits and Clan Identities in New Guinea

Nearly all New Guinea societies are organized around families and groups of families that belong to the same clan, and these clans are typically associated with particular kinds of spirits. The Ningerum of Papua New Guinea, for example, who have a very low population density of seven to fifteen people per square mile and live in the heavily forested upper reaches of the Fly River, are concerned with various clan spirits that inhabit their traditional clan lands. These clan spirits have a full range of human emotions, but they become dangerous when they get jealous or angry, whereupon they can cause sickness or even death to people from other clans or even among the children and elders of their own clans. When they are happy and well attended to by the living with gifts of food, especially pork, they bring good harvests in the gardens, success in hunting, and healthy, prosperous families. All Ningerum rituals, aside from a few very specific and mostly minor healing rites, emphasize dealing with these clan-based spirits, and at major feasts, pigs are sacrificed to these spirits to honor them with a bit of pork and other gifts made to them.

Among the Elema and Purari tribes of the Papuan Gulf, population densities have been much higher. When these societies were first observed and studied in the early twentieth century, each village had several large longhouses, where men lived with their brothers and sons in rooms belonging to particular clans or subclans (Welsch 2006). These clan and subclan groups had various dances at initiation rituals, and the dance costumes depicted various animals that were associated with the particular clan holding the initiation or other ritual, such as crocodiles and geckos (Figure 17.3).

- **Totemism.** A system of thought that associates particular social groups with specific animal or plant species called "totems" as an emblem.

- **Shaman.** A religious leader who communicates with the spirit world about the needs of the living, usually through some form of ritual trance or other altered state of consciousness.

- **Trance.** A semiconscious state typically brought on by hypnosis, ritual drumming, and singing, or hallucinogenic drugs like mescaline or peyote.

These systems of totems are absent among the Ningerum, but they are clearly present in a very simple way among the Elema and Purari tribes.

Totemism in North America

Early anthropologists studying American Indian societies observed that people identified with particular animals, often claiming to be descended from them. These people indicated their clans, lineages, tribes, or other social groups with emblems, usually animals, plants, places, and geographic or meteorological features (Figure 17.4). Anthropologists usually refer to these emblems as totems, and **totemism** as the system of thought that associates particular social groups with specific animal or plant species. Totems help create social cohesiveness by stressing group identity, focusing group and private rituals on totems. Some Native American societies simultaneously employed color symbolism, directional symbols, and species as totems. Until the 1920s, anthropologists interpreted totemism as evidence of a group's limited intellectual capacity, since people could not possibly be descended from eagles, wolves, or pythons.

We see a version of totemism in American culture as well, especially with sports teams or military units named after animals or a particular social group, cultivating among fans and soldiers a sense of belonging to a social order larger than oneself (Linton 1924). But these totems are largely secular in orientation, while traditional tribal societies, such as those along the Northwest Coast of North America, usually understood themselves to be related to the totemic animal in some supernatural way.

Shamanism and Ecstatic Religious Experiences

As early as the sixteenth century, European travelers from Russia and central Europe encountered tribes in Siberia whose religious rituals involved spiritual leaders called **shamans**, religious leaders who communicate the needs of the living with the spirit world, usually through some form of ritual **trance**—a semiconscious state typically brought on by hypnosis, ritual drumming and singing, or hallucinogenic drugs like mescaline or peyote. These specialists were not political leaders but were focused on healing and ensuring the health and prosperity of the community, using drum rituals to connect with the spirits.

These practices are found in one form or another on all continents but especially North and South America, Africa, and Asia. The details of these shamanic traditions vary widely, but they are often associated with small-scale societies with more or less egalitarian political structures. Anthropologist Napoleon Chagnon and Timothy Asch's 1973 film *Magical Death* shows one of the best-known examples of shamanic healing (Chagnon and Asch 2008). In this film, a Yanomami shaman heals his family by ingesting hallucinogenic snuff made from a local plant. As in

Figure 17.3   Eharo Mask.

Figure 17.4   Chiefly Totems. Totemic images identified with the clan and social position of a Kwakiutl chief on Vancouver Island, British Columbia. The main images on the two poles are eagles; other elements associated with the eagle moiety are grizzly bears. The figure at the bottom of the left pole holds a ceremonial copper plaque, suggesting the importance of the chief. These poles capture the social identity, the social position of the chief, and his great accomplishments, all expressed through the carved memorial pole.

- **Spirit familiar.** A spirit that has developed a close bond with a shaman.

- **Speaking in tongues.** The phenomenon of speaking in an apparently unknown language, often in an energetic and fast-paced way.

many shamanic traditions, this shaman is assisted by his **spirit familiar** (a spirit that has developed a close bond with the shaman), who helps him see other spirits and heal his children. In societies more familiar to Americans, such as some Pentecostal and charismatic Christian traditions, the ecstatic religious experience that has long been associated with shamans is fostered by members of the congregation through witnessing, singing, and **speaking in tongues** (the phenomenon of speaking in an apparently unknown language, often in an energetic and fast-paced way).

Whether it is religions like those of the Ningerum, totemism among Native American groups, or shamanism, each of these religious traditions stress group identities and links these identities to various religious symbols.

Figure 17.5   Symbols of Royal Authority in the Benin Kingdom. Bronze figures and reliefs represented royal connections to the gods. The focus of all power in the kingdom was in the center of the palace in the person of the oba. (Hood Museum of Art, Dartmouth College, Hanover, New Hampshire.)

Ritual Symbols That Reinforce a Hierarchical Social Order

Ritual symbols tend to reinforce the social hierarchy and the political order at the same time as they interact with divine beings and powers. In the former kingdom of Benin, in what is now Nigeria in West Africa, for example, the Oba (king) was believed to be divine. The fiercest animal in the region, the leopard, became a symbol of royal power, projecting an image of the Oba's power over his people. One feature of Benin religious practice was the Igwe Festival, which was a cleansing ritual expelling evil from the entire kingdom led by the Oba. This ritual sequence served to strengthen and renew the Oba's divine powers. Benin bronze sculptures and reliefs often depict members of the royal family, offering another way for the Benin to venerate their Oba (Figure 17.5). By strengthening the Oba, the community felt it was maintaining the well-being of the kingdom. Benin rituals and art together provided a model of the divine nature of the ruler, supporting a social order in which the ruler dominated over all others (Bradbury 1957; Dark 1962, 1982; Eboreime 2003).

Polytheism and Monotheism in Ancient Societies

The kingdoms and dynasties of ancient Egypt provided a similar model of the social order being replicated in many of its most important rituals. The pharaoh was a king ruling over a vast empire of people along the Nile and Mediterranean coast and extending into what is now Israel and the Arabian Peninsula. Everything about Egyptian ritual—as well as the construction of great pyramids and structures like the Sphinx—celebrated a complex hierarchy of officials and priests, with the pharaoh as a divine figure at the head of the state and its religious organizations. However, the pharaoh was not the only divine figure; Egyptians held that there was a host of other, more or less powerful deities, making their religion one of **polytheism** (belief in many gods). All of these gods demanded the attention of humans or, it was thought, they might harm the human world with droughts, plagues, locusts, and floods of the Nile River.

Nearly all of the ancient societies in the Middle East and the Mediterranean were polytheistic with complex state rituals that promoted and supported an image of the state and its human leaders as superior to ordinary men. The main exception to polytheism in the ancient world was the ancient Hebrews, whose religion focused on a single god called Yahweh. In all likelihood, Yahweh began as a local deity that was worshiped and venerated by one of the tribes of Israel that became the ancient Hebrews (Armstrong 1994). When the Hebrews established Yahweh as the God of Israel, they began a long-term shift to **monotheism** (belief in a single god). The key feature of monotheism was that it symbolized a single universal faith because the single God was presented as the deity of all, whereas polytheism encouraged different groups to identify with different local gods, in much the same way that totemism works.

- **Polytheism.** A type of religion with many gods.

- **Monotheism.** The belief in a single god.

World Religions and Universal Understandings of the World

Most of us are more familiar with the universal monotheistic **world religions**—or religions that claim to be universally significant to all people—of Judaism, Christianity, and Islam than with the small-scale religions discussed previously. All three of these monotheistic world religions provided a general message that was applicable to all people, not just the members of a small clan or social group. For the most part, all three provided a positive, uplifting message for adherents, and all three also became state religions, whose religious message and ritual supported the government of the state.

- **World religions.** Religions that claim to be universally significant to all people.

Islam illustrates the ways a local monotheistic religion can become universalized through a set of beliefs and social order. Islam emerged during the seventh century in the Arabian Peninsula when the Prophet Muhammad received holy scripture in the form of poetry from a single, universal God—called Allah in classical Arabic. Most non-Muslims are startled to learn that the Prophet had one Christian wife and lived peaceably among a mix of Muslims, Jews, and Christians in Medina, until members of one of the Jewish tribes attempted to assassinate him. Jesus, Mary, John the Baptist, Moses, Abraham, and Adam, among others, are discussed at some length in the **Quran**, and all are considered prophets. From a Muslim point of view, Muslims, Christians, and Jews are all "people of the book," meaning that each has scripture received through prophets from God. But followers of Islam, which is the newest of these three religions, believe that God's message was most accurately received by the Prophet Muhammad and that Christians and Jews didn't get the entire message from God.

- **Quran.** The main body of scripture in Islam, consisting of verses of classical Arabic poetry understood to be revealed to the Prophet Muhammad by Allah, often in dreams or in the midst of other activities. These verses were memorized by Muhammad's followers and written down after his death.

Asia has also produced important world religions that reflect particular histories of social stratification and universalistic belief. Hinduism was a polytheistic religion that emerged in India thousands of years ago. Like the polytheistic religions of the Middle East, Hinduism supported the authority of local princes and kings, and it focused on achieving good relations between people and various gods. Sometime in the fourth to sixth centuries BCE, a man named Siddhartha Gautama emerged as the founder of a new faith called Buddhism in reaction to Hinduism. According to Buddhist traditions, after selfishly pursuing his own pleasure through licentious living, Gautama was mysteriously awakened to his misdeeds and promoted a life of reflection and active commitment to the Buddhist path, accepting the Buddha, the *Dharma* (the Buddha's teachings), and the *Sangha* (the Buddhist community). Unlike most other religions, Buddhism encourages its members to strive toward greater enlightenment. In this sense, Buddhism is neither monotheistic nor polytheistic, but is more like a moral code of conduct. The rituals often involve meditation and devotional acts aimed at turning people from worldly desires (wealth, sex, power, etc.) to concern for other people and all other creatures, and a state of enlightenment called *Nirvana*.

The Localization of World Religions

In spite of their universalistic claims and aspirations, world religions have spread dramatically because their actual practice is highly flexible and adaptable to local interests, beliefs, and social practices. To take an extreme example, consider the example of serpent handling among certain minority Pentecostal Christian sects in the Appalachian region of the United States. It may come as a surprise to most Americans that their compatriots might handle venomous serpents during rituals that are characterized by loud music and dancing that would seem to agitate snakes. Indeed, most Christians would judge this practice harshly as backward or ignorant, even though a Bible passage in the Book of Mark notes that a sign of God's grace is the handling of serpents among his followers.

This issue came to light during 2014, when a famous Pentecostal preacher, Pastor Jamie Coots from the congregation of the Full Gospel Tabernacle in Jesus Name of Middleboro, Kentucky, was bitten by a venomous snake during a snake-handling service and later died after refusing medical intervention (Bacon 2014; Estep 2014). Adherents in serpent-handling churches believe their faith in God protects them from being bitten by the rattlesnakes or copperheads they repeatedly handle without any protective covering. In their belief, each individual's faith directs God's power over the serpents, preventing them from biting the adherent. That so many of the serpent handlers are not bitten by the snakes gives ritual evidence that God is protecting the faithful (Adair 1967a, 1967b; Kimbrough 2002). And when someone dies, as happens every couple of years in the United States, snake handling churches typically do not give up their ritual practice. The act of handling a snake—the snake being a meaningful biblical symbol often associated with eternity and rebirth—turns the world these people live in symbolically upside-down: it shows that, when they literally take their lives in their hands, the dispossessed, poor, and marginalized can demonstrate that they are living a more virtuous and faithful Christian life than other, more mainstream Christians.

How Does Atheism Fit in the Discussion?

Finally, we must ask if atheists, agnostics, and nonbelievers have a religion. This question has been a worrisome issue for anthropologists, because traditionally anthropologists have defined religion in terms of a belief in the supernatural, which means that these beliefs have little basis in empirical fact. And many anthropologists think of themselves as agnostics (though all are not, as we explore in "The Anthropological Life: Is Anthropology Compatible with Religious Faith?").

But taking a step back, if all humans have some sort of worldview, then everyone has some sort of perspective on life analogous to religion. Secular people must also have symbolic systems that give meaning and purpose to their lives. We saw this secular system of meaning enacted in the solidarity marches in Paris on January 11, 2015, and when the forty world leaders stood arm in arm on a Paris street to show solidarity in their defense of free speech after Muslim terrorists attacked the offices of the magazine *Charlie Hebdo* in Paris. Although many Parisians are only nominally Christian, and the many world leaders came from various religious and secular backgrounds, the marching in the streets of Paris was a secular ritual to promote free speech and civility among nations (see Haugerud 2016) (see Figure 17.6). For some, secular rituals that celebrate the state or nation, particular occupations, or other identities may achieve many of the same ends as religious rituals. For others, practicing scientific research may construct a worldview similar to that of people with more traditional religious beliefs. Furthermore, every time "secular" people knock on wood,

The Anthropological Life
Is Anthropology Compatible with Religious Faith?

Many cultural anthropologists are not active members of organized churches. For the most part this is because most religious institutions give a strong preference to their own community's cultural practices and beliefs and dismiss those of non-believers and other groups.

Mary Douglas was one of the most celebrated British anthropologists in the post–World War II era. She was a student of E. E. Evans-Pritchard at Oxford University, who was perhaps the leading British social anthropologist of his generation, and like Douglas was a practicing Roman Catholic. As religious minorities in Anglican Great Britain, both scholars were sensitive to the religious beliefs they encountered in the African societies they studied. Evans-Pritchard (1976) had first studied witchcraft, magic, and religious beliefs among the Azande of southwestern Sudan. Later, he observed ritual practices among Nuer (Evans-Pritchard 1940, 1956) of what is now South Sudan. In the 1950s Douglas (2005) conducted fieldwork among the Lele people of Belgian Congo (today the Democratic Republic of the Congo). All three societies had complex religious ideas and in all three the anthropologists were striving to view the world "from the native's point of view," to borrow a phrase from Bronislaw Malinowski, one of Evans-Pritchard's teachers.

There is no reason to believe that having religious beliefs should prevent an anthropologist from understanding the religious and spiritual beliefs of people in another society. When writing about her beliefs as a practicing Catholic, Douglas (2005) wrote about how her own deeply held beliefs allowed her to understand similarly deeply held beliefs among the Lele, even though both sets of beliefs were different in content. She initially focused on Lele social and political organization, but she was soon dragged into the middle of tensions within the village that involved fundamental religious beliefs, especially Lele ideas about magic and sorcery (Douglas 1999). Douglas's contributions to our understanding of the role of ritual and religious beliefs and how they play out in a society appear in her explanations of why certain classes of people

🌱 **Mary Douglas.**

were likely to be accused of witchcraft and sorcery, while others would largely be exempt. Douglas (1970) focused on how these fundamental categories get projected onto natural species and categories of people within the community.

Douglas often remarked in private that her teacher, Evans-Pritchard, saw a strict social hierarchy among the Nuer that mimicked many aspects of his own Roman Catholicism. She recognized that this was one possible weakness in the way she and Evans-Pritchard viewed the religions and the worldviews of the communities they studied, and her work was often structured to temper such tendencies. Douglas would argue—and we would concur—that there is nothing inherent in anthropology in conflict with personal faith. But it must not blind the researcher from being able to observe what is actually happening in real communities.

throw spilled salt over their shoulders, make a wish while blowing out birthday candles, or pick up a "lucky" penny, they are drawing on the same kinds of magical beliefs and rationalities that are common in religious communities (see Magical Thought in Non-Western Cultures). Geertz's definition of religion was specifically designed to be as useful for secular worldviews with a rich array of secular symbols as it is for more traditional religions.

Figure 17.6 World Leaders March in Solidarity for Freedom of Speech in Paris, January 11, 2015.

THINKING LIKE AN ANTHROPOLOGIST: RELIGION

Consider any three different societies we have discussed in this book. Discuss the extent to which the scale of the society—measured in terms of population or number of people within the same administrative or governing body—is reflected in the complexity of technology and the complexity of religious concepts. How do these three measures of complexity—population size, technological complexity, and sophistication of religious ideas—match up? What does this kind of comparison tell us about evolutionary models of society?

17.3 How Do Rituals Work?

All rituals have certain key features, including that they are repetitive (happening at set times or before or after certain events) and stylized (following a set order of words or actions). What distinguishes religious ritual from daily habits such as brushing one's teeth (which some of you might think of as a "ritual") is that nobody invests special significance in tooth brushing. Some rituals, such as rites of passage (discussed later in the chapter), are especially significant in a person's life. But, before we explain why and how they work, it is important to note that anthropologists have long understood that at the heart of all ritual action exists a particular mode of thought that we call "magical." What do we mean?

Magical Thought in Non-Western Cultures

- **Magic.** An explanatory system of causation that does not follow naturalistic explanations, often working at a distance without direct physical contact.

When anthropologists talk of **magic**, they discuss it as an explanatory system of causation that does not follow naturalistic explanations—such as being struck by a weapon or infected by some virus—often working at a distance without direct physical contact. Informants nearly always accept magical explanations as real, and they often believe deeply that such manifestations are frightening or dangerous.

Magic can have many goals, usually goals that are out of reach through an individual taking direct action. The practitioner may want his or her gardens to flourish or his hunt to be successful. She may want the food at her feast to go further than it normally would, or to attract the affections of a handsome young man in a neighboring hamlet. Techniques may involve incantations, spells, unusual behaviors, and the manipulation of any number of special objects, all in an effort to cause some desired event to occur. For anthropologists, the point is not necessarily whether magical practices actually bring about their desired ends or not. It is usually enough to understand that members of a community accept that these processes occur. But why do these puzzling practices make sense to the people who practice magic?

Sympathetic Magic: The Law of Similarity and the Law of Contagion

The English anthropologist Sir James G. Frazer (1854–1941) coined the term **sympathetic magic** to refer to any magical rite that relies on supernatural powers to produce its outcome without working through a specific supernatural being such as a spirit, demon, or deity. Frazer was the original armchair anthropologist who never conducted fieldwork himself, instead drawing upon examples from around the world observed and recorded by others. Frazer argued that sympathetic magic works on two principles that he called the "law of similarity" and the "law of contagion." Both involved sympathetic magic because the person or object acted upon did so "in sympathy" with the magical actions. The power of Frazer's terminology is that it offered a succinct tool for making sense of how people come to believe the non-empirical. Frazer's two laws were not "laws" per se, but a description or characterization of how people in one or another society might understand magic to work.

Frazer (1890, 1911–1915) described the law of similarity as beginning with some point of similarity between an aspect of the magical rite and the desired goal. A good illustration is a "voodoo doll," which is an image that represents the maker's enemy, often marked by some small possession or piece of cloth that was once in intimate contact with the intended victim. By poking or stabbing the image, they hope to produce pain in the corresponding part of the victim's body. For the Inuit, this same principle of similarity also applies to charms or fishhooks that represent a seal and allow fishermen or hunters to catch fish as easily as a seal does. Today, anthropologists often speak of these similarities as metaphors, since the charm or fishhook carved as a seal is not really a seal but merely an object that resembles a seal (Figure 17.7). Nevertheless, the thought behind this magical association is that seals are good at catching fish, and so the seal-like charm attached to the hook will attract fish.

Alternatively, a magical rite could follow the law of contagion, in which things that had once been in physical contact with one another could have an effect even when they were no longer in contact. According to the law of contact, mundane objects we've touched or produced as individuals, such as a cigarette butt, a scrap of partly eaten food, hair, nail clippings, sweat, urine, and feces, carry part of our essence, and harmful things done to them by an ill-intentioned magician can by extension hurt us (Figure 17.8).

Applying These Principles to Religious Activities

Although Frazer depicted these two types of magical principles as occurring in separate situations, they often occur together, drawing simultaneously on the similarities and the previous contact. And while Frazer saw magic as distinct and separate from religion, most anthropologists now recognize that magical principles are often invoked in religious rituals.

• **Sympathetic magic.** Any magical rite that relies on the supernatural to produce its outcome without working through some supernatural being such as a spirit, demon, or deity.

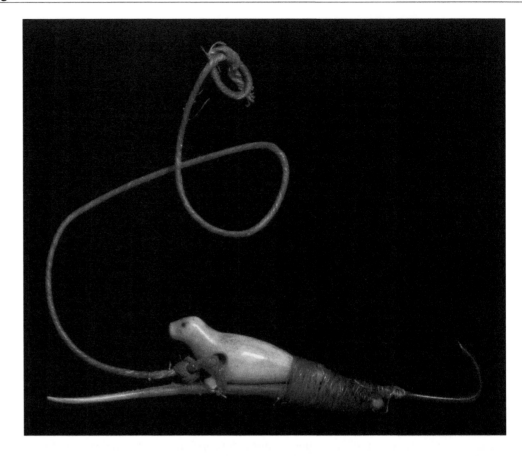

Figure 17.7   Sympathetic Magic Among the Inuit. Attached to this fishhook is a charm carved of ivory in the shape of a seal. The charm is meant to ensure that the hook will be successful in catching fish like a seal is successful in catching fish. (Hood Museum of Art, Dartmouth College, Hanover, New Hampshire.)

Figure 17.8   Contagious Magic in Papua New Guinea. A Ningerum man in Papua New Guinea prepares for a pig feast by anointing a pig lengthwise with sago flour in the belief that this rite will make the food go further. When their guests eat just a little of the pork, they will quickly feel full. Anointing the pig uses contagious magic.

For example, the Christian ritual of communion embodies both principles of magic simultaneously. The elements used in the rite—the bread and the wine—are consecrated by the priest or pastor and intended to be consumed by members of the congregation. This ritual imitates the Last Supper, when Jesus is said to have shared bread and wine with his most devoted followers, declaring the bread to be his "body" and the wine to be his "blood." The Last Supper was held at the start of the Jewish feast of Passover, which reenacts the story of the Jewish exodus from Egypt. Because the meal was part of the Passover, the bread was unleavened and flat, similar to the unleavened matzoh bread that is commonly produced today as large flat wafers.

Some Protestant congregations in the United States prefer loaves of bread to the matzoh-like wafers most typically used by Catholics, Episcopalians, and Lutherans. By using leavened loaves of bread and breaking off a piece for each participant in the ritual, this congregation is emphasizing the communal sharing of a ritual meal to bind the active community together, rather than the "historic" details that would have been present at any Passover meal in ancient Jerusalem as described in the Gospels.

Jesus himself is using a metaphor when he announces that the bread "is my body" and that the wine "is my blood." The wine— most commonly red wine—is an appropriate element because it resembles blood in color—law of similarity. The wafer resembles the unleavened bread of the Passover meal, which in turn is a symbol for Jesus's flesh. When congregants each eat a consecrated wafer and drink a sip of wine, they are linked together as a congregation because they have shared the same wafers and wine—law of contact (Figure 17.9).

Figure 17.9   The Christian Eucharist or Communion. The similarity of red wine to blood and wafers to flesh establishes the similarities between the ritual objects and their meaning. Consuming them during the ritual invokes the law of contagion to spread the blessings of God among all the people.

Magic in Western Societies

Americans tend to believe that modernization has eliminated magical thought in our own culture. Yet many of the elements observed in non-Western societies also occur in contemporary America. In his study of baseball players, for example, anthropologist George Gmelch (1978) noted that players often have lucky jerseys, good luck fetishes, or other objects that become charms. For these players, ordinary objects acquire power by being connected to exceptionally hot batting or pitching streaks. These charms follow the law of similarity. For three months during a winning season, one pitcher Gmelch interviewed followed the exact same routine: at lunch he went to the same restaurant, had two glasses of iced tea and a tuna fish sandwich, and for an hour before the game wore the same sweatshirt and jock strap he had worn the first day of the streak. He was afraid that changing anything he had done before the first winning game might produce a bad result. The broader point here is that magical beliefs and practices are an intrinsic dimension of any society's worldview. As a distinctive mode of rationality, magic coexists and interpenetrates with other modes of rationality, including scientific and secular worldviews.

Rites of Passage and the Ritual Process

The most important type of ritual is a **rite of passage**, a life cycle ritual that marks a person's or group's transition from one social state to another. In 1909, French sociologist Arnold van Gennep (1960) outlined the structure of rituals that marked the passage of individuals from one status to another. Rites of passage include marriage rituals, in which individuals change status from being single to being married, and rituals that mark the transition from childhood to adulthood. Initiations are common around the world, even in industrial societies such as ours that carry out such rituals in "sweet sixteen parties" for young women, school graduation, and the like. Funerals

● **Rite of passage.** Any life-cycle rite that marks a person's or group's transition from one social state to another.

A World in Motion
Contemporary Pilgrimage and the Camino de Santiago

Tourism is the world's largest industry, moving people by the hundreds of millions every year across borders. Although much of that tourism is focused on secular pursuits, religious tourism is an important transnational phenomenon. In fact, it has been for a long time, but we haven't called it "tourism." We have called it pilgrimage.

During the Middle Ages, thousands of Europeans made spiritual journeys to religious shrines and sacred sites scattered across the continent and the Middle East. Pilgrims set off on these personal journeys for personal religious enlightenment, completion of doctrine, and increasing one's ritual status at home on one's return. The Camino de Santiago de Compostela (the Way of St. James) in northern Spain is one of the most important pilgrimage routes in Christendom, connected with all of Europe through numerous smaller pilgrim paths. Today, the Camino de Santiago is perhaps the best-known pilgrimage in Europe. The year before the COVID-19 pandemic shut much of Europe down for more than a year, more than 300,000 pilgrims walked some part of the Camino.

Increasingly contemporary pilgrims are coming to the Camino not for the traditional pilgrim's spiritual journey, but to achieve some personal growth and a feeling of accomplishment. 500 miles is a long walk by anyone's standards and most pilgrims achieve a great sense of accomplishment when they mount the steps to the Cathedral of St. James. Such secular pilgrims are often on their own personal journey of reflection and contemplation. Nevertheless, whether the pilgrimage is for traditional religious purposes or for secular ones, thousands of pilgrims walk the "pilgrim's path" each year before returning to their workaday lives back home after climbing the steps of the Cathedral of Santiago.

Throughout their journey, pilgrims are armed with guidebooks and smartphones that allow them to book rooms each night along the Camino. But between these nightly punctuations of sociality and the chance to rest, eat, and drink beer or wine with others they have met along the way, most modern pilgrims report the experience in deeply personal terms of self-revelation and exploration. It is as if the miles of walking are aimed at reaching someplace within oneself, rather than reaching the cathedral at the end of the road. We have met some pilgrims who never climbed the steps of the cathedral, suggesting that it was the journey rather than reaching the cathedral that was more important. The miles of quietude and solitude, even monotony, allow people to connect with themselves in ways that modern life does not. At its core, walking the Camino is a ritual experience whether the goal is spiritual awakening, personal renewal, or an individual's quest to know themselves more fully (Challenger 2016).

Camino de Santiago Modern pilgrims walking on the Camino de Santiago in northern Spain. Walking hundreds of miles across rustic landscapes, the modern pilgrim's days are largely spent in collective solitude. Each pilgrim explores hundreds of miles of the Camino in a collective act that is usually individual during the day, congregating for meals in the evening.

represent another rite of passage that focuses on the deceased but is largely about the transition survivors will experience.

For anthropologist Victor Turner (1967, 1969), all rituals invoke symbols that can convey the underlying meanings of the ritual. Ritual symbols can consist of objects, colors, actions, events, or words. **Pilgrimage**, which is a type of ritual in which a

• **Pilgrimage.** A type of ritual in which a journey is made to a destination of spiritual importance.

journey is made to a destination of spiritual importance, involves embodied movement over a long distance (see "A World in Motion: Contemporary Pilgrimage and the Camino de Santiago"). Often the symbols at the heart of rituals point to, suggest, or take meaning from myths or sacred texts known to participants, such as the cross or the wine and wafers in Christian church services. When American brides wear white, they are symbolically expressing their purity, whereas when Chinese wear white at a funeral, they are expressing their grief. What is common throughout these examples is that rituals create solidarity and meaning for participants and represent tradition for a group of people.

THINKING LIKE AN ANTHROPOLOGIST: RELIGION

Compare the ritual symbols used in a televised Sunday morning service conducted by a Protestant televangelist with those used in a televised Sunday morning Roman Catholic mass. Although both services are religious rituals for Christian sects, they look very different. How do the different structures in the two services suggest different meanings derived from the same scripture?

17.4 How Is Religion Linked to Political and Social Action?

Time magazine's cover for April 8, 1966, asked the provocative question, "Is God Dead?" (*Time* 1966). Playing off the nineteenth-century German philosopher Friedrich Nietzsche's famous claim that "God is dead"—suggesting that the **secular worldview**, or a worldview that does not accept the supernatural as influencing current people's lives, had finally overtaken the religious one in Europe—*Time* was asking whether the same secularizing trend was at work in America. Formal church membership in Europe had declined sharply, to fewer than 10 percent of the population in some countries, and *Time* was suggesting that perhaps religion would no longer play a role in political action, as it had played in the abolition movement of the nineteenth century and has played in the civil rights movement. *Time* was so wrong. More than fifty years later, we can see the persistent power of religion in the United States, in politics, in social discourse, in civil rights, and on TV. Between the 1940s and 2000, American church membership rose gradually to about 70 percent of American adults. Today church membership has gradually declined to just below 50 percent. Church attendance has clearly been in decline over the past thirty years, but it definitely does not mean that religion is dead (Jones 2021). So, why was *Time* magazine so wrong?

The main reason is the magazine's false assumption that as a society "modernizes," it begins to value scientific knowledge and reason over religious values and practices. The *Time* authors assumed that secularization would continue to grow, but American churches responded to social change not by ignoring it but by challenging it. Churches and other religious organizations became increasingly political, often supporting one political party or the other. In nearly every society, political and religious institutions are not only engaged with one another, they are frequently the same institutions. The broader point here is that religious values, symbols, and beliefs typically either

• **Secular worldview.** A worldview that does not accept the supernatural as influencing current people's lives.

challenge or uphold a particular social order. We illustrate this point by considering the forceful rise of religious fundamentalisms around the world.

The Rise of Fundamentalism

Since the 1960s, the most significant change in US religion has been how much more active religious organizations have become in public life, particularly among the conservative churches that call themselves **fundamentalist**, people belonging to conservative religious movements that advocate a return to fundamental or traditional principles. Fundamentalist TV preachers have expanded their broadcasting since the early 1980s, and conservative religious groups and religious organizations have been as deeply involved in elections and politics as ever. The rise of fundamentalism is not unique to the United States, either. Across the world, conservative groups have turned to fundamentalism to make sense of and confront changes that are happening all around them. As in the United States, fundamentalist religion and conservative politics are deeply engaged with one another in other societies as well (Berger 1999).

Understanding Fundamentalism

Scholars have had difficulty agreeing on a definition of fundamentalism. Traditionally, **fundamentalism** in America has been associated with extremely literal interpretation of scripture, particularly prophetic books in the Bible. Recently, the American media has often associated fundamentalism with Islam, violence, extremism, and terrorism, but both views are far too narrow and biased, because most of the world's religions have their own conservative, "back to fundamentals" branches, and most are not so outwardly violent.

To correct these biases, in the 1990s a team of researchers working on the Fundamentalism Project at the University of Chicago studied conservative religious movements within Christianity, Islam, Zionist Judaism, Buddhism, Hinduism, Confucianism, and Sikhism (Marty and Appleby 1991; Almond, Appleby, and Sivan 2003). Not all of these diverse movements rely on literal readings of scripture, and for some groups, sacred writings are of little consequence. Nor do fundamentalist groups necessarily reject everything modern. Most have embraced television, computers, the internet, and other digital technologies to get the word out. And conservative Arab Muslims celebrate the medieval Islamic origins of modern science and technology.

The Fundamentalism Project (Marty and Appleby 1991:viii–x) found several key themes common to all of these conservative religious movements. These include the following:

- They see themselves as fighting back against the corrosive effects of secular life on what they envision as a purer way of life. They fight for a worldview that prescribes "proper" gender roles, sexualities, and educational patterns. Their interpretation of the purer past becomes the model for building a purer, godlier future.
- They are willing to engage in political, even military, battles to defend their ideas about life and death, including issues that emerge in hospitals and clinics dealing with pregnancy, abortion, and the terminally ill.
- They work against others, whether infidels, modernizers, or moderate insiders, in the process reinforcing their identity and building solidarity within their community.
- They have passion, and the most passionate are those who "are convinced that they are called to carry out God's or Allah's purposes against challengers" (Marty and Appleby 1991:x).

• **Fundamentalist.** A person belonging to a religious movement that advocates a return to fundamental or traditional principles.

• **Fundamentalism.** Conservative religious movements that advocate a return to fundamental or traditional principles.

Political action among fundamentalists has sometimes taken a more violent course, as suggested by recent jihadist attacks in the West, and by militant Sikhs' armed combat and insurrection against the government in India. Anthropologist Cynthia Keppley Mahmood (1997) studied the role of religion in conflict between different religious groups on the Indian subcontinent. We usually think of religious tension on the subcontinent as being focused on Hindus and Muslims, but Mahmood was concerned with another religious minority, people who are members of the Sikh religion in the northwestern Indian state of Punjab. From 1980 onward, a group of ethnic Sikhs, whose religion differs from Hinduism, Islam, Buddhism, and Christianity, have been engaged in an insurrection against the Indian government seeking to establish a sovereign nation called Khalistan ("Land of the Pure") (Figure 17.10).

Figure 17.10   A Sikh Temple in India. The vast majority of Sikhs are not militant or violent, just as most Christians, Jews, Muslims, Hindus, and Buddhists are non-violent.

We often think of religious organizations as being focused on peace, but the Sikh insurgency has used a militant strategy to support their religious beliefs as they attempt to maintain their own ethnic and religious sect. Khalistanis identify themselves through both their ethnic identity as Sikhs and their distinctive religious identity. In certain respects, her research on religion and violence was fraught with a variety of ethical issues because the group she was studying were actively engaged in violence. Other Sikhs, whom she also interviewed and whose lives and religion she studied, were less violent. She found a wide variety of views about the role of violence in religious action. Mahmood's research demonstrates that religious ideologies can be intimately linked to social action, but at least in some communities there can often be a wide range of responses to violence (Mahmood 1997).

The broader point here is that fundamentalists are not isolated from the world of politics but actively engaged in it. Unlike religion in most small-scale societies, fundamentalism does not typically support the existing political order but fights against it. We can see this in the active involvement of Evangelical Christians in presidential elections and national politics beginning in the 1980s, supporting conservative candidates. In recent decades, these groups have stood in vocal opposition to non-conservative candidates, often asserting their influence in state legislatures, city councils, planning boards, and school boards.

What we do see in fundamentalism is that membership and a sense of belonging to a community is an important feature of religious organizations in industrial societies where it is easy for individuals to feel anonymous. And while fundamentalism has seen a resurgence in India, a number of Muslim countries, and Israel, it has seen a strong resurgence in the United States thanks to the close alignment of fundamentalists with the contemporary Republican Party in the US. Indeed, part of the power of any religious organizations (churches, synagogues, mosques, and other religious centers) is that they bring people together, provide them social support, and give them an identity within a broader secular world. Anthropologists have long understood that this process of belonging and the social action associated with group membership is bolstered by important symbols.

THINKING LIKE AN ANTHROPOLOGIST: RELIGION

Consider the Fourth of July ritual that takes place in your home town. How do the parades and the speeches and fireworks build symbolic support for the state and federal governments and for the US military? How do the symbols support the existing government?

Conclusion

The COVID-19 pandemic has ended. But its effects on people's lives lingers in various ways. It would be a mistake to ignore its effects on people's religious lives. As the research by Inayat Ali on the impact of the pandemic on Pakistani culture and funerary practices shows, religion and the rituals that are key aspects of everyday lives are not isolated domains of human spiritual existence, but shaped by and filtered through sociocultural processes and external events. Such changes in funerals or burial practices do not necessarily transform the significance of funerary practices, but they do tend to change the symbolic import of these rites in a variety of ways. A memorial service held months after a death cannot serve to bring families together in times of grief in the same way that a funeral held two or three days after a death does. And what happens when a year or two after a death the family has either a simple memorial or no memorial service whatsoever?

These are critical issues for the people living through these events, helping them sort through the complex issues that are inherent to human life. The same processes have been at work in the small-scale village societies that anthropologists focused on throughout much of the twentieth century. In those small-scale societies, the play of symbols happened in a much smaller interactive sphere. In contemporary societies, the play of symbols is every bit as active and important. Even so, many of the lessons we have learned from these small-scale societies can be applied to complex societies like our own with its modern technologies, its cosmopolitan cities, and its larger populations. As we have suggested throughout this chapter, meaning is constructed by social interaction, especially through rituals in churches, synagogues, and mosques, but also in public ritual in public spaces like your own graduation, civic ceremonies, and, of course, public and private funerals.

Different societies or different communities may have different understandings of what is most important in life. Whether or not we agree with such perspectives, we can never understand the actions of others without understanding a community's worldview and the powerful moods, motivations, and social actions it creates. These are the benefits of approaching conflicting beliefs from "the native's point of view."

KEY TERMS

Animism p. 481	Polytheism p. 488	Speaking in tongues p. 488
Fundamentalism p. 498	Quran p. 489	Spirit familiar p. 488
Fundamentalist p. 498	Religion p. 481	Sympathetic magic p. 493
Interpretive approach p. 483	Rite of passage p. 495	Totemism p. 487
Magic p. 492	Rituals p. 482	Trance p. 487
Monotheism p. 489	Secular worldview p. 497	World religions p. 489
Pilgrimage p. 496	Shaman p. 487	Worldview p. 483

Reviewing the Chapter

Chapter Section	What We Know	To Be Resolved
How should we understand religion and religious beliefs?	Anthropologists have long considered the reasons people have religion and how religions work. While some classic approaches emphasized that religion is about the supernatural, more recent approaches emphasize the symbolic and action-oriented character of religious beliefs.	Many anthropologists accept that we can learn a great deal about the worldviews of the peoples we study, but not all anthropologists believe that we can fully understand how any individual sees and feels about his or her world.
What forms does religion take?	Traditional societies with limited social stratification tend to have simpler religions than the religions of complex societies, but this correlation is not inevitable.	We don't really know what environmental, political, or social conditions produce more complex forms of religious ideas.
How do rituals work?	Rituals use symbols that convey deep meanings about the world and how it should be. All rituals rely on some version of magical thinking. Ritual symbols themselves rely heavily on metaphor and other kinds of resemblances for conveying meaning.	It is not entirely clear why humans in all societies so readily accept ideas and beliefs that can be so easily shown to be incomplete, if not wrong.
How is religion linked to political and social action?	Religions have always been linked to political organizations and the social order. Anthropologists reject the idea that as the world modernized it would become more secular, drawing on the widespread rise of fundamentalism to demonstrate the continuing social and political importance of religion.	There is no real consensus as to how much political institutions can shape religious symbols, rituals, and worldviews, even though it is obvious that groups in power often try to.

READINGS

One of the most important early studies of a traditional, non-Western religion is E. E. Evans-Pritchard's 1937 classic ethnography, *Witchcraft, Oracles, and Magic Among the Azande* (abridged edition, Oxford: Clarendon Press, 1976, originally published in 1937), in which ideas about witchcraft, diviners called "oracles," and magic are described and discussed in their natural context in what is now South Sudan.

Two important studies provide examples of symbolic studies of religion. Clifford Geertz's 1966 article "Religion as a Cultural System" (in Michael Banton, ed., *Anthropological Approaches to the Study of Religion*, pp. 1–46, ASA Monograph 3, London: Tavistock) explores a symbolic definition of religion that sees religion as a "system of symbols." Another essay in the same volume by Victor Turner explores color symbolism among the Ndembu and has become one of the classic analyses of religious symbolism. Victor Turner's book *The Forest of Symbols: Aspects of Ndembu Ritual* (Ithaca, NY: Cornell University Press, 1967) expands on this analysis by offering a series of explorations of just how such a system of symbols might work in a functioning society in southern Africa.

For an anthropological perspective on the interactions between Islam and politics, see Dale F. Eickelman and James P. Piscatori's book *Muslim Politics* (Princeton, NJ: Princeton University Press, 1996). Even though it was written before the post-9/11 world, it offers useful analytical tools to understand the complex intersections of religion and political action in the Muslim world.

If you want to understand the rise of religious fundamentalisms in recent decades, see Martin Marty and R. Scott Appleby's edited volume *Fundamentalisms Observed* (Fundamentalism Project, Volume 1, Chicago: University of Chicago Press, 1991).

Epilogue

Anthropology and the Future of Human Diversity

Beginning around the year 2000, people from many countries began traveling to and buying property in a small village called Bugarach (population 189), which is near the Pyrenees mountains in the far south of France. Calling themselves "esoterics," these individuals had identified a nearby mountain peak as a good place to survive what they predicted was going to be a cataclysmic transformation of the world that would take place on December 21, 2012. They had come to this conclusion based on a reading of the Mesoamerican Long Count calendar, one of several calendars used by the ancient Maya that traces back to mythical creation times. They believed that the calendar marked that particular day in 2012 as a special moment of cosmic transformation, provoking the destruction of the world as we know it, but also ushering in a great spiritual awakening for humankind. The mountain near Bugarach, it was thought, was occupied by an alien spaceship that could transport survivors to safety.

Over the next decade, thousands of people poured into the area, many of them to climb the peak and some of them to settle there. As 2012 approached, many locals were growing exasperated with the chaos caused by all the activity, and the village's mayor threatened to call in the army. Not long before that fateful day arrived, police showed up and began limiting access to the mountain. Finally, the day came. . . . And there was no cosmic cataclysm. This fact didn't lead most of the esoterics to ditch their predictions of big changes to come but only to reassess when these things will occur, and many of them remained in the Bugarach area.

Uncertain Futures. Based on predictions that the world would come to an end on December 21, 2012, "esoterics" began traveling to Bugarach, France, where they hoped an alien spaceship in the mountain pictured here might transport them to safety and a new spiritual awakening. Even though their predictions did not come true, many esoterics still believe that big changes are going to come. Like people everywhere, they want to know what the uncertain future will bring so they can prepare themselves for it.

For many of you reading this book, the beliefs and motivations of the esoterics seem strange, exotic, and difficult to understand, maybe even ridiculous. And yet there is something deeply human that drove the esoterics to put so much stock in the Maya calendar in their quest to create meaningful lives, and that is the desire to know what the future holds. Wanting to predict the future is a very common human desire. We all want to understand what is likely to happen to us, of course. Sometimes it is driven by simple curiosity about how things taken for granted today might differ in the future. But more often than not, there is a pragmatic concern of wanting to know what to do in the present to prepare for what is to come.

Across the world, people have developed many esoteric bodies of knowledge to explore and satisfy this urge, and those who can gain access to that special wisdom often carry great social authority. The list includes diviners, oracles, seers, soothsayers, prophets, healers, and fortune tellers. It also includes scientists in disciplines like climatology, physics, and medicine, and a few in social science fields like economics, behavioral psychology, and political science. Although we tend to separate the first group from the second because of the latter's use of the scientific method, in the specific cultural contexts in which they operate, all of these actors can make useful and sometimes highly reliable predictions about what is to come. People regularly take action as a result of their pronouncements.

But as Yoda, that iconic source of wisdom in popular culture, once observed, "Difficult to see. Always in motion is the future." Few anthropologists are likely to consider *The Empire Strikes Back*—the movie in the *Star Wars* franchise in which Yoda makes this observation—to be a source of authoritative and rigorous cultural insight (with all due respect to *Star Wars* creator George Lucas, who studied cultural anthropology in college). Yoda's observation nevertheless does align strongly with what we know about human social complexity. It also relates to one of the reasons anthropologists are deeply hesitant to offer predictions about the future, although we as individuals may be as keen as anybody to know what is to come. The human future *is* always in motion. People are not robots, programmed to carry out codes instilled in them by their upbringing and enculturation. One of the things every cultural anthropologist doing fieldwork eventually experiences is that people will *tell* you one thing, only to *do* something different. Usually they are not doing this because they are lying or simply saying what they think the anthropologist wants to hear, or because they are irrational and cannot think straight. They do it because human action is fluid, situational, and context-dependent.

If we apply this insight to the trajectory that the human species as a whole is currently on, the ability to predict our future becomes even more uncertain. One reason is that, even as our knowledge of ancient primates and the hominin family tree has been growing by leaps and bounds in recent years due to fortuitous field discoveries, our understanding of the specifics of how and why contemporary humans emerged is still very much unsettled (Chapter 6). How can we understand where we are headed as a species if we still do not grasp with precision our own past? Moreover, thanks to advances in genomic science, tantalizing details have recently come to light about interbreeding and gene flow between our ancestors, Neanderthals, and Denisovans, suggesting that any assumptions about the specialness and uniqueness of ourselves as *Homo sapiens* are, at the very least, problematic, because they have not taken into account the fluidity and contextual dynamics that may have brought together distinct hominin populations several hundred thousand years ago. Add to all of this recent developments in evolutionary theory presented in Chapters 3, 7, and 8 that consistently tell us that biology and culture jointly and integratively shape human bodily experiences and evolutionary trajectories, and it's clear that things have gotten exponentially more complicated!

Nevertheless, anthropology has developed many strategies, among them holistic and cross-cultural perspectives (Chapter 1) and a diverse and effective toolkit of field-work and laboratory methods that enable us to understand and contextualize the complexity and fluidity of human thought, social action, language, biocultural evolution, and prehistory. We have explored this toolkit for you in a series of "Methods Memos." Each of anthropology's four branches has its own distinctive methodologies, and new ones emerge all the time. We see the greatest change in methods in the ways biological anthropologists and archaeologists study the relationship among different species and among different prehistoric communities. Linguistic anthropology has seen significant enhancements in their methods over the past quarter-century, especially around the performative and ideological aspects of language use. Cultural anthropologists tend to use the same traditional method of participant observation that has been in vogue for the past century, although they too have seen new methods emerge to study cross-border dynamics and globalization.

At the heart of all of these methodological approaches and innovations is continued commitment to the culture concept—which we have defined here as those collective processes through which we construct and naturalize certain meanings and actions as normal and even necessary (Chapter 2)—to frame and inform investigation in all of anthropology's branches. While many animal species, especially primates, can use tools and demonstrate behavioral variation, intergenerational learning, and intensive social cooperation, no other species does these things to the extent or in the same ways that we do (Chapter 5). Our capacity for symbolic abstraction and the creation of collective meaning, mediated through language, is undoubtedly a major factor in helping us interact with the world in distinctive ways and gives us the capacity to imagine and construct other worlds.

Cultures of course are themselves as dynamic, emergent, and changing (Chapter 2). And our languages seem every bit as fluid as our cultures (Chapter 12). No group of people has ever been totally static and homogeneous, not least for the reason that every society and cultural group contains different individuals who have different life experiences due to their particularities of age, gender, social identity, and other factors, as well as distinct social expectations about how to communicate with others (Chapter 12). Creativity, uncertainty, and social conflict are key aspects of everyday social relations everywhere as people work toward a collective understanding of their individual experiences of the world and with others in their communities. As humans, we express those understandings through fairly stable forms of symbolic communication, values, behavioral norms, and social traditions. But thanks to the widening scale of social relationships associated with intercultural, globalizing, and transnational interconnections (Chapter 4), the processes of cultural dynamism seem to have intensified and now manifest themselves in almost all aspects of people's lives in the contemporary world.

This dynamism is present in what we may think of as the material aspects of life (Chapter 9), in relationships of sustainability (Chapter 14), and in economic activity and political relationships (Chapters 13 and 15). Even though some aspects of human life seem stable and fixed, no society is entirely static in matters of social identity, kinship, and gender, kinship being one of the most traditional topics anthropologists have studied since 1870 (Chapter 16). Finally, we can see dynamic processes in our religious beliefs and activities (Chapter 17).

For the better part of the twentieth century, the social sciences and many anthropologists emphasized the stability of social configurations, viewing change as abnormal and troubling to the theoretical perspectives on humanity they were developing. We have obviously taken the opposite view, which reflects the latest thinking of our discipline. Nowhere is the dynamism of the human species so visible as when we look at the tremendous changes our species has experienced since the emergence of anatomically contemporary humans, and especially after we began to control our own food supplies through horticulture and herding, which later would become full-blown agriculture (Chapter 10). Human control over our own food supply was truly revolutionary, except that we could not always control other human groups. These interactions in the Neolithic era forced our species to come up with ways to interact with people in other groups and to organize how to interact within their own group (Chapters 4 and 10), eventually leading to greater levels of social complexity (Chapter 11).

Having said all this, there is one thing anthropologists are reasonably certain about as we look to the future, and that is the persistence of human diversity. Diversity, understood by anthropologists as variety and multiplicity, is a basic pattern of nature and the basis upon which natural systems—oceans, forests, mountain ecosystems, and so on—and the species within them thrive.

We can appreciate these patterns among people simply by recognizing the sheer variety of ways of being human in the world. Processes of globalization do appear to contribute to some kinds of cultural convergences around the world. We see it especially in the alignment of certain kinds of economic activity and consumption patterns. But the archaeological and cultural anthropological record is also full of fascinating details about how, through the processes of culture, people everywhere turn alien cultural imports into something more familiar to them, and less familiar to the communities from which they received them. Although there is still debate in the field about how and why these processes play out as they do, most anthropologists have come to accept that human diversity persists because of, not in spite of, interconnections across cultures (Chapters 4 and 9).

Anthropology also offers a useful reminder that knowing what to do and making a difference in the present do not require being able to predict the future. Anthropologists are experts at identifying the causes of many different kinds of social problems. Whether it is helping craft a new constitution in Ghana or figuring out ways to address food justice in black urban communities (Chapters 14 and 15), anthropologists have offered effective problem-solving strategies for policymakers and corporations as well as vulnerable communities and social movements struggling to make social change. The variety of practical issues anthropologists have taken on is as diverse as the human condition and reflects engagement with the big issues most of us are worried about in the contemporary world: improving human health and well-being; addressing difficulties of cross-cultural communication; adapting to the challenges of environmental sustainability; handling tensions around international relations, terrorism, and violence; understanding the effects of religious fundamentalism; and moving toward the construction of social justice; among others.

What unites all of these diverse scholars with distinct anthropological approaches are certain shared intellectual orientations and assumptions. Some of those orientations are very concrete, including appreciation of the persistence of human diversity, the holistic perspective, critical relativism, and a rejection of ethnocentrism. Some are less tangible but no less critical. Foremost among these is the ability to "think like an anthropologist," a point we assert at the end of every major section of each chapter. To a large extent this has to do with how we pose questions, rooted in recognizing that 99 percent of a good answer is asking a good question. Doing anthropology means being habitually curious about how and why people do and have done the things they do in their everyday lives, and gaining the skills and confidence to ask useful questions—to ourselves as thought experiments, and to others in empirical research—that help focus attention not just on what is happening but on how to interpret it.

Each of the three of us authors naturally use our anthropological perspectives all the time, and not just in our research but in our everyday lives as well. We have seen how many of our best students who pursue careers in the health sciences, business, non-profit work, education, and other professions have also benefited greatly from internalizing anthropological thinking as a way of understanding their jobs, their social networks, their neighborhoods, and the world we hear about on the news. To highlight how anthropology can be useful for everyone, we have included a series of "The Anthropological Life" boxes that discuss how some anthropological thinking can enhance one's life and career.

Another key element of anthropological thinking is recognizing that our disciplinary forebears have been asking rigorous questions about human diversity for over a century. Many of those classic questions and the answers to them have constituted anthropology's contributions to knowledge. Anthropologists have learned a great deal about human diversity, and it is often useful to bring those classic examples, debates, and analyses to bear on contemporary problems. At the same time, many debates remain unresolved, new questions emerge all the time, and anthropology's relationships and intersections with many other disciplines in the humanities, natural sciences, and social sciences make for a lot of cross-fertilization that constantly brings new issues into consideration. All of these factors contribute to the creation of a dynamic and engaged discipline.

We hope it is clear by now that it is not necessary to be a professional anthropologist to appreciate all these things. With some effort and an open mind, anybody can realize that there is great value and lifelong relevance in learning how to be curious, observe and listen to others, ask meaningful questions, record accurate information, recognize several truths at once, and establish and maintain ethical and collaborative relationships with diverse kinds of people. We feel that there is much to be gained—for a successful career, a meaningful life, or both—for those of you who make the effort to incorporate these activities and approaches into your daily encounters with those around you. While the future of human diversity as a whole does not necessarily depend on *your* doing these things, it will make your understanding of the diverse world in which you live much richer and your navigation through it more fluid.

Glossary

Absolute dating (or chronometric dating). Any dating method that determines an age of a fossil, rock, artifact, or archaeological feature on some specified time scale.

Acephalous society. A society without a governing head, generally with no hierarchical leadership.

Acheulian tools. A more complex and diverse stone-toolkit than earlier Olduwan tools. The main characteristic was bifacial flaking, a process that produced strong, sharp edges.

Action research. Fieldwork done in collaboration with a community affected by a social problem to create change or to empower the community.

Action theory. An approach in the anthropological study of politics that closely follows the daily activities and decision-making processes of individual political leaders, emphasizing that politics is a dynamic and competitive field of social relations in which people are constantly managing their ability to exercise power over others.

Adaptation. The development of a trait that plays a functional role in the ability of a life form to survive and reproduce.

Adjudication. The legal process by which an individual or council with socially recognized authority intervenes in a dispute and unilaterally makes a decision.

Affiliation. A relationship between individuals who are frequently in close association based on tolerance, even friendliness.

Age-grades. Groupings of age-mates, who are initiated into adulthood together.

AIM (American Indian Movement). The most prominent and one of the earliest Native American activist groups, founded in 1968.

Alleles. The variants in the DNA sequences for a given gene.

Alloparenting. A practice in which the role of parenting is performed by individuals who are not the biological parents of children.

Alluvial soil. Rich, fine-grained soils deposited by rivers and streams.

Altruism. Seemingly "selfless" acts that have a net loss of energy to the actor but a net gain in energy to the receiver.

Analogous. Similar in appearance or function, not the same due to shared ancestry.

Analyzing secondary materials. Field notes are primary data because they are produced by the anthropologist. Anthropologists also use secondary data, which are published and unpublished materials produced by others, including newspaper clippings, government reports, institutional memos, and so on.

Animal husbandry. The breeding, care, and use of domesticated herding animals such as cattle, camels, goats, horses, llamas, reindeer, and yaks.

Animism. The belief that inanimate objects such as trees, rocks, cliffs, hills, and rivers were animated by spiritual forces or beings.

Anthropocene. Refers to the geological epoch defined by substantial human influence over ecosystems.

Anthropogenic landscape. A landscape modified by human action in the past or present.

Anthropoid. A primate superfamily that includes monkeys, apes, and humans.

Anthropological linguistics. The branch of anthropology that studies human beings through their languages.

Anthropology. The study of human beings, their biology, their prehistory and histories, and their changing languages, cultures, and social institutions.

Anthropology at a distance. A research strategy when disruptions such as war prevent an anthropologist from doing fieldwork in a community. It relies on previously published research and interviews with individuals who have migrated out of the community.

Anthropology of development. The field of study within anthropology concerned with understanding the cultural conditions for proper development, or, alternatively, the negative impacts of development projects.

Anthropometry. The measurement of body parameters that assess physical variation and the relative contributions of particular body parts to overall body shape.

Applied anthropology. Anthropological research commissioned to serve an organization's needs.

Appropriation. The process of taking possession of an object, idea, or relationship.

Arboreal. Living in the trees.

Archaeology. The study of past cultures, by excavating sites where people lived, worked, farmed, or conducted some other activity.

Assemblage. A group or collection of objects found together at a site or excavation.

Australopithecines. A word that refers to the genus *Australopithecus*.

Balanced reciprocity. A form of reciprocity in which the giver expects a fair return at some later time.

Band. A small, nomadic, and self-sufficient group of anywhere from 25 to 150 individuals with face-to-face social relationships, usually egalitarian.

Behavioral ecology. The study of behavior from ecological and evolutionary perspectives.

Behavioral system of inheritance. The types of patterned behaviors that parents and adults pass to young members of their group by way of learning and imitation.

Binomial nomenclature. A taxonomic system that assigns two names to organisms.

Biocultural. The complex intersections of biological, psychological, and cultural processes.

Biocultural evolution. The interaction of cultural capacity and biology to meet selective demands.

Biological anthropology. The study of the biological and biocultural aspects of the human species, past and present, along with those of our closest relatives, the non-human primates.

Bipedal locomotion. The use of two legs rather than four for movement.

Blood types. Sets of proteins that coat the red blood cells, which serve a variety of functions in the human body, including delivering oxygen to tissues and producing antibodies as an immune response.

Breccia. A rock composed of broken fragments or minerals cemented together by a fine-grained matrix.

Bridewealth. Exchange of gifts or money to compensate another clan or family for the loss of one of its women along with her productive and reproductive abilities in marriage. Sometimes known as "bride price."

Call systems. A manner of communication that features patterned sounds or utterances that express meaning.

Canine/Premolar-3 shearing complex. A condition in which the lower first premolar tooth is somewhat sharpened or flattened from rubbing against the upper canine as the mouth closes.

Capitalism. An economic system based on private ownership of the means of production, in which prices are set and goods distributed through a market.

Carbon-14 dating. A dating method that establishes the date or period of an organic artifact or feature from the relative proportions of radioactive carbon to non-radioactive isotopes.

Carrying capacity. The population an area can support.

Centralized political system. A political system, such as a chiefdom or a state, in which certain individuals and institutions hold power and control over resources.

Chiefdom. A political system with a hereditary leader who holds central authority, typically supported by a class of high-ranking elites, informal laws, and a simple judicial system. The population often numbers in the tens of thousands with the beginnings of intensive agriculture and some specialization.

Chronometric dating. Any dating method that determines the age of a fossil, rock, artifact, or archaeological feature on some specified time scale.

City. A relatively large and permanent settlements, usually with a population of at least several thousand inhabitants.

City-state. An autonomous political entity that consisted of a city and its surrounding countryside.

Clan. A group of relatives who claim to be descended from a single ancestor.

Clinal variation. A type of variation in which change is gradual across groups and in which traits shade and blend into each other.

Clinical therapeutic process. The healing process that involves the use of medicines that have some active ingredient that is assumed to address either the cause or the symptom of a disorder.

Code switching. Alternating between two or more different languages during a conversation.

Cognate words. Words in two languages that show the same systematic sound shifts as other words in the two languages, usually interpreted by linguists as evidence for a common linguistic ancestry.

Collapse. The rapid loss of a social, political, and economic order or complexity.

Colonialism. The historical practice of more powerful countries claiming possession of less powerful ones.

Commodities. Mass-produced and impersonal goods with no meaning or history apart from themselves.

Commodity money. Money that has another value beyond itself, such as gold, which can be used as jewelry.

Comparative method. A research method that derives insights from careful comparisons of aspects of two or more cultures or societies.

Complex society. A society in which socioeconomic differentiation, a large population, and centralized political control are pervasive and defining features.

Constructivist approach. A theoretical approach emphasizing that a core dynamic of human biology and culture is processes of construction: the building of meanings, social relationships, ecological niches, and developing bodies.

Consumers. People who rely on goods and services not produced by their own labor.

Consumption. The act of using and assigning meaning to a good, service, or relationship.

Cormic index. Standing height divided by sitting height.

Corporate groups. Groups of real people who work together toward common ends, much like a corporation does.

Costs and benefits. An analytical approach that considers the caloric cost of obtaining food and the calories obtained.

Creole language. A language of mixed origin that has developed from a complex blending of two parent languages that exists as a mother tongue for some part of the population.

Critical relativism. Taking a stance on a practice or belief only after trying to understand it in its cultural and historical context.

Cross-cultural perspective. Analyzing a human social phenomenon by comparing that phenomenon in different cultures.

Cultigen. Any plant that is intentionally grown for human use.

Cultural anthropology. The study of the social lives of living communities.

Cultural appropriation. The unilateral decision of one social group to take control over the symbols, practices, or objects of another.

Cultural construction. The meanings, concepts, and practices that people build out of their shared and collective experiences.

Cultural determinism. The idea that all human actions are the product of culture, which denies the influence of other factors, like physical environment and human biology, on human behavior.

Cultural economics. An anthropological approach to economics that focuses on how symbols and morals help shape a community's economy.

Cultural imperialism. The promotion of one culture over others, through formal policy or less formal means, like the spread of technology and material culture.

Cultural landscape. The culturally specific images, knowledge, and concepts of the physical landscape that help shape human relations with the landscape.

Cultural relativism. The moral and intellectual principle that one should withhold judgment about seemingly strange or exotic beliefs and practices.

Cultural resource management (CRM). Research and planning aimed at identifying, interpreting, and protecting sites and artifacts of historic or prehistoric significance.

Culturally constructed concept of race. A set of cultural or ethnic factors combined with easily perceived morphological traits (e.g., skin reflectance, body shape, cranial structure) in an artificial "biologized" category.

Culture. The taken-for-granted notions, rules, moralities, and behaviors within a social group.

Culture-bound syndrome. A mental illness unique to a culture.

Culture and personality movement. A school of thought in early and mid-twentieth-century American anthropology that studied how patterns of childrearing, social institutions, and cultural ideologies shape individual experience, personality characteristics, and thought patterns.

Culture of migration. The cultural attitudes, perceptions, and symbolic values that shape decision-making processes around, and experiences of, migration.

Customs. Long-established norms that have a codified and law-like aspect.

Delayed reciprocity. A form of reciprocity that features a long lag time between giving and receiving.

Deoxyribonucleic acid (DNA). Spiral-shaped molecule strands that contain the biological information for the cell.

Derived characteristics. Traits unique to a species that evolved after two or more species who have shared a common ancestor diverged.

Descriptive linguistics. The systematic analysis and description of a language's sound system and grammar.

Development anthropology. The application of anthropological knowledge and research methods to the practical aspects of shaping and implementing development projects.

Developmental bias. The idea that not all variations are random but are a function of the developmental processes organisms undergo during their lives that tend to generate certain forms more readily than others.

Developmental systems theory (DST). An approach that combines multiple dimensions and interactants toward understanding the development of organisms and systems and their evolutionary impact.

Diffusionists. Early twentieth-century Boasian anthropologists who held that cultural characteristics result from either internal historical dynamism or a spread (diffusion) of cultural attributes from other societies.

Discrimination. Negative or unfair treatment of a person because of his or her membership in a particular social group or category.

Discourse analysis. An approach that closely analyzes the content, sociopolitical significance, and effects of semiotic practices beyond individual speech events to show how these practices are involved in and shape social processes.

Disease. The purely physiological condition of being sick, usually determined by a physician.

Dispersal. A pattern of one sex leaving the group they were born into at about the time of reproductive maturity.

Diversity. The sheer variety of ways of being human around the world.

Division of labor. The cooperative organization of work into specialized tasks and roles.

Domestication. The converting of wild plants and animals to human uses by making plants able to be grown for food or other uses, or taming animals or turning them into herds that can be raised for meat or milk.

Dominance hierarchy. The ranking of access to desired resources by different individuals relative to one another.

Dowry. A large sum of money or in-kind gifts given to a daughter to ensure her well-being in her husband's family.

Ecological footprint. A quantitative tool that measures what people consume and the waste they produce. It also calculates the amount of biologically productive land and water area needed to support those people.

Economic anthropology. The branch of anthropology concerned with how people make, share, and buy things and services.

Economic system. The structured patterns and relationships through which people exchange goods and services.

Embodiment. A concept that refers to how people literally incorporate, biologically, the material and social worlds in which they live, from conception to death.

Empirical. Verifiable through observation rather than through logic or theory.

Enculturation. The process of learning the social rules and cultural logic of a society.

Environmental anthropology. The branch of anthropology that studies how different societies understand, interact with, and make changes to nature and natural ecosystems.

Environmental justice. A social movement addressing the linkages between racial discrimination and injustice, social equity, and environmental quality.

Epigenetic system of inheritance. The biological aspects of bodies that work in combination with the genes and their protein products, such as the machinery of the cells, the chemical interactions between cells, and reactions between types of tissue and organs in the body.

Essentialism. The philosophical position that dictates that each organism has a true, ideal form, and that all living representatives of that organism are slight deviations from the ideal type.

Ethics. Moral questions about right and wrong and standards of appropriate behavior.

Ethnobiology. The branch of ethnoscience that studies how people in non-Western societies name and codify living things.

Ethnocentrism. The assumption that one's own way of doing things is correct, while dismissing other people's practices or views as wrong or ignorant.

Ethnographic method. A prolonged and intensive observation of and participation in the life of a community.

Ethnography of speaking. An anthropological approach to language that distinguishes the ways that people actually speak from the ideal ways that people in any culture are supposed to speak.

Ethnopoetics. A method of recording oral poetry, stories, ritual language, and nearly any narrative speech act as verses and stanzas rather than as prose paragraphs in order to capture the format and other performative elements that might be lost in written texts.

Ethnohistory. Combining historical and ethnographic approaches to understand culture change, especially in societies with few or no written records.

Ethnoprimatology. The study of the interface between human and ape communities.

Ethnoscience. The study of how people classify things in the world, usually by considering some range or set of meanings.

Eugenics. The study of genetics with the notion of improving human biology and biological potential; often associated with simplistic, erroneous assumptions about the relationship of behavior or cultural traits to simple genetic systems.

Evolution. The adaptive changes in populations of organisms across generations.

Exchange. The transfer of objects and services between social actors.

Exiles. People who are expelled by the authorities of their home countries.

Exogamous. A social pattern in which members of a clan must marry someone from another clan, which has the effect of building political, economic, and social ties with other clans.

Explanatory model of illness. An explanation of what is happening to a patient's body, by the patient, by his family, or by a healthcare practitioner, each of whom may have a different model of what is happening.

Extended evolutionary synthesis. The view of evolution that accepts the existence of not just genetically based, but also non-genetically based, processes of evolution: developmental bias, plasticity, niche construction, and extra-genetic inheritance.

Extended families. Larger groups of relatives beyond the nuclear family, often living in the same household.

Extra-genetic inheritance. The socially transmitted and epigenetic factors that can aid in the adaptive success of organisms.

Feature. An attribute found in an excavation, such as a pit, a crude fireplace, or a wall, that was formed, created, or modified by humans.

Fiat money. Money created and guaranteed by a government.

Field notes. Any information that the anthropologist writes down or transcribes during fieldwork.

Fieldwork. Long-term immersion in a community, normally involving firsthand research in a specific study community or research setting where people's behavior can be observed and the researcher can have conversations or interviews with members of the community.

Foodways. Structured beliefs and behaviors surrounding the production, distribution, and consumption of food.

Foraging. Obtaining food by searching for it, as opposed to growing or raising the plants and animals people eat.

Foramen magnum. The opening at the base of the skull (cranium) where the spinal cord enters and connects to the brain

Forensic analysis. The identification and description of dead people.

Formal economics. The branch of economics that studies the underlying logic of economic thought and action.

Fossilization. The process by which hard tissues like bone and teeth slowly turn to stone as molecule by molecule the hard tissues become rock, keeping the shape of the original bone.

Founder effect. A form of genetic drift that is the result of a dramatic reduction in population numbers so that descendant populations are descended from a small number of "founders."

Functionalism. A perspective that assumes that cultural practices and beliefs serve social purposes in any society.

Fundamentalism. Conservative religious movements that advocate a return to fundamental or traditional principles.

Fundamentalist. A person belonging to a religious movement that advocates a return to fundamental or traditional principles.

Gender. The complex and fluid intersections of biological sex, internal senses of self, outward expressions of identity, and cultural expectations about how to perform that identity in appropriate ways.

Gender/sex systems. The ideas and social patterns a society uses to organize males, females, and those who do not fit either category.

Gender variance. Expressions of sex and gender that diverge from the male and female norms that dominate in most societies.

Gene. A segment of DNA that contains the code for a protein.

Gene flow. The movement of genetic material within and between populations.

Genealogical amnesia. Structural process of forgetting whole groups of relatives, usually because they are not currently significant in social life.

Genealogical method. A system of notation for naming individuals in a community in relation to a key informant—such as "mother," "mother's brother," and so on. It is a key tool for understanding relationships in non-industrial societies where kinship relations are central to political and economic life.

General purpose money. Money that is used to buy nearly any good or service.

Generalized foraging model. A model that asserts that hunter-gatherer societies have five basic characteristics.

Generalized reciprocity. A form of reciprocity in which gifts are given freely without the expectation of return.

Genetic drift. A change in genetic variation across generations due to random factors.

Geneticization. The use of genetics to explain health and social problems rather than other possible causes.

Genome. The complete set of an organism's DNA.

Genotype. An organism's genetic component.

Geographical Information System (GIS). A computerized methodology that brings together data from several sources and integrates them with a geographic reference map.

Globalization. The widening scale of cross-cultural interactions caused by the rapid movement of money, people, goods, images, and ideas within nations and across national boundaries.

Government. A separate legal and constitutional domain that is the source of law, order, and legitimate force.

Gracile. A body of slender build.

Green Revolution. The transformation of agriculture in the developing world that began in the 1940s, through agricultural research, technology transfer, and infrastructure development.

Grooming. Touching another individual to remove dirt, insects, and debris, usually as a way for individuals to bond.

Habitation sites. A place where people lived at some time in the past, perhaps repeatedly over a number of seasons

Haplorrhini. The infraorder of primates including monkeys, apes, and humans.

Holism. Efforts to synthesize distinct approaches and findings into a single comprehensive interpretation.

Holistic perspective. A perspective that aims to identify and understand the whole—that is, the systematic connections between individual cultural beliefs and practices—rather than the individual parts.

Hominidae. A family of primates that includes the Hominids, namely, humans and their ancestors.

Homininae. The African subfamily of the Family Hominidae, which includes humans, chimpanzees, and gorillas.

Hominine. The division (called a tribe) in the superfamily Hominoidea that includes humans and our recent ancestors.

Hominini. The tribe to which humans and our direct human ancestors belong, who are referred to as hominins.

Hominoid. The primate superfamily Hominoidea that includes all the apes and the humans.

Homologous. The characteristic of being similar due to shared ancestry.

Horizontal stratigraphy. The study of layers of soil or rock and how they were deposited.

Horticulture. The cultivation of gardens or small fields to meet the basic needs of a household.

Human biodiversity. The similarities and differences within and across human groups that have biological dimensions.

Human Genome Pinroject. An international scientific research project between 1990 and 2003 whose goal was to identify all the genetic material in humans.

Human leukocyte antigen system (HLA). A series of proteins on the surface of white blood cells that recognize foreign particles or infectious agents.

Hybridization. Persistent cultural mixing that has no predetermined direction or end-point.

Hydraulic despotism. Denotes empires built around the control of water resources by despotic, or all-powerful, leaders.

Illness. The psychological and social experience a patient has of a disease.

Immigrants. People who enter a foreign country with no expectation of ever returning to their home country.

Incest taboo. The prohibition on sexual relations between close family members.

Industrial agriculture. The application of industrial principles and methods to farming.

Industrialization. The economic process of shifting from an agricultural economy to a factory-based one.

Informants. People an anthropologist gets data from in the study community, especially people interviewed or who provide information about what he or she has observed or heard.

Intensification. The use of certain preparation, management, and cultivation processes to increase yields.

Intermembral index. The ratio of arm length to leg length.

Interpretive approach. A kind of analysis that interprets the underlying symbolic and cultural interconnections within a society.

Interpretive theory of culture. A theory that culture is embodied and transmitted through symbols.

Intersex. Individuals who exhibit sexual organs and functions somewhere between male and female elements, often including elements of both.

Intersubjectivity. The realization that knowledge about other people emerges out of relationships and perceptions individuals have with each other.

Interviews. Systematic conversations whose purpose is to collect field research data, ranging from a highly structured set of questions to the most open-ended ones.

Kin selection. The behavioral favoring of your close genetic relatives.

Kinship. The social system that organizes people in families based on descent and marriage.

Kinship chart. A visual representation of family relationships.

Language. A system of communication consisting of sounds, words, and grammar.

Language ideology. Widespread assumptions that people make about the relative sophistication and status of particular dialects and languages.

Laws. Sets of rules established by some formal authority.

Levallois technique. Stone tool-making technique that involves complex preparation of the stone and provides a higher quality toolkit than previous types, with more uses.

Life histories. Interviews that focus on an individual's phases of life, to understand how social patterns have changed or how age affects social position

Limited purpose money. Objects that can be exchanged only for certain things.

Lineage. A group composed of relatives who are directly descended from known ancestors.

Linguistic anthropology. The study of how people communicate with one another through language and how language use shapes group membership and identity.

Linguistic relativity. The idea that people speaking different languages perceive or interpret the world differently because of differences in their languages.

Localization. The creation and assertion of highly particular, often place-based, identities and communities.

Macaca. The genus of macaque monkeys.

Magic. An explanatory system of causation that does not follow naturalistic explanations, often working at a distance without direct physical contact.

Maize. The indigenous species of corn that was first domesticated in Mexico—the term is often used for any variety of corn, since all current varieties are thought to have been derived from this early version of so-called Indian corn.

Market. A social institution in which people come together to exchange goods and services.

Masculinity. The ideas and practices of manhood.

Material culture. The objects made and used in any society; traditionally, the term referred to technologically simple objects made in pre-industrial societies, but material culture may refer to all of the objects or commodities of modern life as well.

Materiality. Having the quality of being physical or material.

Matrifocal unit. A cluster of individuals generally made up of related females.

Means of production. The machines and infrastructure required to produce goods.

Mediation. The use of a third party who intervenes in a dispute to help the parties reach an agreement and restore harmony.

Medical pluralism. The coexistence and interpenetration of distinct medical traditions with different cultural roots in the same cultural community.

Medicalization. The process of viewing or treating as a medical concern conditions that were not previously understood as medical problems.

Megadontia. The characteristic of having large molar teeth relative to body size.

Meiosis. The process of gamete production.

Melanin. A complex polymer that is the main pigment in human skin, occurring in two colors: black and brown.

Mesolithic. The period from the end of the last ice age until the beginning of agriculture. During this period, a number of hunter-gatherer-forager groups established lakeside or seaside settlements that seem to have been year-round sites.

Migrants. People who leave their homes to work for a time in other regions or countries.

Mind. Emergent qualities of consciousness and intellect that manifest themselves through thought, emotion, perception, will, and imagination.

Mitosis. The process of cell division and replication.

Modern synthesis. The view of evolution that accepts the existence of four genetically based processes of evolution: mutation, natural selection, gene flow, and genetic drift.

Modes of subsistence. The social relationships and practices necessary for procuring, producing, and distributing food.

Money. An object or substance that serves as a payment for a good or service.

Monotheism. The belief in a single god.

Morphology. The structure of words and word formation in a language.

Mousterian industry. A disk-core technique of stone toolmaking that allowed the toolmakers to produce many good flakes with little effort and then turn those flakes into a wide variety of fine tools. Associated with the Neanderthals.

Multiple dispersals model (MD). Incorporates complexities in genetic datasets to argue that humans left Africa in multiple waves.

Multiregional evolution model (MRE). Modern humans are only the most recent version of a single species, *Homo sapiens*, that had been in Africa, Asia, and Europe for nearly 2 million years.

Mutation. Change at the level of the DNA (deoxyribonucleic acid).

mya. Million years ago.

NAGPRA (Native American Graves and Repatriation Act). In the United States, the 1990 law that established the ownership of human remains, grave goods, and important cultural objects as belonging to the Native Americans, whose ancestors once owned them.

Natal family. The family into which a person is born and (usually) raised.

Nation-state. An independent state recognized by other states, composed of people who share a single national identity.

Natural selection. The process through which certain heritable traits become more or less common in a population related to the reproductive success of organisms interacting with their environments.

Naturalize. To make part of the natural order of things through the production of scientific theories, schemes, and typologies.

Negative reciprocity. A form of reciprocity in which the giver attempts to get something for nothing, to haggle one's way into a favorable personal outcome.

Negotiation. A form of dispute management in which parties themselves reach a decision jointly.

Neoclassical economics. Economic theories and approaches that study how people make decisions to allocate resources like time, labor, and money in order to maximize their personal satisfaction.

Neolithic Revolution. The "New" Stone Age when humans began to produce their food (growing crops and raising animals) rather than relying exclusively on foraging, but using a stone-tool technology.

Niche construction. When organisms play an active role in their evolution by reshaping the environment to suit their own needs.

Nocturnal. Active during the nighttime.

Non-centralized political system. A political system, such as a band or a tribe, in which power and control over resources are dispersed among members of the society.

Norms. Typical patterns of actual behavior as well as the rules about how things should be done.

Nuclear family. A domestic family group formed by a couple and their children.

Nutrition transition. The combination of changes in diet toward energy-dense foods (high in calories, fat, and sugar) and declines in physical activity.

Obesity. Having excess body fat to the point of impairing bodily health and function.

Olduwan tools. Rocks that were modified to produce sharp flakes and edged choppers.

Optimal foraging strategy. A foraging lifestyle wherein people capture just enough calories from the environment as they (and their families) need to survive comfortably.

Othering. Defining colonized peoples as different from, and subordinate to, Europeans in terms of their social, moral, and physical norms.

Overweight. Having an abnormally high accumulation of body fat.

Paleoanthropologists. Physical anthropologists and archaeologists who study the fossilized remains of ancient primates and humans to understand their biological and behavioral evolution.

Paleoethnobotany. The study of ancient plant remains in order to reconstruct a picture of prehistoric environments and human-plant interactions.

Paleolithic. Literally "old stone," refers to a long epoch in human prehistory from about 2.5 mya to 10,000 years ago, and roughly corresponds with the Pleistocene geological epoch.

Pan. The genus of chimpanzees.

Participant observation. The standard research method used by sociocultural anthropologists that requires the researcher to live in the community he or she is studying to observe and participate in day-to-day activities.

Pastoralism. The practice of animal husbandry, which is the breeding, care, and use of domesticated herding animals such as cattle, camels, goats, horses, llamas, reindeer, and yaks.

Pastoralist society. A group of people who live by animal husbandry.

Patrilocal bands. Small groups in which men controlled resources and hunting territories.

Phenotype. The observable and measurable traits of an organism.

Philology. Comparative study of ancient texts and documents.

Phonology. The systematic pattern of sounds in a language, also known as the language's sound system.

Phylogeny. A graphic representation that traces evolutionary relationships and identifies points when an evolutionary event or change occurred, such as the creation of a new species.

Pidgin language. A mixed language with a simplified grammar, typically borrowing its vocabulary from one language but its grammar from another.

Pilgrimage. A type of ritual in which a journey is made to a destination of spiritual importance.

Placebo effect. A healing process that works by persuading a patient that he or she has been given a powerful medicine, even though the "medicine" has no active medical ingredient.

Plasticity. A particular form of developmental bias in which an organism responds to its environment by changing during its lifetime.

Political ecology. The field of study that focuses on the linkages between political-economic power, social inequality, and ecological destruction.

Political power. The process by which people create, compete, and use power to attain goals that are presumed to be for the good of a community.

Politics. Those relationships and processes of cooperation, conflict, and power that are fundamental aspects of human life.

Polyandry. When a woman has two or more husbands at one time.

Polygamy. Any form of plural marriage.

Polygyny. When a man is simultaneously married to more than one woman.

Polytheism. A type of religion with many gods.

Ponginae. The Asian derived subfamily of Hominidae to which the Orangutan belongs

Population. A cluster of individuals of the same species whose members share a common geographical area and find their mates more often in their own cluster than in others.

Postcolonialism. The field that studies the cultural legacies of colonialism and imperialism.

Postorbital constriction. An indentation of the sides of the cranium behind the eyes.

Potlatches. Opulent ceremonial feasts intended to display wealth and social status by giving away or destroying valuable possessions like carved copper plates, button blankets, and baskets of food. These were characteristic of the communities on the northwestern coast of North America.

Practicing anthropology. Anthropological work involving research as well as involvement in the design, implementation, and management of some organization, process, or product.

Prehensile. The ability to grasp things, usually referring to hands or tails.

Prejudice. Preformed, usually unfavorable opinions that people hold about people from groups that are different from their own.

Prestige economies. Economies in which people seek high social rank, prestige, and power instead of money and material wealth.

Protein synthesis. How DNA assists in the creation of the molecules that make up organisms (proteins).

Proto-language. A hypothetical common ancestral language of two or more living languages.

Push-pull factors. The social, economic, and political factors that "push" people to migrate from their homes and that "pull" them to host countries.

Qualitative method. A research strategy producing an in-depth and detailed description of social activities and beliefs.

Quantitative method. A methodology that classifies features of a phenomenon, counting or measuring them, and constructing mathematical and statistical models to explain what is observed.

Quran. The main body of scripture in Islam, consisting of verses of classical Arabic poetry understood to be revealed to the Prophet Muhammad by Allah, often in dreams or in the midst of other activities. These verses were memorized by Muhammad's followers and written down after his death.

Race. A system that organizes people into hierarchical groups based on specific physical traits that are thought to reflect fundamental and innate differences that are rooted in genetic and biological differences.

Racialization. The social, economic, and political processes of transforming populations into races and creating racial meanings.

Racism. The repressive practices, structures, beliefs, and representations that uphold racial categories and social inequality.

Rapid appraisals. Short-term and highly focused fieldwork, typical of applied anthropology projects.

Recent African origin model (RAO). Modern humans arose as a new species in Africa about 150,000 years ago, during the late Pleistocene.

Reciprocity. The give-and-take that builds and confirms relationships.

Redistribution. The collection of goods in a community and then the further dispersal of those goods among members.

Refugees. People who migrate because of political oppression or war, usually with legal permission to stay in a different country.

Relative dating. Any dating technique that provides a rough assessment of the age of a fossil, artifact, or archaeological feature relative to other fossils, rocks, artifacts, or features.

Religion. A symbolic system that is socially enacted through rituals and other aspects of social life that relate to ultimate issues of humankind's existence.

Repatriation. The return of human remains or cultural artifacts to the communities of descendants of the people to whom they originally belonged.

Replication. The process by which DNA makes copies of itself.

Reproductive success. Measured by how many surviving offspring an organism has.

Residue analysis. Microscopic analysis of the residues of plant and animal foods, especially starches, on pottery or tools.

Resilience. The ability of a social system to absorb changes and still retain certain basic cultural processes and structures, albeit in altered form.

Rite of passage. Any life-cycle rite that marks a person's or group's transition from one social state to another.

Rituals. Stylized performances involving symbols that are associated with social, political, and religious activities.

Ruralization. Process in which the countryside was configured as a contested no-man's land lying between competing city-states.

Sagittal crest. A ridge running along the top of the cranium, usually representing increased bone area for the attachment of chewing muscles.

Sagittal keel. A raised area in the mid-cranium.

Salvage paradigm. The paradigm which held that it was important to observe indigenous ways of life, interview elders, and assemble collections of objects made and used by indigenous peoples.

Scientific concept of race. A population or group of populations within a species that has measurable, defining biological characteristics and low statistical measures of similarity.

Scientific method. The standard methodology of science that begins from observable facts, generates hypotheses from these facts, and then tests these hypotheses.

Secular worldview. A worldview that does not accept the supernatural as influencing current people's lives.

Sedentism. Year-round settlement in a particular place.

Sex. The reproductive forms and functions of the body.

Sexual dimorphism. A difference between the sexes of a species in body size or shape.

Sexuality. Sexual preferences, desires, and practices.

Shaman. A religious leader who communicates with the spirit world about the needs of the living, usually through some form of ritual trance or other altered state of consciousness.

Shared characteristics. Traits or structures that are shared by all or most species in a group because they are inherited from a common ancestral species.

Shared derived characteristics. Traits that evolved after all the species being compared shared a common ancestor, but prior to some more recent speciation events.

Sick role. The culturally defined agreement between patients and family members to acknowledge that a patient is legitimately sick, which involves certain responsibilities and behaviors that caregivers expect of the sick.

Social complexity. A society that has many different parts organized into a single social system.

Social institutions. Organized sets of social relationships that link individuals to each other in a structured way in a particular society.

Social sanction. A reaction or measure intended to enforce norms and punish their violation.

Social support therapeutic process. A healing process that involves a patient's social networks, especially close family members and friends, who typically surround the patient during an illness.

Sociolinguistics. The study of how sociocultural context and norms shape language use and the effects of language use on society.

Speaking in tongues. The phenomenon of speaking in an apparently unknown language, often in an energetic and fast-paced way.

Spheres of exchange. Bounded orders of value in which certain goods can be exchanged only for others.

Spirit familiar. A spirit that has developed a close bond with a shaman.

State. The most complex form of political organization, associated with societies that have intensive agriculture, high levels of social stratification, and centralized authority.

States. Societies with forms of political and economic control over a particular territory and the inhabitants of that territory.

Stelae. Carved limestone slabs.

Stops. Sounds that are formed by closing off and reopening the oral cavity so that it stops the flow of air through the mouth, such as the consonants *p*, *b*, *t*, *d*, *k*, and *g*.

Strategy. A set of behaviors that has become prominent in a population as a result of natural selection.

Strepsirrhini. The infraorder of primates including lemurs, galagos, and lorises.

Structural power. Power that not only operates within settings but also organizes and orchestrates the settings in which social and individual actions take place.

Structural-functionalism. An anthropological theory that the different structures or institutions of a society (religion, politics, kinship, etc.) function to maintain social order and equilibrium.

Subspecies. A population that meets the criteria defined within the scientific concept of race.

Substantive economics. A branch of economics, inspired by the work of Karl Polanyi, that studies the daily transactions people engage in to get what they need or desire.

Surface collection. A collection of pottery and stone artifacts made from the surface of the soil around a possible site.

Surplus value. The difference between what people produce and what they need to survive.

Swidden agriculture. A farming method in tropical regions in which the farmer slashes (cuts down trees) and burns small patches of forest to release plant nutrients into the soil. As soil fertility declines, the farmer allows the plot to regenerate the forest over a period of years.

Symbol. Something—an object, idea, image, figure, or character—that represents something else.

Symbolic system of inheritance. The linguistic system through which humans store and communicate their knowledge and conventional understandings using symbols.

Symbolic therapeutic process. A healing process that restructures the meanings of the symbols surrounding the illness, particularly during a ritual.

Sympathetic magic. Any magical rite that relies on the supernatural to produce its outcome without working through some supernatural being such as a spirit, demon, or deity.

Syndemic. A concept that refers to epidemics or adverse health events that involve the clustering of diseases, adverse interactions between these diseases, and socio-environmental conditions that exacerbate the effects of diseases or make people more vulnerable.

Syntax. Pattern of word order used to form sentences and longer utterances in a language.

Taste. A concept that refers to the sense that gives humans the ability to detect flavors; taste can also refer to the social distinction and prestige associated with certain foodstuffs.

Taxonomy. A system of naming and classifying organisms.

Terrestrial. Living on the ground.

Test pit. A preliminary excavation, usually of a single 1 m × 1 m square (or a half meter square) to see if artifactual material exists at the site and to assess the character of the stratigraphy.

Theory. A tested and repeatedly supported hypothesis.

Totemism. A system of thought that associates particular social groups with specific animal or plant species called "totems" as an emblem.

Trace fossils. Soft tissues such as organs, skin, and feathers that do not fossilize but sometimes leave impressions, or traces, on the sedimentary rock that forms around them.

Tradition. Practices and customs that have become most ritualized and enduring.

Traditional ecological knowledge. Indigenous ecological knowledge and its relationship with resource management strategies.

Trance. A semiconscious state typically brought on by hypnosis, ritual drumming, and singing, or hallucinogenic drugs like mescaline or peyote.

Transactional orders. Realms of transactions a community uses, each with its own set of symbolic meanings and moral assumptions.

Transhumance. The practice of moving herds to different fields or pastures with the changing seasons.

Transnational. Relationships that extend beyond nation-state boundaries but do not necessarily cover the whole world.

Transnational community. A spatially extended social network that spans multiple countries.

Tribe. A type of pastoral or horticultural society with populations usually numbering in the hundreds or thousands in which leadership is more stable than that of a band, but usually egalitarian, with social relations based on reciprocal exchange.

Urbanization. Process by which towns grew as residential centers as opposed to being trading centers.

Use-wear. Patterns of wear and tear on an artifact that is presumed to be due to use.

Value. The relative worth of an object or service that makes it desirable.

Values. Symbolic expressions of intrinsically desirable principles or qualities.

Violence. The use of force to harm someone or something.

World culture. Norms and values that extend across national boundaries.

World Heritage Site program. A program that provides financial support to maintain sites deemed by the World Heritage Committee to be of cultural or natural importance to humanity.

World religions. Religions that claim to be universally significant to all people.

World systems theory. The theory that capitalism has expanded on the basis of unequal exchange throughout the world, creating a global market and global division of labor, dividing the world between a dominant "core" and a dependent "periphery."

Worldview. A general approach to or set of shared unquestioned assumptions about the world and how it works.

References

Adair, Peter. 1967a. *Holy Ghost People*. Documentary film available on DVD and Amazon Prime. Accessed December 4, 2019: https://www.amazon.com/Holy-Ghost-People-Peter-Adair/dp/B07BFK9G95/ref=sr_1_1?keywords=holy+ghost+people&qid=1575467888&sr=8-1.

Adair, Peter. 1967b. Snake Handling Scene from *The Holy Ghost People*. Accessed December 4, 2019: https://www.youtube.com/watch?v=hM2eFXsbToM.

Adams, Robert McC. 1974. Anthropological Perspectives on Ancient Trade. *Current Anthropology* 15(3):141–60.

Adultery. 2009. "Adultery: Criminal Laws, Enforcement of Statutes, as a Defense, Divorce, Cross-Reference." Accessed on 8/18/2009: http://law.jrank.org/pages/4112/Adultery.html.2

Agro, Charlsie and Luke Denne. 2019. "Twins get some 'mystifying' results when they put 5 DNA ancestry kits to the test." CBC News, January 18, 2019. Accessed on April 12, 2022: https://www.cbc.ca/news/science/dna-ancestry-kits-twins-marketplace-1.4980976

Ahlstrom, Richard V. N., Carla R. Van West, and Jeffrey S. Dean. 1995. Environmental and Chronological Factors in the Mesa Verde–Northern Rio Grande Migration. *Journal of Anthropological Archaeology* 14:125–42.

Aiello, L. C., and J. C. K. Wells. 2002. Energetics and the Evolution of the Genus *Homo*. *Annual Review of Anthropology* 31:323–38.

Aitken, M. J. 1985. *Thermoluminescence Dating*. New York: Academic Press.

Ali, Inayat. 2021a. From Normal to Viral Body: Death Rituals During Ordinary and Extraordinary Covidian Times in Pakistan. *Frontiers in Sociology*, February16, 2021. Accessed April 20, 2022: https://doi.org/10.3389/fsoc.2020.619913.

Ali, Inayat. 2021b. Rituals of Containment: Many Pandemics, Body Politics, and Social Dramas During Covid in Pakistan (Brief Research Report). Frontiers in Sociology. April 30, 2021. Accessed April 20, 2022: https://www.frontiersin.org/articles/10.3389/fsoc.2021.648149/full.

Allen, Theodore W. 1997. *The Invention of the White Race*. Vol. 2. London: Verso.

Allport, Gordon. 1958. *The Nature of Prejudice*. Abridged edition. New York: Doubleday Anchor Books.

Almond, Gabriel, A., R. Scott Appleby, and Emmanuel Sivan. 2003. *Strong Religion: The Rise of Fundamentalisms Around the World*. Chicago: University of Chicago Press.

Alverez, Fernando, David Argente, and Diana Van Patten. 2022. Working Paper 29968, National Bureau of Economic Research (Cambridge, MA). Accessed May 24, 2022:https://www.nber.org/papers/w29968

Alvarez, Priscilla. 2019. "What Happened to the Migrant Caravans?" CNN. Accessed July 8, 2020: https://www.cnn.com/2019/03/04/politics/migrant-caravans-trump-immigration/index.html.

Alvarez Astacio, Patricia. 2013. "Screening Room: Savage Memory." Visual and New Media Review, *Fieldsights*, July 10. Accessed July 15, 2022:https://culanth.org/fieldsights/screening-room-savage-memory.

American Academy of Arts and Sciences. 2018. The State of the Humanities 2018: Graduates in the Workforce & Beyond. Accessed October 15, 2018: https://www.amacad.org/multimedia/pdfs/publications/researchpapersmonographs/HI_Workforce-2018.pdf.

American Anthropological Association. 2015. Race: Are We So Different? Accessed December 21, 2015: https://understandingrace.org/.

American Psychiatric Association. 1994. *Diagnostic and Statistical Manual of Mental Disorders: DSM-IV*. Fourth Edition. Washington, D.C.: American Psychiatric Association.

Ames, Michael. 1999. How to Decorate a House: The Re-negotiation of Cultural Representations at the University of British Columbia Museum of Anthropology. *Museum Anthropology* 22(3):41–51.

Amnesty International. 2019. "Torture." Accessed January 29, 2020: https://www.amnesty.org/en/what-we-do/torture/.

Anand, Nikhil. 2017. *Hydraulic City: Water and the Infrastructures of Citizenship in Mumbai*. Durham. NC: Duke University Press.

Anderson, Eugene N. 2005. *Everyone Eats: Understanding Food and Culture*. New York: New York University Press.

Anyon, Roger, T. J. Ferguson, and John R. Welch. 2000. "Heritage Management by American Indian Tribes in the Southwestern United States." In F. O. McManamon and A. Hatton, eds., *Cultural Resource Management in Contemporary Society: Perspectives on Managing and Presenting the Past*, pp. 142–59. London: Routledge.

Appadurai, Arjun, ed. 1986. *The Social Life of Things: Commodities in Cultural Perspective*. Cambridge: Cambridge University Press.

Armstrong, Karen. 1994. *A History of God: The 4,000-Year Quest of Judaism, Christianity and Islam*. New York: Ballantine Books.

Arnold, Jeanne. 1996. The Archaeology of Complex Hunter-Gatherers. *Journal of Archaeological Method and Theory* 3(1):77–126.

Arnold, Kate, and Filippo Aureli. 2007. "Postconflict Reconciliation." In Christina J. Campbell, Agustín Fuentes, Katherine C. MacKinnon, Melissa Panger, and Simon K. Bearder, eds., *Primates in Perspective*, pp. 592–608. New York: Oxford University Press.

Arsuaga, J. L., J. M. Bermudez de Castro, and E. Carbonell, eds. 1997. The Sima de los Huesos Hominid Site. *Journal of Human Evolution* 33:105–421.

Arthur, Wallace. 2004. *Biased Embryos and Evolution*. Cambridge: Cambridge University Press.

Asfaw, B., T. White, O. Lovejoy, B. Latimer, S. Simpson, and G. Suwa. 1999. *Australopithecus garhi*: A New Species of Early Hominid from Ethiopia. *Science* 284:629–35.

Atran, Scott. 2001. "The Vanishing Landscape of the Petén Maya Lowlands: People, Plants, Animals, Places, Words, and Spirits." In Lisa Maffi, ed., *On Biocultural Diversity: Linking Language, Knowledge, and the Environment*, pp. 157–76. Washington, DC: Smithsonian Institution Press.

Avruch, Kevin. 1998. *Culture and Conflict Resolution*. Washington, DC: United States Institute of Peace.

Bacon, John. 2014. Reality Show Snake Handler Dies From Snakebite. *USA Today*, February 16, 2014. Accessed December 4, 2019: https://www.usatoday.com/story/life/tv/2014/02/16/snake-salvation-pastor-dead/5532531/.

Bahuchet, Serge. 1988. "Food Supply Uncertainty Among the Aka Pygmies." In I. de Garine and G. A. Harrison, eds., *Coping with Uncertainty in Food Supply*, pp. 118–49. Oxford: Clarendon Press.

Bailey, F. G. 1969. *Stratagems and Spoils: A Social Anthropology of Politics*. London: Basil Blackwell.

Bakalar, Nicholas. 2013. "A Village Invents a Language All Its Own." New York Times. Accessed July 19, 2019: https://www.nytimes.com/2013/07/16/science/linguist-finds-a-language-in-its-infancy.html.

Ball, H. L., Tomori, C. and McKenna, J. J. (2019). Toward an Integrated Anthropology of Infant Sleep. American Anthropologist, 121:595–612. https://doi.org/10.1111/aman.13284.

Balter, Michael. 2014b. World's Oldest Stone Tools Discovered in Kenya. *Science*, April 20. Accessed May 8, 2015: http://news.sciencemag.org/africa/2015/04/world-s-oldest-stone-tools-discovered-kenya.

Bannister, Bryant, and William J. Robinson. 1975. Tree-Ring Dating in Archaeology. *World Archaeology* 7(2):210–25.

Barbash, Ilisa, and Lucien Taylor. 1992. *In and Out of Africa*. An Ethnographic film. Berkeley, CA: University of California Extension, Center for Media and Independent Learning.

Barnes, Jessica, and Michael Dove. 2015. *Climate Cultures: Anthropological Perspectives on Climate Change*. New Haven, CT: Yale University Press.

Barr, W. Andrew, Briana Pobiner, John Rowan, and J. Tyler Faith. 2022. "No sustained increase in zooarchaeological evidence for carnivory after the appearance of *Homo erectus*." PNAS 19(5). https://doi.org/10.1073/pnas.2115540119.

Bartlett, Robert. 1982. *Gerald of Wales, 1146–1223*. Oxford: Oxford University Press.

Basch, Linda, Nina Glick Schiller, and Cristina Szanton Blanc. 1993. *Nations Unbound: Transnational Projects, Postcolonial Predicaments, and Deterritorialized Nation-States*. Basel: Gordon and Breach.

Basu, Amitra, ed. 2010. *Women's Movements in the Global Era: The Power of Local Feminisms*. Boulder, CO: Westview Press.

Bates, Daniel G. 2005. *Human Adaptive Strategies: Ecology, Culture, and Politics*. 3rd edition. Boston: Pearson Allyn and Bacon.

Begley, Chris. 2021. *The Next Apocalypse: The Art and Science of Survival*. New York: Basic Books.

Begun, David R. 1999. "Hominid Family Values: Morphological and Molecular Data on the Relations Among the Great Apes and Humans." In Sue Taylor Parker, Robert W. Mitchell, and H. Lyn Miles, eds., *The Mentalities of Gorillas and Orangutans: Comparative Perspectives*, pp. 3–42. Cambridge: Cambridge University Press.

Belluz, Julia. 2019. Tiny Samoa Has Had Nearly 5,000 Measles Cases. Here's How It Got So Bad. Vox.com, December 18, 2019. Accessed January 31, 2020: https://www.vox.com/2019/12/18/21025920/measles-outbreak-2019-samoa.

Bellwood, Peter. 2005. *First Farmers: The Origins of Agricultural Societies*. Malden, MA: Blackwell.

Bender, Barbara. 1978. Gatherer-Hunter to Farmer: A Social Perspective. *World Archaeology* 10(2):204–22.

Benefit, Brenda R., and Monte L. McCrossin. 1995. Miocene Hominoids and Hominid Origins. *Annual Review of Anthropology* 24:237–56.

Benn Torres, Jada. 2019. Anthropological Perspectives on Genomic Data, Genetic Ancestry, and Race. *Yearbook of Physical Anthropology* 171(Supp. 70):74–86. DOI: 10.1002/ajpa.23979.

Benn Torres, Jada. 2018. "Reparational" Genetics: Genomic Data and the Case for Reparations in the Caribbean. *Genealogy* 2(1):7.

Benn Torres, Jada, and Gabriel A. Torres Colón. 2021. *Genetic Ancestry: Our Stories, Our Pasts*. New York: Routledge.

Berger, Lee, Darryl de Ruiter, Steven Churchill, Peter Schmid, Kristan Carlson, Paul Dirks, and Job Kibii. 2010. *Australopithecus sediba*: A New Species of *Homo*-like Australopith from South Africa. *Science* 328(2010):195–204.

Berger Lee R., J. Hawks, D. J. de Ruiter, S. E. Churchill, P. Schmid, L. K. Delezene, T. L. Kivell, H. M. Garvin, S. A. Williams, J. M. DeSilva, M. M. Skinner, C. M. Musiba, N. Cameron, T. W, Holliday, W. Harcourt-Smith, R. R, Ackermann, M. Bastir, B. Bogin, D. Bolter, J. Brophy, Z. D. Cofran, K. A. Congdon, A. S. Deane, M. Dembo, M. Drapeau, M. C. Elliott, E. M. Feuerriegel, D. Garcia-Martinez, D. J. Green, A. Gurtov, J. D. Irish, A. Kruger, M. F. Laird, D. Marchi, M. R. Meyer, S. Nalla, E. W. Negash, C. M. Orr, D. Radovcic, L. Schroeder, J. E. Scott, Z. Throckmorton, M. W. Tocheri, C. VanSickle, C. S. Walker, P. Wei, and B. Zipfel. 2015. "Homo naledi, A New Species of the Genus Homo from the Dinaledi Chamber, South Africa." *Elife*. September 10, 2015. 4:e09560. doi: 10.7554/eLife.09560.

Berger, Lee R, Makhubela Tebogo, Molopyane Keneiloe, Krüger Ashley, Randolph-Quinney Patrick, Elliott Marina, Peixotto Becca, Fuentes Agustín, Tafforeau Paul, Beyrand Vincent, Dollman Kathleen, Jinnah Zubair, Brewer Gillham Angharad, Broad Kenneth, Brophy Juliet, Chinamatira Gideon, Dirks Paul H. M., Feuerriegel Elen, Gurtov Alia, Hlophe Nompumelelo, Hunter Lindsay, Hunter Rick, Jakata Kudakwashe, Jaskolski Corey, Morris Hannah, Pryor Ellie, Ramaphela Maropeng, Roberts Eric, Smilg Jacqueline S., Tsikoane Mathabela, Tucker Steven, van Rooyen Dirk, Warren Kerryn, Wren Colin D., Kissel Marc, Spikins Penny, Hawks John. 2023 "Evidence for deliberate burial of the dead by *Homo naledi*." *eLife* 12:RP89106. https://doi.org/10.7554/eLife.89106.1.

Berger, Peter L., ed. 1999. *The Desecularization of the World: Resurgent Religion and World Politics*. Washington, DC: Ethics and Public Policy Center.

Bergmann, J. F., O. Chassany, J. Gandiol, P. Deblois, J. A. Kanis, J. M. Segresta, C. Caulin, and R. Dahan. 1994. A Randomized Clinical Trial of the Effect of Informed Consent on the Analgesic Activity of Placebo and Naproxen in Cancer Pain. *Clinical Trials Meta-Analysis* 29:41–47.

Berlin, Brent. 1973. Folk Systematics in Relation to Biological Classification and Nomenclature. *Annual Review of Systematics and Ecology* 4:259–71.

Berlin, Brent, and Paul Kay. 1969. *Basic Color Terms: Their Universality and Evolution*. Berkeley: University of California Press.

Bermudez de Castro, J. M., J. L. Arsuaga, E. Carbonell, A. Rosas, I. Martinez, and M. Mosquera. 1997. A Hominid from the Lower Pleistocene of Atapuerca, Spain: Possible Ancestor to Neanderthals and Modern Humans. *Science* 276:1392–95.

Bernard, Russell H. 2011. *Research Methods in Anthropology: Qualitative and Quantitative Approaches*. Lanham, MD: AltaMira Press.

Berwick, Robert C., Angela D. Friederici, Noam Chomsky, and Johan J. Bolhuis. 2013. Evolution, Brain, and the Nature of Language. *Trends in Cognitive Science* 17(2):89–98.

Beta Analytic Testing Laboratory. 2018. Accelerator Mass Spectrometry (AMS) Dating. Accessed January 3, 2019: https://www.radiocarbon.com/accelerator-mass-spectrometry.htm.

Binford, Lewis. 1968. "Post-Pleistocene Adaptations." In S. R. Binford and L. Binford, eds., *New Perspectives in Archaeology*, pp. 313–41. Chicago: Aldine.

Bird-David, Nurit. 1992. Beyond the "Original Affluent Society": A Culturalist Reformulation. *Current Anthropology* 33(1):25–47.

Bird-David, Nurit. 1993. "Tribal Metaphorization of Human-Nature Relatedness: A Comparative Analysis." In K. Milton, ed., *Environmentalism: The View from Anthropology*, pp. 112–25. London: Routledge.

Blake, Michael. 2015. *Maize for the Gods: Unearthing the 9,000-Year History of Corn*. Berkeley: University of California Press.

Blakey, Michael L. 1998. The New York African Burial Ground Project: An Examination of Enslaved Lives, a Construction of Ancestral Ties. *Transforming Anthropology* 7(1):53–58.

Blim, Michael. 2000. Capitalisms in Late Modernity. *Annual Reviews of Anthropology* 29:25–38.

Boas, Franz, ed. 1911. *Handbook of North American Indian Languages*. Bulletin of the Bureau of American Ethnology, No. 40. Washington, DC: Government Printing Office for the Smithsonian Institution.

Boas, Franz. 1940. *Race, Language, and Culture*. New York: Macmillan.

Bodley, John. 1999. *Victims of Progress*. 4th edition. New York: McGraw-Hill.

Boellsdorff, Tom. 2021. Why English Might Let Go of "He" and "She." *Sapiens* November 3, Accessed 13 April 2022:https://www.sapiens.org/language/they-pronoun/.

Boggs, Stephen T., and Malcolm Naea Chun. 1990. "Ho'oponopono: A Hawaiian Method of Solving Interpersonal Problems." In Karen Ann Watson-Gegeo and Geoffrey White, eds., *Disentangling: Conflict Discourse in Pacific Societies*, pp. 123–53. Stanford, CA: Stanford University Press.

Bohannon, Paul, and Laura Bohannon. 1968. *Tiv Economy*. Evanston, IL: Northwestern University Press.

Bolnick, Deborah, Duana Fullwiley, Troy Duster, Richard Cooper, Joan Fujimura, Jonathan Kahn, Jay S. Kaufman, Jonathan Marks, Ann Morning, Alondra Nelson, Pilar Ossorio, Jenny Reardon, Susan Reverby, and Kimberly TallBear. 2007. The Science and Business of Genetic Ancestry Testing. *Science* 318:399–400.

Boseley, Sarah. 2012. "World Bank's Jim Yong Kim: 'I Want to Eradicate Poverty.' *The Guardian*. 25 July 2012. Accessed February 17, 2017: https://www.theguardian.com/global-development/2012/jul/25/world-bank-jim-yong-kim-eradicate-poverty.

Boserup, Ester. 1965. *The Conditions of Agricultural Growth: The Economics of Agrarian Change Under Population Pressure*. London: G. Allen and Unwin.

Bradbury, R. E. 1957. *The Benin Kingdom and the Edo-speaking Peoples of South-Western Nigeria*. London: International African Institute.

Braidwood, Robert. 1952. *The Near East and the Foundations for Civilization: An Essay in Appraisal of the General Evidence*. Eugene: Oregon State System of Higher Education.

Brakefield, P. M. 2006. Eco-Devo and Constraints on Selection. *Trends in Ecology and Evolution* 21(7):362–68.

Bramble, Dennis, and Daniel Lieberman. 2004. Endurance Running and the Evolution of *Homo*. *Nature* 432:345–52.

Brettell, Caroline. 2003. *Anthropology and Migration: Essays on Transnationalism, Ethnicity, and Identity*. Lanham, MD: Rowman and Littlefield.

Brettell, Caroline B., and Carolyn F. Sargent, eds. 2001. *Gender in Cross-Cultural Perspective*. 3rd edition. Upper Saddle River, NJ: Prentice Hall.

Brewis, Alexandra. 2011. *Obesity: Cultural and Biocultural Perspectives*. New Brunswick, NJ: Rutgers University Press.

Bridges, K., and W. McClatchey. 2009. Living on the Margin: Ethnoecological Insights from Marshall Islanders at Rongelap Atoll. *Global Environmental Change* 19:140–46.

Bringa, Tone. 2005. "Haunted by Imaginations of the Past: Robert Kaplan's Balkan Ghosts." In Katherine Besteman and Hugh Gusterson, eds., *Why America's Top Pundits Are Wrong: Anthropologists Talk Back*, pp. 60–82. Berkeley: University of California Press.

Brockington, Dan. 2002. *Fortress Conservation: The Preservation of the Mkomazi Game Reserve*. Bloomington: Indiana University Press.

Brookfield, Harold C., and J. Peter White. 1968. Revolution or Evolution in the Prehistory of the New Guinea Highlands: A Seminar Report. *Ethnology* 7(1):43–52.

Brown, Michael. 2003. *Who Owns Native Culture?* Cambridge, MA: Harvard University Press.

Brown, P., T. Sutikna, M. J. Morwood, R. P. Soejono, Jatmiko, E. Wayhu Saptomo, and Rokus Awe Due. 2004. A New Small-Bodied Hominin from the Late Pleistocene of Flores, Indonesia. *Nature* 431(7012):1055–61.

Brown, Peter J. 1991. Culture and the Evolution of Obesity. *Human Nature* 2(1):31–57.

Brownell, K. D. 2002. "The Environment and Obesity." In C. G. Fairburn and K. D. Brownell, eds., *Eating Disorders and Obesity: A Comprehensive Handbook*. 2nd edition, pp. 433–38. New York: Guilford Press.

Jarrod. 2014. Junction Group: Magnetic Re-Survey of Junction Group Archaeological Preserve. *Archaeological Conservancy Blog*, November 12. Accessed May 1, 2019: https://www.archaeologicalconservancy.org/magnetic-re-survey-junction-group-archaeological-preserve/.

Burling, Robbins. 1971. *Man's Many Voices: Language in Its Cultural Context*. New York: Holt, Rinehart and Winston.

Cameron, Catherine M. 1995. Migration and the Movement of Southwestern Peoples. *Journal of Anthropological Archaeology* 14(2):104–24.

Campbell, Christina J., Agustín Fuentes, Katherine C. MacKinnon, Simon K. Bearder, and Rebecca M. Stumpf. 2011. *Primates in Perspective*. 2nd edition. New York: Oxford University Press.

Cann, Rebecca L., Mark Stoneking, and Allan C. Wilson. 1987. Mitochondrial DNA and Human Evolution. *Nature* 325:31–36.

Caplan, Pat, ed. 1995. *Understanding Disputes: The Politics of Argument*. Oxford: Berg.

Carey, Benedict. 2007. Brainy Parrot Dies, Emotive to the End. *New York Times*, September 11, 2007. Accessed July 20, 2010: https://www.nytimes.com/2007/09/11/science/11parrot.html?_r=1.

Carneiro, Robert L. 1974. "Slash-and-Burn Cultivation Among the Kuikuru and Its Implications for Cultural Development." In Patricia J. Lyon, ed., *Native South Americans*, pp. 73–91. Boston, MA: Little, Brown.

Carrier, James. 1995. *Gifts and Commodities: Exchange and Western Capitalism Since 1700*. London: Routledge.

Carrier, James. 1996a. "Exchange." In Alan Barnard and Jonathan Spencer, eds., *Encyclopedia of Social and Cultural Anthropology*, pp. 218–21. London: Routledge.

Carrier, James. 1996b. "Consumption." In Alan Barnard and Jonathan Spencer, eds., *Encyclopedia of Social and Cultural Anthropology*, pp. 128–29. London: Routledge.

Carrier, Joseph M. 1976. Family Attitudes and Mexican Male Homosexuality. *Urban Life* 5(3):359–75.

Carroll, John B., ed. 1956. *Language, Thought, and Reality: Selected Writings of Benjamin Lee Whorf*. Cambridge, MA: Technology Press of MIT.

Casana, Jesse. 2020. "Remote Sensing-based Approaches to Site Morphology and Historical Geography in the Northern Fertile Crescent." In Dan Lawrence, Mark Altaweel, and Graham Philip, eds. *New Agendas in Remote Sensing and Landscape Archaeology in the Near East: Studies in Honor of Tony J. Wilkinson*, pp. 154–74. Oxford: Archaeopress Publishing.

Castañeda, Quetzil E. 1996. *In the Museum of Maya Culture: Touring Chichén Itzá*. Minneapolis: University of Minnesota Press.

Castrì, Loredana, Flory Otárola, Mwenza Blell, Ernesto Ruiz, Ramiro Barrantes, Donata Luiselli, Davide Pettener, and Lorena Madrigal. 2007. Indentured Migration and Differential Gender Gene Flow: The Origin and Evolution of the East-Indian Community of Limón, Costa Rica. *American Journal of Physical Anthropology* 134(2):175–89.

Chagnon, Napoleon. 1968. *Yanomamö: The Fierce People*. New York: Holt, Rinehart and Winston.

Chagnon, Napoleon and Timothy Asch. 1997. *The Feast*. Videocassette. Watertown, MA: Documentary Educational Resources. (Released 1970 as 16 mm film.)

Chagnon, Napoleon and Timothy Asch. 2008. *Magical Death*. DVD. Watertown, MA: Documentary Educational Resources. (Released 1973 as 16 mm film.)

Challenger, Douglas. 2016. Walking the Camino in the Age of Wi-Fi. The On Being Project. Accessed January 30, 2020: https://onbeing.org/blog/walking-the-camino-in-the-age-of-wi-fi/.

Chambers, Robert. 1997. *Whose Reality Counts? Putting the Last First*. 2nd edition. London: Intermediate Technology.

Chapin, Mac. 2004. "A Challenge to Conservationists." *World Watch Magazine* November/December 2004:17–31.

Chappell, Sally A. Kitt. 2002. *Cahokia: Mirror of the Cosmos*. Chicago: University of Chicago Press.

Childe, V. Gordon. 1936. *Man Makes Himself*. London: Watts.

Choquet, Hélène, and David Meyre. 2011. Genetics of Obesity: What Have We Learned? *Current Genomics* 12(3):169–79.

Chossudovsky, Michel. 1997. *The Globalization of Poverty: Impacts of IMF and World Bank Reforms*. Atlantic Highlands, NJ: Zed Books.

Clifford, James, and George Marcus, eds. 1986. *Writing Culture: The Poetics and Politics of Ethnography*. Berkeley: University of California Press.

Codere, Helen. 1950. *Fighting with Property: A Study of Kwakiutl Potlatching and Warfare*. New York: J. J. Augustin.

Cohen, Jeffrey. 2004. *The Culture of Migration in Southern Mexico*. Austin: University of Texas Press.

Cohen, Mark Nathan. 1977. *The Food Crisis in Prehistory: Overpopulation and the Origins of Agriculture*. New Haven, CT: Yale University Press.

Cohen, Mark Nathan. 1998. *Culture of Intolerance: Chauvinism, Class, and Racism in the United States*. New Haven, CT: Yale University Press.

Cohen, Mark Nathan, and Gillian M. M. Crane-Kramer. 2007. *Ancient Health: Skeletal Indicators of Agricultural and Economic Intensification*. Gainesville: University of Florida Press.

Colchester, Marcus. 2003. "The Fifth World Parks Congress: Parks for People or Parks for Business?" *World Rainforest Movement Bulletin No. 75*, October 2003. Accessed February 15, 2005: https://www.wrm.org.uy/other-information/the-vth-world-parks-congress-parks-for-people-or-parks-for-business.

Cole, Douglas. 1985. *Captured Heritage: The Scramble for Northwest Coast Artifacts*. Seattle: University of Washington Press.

Collier, Jane, and Sylvia Yanagisako, eds. 1987. *Gender and Kinship: Essays Toward a Unified Analysis*. Stanford, CA: Stanford University Press.

Conkey, Margaret W., and Janet D. Spector. 1984. Archaeology and the Study of Gender. *Advances in Archaeological Method and Theory* 7:1–38.

Connor, Linda. 1982. Ships of Fools and Vessels of the Divine: Mental Hospitals and Madness, A Case Study. *Social Science and Medicine* 16:783–94.

Conroy, Glenn C. 1997. *Reconstructing Human Origins: A Modern Synthesis*. New York: W. W. Norton.

Coon, C. S., S. M. Garn, and J. B. Birdsell. 1950. *Races*. Springfield, IL: Thomas.

Cooper, Merian, Ernest Schoedsack, and Marguerite Harrison. 1999. *Grass: A Nation's Battle for Life*. DVD. New York: Milestone Film and Video (Orig. released 1925).

Corbin, J. H., U. E. Oyene, E. Manoncourt, H. Onya, M. Kwamboka, M. Amuyunzu-Nyamongo, K. Sørensen, O. Mweemba, M. M. Barry, D. Munodawafa, Y. V. Bayugo, Q. Huda, T. Moran, S. A. Omoleke, D. Spencer-Walters, and S. Van den Broucke. 2021. A Health Promotion Approach to Emergency Management: Effective Community Engagement Strategies from Five Cases. *Health Promotion International*, 36 (Supplement 1), i24–i38. Accessed June 3, 2022:https://doi.org/10.1093/heapro/daab152.

Counihan, Carole. 1999. *The Anthropology of Food and Body: Gender, Meaning, and Power*. New York: Routledge.

Counihan, Carole, and Penny Van Esterik, eds. 1997. *Food and Culture: A Reader*. New York: Routledge.

Counts, Dorothy A. 1980. Fighting Back Is Not the Way: Suicide and the Women of Kaliai. *American Ethnologist* 7:332–51.

Crate, Susan. 2008. Gone the Bull of Winter? Grappling with the Cultural Implications of and Anthropology's Role(s) in Global Climate Change. *Current Anthropology* 49:569–95.

Crate, Susan, and Mark Nuttall, eds. 2016. *Anthropology and Climate Change: From Encounters to Actions*. 2nd edition. London: Routledge.

Csordas, Thomas, and Arthur Kleinman. 1996. "The Therapeutic Process." In Carolyn F. Sargent and Thomas M. Johnson, eds., *Medical Anthropology: Contemporary Theory and Method*. Revised edition, pp. 3–20. Westport, CT: Praeger.

Curtis, Garniss H. 1975. Improvements in Potassium-Argon Dating: 1962–1975. *World Archaeology* 7(2):198–209.

Dakowski, Bruce. 1990. "Everything Is Relatives: W. H. R. Rivers." In *Pioneers of Social Anthropology: Strangers Abroad* (Documentary Film Series). Videorecording. Princeton, NJ: Films for the Humanities and Sciences.

Dalan, Rinita A., George R. Holley, William I. Woods, Harold W. Watters, Jr., and John A. Koepke. 2003. *Envisioning Cahokia: A Landscape Perspective*. DeKalb: Northern Illinois University Press.

Daltabuit, Magalí, and Thomas Leatherman. 1998. "The Biocultural Impact of Tourism of Mayan Communities." In Alan Goodman and Thomas Leatherman, eds., *Building a New Biocultural Synthesis: Political-Economic Perspectives on Human Biology*, pp. 317–38. Ann Arbor: University of Michigan Press.

D'Andrade, Roy. 1995. *The Development of Cognitive Anthropology*. Cambridge: Cambridge University Press.

Dark, Philip J. C. 1962. *The Art of Benin: A Catalogue of an Exhibition of the A. W. F. Hoierr and Chicago Natural History Museum Collections of Antiquities from Benin, Nigeria*. Chicago: Chicago Natural History Museum.

Dark, Philip J. C. 1982. *An Illustrated Catalogue of Benin Art*. Boston: G. K. Hall.

Darnell, Regna. 2000. *And Along Came Boas: Continuity and Revolution in Americanist Anthropology*. Amsterdam: John Benjamins.

Darnell, Regna, and Judith T. Irvine. 1997. Edward Sapir: January 26, 1884–February 4, 1929. *Biographical Memoirs* 71:280–99.

Darwin, Charles. 1859. *On the Origin of Species by Means of Natural Selection: Or, The Preservation of Favoured Races in the Struggle for Life*. London: J. Murray.

Darwin, Charles. 2003. *The Origin of Species*. 150th anniversary edition. New York: Signet.

David, Ariel. 2021. "Study Reveals Role of Climate Change in Human Agricultural Revolution." *Haaretz*. November 22, 2021. Accessed January 5, 2022: https://www.haaretz.com/archaeology/2021-11-22/ty-article/study-reveals-how-end-of-ice-age-led-prehistoric-humans-to-settle-down/0000017f-efac-df98-a5ff-efadcc2b0000.

Davidheiser, Mark. 2007. Overview of Peace and Conflict Resolution Study and Practice. *Anthropology News*, October 11–12.

de Beauvoir, Simone. 2010. *The Second Sex*. Trans. Constance Borde and Sheila Malvany-Chevallier. New York: Alfred A. Knopf. (Orig. published 1949.)

de Heinzelin, J, J. Desmond Clark, T. White, et al. 1999. Environment and Behavior of 2.5 Million Year Old Bouri Hominids. *Science* 284:625–29.

De León, Jason. 2015. *The Land of Open Graves: Living and Dying on the Migrant Trail*. Oakland: University of California Press.

de Mille, Cecil B., director. 1956. *The Ten Commandments*. Hollywood, CA: Paramount Pictures.

de Waal, Frans. 2001. *The Ape and the Sushi Master: Cultural Reflections of a Primatologist*. New York: Basic Books.

de Waal, Frans. 2013. *The Bonobo and the Atheist: In Search of Humanism Among the Primates*. New York: W. W. Norton.

Deloria, Vine Jr. 1969. *Custer Died for Your Sins: An Indian Manifesto*. New York: Macmillan.

deMenocal, P., and C. Stringer. Climate and the Peopling of the World. *Nature* 538:49–50. https://doi.org/10.1038/nature19471.

Dennell, Robbin. 1997. The World's Oldest Spears. *Nature* 385:767–68. Accessed June 9, 2022: https://www.nature.com/articles/385767a0.

Dentan, Robert Knox. 1968. *The Semai: A Non-Violent People of Malaya*. New York: Holt, Rinehart, and Winston.

Dettwyler, Katherine A. 2013. *Dancing Skeletons: Life and Death in West Africa*. 2nd edition. Prospect Heights, IL: Waveland.

Diamond, Jared. 2002. Evolution, Consequences and Future of Plant and Animal Domestication. *Nature* 418(6898):700–707.

Diamond, Jared. 2005. *Collapse: How Societies Choose to Fail or Succeed*. New York: Viking Books.

Dick, H. P. and Nightlinger, J. 2020. "Discourse Analysis." In J. Stanlaw, ed., *The International Encyclopedia of Linguistic Anthropology*., Wiley Online Library. https://doi.org/10.1002/9781118786093.iela0103.

Dietrich, Oliver, Manfred Heun, Jens Notroff, Klaus Schmidt, and Martin Zamkow. 2012. The Role of Cult and Feasting in the Emergence of Neolithic Communities: New Evidence from Göbekli Tepe, South-Eastern Turkey. *Antiquity* 86(333):674–95.

Digangi, Elizabeth, and Jonathan Bethard. 2021. Uncloaking a Lost Cause: Decolonizing ancestry estimation in the United States. *American Journal of Physical Anthropology*. 175(4):1–15. DOI 10.1002/ajpa.24212.

Dirks, Paul H. G. M, Eric M. Roberts, Hannah Hilbert-Wolf, et al. 2017. The Age of *Homo naledi* and Associated Sediments in the

Rising Star Cave, South Africa. *eLife* 2017;6:e24231. Accessed May 1, 2019: https://elifesciences.org/articles/24231.

Dixon, J. E., J. R. Cann, and Colin Renfrew. 1968. Obsidian and the Origins of Trade. *Scientific American* 218(3):38–47.

Dongoske, K., M. Yeatts, T. Ferguson, and L. Jenkins. 1995. Historic Preservation and Native American Sites. *SAA Bulletin* 13(4):13, 39.

Dore, Kerry, Erin Riley, and Agustín Fuentes. 2017. *Ethnoprimatology: A Practical Guide to Research at the Human-Nonhuman Primate Interface.* Cambridge Studies in Biological and Evolutionary Anthropology. Cambridge: Cambridge University Press.

Dorsey, George Amos. 1909. "Studies Sources of Immigration." *Chicago Tribune*, November 14, 1909, p. 5.

Douglas, A. E. 1919. *Climatic Cycles and Tree Growth.* Vol. 1. Washington, DC: Carnegie Institution of Washington.

Douglas, Mary. 1966. *Purity and Danger: An Analysis of the Concepts of Pollution and Taboo.* New York: Praeger.

Douglas, Mary. 1970. *Natural Symbols: Explorations in Cosmology.* New York: Pantheon Books.

Douglas, Mary. 1999. *Implicit Meanings: Selected Essays in Anthropology.* London: Routledge and Kegan Paul.

Douglas, Mary. 2005. "A Feeling for Hierarchy." In James L. Heft, ed., *Believing Scholars: Ten Catholic Intellectuals.* New York: Fordham University Press.

Douglas, Mary, and Baron Isherwood. 1978. *The World of Goods.* Harmondsworth: Penguin.

Dressler, William. 2005. What's Cultural About Biocultural Research? *Ethos* 31(1):20–45.

Dreyer, Edward L. 2007. *Zheng He: China and the Oceans in the Early Ming Dynasty, 1405–1433.* New York: Pearson Longman.

Drucker, Philip, and Robert F. Heizer. 1967. *To Make My Name Good: A Reexamination of the Southern Kwakiutl Potlatch.* Berkeley: University of California Press.

Dunning, Nicholas, and Timothy Beach. 2000. "Stability and Instability in Prehispanic Maya Landscapes." In David L. Lentz, ed., *Imperfect Balance: Landscape Transformations in the Pre-Columbian Americas*, pp. 179–202. New York: Columbia University Press.

Eboreime, Joseph. 2003. *The Installation of a Benin Monarch: Rite de Passage in the Expression of Ethnic Identity in Nigeria.* Paper from the ICOMOS 14th General Assembly. Accessed March 3, 2005: http://openarchive.icomos.org/id/eprint/500.

Edgar, Heather, and Keith Hunley. 2009. Race Reconciled? How Biological Anthropologists View Human Variation. *American Journal of Physical Anthropology* 139(1):1–4.

Edwards, Carolyn P. 1993. "Behavioral Sex Differences in Children of Diverse Cultures: The Case of Nurturance to Infants." In Michael E. Pereira and Lynn A. Fairbanks, eds., *Juvenile Primates: Life History, Development, and Behavior*, pp. 327–28. New York: Oxford University Press.

Edwards, Sophie. 2019. "As Jim Kim Steps Down, a Tumultuous World Bank Presidency Comes to an End." *Devex.* Accessed February 23, 2020: https://www.devex.com/news/as-jim-kim-steps-down-a-tumultuous-world-bank-presidency-comes-to-an-end-94247.

Ehrlich, Paul R. 1968. *Population Bomb.* New York: Ballantine Books.

Eickelman, Dale F., and James Piscatori. 1996. *Muslim Politics.* Princeton, NJ: Princeton University Press.

Eisenberg, Leon. 1977. Disease and Illness: Distinctions Between Professional and Popular Ideas of Sickness. *Culture, Medicine and Psychiatry* 1(1):9–23.

Eller, Jack David. 2006. *Violence and Culture: A Cross-Cultural and Interdisciplinary Approach.* Belmont, CA: Thomson Wadsworth.

Ellis, E. C., N. Gauthier, K. Klein Goldewijk, R. Bliege Bird, N. Boivin, S. Díaz, D.Q. Fuller, J. L. Gill, J. O. Kaplan, N. Kingston, H. Locke, C. N. H. McMichael, D. Ranco, T. C. Rick, M. R. Shaw, L. Stephens, J.-C. Svenning, J. E. M. Watson. 2021. People Have Shaped Most of Terrestrial Nature for at least 12,000 Years. *Proceedings of the National Academy of Science* 118. Article e2023483118.

Ellwanger, Nicholas. 2011. Primatology as Anthropology. *Anthropologies: A Collaborative Online Project*, August 1. Accessed April 10, 2015: http://www.anthropologiesproject.org/2011/08/primatology-as-anthropology.html.

Erickson, Clark. 2000. An Artificial Landscape-Scale Fishery in the Bolivian Amazon. *Nature* 408:190–93.

Errington, Frederick, Tatsuro Fujikura, and Deborah Gewertz. 2013. *The Noodle Narratives: The Global Rise of an Industrial Food into the Twenty-First Century.* Berkeley: University of California Press.

Escobar, Arturo. 1991. Anthropology and the Development Encounter: The Making and Marketing of Development Anthropology. *American Ethnologist* 18:658–82.

Escobar, Arturo. 1995. *Encountering Development: The Making and Unmaking of the Third World.* Princeton, NJ: Princeton University Press.

Eshed, Vered, Avi Gopher, Ron Pinhasi, and Israel Hershkovitz. 2010. Paleopathology and the Origin of Agriculture in the Levant. *American Journal of Physical Anthropology* 143(1):121–33.

Estep, Bill. 2014. Ky. Snakebite Victim's Family Refuses Help. *Firehouse* Feb 17, 2014. Firehouse. Accessed July 12, 2023. https://www.firehouse.com/home/news/11313418/ky-snakebite-victim-sends-ems-away.

Esteva, Gustavo. 1992. "Development." In Wolfgang Sachs, ed., *The Development Dictionary*, pp. 6–25. London: Zed Books.

Estrada, A., P. A. Garber, R. A. Mittermeier, S. Wich, S. Gouveia, R. Dobrovolski, K. A. I. Nekaris, V. Nijman, A. B. Rylands, F. Maisels, E. A. Williamson, J. Bicca-Marques, A. Fuentes, L. Jerusalinsky, S. Johnson, F. Rodrigues de Melo, L. Oliveira, C. Schwitzer, C. Roos, S. M. Cheyne, M. C. Martins Kierulff, B. Raharivololona, M. Talebi, J. Ratsimbazafy, J. Supriatna, R. Boonratana, M. Wedana, and A. Setiawan. 2018. Primates in Peril: The Significance of Brazil, Madagascar, Indonesia and the Democratic Republic of the Congo for Global Primate Conservation. *PeerJ* 6:e4869. https://doi.org/10.7717/peerj.4869.

Estrada, Alejandro, Paul A. Garber, Anthony B. Rylands, et al. 2017. Impending Extinction Crisis of the World's Primates: Why Primates Matter. *Science Advances* 3:e1600946.

Evans-Pritchard, E. E. 1940. *The Nuer: A Description of the Modes of Livelihood and Political Institutions of a Nilotic People.* Oxford: Oxford University Press.

Evans-Pritchard, E. E. 1956. *Nuer Religion.* Oxford: Clarendon Press.

Evans-Pritchard, E. E. 1961. *Anthropology and History: A Lecture Delivered at the University of Manchester with Support of the Simon Fund for the Social Sciences.* Manchester: Manchester University Press.

Evans-Pritchard, E. E. 1976. *Witchcraft, Oracles, and Magic Among the Azande.* Abridged edition. Oxford: Clarendon Press. (Orig. published 1937.)

Fabian, Johannes. 2001. *Anthropology with an Attitude: Critical Essays.* Palo Alto, CA: Stanford University Press.

Fabian, Johannes. 2014. Ethnography and Intersubjectivity: Loose Ends. *Hau: Journal of Ethnographic Theory* 4(1):199–209. Accessed June 6, 2022.: https://www.journals.uchicago.edu/doi/epdf/10.14318/hau4.1.008.

Fadiman, Anne. 1997. *The Spirit Catches You and You Fall Down: A Hmong Child, Her American Doctors, and the Collision of Two Cultures.* New York: Farrar, Straus and Giroux.

Fagan, Brian M. 2005. *A Brief History of Archaeology: Classical Times to the Twenty-First Century.* Upper Saddle River, NJ: Pearson Prentice Hall.

Fairhead, James, and Melissa Leach. 1996. *Misreading the African Landscape: Society and Ecology in a Forest-Savanna Mosaic.* Cambridge: Cambridge University Press.

Farmer, Paul. 1992. *AIDS and Accusation: Haiti and the Geography of Blame.* Berkeley: University of California Press.

Farmer, Paul. 2004. *Pathologies of Power: Health, Human Rights, and the New War on the Poor*. Berkeley: University of California Press.

Fausto-Sterling, Anne. 1992. Why Do We Know So Little About Human Sex? *Discover Magazine*, June. Accessed August 19, 2009: https://www.discovermagazine.com/health/why-do-we-know-so-little-about-human-sex.

Fausto-Sterling, Anne. 2000. *Sexing the Body: Gender Politics and the Construction of Sexuality*. New York: Basic Books.

Fazioli, K. Patrick. 2014. The Erasure of the Middle Ages from Anthropology's Intellectual Genealogy. *History and Anthropology* 25(3):336–55.

Fedigan, Linda Marie. 2010. Ethical Issues Faced by Field Primatologists: Asking the Relevant Questions. *American Journal of Primatology* 71:1–18.

Ferguson, James. 1994. *The Anti-Politics Machine: "Development," Depoliticization, and Bureaucratic Power in Lesotho*. Minneapolis: University of Minnesota Press.

Ferguson, R. Brian. 1995. *Yanomami Warfare: A Political History*. Santa Fe: School of American Research Press.

Field, Les, and Richard G. Fox. 2007. "Introduction: How Does Anthropology Work Today?" In Les Field and Richard G. Fox, eds., *Anthropology Put to Work*, pp. 1–19. Oxford: Berg.

Finney, Ben R. 2004. *Sailing in the Wake of the Ancestors: Reviving Polynesian Voyaging*. Honolulu: Bishop Museum Press.

Fischer, Edward. 2014. The Good Life: Aspiration, Dignity, and the Anthropology of Well-Being. Stanford: Stanford University Press.

Fisher, Christopher T., Helen P. Pollard, Isabel Israde-Alcántara, Victor H. Garduño-Monroy, and Subir K. Banerjee. 2003. A Reexamination of Human-Induced Environmental Change Within the Lake Pátzcuaro Basin, Michoacán, Mexico. *PNAS* 100(8):4957–62.

Flannery, Kent. 1969. "Origins and Ecological Effects of Early Domestication in Iran and the Near East." In P. Ucko and G. W. Dimbleby, eds., *The Domestication and Exploitation of Plants and Animals*, pp. 73–100. London: Duckworth.

Fluehr-Lobban, Carolyn. 2003. *Ethics and the Profession of Anthropology: Dialogue for Ethically Conscious Practice*. Walnut Creek, CA: AltaMira Press.

Foley, William. 1997. *Anthropological Linguistics: An Introduction*. Malden, MA: Blackwell.

Food and Agriculture Organization of the United Nations (FAO). 2012. Undernourishment Around the World in 2012. Accessed September 11, 2013: www.fao.org/docrep/016/i3027e/i3027e02.pdf.

Foster, Robert J. 2008. *Coca-Globalization: Following Soft Drinks from New York to New Guinea*. New York: Palgrave Macmillan.

Foucault, Michel. 1978. *The History of Sexuality*, Vol. 1. *An Introduction*. Trans. Robert Hurley. New York: Vintage Books.

Frazer, James G. 1890. *The Golden Bough: A Study in Comparative Religion*. 1st edition. 2 Vols. London: Macmillan.

Frazer, James G. 1911–1915. *The Golden Bough: A Study in Magic and Religion*. 3rd edition. 12 Vols. London: Macmillan.

Freidson, Eliot. 1970. *Profession of Medicine: A Study of the Sociology of Applied Knowledge*. New York: Dodd, Mead.

Friedman, Jonathan. 1994. *Cultural Identity and Global Process*. London: Sage.

Friedman, Jonathan. 1999. "The Hybridization of Roots and the Abhorrence of the Bush." In Michael Featherstone and Scott Lash, eds., *Spaces of Culture: City-Nation-World*, pp. 230–55. London: Sage.

Fry, Douglas. 2006. *The Human Potential for Peace: An Anthropological Challenge to Assumptions About War and Violence*. New York: Oxford University Press.

Fuentes, Agustín. 2007. *Core Concepts in Biological Anthropology*. 1st edition. New York: McGraw-Hill.

Fuentes, Agustín. 2012. Ethnoprimatology and the Anthropology of the Human-Primate Interface. *Annual Reviews of Anthropology* 41:101–17.

Fuentes, Agustín. 2014a. Human Evolution, Niche Complexity, and the Emergence of a Distinctively Human Imagination. *Time and Mind* 7(3):241–57.

Fuentes, Agustín. 2014b. "There's a Monkey in My Kitchen (and I Like It): Fieldwork with Macaques in Bali and Beyond." In Karen B. Strier, ed., *Primate Ethnographies*, pp. 151–62. Boston: Pearson.

Fuentes, Agustín. 2014c. The Troublesome Ignorance of Nicholas Wade. Huffington Post 10 July 2014. Accessed June 8, 2022: https://www.huffpost.com/entry/the-troublesome-ignorance-of-nicholas-wade_b_5344248.

Fuentes, Agustín. 2017. *The Creative Spark: How Imagination Made Humans Exceptional*. New York: Dutton

Fuentes, Agustín. 2018a. *Core Concepts in Biological Anthropology*. 3rd edition. New York: McGraw-Hill.

Fuentes, Agustin. 2018b. "How Humans and Apes are Different, and Why it Matters." Journal of Anthropological Research 74(2): 151–67.

Fuentes, Agustín. 2019. *Why We Believe: Evolution and the Human Way of Being*. New Haven, CT: Yale University Press.

Fuentes, Agustin. 2020. A (Bio)anthropological View of the COVID-19 Era Midstream: Beyond the Infection, *Anthropology Now* 12:1, 24–32,

Fuentes, Agustin. 2022a. "I Put a Camera on a Monkey. Here's How It Shook My Understanding of Humanity." The Well—March 18, 2022. Accessed on March 30, 2022: https://bigthink.com/the-well/awe-animals-humanity/.

Fuentes, Agustin. 2022b. *Race, Monogamy, and Other Lies They Told You: Busting Myths About Human Nature*. 2nd edition. Berkeley: University of California Press.

Fuentes, Agustin, Kissel Marc, Spikins Penny, Molopyane Keneiloe, Hawks John, Berger Lee R. 2023. "Burials and engravings in a small-brained hominin, Homo naledi, from the late Pleistocene: contexts and evolutionary implications." *eLife* 12:RP89125. https://doi.org/10.7554/eLife.89125.1.

Fuentes, Agustin and Jeffrey V. Peterson. 2021. Social Media and Public Perception as Core Aspect of Public Health: The Cautionary Case of @realdonaldtrump and Covid-19. *PLoS ONE* 16(5):e0251179 Accessed June 9, 2022: https://doi.org/10.1371/journal.pone.0251179.

Fuentes, Agustín, and Carolyn Rouse. 2016. New Articulations of Biological Difference in the 21st Century: A Conversation. *Anthropology Now* 8:14–25.

Fuentes, Agustín and Polly Weissner. 2016. "Reintegrating Anthropology: From Inside Out." Current Anthropology 57(S13): S3–S12.

Fuentes, Agustín, Matthew Wyczalkowski, and Katherine MacKinnon. 2010. A Nonlinear Dynamics Contribution to Modeling Facets of the Evolutionary History in the Genus *Homo*. *Current Anthropology* 51(3):435–44.

Fullagar, Richard. 2005. "Residues and Usewear." In J. Balme and A. Patterson, eds., *Archaeology in Practice: A Student Guide to Archaeological Analyses*, pp. 207–34. Malden, MA: Blackwell.

Gal, Susan, and Judith T. Irvine. 2019. *Signs of Difference: Language and Ideology in Social Life*. Cambridge: Cambridge University Press.

Galbraith, John Kenneth. 1958. *The Affluent Society*. Boston: Houghton Mifflin.

Gallagher, Nancy L. 1999. *Breeding Better Vermonters: The Eugenics Project in the Green Mountain State*. Hanover, NH: University Press of New England.

Garber, Paul A., and Robert W. Sussman. 2011. "Cooperation and Competition in Primate Social Interactions." In Christina J. Campbell, Agustín Fuentes, Katherine C. MacKinnon, Melissa Panger, and Simon K. Bearder, eds., *Primates in Perspective*, pp. 587–99. New York: Oxford University Press.

García Canclini, Nestor. 1995. *Hybrid Cultures: Strategies for Entering and Leaving Modernity*. Minneapolis: University of Minnesota Press.

Gardner, R. Allen, Beatrix T. Gardner, and Thomas E. van Cantfort, eds. 1989. *Teaching Sign Language to Chimpanzees*. Albany: State University of New York Press.

Gardner, Robert. 2004. *Dead Birds*. DVD. Cambridge, MA: Harvard University, Peabody Museum of Archaeology and Ethnology, Film Study Center.

Gardner, Robert, and Karl G. Heider. 1969. *Gardens of War: Life and Death in the New Guinea Stone Age*. New York: Random House.

Garn, Stanley. 1961. *Human Races*. Springfield, IL: C. C. Thomas.

Geertz, Clifford. 1960. *The Religion of Java*. Glencoe, IL: Free Press.

Geertz, Clifford. 1963. *Agricultural Involution: The Processes of Ecological Change in Indonesia*. Berkeley: University of California Press.

Geertz, Clifford. 1966. "Religion as a Cultural System." In Michael Banton, ed., *Anthropological Approaches to the Study of Religion*, pp. 1–46. ASA Monograph 3. London: Tavistock.

Geertz, Clifford. 1968. *Islam Observed: Religious Development in Morocco and Indonesia*. Chicago: University of Chicago Press.

Geertz, Clifford. 1973. *The Interpretation of Cultures: Selected Essays*. New York: Basic Books.

Geertz, Clifford. 1980. *Negara: The Theatre State in Nineteenth Century Bali*. Princeton, NJ: Princeton University Press.

Gellner, Ernest. 1983. *Nations and Nationalism*. Ithaca, NY: Cornell University Press.

Gennep, Arnold van. 1960. *The Rites of Passage*. Trans. Monica B. Vizedom and Gabrielle L. Caffee. Chicago: University of Chicago Press. (Orig. published 1909 in French.)

Genz, Joseph. 2011. "Navigating the Revival of Voyaging in the Marshall Islands: Predicaments of Preservation and Possibilities of Collaboration." *Contemporary Pacific* 23:1–34.

Gero, Joan, and Margaret Conkey, eds. 1991. *Engendering Archaeology: Women and Prehistory*. Oxford: Blackwell.

Gibbon, Edward. 1784. *Decline and Fall of the Roman Empire*. 12 Vols. Dublin, Ireland: W. Wilson.

Gibbs, James L.,Jr. 1963. The Kpelle Moot. *Africa* 33(1):1–11.

Gilfoyle, Daniel. 2020. The Voyage of the Dolphin: The First Europeans on Tahiti. National Archives blog (21 July 2020). Accessed on April 16, 2022: https://blog.nationalarchives.gov.uk/the-voyage-of-hms-dolphin-the-first-europeans-on-tahiti/.

Gill, Richardson B. 2000. *The Great Maya Droughts: Water, Life, and Death*. Albuquerque: University of New Mexico Press.

Gillespie, Thomas R., and Fabian H. Leendertz. 2020. "Covid 19: Protect Great Apes During Human Pandemics." Nature 579(497). https://www.nature.com/articles/d41586-020-00859-y.

Glaskin, Katie, and Richard Chenhall, eds. 2013. *Sleep Around the World: Anthropological Perspectives*. New York: Palgrave MacMillan.

Glauziusz, Josie, 2021. "What Drove *Homo Erectus* Out of Africa?" *Sapiens*, 14 October 2021. Accessed April 26, 2022: https://www.sapiens.org/archaeology/ubeidiya-homo-erectus/.

Gledhill, John. 2000. *Power and Its Disguises: Anthropological Perspectives on Politics*. London: Pluto Press.

Global Justice Now. 2016. 10 Biggest Corporations Make More Money Than Most Countries in the World Combined. Accessed February 17, 2017: http://www.globaljustice.org.uk/news/2016/sep/12/10-biggest-corporations-make-more-money-most-countries-world-combined.

Gmelch, George. 1978. Baseball Magic. *Human Nature* 1(8):32–39.

Godelier, Maurice. 1999. *The Enigma of the Gift*. Chicago: University of Chicago Press.

Golitko, Mark, Matthew Schauer, and John Edward Terrell. 2013a. Identification of Fergusson Island Obsidian on the Sepik Coast of Northern Papua New Guinea. *Archaeology in Oceania* 47:151–56.

Golitko, Mark, Matthew Schauer, and John Edward Terrell. 2013b. Obsidian Acquisition on the Sepik Coast of Northern Papua New Guinea During the Last Two Millennia. In Glenn Summerhayes and H. Buckley, eds., *Pacific Archaeology: Documenting the Past 50,000 Years*, pp. 43–57. Otago, NZ: University of Otago.

Gonzalez, Roberto. 2001. *Zapotec Science: Farming and Food in the Northern Sierra of Oaxaca*. Austin: University of Texas Press.

Gonzalez, Sara L., Ian Kretzler, and Briece Edwards. 2018. Imagining Indigenous and Archaeological Futures: Building Capacity with the Confederated Tribes of Grand Ronde. *Archaeologies: Journal of the World Archaeological Congress* 14(1):85–114.

Good, Mary-Jo DelVecchio, Paul E. Brodwin, Byron J. Good, and Arthur Kleinman. 1992. *Pain as Human Experience: An Anthropological Perspective*. Berkeley: University of California Press.

Goodall, Jane. 1971. *In the Shadow of Man*. Boston: Houghton Mifflin.

Goodall, Jane. 1986. *The Chimpanzees of Gombe: Patterns of Behavior*. Cambridge, MA: Belknap Press of Harvard University Press.

Goodby, Robert G., Paul Bock, Edward Bourras, Christopher Dorion, A. Garrett Evans, Tonya Largy, Stephen Pollock, Heather Rockwell, and Arthur Spiess. 2014. "The Tenant Swamp Site and Paleoindian Domestic Space in Keene, New Hampshire." *Archaeology of Eastern North America* 42:129–64.

Goodenough, Ward. 1965. Yankee Kinship Terminology: A Problem in Componential Analysis. *American Anthropologist*, New Series, Vol. 67, No. 5, Part 2: Formal Semantic Analysis (October, 1965), pp. 259–87.

Gould, Stephen Jay. 1983. *Hen's Teeth and Horse's Toes: Further Reflections on Natural History*. New York: W. W. Norton.

Gould, Stephen Jay. 1996. *The Mismeasure of Man*. New York: W. W. Norton.

Gow, David. 1993. Doubly Damned: Dealing with Power and Praxis in Development Anthropology. *Human Organization* 52(4):380–97.

Graeber, David. 2008. Hope in Common. The Anarchist Library. Originally published in slash.autonomedia.org. Accessed June 1, 2022: https://theanarchistlibrary.org/library/david-graeber-hope-in-common.

Graeber, David. 2011. *Debt: The First 5,000 Years*. Brooklyn, NY: Melville House.

Graham, Laura R. 2012. Review of Defying Maliseet Language Death: Emergent Vitalities of Language, Culture, and Identity in Eastern Canada, by Bernard Perley. *Language* 88(4):914–17.

Grant, Bob. 2007. Do Chimps Have Culture? *The Scientist*. Accessed April 12, 2015: https://www.the-scientist.com/uncategorized/do-chimps-have-culture-46242.

Graves, Joseph Jr. 2015. "Why the Nonexistence of Biological Races Does Not Mean the Nonexistence of Racism." *American Behavioral Scientist* 59(11):1474–95.

Graves, Joseph L., and Alan H. Goodman. 2021. Racism, Not Race: Answers to Frequently Asked Questions. New York: Columbia University.

Gravlee, Clarence. 2009. How Race Becomes Biology: Embodiment of Social Inequality. *American Journal of Physical Anthropology* 139(1):47–57.

Gravlee, Clarence. 2020. Systemic Racism, Chronic Health Inequities, and COVID-19: A Syndemic in the Making? *American Journal of Human Biology: The Official Journal of the Human Biology Council* 32(5), e23482. https://doi.org/10.1002/ajhb.23482.

Gregory, Steven, and Roger Sanjek, eds. 1994. *Race*. New Brunswick, NJ: Rutgers University Press.

Grimm, Jakob. 1822. *Deutsche Grammatik*. Göttingen: Dieterichsche Buchhandlung.

Grose, Jessica. "School's Out: Parental Burnout Isn't Going Away." *New York Times*, June 23, 2020. https://www.nytimes.com › 2020 › 06 › 23 › parenting › parental-burnout-coronavirus.html.

Grove, Richard. 1995. *Green Imperialism: Colonial Expansion, Tropical Island Edens and the Origins of Environmentalism, 1600–1860*. Cambridge: Cambridge University Press.

Gruen, Lori, Amy Fultz, and Jill Pruetz. 2013. Ethical Issues in African Great Ape Field Studies. *ILAR Journal* 54(1):24–32.

Grün, Rainier. 2008. "Electron Spin Resonance Dating." In Deborah Pearsall, ed., *Encyclopaedia of Archaeology*, pp. 153–99. Oxford: Elsevier Science and Technology.

Gudeman, Stephen. 1986. *Economics as Culture: Models and Metaphors of Livelihood*. London: Routledge and Kegan Paul.

Gudeman, Stephen. 2001. *The Anthropology of Economy: Community, Market, and Culture*. Oxford: Blackwell.

Guha, Ramachandra. 2000. *Environmentalism: A Global History*. New York: Longman.

Gulliver, Phillip H. 1979. *Disputes and Negotiations: A Cross-Cultural Perspective*. New York: Academic Press.

Gutmann, Matthew C. 1997. Trafficking in Men: The Anthropology of Masculinity. *Annual Review of Anthropology* 26:385–409.

Haas, Jonathan. 1990. *The Anthropology of War*. Cambridge: Cambridge University Press.

Haenn, Nora, and Richard Wilk. 2005. *The Environment in Anthropology: A Reader in Ecology, Culture, and Sustainable Living*. New York: New York University Press.

Haugerud, Angelique. 2016. Public Anthropology in 2015: *Charlie Hebdo*, Black Lives Matter, Migrants, and More. *American Anthropologist* 118(3):585–601.

Haile-Selassie, Yohannes. 2001. Late Miocene Hominids from the Middle Awash, Ethiopia. *Nature* 412:178–81.

Haile-Selassie, Yohannes, Luis Gibert, Stephanie M. Melillo, et al. 2015. New Species from Ethiopia Further Expands Middle Pliocene Hominin Diversity. *Nature* 512:483–88.

Hakiwai, Arapata, and John Terrell. 1994. *Ruatepupuke: A Maori Meeting House*. Field Museum Centennial Collection. Chicago: Field Museum.

Hale, Kenneth L. 1992. On Endangered Languages and the Safeguarding of Diversity. *Language* 68(1):1–3.

Hamilton, W. D. 1964. The Genetical Evolution of Social Behavior, I and II. *Journal of Theoretical Biology* 7:1–52.

Hanlon, Joseph. 1996. Strangling Mozambique: International Monetary Fund "Stabilization" in the World's Poorest Country. *Multinational Monitor* 17(7–8): 17–21.

Haraway, Donna. 1989. *Primate Visions: Gender, Race, and Nature in the World of Modern Science*. New York: Routledge.

Harmand, Sonia; Lewis, Jason E.; Feibel, Craig S.; Lepre, Christopher J.; Prat, Sandrine; Lenoble, Arnaud; Boes, Xavier; Quinn, Rhonda L.; Brenet, Michel; Arroyo, Adrian; Taylor, Nicholas; Clement, Sophie; Daver, Guillaume; Brugal, Jean-Philip; Leakey, Louise; Mortlock, Richard A.; Wright, James D.; Lokorodi, Sammy; Kirwa, Christopher; Kent, Dennis V.; Roche, Helene. 2015. "3.3-million-year-old stone tools from Lomekwi 3, West Turkana, Kenya." *Nature* 521, 320–325.

Harris, Marvin. 1979. *Cultural Materialism*. New York: Random House.

Harrison, Faye V. 1998. Introduction: Expanding the Discourse on "Race." *American Anthropologist* 100(3):609–31.

Hart, Donna, and Robert W. Sussman. 2005. *Man the Hunted: Primates, Predators, and Human Evolution*. New York: Westview Books.

Hartigan, John Jr. 2006. Saying "Socially Constructed" Is Not Enough. *Anthropology News* 47(2):8.

Harvard University Skeletal Biology Lab. 2015. Biomechanics of Foot Strikes and Applications of Running Barefoot or in Minimal Footwear. Accessed April 20, 2015: https://anabolicminds.com/ community/threads/biomechanics-of-foot-strikes-applications-to-running-barefoot-or-in-minimalfootwear.197421/.

Harvey, L. P. 2007. *Ibn Batuta*. London: I. B. Tauris and Oxford Centre for Islamic Studies.

Hastorf, Christine. 1988. "The Use of Paleoethnobotanic Data in Prehistoric Studies of Crop Production, Processing, and Consumption." In Christine Hastorf and Virginia Popper, eds., *Current Paleoethnobotany: Analytical Methods and Cultural Interpretations of Archaeological Plant Remains*, pp. 119–44. Chicago: University of Chicago Press.

Hastrup, Kirsten, and Peter Elass. 1990. Anthropological Advocacy: A Contradiction in Terms. *Current Anthropology* 31(3):301–11.

Haugerud, Angelique. 2016. Public Anthropology in 2015: Charlie Hebdo, Black Lives Matter, Migrants, and More. *American Anthropologist* 118:585–601.

Hawks, John. 2013. Significance of Neandertal and Denisovan Genomes in Human Evolution. *Annual Review of Anthropology* 42:433–49.

Hawks, John. 2019. "New Hominin Shakes the Family Tree—Again." *Sapiens*, April 10, 2019. Accessed July 1, 2022:https://www.sapiens .org/biology/homo-luzonensis-discovery/.

Hayden, Brian. 2003. Were Luxury Foods the First Domesticates? Ethnoarchaeological Perspectives from Southeast Asia. *World Archaeology* 34(3):458–69.

Heckenberger, Michael J. 2005. *Ecology of Power: Culture, Place, and Personhood in the Southern Amazon, A.D. 1000–2000*. New York: Routledge.

Heckenberger, Michael J., Afukaka Kuikuro, Urissapá Tabata Kuikuro, I. Christian Russell, Morgan Schmidt, Carlos Fausto, and Bruna Franchetto. 2003. Amazonia 1492: Pristine Forest or Cultural Parkland? *Science* 301(5640):1701–14.

Herbert, Louis. 2011. The Functions of Language. Signo: Theoretical Semiotics on the Web. Accessed June 13, 2022: http://www .signosemio.com/jakobson/functions-of-language.asp#:~:text= Jakobson's%20model%20of%20the%20functions,code%20 and%20(6)%20message.

Herdt, Gilbert H. 1981. *Guardians of the Flutes: Idioms of Masculinity*. New York: McGraw-Hill.

Herdt, Gilbert H. 1994a. "Introduction: Third Sexes and Third Genders." In Gilbert Herdt, ed., *Third Sex, Third Gender: Beyond Sexual Dimorphism in Culture and History*, pp. 21–81. New York: Zone Books.

Herdt, Gilbert H., ed. 1994b. *Third Sex, Third Gender: Beyond Sexual Dimorphism in Culture and History*. New York: Zone Books.

Hershbein, Brad, and Melissa Kearney. 2014. Major Decisions: What Graduates Earn Over Their Lifetimes. Accessed October 15, 2018: https://www.hamiltonproject.org/assets/legacy/files/downloads_ and_links/Major_Decisions_Lifetime__Earnings_by_Major.pdf.

Heyerdahl, Thor. 1958. *Kon-Tiki: Across the Pacific by Raft*. Chicago: Rand McNally.

Hill, Jane H. 1978. Apes and Language. *Annual Review of Anthropology* 7:89–112.

Hill, Jane H. 2008. *The Everyday Language of White Racism*. Malden, MA: Wiley-Blackwell.

Himpele, Jeffrey D., and Quetzil E. Castañeda. 2004. *Incidents of Travel in Chichén Itzá*. Videorecording. Watertown, MA: Documentary Educational Resources.

Hinsley, Curtis M., and David R. Wilcox, eds. 2016. *Coming of Age in Chicago: The 1893 World's Fair and the Coalescence of American Anthropology*. Lincoln: University of Nebraska Press.

Ho, Karen. 2009. *Liquidated: An Ethnography of Wall Street*. Durham, NC: Duke University Press.

Hobbes, Thomas. 1909. *Leviathan*. Oxford: Clarendon Press. (Orig. published 1651.)

Hoben, Alan. 1995. Paradigms and Politics: The Cultural Construction of Environmental Policy in Ethiopia. *World Development* 23(6):1007–21.

Hobsbawm, Eric, and Terence Ranger, eds. 1983. *The Invention of Tradition*. Cambridge: Cambridge University Press.

Hodder, Ian. 1982a. Theoretical Archaeology: A Reactionary View. In Ian Hodder, ed., *Symbolic and Structural Archaeology*, pp. 1–16. Cambridge: Cambridge University Press.

Hodder, Ian, ed. 1982b. *Symbolic and Structural Archaeology*. Cambridge: Cambridge University Press.

Hodder, Ian. 1982c. *Symbols in Action: Ethnoarchaeological Studies of Material Culture*. Cambridge: Cambridge University Press.

Hodder, Ian. 2006. *The Leopard's Tale: Revealing the Mysteries of Çatalhöyük*. New York: Thames and Hudson.

Hoffman, Carl L. 1984. "Punan Foragers in the Trading Networks of Southeast Asia." In C. Shrire, ed., *Past and Present in Hunter Gatherer Studies*, pp. 123–49. Orlando, FL: Academic Press.

Hoijer, Harry. 1961. "Anthropological Linguistics." In Christine Mohrmann, Alf Sommerfelt, and Joshua Whatmough, eds., *Trends in European and American Linguistics 1930–1960*, pp. 110–27. Utrecht and Antwerp: Spectrum.

Horn, David. 1994. *Social Bodies: Science, Reproduction, and Italian Modernity.* Princeton, NJ: Princeton University Press.

Howe, K. R. 1984. *Where the Waves Fall: A New South Sea Islands History from Its First Settlement to Colonial Rule.* Honolulu, HI: University of Hawaii Press.

Hrdy, Sarah Blaffer. 2009. *Mothers and Others: The Evolutionary Origins of Mutual Understanding.* Cambridge, MA: Belknap Press, 2009.pp. 30–31.

Hsu, Francis L. K. 1972. "Psychological Anthropology in the Behavioral Sciences." In F. L. K. Hsu, ed., *Psychological Anthropology*, pp. 1–19. Cambridge, MA: Schenkman.

Hulme, Mike. 2017. *Weathered: Cultures of Climate.* Thousand Oaks, CA: Sage.

Humphrey, Caroline. 2002. *The Unmaking of Soviet Life: Everyday Economies After Socialism.* Ithaca, NY: Cornell University Press.

Hunley, Keith L., Graciela S. Cabana, and Jeffrey C. Long. 2016. "The Apportionment of Human Diversity Revisited," *American Journal of Physical Anthropology* 160: 561–69,

Hymes, Dell H. 1962. "The Ethnography of Speaking." In Thomas Gladwin and William C. Sturtevant, eds., *Anthropology and Human Behavior*, pp. 13–53. Washington, DC: Anthropological Society of Washington.

Hymes, Dell H. 1972. "Toward Ethnographies of Communication." In Pier Paolo Giglioli, ed., *Language and Social Context,* pp. 21–44. Baltimore, MD: Penguin Books.

Hymes, Dell H. 1973. *Toward Linguistic Competence.* Texas Working Papers in Sociolinguistics, No. 16. (Later translated as *Vers la competence de communication*, Paris: Hatier, 1991.)

ICOMOS (International Council on Monuments and Sites). 1987. Recommendation on Chichén Itzà. Accessed December 21, 2015: http://whc.unesco.org/archive/advisory_body_evaluation/483.pdf.

Igoe, James. 2004. *Conservation and Globalization: A Study of National Parks and Indigenous Communities from East Africa to South Dakota.* Belmont, CA: Wadsworth.

Inda, Jonathan, and Renato Rosaldo, eds. 2002. *The Anthropology of Globalization: A Reader.* Malden, MA: Blackwell.

International Obesity Task Force (IOTF). 2013. Obesity: The Global Epidemic. World Health Organization Fact Sheet. Accessed September 10: 2013. http://www.iaso.org/iotf/obesity/obesitytheglobalepidemic/.

Internet World Stats. 2018. Internet Users in the World by Region – June 30,30 Jun 2018. Accessed January 4, 2019: https://www.internetworldstats.com/stats.htm.

"Is God Dead?" 1966. *Time* 87(14):cover.

Iyer, Pico. 2001. *The Global Soul: Jet Lag, Shopping Malls, and the Search for Home.* New York: Vintage.

Jablonka, Eva, and Marion Lamb. 2005. *Evolution in Four Dimensions: Genetic, Epigenetic, Behavioral, and Symbolic Variation in the History of Life.* Cambridge, MA: MIT Press.

Jablonski, Nina G. 2004. The Evolution of Humatsingn Skin and Skin Color. *Annual Review of Anthropology* 33:585–623.

Jablonski, Nina G. 2006. *Skin: A Natural History.* Berkeley: University of California Press.

Jablonski, Nina, and George Chaplin. 2000. The Evolution of Human Skin Color. *Journal of Human Evolution* 39:57–106.

Jackson, Michael. 2005. At Home in the World. Durham, NC: Duke University Press.

Jantz, Richard L., and L. Meadows Jantz. 2000. Secular Change in Craniofacial Morphology. *American Journal of Human Biology* 12:327–38.

Jennings, Justin. 2011. *Globalizations and the Ancient World.* Cambridge: Cambridge University Press.

Johnston, Francis E. 2004. Race and Biology: Changing Currents in Muddy Waters. Paper presented at the conference "Race and Human Variation: Setting an Agenda for Future Research and Education," September 12–14, Alexandria, Virginia. Accessed

May 1, 2019: https://understandingrace.org/pdf/myth_reality/johnston.pdf.

Jones, Jeffrey. 2021. U. S. Church Membership Falls Below Majority For First Time. Gallup.com Accessed July 12, 2023. https://news.gallup.com/poll/341963/church-membership-falls-below-majority-first-time.aspx.

Kalipeni, Ezekiel. 2004. *HIV and AIDS in Africa: Beyond Epidemiology.* Malden, MA: Blackwell.

Kan, Sergei. 1989. *Symbolic Immortality: The Tlingit Potlatch of the Nineteenth Century.* Washington, DC: Smithsonian Institution Press.

Kangas, Beth. 2010. Traveling for Medical Care in a Global World. *Medical Anthropology* 29(4):344–62.

Kaplan, David, and Robert A. Manners. 1972. *Culture Theory.* Prospect Heights, IL: Waveland Press.

Kaptchuk, Ted J. 2001. The Double-Blind, Randomized, Placebo-Controlled Trial: Gold Standard or Golden Calf? *Journal of Clinical Epidemiology* 54:541–49.

Katz, Sarah R. 2006. *Redesigning Civic Memory: The African Burial Ground in Lower Manhattan.* Master's Thesis, University of Pennsylvania.

Kearney, Michael. 1995. The Local and the Global: The Anthropology of Globalization and Transnationalism. *Annual Review of Anthropology* 24:547–65.

Kearney, Michael. 1996. *Reconceptualizing the Peasantry: Anthropology in Global Perspective.* Boulder, CO: Westview Press.

Keeley, Lawrence H. 1980. *Experimental Determination of Stone Tool Uses: A Microwear Analysis.* Chicago: University of Chicago Press.

Kelley, Tom. 2006. *The Ten Faces of Innovation: IDEO's Strategies for Beating the Devil's Advocate and Driving Creativity Throughout Your Organization.* New York: Crown Publishing Group. See also https://www.ideo.com/post/the-ten-faces-of-innovation.

Kelly, Robert L. 1995. *The Foraging Spectrum: Diversity in Hunter-Gatherer Lifeways.* Washington, DC: Smithsonian Institution Press.

Kelly, Robert L. 2013. *The Lifeways of Hunter Gatherers: The Foraging Spectrum.* Cambridge: Cambridge University Press.

Kennicott, Philip. 2011. "Yo-Yo Ma, a Virtuoso at More than Cello." *Washington Post*, December 2, 2011. Accessed May 1, 2019: https://www.washingtonpost.com/lifestyle/style/yo-yo-ma-a-virtuoso-at-more-than-the-cello/2011/11/22/gIQAkvNnKO_story.html?utm_term=.e9e29632760c.

Khanmohamadi, S. 2008. The Look of Medieval Ethnography: William of Rubruck's Mission to Mongolia. *New Medieval Literatures* 10(1):87–114.

Khazan, Olga. 2013. "How the World's Newest 'Mixed' Language Was Invented." *The Atlantic*, June 18, 2013. Accessed August 26, 2021: https://www.theatlantic.com/international/archive/2013/06/how-the-worlds-newest-mixed-language-was-invented/276981/.

Kidder, Tracy. 2003. *Mountains Beyond Mountains.* New York: Random House.

Kidwell, Claudia Brush, and Valerie Steele, eds. 1989. *Men and Women: Dressing the Part.* Washington, DC: Smithsonian Institution Press.

Kildea, Gary, and Jerry Leach. 1975. *Trobriand Cricket: An Ingenious Response to Colonialism.* DVD. Berkeley, CA: Berkeley Media.

Kimbrough, David L. 2002. *Taking Up Serpents: Snake Handlers of Eastern Kentucky.* Macon, GA: Mercer University Press.

King, Charles. 2019. *Gods of the Upper Air: How a Circle of Renegade Anthropologists Reinvented Race, Sex, and Gender in the Twentieth Century.* New York: Doubleday.

Kingsolver, Ann. 1996. "Power." In Alan Barnard and Jonathan Spencer, eds., *Encyclopedia of Social and Cultural Anthropology*, pp. 445–48. London: Routledge.

Kinsey, Alfred. 1948. *Sexual Behavior in the Human Male.* Philadelphia: W. B. Saunders.

Kissel, Marc. 2018. Non-Modern Humans Were More Complex—and Artistic—Than We Thought. *Anthropology News* 59(5):14–17.

Kittles, Rick A., and Kenneth M. Weiss. 2003. Race, Genes and Ancestry: Implications for Defining Disease Risk. *Annual Review of Genomics and Humans Genetics* 4:33–67.

Kleinman, Arthur. 1980. *Patients and Healers in the Context of Culture: An Exploration of the Borderland Between Anthropology, Medicine, and Psychology.* Berkeley: University of California Press.

Kluckhohn, Clyde. 1959. "The Role of Evolutionary Thought in Anthropology." In Betty J. Meggers, ed., *Evolution and Anthropology: A Centennial Appraisal,* pp. 144–57. Washington, DC: Anthropological Society of Washington.

Koos, Earl Lomon. 1954. *The Health of Regionville.* New York: Columbia University Press.

Korten, David. 1995. *When Corporations Rule the World.* West Hartford, CT: Kumarian Press.

Kowalewski, Stephen A. 1990. The Evolution of Complexity in the Valley of Oaxaca. *Annual Review of Anthropology* 19:39–58.

Krech, Shepard. 1999. *The Ecological Indian: Myth and History.* New York: W. W. Norton.

Krieger, N. 2019. Measures of Racism, Sexism, Heterosexism, and Gender Binarism for Health Equity Research: From Structural Injustice to Embodied Harm—An Ecosocial Analysis. *Annual Review of Public Health* 41, 4.1–4.26.

Krieger, Nancy. 2005. Embodiment: A Conceptual Glossary for Epidemiology. *Journal of Epidemiology and Community Health* 59:350–55.

Kroeber, A. L. 1916. Zuni Cultural Sequences. *Proceedings of the National Academy of Sciences* 2(1):42–45.

Kroeber, Theodora. 1961. *Ishi in Two Worlds: A Biography of the Last Wild Indian in North America.* Berkeley: University of California Press.

Kroskrity, P. V. (2021), Covert Linguistic Racisms and the (Re-)Production of White Supremacy. *Journal of Linguistic Anthropology* 31: 180–93. https://doi.org/10.1111/jola.12307.

Kuklick, Henrika, ed. 2007. *A New History of Anthropology.* Malden, MA: Wiley-Blackwell.

Kulick, Don. 1998. *Travesti: Sex, Gender, and Culture Among Brazilian Transgendered Prostitutes.* Chicago: University of Chicago Press.

Kuper, Adam. 2000. *Culture: The Anthropologists' Account.* Cambridge, MA: Harvard University Press.

Kurtz, Donald V. 2001. *Political Anthropology: Paradigms and Power.* Boulder, CO: Westview Press.

Kusimba et al. 2020. Mtwapa, Betwixt in Between Land and Sea: Foundings of an African City State. In Stephanie Wynne-Jones and Adria LaViolette, eds., *The Swahili World.* London: Routledge

Kusimba, C. M., and S. B. Kusimba. 2005. Mosaics and Interactions: East Africa, 2000 B.P. to the Present. In A. B. Stahl, ed., *Mosaics and Interactions: East Africa, 2000 B.P. to the Present,* pp. 392–419. Oxford: Blackwell Publishers.

Kusimba, Chapurukha. 1999. *The Rise and Fall of Swahili States.* Walnut Creek, CA: AltaMira Press.

Kusimba, Chapurukha. 2018. Ancient Connections Between China and East Africa. *In* Akshay Sarathi, ed., *Early Maritime Cultures in East Africa and the Indian Ocean: Papers from a Conference Held at the University of Wisconsin-Madison (African Studies Program) 23–24 October 2015, with Additional Contributions,* pp. 83–102. Oxford: Archaeopress.

Labov, William. 1990. Intersection of Sex and Social Class in the Course of Linguistic Change. *Language Variation and Change* 2(2):205–54.

Labov, William, Sharon Ash, and Charles Boberg. 2006. *The Atlas of North American English: Phonetics, Phonology, and Sound Change: A Multimedia Reference Tool.* Berlin: Mouton de Gruyter.

Lahsen, Myanna. 2015. "Digging Deeper Into the Why: Cultural Dimensions of Climate Change Skepticism Among Scientists." In Jessica Barnes and Michael Dove, eds., *Climate Cultures: Anthropological Perspectives on Climate Change,* pp. 221–48. New Haven, CT: Yale University Press.

Lakoff, George. 1980. *Metaphors We Live By.* Chicago: University of Chicago Press.

Lakoff, Robin. 1975. *Language and Woman's Place.* New York: Harper and Row.

Laland, K. N., T. Uller, M. W. Feldman, K. Sterelny, G. B. Muller, A. Moczek, E. Jablonka, and F. J. Odling-Smee. 2014. Does Evolutionary Theory Need a Rethink? *Nature* 514:161–64.

Lancaster, Roger. 1992. *Life Is Hard: Machismo, Danger, and the Intimacy of Power in Nicaragua.* Berkeley: University of California Press.

Lancaster, Roger. 1997. On Homosexualities in Latin America (and Other Places). *American Ethnologist* 24(1):193–202.

Lancaster, Roger. 2004. The Place of Anthropology in a Public Culture Shaped by Bioreductivism. *Anthropology News* 45(3):4–5.

Langgut, Dafna, Rachid Cheddadi, and Gonen Sharon. 2021. "Climate and Environmental Reconstruction of the Epipaleolithic Mediterranean Levant (22.0–11.9 ka cal. BP)." *Quaternary Science Reviews,* Vol. 270, 2021.

Larner, John. 1999. *Marco Polo and the Discovery of the World.* New Haven, CT: Yale University Press.

Larson, Heidi. 2020. Stuck: How Vaccine Rumors Start—and Why They Don't Go Away. New York: Oxford University Press.

Latinis, D. Kyle. 2000. The Development of Subsistence System Models for Island Southeast Asia and Near Oceania: The Nature and Role of Arboriculture and Arboreal-Based Economies. *World Archaeology* 32(1):41–67.

Leacock, Eleanor. 1981. *Myths of Male Dominance.* New York: Monthly Review.

Leakey M. G., C. S. Feibel, I. McDougal, and A. Walker. 1995. New Four-Million-Year-Old Hominid Species From Kanapoi and Allia Bay, Kenya. *Nature* 376:565–71.

Leakey, M. G., C. S. Feibal, I. McDougall, C. Ward, and A. Walker. 1998. New Specimens and Confirmation of an Early Age for *Australopithecus anamensis. Nature* 393:62–67.

Leakey, M. G., F. Spoor, F. H. Brown, P. N. Gathogo, C. Kiarie, L. N. Leakey, and I. McDougall. 2001. New Hominin Genus from Eastern Africa Shows Diverse Middle Pliocene Lineages. *Nature* 410:433–40.

Lechner, Frank, and Boli, John. 2005. *World Culture: Origins and Consequences.* Malden, MA: Blackwell.

Lee, Richard B. 1968. "What Hunters Do for a Living, or, How to Make Out on Scarce Resources." In R. B. Lee and I. DeVore, eds., *Man the Hunter,* pp. 30–43. Chicago: Aldine.

Lee, Richard B. 1969. "!Kung Bushmen Subsistence: An Input-Output Analysis." In Andrew P. Vayda, ed., *Environment and Cultural Behavior,* pp. 47–79. Garden City, NY: Natural History Press.

Lee, Richard B. 2012. *The Dobe Ju/'Hoansi.* Case Studies in Anthropology. Boston, MA: Cengage Learning.

Lee, Richard B., and Irven DeVore, eds. 1968. *Man the Hunter.* Chicago: Aldine.

Lee, Sang-Hee. 2018. Where Do We Come From? *Anthropology News* 58(5):18–20.

Lekson, Stephen H., and Catherine M. Cameron. 1995. The Abandonment of Chaco Canyon, the Mesa Verde Migrations, and the Reorganization of the Pueblo World. *Journal of Anthropological Archaeology* 14:184–202.

Lende, Daniel. 2008. Successful Weight Loss. *Neuroanthropology Blog,* April 5. Accessed May 18, 2015: https://neuroanthropology. net/2008/04/05/successful-weight-loss/.

Lentz, Carola. 1999. "Changing Food Habits: An Introduction." In Carola Lentz, ed., *Changing Food Habits: Case Studies from Africa, South America, and Europe,* pp. 1–25. Newark, NJ: Harwood Academic.

Leonard, William R. 2002. Food for Thought: Dietary Change was a Driving Force in Human Evolution. *Scientific American* 287(6): 106–15.

Leone, M. P. 1973. "Archeology as the Science of Technology: Mormon Town Plans and Fences." In C. L. Redman, ed., *Research and Theory in Current Archeology,* pp. 125–50. New York: Wiley.

Lepper, Bradley T. 2005. *Ohio Archaeology: An Illustrated Chronicle of Ohio's Ancient American Indian Cultures: The Companion Book to the Ohio Archaeology Media Project*. Wilmington, OH: Orange Frazer Press.

Lévi-Strauss, Claude. 1961. "The Effectiveness of Symbols." In *Structural Anthropology*, pp. 186–205. New York: Basic Books.

Lévi-Strauss, Claude. 1969. *The Elementary Structures of Kinship*. Boston: Beacon Press. (Originally published in French, 1949.)

Lewellen, Ted C. 1983. *Political Anthropology: An Introduction*. 1st edition. South Hadley, MA: Bergin and Garvey.

Lewellen, Ted C. 2003. *Political Anthropology: An Introduction*. 3rd edition. Westport, CT: Praeger.

Lewin, Ellen, and William L. Leap, eds. 1996. *Out in the Field: Reflections of Lesbian and Gay Anthropologists*. Urbana: University of Illinois Press.

Lewin, Ellen, and William L. Leap, eds. 2009. *Out in Public: Reinventing Lesbian/Gay Anthropology in a Globalizing World*. Malden, MA: Wiley-Blackwell.

Lewis, Anna, Santiago Molina, Paul Appelbaum, Bege Dauda, Anna Rienzo, Agustin Fuentes, Stephanie Fullerton, Nanibaa Garrison, Nayanika Ghosh, Evelynn Hammonds, David Jones, Eimear Kenny, Peter Kraft, Sandra Lee, Madelyn Mauro, John Novembre, Aaron Panofsky, Mashaal Sohail, Benjamin Neale, and Danielle Allen. 2022. Getting Genetic Ancestry Right for Science and Society. *Science* 376(6590):250–52. DOI: 10.1126/science.abm7530.

Lewontin, R. C. 1972. The Apportionment of Human Diversity. *Evolutionary Biology* 6:381–98.

Libby, Willard F. 1960. "Radiocarbon Dating." Nobel Lecture, December 12, 1960. Accessed January 17, 2019: https://www.nobelprize.org/uploads/2018/06/libby-lecture.pdf.

Lieberman, Daniel. 2020. Exercised: How Something We Never Evolved to Do Is Healthy and Rewarding. New York: Pantheon Books.

Lifton, Robert Jay. 1986. *The Nazi Doctors: Medical Killing and the Psychology of Genocide*. New York: Basic Books.

Linton, Ralph. 1924. Totemism and the A. E. F. *American Anthropologist* 26:296–300.

Lipe, William D. 1995. The Depopulation of the Northern San Juan: Conditions in the Turbulent 1200s. *Journal of Anthropological Archaeology* 14:143–69.

Lippman, Abby. 2001. The Power of Naming Things Genetic. Review of "Sociological Perspectives on the New Genetics." *Second Opinion* 7:99–100.

Little, Peter, and Michael Painter. 1995. Discourse, Politics, and the Development Process: Reflections on Escobar's "Anthropology and the Development Encounter." *American Ethnologist* 22(3):602–609.

Lizot, Jacques. 1985. *Tales of the Yanomami: Daily Life in the Venezuelan Forest*. Trans. Ernest Simon. Cambridge: Cambridge University Press.

Locke, John. 2003. *Two Treatises on Government: And a Letter Concerning Toleration*. New Haven, CT: Yale University Press. (Orig. published 1690.)

Lockwood, William G. 1975. *European Moslems: Economy and Ethnicity in Western Bosnia*. New York: Academic.

Loewen, James. 1995. *Lies My Teacher Told Me: Everything Your American History Textbook Got Wrong*. New York: Simon and Schuster.

Lonely Planet. 2014. "Why Are Hearts the Symbol for a Rustic Toilet in Swedish Countryside?" *Thorn Tree Forum*. Country Forums: Scandinavia and the Nordics: Sweden. Accessed August 2014: https://www.lonelyplanet.com/thorntree/forums/europe-scandinavia-the-nordics/topics/why-are-hearts-the-symbol-for-a-rustic-toilet-in-swedish-countryside.

Long, Jeffrey. 2003. Human Genetic Variation: The Mechanisms and Results of Microevolution. Paper presented at the American Anthropological Association 2003 annual meeting, November 21, Chicago. Accessed May 24, 2007: https://understandingrace.org/pdf/myth_reality/long.pdf.

Long, Jeffrey C., Jie Li, and Meghan E. Healy. 2009. Human DNA Sequences: More Variation and Less Race. *American Journal of Physical Anthropology* 139(1):23–34.

Love, Michael. 1999. "Ideology, Material Culture, and Daily Practice in Pre-Classic Mesoamerica: A Pacific Coast Perspective." In David C. Grove and Rosemary A. Joyce, eds., *Social Patterns in Pre-Classic Mesoamerica*, pp. 127–53. Washington, DC: Dumbarton Oaks Research Library and Collection.

Lovgren, Sven. 2003. "Map Links Healthier Ecosystems, Indigenous Peoples." *National Geographic News*, February 27. Accessed May 15, 2005: http://news.nationalgeographic.com/news/2003/02/0227_030227_indigenousmap.html.

Lyell, Charles. 1830. *Principles of Geology*. London: John Murray.

Lyons, Andrew P., and Harriet D. Lyons. 2004. *Irregular Connections: A History of Anthropology and Sexuality*. Lincoln: University of Nebraska Press.

MacBeth, Helen. 1997. *Food Preferences and Taste: Continuity and Change*. New York: Berghahn Books.

MacNeish, Richard S. 1967. A Summary of Subsistence. In D. S. Byers, ed., *The Prehistory of the Tehuacan Valley*, Vol. 1, pp. 290–310. Austin: University of Texas Press.

Magesh, S, John D, Li WT, et al. 2021. "Disparities in COVID-19 Outcomes by Race, Ethnicity, and Socioeconomic Status: A Systematic Review and Meta-Analysis." *JAMA Netw Open*. 2021;4(11):e2134147.

Mahmood, Cynthia Keppley. 1997. *Fighting for Faith and Nation: Dialogues with Sikh Militants*. Philadelphia: University of Pennsylvania Press.

Mair, Lucy. 1969. *Anthropology and Social Change*. New York: Humanities Press.

Malinowski, Bronislaw. 1922. *Argonauts of the Western Pacific: An Account of Native Enterprise and Adventure in the Archipelagoes of Melanesian New Guinea*. London: Routledge and Kegan Paul.

Malinowski, Bronislaw. 1948. *Magic, Science and Religion and Other Essays*. Boston: Beacon Press.

Malone, Nicolas M. 2021. The Dialectical Primatologist: The Past, Present, and Future of Life in the Hominoid Niche. New York: Routledge.

Malotki, Ekkehardt. 1983. *Hopi Time: A Linguistic Analysis of the Temporal Concepts of the Hopi Language*. Berlin: Mouton.

Malthus, Robert. 1798. *An Essay on the Principle of Population, as It Affects the Future Improvement of Society*. London: J. Johnson.

Mamdani, Mahmood. 1972. *The Myth of Population Control: Family, Caste, and Class in an Indian Village*. New York: Monthly Review Press.

Marcus, George, and Michael M. J. Fisher. 1986. *Anthropology as Cultural Critique: An Experimental Moment in the Human Sciences*. Chicago: University of Chicago Press.

Mares, Teresa. 2019. *Life on the Other Border: Farmworkers and Food Justice in Vermont*. Berkeley: University of California Press.

Marino, Elizabeth. 2015. *Fierce Climate, Sacred Ground: An Ethnography of Climate Change in Shishmaref, Alaska*. Fairbanks: University of Alaska Press.

Marks, Jonathan. 1995. *Human Biodiversity: Genes, Race, and History*. New York: Aldine de Gruyter.

Marks, Jonathan. 2012. The Biological Myth of Human Evolution. *Contemporary Social Science* 7(2):139–62.

Marks, Jonathan. 2015. *Tales of the Ex-Apes: How We Think About Human Evolution*. Berkeley: University of California Press.

Marshall, John, and Adrienne Miesmer. 2007. *N!ai, Story of a !Kung Woman*. DVD. Watertown, MA: Documentary Educational Resources. (Orig. published 1980.)

Marty, Martin E., and R. Scott Appleby, eds. 1991. *Fundamentalisms Observed*. The Fundamentalism Project, Vol. 1. Chicago: University of Chicago Press.

Marx, Karl. 1990. *Capital: A Critique of Political Economy*. New York: Penguin. (Orig. published in 1867 in German.)

Massey, Douglas, Joaquin Arango, Graeme Hugo, Ali Kouaouci, Adela Pellegrino, and J. Edward Taylor. 1993. Theories of International Migration: A Review and Appraisal. *Population and Development Review* 19(3):431–66.

Mauss, Marcel. 1973. Techniques of the Body. *Economy and Society* 2(1)70–88. (Orig. published 1934 in French.)

Mauss, Marcel. 2000. *The Gift: The Form and Reason for Exchange in Archaic* Societies. Trans. W. D. Halls. New York: W. W. Norton. (Orig. published 1924 in French; the classic English translation was published in 1954.)

Mayr, Ernst. 2002. *What Evolution Is.* New York: Basic Books.

McAnany, Patricia A., and Tomás Gallareta Negrón. 2010. "Bellicose Rulers and Climatological Peril? Retrofitting Twenty-First Century Woes on Eighth-Century Maya Society." In Patricia A. McAnany and Norman Yoffee, eds., *Questioning Collapse: Human Resilience, Ecological Vulnerability, and the Aftermath of Empire,* pp. 142–75. Cambridge: Cambridge University Press.

McAnany, Patricia A., and Norman Yoffee, eds. 2010a. *Questioning Collapse: Human Resilience, Ecological Vulnerability, and the Aftermath of Empire.* Cambridge: Cambridge University Press.

McAnany, Patricia A., and Norman Yoffee. 2010b. "Why We Question Collapse and Study Human Resilience, Ecological Vulnerability, and the Aftermath of Empire." In Patricia McAnany and Norman Yoffee, eds., *Questioning Collapse: Human Resilience, Ecological Vulnerability, and the Aftermath of Empire,* pp. 1–20. Cambridge: Cambridge University Press.

McCabe, Terrence. 1990. Turkana Pastoralism: A Case Against the Tragedy of the Commons. *Human Ecology* 18(1):81–103.

McCulloch, Gretchen. 2019. *Because Internet: Understanding the New Rules of Language.* New York: Riverhead Books.

McDade, Thomas. 2001. Lifestyle Incongruity, Social Integration, and Immune Function in Samoan Adolescents. *Social Science and Medicine* 53(10):1351–62.

McDade, Thomas, J. Stallings, and Carol Worthman. 2000. Culture Change and Stress in Western Samoan Youth: Methodological Issues in the Cross-cultural Study of Stress and Immune Function. *American Journal of Human Biology* 12(6):792–802.

McDougall, Christopher. 2011. *Born to Run: A Hidden Tribe, Superathletes, and the Greatest Race the World Has Never Known.* New York: Vintage Books.

McElhinny, Bonnie. 2003. "Theorizing Gender in Sociolinguistics and Linguistic Anthropology." In Janet Holmes and Miriam Myerhoff, eds., *The Handbook of Language and Gender,* pp. 21–42. Malden, MA: Blackwell.

McGrath, J. W., C. B. Rwabukwali, D. A. Schumann, J. Pearson-Marks, R. Mukasa, B. Namande, S. Nakayiwa, and L. Nakyobe. 1992. Cultural Determinants of Sexual Risk Behavior Among Baganda Women. *Medical Anthropology Quarterly* 6(2):153–61.

McHenry, Henry M., and Katherine Coffing. 2000. Australopithecus to Homo: Transformations in Body and Mind. *Annual Review of Anthropology* 29:125–46.

McIntosh, Roderick. 2015. "Climate Shock and Awe: Can There Be an 'Ethno-science' of Deep-Time Mande Paleoclimate Memory?" In Jessica Barnes and Michael Dove, *Climate Cultures: Anthropological Perspectives on Climate Change,* pp. 273–88. New Haven, CT: Yale University Press.

McIntyre, Matthew H., and Carolyn Pope Edwards. 2009. The Early Development of Gender Differences. *Annual Review of Anthropology* 38:83–97.

McKenna, James J. 1993. An Evolutionary Analysis of Infant Sleep. *Sleep* 16(3):264–69.

McKenna, James J. 1996. Sudden Infant Death Syndrome in Cross-Cultural Perspective: Is Infant-Parent Cosleeping Protective? *Annual Review of Anthropology* 25:201–16.

McManamon, Francis P., and Alf Hatton, eds., 2000. *Cultural Resource Management in Contemporary Society: Perspectives on Managing and Presenting the Past.* London: Routledge.

McNeil, William. 1976. *Plagues and People.* Garden City, NY: Anchor Books.

Mead, Margaret. 1928. *Coming of Age in Samoa: A Psychological Study of Primitive Youth for Western Civilization.* New York: William Morrow.

Mead, Margaret. 1930a. *Growing Up in New Guinea: A Comparative Study of Primitive Education.* New York: William Morrow.

Mead, Margaret. 1930b. *Social Organization of Manu'a.* Honolulu, HI: Bishop Museum Press.

Mead, Margaret. 1963. *Sex and Temperament in Three Primitive Societies.* New York: William Morrow. (Orig. published 1935.)

Meggers, Betty J. 1971. *Amazonia: Man and Culture in a Counterfeit Paradise.* Chicago: Aldine, Atherton.

Meigs, Anna. 1997. "Food as a Cultural Construction." In Carole Counihan and Penny Van Esterik, eds., *Food and Culture: A Reader,* pp. 95–106. New York: Routledge.

Meltzer, David J. 1985. North American Archaeology and Archaeologists, 1879–1934. *American Antiquity* 50(2):249–60.

Menzies, Gavin. 2002. *1421: The Year China Discovered America.* London: Transworld.

Merry, Sally Engle. 2003. Human Rights Law and the Demonization of Culture. *Anthropology News* 44(2):4–5.

Mihesuah, Devon A. 2000. *Repatriation Reader: Who Owns American Indian Remains?* Lincoln: University of Nebraska Press.

Miller, Daniel. 1987. *Material Culture and Mass Consumption.* Oxford: Basil Blackwell.

Miller, Daniel, ed. 1995. *Acknowledging Consumption: A Review of New Studies.* London: Routledge.

Miller, Daniel, ed. 1998. *Material Cultures: Why Some Things Matter.* Chicago: University of Chicago Press.

Miller, Todd. 2017. Storming the Wall: Climate Change, Migration, and Homeland Security. San Francisco: City Lights.

Minnich, E. 1982. A Devastating Conceptual Error: How Can We Not Be Feminist Scholars? *Change: The Magazine of Higher Learning* 14(3):7–9.

Mitchell, Peter. 2005. *African Connections: Archaeological Perspectives on Africa and the Wider World.* Walnut Creek, CA: Altimira.

Mithen, Steven. 2007. Did Farming Arise from a Misapplication of Social Intelligence? *Philosophical Transactions of the Royal Society B: Biological Sciences* 362(1480):705–18.

Mohanty, Chandra Talpade. 1991. "Under Western Eyes: Feminist Scholarship and Colonial Discourses." In Chandra Talpade Mohanty, Ann Russo, and Lourdes Torres, eds., *Third World Women and the Politics of Feminism,* pp. 333–58. Indianapolis: Indiana University Press.

Molla, Rani. 2020. Why DNA Tests Are Suddenly Unpopular. Vox Recode. Accessed March 20, 2022: https://www.vox.com/recode/2020/2/13/21129177/consumer-dna-tests-23andme-ancestry-sales-decline.

Money, John. 1985. *Destroying Angel: Sex, Fitness, and Food in the Legacy of Degeneracy Theory, Graham Crackers, Kellogg's Corn Flakes, and American Health History.* Buffalo, NY: Prometheus Books.

Montagu, Ashley. 1997. *Man's Most Dangerous Myth: The Fallacy of Race.* 6th edition. Walnut Creek, CA: AltaMira. (Orig. published 1942.)

Moore, Francis, Justin Mankin, and Austin Becker. 2015. "Challenges in Integrating the Climate and Social Sciences for Studies of Climate Change and Adaptation." In Jessica Barnes and Michael Dove, eds., *Climate Cultures: Anthropological Perspectives on Climate Change,* pp. 169–95. New Haven, CT: Yale University Press.

Morgan, Edmund. 1975. *American Slavery, American Freedom.* New York: W. W. Norton.

Morgan, Lewis Henry. 1871. *Systems of Consanguinity and Affinity of the Human Family.* Washington, DC: Smithsonian Institution.

Morgan, Lewis Henry. 1877. *Ancient Society, or Researches in the Line of Human Progress from Savagery Through Barbarism to Civilization.* Chicago: C. H. Kerr.

Morris, Rosalind C. 1995. All Made Up: Performance Theory and the New Anthropology of Sex and Gender. *Annual Review of Anthropology* 24:567–92.

Munson, Barbara. 1999. Not for Sport. *Teaching Tolerance*. Accessed April 16, 2019: http://www.tolerance.org/magazine/spring-1999/not-for-sport.

Murray, Gerald. 1987. "The Domestication of Wood in Haiti: A Case Study in Applied Evolution." In R. M. Wulff and S. J. Fiske, eds., *Anthropological Praxis: Translating Knowledge into Action*, pp. 223–40. Boulder, CO: Westview Press.

Myers, P. Z. 2014. Developmental Plasticity Is Not Lamarckism. Accessed March 24, 2015: https://scienceblogs.com/pharyngula/2014/08/28/developmental-plasticity-is-not-lamarckism.

Nabhan, Gary Paul. 1997. *Cultures of Habitat: On Nature, Culture, and Story*. Washington, DC: Counterpoint.

Nadasdy, Paul. 2005. The Anti-Politics of TEK: The Institutionalization of Co-Management Discourse and Practice. *Anthropologica* 47(2):215–32.

Nader, Laura. 1990. *Harmony Ideology: Justice and Control in a Zapotec Mountain Village*. Stanford, CA: Stanford University Press.

Nader, Laura. 1995. "Civilization and Its Negotiators." In Pat Caplan, ed., *Understanding Disputes: The Politics of Argument*, pp. 39–63. Oxford: Berg.

Nader, Laura, ed. 1996. *Naked Science: Anthropological Inquiry into Boundaries, Power, and Knowledge*. New York: Routledge.

Nader, Laura. 2001. The Underside of Conflict Management—In Africa and Elsewhere. *IDS Bulletin* 32(1):19–27.

Nader, Laura, and Harry F. Todd, eds. 1978. *The Disputing Process—Law in Ten Societies*. New York: Columbia University Press.

Nagengast, Carole, and Michael Kearney. 1990. Mixtec Ethnicity: Social Identity, Political Consciousness, and Political Activism. *Latin American Research Review* 25(2):61–92.

Nanda, Serena. 1994. "Hijras: An Alternative Sex and Gender Role in India." In Gilbert Herdt, ed., *Third Sex, Third Gender: Beyond Sexual Dimorphism in Culture and History*, pp. 373–417. New York: Zone Books.

Nanda, Serena. 1999. *Neither Man nor Woman: The Hijras of India*. 2nd edition. Boston: Cengage.

Nanda, Serena. 2000. *Gender Diversity: Crosscultural Variations*. Prospect Heights, IL: Waveland Press.

Naranjo, Tessie. 1995. Thoughts on Migration by Santa Clara Pueblo. *Journal of Anthropological Archaeology* 14:247–50.

Nash, June. 1981. Ethnographic Aspects of the World Capitalist System. *Annual Review of Anthropology* 10:393–423.

Nash, June. 2007. Consuming Interests: Water, Rum, and Coca-Cola from Ritual Propitiation to Corporate Expropriation in Highland Chiapas. *Cultural Anthropology* 22(4):621–39.

Nash, Manning. 1958. *Machine Age Maya*. Glencoe, IL: Free Press.

Natcher, David C., Susan Hickey, and Clifford G. Hickey. 2005. Co-Management: Managing Relationships, Not Resources. *Human Organization* 64(3):240–50.

National Collegiate Athletic Association (NCAA). 2005. "NCAA Executive Committee Issues Guidelines for Use of Native American Mascots at Championship Events." (Released August 5). NCAA Press Release Archive. Accessed August 8, 2014: http://fs.ncaa.org/Docs/PressArchive/2005/Announcements/NCAA%2BExecutive%2BExecutive%2BCommittee%2BIssues%2BGuidelines%2Bfor%2BUse%2Bof%2BNative%2BAmerican%2BMascots%2Bat%2BChampionship%2BEvents.html.

National Public Radio (NPR). 2007. Unearthing New York's Forgotten Slavery Era. Broadcast. *News and Notes*, NPR, October 11. Accessed December 4, 2015: https://www.npr.org/templates/story/story.php?storyId=15187759.

Nederveen Pieterse, J. 2004. *Globalization and Culture: Global Mélange*. Lanham, MD: Rowman and Littlefield.

Neel, James. 1962. Diabetes Mellitus: A "Thrifty" Genotype Rendered Detrimental by Progress? *American Journal of Human Genetics* 14:353–62.

Nekaris, Anna, and Simon Bearder. 2011. "The Lorisiforme Primates of Asia and Mainland Africa." In Primates in Perspective. 2nd edition, edited by Christina Campbell, Agustin Fuentes, Katherine MacKinnon, Simon Bearder, and Rebecca Stumpf, pp. 34–54. New York: Oxford University Press.

Nelson, Robin G. 2020. Beyond the Household: Caribbean Families and Biocultural Models of Alloparenting. *Annual Review of Anthropology* 49:355–72.

Nengo, Isaiah. 2018. "Great Ape Haters." *Anthropology News* 59(5):3–5.

Nevalainen, Terttu, and Helena Raumolin-Brunberg. 2017. *Historical Sociolinguistics: Language Change in Tudor and Stuart England*. 2nd edition. London: Routledge.

Nevins, Marybeth. 2013. *Lessons From Fort Apache: Beyond Language Endangerment and Maintenance*. Hoboken, NJ: Wiley-Blackwell.

Nevins, Marybeth. 2017. *Worldmaking Stories: Maidu Language and Community Renewal on a Shared California Landscape*. Lincoln: University of Nebraska Press.

Nichols, Bill. 1997. Film Review Essay. Dislocating Ethnographic Film: *In and Out of Africa* and Issues of Cultural Representation. *American Ethnologist* 99(4):810–24.

Norberg, Johan. 2006. How Globalization Conquers Poverty. Accessed November 19, 2006: http://www.cato.org/special/symposium/essays/norberg.html.

Nordstrom, Carolyn R. 1988. Exploring Pluralism: The Many Faces of Ayurveda. *Social Science and Medicine* 27(5):479–89.

Nyamwaya, D. O. 1993. Anthropology and HIV/AIDS Prevention in Kenya: New Ways of Cooperation. *AIDS and Society* 4(4):4, 8.

Oakley Kenneth P. 1956. *Man the Tool-Maker*. London: British Museum.

Oakley, Kenneth. 1964. *Frameworks for Dating Fossils*. New Brunswick, NJ: Aldine Transaction.

Oberschall, Anthony. 2000. The Manipulation of Ethnicity: From Ethnic Cooperation to Violence and War in Yugoslavia. *Ethnic and Racial Studies* 23(6):982–1001.

O'Connell, J. F., K. Hawkes, K. D. Lupo, and N. G. Blurton-Jones. 2002. Male Strategies and Plio-Pleistocene Archeology. *Journal of Human Evolution* 43:831–72.

Odling-Smee, F. John, Kevin N. Laland, and Marcus W. Feldman. 2003. *Niche Construction: The Neglected Process in Evolution*. Monographs in Population Biology 37. Princeton, NJ: Princeton University Press.

Ofri, Danielle. 2021. Covid Vaccination: The Last Mile. Accessed June 9, 2022: https://danielleofri.com/covid-vaccination-last-mile/

O'Hanlon, Michael, and Robert L. Welsch, eds. 2000. *Hunting the Gatherers: Ethnographic Collectors, Agents and Agency in Melanesia, 1870s–1930s*. New York: Berghahn.

Omi, Michael, and Howard Winant, eds. 1996. *Racial Formation in the United States*. 2nd edition. New York: Routledge.

Ong, Aihwa. 1988. The Production of Possession: Spirits and the Multinational Corporation in Malaysia. *American Ethnologist* 15(1):28–42.

Ong, Aihwa. 1999. *Flexible Citizenship: The Cultural Logics of Transnationality*. Durham, NC: Duke University Press.

Ong, Aihwa. 2006. *Neoliberalism as Exception: Mutations in Citizenship and Sovereignty*. Durham, NC: Duke University Press.

Orlove, Ben. 2005. Human Adaptation to Climate Change: A Review of Three Historical Cases and Some General Perspectives. *Environmental Science and Policy* 8:589–600.

Ortner, Sherry B. 1971. On Key Symbols. *American Anthropologist* 75:1338–46.

Ortner, Sherry B. 1974. "Is Female to Male as Nature Is to Culture?" In Michelle Rosaldo and Louise Lamphere, eds., *Woman, Culture, and Society*, pp. 67–88. Stanford, CA: Stanford University Press.

Ortner, Sherry B. 1989. *High Religion: A Cultural and Political History of Sherpa Buddhism*. Princeton, NJ: Princeton University Press.

Ortner, Sherry B. 1996. *Making Gender: The Politics and Erotics of Culture*. Boston: Beacon Press.

Osburg, John. 2013. *Anxious Wealth: Money and Morality Among China's New Rich*. Stanford, CA: Stanford University Press.

Owusu, Maxwell. 1992. Democracy and Africa: A View from the Village. *Journal of Modern African Studies* 30(3):369–96.

Owusu, Maxwell. 1996. Tradition and Transformation: Democracy and the Politics of Popular Power in Ghana. *Journal of Modern African Studies* 34(2):307–43.

Oyama, Susan, Paul E. Griffiths, and Russell D. Gray. 2001. "Introduction: What Is Developmental Systems Theory?" In Susan Oyama, Paul E. Griffiths, and Russell D. Gray, eds., *Cycles of Contingency: Developmental Systems and Evolution*, pp. 1–12. Cambridge, MA: MIT Press.

Parent, Anthony S. Jr. 2003. *Foul Means: The Formation of Slave Society in Virginia, 1660–1740*. Chapel Hill: University of North Carolina Press.

Park, Michael. 2003. *Introducing Anthropology: An Integrated Approach*. New York: McGraw-Hill.

Parker, Richard. 1989. Acquired Immunodeficiency Syndrome in Urban Brazil. *Medical Anthropology Quarterly* 1(2):155–75.

Parker, Richard G. 2009. *Bodies, Pleasures, and Passions: Sexual Culture in Contemporary Brazil*. 2nd edition. Nashville, TN: Vanderbilt University Press.

Parkin, David, and Stanley Ulijaszek, eds. 2007. *Holistic Anthropology: Emergence and Convergence*. New York: Berghahn Books.

Parry, Jonathan, and Maurice Bloch, eds. 1989. *Money and the Morality of Exchange*. Cambridge: Cambridge University Press.

Parsons, Talcott. 1951. *The Social System*. Glencoe, IL: Free Press.

Partners in Health. 2010. *Partners in Health* web page. Accessed May 18, 2017: http://www.pih.org/.

Patel, Raj. 2008. *Stuffed and Starved: The Hidden Battle for the World Food System*. London: Melville House.

Patterson, Penny, director. 2003. *Koko and Friends*. Videorecording, produced by the Gorilla Foundation, distributed by Dave West, Utah Film and Video.

Pauketat, Timothy R. 1994. *The Ascent of Chiefs: Cahokia Mississippian Politics in Native North America*. Tuscaloosa: University of Alabama Press.

Pauketat, Timothy R. 2010. *Cahokia: Ancient America's Great City on the Mississippi*. New York: Penguin Books.

Pauketat, Timothy R., and Thomas E. Emerson. 1997. *Cahokia: Domination and Ideology in the Mississippian World*. Lincoln: University of Nebraska Press.

Payscale. 2022. Bachelor of Arts (BA), Anthropology Degree. Accessed June 12, 2022: http://www.payscale.com/research/US/Degree=Bachelor_of_Arts_(BA)%2C_Anthropology/Salary.

Pearson, M. N. 2003. *The Indian Ocean*. London: Routledge.

Pendle, Naomi. 2014. Interrupting the Balance: Reconsidering the Complexities of Conflict in South Sudan. *Disasters* 38(2):227–48.

Peregrine, Peter N., Carol R. Ember, and Melvin Ember. 2003. Cross-cultural Evaluation of Predicted Associations Between Race and Behavior. *Evolution and Human Behavior* 24(5):357–64.

Perley, Bernard C. 2011. *Defying Maliseet Language Death: Emergent Vitalities of Language, Culture, and Identity in Eastern Canada*. Lincoln: University of Nebraska Press.

Peterson, Jane. 2002. *Sexual Revolutions: Gender and Labor at the Dawn of Agriculture*. Gender and Archaeology Series. Walnut Creek, CA: AltaMira Press.

Petrie, William Flinders. 1891. *Tell el Hesy (Lachish)*. London: Watt (for Palestine Exploration Fund).

Petrie, William Flinders. 1899. Sequences in Prehistoric Remains. *Journal of the Anthropological Institute* 29:295–301.

Pinker, Steven. 1994. *The Language Instinct*. New York: W. Morrow.

Pinker, Steven. 1997. *How the Mind Works*. New York: W. W. Norton.

Piot, Charles. 1999. *Remotely Global: Village Modernity in West Africa*. Chicago: University of Chicago Press.

Piperno, D. R., and K. V. Flannery. 2001. The Earliest Archaeological Maize (*Zea mays* L.) from Highland Mexico: New Accelerator. Mass Spectrometry Dates and Their Implications. *Proceedings of the National Academy of Science* 98(4):2101–103.

Pobiner, Briana. 2017. Top Five Human Evolution Discoveries of 2017. *SciComm (PLOS Blog)*. Accessed January 8, 2019: https://blogs.plos.org/scicomm/2017/12/07/top-5-human-evolution-discoveries-of-2017/.

Polanyi, Karl. 1975. *The Great Transformation*. New York: Octagon Books. (Orig. published 1944.)

Pollard, Helen Perlstein. 1993. *Taríacuri's Legacy: The Prehispanic Tarascan State*. Norman: University of Oklahoma Press.

Pollard, Helen Perlstein. 2003a. "Development of a Tarascan Core: The Lake Patzcuaro Basin." In Michael E. Smith and Frances F. Berdan, *The Post-Classic Mesoamerican World*, pp. 227–37. Salt Lake City: University of Utah Press.

Pollard, Helen Perlstein. 2003b. "The Tarascan Empire." In Michael E. Smith and Frances F. Berdan, eds., *The Post-Classic Mesoamerican World*, pp. 78–86. Salt Lake City: University of Utah Press.

Post, Lennart von. 1946. The Prospect for Pollen Analysis in the Study of the Earth's Climatic History. *New Phytologist* 45(2):193–217.

Potts, R., and J. T. Faith. 2015. "Alternating High and Low Climate Variability: The Context of Natural Selection and Speciation in Plio-Pleistocene Hominin Evolution." *J. Hum. Evol.* 87, 5–20 (2015).

Powdermaker, Hortense. 1933. *Life in Lesu: The Study of a Melanesian Society*. New York: W. W. Norton.

Powdermaker, Hortense. 1944. *Probing Our Prejudices: A Unit for High School Students*. New York: Harper and Brothers.

Purtill, James. 2019. Samoan Anti-Vaxxer with Links to Australia Arrested after Spreading Conspiracy Theories. ABC (Australian Broadcasting Corporation), December 5, 2019, Accessed January 31, 2019: https://www.abc.net.au/triplej/programs/hack/samoan-measles-anti-vaxxer-edwin-tamasese-arrested/11751204.

Radcliffe-Brown, Alfred R. 1941. The Study of Kinship Systems. *Journal of the Royal Anthropological Institute of Great Britain and Ireland* 71(1/2):1–18.

Radcliffe-Brown, Alfred R. 1952. *Structure and Function in Primitive Society: Essays and Addresses*. Glencoe, IL: Free Press.

Radcliffe-Brown, Alfred R., and Daryl Forde. 1950. *African Systems of Kinship and Marriage*. London: Oxford University Press.

Radin, Paul. 1927. *Primitive Man as Philosopher*. New York: D. Appleton.

Radovčić, Davorka, Ankica Oros Sršen, Jakov Radovčić, and David W. Frayer. 2015. Evidence for Neandertal Jewelry: Modified White-Tailed Eagle Claws at Krapina. *PLoS ONE* 10(3):e0119802.

Raff, Jennifer. 2022. *Origin: A Genetic History of the Americas*. New York: Twelve Books.

Rahnema, Majid, and Victoria Bawtree. 1997. *The Post-Development Reader*. London: Zed Press.

Rappaport, Roy. 1984. *Pigs for the Ancestors: Ritual in the Ecology of a New Guinea People*. 2nd edition. Prospect Heights, IL: Waveland Press.

Rasmussen, Susan. 1991. Modes of Persuasion: Gossip, Song, and Divination in Tuareg Conflict Resolution. *Anthropological Quarterly* 64(1):30–46.

Reese, Ashanté. 2019. Black Food Geographies. Race, Self-Reliance, and Food Access in Washington, D.C. Chapel Hill: University of North Carolina Press.

Reeves, Dache M. 1936. Aerial Photography and Archaeology. *American Antiquity* 2(2):102–107.

Relethford, John H. 1997. Hemispheric Differences in Human Skin Color. *American Journal of Physical Anthropology* 104(4):449–57.

Relethford, John H. 2002. Apportionment of Global Human Genetic Diversity Based on Craniometrics and Skin Color. *American Journal of Physical Anthropology* 118(4):393–98.

Relethford, John H. 2009. Race and Global Patterns of Phenotypic Variation. *American Journal of Physical Anthropology* 139(1):16–22.

Renfrew, Colin, and Paul Bahn. 2004. *Archaeology: Theory, Methods, and Practice*. 4th edition. London: Thames and Hudson.

Rice, Andrew. 2016. "Is Jim Kim Destroying the World Bank?" *Foreign Policy*, April 27, 2016. Accessed January 17, 2017: https://foreignpolicy.com/2016/04/27/is-jim-yong-kim-destroying-the-world-bank-development-finance.

Richards, Paul. 1996. *Fighting for the Rainforest*. London: James Currey.

Richardson, Jane, and Alfred L. Kroeber. 1940. Three Centuries of Women's Dress Fashions: A Quantitative Analysis. *University of California Anthropological Records* 5(2):i–iv, 100–53.

Riches, David. 1986. "The Phenomenon of Violence." In David Riches, ed., *The Anthropology of Violence*, pp. 1–27. Oxford: Basil Blackwell.

Riches, David, ed. 1986. *The Anthropology of Violence*. Oxford: Basil Blackwell.

Riley, Erin P., Linda D. Wolfe, and Agustín Fuentes. 2011. "Ethnoprimatology: Contextualizing Human and Nonhuman Primate Interactions." In Christina J. Campbell, Agustín Fuentes, Katherine C. MacKinnon, Melissa Panger, and Simon K. Bearder, eds., *Primates in Perspective*, pp. 676–86. New York: Oxford University Press.

Rindos, David. 1984. *The Origins of Agriculture: An Evolutionary Perspective*. Orlando, FL: Academic Press.

Rivers, W. H. R. 1906. *The Todas*. London: Macmillan.

Robarchek, Clayton A., and Robert Knox Dentan. 1987. Blood Drunkenness and the Bloodthirsty Semai: Unmaking Another Anthropological Myth. *American Anthropologist* 89(2):356–65.

Robben, Antonius. 1989. *Sons of the Sea Goddess: Economic Practice and Discursive Conflict in Brazil*. New York: Columbia University Press.

Robbins, Richard. 2001. *Cultural Anthropology: A Problem-Based Approach*. 3rd edition. Itasca, IL: F. E. Peacock.

Robbins, Richard, and Rachel Dowty. 2019. *Global Problems and the Culture of Capitalism*. 7th edition. New York: Pearson Education.

Roberts, D. F. 1968. Genetic Fitness in a Colonizing Human Population. *Human Biology* 40:494–507.

Rodman, Deborah. 2017. Why Anthropologists Make Great Politicians. *Huffington Post*, March 29. Accessed October 30, 2018: https://www.huffingtonpost.com/entry/why-anthropologists-make-great-politicians_us_58dbb53fe4b0f087a3041e71.

Roosevelt, Anna C. 1999. The Development of Prehistoric Complex Societies: Amazonia, a Tropical Forest. *Archaeological Papers of the American Anthropological Association* 9(1):13–33.

Rosaldo, Renato. 1989. *Culture and Truth: The Remaking of Social Analysis*. Boston: Beacon Press.

Roscoe, Will. 1994. "How to Become a Berdache: Toward a Unified Analysis of Gender Diversity." In Gilbert Herdt, ed., *Third Sex, Third Gender: Beyond Sexual Dimorphism in Culture and History*, pp. 329–72. New York: Zone Books.

Rouse, Roger. 1991. Mexican Migration and the Social Space of Post Modernism. *Diaspora: A Journal of Transnational Studies* 1(1):8–23.

Rowe, Noel. 2015. How and Why All the World's Primates Project Began. Accessed June 16, 2018: https://alltheworldsprimates.org/About.aspx.

Rowlands, M., and J. P. Warnier. 1988. "Sorcery, Power and the Modern State in Cameroon." *Man* (n.s.) 23:118–32.

Royal, C. D., J. Novembre, S. M. Fullerton, D. B. Goldstein, J. C. Long, M. J. Bamshad, and A. G. Clark. 2010. Inferring Genetic Ancestry: Opportunities, Challenges, and Implications. *American Journal of Human Genetics* 86(5):661–73.

Ruff, Christopher. 2002. Variation in Human Body Size and Shape. *Annual Review of Anthropology* 31:211–32.

Sahlins, Marshall. 1965. "On the Sociology of Primitive Exchange." In M. Banton, ed., *The Relevance of Models for Social Anthropology*, pp. 123–236. ASA Monographs, 1. London: Tavistock.

Sahlins, Marshall. 1968. "Notes on the Original Affluent Society." In R. B. Lee and I. DeVore, eds., *Man the Hunter*, pp. 85–89. Chicago: Aldine.

Sahlins, Marshall. 1972. *Stone Age Economics*. Chicago: Aldine-Atherton.

Sahlins, Marshall. 1976. *Culture and Practical Reason*. Chicago: University of Chicago Press.

Sahlins, Marshall. 1999. Two or Three Things That I Know About Culture. *Journal of the Royal Anthropological Institute* 5(3):399–421.

Sahlins, Marshall, and Elman Service. 1960. *Evolution and Culture*. Ann Arbor: University of Michigan Press.

Said, Edward. 1978. *Orientalism*. New York: Pantheon Books.

Salmond, Anne. 2010. *Aphrodite's Island: The European Discovery of Tahiti*. Berkeley: University of California Press.

Sankararaman Sriram, Nick Patterson, Heng Li, Svante Pääbo, and David Reich. 2012. The Date of Interbreeding Between Neandertals and Modern Humans. *PLoS Genetics* 8(10):e1002947.

Sapir, Edward. 1921. *Language: An Introduction to the Study of Speech*. New York: Harcourt, Brace.

Sapir, Edward. 1929. The Status of Linguistics as a Science. *Language* 5(4):207–14.

Saussure, Ferdinand de. 1986. *Course in General Linguistics*. LaSalle, IL: Open Court. (Orig. published in French in 1916.)

Sayer, Andrew. 2000. Moral Economy and Political Economy. *Studies in Political Economy* (Spring):79–103.

Scheper-Hughes, Nancy. 1995. The Primacy of the Ethical: Propositions for a Militant Anthropology. *Current Anthropology* 15:227–83.

Schneider, David M. 1968. *American Kinship: A Cultural Account*. Englewood Cliffs, NJ: Prentice-Hall.

Schildkrout, Enid, and Curtis A. Keim. 1998. *The Scramble for Art in Central Africa*. Cambridge, UK: Cambridge University Press.

Scott, James. 2009. *The Art of Not Being Governed: An Anarchist History of Upland Southeast Asia*. New Haven, CT: Yale University Press.

Segal, Charles M., and David C. Stineback. 1977. *Puritans, Indians, and Manifest Destiny*. New York: Putnam.

Segal, Daniel A., and Sylvia J. Yanagisako, eds. 2005. *Unwrapping the Sacred Bundle: Reflections on the Disciplining of Anthropology*. Durham, NC: Duke University Press.

Seligman, Rebecca. 2005. Distress, Dissociation, and Embodied Experience: Reconsidering the Pathways to Mediumship and Mental Health. *Ethos* 33(1):71–99.

Senut, B., M. Pickford, D. Gommery, et al. 2001. First Hominid from the Miocene (Lukeio Formation, Kenya). *C. R. Academy of Science Paris* 332:137–44.

Sheridan, Michael. 2006. "Linguistic Models in Anthropology 101: Give Me the Cup." In P. Rice and D. McCurdy, eds., *Strategies in Teaching Anthropology*. 4th edition, pp. 54–56. Upper Saddle River, NJ: Prentice Hall Professional.

Shetrone, Henry Clyde. 2004. *The Mound-Builders*, with a new introduction by Bradley T. Lepper. Tuscaloosa: University of Alabama Press.

Shieffelin, Bambi B., Kathryn A. Woolard, and Paul V. Kroskrity, eds., 1998. *Language Ideologies: Practice and Theory*. New York: Oxford University Press.

Shore, Bradd. 1996. *Culture in Mind: Cognition, Culture, and the Problem of Meaning*. New York: Oxford University Press.

Shorris, Earl. 1992. *Latinos: A Biography of the People*. New York: W. W. Norton.

Silverblatt, Irene. 1988. "Political Memories and Colonizing Symbols: Santiago and the Mountain Gods of Colonial Peru." In Jonathan Hill, ed., *Rethinking History and Myth: Indigenous South American Perspectives on the Past*, pp. 174–94. Urbana: University of Illinois Press.

Simpson, Scott W. 2002. "*Australopithecus afarensis* and Human Evolution." In P. N. Peregrine, C. R. Ember, and M. Ember, eds., *Physical Anthropology: Original Readings in Method and Practice*, pp.103–23. Upper Saddle River, NJ: Prentice-Hall.

Singer, Merill, Nicola Bulled, Bayla Ostrach, and Shir Lerman Ginzburg. 2021. Syndemics: A Cross-Disciplinary Approach to Complex Epidemic Events Like COVID-19. Annual Review of Anthropology 50(1):41–58.

Sivo, Ellen. 2005. The DOs and DON'Ts of College Romance. *Vermont Cynic*, November 29. Accessed June 3, 2017: https://vtcynic.com/36166/life/the-dos-and-donts-of-college-romance/.

Sloane, Patricia. 1999. *Islam, Modernity, and Entrepreneurship Among the Malays*. New York: St. Martin's Press.

Small, Meredith. 1998. *Our Babies, Ourselves: How Biology and Culture Shape How We Parent*. New York: Anchor Books.

Smay, Diana B., and George J. Armelagos. 2000. Galileo Wept: A Critical Assessment of the Use of Race in Forensic Anthropology. *Transforming Anthropology* 9(2):19–40.

Smedley, Audrey. 2007a. The History of the Idea of Race . . . And Why It Matters. Paper presented at the conference "Race, Human Variation and Disease: Consensus and Frontiers," Warrenton, Virginia, March 14–17. http://www.understandingrace.com/resources/papers_author.html.

Smedley, Audrey. 2007b. *Race in North America: Origin and Evolution of a Worldview*. 3rd edition. Boulder, CO: Westview Press.

Smith, Adam. 1976. *An Inquiry into the Nature and Causes of the Wealth of Nations*. Chicago: University of Chicago Press. (Orig. published 1776.)

Smith, M. Estellie. 2000. *Trade and Tradeoffs: Using Resources, Making Choices, and Taking Risks*. Long Grove, IL: Waveland Press.

Soba, Elisa J. 2021a. Conspiracy Theories in Political-economic Context: Lessons from Parents with Vaccine and Other Pharmaceutical Concerns. *Journal for Cultural Research* 25(1):51–68.

Soba, Elisa J. 2021b. Vaccination Against Their Religion? *Bloomsbury Religion in America*. London: Bloomsbury Academic. Theology and Religion Online. Accessed June 9, 2022: DOI: 10.5040/9781350971097.005.

Society for Medical Anthropology. 2014. What Is Medical Anthropology? Accessed June 1, 2014: https://medanthro.net/9/.

Spencer, Herbert. 1874. *The Principles of Sociology*. London: Williams and Norgate.

Spiro, Melford E. 1958. *Children of the Kibbutz*. Cambridge, MA: Harvard University Press.

Spittler, Gerd. 1999. "In Praise of the Simple Meal: African and European Food Culture Compared." In Carola Lentz, ed., *Changing Food Habits: Case Studies from Africa, South America, and Europe*, pp. 27–42. Newark, NJ: Harwood Academic.

Spitulnik, Debra. 1998. "Mediating Unity and Diversity: The Production of Language Ideologies in Zambian Broadcasting." In Bambi B. Shieffelin, Kathryn A. Woolard, and Paul V. Kroskrity, eds., *Language Ideologies: Practice and Theory*, pp. 163–88. New York: Oxford University Press.

Stack, Carol. 1997. *All Our Kin*. New York: Basic Books.

Starr, Paul. 1982. *The Social Transformation of American Medicine*. New York: Basic Books.

Steiner, Christopher B. 1994. *African Art in Transit*. Cambridge: Cambridge University Press.

Stephens, John L. 1843. *Incidents of Travel in Yucatan*. New York: Harper and Brothers.

Stern, Jack T. 2000. Climbing to the Top: A Personal Memoir of *Australopithecus afarensis*. *Evolutionary Anthropology* 9:113–33.

Steward, Julian. 1955. *Theory of Culture Change: The Methodology of Multilinear Evolution*. Urbana: University of Illinois Press.

Stocking, George W. Jr. 1968, *Race, Culture, and Evolution: Essays in the History of Anthropology*. Chicago: University of Chicago Press.

Stocking, George W. Jr., ed. 1985. *History of Anthropology*, Vol. 3. *Objects and Others: Essays on Museums and Material Culture*. Madison: University of Wisconsin Press.

Stoffle, Richard, Rebecca Toupal, and Nieves Zedeño. 2003. "Landscape, Nature, and Culture: A Diachronic Model of Human-Nature Adaptations." In H. Selin, ed., *Nature Across Cultures: Views of Nature and the Environment in Non-Western Cultures*, pp. 97–114. London: Kluwer Academic.

Stonich, Susan. 1993. *I Am Destroying the Land! The Political Ecology of Poverty and Environmental Destruction in Honduras*. Boulder, CO: Westview Press.

Strang, Veronica, and Mark Busse, eds. 2011. *Ownership and Appropriation*. New York: Berg.

Strathern, Marilyn. 1988. *The Gender of the Gift: Problems with Women and Problems with Society in Melanesia*. Berkeley: University of California Press.

Strier, Karen B. 2003. *Primate Behavioral Ecology*. 2nd edition. Boston: Allyn and Bacon.

Strier, Karen B., ed. 2014. *Primate Ethnographies*. Boston: Pearson.

Strong, Pauline. 1996. Animated Indians: Critique and Contradiction in Commodified Children's Culture. *Cultural Anthropology* 11(3):405–24.

Stuart, Zachary, and Kelly Thomson. 2011. *Savage Memory*. Available at IMDB https://www.imdb.com/title/tt1796606/.

Stuart, Zachary and Kelly Thompson. 2011. *Savage Memory*. Indie Rights, Distributor. https://www.imdb.com/title/tt1796606/.

Students Review. 2018. Job Satisfaction by Major. Accessed October 15, 2018: https://www.studentsreview.com/satisfaction_by_major.php3.

Stumpf, Rebecca M. 2011. "Chimpanzees and Bonobos: Inter- and Intraspecies Diversity." In Christina J. Campbell, Agustín Fuentes, Katherine C. MacKinnon, Simon K. Bearder, and Rebecca M. Stumpf, *Primates in Perspective*. 2nd edition, pp. 340–56. New York: Oxford University Press.

Sturtevant, William. 1964. "Studies in Ethnoscience." In A. Kimball Romney and Roy G. D'Andrade, eds., *Transcultural Studies of Cognition*, pp. 99–131. Menasha, WI: AAA.

Sussman, Robert W. 2011. "A Brief History of Primate Field Studies." In Christina J. Campbell, Agustín Fuentes, Katherine C. MacKinnon, Simon K. Bearder, and Rebecca M. Stumpf, *Primates in Perspective*. 2nd edition, pp. 6–11. New York: Oxford University Press.

Sussman, Robert W. 2014. "The Lure of Lemurs to an Anthropologist." In Karen B. Strier, ed. *Primate Ethnographies*, pp. 34–45. Boston: Pearson.

Tainter, Joseph. 2006. Archaeology of Overshoot and Collapse. *Annual Review of Anthropology* 35:59–74.

Tainter, Joseph. 2008. Collapse, Sustainability, and the Environment: How Authors Choose to Fail or Succeed. *Reviews in Anthropology* 37:342–71.

Tannen, Deborah. 1994. *Talking From 9 to 5: How Women's and Men's Conversational Styles Affect Who Gets Hired, Who Gets Credit, and What Gets Done at Work*. New York: W. William Morrow.

Target Jobs. 2022. Archaeologist: Job Description. Accessed June 3, 2022: https://targetjobs.co.uk/careers-advice/job-descriptions/archaeologist-job-description.

Tattersall, Ian. 2012. *Masters of the Planet: Seeking the Origins of Human Singularity*. New York: Palgrave Macmillan.

Taylor, R. E. 1975. Fluorine Diffusion: A New Dating Method for Chipped Lithic Materials. *World Archaeology* 7(2):125–35.

Tedlock, Dennis. 1972. "Pueblo Literature: Style and Verisimilitude." In Alfonso Ortiz, ed., *New Perspectives on the Pueblos*, pp. 219–42. Albuquerque: University of New Mexico Press.

Tedlock, Dennis. 1988. "Ethnography as Interaction: The Storyteller, the Audience, the Fieldworker, and the Machine." In Regna Darnell and Michael K. Foster, eds., *Native North American Patterns*, pp. 80–94. Papers of the Canadian Ethnology Service 112. Hull, Quebec: Canadian Museum of Civilization.

Tedlock, Dennis. 1993. *Breath on the Mirror: Mythic Voices and Visions of the Living Maya*. San Francisco, CA: HarperSanFrancisco.

Tedlock, Dennis. 1999. *Finding the Center: Art of the Zuni Storyteller*. 2nd edition, revised and expanded. Lincoln: University of Nebraska Press.

Teeter, Karl V. 1964. "Anthropological Linguistics" and Linguistic Anthropology. *American Anthropologist* 66(4), Part 1:878–79.

Templeton, Alan R. 1998. Human Races: A Genetic and Evolutionary Perspective. *American Anthropologist* 100(3):632–50.

Templeton, Alan R. 2002. Out of Africa Again and Again. *Nature* 416:45–51.

Templeton, Alan R. 2013. Biological Races in Humans. *Studies in History and Philosophy of Biological and Biomedical Sciences* 44(3):262–71.

Terrell, John, and Robert L. Welsch. 1990. Trade Networks, Areal Integration, and Diversity Along the North Coast of New Guinea. *Asian Perspectives* 29:156–65.

Terrell, John Edward, and Esther Schechter, eds. 2011. Archaeological Investigations on the Sepik Coast of Papua New Guinea. Archaeology in Oceania. *Fieldiana: Anthropology* 42:5–19.

Thierry, Bernard. 2007. "The Macaques: A Double Layered Social Organization." In Christina J. Campbell, Agustín Fuentes, Katherine C. MacKinnon, Melissa Panger, and Simon K. Bearder, eds., *Primates in Perspective*, pp. 224–39. New York: Oxford University Press.

Thin, Neil. 2009. "Why Anthropology Can Ill Afford to Ignore Well-Being." In Gordon Matthews and Carolina Izquierdo, eds., pp. 23–44. *Pursuits of Happiness: Well-Being in Anthropological Perspective*. New York: Berghahn Books.

Thomas, David Hurst. 2000. *The Skull Wars: Kennewick Man, Archaeology, and the Battle for Native American Identity*. New York: Basic Books.

Thomas, Mark. 2008. *Belching Out the Devil: Global Adventures with Coca-Cola*. London: Ebury.

Thomas, Wesley. 1997. "Navajo Cultural Constructions of Gender and Sexuality." In Sue-Ellen Jacobs, Wesley Thomas, and Sabine Lang, eds., *Two-Spirit People: Native American Gender Identity, Sexuality, and Spirituality*, pp. 156–73. Urbana: University of Illinois Press.

Thomson, Rob, Tamar Murachver, and James Green. 2001. Where Is the Gender in Gendered Language? *Psychological Science* 12:171–75.

Thorne, A. G., and M. H. Wolpoff. 1992. The Multiregional Evolution of Humans. *Scientific American* 266(4):76–83.

Tibon, Jorelik. n.d. What Is "Mo"? Traditional Conservation Sites in the Marshall Islands. Republic of the Marshall Islands Biodiversity Clearinghouse Mechanism. Accessed February 17, 2017: http://biormi.org/index_navmap.shtml?en/community.html.

Tierney, Patrick. 2002. *Darkness in El Dorado: How Scientists and Journalists Devastated the Amazon*. New York: W. W. Norton.

Timmermann, A., and T. Friedrich. 2016. Late Pleistocene Climate Drivers of Early Human Migration. *Nature* 538:92–95. https://doi.org/10.1038/nature19365.

Toren, Christina. 1996. "Psychological Anthropology." In Alan Barnard and Jonathan Spencer, eds., *Encyclopedia of Social and Cultural Anthropology*, pp. 456–61. London: Routledge.

Townsend, Patricia. 2008. *Environmental Anthropology: From Pigs to Policies*. 2nd edition. Long Grove, IL: Waveland Press.

Trautmann, Thomas. 2008. *Lewis Henry Morgan and the Invention of Kinship*. Lincoln: University of Nebraska Press.

Trevor-Roper, Hugh R. 1983. "The Invention of Tradition: The Highland Tradition of Scotland." In Eric Hobsbawn and Terence Ranger, eds., *The Invention of Tradition*, pp. 15–41. Cambridge: Cambridge University Press.

Trigger, Bruce G. 2006. *A History of Archaeological Thought*. 2nd edition. Cambridge: Cambridge University Press.

Truman, Harry S. 1949. Inaugural Address, January 20. Accessed June 3, 2014: http://www.bartleby.com/124/pres53.html.

Tsing, Anna Lowehaupt. 2005. *Friction: An Ethnography of Global Connection*. Princeton, NJ: Princeton University Press.

Tuhiwai Smith, Linda. 2012. *Decolonizing Methodologies: Research and Indigenous Peoples*. 2nd edition. London: Zed Books.

Turner, Victor. 1967. *The Forest of Symbols: Aspects of Ndembu Ritual*. Ithaca, NY: Cornell University Press.

Turner, Victor. 1969. *The Ritual Process: Structure and Anti-Structure*. Chicago: Aldine.

Twain, Mark (Samuel Clemens). 1894. *The Tragedy of Pudd'nhead Wilson*. Hartford, CT: American Publishing.

Tylor, E. B. 1871. *Primitive Culture: Researches Into the Development of Mythology, Philosophy, Religion, Art, and Custom*. London: John Murray.

Ulijaszek, Stanley. 2007. "Bioculturalism." In David Parkin and Stanley Ulijaszek, eds., *Holistic Anthropology: Emergence and Convergence*, pp. 21–51. New York: Berghahn Books.

Ulijaszek, Stanley J., and Hayley Lofink. 2006. Obesity in Biocultural Perspective. *Annual Review of Anthropology* 35:337–60.

United Nations. 2016. *International Migration Report 2015*. Department of Economic and Social Affairs. United Nations, New York. Accessed February 17, 2017: http://www.un.org/en/development/desa/population/migration/publications/migrationreport/docs/MigrationReport2015_Highlights.pdf.

US Bureau of Labor Statistics. 2021. Anthropologists and Archaeologists. *Occupational Outlook Handbook. Anthropologists and Archaeologists*. Accessed June 12, 2022:https://www.bls.gov/ooh/Life-Physical-and-Social-Science/Anthropologists-and-archeologists.htm.

Van Keuren, Scott. 2006. Decorating Glaze-Painted Pottery in East-Central Arizona. In Judith Habicht-Mauche, Suzanne Eckert, and Deborah Huntley, eds., *The Social Life of Pots: Glaze Wares and Cultural Dynamics in the Southwest, AD 1250–1680*, pp. 87–104. Tucson: University of Arizona Press.

van Schaik, C. P. 1989. "The Ecology of Social Relationships Among Females." In V. Standee, and R. A. Foley, eds., *Comparative Socioecological: The Behavioral Ecology of Humans and Other Mammals*, pp. 195–218. Oxford: Blackwell Scientific Press.

Vanstone, James W. 1972. New Evidence Concerning Polar Eskimo Isolation. *American Anthropologist* 74(5):1062–65.

Verdery, Katherine. 1996. *What Was Socialism? What Comes Next?* Princeton, NJ: Princeton University Press.

Vergano, Dan. 2014. Cave Paintings in Indonesia Redraw Picture of Earliest Art. *National Geographic*, October 8. Accessed May 26, 2015: http://news.nationalgeographic.com/news/2014/10/141008-cave-art-sulawesi-hand-science/.

Verini, James. 2014. How the World's Youngest Nation Descended Into Bloody Civil War: Fighting Between Its Two Main Tribal Groups Threatens to Tear South Sudan Apart. *National Geographic*, Special Feature. Accessed December 20, 2015: http://news.nationalgeographic.com/news/special-features/2014/10/141001-south-sudan-dinka-nuerethiopia-juba-khartoum/.

Veseth, Michael. 2005. *Globaloney: Unraveling the Myths of Globalization*. Lanham, MD: Rowman and Littlefield.

Vincent, Joan. 1978. Political Anthropology: Manipulative Strategies. *Annual Review of Anthropology* 7:175–94.

Viswesaran, Kamala. 1997. Histories of Feminist Ethnography. *Annual Review of Anthropology* 26:591–621.

Vivanco, Luis. 2006. *Green Encounters: Shaping and Contesting Environmentalism in Rural Costa Rica*. New York: Berghahn Books.

Vivanco, Luis. 2013. *Reconsidering the Bicycle: An Anthropological Perspective on a New (Old) Thing*. New York: Routledge.

Vivanco, Luis. 2016. *Fieldnotes: A Guided Journal for Doing Anthropology*. New York: Oxford University Press.

Voegelin, C. F. 1965. Sociolinguistics, Ethnolinguistics, and Anthropological Linguistics. *American Anthropologist* 67(2):484–85.

Vonnegut, Kurt. 2016. "The Secret Ingredient in My Books Is, There Has Never Been a Villain." *Chicago Tribune*, April 22, 2018. Accessed October 20, 2018: https://www.chicagotribune.com/news/opinion/commentary/ct-kurt-vonnegut-city-news-bureau-university-chicago-perspec-0425-jm-20160422-story.html.

Wackernagel, Mathis, Larry Onisto, Alejandro Callejas Linares, Ina Susana López Falfán, Jesús Méndez García, Ana Isabel Suárez Guerrero, et al. 1997. *The Ecological Footprints of Nations: How Much Nature Do They Use? How Much Nature Do They Have?* Report manuscript. Toronto: International Council for Local Environmental Initiatives.

Wagner, G. A., and P. Van den Haute. 1992. *Fission Track-Dating*. Dordrecht: Kluwer Academic.

Wagner, Roy. 1967. *The Curse of Souw: Principles of Daribi Clan Definition and Alliance*. Chicago: University of Chicago Press.

Wagner, Roy. 1969. "Marriage Among the Daribi." In R. M. Glasse and M. J. Meggitt, eds., *Pigs, Pearlshells, and Women: Marriage in the New Guinea Highlands*, pp. 56–76. Englewood Cliffs, NJ: Prentice Hall.

Wagner, Roy. 1975. *The Invention of Culture*. Englewood Cliffs, NJ: Prentice-Hall.

Wallace, Anthony F. C. 1956. Revitalization Movements: Some Theoretical Considerations for Their Comparative Study. *American Anthropologist* 58:264–81.

Wallace, Anthony F. C. 1966. *Religion: An Anthropological View*. New York: Random House.

Wallace, Anthony F. C. 1970. *The Death and Rebirth of the Seneca*. New York: Knopf.

Wallman, Joel. 1992. *Aping Language*. Cambridge: Cambridge University Press.

Walmsey, A. 2000. Production, Exchange, and Regional Trade in the Islamic East Mediterranean: Old Structures, New Systems? *In* L. L. Hanson and C. Wickham, eds. *The Long Eighth Century*, pp. 265–343. Leiden: Brill.

Walsh, Lorena. 2013. Development of Slavery in the 17th-century Chesapeake. Accessed June 2, 2017: https://www.historyisfun.org/video/development-slavery/.

Ward, C. V., M. G. Leakey, and A. Walker. 2001. Morphology of *Australopithecus anamensis* from Kanapoi and Allia Bay. *Journal of Human Evolution* 41(4):255–368.

Warmington, E. H. 1974. *The Commerce Between the Roman Empire and India*. New Delhi, India: Vikas Publishing.

Warren, Kay. 1998. *Indigenous Movements and Their Critics: Pan-Maya Activism in Guatemala*. Princeton, NJ: Princeton University Press.

Washburn, Sherwood L. 1951. The New Physical Anthropology. *Transactions of the New York Academy of Sciences*, Series III 13(7): 298–304.

Washburn, Sherwood L. 1961. *The Social Life of Early Man*. Chicago: Aldine.

Watson, James B. 1965. From Hunting to Horticulture in the New Guinea Highlands. *Ethnology* 4(3):295–309.

Watson, James B. 1977. Pigs, Fodder, and the Jones Effect in Postipomoean New Guinea. *Ethnology* 16:57–70.

Watson-Gegeo, Karen Ann, and Geoffrey White, eds. 1990. *Disentangling: Conflict Discourse in Pacific Societies*. Stanford, CA: Stanford University Press.

Watters, Ethan. 2011. *Crazy Like Us: The Globalization of the American Psyche*. New York: Free Press.

Webster, D. 2002. *The Fall of the Ancient Maya: Solving the Mystery of the Maya Collapse*. London: Thames and Hudson.

Weiner, Annette B. 1992. *Inalienable Possessions: The Paradox of Keeping While Giving*. Berkeley: University of California Press.

Welsch, Robert L. 1983. "Traditional Medicine and Western Medical Options Among the Ningerum of Papua New Guinea." In Lola Romanucci-Ross, Daniel E. Moerman, and Laurence R. Tancredi, eds., *The Anthropology of Medicine: From Culture Toward Medicine*, pp. 32–53. New York: Praeger.

Welsch, Robert L. 1996. Collaborative Regional Anthropology in New Guinea: From the New Guinea Micro-Evolution Project to the A. B. Lewis Project and Beyond. *Pacific Studies* 19(3):143–86.

Welsch, Robert L. 1999. Historical Ethnology: The Context and Meaning of the A. B. Lewis Collection. *Anthropos* 94:447–65.

Welsch, Robert L. 2006. "Coaxing the Spirits to Dance." In Robert L. Welsch, Virginia-Lee Webb, and Sebastine Haraha, eds., *Coaxing the Spirits to Dance: Art and Society in the Papuan Gulf of New Guinea*, pp. 4–44. Hanover, NH: Hood Museum of Art.

Welsch, Robert L., and John Terrell. 1998. "Material Culture, Social Fields, and Social Boundaries on the Sepik Coast of New Guinea." In Miriam Stark, ed., *The Archaeology of Social Boundaries*, pp. 50–77. Washington, DC: Smithsonian Institution Press.

Wengrow, David. 2010. *What Makes Civilization? The Ancient Near East and the Future of the West*. New York: Oxford University Press.

Werner, Cynthia, and Duran Bell, eds. 2004. *Values and Valuables: From the Sacred to the Symbolic*. Lanham, MD: Rowman Altamira.

West-Eberhard, M. J. 2003. *Developmental Plasticity and Evolution*. Oxford: Oxford University Press.

Weston, Kath. 1993. Lesbian/Gay Studies in the House of Anthropology. *Annual Review of Anthropology* 22:339–67.

Wheatley, Bruce P. 1999. *The Sacred Monkeys of Bali*. Long Grove, IL: Waveland Press.

White, A. M., I. P. Castle, P. A. Powell, R. W. Hingson, and G. F. Koob. 2022. Alcohol-Related Deaths During the COVID-19 Pandemic. *Journal of the American Medical Association* 327(17):1704–706. doi:10.1001/jama.2002.4308.

White, Leslie. 1949. *The Science of Culture: A Study of Man and Culture*. New York: Farrar, Straus and Giroux.

Whitehead, Neil L. 2004. "Cultures, Conflicts, and the Poetics of Violent Practice." In Neil Whitehead, ed., *Violence*, pp. 3–24. Santa Fe, NM: School of American Research.

Whiten, A., J. Goodall, W. C. Mcgrew, T. Nishida, V. Reynolds, Y. Sugiyama, C. E. G. Tutin, R. W. Wrangham, and C. Boesch. 1999. Cultures in Chimpanzees. *Nature* 399:682–85.

Whiten, Andrew. 2021. "The Burgeoning Reach of Human Culture." *Science* 372(6537): DOI: 10.1126/science.abe6514.

Wilcox, Michael. 2010. "Marketing Conquest and the Vanishing Indian: An Indigenous Response to Jared Diamond's Archaeology of the American Southwest." In Patricia A. McAnany and Norman Yoffee, eds., *Questioning Collapse: Human Resilience, Ecological Vulnerability, and the Aftermath of Empire*, pp. 113–41. Cambridge: Cambridge University Press.

Wilk, Richard, and Lisa Cliggett. 2007. *Economies and Cultures: Foundations of Economic Anthropology*. 2nd edition. Boulder, CO: Westview Press.

Wilkinson 2003. Civilizations as Networks: Trade, War, Diplomacy, and Command Control. *Complexity* 8:82–86.

Willey, Gordon R., and Jeremy A. Sabaloff. 1993. *A History of American Archaeology*. 3rd edition. New York: W. H. Freeman.

Winterhalder, Bruce. 1993. Work, Resources and Population in Foraging Societies. *Man* 28(2):321–40.

Winterhalder, Bruce, and Eric A. Smith, eds. 1981. *Hunter-Gatherer Foraging Strategies*. Chicago: University of Chicago Press.

Wolf, Eric. 1984. *Europe and the People Without History*. Berkeley: University of California Press.

Wolf, Eric. 2001. *Pathways of Power: Building an Anthropology of the Modern World*. Berkeley: University of California Press.

Wong, Kate. 2023. "This Small-Brained Human Species May Have Buried Its Dead, Controlled Fire and Made Art." *Scientific American*. June 5, 2023. Accessed on June 10, 2023: https://www.scientificamerican.com/article/this-small-brained-human-species-may-have-buried-its-dead-controlled-fire-and-made-art/.

Wood, Bernard. 2006. *Human Evolution: A Very Short Introduction*. New York: Oxford University Press.

Wood, Bernard. 2010. Reconstructing Human Evolution: Achievements, Challenges, and Opportunities. *Proceedings of the National Academy of Sciences* 107 (Suppl. 2):8902–909.

Wood, B., and Boyle, E. 2016. "Hominin Taxic Diversity: Fact or Fantasy?" *Yearbook of Physical Anthropology* 159:S37–S78.

Wood, B., and M. Collard. 1999. "The Changing Face of the Genus Homo." *Evolutionary Anthropology* 8:195-207.

Woolard, Kathryn A. 1998. "Introduction: Language Ideology as a Field of Inquiry." In Bambi B. Shieffelin, Kathryn A. Woolard, and Paul V. Kroskrity, eds., *Language Ideologies: Practice and Theory*, pp. 3–47. New York: Oxford University Press.

Work.Chron.com. 2018. Duties for an Archaeologist. Accessed June 3, 2022: https://work.chron.com/duties-archaeologist-13263.html.

World Bank. 2018. Decline of Global Poverty Continues but Has Slowed: World Bank. *The World Bank IBRD—IDA* web page. Accessed January 4, 2019: https://www.worldbank.org/en/news/press-release/2018/09/19/decline-of-global-extreme-poverty-continues-but-has-slowed-world-bank.

World Health Organization. 2022. "Constitution." Accessed April 22, 2022:https://www.who.int/about/governance/constitution.

World Instant Noodles Association. 2019. Global Demand for Instant Noodles updated May 9, 2019. Accessed November 17, 2019: https://instantnoodles.org/en/noodles/market.html.

Wortham, Stanton, and Angela Reyes. 2020. *Discourse Analysis: Beyond the Speech Event*. 2nd edition. New York: Routledge.

Worthman, Carol. 2007. After Dark: Evolutionary Ecology of Human Sleep. In Wenda Travathan, E. O. Smith, and James McKenna, eds., *Evolutionary Medicine and Health: New Perspectives*, pp. 291–313. New York: Oxford University Press.

Worthman, Carol. 2012. "Anthropology of Sleep." In Dierdre Barrett and Patrick McNamara, eds., *Encyclopedia of Sleep and Dreaming:*

The Evolution, Function, Nature, and Mysteries of Slumber, pp. 45–49. Santa Barbara, CA: Greenwood.

Worthman, Carol M. 1995. "Hormones, Sex, and Gender." *Annual Review of Anthropology* 24:593–616.

Wrangham, Richard. 2009. *Catching Fire: How Cooking Made Us Human*. New York: Basic Books.

Wrangham, Richard, and Dale Peterson. 1996. *Demonic Males: Apes and the Origins of Human Violence*. Boston: Houghton, Mifflin.

Yoffee, Norman. 1995. Political Economy in Early Mesopotamian States. *Annual Review of Anthropology* 24:281–311.

Zimmer, Carl. 2015. The Human Family Tree Bristles with New Branches. *New York Times*, May 27. http://www.nytimes.com/2015/06/02/science/adding-branches-to-the-human-family-tree.html?_r=0.

Zohary, Daniel, and Maria Hopf. 2000. *Domestication of Plants in the Old World*. 3rd edition. Oxford: Oxford University Press.

Zvelebil, Marek, and Peter Rowley-Conwy. 1984. Transition to Farming in Northern Europe: A Hunter-Gatherer Perspective. *Norwegian Archaeological Review* 17(2):104–28.

Credits

rights reserved; **Figure 5.10:** Devi Snively; **Figure 5b:** Gunter Ziesler/Getty Images; **Figure 5.11a:** Dean Pennala/Shutterstock; **Figure 5.11b:** Steve Meese/Shutterstock; **Figure 5.12:** USO/iStockphoto; **Figure 5.13:** Steve Bloom Images/Alamy Stock Photo; **Figure 5d:** Photo by © Ted Streshinsky/CORBIS/Corbis via Getty Images.

CHAPTER 6

Figure 6.1: Courtesy of Augustin Fuentes; **Figures 6b, 6c, 6d:** Raúl Martín/MSF/Science Source; **Figure 6.3:** The Natural History Museum/Alamy Stock Photo; **Figure 6t:** Courtesy of Briana Probiner; **Figure 6u:** FCG/Shutterstock; **Figure 6v:** Courtesy of Sarah Blaffer Hrdy from Mother Nature: Maternal Instincts and How They Shape the Human Species © 1999; **Figure 6.4a:** © Bone Clones, www.boneclones.com; **Figure 6.4b:** The Natural History Museum/Alamy Stock Photo; **Figure 6.5:** Photo (c) 2001 David L. Brill, humanoriginsphotos.com; **Figure 6dd:** Callao Cave Archaeology Project, Philippines. *New Atlas*, April 10, 2019; Gizmg Pty Ltd.; **Figure 6.6:** Heritage Image Partnership Ltd/Alamy Stock Photo; **Figure 6.7a:** Courtesy of Augustin Fuentes; **Figure 6.7b:** Based on: Bordes, Francois The Old Stone Age. Copyright © 1969 by Francois Bordes, McGraw-Hill; **Figure 6.8:** Javier Trueba/MSF/Science Source; **Figure 6.9:** Hercules Milas/Alamy Stock Photo.

CHAPTER 7

Figure 7a: MariaX/Shutterstock; **Figure 7.1:** Archive Farms Inc/Alamy Stock Photo; **Figure 7.2:** Courtesy of Augustin Fuentes; **Figure 7.3:** Courtesy of Augustin Fuentes; **Figure 7.4:** Courtesy of Augustin Fuentes; **Figure 7.5a:** Getty; **Figure 7.5b:** Alamy; **Figure 7.6:** Courtesy of Augustin Fuentes; **Figure 7.8:** Harper's Weekly; **Figure 7.9:** Book from the collections of Harvard University. Publisher Philadelphia: Lippincott, Grambo & Co. 1854. Public domain; **Figure 7c:** AP Photo; **Figure 7.10:** Courtesy of Augustin Fuentes; **Figure 7d:** Kumar Sriskandan/Alamy Stock Photo.

CHAPTER 8

Figure 8a: Chikara Yoshida/Getty Images; **Figure 8.1:** By Permission of DER; **Figure 8.2:** YASUYOSHI CHIBA/AFP/Getty Images; **Figure 8.3:** AP Photo/Jerome Delay; **Figure 8.4:** Image Source/iStockphoto; **Figure 8.5a:** Prints and Photographs Division, Library of Congress, LC-USZ62019404; **Figure 8.5b:** Bain Collection, Prints and Photographs Division, Library of Congress, LC-DIG-ggbain-09893; **Figure 8b:** Courtsey of Heidi Larsen; **Figure 8.7b:** Arkansas Foundation for Medical Care; **Figure 8.8:** Minnesota Historical Society/CORBIS/Corbis via Getty Images; **Figure 8.9:** Photo courtesy of Robert Welsch; **Figure 8.10:** After Bergmann, J.F., O. Chassany, J. Gandiol, J.A. Kanis, J.M. Segresta, C. Caulin, R. Dahan. 1994. "A Randomized Clinical Trial of the Effect of Informed Consent on the Analgesic Activity of Placebo and Naproxen in Cancer Pain." Clinical Trials Meta-Analysis 29:41-47; **Figure 8.11:** Jochen Tack/Alamy Stock Photo; **Figure 8c:** REUTERS/Alamy Stock Photo.

CHAPTER 9

Figure 9a: Maria Munad; **Figure 9.1:** Field Museum via author; **Figure 9.2a:** Hood Museum; **Figure 9.2b:** Hood Museum; **Figure 9.3:** Courtesy of Luis Vivanco; **Figure 9.4:** Hood Museum of Art, Dartmouth: Purchased through the Robert J. Strasenburgh II 1942 Fund; **Figure 9.5:** Photo Courtesy of Robert Welsch; **Figure 9.6:** Paradigm PR; **Figure 9.7:** Private Collection/The Stapleton Collection/Bridgeman Images; **Figure 9.8:** AP Photo/Bebeto Matthews; **Figure 9.9:** STAN HONDA/AFP/Getty Images; **Figure 9.10:** BornaMir/iStockphoto; **Figure 9c:** UC Berkeley Public Affairs.

CHAPTER 10

Figure 10a: © Jack Golson; **Figure 10.2:** PVDE/Bridgeman Images; **Figure 10b:** AP Photo; **Figure 10.6:** © Robert S. Peabody Institute of Archaeology, Phillips Academy, Andover, Massachusetts. All Rights Reserved; **Figure 10.7:** AP Photo/Ben Curtis; **Figure 10.8:** Smithsonian American Art Museum, Washington, D.C./ Alamy Stock Photo.

CHAPTER 11

Figure 11a: National Geographic Image Collection/Alamy Stock Photo; **Figure 11b:** Bernd Bölscher/Alamy Stock Photo; **Figure 11.2:** WitR/Shutterstock; **Figure 11.3:** Hood Museum of Art, Dartmouth:

Gift of Sir Henry Rawlinson through Austin H. Wright, Class of 1830; **Figure 11.4:** Harvard Semitic Museum; **Figure 11.6:** Brian Overcast/Alamy Stock Photo; **Figure 11c:** CC0 1.0 Universal/Public domain; **Figure 11.7:** Jeffrey M. Frank/Shutterstock; **Figure 11.8:** Scott Van Keuren; **Figure 11.9:** urf/Deposit Photos.

CHAPTER 12

Figure 12a: Monkey Business Images/Shutterstock; **Figure 12.1:** Courtesy of Ron Cohn photographer and The Gorilla Foundation (www.koko.org); **Figure 12.4:** Tsuji/Getty Images; **Figure 12.5:** Jake Warga/Getty Images; **Figure 12.6:** AP Photo/Pablo Martinez Monsivais; **Figure 12.7:** Zoe Cormack; **Figure 12b:** Wikipedia/public domain; **Figure 12.8:** Historical Picture Archive/CORBIS/Corbis via Getty Images; **Figure 12.9:** World Color Survey, WCS Data Archives, http://www.icsi.berkeley.edu/wcs/data.html.; **Figure 12c:** Courtesy Greg Dickson; **Figure 12.10:** Material republished with the express permission of: Montreal Gazette, a division of Postmedia Network Inc.; **Figure 12d:** Courtesy of Bernard Perley.

CHAPTER 13

Figure 13a: Sim Chi Yin/Magnum Photos; **Figure 13.1:** Spontoon Pipe Tomahawk from ANTIQUES ROADSHOW. © 1997–2018 WGBH Educational Foundation; **Figure 13.2:** Photo by Richard McGuire; **Figure 13.3:** AP Photo/Brett Deering, File; **Figure 13b:** Ullstein Bild/Getty Images; **Figure 13.5:** AP Photo/Peter Kramer; **Figure 13.6:** National Anthropological Archives, Smithsonian Institution, NAA INV 05097700; **Figure 13.7a:** Daderot/Wikipedia; **Figure 13.7b:** Photo by James Leynse/Corbis via Getty Images; **Figure 13.8:** AP Photo/Richard Drew; **Figure 13c:** Debby Wong/Shutterstock.

CHAPTER 14

Figure 14a: ISAAC MARTY/AFP/Getty Images; **Figure 14.1:** Drawn after "Pueblos Indigenas y Ecosistemas Naturales en Centroamerica y el Sur de Mexico," National Geographic/Center for the Support of Native Lands; **Figure 14.2:** ART Collection/Alamy Stock Photo; **Figure 14b:** Roy Rappaport Papers, MSS 516, Special Collections & Archives, UC San Diego https://library.ucsd.edu/dc/object/bb00355714; **Figure 14.3a:** Photo Courtesy of Robert Welsch; **Figure 14.3b:** Photo Courtesy of Robert Welsch; **Figure 14.3c:** Photo Courtesy of Robert Welsch; **Figure 14.4:** National Geographic; **Figure 14.5:** © 68/Ocean/Corbis; **Figure 14.6:** Photo by: Universal History Archive/UIG via Getty Images; **Figure 14.7:** Courtesy of Luis Vivanco; **Figure 14c:** Courtesy of Ashanté M. Reese; **Figure 14d:** Lexie Harrison-Cripps/Alamy Stock Photo; **Figure 14.10:** Bettmann/Getty Images.

CHAPTER 15

Figure 15a: The Funabulist Magazine; **Figure 15.1:** Photo by Christophe COURTEAU/Gamma-Rapho via Getty Images; **Figure 15.2:** artist Apa Hugo; **Figure 15b:** Courtesy of Maxwell Owusu, photo by Shafica Ahmed; **Figure 15.3:** Howard Pyle/Wikipedia; **Figure 15.4:** from *Puddn'head Wilson and Those Extraordinary Twins* by Mark Twain (1894) via HathiTrust—public domain; **Figure 15.5:** Image Still from *The Ax Fight* by Timothy Asch and Napoleon Chagnon, 1975, courtesy of Documentary Educational Resources; **Figure 15.6:** Associated Press; **Figure 15.7:** Photo by Craig Barritt/Getty Images for Electus Digital/WatchLOUD.

CHAPTER 16

Figure 16a: Photo by Edgar Negrete/Clasos.com/LatinContent/Getty Images; **Figure 16.2a:** James Willard Schultz, Photographer. Merrill G. Burlingame Special Collections at Montana State University Libraries; **Figure 16.2b:** Photo Courtesy of Robert Welsch; **Figure 16.4a:** Photograph Collection, Prints and Photographs Division, Library of Congress, LC-DIG-ppmsca-13196; **Figure 16.4b:** GEORGE FREY/AFP/Getty Images; **Figure 16.5:** antoniodiaz/Shutterstock; **Figure 16b:** George Rose/Getty Images; **Figure 16.6:** Sarah Jane Rhee; **Figure 16.7:** Photo courtesy of Kirk and Karen Endicott; **Figure 16.8a:** Keystone/Getty Images; **Figure 16.8b:** Photo by David Fenton/Getty Images; **Figure 16.9:** Jonatan Fernstrom/Getty Images; **Figure 16.10:** Pride Foundation/Photo by David Victor; **Figure 16.11:** INDRANIL MUKHERJEE/AFP/Getty Images; **Figure 16.12:** Photo by Arthur Siegel/The LIFE Images Collection/Getty Images.

CHAPTER 17

Figure 17a: NADEEM KHAWAR/EPA-EFE/Shutterstock; **Figure 17.1:** National Archives (NARA), American West Photographs (111-SC-87767); **Figure 17b:** Courtesy of Institute for Advanced Study; **Figure 17.2a:** Dan Kitwood/Getty Images; **Figure 17.2b:** AP Photo/Jessica Kourkounis; **Figure 17.3:** Hood Museum of Art, Dartmouth: Acquired by exchange from the Fairbanks Museum and Planetarium; **Figure 17.4:** Library of Congress Prints and Photographs Division Washington, D.C. 20540 USA; **Figure 17.5:** Hood Museum of Art; **Figure 17.6:** AP Photo/Michel Euler; **Figure 17c:** © Mayotte Magnus/National Portrait Gallery, London; **Figure 17.7:** Hood Museum of Art; **Figure 17.8:** Photo Courtesy of Robert Welsch; **Figure 17.9:** AP Photo/Chris Clark; **Figure 17d:** Gena Melendrez/Shutterstock; **Figure 17.10:** Frank Bienewald/LightRocket via Getty Images.

BACK MATTER

Figure MM3.1: "Australian Paleoanthropology" in *History of Physical Anthropology: An Encyclopedia, vols. 1 & 2.* Frank Spencer. ed. New York: Garland Publishing, 1997; **Figure MM3.2.:** Jim Zuckerman/Getty Images; **Figure Epilogue A:** Tim Sambrook/Alamy Stock Photo.

Index

Page numbers followed by *b*, *f*, and *t* refer to boxes, figures, and tables, respectively.

Abenaki Indians, 209
aboriginal overkill, 419–20
absolute dating, 140, 141*t*
accelerator mass spectrometer (AMS), 82, 275, 276
accents, 350–51
accuracy, 23*b*
acephalous societies, 427
Acheulian tools, 173, 173*f*, 180
action research, 370
action theory, 431
adaptability, 3, 6, 23*b*, 168, 180, 336, 407, 419
adaptation (evolutionary), 54–55, 55*f*
adaptational approach to racial classification, 203
adaptive behavior patterns, 74–75
Adena mound site, 84
adjudication, 445
adolescent sexuality, 457
adultery laws, 474
Adventures of Ozzie and Harriet, The (TV show), 453
aerial surveys, 245
aesthetics, 260–62
affiliation, 122
Affluent Society, The (Galbraith), 285
Affordable Care Act, 224
Africa and Africans:
    archaic humans, 169
    art, 261*f*, 267*b*
    genetic diversity, 190
    HIV/AIDS pandemic, 70, 237–38
    hominin fossils, 148–49
    Homo erectus, 167, 168
    human evolution within, 174*t*
    internet access in, 86
    Miocene transitional hominines, 150*t*
    Pliocene epoch, 149
    Plio-Pleistocene hominin evolution, 154*t*
    polygyny, 460
    racial "science," 202*f*
    Recent African origin model, 172
    Rift Valley of, 276
    sickle cell anemia, 194
    structural-functionalism, 428
    tracing ancestry to, 188
African Americans:
    in Black Lives Matter movement, 364–65
    claiming of past for, 268–69
    discrimination against, 201*f*
    environmental justice for, 421*f*
    kinship studies with, 458*b*
    life expectancy of, 209
    "one-drop rule" for, 439, 439*f*
    urban food justice for, 414*b*
African apes, 115, 116
African Burial Ground National Monument, 268–69, 269*f*
age-grades, 428

aggression, 131, 131*f*, 132, 442–47
agnosticism, 490
agriculture:
    in Amazon River basin, 300*b*
    for Ancestral Pueblo people, 332
    archaeological studies of, 8
    and Cahokia society, 311, 312
    community-supported, 93
    drivers of, 289–95
    early (*See* Neolithic Revolution)
    in Fertile Crescent, 291*f*
    Green Revolution of, 413
    hilly flanks hypotheses, 291–93
    hunter-gatherers' contact with, 289
    impact of, on daily life, 301–4
    industrial, 5, 407, 407*f*, 412–16
    intensive, 406–7
    by Maya people, 335
    in Mesopotamia, 323, 324
    methods of raising food, 295–300
    in New Guinea, 16*b*, 278*f*, 279–81
    population growth and, 134
    sedentism and, 302–4
    social relationships and, 243
    subsistence, 405, 415
    swidden, 405–6
    in Tarascan empire, 327
    traditional knowledge about, 411
Aguililla, Mexico, 92
AIDS and Accusation (Farmer), 239*b*
AIDS Memorial Quilt, 252
AIM (American Indian Movement), 255
Aitape people, 83, 390
alcoholism, 12–13, 231, 231*f*
Alex (African Grey Parrot), 345
Alexander the Great, 332
Ali, Inayat, 479–80
alien spaceship, 502*f*, 503–4
alleles, 61, 71, 74, 188
alliances, 122
allocation of political power, 430
alloparenting, 210, 211*b*, 211*f*
Allport, Gordon, 439, 441
alluvial soil, 247
Altamira caves, 183
alternative dispute management, 447
altruism, 124
Amazon River basin, 299, 300*b*
American Anthropological Association, 14, 24, 317*b*
American English language, 351, 352*b*
American exceptionalism, 4
American Indian Movement (AIM), 255
American Indians and Native Americans:
    adaptability of, 7
    ancestral, 171*b*
    collaborative archaeology with, 21–22
    cultural appropriation from, 44, 46
    cultural resource management by, 256
    gender variance for, 468–69, 469*f*

green stereotypes for, 419*f*
    kinship terminologies, 455
    material culture from, 253
    morbidity/mortality for, 209
    NAGPRA, 45*b*, 255–56, 288*b*
    potlatches of, 287, 287*f*
    religious beliefs of, 482, 487
    rights to land for, 254–55
    in salvage paradigm, 340
    sports mascots portraying, 29–30, 35, 39
Americanization, 100
American Medical Association, 227
American Museum of Natural History, 37*f*, 253
American Samoa, 255, 457
American Sign Language (ASL), 345–46
Ames, Michael M., 45*b*, 45*f*
AMS (*See* accelerator mass spectrometer)
Amuyunzu-Nyamongo, Mary, 21, 21*f*
Analects (Confucius), 4
analogous social patterns, 132
ancestral humans:
    bipedalism and neurobiological complexity of, 162–66
    cultural capacity of, 173–83
    earliest possible, 147–61
    emergence and dispersal patterns of, 167–72
    evolution of, 150*t*, 154*t*, 174*t*
    with most direct lineage, 153, 161
    paleoanthropology as study of, 160*b*
    See also archaic humans; hominins
Ancestral Pueblo people, 332–34
ancestry determinations, 186*f*, 187–88
Andalucía region, Spain, 409
Andaman Islands, 32
Andes, 38, 419
Angkor Wat, 265
Anglicization, 361
animal husbandry, 295, 406
animals:
    communication by, 345–46
    domestication of, 289–95, 298–99, 301–4, 405
    herding, 298–99, 301, 406, 406*f*
animism, 481–82
Anthropocene, 67
anthropogenic landscapes, 420
anthropoid primates, 116, 117
anthropological linguistics, 340
anthropologists:
    characteristics of, 23*b*
    ethical obligations of, 24–26
    ethnographic methods of, 368–71
    female and minority, 13–14
    human and primate biological studies by, 108–9
    as innovators, 20*b*
    language–culture relationship for, 340–41

541